978.3
CORNCO Corncob fuel and cold
prairie winters : tales
from the good old days in

Hometown Memories . . .

Corncob Fuel
and
Cold Prairie Winters
Tales from the Good Old Days
in Eastern and Northeastern South Dakota

A TREASURY OF 20TH CENTURY MEMORIES

At Hometown Memories, our mission is to save and share the memories of days gone by...before they are lost forever. As of this publication, we have created 80 books of memories, and saved and shared over 20,000 stories and 10,000 pictures.
We hope you enjoy them!

Hometown Memories . . .

Corncob Fuel
and
Cold Prairie Winters
Tales from the Good Old Days
in Eastern and Northeastern South Dakota
A TREASURY OF 20TH CENTURY MEMORIES
Compiled and edited by Todd Blair and Karen Garvey

HOMETOWN MEMORIES, LLC
Hickory, North Carolina

Corncob Fuel and Cold Prairie Winters

Publisher: Todd Blair
Lead Editor: Karen Garvey
Design and Graphic Arts Editor: Karen Garvey and Laura Montgomery
Office Services Assistant: Laura Montgomery and Tim Bekemeier
Warehouse Manager: Tim Bekemeier
Assistant Editors: Monica Black, Lisa Hollar, Jodi Black, Greg Rutz, Heather Garvey, Brianne Mai, Reashea Montgomery, Hannah Pletcher, Cathy Elrod, and Tiffany Canaday

ISBN 978-1-940376-08-0
Copyright © 2014

Published by

Hometown Memories, LLC
2359 Highway 70 SE, Suite 350
Hickory, N. C. 28602
(877) 491-8802

Printed in the United States of America

SUSTAINABLE
FORESTRY
INITIATIVE
Certified Fiber Sourcing
www.sfiprogram.org

Acknowledgements

To those Eastern and Northeastern South Dakota (and to those few who "ain't from around here") who took the trouble to write down your memories and mail them in to us, we offer our heartfelt thanks. And we're sure you're grateful to each other, because together, you have created a wonderful book.

To encourage participation, the publisher offered cash awards to the contributors of the most appealing stories. These awards were not based upon writing ability or historical knowledge, but rather upon subject matter and interest. The winners were: Lola Gelling of Frederick, SD; Raymond C. Ernster of Redfield, SD; Dorothy Bierwagen of Greenley CO. We would also like to give honorable mention to the contributions from Elaine McDaniels of Bryant, SD and Nadine Huwe Sauer of Webster, SD. The cash prizewinner for the book's cover photo goes to Vincent Leemhuis of Castlewood, SD (you'll find their names and page numbers in the table of contents). Congratulations! It was extremely difficult to choose these winners because every story and picture in this book had its own special appeal.

Associate Editors

David G. Anderson
Patricia Anderson
Mary Lou Fluegel Beath
Bob Boardman
Melba Pierce Brown
Donald R. Bye
Josephine Christopherson
Verl Cutler
Ardis Dragsten
Hazel Erickson
Paul Erschens
Wilfred "Buzz" Greening
Margaret L. Grottke
Stephen J. Grottke
Lois Hagemann
Philipina (Phil) Heintzman
Delores Henning
Pat Herr
Calvin C. Huber
Mary Hymans
Carol M. Joffer
Laura M. Jones
Ronald E. Kangas
Bonnie Kirchmeier
Ramona Kirkeby

Beverly Kluess
Gloria Langager
Herbert Lokken
Joe Malheim
Arlene Mardian
Paul Mardian
Eugene McMillan
Les Patton
Loran Perry
Marvin H. Perry
Raiden V. Peterson
Beverly M. Prostrollo
D. Ransom
Devon M. Reeve
Steve Reidel
Gail Roe
Leland Roe
Nadine Sievers
Devona J. Simonson
Norm Sparby
Warren Thomas
Jelene Tilden
Betty J. Voight
Nancy Volkart
John S. Wangberg
Molly Williams

INTRODUCTION

We know that most folks don't bother to read introductions. But we do hope you (at least eventually) get around to reading this one. Here's why:

First, the creation of these books is in its fifth generation after we took over the responsibilities of Hometown Memories Publishing from its founders, Bob Lasley and Sallie Holt. After forty nine books, they said goodbye to enjoy retirement, and each other. Bob and Sallie had a passion for saving these wonderful old tales from the good old days that we can only hope to match. We would love to hear your thoughts on how we are doing.

Second—and far more important—is the who, what, where, when, why and how of this book. Until you're aware of these, you won't fully enjoy and appreciate it.

This is a very unusual kind of history book. It was actually written by 434 South Dakota old-timers and not-so-old-timers who remember what life was really like back in the earlier years of the 20th century in Eastern and Northeastern South Dakota. These folks come from all walks of life, and by voluntarily sharing their memories (which often include their emotions, as well), they have captured the spirit and character of a time that will never be seen again.

Unlike most history books, this one was written from the viewpoint of people who actually experienced history. They're familiar with the tribulations of the Great Depression; the horrible taste of castor oil; "outdoor" plumbing; party line phones; and countless other experiences unknown to today's generation.

We advertised all over Eastern and Northeastern South Dakota to obtain these stories. We sought everyday folks, not experienced authors, and we asked them to simply jot down their memories. Our intention was by no means literary perfection. Most of these folks wrote the way they spoke, and that's exactly what we wanted. To preserve story authenticity, we tried to make only minimal changes to written contributions. We believe that an attempt at correction would damage the book's integrity.

We need to include a few disclaimers: first, many important names are missing in many stories. Several folks revealed the names of their teachers, neighbors, friends, even their pets and livestock, but the identities of parents or other important characters weren't given. Second, many contributors did not identify pictures or make corrections to their first draft copies. We're sure this resulted in many errors (and perhaps lost photographs) but we did the best we could. Third, each contributor accepts full responsibility for his or her submission and for our interpretation of requested changes. Fourth, because some of the submitted photographs were photocopied or "computer printed," their quality may be very poor. And finally, because there was never a charge, "fee," or any other obligation to contributors to have their material included in this book, we do not accept responsibility for any story or other material that was left out, either intentionally or accidentally.

We hope you enjoy this unique book as much as we enjoyed putting it together.

The Hometown Memories Team
August 2014

TABLE OF CONTENTS

The Table of Contents is listed in alphabetical order by the story contributor's last name.

To search for stories by the contributor's hometown or year of birth, see indexes beginning on page 531.

Peggy Kasten	359	Elaine McDaniels	22
Janet Keenan-Hauck	282	Eugene McMillan	275
Jeff (Hub) Keiser	51	Margaret McPeek	200
Jack Kennedy	362	Janet Elaine Meehan	48
Lorraine Kightlinger	195	Martha Mehlhaff	277
Bonnie Kirchmeier	115	Dee Melicher	426
Ramona Kirkeby	196	Alice M. (Stegeman) Mentzel	348
Mark Kisely	125	Aloyce "Al" Menzia	448
William W. Klucas	47	Danna Garber Mercer	263
Beverly Kluess	237	Helyn Mertens	463
Duane J. Knebel	55	Phyllis Meseberg	299
Merle (Nick) Kneebone	444	Joyce Meyer	353
Erma Knutson	190	Lyle L. Meyers	158
Doris Struckman Koisti	390	Nadine Mikel	336
Darlene Konrad	224	Judy Miles	298
Merlon Kotila	465	Alice Mae Bjerke Miller	370
Clarice W. Kranz	215	Luella Miller	277
Joyce Krokel	424	Dorothy Moe	85
Ellen Lehmkuhl Kub	497	Eleanore R. Moe	169
James P. Kurkowski	155	Edward A. Moeller	191
Pat La Mee	145	Ruth A. Moller	400
Rose Lamb	135	Gene Monahan	382
Edward H. Lamers	100	Lois (Kannegieter) Monahan	367
Gloria Langager	84	Raeburn Moore	235
Beverly Langner	330	Sheral (Sievers) Morrill	398
Selma Lapp	385	Ruth Myrvold	215
Roger Larsen	179	Dorene Nelson	210
Connie Lehmkuhl Larson	507	Lois Nelson	80
John Larson	172	Phyllis E. Nelson	375
Duane W. Laufmann	467	Violet Nelson	303
Mary Louise Lechner	472	Shirley A. Neshiem	228
Jacqueline Lee	191	Mathilda Nipper	104
Vincent Leemhuis	24	Gladys Noack	174
Bernice Lemley	516	Edith M. Noeldner	147
Donna Lewandowski	331	Marion (Bunting) Nordquist	291
Dorothy Lichty	449	Gene Norton	45
Virgil Likness	387	Joseph Nuhsbaumer	287
Verla Lindblad	313	Donna O'Connell	388
Pauline Lloyd-Davies	462	Virginia O'Connor	213
Clarice Logan	329	Alice M. Olson	486
Herbert Lokken	228	Glenn Olson	385
Vivian Lundgren	444	H. Lynette Olson	301
John R. Maciejewski	213	Harland F. Olson	427
Marvin Madsen	229	Jean P. Olson	436
RuthAnn Major	116	Joyce R. Stanislzus Olson	172
Joe Malheim	81	Leland Olson	246
Mary Lou A. Gasper Malli	527	Dorothy Goodspeed O'Neill	338
Juliana Malsom	183	Joan I. Oster	318
Arlene Mardian	53	Harriet Otto	431
Paul Mardian	411	Ruth Overby	50
Don Markseth	445	Donna (Heald) Pack	413
Vickie (Veeder) Marotz	475	Mae L. Palmer	191
Nadine Matthews	127	LaVern Papka	502
Fred Maxwell	427	Francis Parsey	330

Arlene Parsley	474	Kathy Scharn	287
Mary Jane Patchin	456	Betty Walker Schinkel	264
Dorothy J. Patton	443	James A. Schmidt	300
Les Patton	306	Margaret Schmidt	327
Paul W. Patton	441	Rosalia Schmidt	372
Alma M. Paulson	47	Arlene Schneiderman	61
Evelyn Paulson	340	George Schott	118
Russell H. Payne	491	Donald Schultz	231
Audrey R. Pedersen	517	Luella Schultz	240
Lorraine Peickert	162	William A. Schumacher	470
Lorna Mundhenke Perkins	472	Verna E. Schutt	124
Gail A. Perry	89	Myrle Sederstrom	304
Loran Perry	242	Clarence A. Senftner	519
Murvin H. Perry	314	Lowell Seymour	501
Jerry Otis Peters	331	Carol Shoup	140
Carleton Peters	142	Nadine Sievers	172
Gracene E. Petersen	345	Devona J. Simonson	311
Lawrence L. Peterson	261	Emery Sippel	108
Lois Peterson	206	Virginia Rawlins Skiner	65
Marlyce Peterson	483	Arlyn "Butch" Smith	378
Phyllis A. Bjerke Peterson	406	William F. Smith, Jr.	150
Raiden V. Peterson	48	Les Solberg	94
Carol Pevestorf	476	Barbara Solsaa	156
Beverly Phelps	513	Norm Sparby	200
Jane Jensen Pierce	489	Ervin Spitzer	263
Joyce J. Poppen	495	Cheris St. John	234
Freda Poyet	512	Geraldine Starkey	450
Helen M. Prater	433	Larry L. Steele	105
Robert Pray, Sr.	50	Donna Steenson	505
Beverly M. Prostrollo	95	Joyce Steinle	391
Virginia Pulfrey	369	Donald G. Steward	124
Kathryn Cole Quinones	167	Marge Stewart	375
Arlene Randall	261	Ardyce (Steen) Struck	96
Earl Randall	261	John "Matt" Sutton	248
D. Ransom	219	David Sveum	31
Shirley Reed	153	Lona Swanson	192
Dana Reeve	143	Nadine TeBeest	305
Devon M. Reeve	222	Harold G. Thaden	144
Muriel Reeve	482	Marjorie Thoelke	386
Arlo Remmers	203	Warren Thomas	103
Dorothy Reyelts	504	LaJoy Thompsen	387
Steve Riedel	27	George M.C. Thompson	112
Elaine Ries	230	Marileen Tilberg	74
Gail Roe	26	Jelene Tilden	57
Howard Roe	138	Gail Torrence	336
Leland Roe	44	Helena Townsend	173
Betty Roggenbuck	500	Adeline Rumpza Tracy	311
Bernice B. Rollo	86	Jerry L. Tracy	62
Darlene Rowderdink	42	Mr. Jerry Travis	66
Mavis Royer	76	Leonard Uecker	520
Twila Sanborn Ruden	262	Suzanne Unzen	235
Harlow H. Rudolph	389	Dorothy Van Kempen	274
Leroy Sauer	130	Vernon Vedvei	98
Nadine Huwe Sauer	24	Betty J. Voigt	89

The Tales...

True stories intentionally left just as the contributor wrote them.

A Depression Years Kid
By Lola Gelling of Frederick, South Dakota
Born 1925

Many times when my children asked if I had "this or that" when I was young, my answer was usually, "No." I was a child of the depression years. There are many good and bad memories of those years, but the year of 1930 when we lived on a farm southeast of Frederick for the summer stands out so vividly in my mind. My sister and I loved that summer. We played with the new kittens in the barn and roamed the pastures. We started country school that fall; we only attended two months before we moved to town, but those were wonderful days.

The road that ran by the farm, which was called Sunshine Highway, was the main road to Aberdeen in those days. It was this road that brought experiences we'll never forget. These were the years of the hobos or bums, whichever you want to call them. Many were neither, just poor men with no jobs trying to find any kind of work. The majority were polite and so grateful for the handout they always received from my mother. She never turned any away, even if it was only bread and butter that she had to offer. Scarcely a day went by that we didn't have someone in need of food.

We learned that our house was marked; that meant that it was a home where you always got a handout. To this day, I do not know what the marking was. Many old-timers will tell you this was the gospel truth.

There were a few times we were frightened. Our father ran a shoe repair shop in Frederick, so he left in the mornings and did not return until late in the evening. My mother was left alone with us children. After we started school, she was alone in the daytimes. One hot day, a hobo stopped begging for something to eat. After he ate what my mother could spare, he went down to the barnyard where an old well was. He stripped off his shirt and proceeded to wash it. Only a trickle of water came out—just enough to wet the shirt, but not enough to wash it. He came back to the house very angry, blaming my mother for not telling him about the well. This was one time our mother was very happy for the lock on the door!

One evening as my mother, my sister Lucie, and I were sitting on the back steps, we saw a man coming down the opposite side of the road. He went into the ditch and just stayed. We sat on the steps until nearly dark and then we went into the house and locked all the doors. Later that night when my father came home, his car lights shone on a man sleeping in the ditch on our side of the road just north of our house. After checking on us and making sure all the doors were locked, he drove down to the neighbor south of us and brought the neighbor back with him. As they were coming back, they met the hobo walking down the road, so they watched him until he was long out of sight.

A wagonload of Gypsies stopped once. We children were fascinated by them but our parents did not take their eyes off of them.

One wonders how many men trudged that road those bleak years when the trains came into Frederick. The boxcars were loaded with men. When we see people today with so much and so much waste, we can't help think of those years when a slice of bread was so dear. I believe our generation came out of it stronger and more independent in spirit as well as having a profound appreciation of life.

Train's Coming
In memory, I wander through the years. I hurry back and listen for the whistle of the iron horse on the track. If I could share a special childhood memory with the youth of today, I'd have them turn off their computers, television sets, and video games and come with me down memory lane to when I was a child and we'd watch the train coming down the track into Frederick.

If we stand where the old depot stood (across from the Masonic Hall and now an antique shop), close our eyes, and listen real hard, we'll hear that old whistle as the train comes rolling down the hill from the north. We'd open our eyes and see the black smoke pouring out and the steam hissing from the sides as it came to a screeching stop. What a feeling as the ground under us shakes; it is a sensation you never forget. I can still hear the townspeople hollering to each other, "Train's coming!" and there was always a crowd there to greet it. It came from the south in the morning and back from the north at about 4:30 in the afternoon. It was a very important part of our life in those days, as the mail came by train, farmers shipped their cream by rail, and all freight came by rail instead of trucks.

Many people shopped by catalog in those days, so their orders came by train.

The depot was a second home to my sister Lucie and I, as our childhood playmate was Mary Ellen Cook. Her father, E.W. Cook, was the agent in Frederick for many years. I can still see him briskly walking up the street, always whistling. Many people did not know he had an artificial leg. As a young brakeman in St. Paul, Minnesota, he slipped under a moving train car and his leg was cut off. Many hours we spent playing in the passenger room with its big, long benches and potbellied stove. Sometimes we'd play games up on the window desk in the office. I can still hear the old telegraph clicking out a message. But the grandest place to play was the old freight room. What a great place to play hide and seek! We'd hide in the big, dark coal room. I remember the little Henry boy that always wanted to play with us. Because we were older, we always made him hide his face and then we'd run way down to the park and hide from him! Usually he gave us hunting us and went back home. Shame on us, but back then, we thought it was funny!

Years ago when Emory and I visited Mary Ellen and her husband in Arizona, we had a wonderful time reliving all those old memories of our days at the old depot. She laughed as she told how her dad used the old freight room to teach her sister Dorothy a lesson. The girls' mother was an invalid, so it was their job to keep the house clean. Dorothy was told time and again to pick up her clothes, but as Mary Ellen said, "She always liked to try Pa's patience," so she usually forgot to comply with his orders. One day Dorothy came home from school, bounding up the stairs to where the Cooks lived above the depot. There was a door at the top of the stairs that when opened looked down into the freight room. That day it was opened and as she looked down, she saw all her clothes on the freight house floor! In a fit of anger, she ran down to her dad, demanding to know what her clothes were doing down there. Her dad calmly replied that she had two choices: to pick them up upstairs or in the freight room, whichever she preferred. I asked Mary Ellen if this worked, and she said that it did for a while.

I wish our young people could have met those trainmen. They were so kind to us little girls. Many of them had Irish names, especially the engineers. One day they put us in the engine and gave us a ride down the track a ways. Another time we rode in the caboose up to Ellendale. We went up in the morning and came back on the afternoon train. We really felt grownup. I can remember making mud pies and offering them for sale to the new train crew. With our hands full of pennies, we'd run up to Sleeper's Store. It was hard to decide what to spend them on, as there were so many choices for a penny in those days! Years later, I would smile when I heard my dad tell my son Mike that he'd give him a penny if he'd do something for him. I heard my son reply, "Pennies are no good, Grandpa. They don't buy anything." Today, a quarter hardly buys anything.

There were sad times too at that old depot when Mary Ellen's mother passed away, leaving her without a mother while she was still a child. I'll always remember when Dorothy's little boy Jimmy, about two years old, drowned in a big crock jar of rainwater on the back steps of the freight room. It was my first experience with death. I remember going to Pete Hanson's to see him. He looked like a wax doll.

Remember—isn't it a powerful word? The greatest gift God could give us. Have you noticed that as you grow older, it is hard to remember your appointments and what day it is, yet the past can be so clear? Time never dims my memory of three little girls standing by an old depot, eagerly watching north, just waiting to tell the world, "Train's coming!"

My Little House on the Prairie: Winter 1947
By Raymond C. Ernster of Redfield, South Dakota
Born 1932

It was so cold outside one had to turn their back to the stove to warm. The radio was a priceless link to the outside world. I would hurry on Saturday to finish the outdoor work then listen to the Metropolitan Opera at one o'clock. No telephone, no electricity, and no running water made self-sufficiency very necessary. One learns quickly how to prepare ahead, to eat, and have only the water needed for each day's use. An oversupply would freeze and burst the container when the fire burned low at night.

The sky was so beautiful at night; Northern lights would flash wildly in the distance. The calls of the foxes as they sent out lonely messages to each other would chill your spine. The old farm dog would sit on the haystack and answer them with long, sad, cries of his own lonely life. The little terrier, my only friend and constant companion would become very nervous and beg to go into the house where she could curl up by my feet and sleep. Her 15-pound warm body made a great bed warmer at night, so she shared bed with me most of her life. Cradled in my arms or curled about my feet, she was a great comfort in my long, alone hours. I often pictured myself as a lucky Robinson Crusoe. I had so much more than he.

After about ten days without leaving the farm and needing supplies from town, I hitched the team to the sled early one clear day and loaded the eggs and cream to sell in town. My terrier was so excited when she noticed we were going somewhere. Even the old farm dog danced about with glee in the pure, white snow. The team needed the exercise, so after a feeding of grain and watering, they were hitched to the already loaded wagon box on sled runners and we started the four and a half mile trip to town. The first one and a half miles was rough, going on the ungraded prairie road. No trail had been broken through the deep snow ahead of them. The three mile, ice-glazed, gravel road was easier, so better time was made. It was great to see people again, and the dogs ran gaily about checking every corner and alley for other dogs and cats.

It must have been an interesting sight to the townspeople, but I paid no attention to them. I had much to do before starting home. Darkness comes by five o'clock in the afternoon. I had planned to be home and comfortable by my fire by then. I proudly exchanged my eggs and cream for groceries and checked for mail at the post office. I was informed when I went to the gas station that Dad had called and sent me a message that Mom was improving and he would be home soon to check on the farm. Great joy filled my heart as a 14 year-old boy still misses loving parents around to whom he can nag and complain.

Sugar, flour, coal, salt and some store-bought cookies filled the sled box with my necessary survival supplies. Oh yes, a new set of hinges for the chicken house door was needed at the hardware store. There, I was greeted by a warm and well-fed owner who acted like I could not pay for my selection. "Why aren't you in school?" he questioned. I simply said, "How Much?" I paid for my purchase without answering his question and departed quickly. Five gallons of kerosene at the station and I was finished…so was my money.

The team and dogs were getting cold and restless. After giving each horse an extra treat of oats and corn, we started for home. The last mile and a half of deep snow was tough on the team and the dogs begged a ride with me on the sled. The horses slowly drew us back to our beautiful palace on the hill. The king couldn't have loved his castle more than I loved my house that evening as I enjoyed a meal of steak, fried potatoes, cottage cheese, fresh cream over custard, and those fantastic store-bought cookies. Such sweet satisfaction. After checking the expectant milk cow one more time, a tired, happy, and proud 14-year-old boy went to bed.

By sunrise, there was a new, fresh, blanket of snow on the windowsill smiling at me. Jack Frost on the windowpane built designs that painted pictures your imagination could make into a wonderland. Pain of the quietness grew as reality set in and another hard day of work must begin. The animals depended on me for everything.

Out of bed, the room temperature reads five degrees. Both stoves are filled and after a splash of kerosene, plus the lit match, a roaring fire of corncobs is giving immediate relief. Some leftover food is placed on the stove to warm, and then I added coal to the stove to keep heat in the house through the day. The terrier is pleading to get outside to relieve herself, which I have already done in the five-gallon bucket by the door. A quick word of sympathy, and she is let outside.

The storm is not over, as the ground wind is still moving the snow. Through a clear part of the glass, one can see cattle licking the water, which is frozen again. The pang of responsibility settles on my shoulders—there is work to be done. Bundle up and start another day—there is no time for self-pity or grief when there is so much to do. God give me the strength, and away I go. On that winter day, a struggle for survival surged through me, and the chores were done.

In my hours alone, some of my thoughts were of Eva, a sweet, young neighborhood girl who had not gone to high school. As I sat fantasizing of her beauty and charm, I wrote a most endearing love letter promising that in just four years we would be 18 and could get married. The letter was sealed before my fantasy hit reality and the hungry flames of the stove quickly consumed an afternoon dedicated to promises of eternal love and companionship. Fortunately, the urge to write such a letter did not fall upon me again that winter.

A pleasant afternoon was spent when a brief warming trend made walking quite easy. An empty school just a quarter of a mile away contained two old pedal-pump style organs. The dogs and I walked to the school and we slipped in through a basement window. I needed an audience, so the dogs most eagerly came in the same way that I did. You have never heard a more memorable performance of "The old Rugged Cross" or "In the Gloaming" than was played that day with the two dogs howling most sadly out of tune. What I would give to hear a recording of that performance today.

Spring came as it always does. Mom and Dad came home in April and all was well with the work. A mom was never more loved and pampered by a son than my mom that spring on that wonderful prairie. We had walks and talks and conversations about everything were shared. There was always her beautiful, warm smile, and an assuring touch upon the arm. She was the most beautiful and warm lady. I wanted everyone to know that she is my Mom. She is the best.

Time would pass before I visited the farm on June 15, 1977. It was quiet and beautifully green. The old prairie road is the same, but a little less worn. The buildings are gone, the windmill is gone, and just an open well remains. The one beautiful and cool shade tree has died and stands grey and ghost-like against the blue, summer sky. Mom and Dad are gone, at rest. Loneliness lingers on the hill. Memories of laughter, love, pain, and sadness run by my mind, but most of all my pride that says; *it was here that I became a man when I was 14 years old.* The pride and love are all that remain. I did finish high school. I did serve in the army. I did graduate from college

twice and became a classroom teacher and speech therapist. It took 32 years to get all of this into proper perspective. I thank God my three boys had a different way of becoming men, but I very much treasure the experiences and memories of "my little house on the prairie."

The Uncontrollable
By Dorothy Bierwagen of Greeley, Colorado
Born 1929

I wrote this as an English assignment as a freshman in high school. We were to write of a real life incident that we had heard of. I remember of my mother telling me and showing me pictures of a tornado that destroyed her parent's farm. This took place July 4, 1928 on a farm between Miller, South Dakota and Highmore, South Dakota, in eastern South Dakota.

The forces of nature are free from man's power. The raging floodwater, the blinding blizzards, and the soaring winds are as uncontrollable today as they were during our grandparent's time. It is against one of these forces that my grandparents' courage was tested. Grandfather Speirs was a tall, well-built man, with a clear-keen mind and a brown bushy mustache. He was a kind-hearted soul, but a very stubborn person, too. Perhaps it was this stubbornness; this unwillingness to let himself be overcome that had helped him to accomplish so much. He was the kind of man that would work hard to accomplish great

John Riley Speirs and Mary Elizabeth Zepp

20

things, and then would sit back and view, with pleasure, what he had done. Often times you would see him making the round of his farm with his hat perched on the back of his head, a cigar in his mouth, and his thumbs in his suspenders. He disliked having anything interfere with his plans; perhaps that is why what happened to his life's work was such a blow to him. The Speirs family had come to South Dakota in 1905 and by the year 1928, they had built up one of the finest farms in the state. On the farm were two residents, two large stock barns, and a number of smaller buildings. It is on this farm that my story takes place.

It was an ordinary day in July of the year 1928. The heat of the afternoon was growing less as early evening drew near. As they went about their evening chores Grandfather and Grandmother Speirs watched the western sky, at first casually, and then anxiously as dark clouds mounted higher and higher. As they came closer, hurried preparations were begun, but all too late for in a sweep of fury the storm broke, not an ordinary storm, but a tornado at its fullest force.

Grandfather and grandmother were in the kitchen when they saw it swooping down upon them. They thought at once of the cave, or fruit cellar, near the house. Mrs. Speirs headed for the cave calling over her shoulder, "Hurry John! We will never make it!" "I'm coming, you hurry on." Mrs. Speirs reached the cave safely. Mr. Speirs was close behind her, but as he was passing through the doorway, the door blew shut, catching one leg, and throwing him to the floor where he lay, between the wall and a large stone jar. They had hardly reached the cellar when the house was blown to pieces. Debris of every kind was showered on them. Both grandfather and grandmother were bruised painfully by flying articles. How they escaped death is a miracle.

As the elderly couple sat petrified together in the cave, it seemed as if centuries passed while they waited for the storm to cease. The strained, scared conversation of the two old people comforting each other and bemoaning what they assumed was taking place outside, did little to make the time go faster. Grandmother sat clenching and unclenching her hands and muttering through anxious lips, "Oh John, what will happen to us! What can we do! What can we do?" Grandfather, struggling

John and Mary Speirs in 1928

to keep courage in his voice, gravely replied, "It won't last long, mother. But, oh how hard the wind is blowing!"

Their thoughts of what must be happening outside did not half measure up to what actually was taking place. It seemed that the outlawed wind had no mercy what so ever on this farm. In turn as it reached each building, it would pick it up and whirl it to pieces and in place of a well-stabled building, scraps of lumber would be strewed in all directions. The work of years was wiped out in the blink of an eye.

The little pool at the end of the orchard did not seem to half satisfy the thirsty demands of the whirling winds, as in a matter of seconds, not even a little trickle of water was left. Huge trees, which had surrounded the buildings,

21

Horse barn on the Speirs farm

were stripped clean of leaves and branches and many of them were de-barked. Straws and splinters were blows into trees so far that they resisted efforts to be pulled out. Every bit of furniture was demolished and the family's personal belongings were scattered and torn by the fury of the wind. A more desolate picture could not be imagined. Blast upon blast of the outlawed wind tore over everything, leaving little hope in the hearts of either.

When the storm finally subdued, grandmother and grandfather came out to look at the remains. With the shock of the demolished scene, grandmother at once broke down when seeing her home in ruins. Grandfather walked around heartlessly, picking up bits of the ruin and thinking how everything he had worked for, lived for, and loved, was gone. Not one building or part of one was left standing. The large house was so completely swept away that were it not for the foundation, there would have been difficulty in placing its location. The buildings and trees were as completely destroyed as though consumed by a fire. As they walked about the ruins, leaving the pains of this terrible destruction, they could not make themselves believe that their eyes told them. How could this happen to them? Why was life so cruel? These were the pleading questions asked by the dismayed couple.

One of the children's ragdolls was found sitting in one of the remaining trees. In the mass of wreckage, where nearly everything else had been smashed, stood a white china water pitcher, not even chipped. An egg was found unbroken in the wreckage of the horse barn. In the reminiscence of one building, Grandfather Speirs found his ever-faithful

friend, his dog, Tippy. A piece of timber had been driven into his head. Grandfather and grandmother then realized how fortunate they were to have been spared with their lives. They knew it was only by God's will that they were still alive. Grandmother and Grandfather Speirs kept scars from this blow years afterwards, but it didn't stop them or slow them up. They made new plans, bought a new home, and started a new life together.

The Night the Party Line Helped Us
By Elaine McDaniels of Bryant, South
Dakota
Born 1932

We were living in the days when there were no school buses to the little town of Bryant situated in Hamlin County in eastern South Dakota. For part of the years of high school, I stayed in town during the week from Monday through Friday. My cousin, Rose, and I shared a room at a boarding house.

My dad had bought a used 1929 Model A Ford coupe. He paid $25.00 for it. One like it sold at an auction for $5,000.00 a few years ago. It had a rumble seat. I drove it to school my senior year. In the mornings, I would go to the neighbor's and pick up four children. Three of us sat inside the car and two grade school children sat in the rumble seat on the outside of the car. We would leave them off at a one-room schoolhouse in the country. Then we continued on to Bryant to high school.

Besides being the days of rumble seats and no school buses it was also the day of party lines. Very early one morning, Ted called me to find out what time I would be coming to pick them up for school. As soon as he dialed and heard the voice of an old Swedish neighbor man, he knew he had made a mistake dialing. Without saying a word, he quickly hung up and dialed our number. Ted heard my dad say, "Hello" and then he heard Henning in his Swedish brogue say, "Hello." Ted was horrified when he heard what was taking place. Neither man said any more but only waited for the other one to talk. Finally Dad said, "Pretty nice day.' Henning replied, "Not so bad." There was a long pause, and then Dad tried again. He asked, "Well, what's on your mind?" After a pause, Henning said, "Not much." After a lapse in conversation,

Ted heard a click and then another one as the strange conversation came to an end without even a "goodbye." By now, Ted was hysterical. It was a mystery we all pondered for years. In one house, they had wondered, "Why did Hjalmar call so early, but didn't have anything to say?" At our house we wondered, "What was wrong with Henning when he called and didn't have anything to say? Do you suppose he had been drinking?" Ted didn't reveal his part until many years later. And when he did, he laughed just thinking about it; the party line joke he had played by mistake.

Speaking of party lines, on March 19, 1951 it was a wonderful thing to have a party line. We lived in the country at the end of a long driveway, six miles from the nearest town, which was Bryant, South Dakota. We had been in the midst of a blizzard for three days. The roads were impassable. My sister and her two-year-old son were staying at our house. She was expecting a baby. Velma began to go into labor early in the evening. I got on the phone to try to locate a snowplow to come and open our driveway. To my horror, I heard a voice say, "All snowplows are out except for one which goes five or ten miles an hour." That snowplow was in the town of Hayti, about thirteen miles from our house. So that was out of the question. We needed help very soon.

Right after I hung up, our phone rang three shorts. It was our ring. Lloyd, one of our neighbors, was calling. He had listened on the party line. He said, "If some of the guys in the neighborhood will help, I will come with my tractor and open the road. We can go and get Ellen Paso and bring her to your place." Ellen was a registered nurse who lived near us. Immediately Wesley was getting bundled up to go out into the storm to help.

Our party line was busy all evening. People were concerned and willing to help if they could. Someone got on and told others to get off the phone because there was sickness on the line. Then our phone rang again. One of the neighbors north of us was reporting that she could see the tractor going by their place. Then she called saying they were stuck but telling about their progress. Soon they were out and moving along again. I am certain there were many "rubber necks" and well-wishers listening in that night.

Velma's pains were getting closer. I ran upstairs to look out an upstairs window to see if I might see the tractor lights through the blizzard. Suddenly I did see the lights of the tractor turn down our driveway. With extreme joy I yelled, "Here they come!" But at that same time, I heard different sounds coming from the downstairs bedroom. I flew down the stairs just in time to help deliver a baby

The car that Elaine drove to school

23

girl.

Ellen appeared ten minutes later. She was bundled up like an Eskimo. What a welcome sight she was! She happily took over and did what had to be done. She called someone to get directions on how to make a formula from milk from a cow. The new mother knew she wouldn't be able to nurse the baby. She would have to go back to work soon.

I went into the kitchen, pulled the door shut behind me, and proceeded to make coffee and lunch for the men. Among the men, I saw one of my eighth grade students. He looked so grown up there among the men. I heard the stories of how they plowed through drifts; at times, the blizzard was so bad they could scarcely see the road before them. Some of them had frozen faces. Another neighbor had left earlier to get Ellen in his tractor and wagon. They met Lloyd in his tractor. They had put a tarp over the wagon to make it warmer for Ellen as she rode through the blizzard. Ellen stayed all night because the roads were totally blocked again within half an hour.

It was a night to remember, neighbors taking care of neighbors. It was a gift from God that was sent to us that wintry night. Now after all of my family is gone, I'm still enjoying that gift of long ago: my niece who was born that night. Her big brother, my nephew, who was two years old at that time, lives not far from us. Last night we attended Liz's 63rd birthday celebration at her house just a few blocks from our house. Some of her children and grandchildren were there also.

A lot of changes have taken place in those 63 years and many faces are missing. But with eight of our own children and many grandchildren and great-grandchildren around us, we have much for which to be thankful. They continue to bring us happiness. Sometimes we tell them stories of those days of long ago when we were young.

The Most Perfect Wife
By Nadine Huwe Sauer of Webster, South Dakota
Born 1933

A story that my father Albert Huwe loved to tell was why his mother, my grandmother, was such a wonderful wife. It seems that when Grandpa and Grandma were traveling by horse and buggy home from their wedding ceremony, the horse tripped. Grandpa said, "That's once." After traveling on a ways, the horse tripped again. Grandpa said, "That's twice." Again after a short distance, the horse again tripped. Grandpa said, "That's three times," and got out of the buggy and shot the horse. Grandma was appalled, saying "Rudolph! How mean of you! I had no idea you were so bad tempered! I won't stand for you behaving like that. Grandpa said, "That's once."

The Pecky Kind
When I was a young teenager, I was requested to go out to my oldest sister's farm and help with household and farmyard chores. My sister had just come home from the hospital and needed time to recuperate. I had my best friend Marlene come help me. We were both town kids in Bristol. It must have been at harvest time, as there were many men working there also. At that time, the farm had no electricity, so it was kind of like being in another world.

One of our main chores was to collect the eggs. We went to get the eggs and only brought a very few. When asked where the rest of them were, we replied that the chickens were occupying a lot of the nests. We were then told to reach under them and retrieve the eggs. When my friend and I discussed how to go about this, she sounded very wise when she said, "Some are the 'pecky' kind." So, she decided to take a small stick and bop each one on the beak to see if it was the 'pecky' kind. Yup, sure enough, each one was. After she bopped the beak and found they were, I took a big stick and jacked them up and grabbed the eggs. In a very few days, the chickens didn't seem to produce many eggs. When the truck from Sugar Creek Creamery arrived to pick up cream, he had two passengers with him back to Bristol. Our life as farm helpers was over.

Prohibition Memories
By Vincent Leemhuis of Castlewood, South Dakota
Born 1920

My folks made beer. It was dark and foamy. They made beer quite a bit for several years. It was touchy because it was during prohibition, and making your own alcoholic beverages was illegal, too. It had a different taste than beer you buy now has. They started the beer in a large crock, maybe 15 or 20 gallons. They had it in the closet, and every day they would skim it until it quit working. Then they would bottle and cap it. They would put some in regular bottles and some of it in half-gallon clear glass bottles with caps. The folks had a capper and would buy the caps. Then it was aged more in the bottles. I remember they buried the beer bottles out under some of the shocks in the fields. They put them there because it's pretty hard to go find beer in a 40-acre field unless you go dig under every shock. Many people made their own beer back then.

Folks enjoying prohibition times

My folks had to be really careful. The feds were watching them bad. The reason for this is because my Uncle Barney was bootlegging and the feds were on to him. He would come to our place to get his stash ready to sell. I'm 93 now, born in 1920, and this was during prohibition, so I was a little shaver. There were a lot of bootleggers in my area. I even remember most of their names. Barney would get his moonshine in Saint Cloud, Minnesota. He had a contact there. I remember that guy, too. They would have it hidden in manure piles in small wooden kegs and dig them out. He'd come back in an old coupe car with the kegs in the back. The kegs were never used again because it would be pointless to risk getting caught with empty kegs. I remember breaking them up and using the wooden slats for skis.

The moonshine was a faint yellow and the alcohol was clear, just like water. Barney would "cut" them both using only distilled water. This was done to decrease the alcohol content, which was pretty high, and to make it stretch further. The reason he used distilled water is because if you shook the mixture it would not bubble, so the water was not detectable. I can picture it in my mind. I am still in the kitchen on the farm northeast of Castlewood (South Dakota) watching him fill bottles—half pint and pint. After he bottled it, he sold it. He would get orders sometimes. How he got them I can't tell you. Whether by telephone or messenger, I don't know.

Now, a lot of the roads were dirt. Not even gravel, just dirt. They would "mark" the drop spots. For example, there might be a big rut in the road. Someone would take a rock and put it in a rut on the road and the alcohol would be in the field across from the rock. There were other kinds of marks, too, but I remember the rock ones the best. He never sold from my folk's place, ever. He would always sell elsewhere, like Kranzburg (South Dakota), which was known as a bootleg town.

The feds watched Barney, so that meant they watched our place, too. They could come into a home to search, but they had to be really sure they would find something or it was considered an invasion of privacy. They never came into our house, but I remember them coming on the place. I was questioned twice. I was maybe about six or seven years old. I was coached. "Is your uncle here?" "No." "Where is he?" "I don't know. I haven't seen him." Barney would be sleeping upstairs.

One time after Barney mixed all the stuff in the kitchen at the folks, he accidently left the keg with some in it in the house. He usually took the kegs and got rid of them. My folks didn't know what to do with it. They didn't want to take it outside because they knew the feds might be watching. So, they opened their "mattress," which in those days was just heavy cloth with straw in it. They put the keg in the mattress between them for the night. It was long remembered and made everyone laugh

25

how all night the keg went "glug, glug" every time they rolled over in bed. Not everyone can say they slept with a keg of bootleg liquor!

I remember a pickup one time when Barney stashed some kegs in my folk's straw pile. My Dad found out a friend of Barney's, who was not quite trustworthy, knew about it. As I said, there were quite a few bootleggers in the area, and they all knew each other. They were all more or less friends, but the rule was that a bootlegger was his own friend. Dad said to get rid of the kegs. Barney didn't think there would be a problem, but he did as Dad said. Dad took one keg and hid it, Barney took another, and a different friend took the third with him. The next morning when we got up, the straw pile was completely flat and scattered. The feds had been there in the night.

I liked Barney. He always kept store bought plain ginger ale at our place. I liked it, and that is what I always drank for a treat. I remember once Barney gave me a dollar bill. The bill was larger back then—big and wide. I don't remember what happened to it. Most likely the folks needed it. It was tough times back then. Good times, but tough.

Jennie and the Chicken Thieves
By Gail Roe of Hazel, South Dakota
Born 1944

During the 1930s, every farm wife had a garden, a milk cow, and chickens. The animals were an important economical part of every household, deserving of good care. Traveling salesmen and chicken thieves were also part of the landscape, sometimes combining the sale of bowls with stealing the chickens. Anyway, these salesmen weren't really very smart. Not when it came to dealing with a certain Jennie Lakness, a lady who knew her chicks as well as she knew her two small children.

One day, a nice Model A sedan with two men inside drove into the Lakness farmyard, located south of Henry, South Dakota. The car pulled to a stop in the middle of the yard. One man got out, reached into the car, and brought out some very nice looking glass bowls, the type that any good cook could mix bread in. He went on and on about the merits of the bowls, how pretty and strong they were. He said they could even be dropped on the ground and they wouldn't break. To demonstrate this

wonderful feature, he even dropped one on the ground and by golly, it did not break. Jennie did not buy the demonstration or the bowls.

After these two gentlemen left the yard, Jennie got to thinking as to where the second man had spent his time while the first fellow was doing his sales pitch. She checked the chicken house. Her chickens were gone!

She stuffed the kids into the car and drove like a wild woman the one mile over to the neighbor's farm. Even before the car had come to a complete stop, she hopped right out, ripped the wonderful bowl right out of the hands of the salesman, and smashed it against the fender of his car, sending glass flying everywhere. The other villain was caught in the chicken house, gathering up the neighbor's chickens.

Hell hath no fury like an angry Norwegian lady! Jennie demanded that they give back her chickens and get out of there. The neighbor lady and the salesmen/thieves were so surprised that they couldn't move. Peeling out of the yard, a crate of chickens was left behind for Jennie and the neighbor lady to divide. Perhaps the thieves were "scared straight."

Jennie Lakness was my mother. She was born in 1905 and passed away in 2005, just before her 100th birthday. She told us before her death that she didn't want to be 100; it was just too much work! She died on the same day that my father had died on 32 years earlier. I think she had it all planned!

Farmer's Club in the 1950s
By Clark Hanson of Watertown, South Dakota
Born 1948

Lakeview School District #3 was located in Codington County about seven miles northwest of Watertown, South Dakota. It was a pristine country school with outdoor toilets, an outdoor well from which the drinking water was hand pumped, and a flagpole, which flew Old Glory each day school, was in session. In a single room with 25-35 students, one classroom teacher taught grades one through eight readin,' writin,' 'rithmetic, and the rest of the basic studies of the time.

On alternate Friday nights through the winter months in the late 1950s, the

Lakeview #3's student body in 1954

schoolhouse would be standing room only with the entire neighborhood getting together for an evening of camaraderie and fun. The meetings were called the "Farmer's Club," and the parents and grandparents present at the meetings were the people that Tom Brokaw wrote about in his book "The Greatest Generation." They were hard working, quick to laugh, slow to judge, and would never turn down a stranger in need.

It was at one of these meetings where for the first time in my life I witnessed a grown man break down and cry. He had been presented a neighborhood monetary collection as a result of a terrible fire at his family home. The meeting protocol was always the same: minutes of the last meeting, a short entertainment program presented by one of the member families, and then a grand lunch. There were no store bought goodies at this lunch table—only homemade recipes of treats so delicious that most of the tin pans were emptied in short order. The farmers would talk crops, winter, the newest farm equipment, and one always knew when a good joke was told by the sudden eruption of laughter from the men gathered at the back of the room.

Farmers Club was an exciting time for a ten-year-old boy. Together with my buddies, we played tag in the dusty basement and tried our best to impress the girls from the neighboring country school. The most fun was harassing our older siblings who had gone out to their cars to listen to the local football or basketball team on KWAT radio. Buddy Holley or Elvis could be heard from some of the cars with antennas capable of capturing the great KOMA station out of Oklahoma. It was a wonderful time to grow up in America, and much life learning was taking place for us youngsters—the first crush, the pubescent

feuds, and maybe even that first kiss. The evening would end with our parents coming out the schoolhouse door and making the drive home on snowy, gravel roads.

Our Farmers Club was a snapshot of America at its best and was the realized promise our founding fathers envisioned for their creation. The numbers of the greatest generation are dwindling rapidly. To those of you still living and all that have passed on: we thank you for your guidance and the wonderful example of how to live a life!

A Glimpse Through Grandma's Window
By Steve Riedel of Huron, South Dakota
Born 1954

When my stiff, old fingers tingle, I remember a warm, sunny day on our family farm near Ramona, South Dakota. My older brother and I were playing in my grandparent's large, white farmhouse while Grandma was busy making our noon meal.

"If anyone wants to see the horses hitched one last time, they better come quick," Grandma shouted from the pantry. The excitement in her voice rang all the way into the living room where we boys were playing. Since I had never heard Grandma, a petite and soft-spoken person, do so much as raise her voice before, her shout quickly captured my attention. I looked at my brother. "Let's go!" I said eagerly as I started toward the kitchen.

My brother hesitated. Having worked with the horses many times, he mumbled, "I've seen them enough." I heard his comment and now, torn between Grandma's excitement and my brother's indifference, I froze in my tracks. When Grandma saw that no one went to the window, she was overcome by a sudden sadness. "This is the last time Grandpa is going to work them," she said with a downcast tone in her voice.

For some reason, a reason I could not understand, Grandma wanted us to share in this moment. Her unspoken, "please, come look" drew me away from my brother and into the kitchen, where I was greeted by a cruel twist of fate. Too small to see over the window sill, too small to look down the gentle slope toward the gravel driveway where the horses would be, all I could do was gaze upward into the bright blue sky! Dejected, I stepped hesitantly closer to the window and reaching high, slipped my tiny fingers over the sill. With a tenuous hold, I pulled upward in hopes of getting my eyes high enough to see the horses. My slender arms trembled, and my little fingers lost their hold. My feet hit the floor without me getting as much as a glimpse through Grandma's window.

"I want to see the horses!" I said to myself. More determined than ever, I grabbed the sill again and this time held tighter and pulled even harder. My arm muscles grew tense as my little chin rose. Up and up it went until, sliding over the windowsill and there, like a coat hanger, it helped support my weight. I could see Grandpa's horses!

Coal black and standing only twenty yards beyond Grandma's kitchen window, Dick and Lady looked monstrous. Long leather straps were strung everywhere between them and a wooden wagon filled high with loose prairie hay. While the giant horses stood motionless as if stuck in time under draping fly blankets, I struggled to keep my grip on the sill. All too soon, my arms trembled again and just as my strength faltered, Lady twitched her leg, probably to shoo gathering flies. My chin slipped from the sill and my feet fell back to the floor. A sharp pain tingled in my fingertips.

"What will happen to the horses? Will they be slaughtered?" someone, maybe my mother, asked.

"Oh, no!" Grandma answered. The tone in her voice said that such an ending for Dick and Lady was unthinkable. "Grandpa sold them to a man who still needs a working team out west. Good teams are hard to find, you know."

"Good," someone else said. Even though Grandma had assured us that the horses would be fine, a heavy regret, one beyond a child's understanding, lingered in the farmhouse. A few days later, at a time when I didn't see, the horses disappeared and though there were still cows in the pasture, the green expanse of South Dakota prairie seemed empty to me.

Now, many years later, I understand

Steve's father with a team of horses

the sadness in Grandma's voice. She knew Grandpa had decided to retire along with the horses that day. Shortly after Dick and Lady were sold, my grandparents moved to town and their house became our house. Their time on the family farm had come and gone; an era had passed. Of course, Grandma and Grandpa came to help around the farm from time to time. On those days, I'd rush to Grandpa's lap. If he didn't have a half-stick of Black Jack Gum to give me as a treat, he'd let me fish his railroad watch from the pocket in his bib overalls. I'd hold the shiny pocket watch tight to my ear and listen closely to the rapid "tick, tick, tick, tick." Time flies by so fast. Today, when my old fingers tingle, I remember fondly my glimpse through Grandma's window.

Mama and Her Turkeys
By Mary Lou Fluegel Beath of Evansville, Wisconsin
Born 1934

Mama ordered five hundred baby chicks at the Sioux Falls hatchery along in March each spring. The hatchery would call out to the farm when they had her order ready to fill. We would drive into the city to pick up five big, square, low, flat boxes with air holes and four sections each. Inside were round, little furry cheepers, all fuzzy and sweet. One year as Mama stood counting out her chicken money to pay the bill, a bigger box of furry fowl caught her eye.

28

"What are those?" she asked. "Turkeys," came the answer.

She must have had a few extra dollars and six baby turkeys were boxed up along with the brooders and came on home. They were at least twice the size of a baby chick and twice as ugly! Mama didn't seem to mind, and they got treated even better than the chickens. They had the run of the house yard, something no chickens ever had except setting hens on eggs. They had their own barrels beside the summer kitchen and shared dishes and tidbits with the cats.

Sometime between cute babyhood and adulthood, three of the turkeys didn't survive. That left us with Tom, Dick, and Harriet. They, much like lambs, thought we were their mama and daddy and followed us around the yard, making odd teenaged gobbles. Their downy furry look was soon covered by motley-looking feathers. When we wanted to call down to the guys at the barn, those pesky birds would raise a noise that was impossible to yell over or hear back over. When company would drive up, they would flock to the yard gate and set up such a ruckus the company was held at bay until one of us would come out, shoo away those ugly pugly turks and help the people or person into the safe porch area. We had more of a guard dog than just Major. Now we had guard turkeys!

One day Mother brought a pan of garden lettuce to the cement seat area around the cistern. She pumped up a pan of water and placed the lettuce on her right, the water pan in her lap to wash the lettuce leaf by leaf, and an empty pan on her left to receive the ready to eat lettuce. She went about this often done task without much concern or thought, and her mind was on other things. When she reached the end of the lettuce to be washed, she reached for the cleaned lettuce pan. To her surprise, there wasn't a leaf of lettuce in that pan. She had gotten used to those three turkeys right by her all the time and hadn't noticed what they were pecking away at. What they were doing was taking each leaf of lettuce she put in the 'all clean' pan and putting it one step farther, down on the ground beside the cistern. They were helping her. Some help!

They "helped" me one day, too. During summer time when it was wash day, Mama heated the wash water, filled the machine, and put the white load in first to be rub-a-dubbed around. Then together we would put those sheets, pillow cases, and other whites through the wringer. She would have me guide the clothes into the blue rinse water and during the next step; we would get the rinsed clothes into a wicker laundry basket. Then it was my job, alone, to take the basket out to the clotheslines that were between poles out east of the house. I could barely reach the lines to get the sheets up and push the clothespins down to hold the sheets above the grass. Five sheets seemed like a big job, and then came the easier little stuff. Pretty soon, I went back in to be ready to put the second load of darks through the rinse and into the basket. I carried the second load out the door and looked up with pride at my well-hung whites. But to my dismay, the sheets, pillowcases, dish towels, and white shirts and blouses were all on the ground. There at the very end of one line were the turkeys, up on the wire, pulling out the last few clothespins from the things at that end of the line. They were "helping" me. I nearly cried. Mama had heard my astonished cry and had just caught a glimpse of the turkey caper as she came out to see what was wrong. She laughed until the tears rolled down her cheeks. Those darn turkeys were getting too smart for their britches.

It, of course, had been her intention in the beginning to raise our own Thanksgiving dinner, and maybe have Christmas dinner too. But as more and more stories of those turkey capers piled up and those darned bird brains endeared themselves as pets, it became more and more certain they would never face a hatchet on our chopping block. We purchased a dressed turkey from Piggly Wiggly for our own table and eventually, Mama gave Tom, Dick, and Harriet to willing, non-involved neighbors who had no heartstrings attached. That was the last year, the only year, Mama raised turkeys.

"I Got That Fat Man in the Red Suit Tied Up in the Barn. That Son of a Biscuit Won't Get Away!"
By Dorothy Graves of Aberdeen, South Dakota
Born 1943

I remember a blizzard on the farm at Verdan, South Dakota, I think in early 1950

29

Dorothy's parents, Arlyle and Leland with Dorothy and her sister Connie in 1950

or '49. My dad ran a rope from the barn to the back door of the house. We held on to the rope when we went out to milk the cows twice a day, and feed all the animals that were put in the barn. There were two horses, calves, sheep, and pigs. One time I let go of the rope and panicked, realizing how a person could wander off the path and get lost.

The barn smelled so good from the hay we pushed down the holes and it was warm from all the animals' body heat. We also carried water to the animals. In the house, we had three lambs. Their pens were cardboard boxes and rags for bedding. We took turns feeding them every 2 hours until we could put them back in the barn. The rope stayed up all winter.

My dad was always buying and selling animals. He had a 1949 International pickup with a homemade wooden box to keep cattle from jumping out. He began to tell us he was going to see "a man about a horse" when he left for the sales barn. We had lost Dolly— one of our horses—and wanted a pony so we could raise it. We always got excited when he left and disappointed when he came home

with sheep, pigs, a goat, another cow, or some calves. We (my sister and I) wanted a pony so bad and had heard it about a year, and we were saying, "Ya, right."

We had another horse named Daisy, a big horse. She let 3 of us kids get on her, bareback. She gave us a ride but would only go a mile from home, then turn quick and, of course, all three were in the ditch. Daisy went home and pushed the door open with her nose, and was standing in the stall waiting for oats.

I was painting one of the sheds with red paint. Dad came home and I saw something move in the pickup. Dad called us to come to the pickup. We climbed up and saw a pony, 9 months old, with a large cut from below her right eye to the left nostril. She had been kicked by another horse so Dad washed out the cut, then he let flies lay eggs and stay in the wound. I thought it was terrible and he let it go for a month. One day he put axel grease in the wound and outside the wound, and then he put sulfur in the wound. In 2 months, the pony healed and had no scar. We named her Smoky and Dad paid $9 for the beautiful Tennessee Walker, so no ride on her was ever bad.

When it was Christmas time, there was so much excitement and anticipating with baking and making gifts and shopping at the five and dime stores in Aberdeen, SD: Chaffins, Woolworth, NewBerrys, Kresgies, Sears, and Montgomery Ward's. We would come as a family to shop and would go to the movies while Mom and Dad did some business. Then Mom came to get us, and then we went home. Back on the farm, on Christmas Eve we went to church, and after supper Dad would go to the barn to milk and feed the cows.

We heard bells, and then he came in with

Connie on the big horse, Daisy and Dorothy riding Smokey the smaller horse

the milk to be pasteurized, and announced, "I got that fat man in the red suit tied up in the barn. That son of a biscuit won't get away!" We became upset and begged him to let him go, because all the other kids needed to have their gifts delivered. Come Christmas morning he announced, "He got away." We always would look for reindeer hoof prints, sleigh marks, and Santa's footprints in the snow.

We always, in the spring, had chickens, ducks, and geese. We would get about 3-4 boxes of baby chicks from the Inman Hatchery in Aberdeen and 1 box of ducklings. They were placed in the middle of the back seat between my sister and I. We would stick our fingers in the holes and they nibbled on them. Then they were put in the chicken coop with heat lamps, fresh water, and feed trays. We had a pair of geese, and when it was nesting and mating time, we would be chased by the gander. I hated that but we sure got our exercise running!

One of my jobs was to gather the eggs daily. We had some setting hens, which would bite your arm or hand so I would use a stick to push their head away. In the winter, I wore gloves. Sometimes the chickens, in the summer, would lay eggs under the hayrack or drill or disc, and when I found them 2 days later, they sure stunk and I would throw them into the pigpen with my sister, but we had to break them to not put them in with the good ones. We sold eggs and cream to the town neighbors. We also hauled cream to Conde or Groton to be sold to the creamery. This was family money. I did not get paid for working on the farm.

Experiences, Observations, and Reflections from an Ordinary Life
By David Sveum of Arvada, Colorado
Born 1930

I am the son of parents who were a farmer and farmer's wife and was born at Peabody Hospital in Webster, South Dakota. Herbert Hoover was then President and our country was experiencing the Great Depression. I was born shortly after those Tom Brokaw referred to as being the "greatest generation." I grew to adulthood on my parents' farm about 12 miles south of Webster.

I am indebted to caring parents who had good values that passed them on to me and my siblings. My parents worked hard to earn a living and they encouraged me to do my best in everything that I tried. They also trained me to be a responsible person. I was my grandparents' first grandchild. They lived nearby, so I visited them often while I was in elementary school. They were proud of me and encouraged me during my early formative years. My family makes me proud and affirms my belief that life is good. The good people that I have had the privilege of knowing and spending time with give me faith that things work out for ordinary people who do their best each day.

Each member of our family helped accomplish the farm work when I was growing up. The work was hard but satisfying, and helped me and my three siblings develop good work ethics that served us well later in life. We were so busy during our childhood that we didn't have time to get into any significant trouble. We learned to use it up, wear it out, make it do, or sometimes do without. We were also frugal in selecting the things we purchased. However, we were never so poor that we went without real necessities. Some of this conservatism has stayed with me and serves me well during the current economy. Norwegians are a little stiff and typically didn't show much emotion; that was true for us. We were not a hugging and kissing family, but our actions made it obvious that we cared for each other.

During the years I attended elementary and high schools, our family life outside of studies concentrated on the farm work that needed to be done and the activities my brother and sisters and I participated in. Each of us took part in some farm activities including planting and harvesting, milking, gardening, cooking, cleaning, or other farm chores. There were church and 4-H activities, FFA projects, and other activities requiring the parents' participation.

Being the oldest child in the family had both benefits and disadvantages. I was given lots of responsibility early, but occasionally had to stay home to take care of farm chores while the rest of the family went visiting or on short sightseeing trips. I understood why this arrangement was necessary, but it limited my opportunities to participate in some fun things with the rest of the family.

We enjoyed doing simple, practical things. We had our own eggs, cream and ice in the winter, so we often made ice cream. We used half-milk, half-cream, eggs, sugar and vanilla to make our homemade ice cream. We cut down a small tree from our grove of evergreen trees my grandfather had planted or cut a branch from one of the large trees, which we then decorated to help us celebrate Christmas. This was more practical than buying a tree for Christmas.

I was in elementary school when the United States entered World War II after the Japanese attacked Pearl Harbor on December 7, 1941. Members of our farm community were patriotic and fully supported the war effort. Gas was rationed during the war and it was difficult to buy overalls, sugar, and many other things that make everyday life comfortable. The father of one of my classmates owned a truck, and one Saturday the students from our rural elementary school loaded it with scrap iron from obsolete horse-drawn farm machinery stored in our neighbor's yards. The truckload of scrap iron was then donated to help support the war effort.

Horses played an important role in my early life and I started driving and riding them when I was very young. My father harnessed a team of gentle, well-trained horses and had me drive them mowing hay starting when I was very young. He kept a close eye on me in case I had trouble and needed help. The horses were experienced at pulling the mower and walked next to the standing hay, so they didn't need much steering by me. I rode one of our draft horses for a few years until my father purchased a young, spirited, green broke, riding horse for me when I was in the eighth grade. I never owned a saddle, so I rode horses "bareback" often with friends on Sunday afternoons for inexpensive entertainment.

I drove horses pulling a grain binder and then helped pick up the tied bundles by hand and placed them in shocks. I drove a team of horses hitched to a hayrack and hauled bundles during two threshing seasons when I was 17 and 18 years old. I was the youngest hauler on the crew. The hayrack bottom was 12 feet by 8 feet and had rubber tires mounted on steel rims welded to steel hubs. I loaded the bundles, hauled them to a threshing machine, and then pitched them one at a time into the

David and his sister, Joanne riding the horse with his cousin, John Lee holding the rein

threshing machine feeder. There were ten farms on our threshing run and we all worked together, so I sometimes had to drive the horses a few miles to get to the farm where we were working. Ten of us were bundle haulers and we each hauled about eight loads per day. This was hard work for someone as young as I was. It took some skill to load the bundles into the hayrack so they were parallel to each other. This made them easier to unload. I tried to drive my team of horses so they pulled the rack as close to the feeder as possible without hitting it to make it easier for me to unload my bundles into the feeder. My father purchased a combine the following year, which made harvesting much easier.

So, for my concluding remarks, I want to pass on some values, traditions and guidance based on my life experiences. I have witnessed wars and terrorist activities against our country by evildoers, advances in computing technology from paper and pencil to the slide rule in college, electronic calculators, computers and the internet; a telephone communication system that our farm neighbors owned and operated to several choices of service providers; and the mechanization and demise of the small family farm. During my adult working career, I lived several places. This taught me to be flexible about where to live because different places offer different opportunities. I learned something new at each office where I worked, so these moves made me technically and mentally stronger.

Someone has said your life story is revealed by the way you live and we leave footprints where we have been. Everyone should develop some sort of plan for their life. I have learned a good plan is to get a good education or other training to increase the range of employment opportunities that may become available. My hope and priorities for my children and grandchildren is for them to develop good values, obtain a college education or develop a unique skill, to be happy with peace of mind, and have reasonable financial security. You can learn to enjoy many occupations, so do something that provides a decent living. Sometimes opportunities that you never dreamed about can present themselves if you are goal-oriented and well organized.

Religious faith is the source of meaning and values, so it should provide a framework for living and help you decide what to do. The great UCLA basketball Coach, John Wooden, has defined success as being: the peace of mind that is the direct result of self-satisfaction in knowing you did your best to become the best you are capable of becoming. I realize that I can't change the world in a major way, so I would characterize my philosophy as: be responsible and try to do well in whatever job or activity you choose to participate in, or find something you want to do and work hard at it with enthusiasm. Focus and determination are often more important than brilliance and sometimes ordinary people can do extraordinary things.

I have always retained an interest in farming and ranching, which is evident from what I have written even though I chose a different career. The solid base values of my life were formed while I was growing up and involved with the farm. During retirement, I developed a passion for performing genealogic research based on thoughts expressed by two unknown Authors: *A life undocumented is lost after one generation*, and *A family tree can wither if nobody tends its roots*. I hope this discussion about some experiences, observations, and reflections from an ordinary life have been interesting and encourage you to write your own memoirs someday.

Working and Playing on the Farm
By Roger Goens of Volga, South Dakota
Born 1954

When I was in school we lived on a farm and had no running water. We did have a cistern with a hand pump in a back porch and we also had two other wells on the farm. The cistern we used only for washing clothes and

ourselves. We used water from the wells for drinking and cooking. It was an endless chore hauling water in and then hauling slop pails out. We would always take a bath on Saturday nights. We just had a washtub from the old wringer washer that we would use. We would start with the youngest and go to the oldest. I was lucky because I was the middle of three boys and my dad was lucky because it was just us three boys and my mom ahead of him. Water had to be warmed up on the stove. We had a range, but we also had an old wood stove that always had a teakettle on it for warm water. On bath nights, water was warmed in canners so we would have a little extra. It was a happy day when my Dad brought home an oblong tub that he had bought on an auction sale. Bath day got a little better after that.

Our only bathroom was the outhouse or I guess with all us boys anywhere outside was good. I remember that outhouse wasn't very airtight. In the wintertime after a blizzard you would have to brush the snow off the seat before sitting down. It would be so cold! In the summer it was okay to have a little extra airflow, but then the flies would be so bad. I remember it also getting a little full and that was nasty. My dad or mom would keep putting lye in there to try and eat it down a little, but it was only a matter of time before something had to be done. Dad told us boys to start digging a new hole not too far from the old outhouse. He staked it out and we went to work. It was hard digging, but we wanted to make sure the new one wouldn't fill up in a long time. We ended up digging that hole about 6 feet deep. It took us a while, but we got it done.

One day when we came home from school the outhouse was moved over the new hole and the old hole was leveled and filled in with new dirt. We couldn't have been happier! No more having to witness that mess right under the seat. Six foot down worked for us and we never had another problem. I don't know how my dad got that thing moved in one piece and then had to deal with that old mess. I'm just glad I wasn't there having to help.

I loved life on the farm. This was all back in the late '50s and early '60s. We never lacked for something to do when we weren't working at something for my dad. There was always adventures of some kind. We played in the hay barn a lot when the weather wasn't very good outside. We had loose hay in the barn so we had piles of hay to jump on. It was also a favorite spot for all the farm cats so we would try and find them and sometimes we would find their kittens. They would always be gone the next day though because the mother cat must not have liked us playing with them. We always had horses too, so in the good weather we was always riding them exploring somewhere. Sometimes we would get together with neighbors that had horses and pretend we were buffalo hunters or old west cowboys on a long trail ride. Of course sometimes we would be outlaws and somebody else would be the sheriff and deputies. We would all have quite the imaginations.

Dad was always set in the old ways of doing things, so there was always plenty of work to do on the farm also. We put up all our hay, loose in stacks or loose into the haymow. This was always interesting because we would load the hay on a hayrack by hand. Before we started loading we would put down slings. Then when we got to the barn we would pull the rack under the big barn door. Then we would have to open the big door by hooking the old A John Deere to a long rope that went from one end of the mow to the other and then down into the main barn and then through the barn out the door. We would then have to unhook the big door and back the tractor up real slow so the door wouldn't slam down against the barn. After that we would hook the slings up to the big rope and pull the hay up into the barn. We would pull the first loads way to the back and then there was a way to unhook or trip one side of the sling somehow so the hay would drop out of the sling. That was the fun part. Loading the racks was a lot of work even for us boys when we were quite young. The other hay we would put up in big square stacks.

Us kid's job was to move the hay around and keep everything going up straight. Some people had stack frames to keep everything right, but not at our farm. Then in the fall, we would have a guy come and move the stacks into the yard close to where we would feed them. Our dad was probably the last farmer in Hamlin County to still thresh grain instead of combining. We were helping cut grain with a binder at quite a young age, probably 10 or 11. We would drive the old A John Deere while Dad sat on the binder and run that.

After everything was cut, we would then all go out and shock the grain so it could be threshed later. Since not many farmers harvested this way anymore we would always get plenty of visitors once we started threshing. Dad would put an electric fence around the straw pile to keep the cattle away, but let the pigs go up and tunnel in and around it. That is where our sows would have their little pigs and it seemed to work well. Dad would usually know when a sow had pigs because she would come out to eat and then head right back to the straw pile. A lot of times he would have me crawl into the little tunnel and count how many piglets a sow had. I think I always got this job because my brothers were too afraid the sow would catch them in there. I had faith that my dad wouldn't let that happen so in I would go only staying long enough to count the little pigs. We never knew for sure how many were born and how many were lost, but they seemed to do quite well in the old straw pile.

In the spring, there was always plenty of rock to pick as well as fences to mend and animals to feed and take care of. Another job I didn't care for too much was castrating little pigs and lambs. My job was to hold the little pigs and it seemed like dad always waited too long letting the pigs get too big because it was quite a chore to hang onto them with dad yelling at me to hold them still. Another job I always seemed to get was holding the trouble light while dad was fixing a piece of equipment. I could never seem to get that quite right either because dad was always yelling at me to get the light out of his eyes and get it pointed at whatever he was working on. I did the same things to my kids later on.

When I started 1st grade we went to a little country school. One teacher taught 1st through 8th grades. I remember we walked to school if it was nice enough. Nice enough was above zero and not a lot of wind. It was about 2 ½ miles to school. If the weather was thought to be bad enough my dad or the neighbors would give us a ride to school. I remember a little creek just to the south and down the hill from our schoolhouse. We would spend a lot of time down there during recess. We would skate on the ice and play different games, which I really don't remember anymore. A lot of them were just made up I think. I do remember falling through the ice in the spring one time. I thought I was a goner for sure, but only went up to my waist and I was only in 1st grade so the water wasn't very deep. The teacher wasn't very happy about it either, but she put my desk by the old oil burner stove so I would dry out before it was time to go home. Then I got scolded at home and was told to stay away from that creek.

I also remember the first day of school; I was so proud of all my school supplies. I had a big pink eraser that somehow got knocked off my desk that first morning when I was putting things away and went bouncing up towards the teacher's desk. The teacher caught a glimpse of that eraser out the corner of her eye and jumped clear on top of her desk screaming thinking it was a mouse. She wasn't very happy and wanted to know who threw that eraser. Even at that young age I thought it best to keep my mouth shut, so I lost my nice eraser on the first day of school. It must have really been traumatic for me because I still remember it. The next year they closed that little country school and we had to go to town school. That was a new experience for us. They had indoor plumbing at town school so that took a little getting used to. Overall though it was a good experience, because we got to meet a lot more other kids and make more friends. I wouldn't want to change a thing growing up and working and playing on the farm. It was a great experience!

The Farmhouse
By Betty Jean Fisher of Britton, South Dakota
Born 1933

They're mostly gone now—those venerable, L-shaped, two-storied home structures that farm families called "home." They once dotted the landscape of eastern South Dakota's fertile cropland with farm families living closely enough together to form their own little "township" neighborhoods, complete with rural schools and sometimes churches. These simple, no-nonsense farm homes were constructed as utilitarian shelter against the extreme heat and cold of this prairie environment.

Because of the scarcity of building materials and for heating efficiency, most farmhouses were quite small, the largest room being the kitchen—the "heart of the home." This room required space to accommodate the gathering of family, neighbors, "hired men," as well as the space-consuming wood and corncob-burning cast iron cook stove. The cook stove, which replaced the traditional fireplace, still required a chimney. The heat created by the stove was a comfort in cold weather, but something to be endured in the heat of summer.

In addition to the kitchen, the house was comprised of a smaller living room, often dominated by a space-heating stove, and an even smaller bedroom with room for little more than a bed. To benefit from the living room's stove, these bedrooms were sometimes enclosed by just a curtain.

A narrow, steep, enclosed staircase led to the second floor room, which was usually left unfinished with exposed rafters and wall studs, and which provided additional sleeping space. There was no central heat in these farmhouses, and no indoor plumbing. An outhouse and a chamber pot under the bed had to suffice. And, until the rural areas received electricity, some as late as the 1950s, kerosene lamps, and lanterns served as the sources of light.

My maternal grandparents lived in a house as I just described. By the time I came along, the upstairs contained little of interest except a steamer trunk that my immigrant grandmother had brought from England. As a child, I spent exciting hours exploring its contents, which included beaded purses and a fully beaded Indian moccasin tongue. (I've often wondered what happened to the rest of that moccasin and how that tongue came to be in that trunk.)

I find these old farmhouses, relics of another time, fascinating. As I've wandered through many such homes, long abandoned, floors littered with falling debris and with the smell of decay, I've tried to envision the families once sheltered there. I've wondered how the sometimes large families managed in so little space. I've thought about the laughter and the tears, the struggles and hard work, the celebrations with family and friend that these walls once knew, and I've thought: If only these walls could talk.

As difficult and demanding as rural life could be for these farm families, they did take time to celebrate life, especially in the bleak winter months, fellowshipping together on a regular basis. My husband, who as a child was present at such gatherings, recalls that, taking turns hosting, the neighbors would start out the evening playing cards and would eventually roll up the rug and dance to the fiddle music supplied by his father. There was a lunch provided, which usually included ice cream, as there was no lack of cream or ice. (Each farm family had its own milk cow and cream separator.) The children, when sleepy, curled up on a bed loaded with guests' coats and drifted off to the hum of voices. I, myself, experienced this warm, cozy feeling on a bed of coats when our "town" family was invited to a rural gathering.

Remembering rural life then, these farmhouses speak of the brave, hard-working people who built and lived in them. They are testaments of the hardships these courageous farm families endured, overcoming unbelievable obstacles to settle this often hostile environment, paving the way for future generations. I experience an overwhelming sense of pride and appreciation for their sacrifices, and am challenged, as a daughter of the prairie, to exhibit the same courage and endurance as they exemplified.

Feeling the way I do, it is not hard to understand why I chose to rescue not one, but two such deserted farmhouses. The rescue of the first one came about in an unexpected way:

In the early 1960s, I was driving home from a neighboring town, and there it was! I had passed this way before, but on this day, my attention became focused on a particular abandoned farmhouse. Even in its weathered, unpainted condition, there was something welcoming and stately about it. It was in the "farmhouse" style, but was larger, fully two and a half storied.

In the absence of a "no-trespassing" sign, I stopped the car and eagerly set out to explore it. I found an unlocked downstairs window and climbed through. As I went from room to room, I became more and more excited, as the house contained so many features I value in a home—bay windows, an open stairway, and a large kitchen. The only feature I found lacking was a fireplace.

As my farmer husband and I were expecting our first child, it was time to move from town to the country. I instinctively knew this would be the perfect home for us. My husband was in agreement, and together we sought out the owner, bought the house (for under $2,000.00), and engaged a house mover who moved the house 16 miles to its present location.

It was set down on what was, until then, a bare oat field. It was set back from the highway to be reached by a winding drive. Painted colonial yellow with white trim and black shutters, and with window boxes filled with red geraniums, the house took on new life. Framed by evergreen trees we were quick to plant, it was to become a "Currier and Ives"-type showpiece and landmark, admired by many.

The interior, also, lived up to my expectations, requiring few structural changes. The kitchen cook stove chimney was removed. The basement stairway was moved to a newly-weatherized, back entry, leaving a perfect niche for the kitchen range. Surrounded by brick-patterned wall covering with a shelf above, this niche took on the ambiance of a fireplace, providing a place to display my antique cooking utensils.

Sliding doors separating the living and dining rooms were removed to widen the opening. Such "pocket" doors were designed to close off the "parlor" and were usually opened only for special guests and occasions. A large pantry off the kitchen was converted into a handy bathroom with ample shelving. With the installation of new bathroom fixtures upstairs, and the installation of central heating, the renovation was nearly complete.

The last structural change was the addition of a rosy-brick fireplace on an outside living room wall. This fireplace proved its worth during a fierce three-day spring blizzard that took out the electrical power. We hung a quilt in the doorway to conserve heat, spread mattresses on the floor, and huddled day and night around this fireplace, our only source of heat. My collection an antique cookware was again put to use, cooking over the open fire.

This was not a "cozy" experience, as one might romanticize, but was uncomfortable and even threatening. The fireplace demanded a constant supply of wood, which meant my husband, had to go outside where the howling wind had created a "whiteout." As a safety precaution, he used an attached rope to ensure he'd find his way back. This experience gave me a good taste of life in these farmhouses before central heating—of how the cold creeps in around the edges.

The interior of the house was decorated with fresh paint, wallpaper, curtains, and rugs. Except for the kitchen, the woodwork was painted white, giving the interior a bright, somewhat elegant look. It was furnished with antique and traditional furnishings in keeping with the style and period of the house. The overall effect was one of comfort and coziness, with touches of elegance such as the crystal chandelier my husband and I bought with wedding gift money.

An ample walnut drop-leaf table, which was revealed by prior owners as having come to Dakota in a covered wagon, sat in the center of the kitchen. It was the scene of countless meals, children's homework, visits over coffee and homemade goodies, and much, much more. In the summer, it might have held a brown crockery pitcher of brightly-colored zinnias, and at Christmastime, an old kerosene lantern filled with red fuel and decorated with a green ribbon holding holiday greenery.

A comfortable pressed-wood rocker, to which guest gravitated, sat in the corner. The number of hours spent rocking our four babies in that chair cannot be calculated. Another special kitchen furnishing was an old "Hoosier" cabinet, which held all my baking supplies. It was valued not only for its convenience and charm, but because it had previously sat in my grandparents' farmhouse kitchen. (As a child, I would hopefully check it out for one of my uncle's delicious biscuits.)

Two of the five bedrooms were furnished with antique brass-trimmed iron beds covered with hand-pieced quilts. The one in my daughter's room was found while exploring an abandoned farmhouse on the banks of the James River. (The relatives were located, and they sold it to me for $12.00.)

On an antiquing adventure promoted by my father, I found and rescued an antique oak-mirrored, marble-topped sideboard, which was sold to me by an elderly owner of an abandoned general store. This sideboard graced the dining room, its shelves displaying my collection of plates with hand-painted roses. The dining room also held our annual traditionally-decorated Christmas tree, which was the first thing the children saw and smelled

when they descended the open stairway each morning.

The antique furnishings throughout the house gave it a connection to the past and a sense of permanence, which I found comforting. Once again, this old farmhouse had settled into its role of sheltering a farm family on the Dakota prairie. Once again, its walls echoed with the laughter of children, of music, and the buzz of activity. Once again, the kitchen held the aroma of baking bread, thanksgiving turkey, and gingerbread boys. And if this old house could have talked, I'm sure it would have "smiled" and said, "Thank you."

At this writing, the house is still lived in, still cared for. Our eldest son, the next generation farmer, makes it his home now. He honors its historic value, and makes any necessary changes in keeping with its original design. It still draws compliments, still serves as a landmark—that "big, yellow house on the corner."

And, in case you're wondering about the second farmhouse I rescued, it now serves as the family lake cottage, and is another story for another time…

The Last Years of an Era
By Elroy Dragsten of Buffalo, Minnesota
Born 1925

It seems that when we were young we had more work to do and greater responsibilities than most of the children have today. It may have been a difficult time for our parents during the Depression and drought of the '30s, but for me it was a great time and Wallace, South Dakota was a great place to grow up. We did not have OSHA, child labor laws, 40-hour weeks, child welfare, no driver's license, and we survived just fine.

My father, Peder Dragsten, owned a garage and machine shop. Every fall he would close up the garage to thresh. Dad also had a truck with a tank for hauling water to people's cisterns and steam threshing machines.

My mother, Inga Fiksdal Dragsten, was a stay-at-home mother. She had six children; Brother Arnold died in an accident. She was in poor health due to a gall bladder problem that was not diagnosed until she was older. I

Elroy and his cousin, Pearl Draxten

was the youngest, and when I was born, my mother was very sick and the job of caring for me became the responsibility of my eight-year-old sister, Irene. Brother Monroe was six and sister Ardes was 15 months. This was an awesome amount of responsibility for an eight year old. My ten-year-old brother, Palmer, started driving the water truck when he was nine and was busy working. He was the one who checked how much gasoline was in the tank by lighting a match. He survived but the truck didn't.

One of the earliest recollections that I have involves threshing. My dad was threshing at the Ted Moe farm south of Wallace. It was 1929. I was four years old. I spent the night in the caboose with Dad. The caboose was a bunkhouse on wheels where the engineer and separator man slept. This was a steam threshing machine, and they had to be close by to keep the fire going. I think the reason I remember this is because I was scared.

Every fall from the age of four on, I was involved with threshing. I would always get a chance to spend a couple of days riding with one of the bundle haulers. Usually I would get

to drive the horses or I would get on top of a truckload of grain and ride to the elevator in Wallace.

In 1933, I got my first opportunity to be an actual member of the threshing crew. They needed a truck driver to haul grain. The only one available was my 16-year-old sister, Irene. She protested but it was an emergency, and Dad said she had to. I was eight years old and was her willing and very happy assistant. I didn't understand why anyone would not want to be part of the threshing crew. To be allowed to sit at the same table and eat with the bundle haulers was a dream come true. It was hard work shoveling the grain out of the truck box, but I was proud I could help. The grain truck was a converted 1915 Marmon Limousine. The transmission was not synchronized. The only mishap we had was when we were near the top of a hill, and Irene tried to shift gears and missed. As we started rolling backward, I climbed out on the running board and told her which way to turn the wheel. Irene was shaken but unhurt, and we continued on our way. Incidentally, the brakes were worthless.

South Dakota did not require a driver's license, but I had driver's training. When I was nine years old my 15-year-old brother, Monroe, who I always admired but who was a renegade, came by the house and asked me to go along hauling water. The first thing he did was give me a cigarette. There we were, two kids going down the road smoking cigarettes. I was doing more choking and coughing than smoking. After delivering a tank of water and heading back to the well, Monroe stopped the truck and told me to drive so he could hunt pheasants. The truck was a 1927 Chevrolet with a 3-speed transmission and 2-speed differential. He showed me the shift pattern and then took his shotgun and sat on the front fender. I got the truck going, and Monroe started yelling, "Shift gears, shift gears." I looked down at the gearshift and ran in the ditch. I got back on the road and got it in second gear. He started yelling again, "Shift gears, shift gears." I looked down at the gearshift and again ended up in the ditch. I got back on the road and got the truck in high gear. I will have to say, you learn fast when you have someone with a shotgun hollering at you!

When I was 12 years old, I worked on the farm for my uncle, Andrew Dragsten. I helped with the chores: milking cows, feeding the chickens, and more. My main job was driving his homemade tractor. I did the summer plowing, pulling my uncle on a two-row cultivator and the binder. My uncle and aunt were nice people, but Andrew did have a quick temper and could swear in two languages. He would get mad at me, and he would use all the swear words he knew. When I was pulling the binder I would get even with him. With a little maneuvering I would make sure that the steel bull wheel would hit a lot of rocks. We were traveling about twice as fast as horse would walk. Andrew would bounce in the air and get a good jolt when he came back down on that steel seat. Due to the speed we were traveling the binder made a lot of racket, but I could hear Andrew going through his usual list of swear words. One evening, I overheard him telling his wife, Olga, that his back hurt and that it seemed like we hit every rock in the field, if he only knew. My salary was 25 cents a day. That fall when I was through working, I as happy to be paid $5.50, which was the most money I had ever had.

That fall my dad gave me the good news that I was to drive the water truck. I was to haul water for the Minton Fahen steam threshing machine. It was the last steam threshing machine in the area. The previous year, when I was 11 years old, I felt hurt that my dad had given the job to Russell Fahen. After all, my brother, Palmer, was hauling water to two team rigs when he was nine. But at last I was on my own, working with a threshing crew. The fun of being around all those young men

Elroy and his niece, Mavis Dragsten

who were always happy, joking, telling stories, pulling tricks on one another, and eating those wonderful meals was the best.

The next fall, when I was 13, I was given the job of being the engineer for my Uncle Andrew Dragsten's threshing run. Andrew had a Reeves 30/60 tractor with a 40-inch case separator. When I look at a picture of that tractor with the nine-foot drive wheels it seems it would be fun to drive it, but it was not fun. We worked six days a week, and it was a job with responsibilities. We would get up about 4:00 a.m., do some chores, and then drive to the farm where we were to thresh. The tractor took about 45 gallons of gas, filled five gallons at a time. Once I made sure everything was ready to go, we would go in and eat breakfast. After breakfast, we usually had to reset the machine and have it running by 7:00 a.m. We threshed from 7:00 a.m. to 7:00 p.m. with an hour off at noon. At night we removed all the belts and made any repairs. If we were through threshing at that farm, we would move to the next one. It was a slow move; the tractor traveled at 2 ½ miles an hour. Then we had supper and drove home and did the chores. It was not hard labor. I sat around all day except for some occasional greasing or if we had to reset the machine because of a wind change. But I had to be there, ready at all times to shut it down in case something went wrong. If any threshing machine had a breakdown it would be the talk of the county. It was embarrassing to have a breakdown, and I did not want it to be my fault.

The following spring I became a fulltime employee in my dad's garage. My dad had calendars made that said, "Peder Dragsten and Son Garage." My father proudly showed me the calendar and was disappointed when

Elroy and his uncle, Andrew Dragsten in 1938

I showed no interest in it. That fall when I was 14, I became the engineer for my dad's threshing run. The engine was a Twin City 40/80. The engine sat in line with the frame with bevel gears connected to the crankshaft and a shaft at right angles to the drive pulley.

My dad was never very good at giving instructions. He seemed to think I should know what to do. But he did give me instructions on running the engine. One of the things he told me was to put two handfuls of grease in the bevel gear box every day. I got mixed up and only put in one handful. After a while those gears started to make a grinding noise. He figured out what was wrong, and I corrected my mistake. But it was too late. We made it through the season, but the gears were shot. To eliminate the need for the bevel gears my dad made a frame and fastened the engine crosswise on it. The engine, radiator, and gas tank were all fastened to the frame and could be slid onto a truck. For the truck he used the rear of a well drilling rig and fastened that to the Marmon truck. The well drilling rig had hard rubber tires so a pneumatic tire was added to give it more flotation. It ended up with two transmissions, one from the well driller and the one with the Marmon. The steel wheels on the separator were cut off and rubber tires were added which made moving a lot faster.

After World War II, farmers were buying more tractors and combines started to show up in our area. My dad hated combines and refused to work on them. He could not believe a farmer would spend all that money on a machine that would be used for just a few weeks. Also a combine going up and down those hills around Wallace could not do as good a job as a threshing machine. But it was getting harder to get enough farmers together to make a good threshing run. To offset the lack of manpower, Dad made several machines, but they each had issues that made them difficult to implement. Dad fought to keep the way of life he had known since coming to America from Norway as a 16 year old in 1907. He fought it with his ingenuity, money, and labor. But the farmer no longer had to cooperate with his neighbor to complete the harvest. The great harvest get together was over. The combines were here to stay and the threshing machine was destined for the junk yard. It was the end of an era.

My Life: One Adventure after Another
By Wauneta Holdren of Faulkton, South Dakota
Born 1924

Learning that life had set me in a family of nine kids (six brothers and two sisters) started this girl with not much but love and laughter. Being number eight in that line-up put me with great examples of life patterns to follow. There was always string music, singing, surprising jokes, and laughter.

I had this inner desire for outdoor activities instead of housework. I had figured out that housework had a way of repeating its duties three times a day. Regardless. I started wondering early on, as to how I could get out of the house and be out there when I was busy working? Somehow, my "teenaged" shaped mother understood me. Mom made all my brothers and Dad's shirts, and I feel sure that she invented the first pair of little girls blue jeans ever made. Using material in varied shades of my brother's worn-out jeans, she made her girl some long pants like the boys wore. What a happy, barefooted tomboy I was with those leg-covering blue jeans! A brother brought out my bridled horse. He had tied the long bridle reins together before bringing them over the horses head to hand to me. Maybe I didn't need a saddle, but understand, the horses reins are the rider's steering gear.

I was almost nine years old at the "Old Settler's" yearly picnic. My brothers heard there was to be a horse race at 3 o'clock. Two of them went home to get our white "Cricket" horse. They didn't know that Dad had me over at the kids foot races, putting the winner's "dollar bill" prize in his pocket for every race he put me in.

The boys found me and we hurried to the racetrack. They threw me astride our barebacked white horse. I heard all of them talking about racehorses. At nine, you know little about horse breeds, but you've learned to do as you are told. They slapped Cricket on her hip and told her she better stay in there and run. I was just sitting back checking out the other horses. I couldn't see any kind of difference in these "race horses" than any other horses that we had lined up with and outrun. The two closest riders had saddles so small that I could hardly see them. The rider's knees looked to be up at his waist. Before I

40

got any questions figured out, everyone heard the gun shot signal to go. Cricket almost ran out from under me! She loved to run—almost as much as I loved to ride. What a race! We went over that finish line a full horse length ahead of all three of those racehorses!

A couple of years later, I heard all of the adults talking about the country being overrun with coyotes. With my time at the pasture, putting cows out or bringing them in, I had spent a lot of time preparing for winter coyote hunts in the garage, helping my youngest brother. He had gotten this Model A Ford coupe with a rumble seat behind. I had helped him build the neatest slat-box where the rumble seat had been to; carry his three long-legged greyhounds in. At the front of the dog box above the driver's side, was a space for the "lookout man" to stand. He would use the lever that opened the back of the box to let the dogs out. He could talk to the driver through his rolled-down window.

When he and the neighbor boy went to check out different hunting areas, sometimes I got to go along with them. What an excitement to me! I was invited to go along and share the unexpected events of so many coyote hunts. We always carried water and treats for the dogs, and two gallons of motor oil for the Ford. Sometimes we pulled in home with the motor clanking so loud we knew that there would be motor repair work again! But, we got it done! Last night's snowfall would be a great help. School time and family farm chores really cut into our short winter days of hunting time. The three of us shared work duties. I quickly figured out the "get me" chores, and I had better put the right sized quarter inch tool into the machine's hand that he asked for!

The years sped by. I married the neighbor boy. My youngest brother Clyde married one of my best girlfriends. We lived about three miles apart in this farming area. We two couples spent as much time together as our individual farming needs seemed to allow. When coyote hunting time got around, Ruby asked to stay at home and do the cooking. Perfect! We could take extra for meals, ending our hunt at their place.

This one afternoon it seemed the further south we went, the deeper the snow was getting. My brother Clyde was driving. He had spotted a coyote about halfway across this section of grassland. He had the gas pedal to

the floorboards! Clyde might have seen one-but Jack saw one much closer. He excitedly reached though the open driver's side window, grabbed the steering wheel out of Clyde's hand, and yelled, "The other way! The other way!" as an explanation for such actions of now forcefully becoming our driver!

There were three yelling voices. The hounds joined in with that one kind of excitement yelp. From between their wooden-slated dog box, hounds had spotted our prey. Why wasn't some fool man hitting that door lever to open their crate door and let them out? I honestly wasn't so sure that all four-car wheels were on the ground, going the same direction.

It seemed to me a lot of time had been wasted. I saw the coyote adding on faster running speed. As Clyde and I refocused our shaken-up minds, Jack hit the dog box release. Those three hounds hit the ground at them, "finally," getting to run speed. The fastest blue hound was the flip dog to stop coyote running. Grabbing the coyote by the tail and sending him into the air, his long-legged speed took him past all the commotion. The second dog grabbed the rump end of the coyote, stopping any wild idea of escape. The (hill dog) knew where the throat everything was all over. There were three happy human voices; each overpowering any other's excited words. Then there was instant silence, as hounds and humans became aware of a Model A Ford motor demanding, "more oil"!

Almost as fast as the time of the kill, the oil was in the motor. It stopped that knocking sound. Yes! The whole gallon of oil was used. The motor purred like a kitten again. We were actually going to get by without motor repairs—this time.

Memory loves re-running and comparing hunts—like the time we had additional snowfall covering. The lookout men easily spotted two coyotes. I think I should tell you that none of us ever owned a set of binoculars, which is man's way of saying, "I can see it clearly." We all knew the creek draw was in this section of grassland. All of us were watching out for snowdrifts from last night's wind. I yelled, "We are at the creek. Don't try it." Jack yelled through the driver's window, "You can't make it." But Clyde had that gas pedal to the floorboards! He said, "Our momentum will…" Oh! What a sudden stop! That Ford motor sounded like a big low-flying airplane. Snow flew so high –when it came own it was dark inside the cab. Snow was coming through the driver's side open window, almost covering him up. Do you know he was still trying to say, "Our momentum will carry us there!"

But not today! The weight of the car's load began silently sinking down through that snow, down to the dry dirt of the creek bed. It was very much like an old hen settling down on her nest of hatching eggs. Snow spilled through the open driver's car window. The more the car settled, the more snow came in. As the driver's sideman, my mind is telling me to move, but I can't! My head is making me, one flat-chested snowman driver's companion! But, we both could breathe. Thoughts and actions don't always coordinate when we want them to!

Jack, from his dog box height, could see what was going to happen. He did break the dog box cage board that he was behind. He yelled, "Are you guys okay?" Then grabbed the nearest snow shovel and headed to our rescue. He jumped down from the dog box, landing where the snow was much deeper. He began this eerie sinking process into the snow with the shovel in his hand. What a replica of our national version of the Statue of Liberty he made!

I know laughing is good for the soul's wellbeing, but do you know how long it takes to dig out of a car in that much snow when all you can do is laugh? I can tell you; it takes time!

Our job was to dig that vehicle out of this wide creek bed of drifted snow. Wheels couldn't even touch the dry dirt until we got the snow cleared out beneath the vehicle. We let the dogs out of their crate. Have you ever felt your dog was laughing at you from some dumb stunt? We had three dogs laying out there—watching us, and I know they were laughing on the inside! We found some "cedar posts" to lay in front of the car tires, trying to stop its forward movement. Then we could finally clean out the packed snow holding the car up. What a day!

No coyote hide sale for this weekend. Three people had sore muscles that could have used a couple more bottles of sportsman's rubbing alcohol that night. You may know about sore work muscles, but have you ever considered all the muscles that get used overtime when you can't stop laughing?

Memories like this tell me that dreaming, activities, and laughter are the best gifts that we ever give to ourselves. I'm glad! Like Jimmy Durtante used to say, "I got millions of 'em! They come in very handy, when I do have a bad day, and need a face-lifting smile!"

Growing up in South Dakota
By Darlene Rowderdink of Lancaster,
California
Born 1932

I was born on a farm by Hamlin, South Dakota. The only thing I remember about the house I was born in was a story my Mother told me. She said one day the mailman came up to her and asked if she was looking for some little girls. She said yes. Then he told her that we were playing in the mud and water in the middle of the road.

We didn't have many toys so we would make mud pies with jar lids, we had a wagon and stilts that Dad made for us. I got my first doll when I was in high school. Our aunts were very small ladies so they would send us their old clothes and shoes for us to play dress up in. One time my sisters and I were playing in the small trunk of our car and the trunk latched closed. We were stuck inside and we screamed and screamed for help. When our Mother found us, we were purple from screaming and the lack of oxygen in the trunk. We really got lucky.

For Christmas, all we would get was a sack with an apple, nuts, peanuts, and hard

Picking walnuts at Aunt Josephine's in 1952

candy from our church. My favorite holiday was Easter. We never dyed eggs but when we would wake up on Easter morning the front and the back porch would have eggs hidden everywhere. We found out years later that our neighbors that didn't have any kids would come over early morning and would hide the eggs. We always had an outhouse on all the farms and didn't have running water. We also had what was called a "slop pail," which was a paint pail inside for night. We had a wringer washing machine that ran on gas. We had kerosene lamps and lanterns for the barn and outside. We didn't have a gas stove until the last farm we lived on. We also had an oil-burning stove in the living room for heating. We had to pull water out of cisterns, which was hauled in, from Hayti. We heated it in a boiler; we did that on a wood stove, which was heated by corncobs. We heated water in a teakettle to wash our faces and to do the dishes. There were six of us and we had to bathe in a little round tub, the little ones went first. I made pajamas out of feed sacks, used old pajamas as the pattern.

My Mom listened to Ma Perkins and to the news on the radio. We were not allowed to run the batteries down. The phone had party lines so there were different rings for each family member on the line. Had a storm one day and lightning struck a mile from us and fire came out of the phone. It killed cows where it hit.

Growing up, we only ate chicken, pork, eggs, and the vegetables we grew: corn, beans, carrots, and potatoes. We would also make homemade bread. We only ate meat once a day because that is all we could afford. We didn't eat beef because we would sell it since it was worth a lot of money. I never ate beef until I was in high school. We would can meat for the winter and store it in the cellar, which was just dirt. We would make our homemade ice cream in the winter and would have my Dad's family over for cake and ice cream because four of us had birthdays in December and January

I went to a one-room schoolhouse until the middle of fourth grade. We had a really

Ernest Schaefer's farm in 1945

bad storm that year which took everything but the house, so we had to move. Moved to a farm by Hayti, and went to school from fourth to twelfth grade in Thomas, what a bad time. Our clothes were too old for us (they were hand me downs from our aunts in California,) so we were bullied, but down the line they became our dearest friends (way back then.) We cried every morning waiting for the bus. The bus was a truck with a closed in box with benches on the sides, it had a door on the back and no windows.

We would go to town on Saturday nights to get groceries. All of our meat was kept in a locker in town. Every once in a while we would get ten cents to see a movie. We would go to the big town, Watertown, when my Dad had to get parts, our shoes, and other things.

Then we had to move again because the owners son wanted to farm so that he could avoid the service, he came from California. My folks bought a farm not far from where we were so we got to go to the same school. We got our first lights in 1945 when REA came, which was really something. My youngest sister was born that year in May.

Us three oldest girls milked cows by hand until we got milkers. We had to separate the milk, lift the big pails up into a separator, which had to be washed every day. The cream man came to pick up the cream, which we kept in the cellar. We also had to feed the animals and work in the field. We did all kinds of things. We cut grain with binders then had to shock. My Dad ran the thrashing machine so I had to get up early with him. I would grease one side of the machine and he would grease the other before everyone came, did three families all together. The other two families had boys but they would go to play ball so us girls did the pitching of the bundles into the thrasher. Us three oldest girls did the pitching of the bundles in to the thrasher. Us three oldest girls also picked up potatoes at neighbors so we missed the first week or so of school. This way we were able to make money to buy school clothes. One of us girls had to stay at the house to do the housework while the others worked outside. I drove a tractor and an old Diamond T truck with grain in it to town before I ever drove a car.

We had a car but we weren't supposed to drive it in the field because of rocks, but my sister did and got hung up on a big one. A while later my Dad couldn't figure out how the axel got bent under the car. We were told to never go into the hog house because there were new little pigs. Well we did and the mother killed them all, at least that was what we were told.

My sister and I didn't want the boys to know we worked in the fields so we would cover all exposed skin with cold cream and covered our face with mom's powders, which took a lot of washing to get off, so we wouldn't get tan. We also would wear dad's old long sleeved shirts.

I stayed home one year after graduation to help my Dad on the farm. My Dad got hailed out three years in a row so had to sell the farm. Then I went to town to work and finally got paid. I had an apartment with a bathroom, which had a shower and tub and I loved it.

The first color TV came out when I got married in 1957, but we didn't get one for a couple of years. I was in Lancaster, California when the first man landed on the moon.

Ringing in the New Year of 1900
By Frank Weis of Valley City, North Dakota
Born 1933

This is a story that my dad told his family that happened years ago. I was raised at Tea, South Dakota during the 1930s, '40s, and '50s. Tea is six miles southwest of Sioux Fall, South Dakota. During my watch, Tea had a newspaper called Tea Leaves, a Tea Coffee Shop, and a ladies bowling team called the "Tea Bags."

In 1899, my dad lived with his parents on a farm near Cherokee, Iowa. On December 31, 1899 around 11:30pm, my dad and his dad, my grandpa, hitched up a team of horses, drove to the nearest township intersection, and met some neighbors and friends. They then shot off some black powder at midnight, thus welcoming in the new year of 1900!

One Gutsy First Grader
By Leland Roe of Hazel, South Dakota
Born 1941

My early school days were spent in a one-room country school. As a first grader, my teacher happened to be married to one of my cousins. Perhaps maybe being kind of related to the teacher made me a little too brave, ignoring discipline.

The assignment was to write the numbers from one to one hundred. I had trouble making the number six. It usually turned out backwards, like a lowercase "d." After getting a little more than halfway done, I was tired of it all and took the paper to her desk. She told me to sit back down and finish to 100, and to also change the sixes so that they were correct.

Well, I finished writing to 100 and took it back to her. I told her, "Here it is, but if you want the sixes changed, you'll have to do it yourself."

Spook Light
By Thelma Hayden of De Smet, South Dakota
Born 1929

I was born in 1929, and grew up in Miner County, east central South Dakota near Roswell, in the vicinity of Carthage, Fedora, and Roswell. I never saw the Spook Light, but vividly remember the stories and theories talked about during my childhood.

It was a very bright, white light, and looked like a bonfire bouncing along the ground. It was seen by many in the 1930s, '40s, and '50s. About every other night, it would appear out of nowhere, and then disappear. It always came from the south and looked like it was coming up over the hill. It could change radiance and surge into brighter bursts, reflecting off the farm buildings. Some drove through it, and while others saw it, the driver didn't. It would be seen regularly for periods of time, then not again for weeks. I don't remember anyone being frightened, just curious. It was a mystery that was never solved. It hasn't been seen for years.

Poor as Church Mice
By Bonita Dolney of Bristol, South Dakota
Born 1938

When the Second World War was over, our family (Dad, Mom, my brother, and I) moved into the basement of a former Lutheran church because of a shortage of housing caused by the aftermath of the war. We would go up on the overhead bridge and watch the troop trains pass by. We lived in Bristol, as did the entirety of dad's family. Our bathroom was a chemical toilet located up in the narthex. Our bath was an oval metal tub. We had no formal kitchen, just a two-burner gas stove. Another family lived on the other half of the basement and they had three children. Our space was separated by a wood divider that did not go all the way to the ceiling. A curtain was the door between the two places. I don't remember living there a real long time. My brother and I could always tell people that we were "as poor as church mice."

Sledding
I remember in the late 1940s when a lot of kids in town would go sledding on a hill right off of Main Street. One of the families had a Swedish sled, which had a chair on it, and a person could stand on the back. So, we would have a convoy of sleds going down the hills. No parents were around and no one got hurt. I can still hear the shrieks and laughter from long ago. Also, we made snow tunnels in the huge snow banks. Mother was so worried that we would get buried in them.

Memories from the Family of Jacob and Cecila Boruta Tuchscherer
By Ann J. Cazer of Custer, South Dakota
Born 1936

One-room Schoolhouse
My first grade school memory was while attending Alban # 2. Dad left for work to the Cold Springs Granite Quarry very early in the morning. Mother would bundle me up and send me out the door with my lunch pail to walk to school, as she had no other way of getting me to the school. If I was lucky, I would get to the highway at the time A.O. Schmidt was heading to town to his law office, and he would stop and take me back to school. At that time, there was only eight students, eight grades, and four boys and four girls were enrolled.

Wringer Washer Incident
Mother always brought her wringer washer into the kitchen on Monday, which was always washday. She had her white clothes in the machine, went to wring them out, and felt something squishy in the water. She turned off the machine. At that time, the folks raised toy terrier bulldogs to supplement the income. She waited for Dad to come home from work, as she was thinking it was a puppy that had curled up for a nap in the clothes that she had put into the machine. When Dad came home from work at 3:00pm, he checked the machine, and the mystery article was my snow boot. Mother didn't think of counting the puppies!

Mischief
My sister, who was four of five, always was coming up with something unusual. After dinner, Dad would sit in his rocking chair with his feet on top of the parlor stove and take a nap. One night, Rosemary got the bottle of mentholated out and painted stick man figures on the back of Dad's baldhead. Dad wasn't aware of what she did until the next day when he went to town for a haircut. Everyone in the shop had a good laugh, including the barber. Dad was embarrassed, and of course, he never raised his voice, just asked if Sis she had a good time.

Wringer Washers, Radios, and Record Players
By Gene Norton of Miller, South Dakota
Born 1928

My name is Gene. I was born in 1928, so I am 85 years old now. I was born just west of the Missouri River on a cattle ranch. We never had electricity on the ranch that I was born on.

When I was a young boy in the 1930s, Monday was washday on the ranch. It was my job to take a horse and stone sled with a barrel on it and go to the stock dam and get a barrel of water to wash clothes with. My mother would fill a copper boiler with water and put it on the cook stove to heat. Then, we had an old washing machine that we had to push and pull the handle on the side of it to make it agitate to wash the clothes. We would then put the clothes through the wringer that we had to turn by hand to wring the water out of them. Then it was time to hang them on the clothesline made of #9 wire outside to dry in the sun and wind.

During the '30s, we had a battery-operated Zenith radio that ran off of a car battery. We would have to put it back in the car when it would run down and use a team of horses to pull the car to start and charge it back up. We would only listen to the radio for certain programs, like Ma Perkins, the news, and Judy and Jamie. On Saturday nights, we would get to listen to the Grand Ole Opry from Nashville. The kids got to listen to Jack Armstrong and The Lone Ranger before we did our chores. There were very few channels on the radio. Our main stations were WNAX, Yankton, South Dakota and KSFY, Sioux Falls, South Dakota. We would get the live stock markets from KSFY because that is where we shipped our cattle for marketing.

When I was 15 years old, my dad got sick and sold all of the cattle except 75 heads. My family moved to town and left me on the ranch to take care of them. I was a freshman in high school, and I rode to school 15 miles a day for two years.

I had a good friend who would come and see me at night. We had a Victrola and a large amount of old, thick 78-rpm records. We would sit and play cards and listen to records 'til ten or eleven o'clock. Then, he would get on his horse and go home. This would happen three or four nights a week. I also had a cylinder player that you had to keep cranking while it played.

The Stubborn Pony
By Melba Pierce Brown of Cameron, Missouri
Born 1926

I was born in the country near Raymond, South Dakota in 1926. My dad, Everett Pierce, was trying hard to grow crops and had some milk cows during the Depression years. We all had jobs to do. My brother Glenn and I had the job to walk down to the pasture where a creek ran through to bring up the milk cows when we got home from school.

It was quite a long walk for a six and eight year old, so my father scraped up enough money to buy a Shetland pony named Kewpie for us to ride to get the cows. We were excited the first day we rode her to get the cows. As we started to round up the cows, she bucked us off and ran home! This was a daily routine!

My disappointed dad decided he would teach her a lesson. My long-legged dad rode her a ways to show her who was boss, but the toe of his shoe caught in a gopher hole and pulled him off! She took off and he walked home with the cows!

My brother and I finally decided one of us would lead her and one ride. She finally accepted the job of bringing home the cows. She later had a colt named Goldie.

Melba and Glenn with Kewpie the pony in 1932

Bulls in School and Surprises in the Snow
By Alice Clark of Madison, South Dakota
Born 1923

When I was in fourth grade in school, we lived in the country. One day in the fall, we had a live bull come into the school. It was scary! We all screamed and the teacher tried to chase him out. She did not know what to do, but she rang the school bell and that scared him. He left, but us kids were so scared that most of us cried. Thank goodness for school bells!

When I was about eight years old, we lived in South Dakota. I am 90 years old now. This one winter, I remember we had so much snow. There were great big snowdrifts. Me and my sisters were playing on a big snow bank. We decided to make a big hole in it. After we had made quite a big hole, we saw something in the hole, so we kept digging. Lo and behold, there was a rooster in there. We dug him out and he was still alive. He was kind of froze, so we took him out and home. Mom cleaned him and took all his feathers off. We had him for dinner that night. He really tasted good!

Life in the Country
By Alma M. Paulson of Columbia, South Carolina
Born 1929

I was born in rural Butler, South Dakota on August 23, 1929. I have a twin sister, Thelma, born a half hour before me. We truly enjoyed growing up together. We were the youngest of seven children. Times were very hard at that time financially because of the Great Depression. In fact, my parents lost the farm six years later. Dad was a farmer. We had always had stacks of hay for the animals on the farm. However, a few years later, we had bales of hay stacked up. Now Dad had to buy hay, as the ground was too dry for hay to grow. Thelma and I really enjoyed the bales because we could climb up and down them. At this time, I didn't know what Depression and poverty meant. This was just life.

When Thelma and I were five years old, we each got a doll from my sister's boyfriend shortly before they got married. They were the only dolls we ever had. Mom later made clothes for our dolls, and for Thelma and me, out of the printed sacks that flour came in.

Mom and Dad had the Sears and Roebuck catalog. Thelma and I enjoyed cutting out people and then cutting out other pieces of clothing. We would cut little tacks of paper at the shoulders so that we could put new outfits on the "people." We played "farm" with dominoes, marbles, and stones. We made pastures and buildings out of dominoes. Larger marbles were horses, the smaller marbles were sheep, and the little stones were chickens. One of our brothers who was six years older than us made a play wagon out of old shingles and empty thread spools for the wheels. Boy, we really thought that was great.

When we were old enough for school, we walked a mile and a half to our rural schoolhouse. In our first grade, we had a brother, Ordeen, in the eighth grade. In winter cold days, he hitched a horse to a big, wooden three foot by five-foot box with wooden runners under it. Thelma and I would sit in the box. We were all covered up with a quilt wrapped around us. Ordeen would stand in the front part with a horse linked up to the box, and the reins in his hands. He would direct the horse across the country to the school. He stopped the horse at the school. Thelma and I would get out then. Ordeen turned the sleigh around facing home, tied the reins to the sleigh, got the horse to go, and jumped out. The horse headed for our barn and open door where oats were waiting for him.

We had a great life.

Wintry Railway Troubles
By William W. Klucas of Mobridge, South Dakota
Born 1944

The event that I always remember is the March 3rd through 6th 1966 blizzard in South Dakota. On March 7th, they started to clear the main line on the Milwaukee Railroad. We left Mobridge at 3:00pm and headed west with a wedge plow, two engines, and a caboose with 50 snow shovelers inside.

We got to west of Wakpala and stalled due to the engine traction motors getting wet. They radioed for help and two fresh engines were sent out. We were pulled back to Wakpala with our engines left on a siding. The fresh engines were hooked on the plow and the caboose hooked behind the engines.

By this time, it was 8:00pm, and it was dark. We came up to a drift at the entrance to a cut in the path of the right of way. We hit this drift going 40 mph. The next thing we knew we had four to five feet of snow over the top of the head engine. We were stuck.

There were six men including me buried alive in the head engine cab. The engines never died. Where they got oxygen from I will never know. The head brakeman got the window open and started burrowing upward. I kept the snow from getting near the high voltage cabinet with my shovel. Once we had an air hole, we were okay.

The snow shovelers had to dig us out. It

took nine hours to dig out the plow and engine. It was truly a night to remember. The cut was between 2,000 and 3,000 feet long. The snow was between 20 and 30 feet deep. They had to use dynamite and a rotary plow to clean it out.

Mischief at School
By Raiden V. Peterson of Covina, California
Born 1928

This story is about this postcard. When I showed it to my grandson Ben about two years ago, he looked at it and said, "Grandpa, how did you ever get this card? There is no address." I told him that we lived about three miles north of town and that the mailman knew all the people on his rural route. No farmers had an address at that time.

I was going to Howard High School when this story took place in about 1945. One day after lunch, my buddy Paul and I stopped by his uncle's blacksmith shop and got a small amount of carbide. Our last period was free time, so we asked to go down and practice boxing in the gym. However, we were going to experiment with the carbide. We went to the restroom, put carbide in an empty inkbottle, added some water, put the lid on tight, and went to the other side of the restroom to wait for it to explode. Wouldn't you know it? About the same time it exploded, our coach Mr. Sampson walked in. Wow! There was carbide, ink, and glass all over his suit. Needless to say, we were on detention for two weeks an hour a day after school.

Another story is about the third day that I got a bright idea. The clock on the wall had no glass and it was behind the teacher's desk. Her name was Miss Ward. That day I brought a ruler with me. I reached up while Paul

Howard High School

The Children's Parade post card in 1933

distracted her and moved the clock ahead 15 minutes. At 4:00pm, I told her our hour was up. She thought the hour passed rather quick. I told her that the clock said 3:00pm when we came into the room—which it did!

History Repeats Itself: Storm Atlas Mimics Another Blizzard Over 100 Years Earlier
By Janet Elaine Meehan of Lead, South
Dakota
Born 1952

I remember the blizzards of my youth and young adulthood in South Dakota. Both my mother and mother-in-law perfected a dish similar to a shepherd's pie, but made in an eight by eight inch cake pan—and without any crust.

The dish had been around since the "dirty thirties" and contained layers of browned hamburger and onion, cottage cheese, mashed potatoes, peas and/or shredded carrots, and even a layer of rice. (The Eastern South Dakota or North Dakota women had large families to feed!) The mashed potatoes were the top layer, with maybe a sprinkling of cheese.

In my life, I have seen many blizzards and snowstorms and Nor'easters (on the East Coast) come and go. And, we were always well fed through them. The tradition of the farm stuck with me and my husband. There was always a well-stocked freezer or pantry. (Larder was what it was called in the old days.)

Imagine my surprise when I heard of a big storm coming to Western South Dakota and parts of Wyoming in our 40th year of marriage. They predicted it would be a 944 out of 1000 on the "badness" scale. Off to the store we went with a lengthy grocery list!

When it hit in early October, the ranchers had not brought their cattle in from summer pasture and the animals had not grown their winter coats. They were literally blind-sided by what was dubbed as "Storm Atlas." Chilled to the bone first by many inches of rain, tens of thousands of cattle, horses, and sheep were lost. They were suffocated, drowned, and caught in fence lines when they could find no shelter. The storm was compared to one that swept through the Dakotas, Wyoming, and Montana in 1886 and 1887. At that time, Teddy Roosevelt was still farming in Medora, North Dakota and lost livestock. The giant Swan Land & Cattle Company in Wyoming took a substantial hit, too.

Atlas involved winds up to 80 mph, and our high mountain village of Lead, South Dakota had 56 inches of snow to deal with. There is a hill outside our front door that they block off during snowstorms. It is named Glover's Hill after a famous brick house that Mary Baker Eddy built for a Christmas gift to her son. The snow piled up so high on that hill that my husband, daughter-in-law, and son had to crawl up that hill on their bellies to shovel out vehicles parked at the top of the hill. There was one moment, early on, where the deep snow threatened to swallow up Alexandra, our daughter-in-law.

That was just the start of a very long and grueling winter. The winter of 2013 and 2014 broke 2,400 records for cold temperatures across the United States. There were hundreds of electrical outages and stocks of propane began running low.

Our Family Survived the "Dirty Thirties"
By John S. Wangberg of Sinai, South Dakota
Born 1925

I was born March 24, 1925 on a farm owned by Marcus Gullickson, in Riverview Township near Flandreau, South Dakota. I was the eighth child of Johannes and Astrid Wangberg who had emigrated from Norway in the early 1900s. My father was a meticulous bookkeeper, having learned the trade in Norway, but thought he wanted to be a farmer.

Our family moved to Egan, South Dakota when I was about eight years old and we lived in the Nobe Smith house for several years while Dad farmed 80 acres of land west of town. It was at this time that my younger brother Harold and I put dry grass in a pail and were going to set it on fire behind the chicken house. The owner caught us and spanked us while mother approved.

The next move by horse and wagon brought us to a farm two miles south of Egan, South Dakota on a 160-acre farm with buildings, and known as the Pettigrew Farm. In the ten years following, we experienced one good corn crop with corn selling at ten cents per bushel. Almost every year we were plagued with clouds of grasshoppers or locusts. Then there were the clouds of rolling dirt storms that covered everything. We were usually able to raise good potatoes.

We experienced a few major setbacks during those good old days. Our brooder house caught fire and we lost over 100 baby chicks. We called the Egan Fire Department and their truck came quickly, but they couldn't get up the steep hill to our place. Fortunately, a bread delivery truck came along and pulled the fire truck up the hill. But it was too late to save the brooder house or the chicks within it. While my mother was trying to rescue some of the chicks, she fell and injured her hip. Mother's badly injured hip bothered her the rest of her life.

Another setback involved a young heifer that broke out during a flash flood. She wandered into a neighbor's barnyard, with tracks leading up to the door of a barn owned by a neighbor. However, he refused to let my brothers identify the animal, which now was in his barn. Another time, thieves stole all of our turkeys, which were ready for market after they had poisoned our watchdog.

There was a government program to help farmers who were struggling to keep their families fed. It was called the Public Works Administration. Father and other farmers furnished their own wagons with 24-inch sides and a team of horses to haul gravel to develop the county and township roads. In addition to improving the local roads, this program provided some income for many farm families.

After living over eighty years, I look back on the lessons I have learned from my childhood on farms in Moody County during tough times. It took persistence and cooperation to have a successful home and farm in a good community.

Deep Trouble
By Robert Pray, Sr. of Groton, South Dakota
Born 1924

I went to a country school that was two miles from home for all eight grades. We generally rode a pony when weather was decent. While I was in the eighth grade, two neighbor boys talked me into going with them to a nearby town, six miles to be exact, to deliver a horse for their Dad. We drove in a horse and buggy and trailed the horse we were to deliver. On the way back, our horse was spooked by a rabbit that had crossed ahead of us. I was sitting on the rear of the buggy dangling my feet, so I fell to the ground. Doing so, I ripped a huge hole in my brand new bib overalls. With no permission from my folks or my teacher to even go on this trip, I was in deep trouble.

My Honeymoon
I got married eight years later after a tour in the U.S. Navy. Our honeymoon trip took us to the Black Hills. We drove a 1932 Chevrolet coupe. We spent our first night in Mobridge, South Dakota. The hotel was full, so they sent us to a private home. In the morning, the landlady seen our wedding cake and gave us

Bob and Ruth Pray on their wedding day in 1946

our rent money back, the whole sum of three dollars.

We woke up the next morning to six inches of snow. On the way to the Black Hills, the radiator sprung a leak. In those days, there wasn't any Prestone to speak of, only alcohol, and when you got a whiff of that, it was unbearable. But, we made it to Rapid City and parked behind my brother's cabin where we stayed for a week. We spent the next few days removing the radiator and had it repaired. It was all quite frustrating, but I would give anything to be able to do it all over again.

Ruth and I did all our courting through the mail while I was in the service and will be married 68 years this December 2014.

Bob and Ruth a day before the wedding

Teaching, Learning, and Loving
By Ruth Overby of Mellette, South Dakota
Born 1926

I grew up on a farm and went to country school through the eighth grade. I entered Herreid High School with the freshman class of 1941. I felt like a pebble in a giant pool. I graduated from high school in 1944. World War II was on and teachers were hard to get, as everyone was working in factories for the war. People who wanted to teach could take a test and be qualified to teach in a country school. I passed the test and secured a position at a county school. I was paid one hundred dollars a month. I paid the family I stayed with forty dollars a month for room and board. Some social security was withheld from my check. I saved all I could.

Each school I taught at was grades one through eight with about eight or nine

50

students. I had to do my own janitor work. Most schools had a potbelly stove. Every morning I'd start a fire and bank it in the evenings, hoping there were still hot coals in the morning. Many times there weren't. I had to carry out the ashes every day and clean the blackboards. The students and I all carried our lunches and our drinking water to school. There were two outhouses—one for the boys and one for the girls.

One year I taught at a school near my parents' home. That year I rode my Shetland pony "Dapples" or walked the two miles to school. I pulled items I needed to school on a child's sled.

At Christmas, I had the children do a program. They sang songs and gave skits for their parents and friends. I had my brother dress up as Santa and he gave the children gifts I had purchased. He gave everyone sacks of nuts and candy. The pupils liked to draw names to exchange gifts and each gave a gift worth 25 cents to another child.

I wanted to further my education and began attending Northern State Teachers College in Aberdeen, SD in the summers. I stayed in college the whole school year of 1947-'48. There were six girls in two rooms at the Seymour Hall dorm. I had only 200 dollars in the bank, so I got a part time job in the dining hall on campus. I earned 20 dollars a month. I didn't have much spending money, but two of the girls and I liked to roller skate. On Sunday night, we could roller skate for 50 cents. We took the bus to the roller rink for ten cents. We rented skates that clipped on our shoes for 25 cents. We spent another ten cents for the bus home. I had five cents for a bottle of pop.

I graduated college debt-free in 1948. One summer day in June of 1947, I was a bridesmaid at my cousin's wedding. One of the ushers was a handsome blue-eyed blond. The wedding was on a Sunday afternoon and I had to get back to college from the country church. My cousin arranged for the blond and his brother to take another cousin and I back to Aberdeen. Lo and behold, this handsome gentleman also liked to skate. We would get together at the rink. After a while, he started picking me up to go skating. A year after my cousin's wedding I married my handsome blue eyed blond. We celebrated our 65th wedding anniversary on September 26, 2013.

A Kieser Family Short Story
By Jeff (Hub) Keiser of Wessington Springs, South Dakota
Born 1960

My grandfather wasn't alive for the great blizzard of 1888, but his father often told stories of it. This blizzard is and was of historic proportion and is still talked about today. My grandfather, H. Ward Kieser was born in 1890, but had heard stories of the great blizzard all his early life and mused that he felt as if he had lived right through it.

On the day of the blizzard of 1888, Henry H. and another man had traversed to Woonsocket, some sixteen miles away for supplies. The blizzard, as many have related through the years, came very quickly, turning from an extra nice January day to a ravaging deadly storm in a matter of a few hours. They were caught-up in the middle of the storm on their return trip from Woony.

After fighting with team through the storm, the outline of some buildings came into view, and a light could be seen in a window. They knew not where they were, other than being somewhere on the area of Blaine or maybe the southern edge of Franklin township. H.H. knocked on the door and a man opened it but a crack. He asked for refuge from the storm, but the man answered they had no room for them and for them to go away. Great-grandfather pushed his way in the door and stated they would be staying the night until the storm let up and directed the man with him to put the horses in the barn. He said that he would help the "hosts" prepare them some sustenance and a place to sleep. No trouble was had, and the "host" was never identified. When the storm had relented in the morning H.H. and the man traveling with him took to the trail and went home.

I, of course, cannot remember this story from experiencing it, but was told the story several times by my Grandfather Ward. He loved to tell stories, and did frequently, but they always stayed the same. His father, H.H., was known to be a no nonsense kind of guy and was a respected man in the community of Wessington Springs who also wasn't one to embellish.

My personal storm experiences, though not as dramatic, give me a picture of the ever-present danger of changing Dakota weather

51

and demonstrate how, with the passing of time, the intensity of our violent weather episodes has weakened some. I was very young when the winter of 1962 was making the headlines. I can only remember that on our farm, we had a shelter belt that ran on the north side of the farmstead, from the county road going past our place, to a half mile west, with a slight jog to the south then west again, about a third of the way through. At the jog, we kids and our mother could go sledding on the south side of the shelterbelt that had been planted some eighty years earlier. We would walk all the way up to the treetops that barely protruded through the snow, and sled down to nearly ground level to the south. What fun! That was snow resulting from a two to three day blizzard.

In 1968, we had a two-day blast hit our area on Christmas Eve. We had gone to town in the early evening for the Christmas Eve service at our church and then went home, not having too much difficulty. But, in the night it snowed and blew. For the next two days we were "snowed in" and could only take care of the livestock—no traveling to church, town, or anywhere. About the third day, which I think was a Monday or Tuesday, via the party-line phone line, we found out the county was to plow out the east-west road three miles north of our place, but wouldn't be coming south because they didn't have time to. My dad, Ken, and our next neighbor to the north, Vernon, hatched a plan. They both had good tractors with F-10 Farmhand loaders and heat-housers. They decided that they would dig out the three miles of road themselves. This they did, and by afternoon of the following day, Dad loaded us all up in the '65 Chrysler Newport and we headed towards town, catching Vernon as he dug out the last few feet of road at the three mile intersection.

As a kid, it was quite impressive to see the snow piled about eight to ten feet high on either side of the road, with only about enough room for one car at a time to pass. Those two men had moved a world of snow, or so it seemed! And with *farm* machinery! That whole winter was a rather snowy one, maybe not a record maker, but, then again, this *is* South Dakota. Our average of just about everything is deduced from our extremes, and when it comes to weather, well, that is about all we ever experience—extremes!

The next winter to take place and leave an indelible mark on my memory was the winter of '71/'72. 1972 was a year of record precipitation and that started with a very ferocious winter. Though as time passes we have noticed that the length of these winter storms become shorter, they can still bring major snow and intensity. In February of '72, we had some relatives from Colorado at our farm for a short visit. I can't remember how they managed to come at that time of year, what with two boys in school and all, perhaps being from a large metropolitan area, they were on a spring break or something. Anyway, we had had some rough weather prior to their arrival and there was a great amount of snow on the ground. I had gotten to stay home from school for a day or two to spend time with the cousins that were there. One cousin and myself made plans to walk north a mile or so the next day and snoop around the old abandoned Guerker place. It seemed somewhat spooky and mysterious and we thought it would be fun.

A storm brewed up again overnight and on the day of our planned exploration the weather was bad enough that they called school off. Just great! I was ready to go ahead and walk the mile or so north as planned, but my cousin pooped out! He was too "soft" to go walking in this kind of a storm! He thought I was crazy! Well, just to prove to him that South Dakota boys weren't soft and Colorado boys were, I dressed up and walked the distance myself! Take that, Rocky Mountain High boy! Of course everyone at home thought I was nuts, and maybe I was, but, hey, it wasn't all that cold, certainly it was above zero, maybe even ten or twenty degrees! And the wind was only blowing around 25 or 30 miles per hour! Merely a breeze here in the real world of men! Anyway, I made the trip, my cousin was embarrassed, I was smug, and nothing bad happened.

But, the winter wasn't over yet. We had a lot more snow that winter and a record amount of rain in the spring, so much so that dire measures were to be taken in order to get a crop in the ground that spring. Duals had to be purchased and put on the "big" tractor, a 100 hp, 856 I.H. My brother had to take time off from college to help with the spring planting and both grandfathers were put to work helping in the field where needed.

It was a heck of a wet year and we had tremendous crops. The wheat was good and the yield high. The silage crop grew tall and thick and a new silage chopper and dump wagon were to be purchased in order to get the entire crop in. We even employed the neighbor's son, Royce, who had recently returned from Vietnam, That was a great year.

Let's fast forward to 1986. '86 began as a mild tempered yet wet winter. In early April, we had a major rain and ice storm that took down a lot of trees and really saturated the ground, making calving a nightmare to say the least. By mid to late April, things were getting a little better and there was some farming getting done, albeit late. And then, the *big* one came. Although there was some warning from the national weather service, many chose to ignore the warnings, and that was a huge mistake.

The day the storm hit started out fairly normal. I was drilling spring wheat 'til about four in the afternoon when the rain and mud became too great. By suppertime it was raining in earnest and starting to turn to snow, heavy *wet* snow. The wind picked up in the night and although it wasn't all that cold, over a foot of snow fell by morning and was drifted around pretty badly. It was cold enough too, that ice formed on the power lines, knocking out a lot of power in the region. The storm only lasted a few hours, but the affects were substantial and the loss of livestock, huge.

We had neighbors who had just purchased the farm adjacent to ours. It being so wet where they lived over in eastern Blaine Township, they thought it wise to bring their calved pairs over to their "new" farm where there was plenty of somewhat dry pasture for them to keep dry on. Even with all the warnings of impending snow and wind, they still brought the cattle over the day before the storm hit. Bad plan. The cows, not knowing where they were, took to wandering with the wind during the big blow. The next morning their cows were scattered around for miles with many of them dead from exposure or from getting stuck in fences. They lost nearly a third of that herd. Another neighbor to the west two miles had his small herd wander into a usually dry lakebed that was full of water and drowned nearly the whole herd. The stories were many, and many were all the same. Lots of warning, little heeding, major losses. Even though most of us are of generational ancestry in the area and the Dakotas in general, Mother Nature wins one every once in a while.

There has been several one day and one-half day storms over the last ten or fifteen years or so, but, the intensity that those of us of a "certain" age experienced in our younger years and of the storms told to us by our ancestors doesn't seem to be there anymore. Yes, we have had some bad ones, but not the multiple day things of years past. We have great amounts of snow from individual storms that have choked the region and blocked roads. Roads have been closed for one or maybe two days, but, then again, that is due in part because man has gotten a little bit smarter over the years and we try not to place so much risk at the feet of those who can't seem to grip the thought of safety over want or desire. We are doing a better job of protecting ourselves and our mankind. History is a great teacher if you only pay attention and respect what Mother Nature has presented man with over the years. Life is fragile. Our forefathers knew this and they wrote and told the stories of the tragedies that man suffered because of being ill prepared for her fury. Two, three days and sometimes longer blizzards of our past have become shorter. Perhaps, in another 20-50 years blizzards will amount to six hours or less. Wouldn't that be a wonderful evolvement of nature? We can only hope!

Memories of My Grandparents
By Arlene Mardian of Aberdeen, South Dakota
Born 1940

I remember when my Grandma Alice and Granddad Charles Cunningham lived with my Uncle Joe and Aunt Adeline and Cousins Loretta, Ray, Louie, Roger, and Brent on a farm. The farm was located about nine miles northeast of Onaka, South Dakota. It was a small home with two bedrooms on the main floor and one room upstairs with two beds. When we other grandkids got to stay the night, we would crawl in with either Grandma or Granddad, wherever there was space available. There were no closets or bathroom up there either. Clothes were simply hung on a bar near the wall in the corner.

Behind the clothes, there was a chamber

Alice and Charles Cunningham

loved to tell us stores about how he grew up in Vincennes, Indiana. But most of all, he loved arguing politics. He was an Irish, Catholic, Democrat!

Granddad hand-planted a tree belt on the north and east side of the farmstead. When the trees needed watering he would carry buckets of water to each tree. Fifty years later most of that tree belt is still standing. I remember he also took care of a large garden that grew great watermelons.

In the 1940s and until Granddad died in 1952, Granddad and Grandma would take bus trips to Denver, Colorado and Pasadena, California. In Pasadena they visited Granddad's sisters and would watch the Rose Parade from Aunt Stella's front porch.

Though the home on the farm was not very large and lacked facilities, I cherish the memories of the time I spent there with my aunt, uncle, and cousins. However, the time spent there with Grandma and Granddad is priceless.

pot, commonly referred to today as a bathroom stool. The difference was that this thing did not have a flush handle. Each day this pot had to be carried out and dumped down the outdoor toilet. Grandma also had a card table up there where she would often sit by herself and work on puzzles. The walls and ceiling upstairs were not finished off. I remember the exposed roof rafters with the shingle nails sticking through. In winter, when it was cold, these shingle nails would be white with frost.

In the kitchen, there was a propane stove and a table, with six chairs and a high chair for the babies. Since there was no indoor plumbing water had to be carried in with a bucket from the well outdoors. In one corner of the kitchen stood a small table with a washbasin and the water bucket sitting on it. A dipper was used to put water in the basin for hand washing. The dipper, used by the entire family, was also how you took drinking water.

The living room had the usual sofa, rocking chair and a dining table with chairs around it. In one corner of the room sat a library table. On this table sat a wood-cased radio. Granddad would sit in the rocking chair while listening to his favorite radio program called, The Lone Ranger. Granddad also

Memories of the Blizzard
By Violet Woehl of Aberdeen, South Dakota
Born 1925

My memories of blizzards and cold weather I will never forget. The blizzard of 1966 was a five-day event. It started on March 4th, a Wednesday. Our seven children went on a school bus for 23 miles to school in Ashley, North Dakota. It was already snowing when school let out. The bus driver brought our children home and scraped the windshield at our place. He told us to call the other parents on his route and tell them to meet him on the main road, and they did. The bus driver never made it back to Ashley until five days later.

We lived on a farm and we were milking cows. They were all in the barn. My husband and I went out to milk the cows. We had to hold hands so we didn't get lost. On Friday morning, we were getting dressed for the cold. He opened the door of the house and stepped out and was gone. The door opened inward and there was snow halfway up the door. Then, he came back in. He said, "We are not going out today. You can't see a thing when you are out there." We got snowed in. We melted it and strained it for the water to do dishes and other things. We had no running water back then.

On Saturday morning, we had to go out because we had to milk those cows. The cows were all bellowing when they heard us. They wanted water.

On Sunday, it was getting better, so we started the tractor and started moving snow. We opened the tank for water so we could water the cattle, and then let the cattle out through the calf pen to water them. They all went out one by one because they wanted water so badly. We worked all day just to do chores and move snow away from the front door of the barn and house. For some reason, the roads were not blocked after those five days of snowing that hard! There never was a blizzard that lasted that long since then. I am 88 years old now and I have seen many blizzards since, but none of them ever lasted that long.

Violet, Hilda Nies, and Lenora Buchholz in 1938

The Complete Destruction of the Knebel Farm
By Duane J. Knebel of Watertown, South Dakota
Born 1937

Following is a written story based on verbal and visual accounts that were caused by a tornado that occurred on Saturday, June 17, 1944.

This tornado totally destroyed the farmstead of the Dan Knebel family. Dan and Minda Knebel were renting this farm from the Saga sisters. It was located one mile east and two and a half miles north of Roslyn, South Dakota.

It was a rainy June day. The folks needed to do some shopping, so they decided to journey to Webster, South Dakota. My folks were diversified farmers, raising hogs and chickens, along with grain farming and milking cows. After the morning milking and chores, we were on our way to Webster. Completing our shopping around 4:00, we were getting ready to leave Webster when a neighbor, Paul Schmidt, came by our car on Main Street and wanted Dad to go into the pub and have a glass of beer with him. We (my mother, my sister, and I) waited in the car for Dad until he returned a short time later. We then started our 15-mile journey home. (I refer to it as journey—driving a 1936 Chevrolet on gravel roads.) As we approached Roslyn from the South, we could see storm clouds northeast of Roslyn. About a quarter mile south of Roslyn (it had rained very heavily), we drove through a large water puddle on the gravel road and our car got wet and stopped.

We were sitting in our car; it was very hot and humid, and we had all the windows open. We could hear a loud roar, and Mother suggested it was the train. Dad said, "No, it is Saturday and the train doesn't run on Saturday." Paul Schmidt eventually came behind us and pushed our car into Roslyn to Blank's Garage. They dried out the wires, and we were back on our way. We had to stop at the butcher shop and get some meat from our locker. Julius Monshaugen, the owner of the Butcher shop, looked at dad in a strange way and wanted to know where he was going. Dad told him that we were going home. Julius already knew our farm was destroyed, but didn't know what to say!

We drove the mile east from Roslyn, and as we turned and headed north, there was evidence of strong winds as some trees were blown over in a pasture on the west side of the highway. As we traveled up and down the hilly road, we came over the last hill. That was when our farmstead came into view. At first, the folks thought maybe it was a fire, but quickly realized it was wind. I remember Mom started crying and saying, "Everything that we've worked for is gone." The only building standing was the barn. The barn was one year old, as it was destroyed in a windstorm the previous summer, and had been rebuilt. As we drove the 3/8 of a mile in on the driveway, our neighbors (Ziniels and Storleys) were already at the farm site looking for us, as they did not know we had been gone for the day. Needless to say, they were glad to see us. Everyone was standing around and just looking, not sure what to say or what to do!

In all, six buildings (the house, granary, shed/garage, hog barn, chicken coop, and brooder house) were totally demolished. The buildings weren't just blown over; they were completely gone. Refuse was scattered in a Northeasterly direction up and over a large hill for close to a mile. We salvaged one kitchen chair and the cook stove, but not one piece of clothing. Everything else was just "gone." We had to kill several hogs that had non-survival injuries. Mother raised chickens and sold eggs. She had about 250 leghorn chickens in the brooder house, and the house and chickens were totally "gone." Our guess was that they ended up in a large slough just north of the farmyard. Most of the farm machinery (Dad still farmed with horses) was all wrecked and twisted up. Most of the cattle escaped serious injury, as they were at the far end of the pasture. Our horses were evidently picked up by the tornado and dropped in the pasture about 300 yards north of the farmyard, as we found hoof prints in the sod about six inches deep. We also picked wooden slivers out of the horses' shoulders (when they festered and broke open) throughout the summer.

The Ziniels (our neighbors to the east) saw the tornado approaching their place from the southwest, and ran to their basement. After waiting, they looked out and saw it moving to the northwest. They ran up to the top of their driveway and watched as the tornado had turned to the northwest and was heading straight toward our farmyard. After crossing over a small slough, it crashed the farmyard. As they watched, Math (Ziniel) indicated that it lifted the house straight in the air, and then it was like it exploded. Then they couldn't really distinguish much more.

The house was a large square two-story house that was setting on a rock foundation. It had a "cellar" that was also lined with large rock. Had we been home and gone to the cellar, it probably would have been fatal for all of us, as the cellar was filled with large rocks after the storm. We stayed with my grandparents (Dad's parents) for the remainder of the summer. Their farm was located about six miles north of our farm. With the barn still operational, Dad and Mom commuted back and forth to milk, take care of the livestock, and do the rest of the farm work. This was during World War II, so the Red Cross was very limited for a local help. I remember wearing the same clothes (other than for washing) for a long time.

The two Lutheran congregations, (Fron and Roslyn) had a large community benefit for our family. This was just a tremendous effort by the community, and very much appreciated by the Knebel family. We had a player piano and all we found was the large board with the strings on it. No personal items to speak of were found. There were several oddities that we witnessed. A wooden ladder was lying against the west side of the house, and was still laying there after the storm. I had several cast-iron toys by one end of the ladder and they were gone! Dad had a four-wheel trailer without a box on, and the tornado tipped our new manure spreader on top of the trailer so perfectly that we just hooked onto the trailer and pulled it away. We had a well pump-house between the barn and the hog barn. We had several milk pails hanging over the fence posts that were between the pump house and the hog barn. The hog barn was gone, but the pails were still hanging on the posts. We found the face of the kitchen clock, and the hands had stopped at 6:10pm. Our neighbor said that was the approximate time that the storm hit the farmyard.

Probably the biggest question was; why did our car get wet? Our conclusion was that the good Lord was looking after the Knebel family. In trying to calculate out the time, if Dad would not have stopped for a glass of beer and had our car not gotten wet, we would have been home at the time the storm hit.

Our farm was not the only destruction on that particular Saturday, June 17. Several communities in Northeastern South Dakota also had tornadoes. The small town of Bath, South Dakota, located six miles east of Aberdeen, was one the first communities struck by the storms and received major damage. The storms caused major damage in the Florence and Wilmot communities also. The death toll was 13 with over 50 injured.

For a number of years following the tornado, my sister and I were deathly scared of thunderstorms, after realizing the danger that could accompany them. As I mentioned earlier, the car getting wet was always a topic of conversation and was always a part of our Thanksgiving prayers.

My sister was about 12 years old at the time and I was about seven years old, but the memories and the aftermath of the storm are still very vivid in our minds. All the events/happenings that took place before, during, and after the storm were told many times at family gatherings. At the time, no one thought about taking any pictures, and our camera was long gone. The local newspapers carried a small printed story but no pictures. The area newspaper's major concern was covering World War II.

By the fall of 1944, Dad and Mom rented a farm one mile south and one mile east of Roslyn and basically "started over" farming again. My dad and mom later indicated that is when they should have engaged a different profession. They continued farming until 1957. They moved off the farm and Dad purchased a Standard Service Station in New Effington, South Dakota and continued in the business until 1970, at which time they moved back "home" to Roslyn.

Grandma's House
By Jelene Tilden of Canova, South Dakota
Born 1951

The urgent need to empty my bladder would not allow me to lie in bed any longer. It was warm and comfy in the big, soft bed, weighed down with a pile of heavy, cotton-stuffed comforters. Reluctantly, I pushed my face out from under the heavy quilts. The cold nipped my nose immediately. My eyes opened to an icy gray dawn filtering through the narrow window in Grandma's "spare room." The bed was smothered with quilts so heavy and thick that the heat of my body did not penetrate all the layers. The top quilt was stiff as a board, covered in frost thick enough to scrape with my fingernails.

I had put it off as long as I dared. After a brief struggle to pull the rigid quilts back, I gave up and wriggled up and out from under them. Hoping that my stockings would keep my feet warm, I slid off the high metal-framed bed. The cold, so intense it penetrated the "armor" of socks instantly, made my eyes water. I dashed for the door, which opened,

directly into the living room, where the house's heating system was located. Dad had already built a fire in the big pot-bellied stove. It had not yet driven the cold all the way out of the room. Still, it felt great to me, stepping out of the completely unheated bedroom.

I paused a moment, thinking. I would have to go back into the refrigerated bedroom to dress, just so I could make the dash to the outhouse. The outhouse was located a respectable 20 yards from the house so there was no outhouse aroma noticeable from the

Jelene's father, Louis Frank Lux in 1937

57

porches. Grandma was already comfortably seated in her rocking chair near the stove. A kettle of water that never left the top of the stove was just beginning to puff a thin line of steam. This large teakettle served a dual purpose. It provided on demand hot water and provided humidity to the moisture starved, dry winter air.

Grandma's bedroom was the only "heated" bedroom in the house, in that she didn't close the door at night so any heat from the wood burner bled into her room. She only heated her bedroom, the living room, and the kitchen. Just wasn't necessary to waste wood or coal to heat when all a person was doing was sleeping. No one was allowed to go into Grandma's bedroom.

Grandma's piercing blue eyes studied me knowingly for a moment, a hint of amusement playing slightly at the corners of her mouth. "Good-morning Sweetness," she addressed cheerily. "The chamber pot is in my bedroom there; just open the bottom door of the commode on my side of the bed. " No thanks, Grandma, I would like a little more privacy," my self- conscience seven year old self-advised her.

"It's okay if you close the door for a minute, Sweetness." Grandma's eyes were twinkling with amusement now. She knew how badly I hated the outhouse and how much more I despised the chamber pot. The people that used the chamber pot had to take a turn "taking it out." This involved hauling the full pail of human waste to the cliff and dumping it over without throwing yourself over the edge in the process and not slipping on the treacherous icy snow-pack on the path. A fall would mean dumping the pail on yourself. I knew this because I had seen it happen to the adults. Disgusting! At our house in Mitchell, we had a furnace that ran off fuel oil, and running water with a water heater, and a toilet you could flush.

I contemplated briefly the prospect of using the chamber pot in the forbidden off-limits room, or get dressed and bundled up against the weather. Without bothering to dress, I pulled my parka on, stepped into my boots, and bolted for the outhouse. An icy wind ripped through my thin pajama pants like I wasn't wearing any. The path to the outhouse sloped downhill somewhat, and if I slipped and fell I was afraid I would not be able to hold it.

The outhouse itself was a fearsome structure that was perched right on the edge of a 30-foot cliff overlooking the Missouri river. I lived with the fear that at some point, with the least provocation, it would topple over the edge. Erosion had brought it to this precarious perch. There was no electricity in the outhouse, and because Grandma's house was in town, to protect the user's privacy, there was no window of any kind installed. It also protected the user from being able to see anything inside. Unfortunately, when they built the outhouse, they didn't put two holes in the perch, one lower to the floor for children to use and a higher perch for the adults. I had heard Grandma talk about her aspirations to one-day re-build the outhouse and make it a "two-holer." She would never be wasteful enough to consider doing it before the hole was filled and the outhouse needed to be moved.

To its merit, the outhouse was holding its own against the forces of nature. It actually leaned forward, away from the cliff. This was a bit of a comfort, but due to natural settling of the structure, and the forward leaning, the door was always swung open and refused to close enough to secure it. So the user must be tall enough to sit on the perch and hold the door closed enough to ensure modesty. The inability to close it all the way allowed some daylight to leach in around the gap between the door and the frame.

With watering eyes, I stepped onto the slanted floor and clutched the door with one hand, while struggling with my coat and pajama pants with the other. Finally, I turned and backed up to the perch. Not quite tall enough, I needed both hands to place on either side of the hole, and then, with a little jump, I could be on the perch in the right position. I had to give up the hold on the door, which swung sharply open with a bang. I couldn't reach it without dismounting, and the cold wind caused a spontaneous release from the overextended bladder. I sat there with streaming eyes, miserably hoping   against hope that no one would walk up. Because of the slope of the land, the outhouse itself was somewhat shielded from view, with only the roof being visible from the house and street.

The likelihood of anyone coming within eyesight on a wintery day was pretty remote, but my fear of embarrassment was overpowering. Anxious to get back to the warm living room, I failed to zip my coat and slipped and fell on the sloping path as I stepped off the slanted floor of the outhouse. When I arrived with chattering teeth back in Grandma's kitchen, she chided me for not zipping my parka and prompted me to wash.

"Don't furgit to warsh yer hands, Sweetness." With that, Grandma led me to the washbasin. This consisted of a large round tin bowl with a white chipped enamel coating. There was a glass "pitcher" sitting in the bowl that was kept full of water, so it was at least at room temperature. Grandma poured some into the basin then added a splash of hot water from the teakettle on the stove. I towel dried my hands on a towel hanging on a nail in the side of the small dresser the basin was on.

There was a large pantry/closet room that opened right off the kitchen. "Grandma, you should have indoor plumbing put in. There is room in here." I knowledgably informed her. She and my great-gran and Aunt then had an animated discussion regarding the merits of indoor plumbing. They summarized and finally agreed that indoor toilets were disgusting and unsanitary.

"You should at least put in running water," I persisted, exasperated at their old-fashioned, uninformed, illogical conclusions. As a seven year old in 1959, I was educated in modern technology. We even had a telephone at home and I knew how to use it! Our ring was 2 short bursts. If it rang with any other pattern, I should not pick it up or I would immediately be eavesdropping on the neighbors and Dad would take a very dim view of such improper behavior.

Grandma's eyes were twinkling and her head came up with pride when she informed me "I got indoor running water." She nodded toward the hand pump mounted on the counter in the kitchen. It had a tin cup secured to it with a piece of wire so it would not get lost. This pump had to be primed with a cup of water before it would actually draw water up from the cistern. Without the primer, you could pump all day and only get a good workout. My shoulders slumped in defeat. At least we would be going home soon.

Several years after this visit to Grandma's house, I went to spend the summer with my sister on their "homestead." They didn't have running water, or even a well. We had to gather water in milk cans at the city "run-off easement." So when we finally got a well put in, I was elated that we could walk out to the yard and pump water right there! We never ran out of water. It was then that I realized why Grandma was so proud of her indoor pump.

There was no TV at Grandma's house. For entertainment, we huddled around the potbelly stove, telling stories and gossip, or played cards at the kitchen table or gathered around the radio listening to The Lone Ranger and Sky King. Sometimes we got to listen to the Inner Sanctum. Grandma would ask me or my younger brother to read the newspaper out loud. Grandma could read, but not well enough to enjoy it, and Great-Gran couldn't read at all. It puzzled me how she was able to do her job delivering mail (on horseback) when she couldn't read. I was much older before I realized the significance of Great Gran declaring vehemently, "I put my mark on it, didn't I?"

For summer fun, Great-Gran, Grandma and an assortment of older friends and neighbors would just sit on the porch and smoke, chat, and do nothing at all, simply enjoying the long, cool shadows of the evening after a hot summer day, the kitchen still uncomfortably warm, even with a fan going. For entertainment, Grandma proudly displayed her ability to blow smoke rings. She was equally proud of her skill of rolling her own cigarettes. She sniffed with disdain at auntie's cigarette roller that consistently delivered a cigarette of nearly the same size, perfectly compacted for a perfect "draw."

Great-Gran didn't smoke and was toothless. Instead, she enjoyed "a chaw of tabaccy." There was even a spittoon right beside the porch. Great-Gran prided herself on her ability to hit the inside of the spittoon with accuracy and with just enough force to make it plink, and "nary a dribble one" on the chin.

Grandma's house may not have been long on modern conveniences, but some of my best memories of South Dakota are from those visits. After graduating from Mitchell High, I traveled out of state to work and live. Twenty years later, the wonderful memories of South Dakota brought me home.

Learning to Work, Share, and Save During the War

By Phyllis Arwood of Huron, South Dakota
Born 1935

Growing up during World War II was a real education for my three brothers, my sister, and I. Times were hard. We were poor, but I guess we just didn't realize it. Our mom sewed for us five kids and we always had a change of clothes that was clean and mended. We all learned to work, save, and share, as did everyone in America.

On December 8, 1941, the United States of America declared war on Japan, Germany, and Italy, after Japan attacked Pearl Harbor. Business slowed as factories were used to make war items. Government-fixed prices and rationing began. Every man, woman, and child was issued a book of ration stamps. If shoppers complained they were reminded, "Don't you know there's a war going on?" Many housewives went to work in defense plants. Our mom was a nurse and she volunteered at the local hospital, rolling bandages. Our young men were drafted into the service and fought the war.

Also on the home front were the "Victory Gardens," which were important because food was scarce, very expensive, and rationed. Home canning was a must as tin cans were not available for factory-canned goods. Our family was up before daylight working in our huge three-lot victory garden. At our house, home canning began as soon as the fruits and vegetables were ready to harvest. Many hot summer days were spent washing produce and packing jars for the pressure cooker. After our bath at night, we rubbed our chapped hands with Vaseline and Mom would wrap them with rags so it didn't get onto our bedding as we slept.

All of America learned to save, and even do without. Old newspapers and magazines were saved and bundled. Tin cans were washed; both ends cut out, and flattened for the scrap heap. All my siblings and I were in Scouts and joined with the troops going door-to-door collecting tin cans and papers for the cause. Nothing was thrown away.

At school, Red Cross boxes were to be filled with personal hygiene items by the students, then picked up and sent overseas to our soldiers. Signs appeared in store windows urging us to buy "Victory Bonds." Saving Stamps were sold every Friday at school and all students were asked to buy at least one ten cent stamp. It was a hardship for large families. Carpools were formed in an effort to save on cars, tires, and gasoline. Our dad, a traveling salesman, carpooled with men traveling the same territory with other companies.

Our Nation was awestruck with the dropping of the first atomic bombs on Hiroshima on August 6, 1945, and on Nagasaki, Japan, August 9, 1945, but it did end the war on August 15, 1945. Victory over Europe—V.E. day, and Victory over Japan—V.J. Day were days of celebration for the United States of America. Those of us here in Huron, South Dakota at that time will never forget how the whistles blew, the people honked their car horns and the ringing of church bells. The people yelled and hugged and kissed everyone in sight.

Our family, like many, got into the car and drove uptown to see all the excitement. The streets were jammed with traffic and people running in and out of traffic. The man in the car behind us forgot he was driving a car, I guess, and ran into the back of ours. Our dad had a few "blue words" for him. We then promptly came home.

We kids, being disappointed that we

Phyllis Arwood's family in 1942

60

couldn't be a part of the excitement uptown, decided to do our own celebrating. Cutting up newspaper into confetti, we ran around our barn and chicken house throwing confetti at each other. Our dad came out and made it clear that we were to pick up every scrap of that paper! I can remember vividly wishing we hadn't cut the pieces so small. We all did a lot of giggling as we picked up that confetti.

Later that month our fighting boys came home. Many boys, who left single, came back with "war brides." Our country then faced a critical housing shortage. Having a large seven bedroom, three bath home, our parents rented out rooms with kitchen privileges and our family learned more about sharing. We learned to get along with people of all ethnic backgrounds and to respect other people's property and to mind our own business.

Looking back, as hard as things were, I'm thankful for having learned to work, share, and save.

Rabbit Hunting and Saturday Night Dances

By Arlene Schneiderman of Aberdeen, South
Dakota
Born 1942

These are just a few things that I remember from my childhood growing up in Roscoe, South Dakota. We were some of the first people in Roscoe to get a TV. My father would go on top of the house to the antenna, one of us kids sat by the open window to let him know how the TV looked, and one of us watched the TV to see when the picture was good. Most of that time it was very bad but we were okay with it as long as we could make out the figures. Before we had a TV, we would sit and listen to the Long Ranger and Fibber Mcgee and Molly on the radio.

Around Halloween-time, some of us high school kids would get together and pull a large piece of machinery on top of the city hall. We would always come to Aberdeen to do our shopping, and looked forward to going to the Virginia café to have the best hot beef combo in the area.

Some of us kids would get together and go out rabbit hunting at night. One night we shot a skunk and the owner of the new car threw it into the trunk. The smell never did come out. The boys went to school the next day and got sent home because their shoes still smelled like skunk.

My mom owned a variety store, and as kids, we were not able to just sit idle. Due to the bad snowstorm that we had just had, there was snow up to the telephone poles. We used all our embroidery thread and other supplies to make things with, so my brother and I said we would walk down to the store and get more supplies. He would get stuck in a pile of snow then I would. We took turns pulling each other out.

We lived in an old house while my father built a new house. It had a chemical toilet upstairs and there was always a box of wrappers from peaches standing beside for us to use as toilet paper. I can still smell the wrappers.

We would pool our money to buy gas to go to other towns to dances. Gas was 25 cents at the time. Saturday nights was a big night in town. Five of us girls would call around all week and decide what we were going to wear. Then, we would walk up one side of the street and down the other, hoping the boys would pick us up. If there was a dance close-by, we would get together and go. It was not unusual for 8 or 9 of us to go in one car. There was always a good house party on the weekends. Someone's parents were always gone for the weekend. Many hours were spent playing with our paper dolls. We would cut extra clothes for them out of the Sears catalog.

Our neighbors had an orchard in their backyard. We would go there at night and steal their fruit. There was also an outhouse there, which we would move off the hole. They were smarter than we thought; they never fell in.

One time there was a bad accident on Main Street in Roscoe. A car was hit by the Midnight Flyer (train). Many people in one family were killed.

My father bought some land and made an ice skating rink for all the kids. My brothers would flood it from the fire hydrant that was close by. Dad also put a small building by it so we could use it as a warming house.

Our Saturday baths were always the same; Mom always went first, and then it went from the youngest up. My two brothers got tired of being last, so they put a barrel on top

61

of a building and filled it with water in the morning. When they were ready, the water had already gotten warm, and they had a clean shower. We moved from the farm to town and back many times.

Our water supply in the house came from a cistern next to the house. When the wind blew, we pumped water from the windmill into the cistern. When the water ran out, it was time for one of us to go down the hole and wash the rust off the walls. I was always afraid to go down. I made sure my mom was not mad at me that day so I could come out of the hole again. It would have been easy for them to put the cover on the hole and leave me down there. It is funny how young minds think.

My parents were hard-working people. Mom would take us kids out to the field with her. She would sit us beside a shock and go to work. She would work awhile, and then come back to check up on us. Every spring and fall, we would butcher a pig and a cow. We would make sausage, headcheese, blood sausage, etc. Mom would render the lard and make lye soap. It was sure stinky. In the fall, Dad would take a load of grain to town to sell and buy enough flour and sugar to take us through the winter.

My father went to Firesteel (I think that is the place) and get big junks of coal to burn in our furnace. We had to throw it through the basement window into the coal bin. When the Shrine Circus came to Aberdeen, my friend's parents would let a bunch of us kids get into the back of their pickup, and they would put a tarp over us so we would stay warm. Then, off we would go. We would lay pennies on the railroad tracks so the train would flatten them. Grownups would sit in their cars on Main Street and watch what was going on and visit with other people. I can still see the men leaning up against the cars and talking about the crops, machinery, etc.

Mom's Wise Words
By Jerry L. Tracy of Rapid City, South Dakota
Born 1930

The day started out like any other beautiful early spring day in May 1940. Dad had already left for work on the WPA gang and they were working on the ski-jump west of Pollock. Mom had packed him a couple of leftover pork chops from the previous evening meal for his lunch. Earlier, Dad had gotten the benches in for setting the tubs of water on, and the Thor washing machine was washing white clothes. The copper boiler on the wood stove was spewing out steam and would be ready to receive the white clothes. Already, Mrs. Wright's bluing had been added, and they would come out dazzling white, ready to be hung on the lines in the backyard. The Philco radio was tuned into KFYR and Glen Miller and his orchestra had finished playing "Blueberry Hill" with Ray Eberle on the vocal. The next number was "Perfidia" with Xavier Cugat and his orchestra. Mom had made a boiling pot of cocoa and had a large number of homemade bread toast slices prepared for our devouring. The six of us older Tracy kids enjoyed the breakfast. Lee was too young to appreciate toast and cocoa. We gathered around the round oak table and said a very hurried grace, the same one we still use today. I felt then and feel now that God appreciates short prayers as well as long, drawn-out ones. I fall asleep with long ones uttered by others. Does God?

Pat usually finished first. He had to, as he would rush to the telephone office to open at 8:00. Mom would arrive by 9:00 so he could get to school. I don't think I was into brushing my teeth regularly, so I skipped this chore and emptied some ashes from the wood cook stove and carried out the slop pail. This was gross. Jean and Carol had to do the dishes. Don was getting ready for school and Mom was working on Linda's beautiful long red hair. She would be going with Mom to the telephone office and then go next door to stay with Grandpa and Grandma Tracy. Aunt Marion was there, also.

With the exception of Pat, I guess we all go to school early enough to do what we liked best. I played softball with my friends and classmates Knute and Ole Hoime, Ellef Severson, Jackie Budweiser, Bobby Heckelsmiller, Norlyn Schirber, Albert Whalen, Roger Parrott, Andy Boschker, Myron Liebelt, and others. I have a hard time remembering. I can remember Ruth Joan Parrott watching, and I always thought that she was watching me. I surely did try to show off for her. I must ask her sometime if she ever had the "hots" for me.

The school bell sounded, and, of course, we went to our rooms. Personally, I went to the fifth grade. Miss Fjon would tend to my educational needs. We said the "Pledge," and Yvonne Doorn came around with a can with "YCL" labeled on it. She wanted pennies for Mount Rushmore. I had nothing to contribute this day. Miss Fjon read to us from Swiss Family Robinson. In geography, we had to know all the states and capitols by the end of the year. Miss Rossow, the county superintendent of schools, would not pass us into the sixth grade unless we knew all of them; I had been told this anyway. We had a spelldown later in the morning. I was good at that. School was dismissed, and I rushed home.

When we were all there, Mom had us all eat homemade buns with a Pabst cheese and chow-chow mixture. She had promised us a treat, and so we had cherry nectar for drinks. As we finished lunch, Mother said, "Jerry, would you please remain for a short while?" Now, I thought this was peculiar. After the rest were out of earshot, Mom asked, "You're using the Lord's name in vain, aren't you?" I said, "Not me." She said, "Last night I went upstairs to check on all of you, and I heard these curse words come from your room." I replied, "It must have been Pat." She said, "Oh no. It must have been you because Pat doesn't curse." I started crying, and then she said, "You must use the Lord's name in vain a lot in order for you to say those words in your sleep. Where did you ever learn them? Your father and mother surely don't use them." I said, "I get them from Knute and Ole." Now she said, "You know, I'm sure Mrs. Hoime probably gets the same story, but with it coming from Jerry."

I was really bawling now. Mom put her arm around me and pulled me tight. With a tear in her eye, she said, "You know, son, you really don't have much to say if you must use the Lord's name in vain to reinforce a point or statement. Please taste the words before you use them." I will never forget this two-minute talk that seemed at the time to never end. She ruffled my hair and said, "Now go to school and have a wonderful day and think about our talk."

Over the years, I have thought about this so often, and especially whenever I hear

Seven of the thirteen children at Tracy's in about 1939

people using curse words. I've cursed since then, but I will never forget that talk. I was no doubt humiliated, but didn't realize it as a ten year old. Thinking back now, I'd rather have had Mom catch me doing something I wasn't supposed to be doing, Mrs. Doorn catching me lifting up Yvonne's dress, or Mrs. Schaeffer catching me stealing strawberries from her garden. The ordeals a ten year old must go through to grow up is magnified in so many instances.

I went to school much wiser and caught up to Pat, Jean, Carol, and Don in the alley in the back of Mrs. Wentz's. They were sitting on some stacks of wood, and Pat said, "What did Mom want?" I told the kids, "Mom said Pat's voice sounds so much like mine."

Call Completed
By Evelyn Brand of Redfield, South Dakota
Born 1932

In this era of instant communication with cell phones and text messaging, it's hard to believe that the telephone operator played such an important role in our daily lives.

It was during a raging blizzard that I began my career as a telephone operator in March of 1950. As I walked into the building that now houses the Redfield Press, the switchboard was dotted with blinking lights. I was later to learn the lights were caused by farm lines out of order from the storm. Wearing my headset, which was plugged into the switchboard, I was seated at that panel of blinking lights with a lady instructor seated behind me in what looked like a large high chair. With her control board, she was able to put a light on the board for me to answer. She would place

The switchboard in Redfield, South Dakota in 1962

make-believe calls, local and long distance. After only a few days of that training, I was on my own.

"Number please?" "Thank you." There could be six or eight operators on duty at one time. Most times three or four would handle the local and long distance traffic.

I was soon to learn that "Central," or the operator, was a very important part of small town life. Our town had a population of less than 3,000. We were responsible for placing emergency calls to doctors, ambulances, the fire department, and to the police. On the lighter side, we were depended on by the elderly people who would ask, "What day is it?" and endless calls asking, "Time please?" Few people bothered to look up telephone numbers in our small telephone directories. "Ring Jones' Drug or Bob's Drive In," was a common request. In a few short weeks, an operator knew the frequently called numbers by heart.

We had a chief operator on duty during the day. She was an authority figure and always kind. There were varied shifts: 7:00am to 4:00pm, 8:00am to 5:00pm, 11:00am to 3:00pm, 7:00pm to 11:00pm. The night shift from 11:00pm to 7:00am was usually handled by one operator. I worked all shifts, at one time or another.

We were high on the pay scale for the area and time. In those days, there were no police radios or dispatchers. If a fire was reported, operators were to turn on the siren, which was a larger light switch at the end of the switchboard. There were two switches— one for police and one for fire. In haste, it was easy to turn on the wrong one, so the fire switch was covered with a red leather flap.

Our police number was 260. If no one answered when we called, we then asked the calling party, "Do you want us to turn on the signal?" If they did, we would turn on a switch to activate the signal. The signal was located at the top left corner on the roof of the Harland Packard Hotel on Main Street. The light was to be watched by on-duty police. They would then call the operator and she would tell them whom to contact. As I recall, it wasn't just a light; it made a clanging sound as well. I don't remember how many police officers or firemen we had, but do recall that the firemen (who had red lamps on our switchboard) asked, "Where to?" while the fire siren wailed.

Pheasant hunting was, and still is, a drawing card to our county. It was our busiest time for toll calls. People from all over the United States came to our area to hunt, and they would call home every evening. Unlike today where you can just dial the number anywhere, we had to call several larger cities to route their calls. Sometimes there was a long delay, waiting for lines to clear. Each position of our switchboard was utilized at that time. Since this is an agricultural area, harvest season was another busy time.

There were many bad connections on long-distance calls those days. We were sometimes called on to repeat conversations for our local caller. This information was all recorded on our tickets. We filled out a ticket for each long distance caller, listing the calling number, place and number called, and also time. When the conversation began, the ticket was stamped under a dial at our right. When the caller would hang up, a light would signal us to stamp the ticket again and pull the plugs. Call completed.

Though we were seated while on duty, the stress that we went through was mental. We sat side-by-side and got to know our fellow workers. We shared our sorrows and joys, recipes, and our children's accomplishments. We had a close relationship.

I was married in 1951. My husband was in the service and sent to Korea, and two of my sons were born during the years I worked (March 1950 to February 1963). The telephone office was closed sometime in 1963 when this area changed to dial service.

The Santa Surprise
By Virginia Rawlins Skinner of Watertown,
South Dakota
Submitted by her daughter, Roxanne Hardie

It was Christmas Eve. The ground was covered in a glistening white snow just right for kicking with your boots to make a soft, powdery haze that danced in front of your eyes like miniature fairies in the bright moonlight. The Christmas Eve service at church was over and all the cousins were walking back to Grandma Rawlins's house to wait for Santa's arrival.

My cousins Jean, Jackie, Frank, Bob, and Barb, and of course my little brother were all spending the night at Grandma's with our parents. The excitement we felt was like electricity flying through the air. We knew that this was the year that Santa would bring us just what we wanted. We had been told that he might even pay us a visit before we went to bed. What more could a child want!

Jackets were removed, faces were washed, and pajamas were on. The adults were scattered here and there through the house, but the children were gathered in the living room around the tree just waiting impatiently for the gifts and Santa to arrive.

Then we heard it. The sleigh bells jingling and the feet stomping and we knew—Santa really was there. He came in with a "Ho Ho Ho!" and the little ones nearly fainted with the joy and excitement. He sat down in the big

Helen and Rusty Rawlins on a pheasant hunt

stuffed chair that was Uncle Harold's and told each of us to take turns coming up on his lap to tell him what we wanted for Christmas.

Now to tell this story correctly, you have to understand that each of us kids had nicknames. These names were ones that had been given to them by my father, Rusty. My brother Ron's nickname was Tom. My cousin Bob Gilman went by Rub a Dub. My cousin Barb Gilman was always Babsy. I was Dee Dee, and so on.

Well, as each child sat on Santa's lap, he would ask if we had been good that year and what they wanted for Christmas. This went on through all us kids, one at a time. We were so totally convinced that we were the luckiest children in the whole town because Santa actually visited our house on Christmas Eve.

Then, he got to my cousin Bob. He said "And have you been a good little boy all year?" Bob just stared at him in awe and said "Yes." Then my father said, "What do you want for Christmas, Rub a Dub?" The older ones of us knew, of course, there was no Santa, but until that minute, we didn't know who was playing Santa. However, when he said, "Rub a Dub" we knew, and we started to giggle. We giggled, and that made my dad start to giggle. My Aunt Mabel got angry with him, and the angrier she got the more us kids and my father giggled. There was no saving the situation after that.

Helen and Rusty Rawlins in about 1945

Needless to say, Aunt Mabel and my mother thought he had ruined Christmas for everybody forever. That couldn't be further from the truth. It made it a very special Christmas and a wonderful Christmas memory that we talked about for years at all our family gatherings.

The Carefree Days of My Youth
By Mr. Jerry Travis of Sun City West,
Arizona
Born 1933

I grew up in a tiny town on the Missouri River, about sixty miles south of the North Dakota border during the '30s and '40s. Those were the days of the dustbowl and the Depression, but the bringing up was well worth it with its Midwestern values, parental controls, familial bonding, and youthful freedom.

We always celebrated the end of winter when the ice broke up and the Missouri River again began its southern flow. One moment the river would be solid ice and the next moment it would break up and begin its rush downstream. We always had a town contest to see who could come closest to that moment. Townspeople would gather on the highway bridge to listen to its thunder and feel the massive blows as the blocks of ice crashed into the piers. Often the ice would pile up downstream to form a frozen dam, and river water would flood the plains along the southern and eastern edge of town. Soon the ice melted and decayed enough that the Muddy Missouri could resume its journey, leaving the flood plains enriched with North Dakota silt.

Around mid-March, the robins returned to signal the beginning of spring. But before that, on Valentine's Day, we took our homemade cards to school to deposit in a classroom box. The cards were doled out at the end of the school day, and each of us was hoping to get the most cards, wanting to be everyone's valentine. May 1st marked May Basket Day, a custom that seems to have disappeared from my home as well as the rest of the country. As I remember it, boys and girls made small baskets filled with candy, then delivered them one at a time to favored members of the opposite sex. Knock on the door or ring the

bell, leave the basket, and then run away fast or slow, the speed depending on whether or not you wanted to be caught because, when caught, the pursuer could plant a kiss on the pursued. My first kiss was at the lips of a very speedy little curly-headed girl who lived nearby. I didn't really want her kiss, but my parents insisted I deliver a basket to her, and I fled from her door as though the devil were in hot pursuit. I didn't stand a chance.

I remember the summers, ah, the summers. Each morning we were released to roam wherever we wanted as long as we returned in time for supper (never called it "dinner"). We played endless summer games like Kick the Can, Run Sheep Run, Red Light-Green Light, Mother May I, Hop Scotch, and rubber guns.

I remember going to local gas stations to plead for old inner tubes, to be cut up and made into ammunition for the pistol and rifle and Tommy gun weapons that we fashioned out of discarded lumber and our mother's clip-style clothespins. Endless summer days were spent pursuing each other through the city park, firing our rubber missiles at each other. I don't remember what the rules of the game were, but maybe it was like with modern paintball warfare, anyone rubber-struck was considered dead and out of the game. Maybe we just kept running and shooting; I don't remember.

None of the other games required much equipment, an old tin can for Kick the Can and rickety bikes for Cops and Robbers, or Cowboys and Indians as we sometimes called

Springtime migs

66

it. Forgive us, all you Native Americans. Back then, we didn't know any better. These were days filled with migs (marbles), climbing up on the framework of highway billboards, digging underground tunnels and rooms in one of the many vacant lots, going out on evening crabapple raids, shooting hoops at someone's backyard basket, and playing touch football in the city park.

I remember building cheap drugstore kites that were so flimsy that they didn't last much more than one kite outing in the strong South Dakota winds. These winds had almost nothing to slow them down. The countryside was essentially treeless, and the trees in town weren't numerous enough or tall enough to shelter us from it. The clouds of dust it kicked up from our unpaved streets could at times hide the sun. We had cap guns, usually around the Fourth of July. We had clothespin guns that could shoot and light a farmer match when we released it. I have no idea how we built them only that they worked. We had large buttons from our mothers' sewing baskets that we could wind up on a piece of string and get spinning as we pulled our hands back and forth.

We had little kid telephones we made with empty Pard cans, a line of copper filament running from one can to another. The cans were made of cardboard that held the dry dog food I fed to Rusty, my cocker spaniel pal of my youth. I remember communing with my next-door neighbor, the copper line running from my upstairs bedroom window to his. We had lots of late-night silliness from Pard can to Pard can.

We had Saturday double features at the Mascot Theatre—Hopalong Cassidy, Tim Holt, Tarzan, the Mummy, Gunga Din, and King Kong. As a movie treat we could buy nickel Powerhouse bars, orange or raspberry pushups, fudgesicles, and bags of popcorn. I could go to the library to check out any of the books by Edgar Rice Burroughs and read them and then read them again. These included the Tarzan series, the Mars series, the Venus series, At the Earth's Core, and Pellucidar. However, the books that got me hooked on reading when I was only seven or eight years old were the L. Frank Baum Oz series. Oh, how I loved that enchanted land. I loved those books.

Later, after childhood and into adolescence,

Jerry's siblings on a running board

I and my friends would hike to the river to fish those muddy waters for whatever we could hook. We used green, 50-pound test line purchased at my uncle's hardware store, five or six heavy-duty hooks spaced at four-foot intervals, then anchored with a sinker, a heavy spike we found along the railroad tracks, or a large nut from our fathers' garages. They were called throw lines, and we'd spin the sinkered line overhead and then cast it out into the river. The end of the line was attached to a stick or heavy tree branch that we pushed down into the muddy shore. Then we'd sit and wait to see what kind of creature might take the bait of worms or chicken guts. We would pull the line in and find bullheads, catfish, eels, carp, shiners, and an occasional sturgeon. The river has since been dammed and is now a huge body of water with the best walleye fishing in the world. No more the days of muddy brown water and bullheads and such. Those belonged to my youth.

In those days before the use of too much DDT, the summer streetlights were a swarm with millers, moths, and black beetles. The ugly June bugs would attach themselves to my bedroom screens. I'd finger-flick them off with a vengeance. Sometime in spring or summer the box elder bugs would suddenly appear, their slim red and black bodies seeming to be everywhere. And then, just as suddenly, they'd be gone. Most of the summer nights were claimed by clouds of mosquitoes. These were the days before the many kinds of bug repellants one can now apply. I guess we just got used to slapping them away, putting up with the bite bumps on arms and cheeks. We were not yet aware of encephalitis, West Nile virus, malaria, or yellow fever. We were all youthfully immune to those diseases. Not so with poliomyelitis, that mid-century epidemic that our mothers heard about and dreaded. In 1950, it struck our little town and infected a number of our children, killing two. That black polio cloud may have been the only dark time in our sunny South Dakota youth. It was a great time, a great place in which to grow up.

Getting Electricity
By Patricia Anderson of Redfield, South Dakota
Born 1932

My Father, Frank Dvorak, had two special traits: the love of people, i.e., generosity to help anyone who needed it, and, a gift of humor. We lived on a farm near Ashton in South Dakota. Dad loved to read. His education included eight grades of school and a college agriculture course in Brookings. If he couldn't find anything else to read, he read the dictionary. I think he read it at least four times cover to cover.

Mom and Dad were quite musical. Dad played the violin and Mom the piano. Sometimes they would play for dances. Everything that Dad owned could be used by anyone. Sometimes we would come home from town and a machine was missing, possibly even the tractor. Dad would just say that somebody had needed it and it would be back soon. Mom and Dad thus had many good friends. He always had tricks or jokes that were enjoyed by all. He taught us to have clean fun and to never hurt anyone's feelings, but to always make yourself the clown.

Frank Dvorak

In 1942, the REA (Rural Electric Association) began having meetings in South Dakota. Spink County and Beadle County started out together. Dad went to the meeting in Redfield, and his heart was won over. If the farmers could have electricity, he just knew how much easier their lives would be. Dad had two special friends that felt the same way: Pat Clausen and Ray Fleming. These two and Dad were on the board for REA. (I don't remember the other board members.) In order for REA to become a reality, first came "sign-up time" for the farmers. In order to sign up for REA, farmers were asked to give $5.00. This was just after World War II, and money was tight. A lot of farmers did not have the same dream as Dad. They thought that it would be almost impossible to get electricity to all the farms, and thus, they might never see their $5.00 again.

Getting farmers to sign up also took a lot of time. It was not easy to travel around the County. Summers were hot in South Dakota and cars didn't have air conditioning or radios, and roads were often just dirt roads.

Dad had to do this while trying to work on his own farm as well. Dad's equipment included a Farmall M tractor and a small combine that cut only a six-foot path. Machines were small and work took long hours. However, Dad persevered, and a lot of farmers did sign up, I think partly because they knew Dad and they were his friends.

REA did go through, and they started to build the lines. People started to have their homes wired. The REA put out a little paper, and Dad wrote a column under the pen name of "Frank Kilowatt." It was pretty funny. He used us, especially Mom, to write about using electricity and being safe. Here was a whole county of people—men, women, and children, that were not familiar with electricity. He made up situations about the safety of water and electricity. He would explain what would happen if you plugged too many things into an outlet and blow a fuse. A column might start something like this:

"We got our new electric stove, and Bessie was about to start supper. She put a pan of water on the stove to get hot while she went to the garden to get a couple of potatoes, just like she always did. However, she didn't get out that door before that water was boiling away and splattering all over that stove. It sure heated up quick! Then sometimes she takes the pan off the stove and forgets to shut it off, and boy does that burner ever get red hot! Be sure to remember not to put anything that will catch on fire by those burners!"

People read this column. I think they learned more from the column than if he would have made it more like a lesson or instructions.

Yes, the lines were going up and people were getting lights except for those who had not signed up. Those that signed up first came first. Some people who had not signed up were still getting their homes and buildings wired as the lines were getting close to their homes, but the REA did not hook them up even if they went right by their farms because those who had paid came first. Those that did not sign up were not on the REA's "map." This caused some hard feelings. This was especially true with one farmer who owned a small airplane would not sign up because he didn't want "all those wires around his farm." Because the REA went the closest way to those who had signed up, wires ran on three sides of his farm because his home was not on the REA map.

The REA had hired a manager to do the bookwork. The government became very upset with the board and the manager, for the government thought that some of the money was misused, or even stolen. They were coming to find out what was happening with the money. The government, of course, allowed a certain amount for poles, wires, transmitters, and so on. The records that were given to them did not correspond to the money given to the REA. The hired manager had paid no attention to what the money was for, but used it where he thought he needed it to get the work done the fastest, and he kept very poor records. I remember my Dad saying some records were on the back of matchbook covers.

Of course, the government men were very upset when they came into that meeting. As they all sat down and while the government men were getting ready, the board members began to talk to each other. They each came with a pocket full of change. Dad started with "Pat, where is that nickel you owe me for that cup of coffee?" A nickel rolled across the table with "You owe me a dime, Frank, for that candy bar I bought you, and Ray, you owe me a dime too for the gum I gave you." Ray's turn: "Frank I bought you a pack of cigarettes for a quarter, and Pat, you owe me for the coffee I bought you, too." Soon the nickels, dimes, and quarters were rolling across the table in all ways. The government men started to laugh and understood that it was to show them the money was not lost but all mixed up

Pat and Frank dancing

69

and they would get it straightened out as soon as possible. And so the meeting started in a much better atmosphere.

We had our house wired and had bought an electric refrigerator and stove before the electricity was turned on. People came to our house to see how it was wired. I remember the day I came home and Mom said, "We have lights," and the refrigerator was running. Now there was no more dripping iceboxes and no more putting up ice each winter.

Dad stayed on the REA board for many years. I have a picture of the board after Spink County and Beadle County split up. It was taken in 1950. I have all their names. Dad always said that his greatest thrill was to come over the Clark Hills at night and see the Jim River Valley all lit up and know that he a played a bit in making it happen.

One Stinky Situation
By LeRoy P. Gross of Huron, South Dakota

My wife and I lived on a farm 12 miles northeast of Hitchcock, South Dakota. We milked cows 28 of those years. By springtime, the cow lot beside the barn got pretty deep with manure and snow slush. One day, my tractor got stuck in all the slush. I took a different tractor to take my wife to the stuck tractor to pull it out. We laughed when we decided it would make quite the headlines in the newspaper: *Wife drowns in manure slush.* We got the tractor out!

Party Line Phones
By Rick Herr of Watertown, South Dakota
Born 1952

My Grandfather, Albert Herr, was in the road construction business. He did a lot of business with the Caterpillar dealership in Aberdeen, South Dakota. I believe the name of the dealership was Foster-Bell.

One day when Grandpa was working on some equipment, he needed to call Foster-Bell to see if they had some parts on hand to complete his repair on the equipment. Grandpa lifted the receiver on the phone to make the call only to hear two ladies visiting. He hung the phone up and continued his work. A short time later, he tried the call again; the same

ladies were still talking. Grandpa went back to work. It was now approaching noontime. He tries the call again, and the ladies are still talking.

Grandpa was at his wits end, so he joined the conversation and said, "Lady, your beans are burnin'." The ladies hung up and Grandpa got his parts ordered!

"Eggs"tra Embarrassing
By Ruth Jorgenson of Waubay, South Dakota

When my husband and I were married, we bought land and started farming two and a half miles south of Waubay, South Dakota. It was two miles north of Bitter Lake, also, which was too close, as the farm completely flooded due to rising water. I am now retired in Waubay; my son and his wife lived on the farm until they were forced to leave because of flooding.

My most embarrassing moment that I remember was when we were on the farm, among other animals; we bought baby chicks and raised them for laying hens. Anyone that has done this knows that when they are grown and ready to lay eggs, they will find a place wherever they can to lay their first egg.

I had gone to town and went into the store. I looked out, and people were gathered around my car, laughing. I didn't think my car was that funny! Then, I discovered a chicken had crawled under the hood of the car and had come to town with me! When I stopped, she came down and was running around cackling. She had laid her egg and she was proud! She was a little dizzy, but happy. I was embarrassed! She was caught and taken home where she was supposed to be!

My Teaching Days
By Anastasia Gebhart of Elkton, South Dakota
Born 1932

I am an 82 year old woman that has lived in Brookings County, South Dakota all my life—first in Aurora, and then in Elkton. My husband and I have been married for 62 years. I taught in a rural school three miles south of Aurora, and that is what this story is all about.

It was a large one-story building with no indoor plumbing. There were two outhouses outside for our use. I had 27 students in grades first through the eighth. The subjects that had to be taught were Math, English, Spelling, History, Geography, Music, Art, and Science. Even the first and second grades were taught simple classes in all of them. I had to sweep my own floors, wash the blackboards, start the furnace, and keep it going all day with wood and coal. We had to supervise lunch hour and playtimes. The games the students played were Anti-I-over, Hide and Seek, Kick the Can, and softball.

About a week before Christmas, we put on a program for the parents and community. Santa paid a visit, and each child received an apple, an orange, some peanuts, and candy— all of which the teacher provided. For all of this, the standard pay was $72.00 per month for nine months. This was in 1952, but I enjoyed my students and my teaching. There was one superintendent for the county, and she made her rounds to visit the schools. You didn't know when she was coming. She was very strict on the students and the teachers, but that was okay because then the students were taught right.

A Line from House to Barn
By Molly Williams of Aberdeen, South Dakota
Born 1936

I was one of seven kids raised on a farm six miles from the town of Britton, South Dakota. There were twelve-hundred people there then.

Our school was one mile from our farm. Most days we had to walk to and from school. When there was a great deal of snow on the roads, our dad took us to school piled on our little grey tractor.

We took our lunch to school and set any hot dish we brought on top of the oil-burning heater when we got to school so it would be warm by lunchtime. Sometimes we would lay a Hershey bar on the heater and when it was melted, we ate it with a spoon.

At lunchtime, we would play in the haystacks in the field by the school. By the time the bell rang for school to start again, we were covered with hay, which was so hard to get out of our hair.

After school my siblings and I would run the mile home because whoever got home first got the funny papers to read, which was a big deal back then as it was the only thing we had to read besides schoolbooks.

We had no electricity or indoor plumbing until later on. When we had a bad blizzard, dad would have to run a line from the house to the barn so he wouldn't get lost in the storm. Cows had to be fed and milked no matter what the weather was doing.

On weekends, mom and dad would bundle up the smaller kids and we would walk over to the neighbor's house and the folks would play canasta. I remember being so tired and sleep when it was time to be bundled up again for the walk back home.

Saturday's was always clean the house day. After getting the houses all spic-and-span, we took baths in a big round tub taking turns. Water was heated on the stove and had to be hauled outside and dumped when done. We then went to town to get groceries for the coming week. We always got to get a six-pack of bottled Coke (can't get that size anymore) and ten comic books for a dollar. We would hurry and get supper over then we would make fudge, popcorn and have our Coke and read our comics.

When we were able to listen to the radio, we listened to our favorite program: The Lone Ranger and the Shadow. I truly miss those years and the closeness of our big family.

Dust Storms in the 1930s
By Lucille Brindley of Redfield, South Dakota
Born 1924

This is the story of Mr. and Mrs. Simon Appel and family and how they endured The Dirty Thirties. They had ten children, seven girls, and three boys. Their names were Nellie (Lutter), Maragret (Haider), Bernice (Walz), Doris (Kirrin), Lucille (Brindley), Maxine (Stemper), Marian (Thiel), Edward Appel, Walter Appel and Roger Appel.

The man would come around to the farms and he would have medicines, extracts, everything from house to horse liniments. There was no money, so Mother would have chickens, ducks, or geese dressed out and the man took these as a trade for what she bought.

They would can all their meats back then. The pork, beef, and chicken were canned. When we got sick with a chest cold, mother made a mustard plaster with skunk oil and put it on their chest. In a day or so, we would be getting well. We never went to a doctor.

This is about all the families that survived the dust storms. One family was the Simon and Bertha Appel family. They had ten children and lived on a farm by Cottonwood Lake.

The dust was so bad you could not see in front of you. We lived by Cottonwood Lake, which went dry, no water in it, perfectly dry. You could walk across it. The farmer had no grain or crops because the grasshoppers came and stripped them.

Everyone was on relief. We had to go up to the courthouse to get commodities like flour, sugar, shortening and cod liver oil. My Dad said you have to take one tablespoon of cod liver oil every day because it will make your hair shiny.

They made use of everything. Even the empty flour bags, mom made into under panties for the girls. She always made do. I got the pair that said "Royal Flour" across the behind.

For our shoes dad always took the inter-tube from our tires and traced and cut around it and placed it in the shoes and a cardboard tracing on top of that. Times were very, very hard. Not much groceries.

The man would come with products, spices, medicine, and salve. He would sell his products to all of the farmers. Their products were for cooking in a home. You could buy liniments as well for humans or animals. He would add up the total we bought of his products and we paid him with a live turkey, chicken, or goose. There was no money to give him.

Mom would make mustard plasters would spread on the flannel and would make a pack to place on chest when we had colds. It always worked. They also had cod liver oil, so each of us children had to take one tablespoon of cod liver oil. I hated the stuff! We had to take it and dad would tell us our hair was shiny, but I couldn't see the difference.

Uncle Joe was a bachelor and my uncle.

His name was Joe Ecker, and he lived on a little farm about fifteen miles southwest of Redfield. He did not have a car or anything he could drive but he did have a horse. He rode his horse everyplace. He rode it to all the little towns around. The dust storms were so bad it would blow into the horse's eyes. That was his only transportation.

When we went to school, my dad had a team of horses hitched to the hayrack and dad would put a big iron tub in the middle of the hayrack and start a fire so we kids could stay warm during the winter months on the way to school.

Music in the Chicken House
By Helen Holsing of Cresbard, South Dakota
Born 1933

Bach and Beethoven in the classical era, contemporary musicians like Gershwin, and gospel music singers like Fanny Cosby are all composers. Many more artists wrote music through the centuries and produced beautiful sounds. But have you experienced the sounds of music in the lowly chicken house?

Let me back up. What is a farm chicken? They hatch from an egg and appear soft, downy, and hop and run about. They grow quickly, developing into a young adult covered with feathers. It has a small head, black, beady eyes, and a beak that consumes worms, bugs, and grain. She flaps her wings when necessary. In the early years, farmers raised them in pens. Their purpose? For the chickens to lay eggs for the farmers to sell. Eventually, the birds were eaten. They loved a clean henhouse fresh with straw.

It was my chore in the early evening to check on the flock. Dust settles in the chicken house. Birds have flown on their roosts. A soft clucking sound begins, and is picked up by the whole flock, eventually becoming softer and quieter. Heads tucked under their wings, the hens in the chicken house fall asleep. What peace!

Morning dawns bright and early. These creatures are happy. The world is great in the chicken house. The hens sit in their nests and eventually produce an egg. This is their purpose. Proud of achieving this fete, the bird sings lustily, hops off her nest, and continues

Helen Holsing

with her day's activities. With a large flock, the farmer gains 200-500 eggs. He takes these eggs to town and buys his groceries.

These bundles of feathers make excellent mothers. Pride is shown by the way they care for their brood of eight to ten little chicks. Again, clucking, chucking, and singing, the chicks know their mother and come running. She tucks them under and among her feathers, safe and sound.

Sadly, times have changed. Birds are raised in confinement by corporation for food. Do the fowl still sing happily? I believe this is very questionable!

A '40s and '50s Farm Boy
By Dale T. Bussell of Tucson, Arizona
Born 1936

Our outhouses were a distance from the house, so we had a noticeable path even in the snow. We had a three-holer, one for dad – one for mom – and one for the kids, which was lower. It was always an ordeal when a new hole was stuffed and the old one closed for the season.

Our phone had an alternator that could be removed and then hooked to a chair with wires in it. Then when one sat in this chair, a shock could be felt when the alternator was cranked, much laughs and surprises, especially the one in the chair.

We had a wooden washing machine; in the top lid was an agitator that looked like a low stool with four legs. To make it turn, the lid had cogs and an arm that was mechanically pushed back and forth to create the movement in the tub to get the wash done. Talk about manpower.

I attended seven years in a one-room country school, grades 2 thru 8. New teacher each year, as some teachers only had summer school before they began teaching. Older children helped the younger. Older children stoked the stove and always sat in back.

In wintertime, the younger children were closest to the stove and the older children in the outer side. Everyone wore our coats and hats. In wintertime, we sometimes walked the two miles each way.

Our schoolyard had a barn that could hold four horses. Each side of the barn had one outhouse for girls and one for boys.

My most memorable winter day was when I was going to school on the horse. The temperature was fifty below zero. The horse was smarter than I was, after half a mile, he wanted to go home. I gave in and when I got home, mother said there was no school because it was too cold. Recorded minus was -56 that day.

Our farm chores was the milking of the 12-14 cows. In winter, we had 50 pigs to feed, so in the summer it was 250 pigs to feed each day. It was always busy during farrowing season.

Mom always had 200-250 baby chicks each winter. So we had enough eggs to use and sell. Winter income was eggs and cream to sell twice a week.

Summer harvest was busy as we lived on farm that had a thousand acres of corn each year. Many memories for me.

From twelve years old to eighteen years old, I spent many long days in the field on the tractor. The first tractor that I ever drove had iron wheels before they put rubber tires on it.

I remember going from a two-row cultivator to a four-row one. I could get a hundred acres a day with the four-row machine.

Maturity came early for me. My grandpa and I worked a hayrack and horses one summer to get the grains to the thrashing machine. The combined saved us a lot of work the next year. No more threshing machine.

A lot of people would not believe some things that I could tell them about the '40s and the '50s. Great years for me.

You talk about iceboxes; we had one that held ice in the middle with the compartments on each side and at the bottom. During the winter, the ice from the animal tank was put in to the storage for summer use. One neighbor had an icehouse that got filled from cutting ice from the river; ice cakes at least three feet square. We used straw and saw dust to protect the ice.

In the early '50s, we would have to take the tractor and bobsled to go to town every Saturday to get groceries and supplies. One Saturday it took three hours with three tractors and six people. We had to go thru fields as they had less snow as compared to the roads. It was a long Saturday for us. We had three miles to get to town.

On our farm, each Saturday during the winter we would grind feed for all the animals and this was a good six-hour ordeal. Feed for the hogs, chickens, milk cows. The stock cattle got feed each day with hay and silage. We had 100 head of cows that had new calves each winter. Sometimes we would have to walk in the field with a good food of snow to rescue a new calf. You had to take a gunnysack and be ready to wipe off the calf, then throw the calf over your shoulders and carry it back to the barn with the mother cow following you. Good feeling when the calf grows up.

Life was full of challenges but it was great to have been a farm boy in the '40s and '50s.

My father had pictures of when he was a boy and his father had 28 teams of mules that they farmed with. It was something to see, 28 mules hooked to a header that cut the grain. There would be 5-8 mules on certain pieces of equipment. They farmed in the Beadle County, South Dakota area.

They had a threshing machine. When my father was ten years old, he hauled water for his oldest brother who ran the steam engine. It would take up to 200 gallons of water a day.

One day the boiler on the steam engine got too hot and blew up. It scared everyone including the mules. Grandpa's mules knew the way to town and back home even when he did not know how to get home.

The Duffel Bag That Means a Lot
By Marileen Tilberg of Onida, South Dakota
Born 1950

Two old green duffel bags, purchased at an Army surplus store several years ago, gather dust on the shelf most of the year. Each fall one is pulled out for a hunting trip.

Lynn and the duffel bag

74

As my husband, Darell was getting ready for his elk-hunting trip last month he happened to notice "Lynn S. Hawkins" and a number stamped on one. Why he had never looked at that name before is a mystery. We have known Lynn since we moved to Onida 27 years ago in 1982. Darell asked Rondha Hiller if her dad's middle initial was S. It was, and he was coming to visit for a few days.

When the duffle bag was delivered to Lynn on Sunday, he saw his name and confirmed the military I.D. Number. While examining the bag he commented about the hole that he had patched himself.

"I've wondered where that bag went," he said. He had it filled with his belongings when he was discharged from the Army in 1962. He still has the contents of the bag, but didn't remember if he had loaned it to someone or what. It doesn't matter how it had become lost, now that he has it back. "You don't know how much this means to me," he repeated.

As a nineteen-year-old recruit, he had the duffel bag packed and was ready to deport to Germany for the Berlin Crisis. He was relieved when it was called off and he spent the rest of his three-year, two-month tour of duty in Texas at a top-secret base that was housing hydrogen bombs.

Returning to his hometown of DeSmet, he learned the carpentry and cabinet-building trade, and married Lois, who died shortly after their second son was born. Later, he married Karmen, who had three children of her own. The family purchased Pike Haven Resort in West Sully in 1972, selling it eleven years later.

He farmed with Jerry Zebroski and did carpentry work for Joe Lamb for a few years. Karmen died in a car accident in 1987. Lynn went to work at Black Hills State University in 1989, retiring ten years later.

Lynn and his wife, Val, live in the country north of Sturgis where he keeps busy building frames for Ben Franklin Crafts, plus clocks and furniture for special people. He also collects unusual barbwire. He continues to enjoy fishing and hunting whenever he can, especially with his children.

Clutching the old duffel bag, Lynn said, "This means a lot." It was bringing back old memories.

Dakota Family Reunions
By Nancy Volkart of Watertown, South
Dakota
Born 1952

I am sixty-one years old now. I can remember way back to the age of three years old. I was born and raised in Minnesota, but my Dad's family was in South Dakota. We went to many family reunions in Aberdeen, Scottland, Tripp, and Lesterville.

One of the many reunions, I was eight years old. We had gone to an Aunt and Uncle's and cousin's farm by Scottland. Our Aunt had a German accent. She told my two sisters and me that we were not to go into the house without someone with us. It was a big two-story home.

Well we had to use the restroom so my sisters and I snuck into the house. We got to the front porch and there was a box of baby pigs inside. We walked over the box took a couple of steps and we were in the house.

It was beautiful. It had old furniture, big floor rugs, and lace dollies everywhere. We had to tour the place; we were already in without anyone noticing us. After the tour, we started to sneak back and had to again walk over the box of pigs. The pigs woke up and started to squeal. Oh no, caught in the act! Our parents were embarrassed. We got a lecture, and we told them what we needed to do in the house. All was well after the apology. We ran off back into the yard and played with the cousins.

Outside, our Uncle had a big water tank full of cold well water. Inside it was full of bottles of pop and watermelon. The watermelon was cut into half slices, we sunk our teeth into it, and our cheeks were full of melon. We had a seed-spitting contest.

We played all day with family. That night we slept in the big house, three in a bed, covered up with feather down beds, pillows and quilts.

My sisters and I were like three peas in a pod. We didn't understand that day why our Aunt let pigs into the house and not us three girls. We were clean.

The next day we visited a colony that was nearby. Our Dad was friends to a few families there. I remember the apartment housing. The women were outside busy doing chores. I saw two ladies washing their hair in a rain barrel.

That day we bought feather pillows, honey, and a Blue Diamond straw broom. I think we had that broom all the time up to my Father's death in 2006 and my Mom moved to Watertown.

Dad and Mom, Aunts and Uncles are all gone now. What a wonderful memory I have of the family reunions in South Dakota.

When we have hot summers here in South Dakota, I sometimes go back in time and remember Dad's wonderful German family and remember the fun summers in Dakota. I tell my daughter and son and now their family what fun family reunions meant to me and tell many good stories that I hope will be carried on when I'm gone.

I now live in South Dakota. It has been twenty-five years here. I love this country. It was a wonderful state to raise our children in.

I Remember When: The Bull Story
By Roberta Hilgendorf of Manitowoc, Wisconsin
Born 1949

In 1902, my grandfather, Robert H. Annett (who I called Pa) was working as a hired man near Canby, Minnesota. He was about 20 years old. His brother, Roy, came up from

Roy and Robert Annett

Iowa and made a proposition, "Why don't we start farming together?" They looked around and found a half section of land about four and a half miles southwest of Marietta near the South Dakota border. It was the Jack or John Luedder farm, close to Salt Lake. The owner would rent it to them if they could provide the horses and machinery.

They pooled their resources and bought three cows and one bull, and 10-11 head of horses, enough to pull two plows. They had to break up the sod, which was very hard work for both man and beast. They wanted to get the land broke that fall so it would be ready for spring planting.

One very hot day, not long after they started, one of the horses died right there in the harness. Roy asked, "What are we going to do? We can't afford another horse to pull both plows. How're we gonna get this done this fall?"

Pa thought a minute. "We'll get it done. Go get the bull."

"What! You can't do that," said Roy.

"Sure we can." And off they went to get the bull. Now, a horse can go longer without eating and goes faster than a bull. But a bull is very strong when used as a pulling ox. To see the shorter bull hitched up to the team of horses became the talk of the community, even for many years afterward. However, they made it work. When the bull wouldn't pull anymore, they had to stop and let it graze a while; then it would keep going.

My uncle Robert remembered that even after Pa died in the '60s, when he talked to people from around Marietta, the townspeople remembered that he was Rob Annett's son. They also remembered that he had been the one to hitch the bull up with the horses! After all those years, those old timers remembered.

We Learned Respect and Knew All the Neighbors
By Mavis Royer of Arlington, South Dakota
Born 1925

I was born on a farm near Sinai, South Dakota in 1925. My parents were Detleph and Ella Nelson. I had five brothers, but I was next to the oldest.

I stated school in a one-room schoolhouse. There were twenty-four pupils but I was the only one in the first grade. I didn't have a classmate until the seventh grade. Some of the pupils sat in double desk. There was one teacher for all eight grades. She was also the janitor, carried in the coal and wood, swept the floor etc. We walked a half mile and carried our lunch in a syrup pail. In the fall and spring we played ball, anti-over, or on the merry-go-round. In the winter, we played fox-and-geese and made snow angels.

A new school was built that fall a half mile west. We moved about Christmas time. The desks were hauled in a bobsled. Now we had a basement indoor toilet and a basement to play in when the weather was bad. We took the flag out every morning and pledged to it. We were taught great respect for the flag. Now we had a mile to school, and the North West was awful cold in the mornings.

In the spring and fall when we played ball we got to invite a neighbor school one time a year to play against. We had YCL and someone from the upper class would be President. We had other officers also, and we met once a month I think. They did the planning for a party to celebrate Washington's birthday, Lincoln's birthday, and Valentines. We drew names for the Christmas party and Valentine party. For that, we made a box from a shoebox and decorated it.

In the winter, we brought cocoa in the pint jar and set it on the floor furnace to keep warm. If we forgot to loosen the lid, it would blow off when it was hot. We also brought potatoes and put them in the ash pan in the furnace, they were all sooty, but that was what our hot lunches were.

Back to YCL we had duties. The little kids had to take the erasers out and pound them to clean them. Some washed the black boards, or swept the floors.

Once a month there were PTA meetings. The whole family always came. Baby sitters were unheard of. There was a program, sometimes a speaker, which we kids thought was long! We had lots of good funny readings; someone would make up a "newspaper" and write a joke about someone, all in fun. Young dating couples were a lot of the time the ones.

A couple families served lunch after in the basement. The lunches were in paper sacks, usually a sandwich and cake or cookie. Then they would move the desk to one side and play games like Virginia Reel, London Bridge and Please Oh Please. An adult played the piano. We had gas lanterns and they had to be pumped up several times or they went out. Those games were for the young adults.

We had basket socials once a year. A girl, teenage or older made a box all decorated pretty and put a lunch for two in it. Then it was actioned off. They were to be secret baskets but sometimes a girl wanted a certain guy to buy hers, so she had hinted to him. When he bid some other guy would raise his price. When they got the basket, they ate lunch together.

We had two weeks' vacation a Christmas. We didn't have any other days off. In spring, we had a field day, it was held at Volga. So we went there to run races, three legged races, ball games etc. Girls didn't wear slacks, but we wore long cotton stockings over long legged underwear. It was hard to get them to look nice as the underwear would get all bunched up. In the spring, we would roll up the underwear and roll the stockings down, then make them right when we went home.

We wore the same clothes all week. Clothes were washed once a week, water wasn't plentiful and it had to be heated on the stove after it was carried from outdoors. We hung the washed clothes out doors on lines to dry. No automatic washers or dryers.

When I think back, I think we lived in the best times, it was simpler and we learned respect and knew all the neighbors and enjoyed life.

Collecting 86 Years of Recollection
By Lawrence L. Helwig of Brookings, South Dakota
Born 1928

My maternal and paternal grandparents used the 1862 Homestead Act to secure acreage that would provide a living and a home for them and their following generations. The 480 acres and home place of the paternal grandparents were located between the North shores of Minnewasta Lake and South border of the Waubay Lake Wildlife Refuge in Day County.

In the beginning, the newly broken virgin prairie soils provided good grain and forage crops. A few bad years did occur. Like hail storms and invasion of swarms of grasshoppers. But, the big change was about to happen. The 1929 Great Depression followed by the 30s drought caused many hardships.

A poor market for farm products was the first hardship to occur. It was followed by the drought, which limited the number of products for sale. Livestock was in such poor physical condition that they were either purchased by the government or shot and buried.

The government did supply some help. The WPA and CCC supplied some jobs. Loans were made to buy seed grain and other commodities. The work that was hired to be done paid very low wages. One of our neighbors needed help and hired me for seventy-five cents per week and room and board.

The home place was first occupied by my grandparents, one daughter and six sons. When they married, they would usually move to another place to make their new home. My parents married in 1927, and because the younger siblings didn't marry, they delayed moving until the early 30s. It amounted to four moves. Each was a rented farmstead, and involved a different set of circumstances. However, we attended the same school. The first place involved pumping water for the cattle. The next had two windmills to do the job. Finally, we moved back to the home place.

The late 1930s saw improvement in the dilemma. Better markets and growing condition came along a few years before WWII. However, the war gave way to another situation. The rationing of products like gas, car tires, sugar, and coffee resulted in the issue of government stamps in order to make purchases.

The 1940s resulted in big changes in my life. The first was graduating from grade school, followed by entering and graduating from high school. A three-year enlistment in the Navy brought that decade to an end.

Enrolling in college and securing a B.S. and M.S. degrees in Forestry during the 50s provided a thirty-two year career in three different fields of the profession. In that time frame and up to now, gave way to a sixty-year marriage and a family of one daughter, three sons, several grandchildren and one great-grandchild.

Probably because of the times, there wasn't much literature to read. There was a monthly magazine called "The Farmer," and a weekly newspaper. "The Reporter" and "The Farmer" was delivered to a mailbox located about a mile away. A kind neighbor lady saved a Sunday paper complete with the "funnies" for my reading. The Katzenjammer Kids, Dick Tracy and Blondie and Dagwood were the first to be read. The town library would check out a series of books called "The Adventures of Tom Swift" on a weekly basis.

Heat for the home came from a pot-bellied stove that warmed only the lower level rooms. A Monarch stove cooked the meals and baked the bread. It also had a water reservoir that warmed the water used for personal hygiene. Wood and a cheap soft coal were used for fuel, ignited by dry corncobs.

Clothes to wear came from hand-me-downs. The older family members had first chance, and then passed them to the younger ones. Going bare-footed was usually done in the warm weather. A cheaper so called "canvas shoe" was available in the winter and going to church. Haircuts were done by the mother using hand-operated clippers, scissors and a comb.

In the early years, education was not given a high priority. All members of the eight grades were housed in a one-room building and taught by one teacher. It was located one to two miles away from the farmstead. The school was reached by walking during the warm weather and by a sled in the winter. The sled was topped with a fifty-bushel grain box pulled by a team of horses. A large horsehide covered the passengers as they sat on a hay-covered floor. In that time frame, my attending high school was not mentioned by teachers or others. The John Deer salesman who delivered our tractor and plow that took the place of a five-horse team suggested it.

Upon entering high school, a sport I had not heard of before called basketball caught my attention. Becoming a member of the first five during my junior and senior year increased my self-confidence and acceptance by the student body. After high school graduation, not much thought was given to enrolling in college. Not one member of the class made an attempt to enroll. A few years later, three male members chose to attend. It produced one optician, one engineer and one forester.

Living conditions during the Recession and Drought years, which involved my first fifteen years of life, gave way to improvising or doing without. Basic foods were available, but in many cases required being homemade. There were times when the grocery store manager would allow trading a case of eggs or a sack of potatoes for some of the family needs.

Butter was made by churning cream in a hand-operated-paddle-equipped-churn. All of the bread and most of the baked goods were hand prepared. Jellies were prepared from handpicked fruit. Pork was preserved by heavy salting in a wooden barrel. Beef was cooked in a tightly closed jar. Potatoes and carrots occupied a corner in a cool basement. Ice cream was available only in the winter. If electricity and running water were available in those early years as they are today, many of the inconveniences would have been drastically reduced.

Kerosene lamps did a poor job of providing light in the house and barn. There was no refrigeration to preserve the freshness of the perishables. They were made to last longer by placing them in a bucket with an attached rope and lowering into the coolness of a water well. Drinking and personal use water was carried to the house in a bucket.

Washing the family clothes bordered on cruelty, especially in the wintertime. The buckets of water were lifted and poured into a boiler setting on top of a two-burner kerosene stove and heated. It was transferred into the washing tub containing a corrugated clothes-washing board and rubbed clean. A big step was taken forward when a Maytag washer powered by a one-cylinder gas engine was purchased. Clothes for drying were hung all over the house in the wintertime.

The weather during the drought years was at its worst. There were not shelterbelts to stop the blowing snow. It piled up behind the buildings. The doorways had to be cleared by shoveling. In the summer, the skies were blackened by blowing soil. It too piled up in the protected areas.

Communicating between neighbors was minimal. Some had a boxed telephone that hung on the wall. It had a hand cranked bell that when rung would alert the neighbor by the number of and length of rings.

Travel was usually limited to short distances. A team of horses pulling a steal wheeled wagon or sled topped with a fifty-bushel grain box were often used. If money would permit, a Model A Ford was used.

Amusement and entertainment might be considered a do-it-yourself job. Listening to a radio, powered by a 6-volt car battery was much appreciated. The battery was recharged by a wind-propelled generator.

Dances were popular. They took place on the smooth floor of a hayloft in a large barn. Waltzes, 2-Step and Polkas were played by a local band. Later on dance halls were used by younger groups.

Movies costing eleven cents were attended on Saturday nights. Gene Autry and his singing group were followed by a serial, The Green Hornet.

Carnivals came to town, but because of the shortage of money, attendance suffered.

Some of the activities that occurred might be called unusual because of the age of the involved person. The drought caused a shortage of feed for the livestock. The very limited food in the pastures resulted herding the animals in a nearby field by two boys less than ten years old. Riding horses were provided to them, but without saddles to help in mounting. A nearby fence, piece of equipment or dirt pile would provide the extra height in the mounting.

The dense vegetation inside the nearby wildlife refuge was sought out by large flocks of pheasants. During the winter, a shortage of food forced them to seek other sources. A nearby grain straw pile was visited daily and seemed to satisfy their needs. It was noted that if a hole was dug into the side of the straw pile, it could hide a boy with a .22 caliber rifle. Once inside the hole, straw placed at the entrance would make his presence unknown to the visiting pheasants. As they approached, they would make good targets for the rifle. Roasted pheasants was available for the family throughout the winter.

Also, the nearby lake provided a fishing opportunity. In the winter, a 12'x12' chicken brooder house with 12"x12" holes sawed out of the floor was pulled onto the frozen lake. Corresponding holes were dug into the ice providing a source of fish for the family.

A driver's license was not required in those early years. As a result, a ten-year-old boy could drive a car around the farmstead whenever it was needed. When a tractor was purchased to do the work of the horses, my ten-year-old brother and I operated it most of the time.

Threshing the harvested grain was a neighborhood cooperative effort. Each farmer would furnish the amount of help that was equal to the size of the farm. Hired help would fill in the gap when necessary. WWII came along causing a shortage in the amount of help. This shortage resulted in the farmers giving up threshing, and turning to combines to do the threshing with less help. However, in our case it was decided to purchase a threshing rig. At the age of fifteen, I kept it operational.

Chicken Houses and Pig Pens
By Lois Nelson of Surfside Beach, South Carolina
Born 1935

I was born on a farm near De Smet, South Dakota. I had one brother. We always had neighbors and would help each other. We had a windmill. When the wind didn't blow, then we had to pump the water. That was lots of fun…not. We had lots of cows, pigs, chickens, and sheep. My folks did the milking. If the weather got bad, it was my job to get the chickens in the chicken house; they can really be stubborn! I had to gather the eggs, too. Some of the setting hens can really bite. We didn't have riding horses, just work ones. It was a wonderful day when we got a tractor!

We had lots of bad storms. It was blizzards

Lois Johnson with her baby doll, Judy at age 4

in the winter. My dad would take us to school with horses and a wagon. In the summer, it was bad hail and wind storms. Lots of years, our crops got ruined. One year we had a tornado. We always went to the cellar. We lost the barn, garage, chicken house, and hog house. We also lost every window in the house. I have always been scared since. We live in the south now. It is hard to get used to not having cellars or basements.

We went to country school. They only had one room. We had no running water or indoor plumbing. It was not fun. We played Fox and Geese and other snow games. In the summer, we played softball and had races. Country schools had one teacher and usually 6-16 students. We had eight grades.

In the house, there was one telephone. It was on the wall. There was an operator that you gave the number to. There were usually two to four people on the line. On Saturdays, my dad would bring in the big tub we would take turns bathing. Saturday night everybody went to town. We ate, shopped, etc. It was a fun time.

We had one dog named Babe. I dressed him up and pushed him in the doll carriage. We were best buddies. When I went away for college, he ran away. My dad always said he

Lois Johnson with her dog, Pal at age 1

went to find me.

We had big family reunions. There were seven in my dad's family and 13 children in my mom's. We had lots of cousins. Most of the families had Model A or Model T cars. We had kerosene lamps or lanterns as we called them. We had woodstoves with warming ovens to put coal and cobs in to heat our house. We had huge gardens and did lots of canning for the winter. We got our meat from the farm animals that we butchered and put in lockers. There was no refrigerators, so it was a real treat when it got cold. We could make ice cream, Jell-O, etc. and keep it in the snow banks.

Hide and Seek in the Ice Chest
By Joe Malheim of Forman, North Dakota
Born 1950

To start my story, our family of eight lived on a small farm just a mile from the South Dakota border in the '50s and early '60s. We did most of our trading in South Dakota. We traded farm machinery, and sold most of our livestock in Britton, South Dakota, and we always went to town to buy school clothes. That was like a holiday to us kids. We all felt like kinds or someone special on the first day of school wearing our new shirt and shoes.

I have always loved music, all kinds, but mostly the early country western such as, Hank, Faron Young, Lefty, Earnest Tub, etc. When I was five years old I would get up real early in the morning, sneak outside to my uncle's '53 Chevrolet and turn the radio on to KFYR in Bismarch, North Dakota and listen to "The Old Reb" play country music.

Our farm was located just yards away from the railroad tracks. We were all fascinated by the train. We could hear the whistle blow for miles on a clear day. We would run to the tracks and watch the black smoke roll out of the smoke stack and listen to the clickidy-clack of the rails as the train passed within feet of where we were hiding in the weeds. We must have been hiding a little too close because my dad came out and caught us. He spanked us good! We thought he was mean but he was just trying to keep us alive. It seemed like we were always getting into mischief of some sort.

We were playing hide-and-seek out in the shed behind the hog barn. Dinnertime came around and mom called for us boys to come in and eat. My two older brothers went to dinner and when I did not show up, dad asked what were we doing and where. My older brother told him that we were playing hide-and-seek and dad knew just where I was. He ran out the door right out to the shed and found me hiding in the old ice chest. I was too young to know that the doors did not open from the inside. Life expectancy in one of those old freezers was only about one hour. Dad went back right after dinner with the sledge hammer and broke all of the doors of. That kept us out of the ice chest, but it did not keep us out of trouble.

The neighbor was kind enough to take all of us to the circus in Aberdeen, South Dakota. We were really excited. I was mostly impressed with the way the man taught the lions and tigers to run around the big ring and jump up and sit on the chairs.

I was only five years old at the time and I remember thinking that this could not be too hard to teach the neighbor's dog to do tricks like this. So a few days later, I went over to the neighbor's place and convinced their dog "Buster" to come home with me. I figured that just a few short lessons with a stick and fly swatter, I would have Buster jumping up on the chairs and sitting there.

Somewhere along in the training session, I must have made Buster mad because he bit me several times in the face and on my hands. When mom and dad returned home, I was sitting in the kitchen bleeding from my face in several places. Buster and I were friends by that time, because I had stopped trying to teach him any more tricks. They put poor Buster to sleep for what he had done to me, but it wasn't his fault.

On one other occasion I made my dad upset by walking on his clean floor with my shoes on. Afraid of what may happen to me, I went into mom's closet and hid under a large pile of dirty clothes. I fell asleep.

About five hours later, I awoke from all the noise in the house. When dad finished cleaning the floors, he came looking for me. After an hour or so with no luck finding me, he called the neighbors, who called their neighbors to help find me. We had a lot of water from a large snowmelt that year. They had been searching for me for six hours or so.

It was dark now so everyone thought that I had drowned somewhere close by. Mom was really happy to see me walk out of the closet, wondering why we had so much company in the house.

Living along the railroad tracks, we always had "hobos" or "bums" coming along and asking for handouts, mostly something to eat. We grew up with very little money, but we always had food to eat; fresh vegetables, pork, beef, milk, chicken and eggs. My dad would get upset with my mom because when the "bums" did show up at the door, she would cook a meal fit for a king. I can hear my dad telling my mom, "If you keep feeding them like that, they will never leave!"

In March of 1966, we had a huge blizzard in North Dakota and South Dakota. I recall reading in the paper that Mother Nature dumped thirty-four inches of snow, with winds gusting to seventy-five miles per hour. The scene at the farm was snow drifts sixty to seventy feet tall. The wind had blown so hard that the drifts were as hard as cement. My older brother walked to the barn on ten to thirty foot drifts to check on the cows.

The inside of the barn was covered with snow, every little detail; spider webs, nails, straw, eyelashes and whiskers on the cows. Chickens that were roosting had snow on their combs and beaks. It would have been great pictures for the news people. Life magazine wrote articles on the storm. They had a count of the farm animals that perished in the storm. They needed to update these numbers several times because as the snow melted, they found cows and pigs that were buried were still alive two weeks after the storm was over.

I met the love of my life on the school bus in 1960. I teased her a lot. She told me to leave her alone because she did not like me. To make a very long story short, we have been married forty-five years now, with three daughters and four grandchildren.

My dad died in 1959, which left mom to farm the land and take care of the children. We did alright, but I know that life would have been much different had dad lived. We worked hard to keep the farm going. Mom was a good manager, pinching every penny she could finally call the farm hers.

My two old brothers left to join the service, one in the Army and one in the Navy. My older brother spent 18 months in Vietnam.

He managed to make it home with two Purple Hearts and other "meaningless" medals, as he called them. I had been injured in a car accident, so I was unable to join them. I stayed on the farm for another two years to help with the chores, not any fieldwork because mom rented the land out.

There are thousands of stories out there just like mine, only different. Everyone has a different outlook on the way they grew up. Some good, some bad. I have been asked many times if I could go back to relive my childhood, would I? I would in a minute. I loved growing up on the farm. We worked hard, but we also played hard. I cannot remember a day that I sat in the house wondering what I could do. I was always up to something. And, life goes on!

Moving to the Farm
By Don Dorsman of Garretson, South Dakota
Born 1938

The winter of 1947, my parents bought a farm. My father had worked at the John Morrell meat packing business in the cooler department for 18 years and it was affecting his health. They desired to go farming, and found the farm 11 miles northwest of Canova, South Dakota. On March 1st, we moved from the big city of Sioux Falls, South Dakota to the farm.

My father had purchased ten cows and a bull for $1,000.00 from a farmer near Sioux Falls. The cattle were hauled in a stock truck. The household belongings were loaded into a moving van. My dog Rover and many other possessions that couldn't be hauled in the van were loaded into a two-wheel trailer that was pulled behind the car.

It was a very cold day (I believe around negative 20 degrees). It was about 75 miles to Canova on the existing roads in 1947. We had a 1934 Chevrolet Touring Car. The heater was close to nonexistent. My four sisters, covered with blankets, occupied the back seat. It was very cold in the car, especially for the feet. Dad, Mother, my brother Ronnie, a toddler, and I were in the front. I am sure if anyone had known ahead of time that it was going to be so cold more blankets would have been left out of the van for use in the car. On the entire trip, the only one who was warm was Ronnie because he was wrapped so tightly. Dad nearly froze because he wasn't covered at all. It was a long, cold trip for everyone.

About halfway there, someone looked out the back window and noticed the dog crate was empty. He was nowhere to be seen in the trailer. We were all sure he had fallen out. Dad said we could not go back to look for him, so we would be without a dog. I made everyone's trip more enjoyable by crying over Rover most of the way. Just before we got there, someone noticed him standing in the back of the trailer. Oh, joy! He had evidently crawled behind something to be warmer.

When we reached the farm, the moving van was there waiting for us. The unheated farmhouse was very cold inside. The van driver let us kids sit in the cab of the truck to warm up while Dad set up the oil burner and wood burner, which would heat the house. It was a long, cold day, but ended warm with everyone excited to be on the farm.

Sam and Me
By Verl Cutler of Aberdeen, South Dakota
Born 1927

In February of 1962, my wife and I, from Claremont, South Dakota, decided to visit my uncle and aunt in Bentonville, Arkansas. The first evening we went out for dinner and Uncle Frank invited his neighbors, Sam, and his wife, to eat with us. Before we went out, Uncle Frank said, "Let's stick Sam with the bill tonight. Watch what happens." After a delicious meal, the bill was on the table and Uncle Frank winked at me and shook his head with a no. Soon, Sam picked up the bill, and after reaching for his billfold said, "Frank, I forgot my wallet." Frank knew this would happen, and remarked with, "I'll get it this time."

Sam was a quail hunter, and during the evening, we convinced Sam that the pheasant hunting in South Dakota was number one and that he just had to try it. Lo and behold, that fall Sam and his friend came out to hunt pheasants. They stayed at the Circle Pine Motel at the Groton Corner. They had dinner at Dad and Mother's on the farm at noon, and afterwards we four brothers and Dad took them pheasant hunting. The limit was four male pheasants, so in no time they had their limit, birds dressed and in the deep freeze. The same thing happened the next couple of days. Everything went well, and Sam and his friend went back to Arkansas.

The next year in 1963, Sam called and said they were coming pheasant hunting again if it was okay. "No problem," we replied. This time his friend had a small airplane, so they flew up to Aberdeen and stayed once again at the Circle Pine Motel at Groton Corner. We all ate dinner at Dad and Mother's farm again, and then hunted afterwards, just like before.

At this time, we knew Sam had a hardware store in Bentonville, and one in Rogers, Arkansas. Hunting went as usual the first day. That evening, we decided to take Sam and his friend out for a good South Dakota corn-fed beefsteak dinner. We were eating at Helen's California Kitchen in southern Aberdeen when I got a phone call that my newly purchased west river calves had broken the gate down and were on the loose—all 109 of them. I soon went home and got prepared to start gathering them up at daylight the next morning. My brothers, Dad, and neighbors helped chase them back in, as some got ten miles from home. Sam knew about this and called and said he and his friend would take the plane and fly over the area to look for calves. He said if he found some, he would fly over the farm, dip the plane's wings back and forth, and fly to the stray calves. It worked; before noon, all were gathered except for a half-dozen singles that got into neighbor's herds.

We hunted as usual in the afternoon, got our limit, and had a good hunt. As Sam and his friend were leaving to fly back to Arkansas, I shook Sam's hand and thanked him again for helping locate my calves. He thanked me for a great pheasant hunt. Not everyone can have Sam Walton of Wal-Mart as a hunting friend and helping in rounding up some stray weaned calves!

Thirty years later when Sam Walton flew in his private jet to Aberdeen to dedicate his new Wal-Mart store, he repeated this same story to a friend of mine. Thanks again, Sam, for the help. I wish you would have told me of your future planning of hardware stores!

My, How Times Have Changed!
By Gloria Langager of Sisseton, South
Dakota
Born 1952

Being born in 1952, I would be one of the baby boomers. Looking back and remembering stories from my folks and grandparents I wondered: what would I have to tell my grandchildren?

When I think about it, I guess I have lived through a lot and wouldn't want to trade my childhood with anyone. It was an era of when everyone pretty much lived like everyone else. It was a peaceful time with everyone trusting each other. Many business deals were done by word of mouth and a handshake.

Looking back through my 61 years, I have seen a president be assassinated (John F. Kennedy), seen the first man walk on the moon, and lived through the Vietnam War era. I remember when the Beatles first hit America and lived through the hippie days and flower children and saw women burning their bras. I saw the desegregation of our country and the assassination of Martin Luther King, Jr. I still recall the day that Elvis died; I was devastated. I also remember using the outhouse on cold winter nights, taking baths on Saturday nights in a galvanized tub, and having no TV or phone until I was 16 years old.

Blizzards and bad storms sometimes lasted for three to four days. If you ever got your arm caught in the wringer on the washing machine, you never did it again! That was about the same as putting your tongue on cold metal. I also remember the rotary phone and party lines. My folks owned and operated a café, and our phone number there was 2-W. After I was married, my husband and I lived with a party line phone. Eight of us were on the

Gloria and two of her friends, Arla Aastrom and Kathy Knutson holding a new batch of puppies

same line. Everyone would "rubberneck" on each other's phone calls. My husband's father was a milkman and left real glass bottles on doorsteps of people's houses.

To give you an example of what life was like when I was a kid, we had no childproof lids on medicine bottles, locks on doors or cabinets, and when we rode our bikes, we had baseball caps on, not helmets on our heads. As infants and children, we would ride in cars with no car seats, no booster seats, and no seatbelts. There were no airbags, our tires were bald, and sometimes there wouldn't even be any brakes! Riding in the back of a pickup truck on a warm day was always a special treat. We drank water from a garden hose, not from a bottle. We shared one soft drink with four friends—all from the same bottle. No one died from this. We would leave home in the morning and play all day as long as we were back when the streetlights came on. No one was able to reach us all day…and we were okay.

We did not have PlayStation, Nintendo's, and X-boxes. There were no video games, no 150 channels on cable, no video movies or DVDs, no surround sound or CDs, no cell phones, no personal computers, no internet, and no chat rooms. We had friends and we went outside and found them! We fell out of trees, got cut, broke bones and teeth, and there were no lawsuits from these accidents.

We rode bikes or walked to a friend's house and knocked on the door or rang the doorbell. Sometimes we just walked in and talked to them. Little league had try-outs and

Gloria's parents' cafe

not everyone made the team. Those who didn't had to learn to deal with disappointment. Imagine that! The idea of a parent bailing us out if we broke the law was unheard of. They actually sided with the law.

Yeah, these were the "good ole days." To think, I remember when sex was dirty and the air was clean. Now sex is clean and the air is dirty! My, how times have changed!

Dust Storms and One-Room Schools
By Dorothy Moe of Clear Lake, South Dakota
Born 1927

I was born between Blunt and Harold one mile off Highway 14. My mother gave birth to me at my grandmother's house. I was baptized at the Catholic Church in Blunt ten days later. I weighed 15 pounds. My brother came two years later and he weighed 15 pounds, too.

We lived across the road from my grandmother's house. We moved around quite a lot when I was growing up. We lived in Sioux Falls where my father ran a gas station for three or four years. Then we moved backed to Blunt on the same farm where I was born. My father worked for WPA for several years. This group would work along the riverbank. Later, my father moved to Harold where he operated the Gambles Store. That is where I started school.

I remember getting sick on May 1st and everyone in my grade gave me May baskets. We moved back to that same farm across from grandmother's home. My mother would make me dresses made of printed flour sacks. She would also sew curtains. Back then, you would only have one good dress. When my mother would get a new dress, she would then take her current dress and remodel it just for me. Back then, children did not have many clothes; as soon as we got home, we were made to change so we could use them again. Washday was a lot of work because you would have to haul in water then heat it in a large oval boiler. There was a gas engine on the washing machine.

My brother and I went to one-room country school until the eighth grade. There were nine students in all eight grades. In my brother's grade, there were five students, where as in my grade there were four—three boys and myself. The teacher lived in Canning, which was south and west of Pierre. In the winter, whoever got to school first had to start the fire to heat the building. The school had no basement and the coal stove was in the back of the room. The teacher would build the fire pot up at night to keep a fire going during the night. There was a big water jar with push button on it connected to a basin to wash our hands. Water was hauled in. We had to take it outside to empty it.

We had many dust storms that would last two to three days at times. We had a lot of blackouts where we could not see. The dust blew so hard that the fence posts were not visible and we would walk right over the fence. My brother and I would have to herd our cows in the pasture, as they would walk right over the fences.

The grasshoppers came after that. They would be so thick that it would be nearly dark in the middle of the day. My brother and I would take turns taking a broom outside to brush them off the window so the light would actually be able to shine into the house. The grasshoppers would create slippery roads. My father would plant corn in the middle of the ditches so when it would rain we could get a crop. The grasshoppers would come and eat it off as soon as it would get about six inches high.

My father started to work for a car dealer in Pierre and sold cars both old and new. Sometimes my family and friends would go to the Gray Goose Ballroom Dance Hall. It was the best time of my life. An older couple asked Dad to drive them to San Francisco to their daughter's place. It was very hot here, so we never took coats. When we got there, it was cooler so we had to borrow their kid's coats. We were able to go to the World's Fair. We were from South Dakota where there were very few people, so that was quite an experience to see so many people at one time. I remember riding over the big long bridge where the World's Fair was held. The fair was not about rides—rather samples of foods from all over the world.   After we got back from California, my father had sold the most cars; he won a trip to the World's Fair in New York. However, it was near the time that school was to start. He decided to take the money rather than the trip.

My parent's parted after this time. My mother had to move. My mother found a little place in the southern part of Brookings. My brother got a job at age of 14. I got a job at the café, where I worked for many years. I could go to Pierre and visit my friends on the train. It would cost $5.00 a ticket. I married and we started our life in Brookings then moved to Altamont. We milked 20 cows and had a milk separator in the house porch. We kept the cream can in the basement. When the cream can and egg cases would get full, we would go to town and sell them. The cream can went to town with a load of grain, and my husband would bring back a load of coal and groceries.

Some Sundays, he would hook up the sleigh and put straw bales to sit on, we would wrap up in quilts, and go visiting. When our first child was born, we would go to the movies in town. It would cost 25 cents apiece. When our second child came along, she did not like the movies and did not like to go anywhere, so we stayed home a lot. I had a wringer washer machine with a motor on it. Later, my husband put in 32-volt batteries in the basement. He put a little windmill on top of the house and that kept the batteries charged. He wired the house for lights. I also had a 32-volt iron, refrigerator, and a washing machine. If the wind did not blow, you could not do laundry. After we received coop electricity, we put lights in the barn. We plumbed the house for water using a cistern. The farm had a well with big windmill, but we hauled our drinking water from town. When we did not have wind, we had to hand pump the water for the livestock. Later we got a pump jack that was electric.

My two oldest children went to a one-room country school similar to what I did out near Blunt, however by the time my youngest went to school that era was coming to an end. He went to a two-room school. My husband became a mail carrier and sold the milk cows. We moved to town. The school had a mother's club, which raised money for our school functions and needs. It later became Altamont Community Club after the school closed. We had lunches at farm sales to raise money for children who have medical concerns. We would always serve a turkey dinner on Election Day. We would purchase books for the library and other community needs. Today, out of that the original group,

three of us are left. We still meet once or twice a month to eat.

Our son and his wife own the family farm now and raised their children there. A year after my husband died, I went to live with my oldest daughter for a year. I moved back to the farm where I raised my children and now live in a house across the yard from the big house and can watch my son and his family. Thinking back, there should have been more trees planted when the land was homesteaded to prevent the severity of the dust storms. I see today that people are tearing out the old groves and not replanting more in their place. I hope that we keep planting trees so we can prevent dust storms that were so devastating in my childhood.

The Winter of our Discontent
By Bernice B. Rollo of Aberdeen, South Dakota
Born 1922

It was January of 1932 and I was ten years old. The farm was marooned because of snow and ice. My two sisters and a brother had to

Bernice's parents

86

Royal, Bernice, Thelma, Gladys, and Maynard

get to Ellendale for school 15 miles to the west. My inventive Norwegian father polished the old sleigh runners with a concoction of linseed oil and said, "Let's go to town." He dug out the ancient buffalo robe, threw it on the floor of the wagon, and added hot soap stones that Mom had heated in the Monarch range. I was in the fifth grade and had to tag along so my dad wouldn't have to get me to the country school four miles from the farm.

After considerable packing and making preparations, the old team of horses, Fannie and Bess, was hitched up to the sleigh. Cozily seated under patchwork quilts, we were ready to go. Dad had to face the weather and guide the team. He had planned a route directly west of the farm where roads should have been— but weren't. This plan would save a couple miles and he knew where the old bridge was to cross the Maple River. It was a real "over the river and through the woods" mission!

About halfway there, Dad yelled out "We're crossing on the bridge," and we knew that within a couple hours we would be on the east edge of Ellendale. We had a few housekeeping rooms rented there from an elderly P.M Olson. Once there, we quickly unloaded the food, supplies, and our suitcases of clothes. My older sister Gladys made coffee for Dad, and Fannie and Bess got warm water and a nosebag of oats. Thin icicles hung from their nostrils, but they were used to the cold as had been a trusty farm team for years. Dad was soon on his lonely trip home.

The apartment had few conveniences. A cubbyhole served as a bathroom with only a toilet and a small sink, so it was a sponge bath excursion for us. A dinky mirror and an old clothes rack served well enough. Maynard and I readied ourselves in this room while the girls "preened" at the kitchen sink. The only hot water came from a teakettle in the kitchen. A makeshift refrigerator was an unheated space off one of the bedrooms. An old couch made into a bed. One easy chair and a few folding chairs pretended to be a living room. There were two beds and a small table somewhere in the rambling area. We didn't even have a radio, so we played Chinese checkers, dominoes, and cards until nine o'clock when Mr. Olson turned down the heat.

Sister Gladys was in college at what was then the State Normal and Industrial College. Brother Maynard was in senior high and Sister Thelma also in high school. That left me, the fifth grader, in public school. We thought nothing of walking all those blocks to school. For me, a school day was from 9:00 to 4:00. We walked home for lunch. Gladys had the shortest distance, and somehow had managed to get a schedule so she could have cocoa and sandwiches ready for us or leftovers from last night's supper gleaned from the "fridge."

I had a huge adjustment to make; the country school had a class of 15 and this new school had 35 or more. Violet Peterson was not only a very efficient teacher, but was also very kind to me. She was also the elementary

Bernice's dad, Berntson and grandson Steven Berntson

music teacher and discovered I had a nice singing voice, so I got special attention in that area. Student teachers from the NI helped get me oriented and tutored me in math because I was a bit behind in fractions and protractors.

My mom had made me two new plaid flannel dresses. I also had skirts, blouses, long white stockings, a winter coat made over from one of Mom's, and home-knitted scarves, mittens, and caps. I soon felt like I belonged, but I was lonesome for home, my little brother, and my friends from country school.

Maynard was on the debating team, so he left on Wednesday by train to Minot for a meet. He got back just in time to catch the "Fannie and Bess taxi" home for the weekend. Dad had donned an extra warm overcoat, as it had turned colder than it had been on Sunday. We were on our way by five o'clock and it was almost dark. Dad warmed up a couple times under our quilts because Fannie and Bess seemed to know the way home.

Oh, what a homecoming! Mom's old cook stove set off aromas that I shall never forget. The big kitchen table was set for seven and my four-year-old brother Royal was there waiting for hugs. Dad and Maynard had chores to finish, but it wasn't long before all of us were cuddled down in feather tick beds for the night.

Saturday meant washing clothes in the gasoline-powered Maytag and preparing for the trip back on Sunday, as roads were still not opened. There were no snowplows, only farmers shoveling and using horse-drawn makeshift machinery for clearing paths and lanes. Saturday night was the treat, as we enjoyed a real bath in a tub with water warmed from the kitchen range.

When I think back in hazy memories, I surmise that we thought it wasn't really an unusual January. But right now, I name it "The Winter of our Discontent," to quote John Steinbeck.

Dances at Lake Poinsett Stone Bridge
By Burton Horsted of Sioux Falls, South Dakota
Born 1932

One of the memories of the 1940s and '50s that I remember is of the dances at the Stone Bridge Resort on the north edge of Lake Poinsett. Dances were held in a large pavilion on the lake's edge near the inlet from Dry Lake into Lake Poinsett. In former years, it had been a roller skating rink, so it had a large hardwood dance floor, a stage, and a large front facility where food and drinks were served.

Summer dances were held on Thursday nights, drawing locals from a wide surrounding area including Watertown, college kids from Brookings, and towns and farms for countless miles around. It was the dance hall of the time for that region of the country. It featured a different band each week, playing both old and new-time dances. Many well-known orchestras played there, I'm not sure if Lawrence Welk or Myron Floren was among them, but it is known Lawrence played that area early in his career.

It was a wonderful place for young men and women from different towns to meet. Men looked forward to viewing the current crop of potential girlfriends from other towns. Hopefully they could get a dance or perhaps they could take a girl out to the car for intermission. Maybe they would even take a new girlfriend home! There were certainly couples that came, but largely it seemed boys and girls came separately. Because of this, it was a convenient place for new boyfriend/girlfriend encounters.

For a newcomer, getting a girl to dance required a guy to learn the dancehall customs. The dancehall was wide open with benches along the edge for the ladies to sit. The men stood in groups in the rear or in the bar while the ladies mostly sat on the benches along the edge. When the music started, the men would file down the line of ladies, stopping in front of the lady of choice at which time he would ask for a dance. If the lady declined, the boy had the unpleasant and embarrassing experience of returning back to the rear of the hall, with everyone observing that he had been turned down. It was probably equally embarrassing for all of the ladies that got passed by!

The Stone Bridge Dancehall could be a very wild place, with little law in evidence. Drinking was seemingly wide open for all ages, and fistfights were not uncommon. Old cars were all there was available to get there. Everything from Model A Fords to early V-8s and Chevys came, often from many miles away. They would return home at 1:00 AM or later after the dance was over. And everyone hoped their car would make it back home in the wee hours of morning. For many of the farm boys, it was a short night of sleep before beginning a new hard day of farm work shocking, making hay, or threshing crops the next day.

Progress eventually brought an end to the Lake Poinsett Stone Bridge Dances, but good old memories live on.

Old Stubs
By Gail A. Perry of Piney Flats, Tennessee
Born 1956

My father always told a story about Old Stubs, the family dog. He was a white-collared black mixed breed that was obviously part pit-bull. The family acquired him when dad was only a year old. Dad's father, Grandpa Perry, was employed on a road construction crew during dad's first two years of life.

However, in the spring of 1924, the roadwork played out at Aurora. Grandpa Perry and his father-in-law (Dad's grandfather, Eichel) loaded their families into their Model T cars and headed west to look for work. Grandpa and Grandma Perry and their two sons, two-year-old Murvin (Dad) and six-month-old Lyle, rode in the roadster Grandpa Perry had bought in 1920. The car had been converted into a pickup by substituting a wooden box for the tiny turtle back trunk that came on the car. Grandpa and Grandma Eichel and Grandma Perry's two teenage sisters, Ruby and Nora Eichel, rode in the other vehicle, an earlier model with the rear seat replaced by a wooden box.

They camped in tents along the way, and Stubs usually loped alongside the cars that traveled less than 25 miles an hour. When they broke camp on the third day, Stubs was missing. Reluctantly, they moved on without him. Three days later, he came baying down the railroad they were camped near and joyously rejoined the party.

At the loading ramp of the ferry to cross the Missouri River at Ft. Pierre, the party discussed whether to board the ferry and go on west or to turn back to jobs along the way. They decided to turn back. Great-Grandpa Eichel, who had worked for a Wisconsin railroad when he was young and knew steam

engines, got a job tending the electric light plant in Miller. Grandma was hired as a cook in a restaurant.

The family moved into an apartment above the restaurant. Dad recalls visiting the plant and being frightened by the huge whirring flywheels. However, he was fascinated by the little round balls on a whirling shaft. Grandpa Eichel explained these were the governors that controlled the speed of the engines driving the dynamos that in turn created the electricity. He remembers confusing the whistle the plant blew at noon and evening with the tall smokestack on top of the plant. Grandpa Perry took a job with a wheat farmer near Highmore and the family pitched their tent in the yard of a country school that was closed for the summer. The tent had a bed for Grandpa and Grandma Perry, a couple of campstools, a crude table, a small cast iron laundry stove, and a folding army cot on which Dad and his brother slept.

One sunny summer afternoon when Grandma Perry put Dad down for a nap on the cot, Stubs climbed up on the cot with him. He growled at Grandma when she ordered him off as she watched a gathering storm outside the tent. Shortly Stubs leapt up on the cot and dragged Dad off—just before the tornado struck. Tent stakes pulled loose. The canvas ripped and blew away. The heavy ridgepole crashed down on the cot and smashed it right where Dad had been sleeping.

Where he was working about three miles away, Grandpa Perry secured the horses to the machine he was operating, cranked the old Ford (which had its top blown away), and raced back to the camp. Everything but the stove was gone. He found Grandma Perry huddled behind the stove with an infant son in either arm, being comforted by Stubs. Needless to say, Stubs had a home with the family for the remaining dozen years of his life.

The Hometown Barber
By Betty J. Voigt of Phoenix, Arizona
Born 1931

When growing up in the '30s and '40s, our family lived in a small town in the eastern part of South Dakota. Every Saturday night, a movie was shown at the Legion Hall. As a

Barber, Lorenz Mellom and the butcher, Ivan in the 1940s

teenager, I was impressed with the glamorous lifestyles depicted in cities like New York or Hollywood, which were so different from this "one-horse-town." I didn't realize until later in life that living in that small town would bring experiences and values that would be a rich inheritance, and for that, I can thank my father, Lorenz Mellom.

This was the town where he was born, and he decided it was where he would build his barbershop and raise his own family. My dad's father had been the town banker and his mother a rural schoolteacher. During the Roarin' '20s when Dad was a young man, our country's economy was booming. It was a time for both prosperity and prohibition. My dad was able to buy his first car, a 1928 Chevy. Along with this purchase, he received a small record that played, "Happy Days are Here Again." My sister and I would play that record on a windup RCA Victrola phonograph; we marveled at this technology. Dad told us he married our mother because she was the prettiest girl in the choir and she could really dance the Charleston! After their wedding, they drove the '28 Chevy across the state to the Black Hills for their honeymoon. No motels—they set up a tent and camped!

Times were good until the bank crash in 1929 when my sister was a baby. Three years later, I was born. The depression brought hard times for everyone. Dad decided to attend barber college, and after he completed his

internship, he built his shop on Main Street. Since the hometown bank had closed, my grandparents had moved to a farm, which provided a fun place for us children to play, plus had orchards and gardens for our family's subsistence.

By the time I was in first grade, this small town of 600 people had developed into a self-sufficient community. It all began in the 1880s when many immigrant farmers came from Europe and Scandinavia with the promise of land by the Homestead Act. Our town became incorporated in 1889. At first, there was a creamery, a grain elevator, and eventually a railroad with a passenger depot. The town grew and prospered with every business that adequately met the needs of both farmers and local residents—and of course, a barbershop!

What made this small town remarkable was the vision of many young men who took the risk of starting out a business adventure, and they "made a go of it." It wasn't easy during the depression, but it was a caring community of businessmen and hard-working farmers. Many homes didn't have bathrooms or running water, but no one locked their doors and keys were left in their cars. Even though it was the time of depression, on Saturday nights the whole town came alive. Farmers converged into the town to replenish their supplies and chat with their neighbors at the café. On balmy nights, the men would sit

Betty Mellom Voigt and her dad, Lorenz Mellom

on a bench outside Dad's barbershop waiting their turn while discussing farm markets and politics. The young boys would cruise Main Street as we girls walked down the sidewalks pretending not to notice. My dad worked long hours standing on his feet until after the midnight hour, but for him, barbering was an art and a service that he enjoyed. During those years, the old saying, "Shave and a haircut—two bits" was true for Dad.

During my early years, I remember a horse-drawn carriage that brought milk to our door. I also watched when the dray horse unloaded coal that would slide down a chute into our basement. Some farms still used a horse and plow in their fields and had kerosene lanterns in their homes. In the towns and cities, most everyone had a radio!

One October evening toward sunset, my sister and I were playing games outside with friends when my mother frantically came out of the house screaming, "Go to the barbershop, and tell your dad that the Martians have landed!" Next, my mother ran over to warn our neighbor lady. Her husband was out of town working for the W.P.A. (Work Program Administration). When my mother told her the shocking news, she took off her apron and sighed, "Well, now I won't have to make that pie!" It was October 30, 1938, a little over 75 years ago when Orson Wells' radio program, "War of the Worlds" was aired. There was national panic because many listeners had tuned into the program late and didn't know it was only a fictional drama!

The radio was important for both entertainment and news. I was ten years old when President Roosevelt made the announcement on Sunday morning, December 7, 1941—Pearl Harbor had been bombed. Our young men willingly marched off to war and our community rallied around the war effort. The town's women gathered in homes to wrap bandages for the Red Cross. Families saved grease for glycerin needed in weapons. Most town residents were accustomed to depression living and going without, so it wouldn't be patriotic to complain about the rationing of food, gas, or tires. The newspaper's headlines and front pages reported the progress of the war and newsreels at the movies showed the war action on both the battlefields and in the air. We had a console Philco radio, and Dad would gather the family around the radio

Lorenz Mellom saving his grandson Rick

to listen to President Roosevelt's "Fireside Chats" that he gave to encourage the nation's morale. Our Philco radio had a shortwave band and my Dad would hold his ear close to the speaker so he could hear the news from abroad. One night he heard the name of a missing soldier and he quickly ran over to tell the parents, "Your son has been found; he is no longer missing!"

Despite the economic problems of the depression and World War II, my Dad's concern was always for the success of the town's business. He became active in the Commercial Club that promoted improvement for roads, streetlights, and water. He helped organize town events such as rodeos, dances, and the annual June celebration when Main Street was filled with concession rides. A merry-go-round, Ferris wheel, and vendors were scattered about with their tempting cotton candy and hot dogs. In later years when the economy was better, he was instrumental in organizing a new park with a swimming pool and tennis courts.

It wasn't until the year I traveled home for our State and town Centennial celebration in 1989 that I became aware of my Dad's contributions to the community. Dad was 83 years old and had been the town barber for 60 years. He was given the title, "Grand Marshall" and given the keys to the city. Main Street merchants had dressed their storefronts for the occasion. Crowds gathered and cheered as my dad led the parade down Main Street in a "historical vehicle" with marching bands, clowns, and pioneer horse and buggies.

It seemed my hometown knew my Dad better than I did. He gave toddlers their first haircuts and many seniors their last. The weekend of the centennial, Dad wanted to show me his large pack of index cards with all his customers' names, and said, "I had so many customers in 1960 and now there are so few." As I glanced through the cards, I recognized that most of their names were now engraved on stone in the local cemetery.

When our parents had their 50th wedding anniversary, my husband and I invited Dad to visit us in Phoenix and we sent him a plane ticket. We had a great time showing him the desert scenery and other sites. I asked him if this was his first airplane flight. He said, "No, my first plane trip was with Charles Lindberg." All I could say was "Really!" He went on to explain. "I
was courting your mother then and it cost $10.00 for us both. We got to fly with Lindberg when he was barn storming in the area." At first, I didn't believe him, but Dad was right. A South Dakota history article showed a picture of Lindberg speaking in a field outside of Renner, South Dakota on September 7, 1927. Now I knew something about my Dad that I would bet the people in my hometown never knew about their barber!

A Crop Ruining Storm
By Dr. Richard Baus of Redfield, South Dakota
Born 1932

On the evening of July 3, 1940, my dad, sister, BeAnn, and I attended a talk by our assistant priest, who was returning from a trip to South America. We were driving an old Model A Ford, and on the way into town, we admired the beautiful crops.

Dad was anxious to return home, because a storm was brewing. Two miles out of town, it started to rain and hail. The front passenger window broke, so I jumped into the back seat. Soon that window came in, too. Some hailstones even came through the roof of the old Model A Ford.

The crops that had looked so beautiful on the way to town were ruined upon returning home. We found Mother with a bandage wrapped around one arm. She had been cut by a broken window. This had happened while she was putting on storm windows to cover the broken windows.

My Two Grandpas
By Terry Jackson of Aberdeen, South Dakota
Born 1947

I grew up in the '50s in Mellette, South Dakota. My mother's dad owned the bar. My father's dad had the barbershop. The two were in the same building. I was six or seven and spent most of my time with my granddads. Grandpa Bun would let me have two six-ounce glasses of beer a day, and Grandpa Bob gave me a nickel for the pinball machine. After a couple of weeks, I was getting three to four games off of that one nickel. Grandpa Bun cut off a pool cue to fit me and built a small bench to move around the pool table, and he taught me how to play. I will never forget those days as long as I live. I never had enough time to spend with them before they were gone.

On the James River outside of town was Armadale Park. They used to have dances and car races there. Hear tell they used to have some of the big bands. Sundays were family days, with picnics and games. Small town living was great in the '50s and '60s.

The Fifty-Dollar Ford
By Josephine Christopherson of Wolsey, South Dakota
Born 1928

When my brother graduated from the eighth grade, my grandfather gave him fifty dollars. All of his grandchildren got this. My parents bought my brother a second hand 1929 Model A Ford car with it. My brother used the car to take my sister and me to school and to school activities. He used it to take his girlfriends out, too.

On Sundays, my parents used the car sometimes to visit my older siblings. Two of them lived at Redfield. We had to go over the viaduct between Tulare and Redfield. I was just a little girl then. I was so afraid of going over that viaduct, as my sister and I always had to sit in the rumble seat. When we got close, I would close my eyes and not open them until my sister would say, "Okay, we're over it." I'd sit back on the seat and stop crying.

As my brother got older, he went to the Navy when World War II was on. The car remained on blocks in the barn until he got

Josephine's family in about 1936

arm. Thinking she wanted to go outside, I said, "Tiny, lay down. It is too cold to go out now." She ran to the steps and came back and scratched on me again. I followed her to the steps when she went there again. When I got part way down the steps, I saw that everything downstairs was full of smoke. I woke up my brother-in-law and got the family up and opened the windows. He mustn't have let the fumes burn off as we do but shut the damper off too soon. Thanks so much to Tiny as she saved our lives that night.

Brandy as Medicine

The only medicine I ever remember having at home was a bottle of brandy on the pantry shelf. If we had a cold or sore throat or tummy ache, Dad would warm a glass of water, add a teaspoon of sugar, and maybe about a tablespoon of brandy to it, and we drank it and went to bed. I was the youngest of a family of six and the only one who ever cost my parents a hospital bill – I had my appendix out.

out of the service. He used it again after he was discharged. He courted his wife-to-be in that car, and then his family rode in it after they were married.

Tiny Saves the Day
By Dorothy Even of Watertown, South Dakota
Born 1924

In the 1940s, we lived on a farm in South Dakota. We had a coal-burning heater to heat our home. There were no electric furnaces then. One night my brother-in-law came to stay the night, and so we put a cot in the dining room and closed off the bedroom and the living room, as it was 20 plus below zero. My husband put coal in the heater and told his brother to wait about a half hour so the fumes could get burned off the coal fire, and then he should shut off the damper on the heater. We all went to upstairs to bed.

We had small children then, and we had a little rat terrier dog. At about midnight, the dog came up on our bed and scratched on my

Pride in Paying Taxes
By Lois Chamberlain of Scottsdale, Arizona
Born 1934

My name is Lois Williams Chamberlain and I was born on a farm off Hwy 81, south of Winfred, South Dakota. I am the granddaughter of John and Jennie Williams and Fred and Esther Forsberg. I grew up in the Canova area and attended 12 years of school at Canova. My interesting story (to me anyway) is about my grandfather, Fred Forsberg. He came from Stockholm, Sweden at the age of 17. He could not speak any English and did come through Ellis Island where I have memorialized his name on the wall in the Sweden section. He worked his way through Wisconsin, and then on to Canova where he worked for a farmer, knowing someday he would buy that farm. His wish did come true; he purchased the farm, married, and had eight children there.

My mother, Ellen Forsberg Williams, would tell us four Williams kids about the big tax day when her dad, Fred Forsberg, went to Howard, the county seat, to pay his taxes. He left Sweden because he wanted to own land, and so paying his taxes was a huge privilege. Mother told us he would get up early, get the best horse out, put on the best harness, and hitch up the best buggy. He then got all dressed up in his Sunday best clothes, his top hat, tie, and stickpin, and his handmade woven watch fob made from his wife's hair. Off he would go for the approximately 12-mile ride to Howard. It was a huge day in their life, and he was always so proud to go pay his taxes. Yes, the farm and house are still there, and I think a great-granddaughter now has the hair watch fob. Thanks for reading about a special day in the life of the Fred Forsberg family!

Teacher's "Pet"
By Les Solberg of Clark, South Dakota
Born 1935

I came from a farm family of 6 children: 4 girls and 2 boys. We grew up on a farm 2 ½ miles north of Garden City and all went to a one room, one teacher, school for 8 grades. The school was located a half mile south of the farm and we walked to and from it.

Our teacher lived in Clark but came to the school on Monday and lived there till Friday after school and then went home for the weekend. Her living quarters were in the back of the school, which had no running water. The water came from a cistern with a hand pump on it. She taught all eight grades, which consisted of 10-17 kids, depending on the year.

A couple of years I was the only boy in school so it always seemed like I was the one who got punished when things went wrong. One day when my sisters and I were walking home from school, we came upon a large garder snake and it was a big one. So I caught it and took it back to the schoolhouse, knowing that our teacher would probably be back in her living quarters. I sneaked back into the school and put the snake in one of her desk drawers and then went on home.

I could hardly wait to get to school the next morning and see the look on her face when she opened that drawer. My sisters, knowing what I had done, were also glad to get to school the next morning. We went a little early, played, then the teacher rang the bell and we went in and took our seats. Then we stood and said the Pledge of Allegiance, and sang a song for which our teacher played the piano. Then she

told us to get our pencils and books out of our desk drawers that were located under the seats of our desks. I opened mine and there was the snake that was supposed to be in HER desk!

I raised my hand and she called on me, and I informed her I had found a snake in my desk drawer. She said she couldn't understand how that had gotten in there, but she told me to take it outdoors and turn it loose. It seemed like for the next couple of weeks I kept getting into trouble and the punishment was to stay after school and wash the blackboards. Then I could go home.

To this day, I still would have liked to have been there when she found that snake!

The Storm Cellar
By Shirley Adams of Mitchell, South Dakota
Born 1935

I grew up on a farm in South Dakota, where summer storms on the prairie arrived without warning. These storms turned quickly into tornadoes with devastating winds. Mother was always prepared to handle the storms and keep our family safe. Everywhere we moved, she found a place where we could go to escape the wind and rain that blew so violently across the open prairie during these storms.

One farm that we moved to, one mile north of Plano School in Hanson County, had a huge house and a large red barn, but it did not have a storm cellar. A storm cellar had to be dug. Mother and Norman, my brother, dug a cave for us to escape to in case of a storm. They used hand shovels, and it was difficult work because the ground was so dry that year. When they finished making the hole, they placed timbers across the top and covered that with soil. Next, they made a wooden door to cover the entrance to the cave. When it was finished, Dad said it was a waste of time and that Mother was a "worrywart."

In late August of that year, a summer day became hot and humid. The air was oppressive. Our family was sitting at the table eating supper when Mother sensed a storm brewing. She said we should go out to check the clouds. Alarmed, we all left the table and went outside. The wind had died down to a strange quietness. The atmosphere turned a greenish tint. It was difficult to breathe because the air was so humid and heavy. After making sure that the chickens were safe in the chicken house, Mother herded me and my two sisters, Betty and Jo, into the newly dug storm cellar.

When we entered the cave, Mother lit a kerosene lamp. There were big snakes down there. But when the snakes saw the light, they crawled to the back of the cellar where it was dark. I stayed close beside Mother and her lamp. They were harmless bull snakes, but another fear to think of as the storm raged outside.

Dad and Norman also left the house, but they balked at entering the small cave. They leaned against the lee side of the house next to the cave as the storm approached. Mother and my oldest sister, Betty, pleaded with them, "Please come down, please." At last, when the house began to shake and sway, they both came slipping, sliding, down into the cellar, with the rain coming down around them as the tempest outside increased in intensity. Just as they closed the door behind them, we heard a loud explosion. We thought the house was surely gone.

When the wind and rain subsided somewhat, Dad slowly opened the cellar door and stepped out to view the destruction. He called back, 'The house is standing, but the top half of the barn is gone." Thankfully, we emerged from our hole. The family was safe and our house was intact. Only the roof of the barn was gone. The milk cows and horses were safe in their stalls in the lower part of the barn.

Our family and our farm animals had survived one more episode of life on the prairie.

Soda Jerk Stories from Klein's Drug Store
By Beverly M. Prostrollo of Deadwood,
South Dakota
Born 1928

This is my story. I was born in 1928 in my grandparents' house. I am number nine in a family of twelve. I went through all twelve grades of the public school in Howard, SD. I figured I was born there and would probably die there. I now live in the opposite side of the state, so this probably won't be true.

When I was small I was given a nice doll with hair and I didn't think I would ever get another one, so I hid it outdoors under the porch in the snow, so my little sisters couldn't find it. They didn't, but the dog did and tore it to shreds.

As kids growing up with neighbor kids, we played board games and ice skated in the winter, and in summer played wood tag, anti-I-over the barn in the backyard, and had a bag swing in a neighbor's empty lot, because it had several large trees. The same bunch of kids played softball behind St. John's church. A line drive across second base meant the preacher's tomatoes were in jeopardy. There was also an iron bar at the edge of the lot (probably to tie horses to at one time) that we did gymnastics on while waiting for our turn to bat.

My grandparents' house was right next to ours, which was about half a block from the railroad tracks. This meant we would sometimes have to wait for the train to move so we could go to school. We would always wave or holler to the men working on the train. Living this close to the rail yard meant a short walk for hobos to come to my grandma's back door where she would feed them. Sometimes we would be allowed to visit with them. This same train, in wartime, took many from our town to the war zones. All four of my brothers were in the service at the same time. One gave his life for our country.

When we could earn a dime, it was enough to go to the movie, which we wanted to do every week to see what happened in the next episode of the serial. Did Pearl get loose from being tied to the tracks? We, along with some neighbor kids, had Orphan Annie magic decoders to see what would take place the next day on the radio. We also used these to send notes in school.

My dad bragged about our dog Blackie and the time Rafferty Drug Store had a deal that if you brought an egg in you could get an ice cream cone free. He put an egg in Blackie's mouth and sent him to Rafferty's and they gave him an ice cream cone. He also told of making "home-brew" with a neighbor and the beer bottles blew up under the neighbor's bed, the wife hit the ceiling, and glass and beer were all over the floor. He also had a chance to play catch with Bob Feller, one of the baseball greats. Dad was a pitcher for several local teams for several years. I worked for

Mrs. Feller (Bob's aunt) and ruined one of her blouses, because it got stuck in the wringer on the washing machine.

Every household in Howard washed clothes on Monday and there seemed to be a race to see who would get theirs hung on the line first.

One of my older sisters with her chums followed the town's bootlegger and watched where he hid the stuff he brought back from Canada. When he left, the girls moved it to another place.

I got a job working at Klein's Drug Store as a "soda jerk" when I was a senior in high school. This meant a lot of teasing from classmates when they would come in, usually on Saturday nights. The farmers would come to town Saturdays for supplies and news of local interest. The kids would walk around the block many times while the women gathered some place to visit. We had one old fellow that would wait until about closing time and come in for an ice cream cone, pay for it, put it in his pocket, and leave. He would sit in the doorway of the next building to eat it.

After graduation, I started working in the Miner County Treasurer's office. A couple years later, I married the man I met while at the drug store, moved to Madison (22 miles away), had a family, worked in our bowling center, retired, and moved to the Black Hills of SD.

That's my story and I'm sticking to it.

Snakes Make Me Shake
By Ardyce (Steen) Struck of New Effington, South Dakota
Born 1927

I have always been scared of snakes. Regardless of how large or small, I am simply terrified when I see one. I don't know exactly how it started, but perhaps it was when I first went to Sunday school and heard of Adam and Eve in the Garden of Eden.

The first incident I remember is way back in the early days of no electricity. Indoor plumbing was something in the distant future. The outdoor privy was a necessity. When we said we had to visit Mrs. Jones, we headed out to the little house in the trees. When I was there one morning, to my horror, a snake was slithering in under the door. I started to scream

Ardyce and her twin brother Arlie with a baby chick

and ran out of the door.

My dad and two hired men heard the uproar and came running with pitchforks in hand. All they saw was a scantily dressed little girl screaming and crying. My assailant had slithered off into the grass, but they guessed what I had thought had been so scary and walked away laughing. Many years later whenever I met these two men, they'd smile and ask me if I had been attacked again.

Years later while teaching in a rural school, a six-year-old boy came in and said, "I brought you a present, Teacher." I said, "How nice, Little Tommy," and stretched out my hand expecting an apple or candy. To my horror, he reached in his pocket and pulled out a foot long garter snake. I don't know how I kept from screaming, but I put on my serious face and said "Oh Tommy, you've got to take that baby out to his mother. She's so lonesome and sad." He looked at me so seriously and said, "Okay, I better go find her," and left with his gift still in his pocket. I bet he thought later, my teacher always said to tell the truth, but that time she really told a whopper!

To this day, I never go to a zoo, because I imagine a boa or python might get out of his cage. Silly but true.

Little Flicka
By Lyle Berg of Webster, South Dakota
Born 1932

Once, a young farm boy had a small Shetland pony named Princes who had a little baby. The young farm boy was me, and the little baby was my pet horse, Flicka. The little baby was sorrel with white socks, a white tail, and a white blaze on her forehead, as did the real horse Flicka in the movie. My Flicka was small and was a natural pet with lots of friends. She had a weak understanding of typical rules of behavior for a horse, even a very small horse that was quite worthless except as a pet. Flicka taught me (her also small, incompetent handler) quite a few things. In memory, it seems that she taught me more than I taught her.

One very nice morning as my mother was outside hanging clothes on the line for drying, Flicka, from her restraint-free grazing position in the farmyard, decided she would enter the house. Her nose opened the porch door and she proceeded through the kitchen and living room. She then found the bedroom where a neatly made-up bed with a pretty bedspread was in place over the pillows. Possibly Flicka was thinking of a mid-morning nap. My mother returned into the house and was shocked to find the little horse in the bedroom with the spread pulled back in preparation for occupancy. Yes, Little Flicka did act in her own little way without concern or permission, but she was a cute "little girl." She was cuddly and generally worthless. She got by with about everything she decided to do. Maybe it was Flicka who inspired the later years song, "I Did it My Way."

A Boom-Boomety-Boom Oven
As a young boy in our small house on the farm, my mother stored her portable stovetop baking on the catchall table in the entry porch. That portable oven on the porch table was also a handy place for me, "the young boy" to place the 410-shotgun shell clip of my bolt action Springfield. Of course, a young hunter was taught to not leave a gun loaded when stored in the house. Hence, I removed the clip filled with shells.

One day, my mother carried the oven into the small kitchen and placed it on the wood-burning range to warm up prior to baking an angel food cake. That hot stove activated the gunpowder in the shells in the clip stored on the bottom of the oven. There was a very loud boom-bommety-boom sequence and a reshaped portable oven on the stove. It was good that the oven door was latched and the angel food cake pan wasn't in the oven yet.

I recall the conclusion being a frequently told story with the ending that a portable oven was not a good place to store shotgun shells. That was, of course, after my mother had gathered her wits about what happened!

The Gift
By Bob Boardman of Grenville, South Dakota
Born 1947

It was in the spring of 1951—April I believe. It must have been because I had turned six years old on the 17th. It must have been just another day because I didn't have a party. I remember the snow banks came about two or three feet from the electric wires. The county had given up on trying to keep the roads open. My dad was in Sisseton trying to get a little work.

We lived in a two-room house in Hillhead, South Dakota. Actually, the house belonged to my grandpa and grandma. They had left and moved to St. Paul, Minnesota to find work. We didn't have any electricity or running water. But we had a good well with a good pump on it, just about 50 feet in front of the house—good water. I remember a two-hole outhouse, chicken coop and a small barn.

There were five of us kids. My brother Archie, who was the oldest, had already left home just out of the eighth grade. Next was Shirley; my mother had to farm her out to an older couple. Donna was in the second grade at home. I came next. Barbara is 15 months younger than me.

We had a little oil stove in the room where we slept to keep warm. I have no idea where we got the money to buy oil for it. In the kitchen, we had that big old beautiful wood cook stove. I remember getting some food from the county. At least it kept us from starving, but we had to ration it out each month. Sometimes we would run out of food.

Mom would go without eating so we could have a little food every day.

Mom and I would go down by the creek in front of the house and she would cut that three-cornered slough grass and tie it into a knot. That was what we had to use to burn in the cook stove. Plus we would go out in the neighbor's pasture and pick up dried cow pies. The neighbors would keep and haul the corncobs over after they got done picking the corn. We did have a dirt basement so we would put all the burnable stuff down in that dark hole. Oh yes, it was always my job to go in the dark hole.

Well, like I said, it was after April 17th, because of my birthday. I don't really remember how many days it was after my big day, but Mom told me one morning to hurry up and get dressed to go outside. I asked her "What for?" We looked out the door and she said, "You see all of them black things in the snow?" I told her that I did. Well it had rained that night and well, she told me they were pheasants and they got all wet, then they froze. Mom gave me a big sack and I got as many as I could.

The snow was frozen just hard enough to hold me up. At first, I was scared to pick one up. Then Mom hollered at me that they would be good eating. Well, I must have gotten eight or ten of them. I remember they were very heavy to drag. Mom told me to stay away from the electric wires. At that time, I had no idea what would happen if I touched one wire. Well, I finally got to the house. All this time Mom was standing in the door keeping an eye on me.

What she did to those birds next, I couldn't believe. Of course, she had to kill them and clean them. Well, as I was gathering them up I thought I could make pets out of them. When she killed them, I remember I started to cry and then Barb started to cry. We finally stopped crying. All I know is that we ate like kings and queens for the next few days.

When I was married to my second wife, she told me how poor her family was when she was little. I told her, "With a pasture full of cows and the White River full of fish, and you were poor?" But you know, we didn't realize we were poor, just like so many other people. The pheasants were the gift.

Eternal Communication
By Vernon Vedvei of Hetland, South Dakota
Born 1927

If you take Highway 14 west out of Arlington, you travel about six miles until you see a sign that says Hetland. Turn right and drive slow. Otherwise, you will miss it. There isn't much left of the town: a grain elevator, an old school house, a bank, and a few homes. But, at the north end of Main Street sits an old square building, the original telephone office, built in 1903. A person would have to plug into a switchboard to connect one caller to another. My wife's grandmother was the first telephone operator.

I had the privilege to go to high school in Hetland. When the weather got real bad, I got to stay in town. There were no buses like today. I either stayed at the dorm or at a private home. This was a good deal for me. I didn't have to milk cows before school. There was one catch to all of this, though. I had to call home once a week!

I think there was a telephone in the principal's office, but I never went there except by request! To call home, I would have to spend at least one or two hours waiting for my call to go through. We were on a party line of eight, so it took a long time.

Every time I drive through the old town, I think about those days. Now days, technology includes cell phones, text, e-mail, caller ID, answering machines, and other things. Yet nothing compares to prayer. That is one call we can make, anytime and from any place. The line is never busy, the rates are good, and it is free day and night. God knows who is calling. He always answers prayer, sometimes

The original telephone office built in 1903

right away and sometimes at His appointed time.

This is a song I love to sing:
Central's never busy, Always on the line,
You may hear from Heaven almost any time.
'Tis a royal service, Free to one and all,
When you get in trouble give this royal line a call.
Telephone to glory, O what joy divine!
I can feel the current moving on the line;
Built by God the Father for His loved and own,
We may talk to Jesus thro' this royal telephone.

Life on the Farm
By Nila Weidler of Howard, South Dakota
Born 1927

March 1st was named "moving day," meaning if you were to move to a different farm, this was the day. Many families moved every year. Sometimes it was only across the road. Families were usually large with several children of all ages.

In 1931-32, a small girl (me), Father, and Mother moved to a farm after living in town in Madison for the first two and a half years of her life. Those were the years in the Great Depression, also called the "Dirty Thirties." Lamps were the only form of light aside from the sunlight. Old, dead trees were cut down and into smaller pieces to be carried to the house for heat and cooking. Before dark each day, chores had to be done, such as feeding farm animals, milking cows, and gathering eggs. No brothers of sisters meant no playmates for this young girl.

While playing near the house one day, a friendly dog found her. His former owner had moved somewhere else and the dog had hopes of finding his past home that the loved. This farmer was glad to have a good dog to help keep his cattle in pasture, as they were used to getting out to eat better grass. In a few days, they learned a new boss was in charge there. This dog was a very good cattle dog. He watched open gates, helped the farmer bring milk cows into the barn at chore time.

He was a good pet for the little girl as well. In a few years, she would go to school less than a half mile away. A true friend, the dog would walk with her each day unless schoolchildren with her. Then, he would wait for her to return later in the afternoon with the others. One day at school, she saw their cattle out in the field across from the farm and told the teacher she had to go home and help get the cattle back. The teacher told her no, as she was sure the farmer had let them out to eat. Also, on her first day of school she sat on the edge of her desk and swung her legs and whistled as loud as possible. The rest of the children thought this was funny, but the teacher put a stop to it shortly. The teacher and this family were best friends and neighbors for many years. This teacher passed away a few years ago at the age of 100 years. Both families were forever friends.

In the wintertime when roads were blocked, food was shared. Much ice cream was made and cards were played. My dad started old time dance in Ramona, held every Friday night. Men were charged a quarter; ladies were free. A lunch of a hamburger was a quarter, coffee a nickel. Some winter nights, Mom, Dad, and a neighbor would walk a mile to ride with another neighbor who lived on a better road. One night while dancing, wind came up and a blizzard started. As they got out of the car to start waking, the wind blew out the lantern light and it was nearly impossible to see anything. Out of nowhere, the farmer's good dog came and led the three safely home. Dad said he saved them.

He lived many years until he was poisoned or ate something with poison in it. He didn't die at once, but had a slow, sad death. He was our faithful friend, and we had named him Collie, as he was a beautiful collie dog.

Kansas to South Dakota
In 1911, my dad's family moved from Western Kansas to Eastern South Dakota near Madison. Shortly after getting to the new farm, they noticed that their dog had left. They wrote a letter to the family on their old home in Kansas that their dog had left and could return there. Time passed, and then a letter came from them. Their dog had indeed returned there, but after a few weeks, had left again. Maybe he was on his way back to them. Time passed. He came back to his family. He was very thin; his paws were worn and sore. He stayed this time, but the long miles that he walked with very little to eat or drink was just too much for him. He didn't recover, so he passed away later on. As the saying goes, "Dogs are man's best friend." This saying is very true.

Hired to Work

One winter in the late '30s, the state and country wanted to try to get better roads built. They hired my dad with his good workhorses to work on them. Dad worked long hours in the cold winter. At night, he had chores on the farm to do that Mom couldn't get done, such as milking cows, carrying feed, and feeding the farm animals. He had to brush and care for the good horses that had worked so hard, too. These were improved dirt roads, but were better than before. Gravel roads came later.

Let There Be Lights

In the late '30s, a new act was passed by President Franklin D. Roosevelt to get lights to the farmers and rural areas. Each place would pay a signup fee of $5.00. They would need two places per mile from the main line before they could be hooked up. My dad believed in any new and better thing for farmers. He sent the $5.00 in at once. Other farmers thought he was foolish; they said he would never get REA. Since we lived over a mile from the main line, we didn't it approved because the ones between us and the main line didn't sign up. So, we didn't get REA until 1948. Then, the ones who didn't sign up before though this was a great project and should have been done years ago!

What More Can You Ask For?
By Edward H. Lamers of West Browns Valley, Minnesota
Born 1927

I started school and went through the eighth grade in a one-room school in Becker Township in Roberts County, South Dakota. I was the only one in my class until the 6th grade. We had no electricity and one outhouse

Edwards's family in 1969

for all.

I walked one and a half miles to school, winter, or summer. Anna Bonzlet (we called her "Grandma") and family lived part way and in real cold weather she would have me come in and have hot chocolate, then bundle me up and send me on my way.

In first grade most all our toys were handmade and we carried lunch pails with many times lard on my bread, and sometimes brown sugar on there—what a treat!

My teacher in first grade was Cleo Kelly from Peever, South Dakota. She was my favorite teacher. In 1934, the dust storms were so bad I remember the teacher would light a lamp and keep us until the parents would come with horse and wagon and pick us up on the worst days. Then the winter of 1935-1936, we had heavy snow and we had a big ravine by the farm that filled up with the wind driving it. My dad dug a hole and put straw in it and that was my playground till spring. The roads stayed plugged and we walked to mass on Sundays. My dad and myself, with a lot of farmers out our way, walked 3 ½ miles sometimes on Saturday if we needed groceries or coal. We took the horses and sled to town, cutting across fields if the banks were too high in the road. The post office would stay open on Sunday so folks that walked in for church could get their mail.

We had wood and coal stoves for heat.

I had a pony named Baldy and always rode bareback after the milk cows. The pasture was 1 ½ miles long. One spring a quick thaw one day left the cows caught across the river on the far end. The pony had to swim and I slipped off and hung onto his tail both ways as my dad had told me the cows had to come across the current. I was scared but made it.

I remember school games such as Fox and Geese, Anti Over, a lot of marbles, and Kick the Can. We always had a lot of chores and lots of geese, ducks, and laying hens. Dad had just butchered a hog and used a big iron vat to dip the hog in hot water to scrape the hair off. The folks had gone to town and as a kid; I was going to 'learn' chickens to swim. I had maybe 6 drowned when Dad got home and I got a real licking. Never tried that again.

I remember a few home remedies my mother used for chest colds: mostly skunk grease. I had a lot of boils when I was around 7 or 8 and the doctor had the folks mix sulfur,

Ed on the tractor with a cultivator

honey, and burnt charcoal, and feed that to me. The boils went away, not sure why.

In 1937, I got bucked off a pony on account of riding backwards and broke my left leg. Doctor Bates set it but it swelled up in the cast and they had to cut it off and I had sores all the way. They had 2 big men hold me down to treat the blisters.

In 1936 on the rented farm we lived on they had big sloughs and in there we got a little wheat and oats and that fall Kurrasch from Peever, SD, came with his threshing machine and 6 of the local farmers came with wagons and racks and threshed it. Nobody got a basket full on the racks and I remember we were the only one that had even a little to thresh. After that year, we had the grasshoppers and most of the crops had not much left. I herded cows in 1935 wherever we could find a little grass. From around 1937, I started shocking grain and when 14 I started hauling bundles on the threshing run. The first year Dad hired Ray Metz, Jr., to help me; after that, I was on my own on account of WWII. No help around, and long and hot days, but big meals.

A big memory I have is of a young man's picnics, rodeos, and battery radios listening to boxing, Fibber McGee and Molly, Amos and Andy, Jack Benny, and laughing and no bad language.

Then in 1951, I volunteered for the draft and I served 18 months overseas. I came home to the farm and met shortly after the love of my life, Alvina Lewandowski, and got married in October 1953. We had 3 boys, 2 girls, and we celebrated our 60th wedding in 2013. We loved to dance. We had a great life and family. What more can you ask for? We sold monuments the last 20 years.

The Demise of the Sears Catalog
By Lois Erschens of Elkton, South Dakota
Born 1933

For some strange reason, when I heard that the Sears catalog would be no more, I was suddenly struck with the vision of a pile of magazines and catalogs on the floor of our bathroom. I was also struck with the fact that a walk in the outdoors was necessary to take advantage of the reading materials.

My favorites (if there had to be a favorite) were the *Readers Digest* and the Sears catalog; and, I believe, in that order. It wasn't a dislike for Montgomery Ward's, but it just seemed that Sears had more clear pictures and maybe provided, without a doubt, a tad softer paper. For those who never used an outdoor restroom, no amount of explanation on my part will make you understand what I am talking about. As for my brothers and sister and persons my age, I really need to say no more.

It was in the catalog that everyone, young and old, could wish and dream. Cotton dresses and socket wrench sets, shot guns, dolls, and red wagons were all there. Included was the price, but that was not important because we knew we could not afford them. We just enjoyed looking at and imaging, "What if?" What if we could just have five of anything? What would it be? Not only did the hours fly by, but it might have told us a little bit about ourselves and maybe what we might become.

The Veire mailbox was located about a quarter of a mile west of our place. Some days, almost from the time we left to go get the mail, it was apparent when there was more than just letters and the Sioux Falls Argus Leader. Those packages all wrapped in brown paper and covered with postage stamps were easily the high point of our week—most of all around Christmas.

Oh what a guessing game that would create. Does that look like a big enough box to hold a radio or a phonograph? Was it too heavy for a doll? Too small for a wagon? And on and on.

I suppose we all knew that the fate of the catalogs was inevitable, what with television marketing and the coming of the shopping malls. Yet, don't you wonder as we shop in these malls and outlet stores just how much we have lost, most of all the young people?

There is not much of anything left to the imagination, but we can say that about most everything nowadays. Just an added thought: in my married life, Paul always told me, "If I want something, I think about it. If I need something, go ahead and get it." I tried to tell my children this, but it must have fallen on deaf ears.

Anyway, thanks to the people who put out the Sears catalogs. It was a very important part of a very special time.

Peach season in the summer time was a real treat. The peaches came all wrapped individually in tissue paper; they were much softer than the catalog and went immediately to the outhouse.

Change by the Cup

I remember that in the 1940s and 1950s the S&L Store, Montgomery Store, and JC Penney Store had a system of making change for their customers. When the customer had made a purchase, the clerk made out a handwritten ticket and placed it in a twist-on cup along with the money. The cup was then attached to a trolley, which rode on a wire leading to the cashier's office on a second level. A pull on the rope, would send the trolley up to the cashier, who would place the proper change into the cup along with the receipt. The cup would return by gravity to the clerk who sent it.

Our Neighbors

In the late '40s and early '50s, Hans and Leona DeBoer lived west across the road from our place. Leona had inherited the farm from her father and Hans farmed it. They were good neighbors and lots of fun to visit with. Hans was a big fat Dutchman and not real ambitious. He pumped water for his cattle with a windmill. After a bad ice storm one winter, his windmill froze up and wouldn't turn. Paul was doing chores and heard, BANG, BANG, BANG. Hans was trying to shoot the ice off the gears of his windmill with his shotgun.

Pretty soon, there was a phone call from Hans wanting to know if Paul would climb his windmill and knock the ice off. He went over because he was young and foolish. He said he wouldn't do it for anyone but Hans. It was 60 feet tall and he had to take a hammer along and Pound the ice off of every step all the way to the tower. Paul finally got his windmill turning so he could water his cattle. Paul's reward was a good drink of booze that Hans always had handy. Paul wouldn't take anything for his services.

This was the same Hans that took Paul ice fishing the week before he left for the army. That was his going away present for him. He had a fish house on the lake and he had a heater in it. We spent all afternoon and never caught a fish, but boy did we get drunk!

Spring: The Time for Baby Chicks and other Jobs

For us who grew up on the farm and for those of who that did not, here is a story of the arrival of baby chicks. This happened in March or April at our place and there was a lot to do to get ready for the little peepers arrival from the hatchery. There was the brooder house to clean, a bale of peat to scatter for bedding, and the brooder lights were checked. Everything had to be ready for the warmth and safety of the chicks.

Then we went to town to get the boxes full of chicks and take them home. The little fuzz balls were taken out of the boxes very carefully and put under the brooder hood. Our mother was sure of not letting anyone help her. We might hurt the tiny little fur balls. After the chicks got bigger, we could help with the feeding and cleaning the pen.

The days when every farm had a flock of chickens are long gone. People just don't want to take the time for that kind of thing anymore. It is too bad. Feeding the chickens gave kids something to do and a chance to develop a little responsibility. The gathering of the eggs was another story. The hens didn't really like giving up their eggs all the time. The real mean ones we called cluck hens, and they were soon made into soup, or Sunday dinner. Another unpleasant thing to do was to clean out the chicken house. That was a job that the boys had to do, and sometimes the girls had a chance to do also. The reason the job was unpleasant was the odor was awful; it smelled of ammonia.

When fall came, the job of getting all the chickens out of the trees and into the hen house was not an easy task. We had to wait until dark to get the chickens down from the trees and carry them into the hen house. It always seemed to be the coldest and rainiest night. We knew it was something we had to do and glad when it was over. I am sure there are times when we all think of our life on the farm. I sure do.

Water Witching

One of our neighbors, Sigurd Vick, had a reputation for witching water wells, so we had him come over to tell us where to dig, as we had planned to dig a new well for our house. Two nephews of mine had come to visit us from California and they were at the farm when the witching was going on. They had never heard of witching for water before and I couldn't help feeling they were a bit skeptical about it all. Sig told them that he had been witching for several years. Someone had shown him how and he discovered he could do it.

Some people can do it and some can't. He had found water wells for himself, his father, and several others. "No!" he said, "It isn't hard. A branch from a willow or ash tree works. Some use peach, apple, and other woods also." Sig used a number nine wire with a hand held on the end as he walked around the yard. The boys followed him and peppered him with questions. As he walked, Sig held the witching wire or rod in front of him pointing upward. He began to walk a brisk pace across our yard. Suddenly, the end tipped and pointed down, "Vein along here." I watched as the two boys mouths opened. Sig then backed off and approached from another direction. Once again, the point pointed downward. "Here is where it's closest to the surface." Sig marked the spot.

My nephews wondered if Aunt Lois and Uncle Paul could possibly be putting them on. Sig seemed to read their thoughts. "Here, try it." Aunt Lois was shown how to hold the rod with both hands. Slowly, I started walking, but nothing happened. I came to the spot Sig had marked, still nothing, "It's not working for me," I said. "Try holding it tighter." Still nothing. "Let Paul try." We saw the tip of the rod tilt, twist, pull down. "You are faking it," he was accused. So both of the boys tried their hand at it; still nothing. Without a word, Paul opened his hands. Yes sir, his skin was red, "That's really something," Sig laughed. "Yep, that's the way it works, some got it and some ain't. But no one seems to know why. Obviously, there is nothing supernatural about it, just some law of nature going about its business." My nephew asked us some time later, "How far down did you have to dig?" The answer was, "18 feet to the water vein and 50 feet deep to get enough room to store the water in." "Well," my nephew inquired, "wouldn't you hit water anywhere at that depth?" "Not around here; one of our neighbors has a 550 foot well. It is the darnedest thing and you may think we've got to be just a might peculiar to find water with a No.9 wire." At that time, the cost to dig wells was $4.00 per foot, and you couldn't afford to dig many dry holes looking for water.

Sig never did charge us for his efforts. His usual charge was $25.00; that is what he called his low overhead operation. The only water-witching guarantee was if dig a well and don't find water, you get a refund. Water witching is not only a knack, you have to have talent. The summer of 1968, the new well was dug by Tony Rust, 50 feet deep. It cost $205.00. The well had water in it, but if it didn't rain very much, it dried up. Every December through March, we were always short on water. From April through November we had enough water for our house. In 1977, we paid $145.00 for membership in Brookings-Deuel Water System. We piped in water and now use 2,000 gallons a month at a cost of $22.00. At this time, our first automatic washer was installed.

Toilet Habits of Yesteryear
By Warren Thomas of Forestburg, South Dakota
Born 1929

It was only a two-holer, which may have suggested we were poor back then. Or perhaps Dad's carpenter skills did not extend to a larger three-holer. Or maybe a two-holer was sufficient for a family of five. One hole was large, one was small. Both were neatly sawed with properly beveled edges.

Whatever the particulars of construction, that old outhouse was our personal restroom, bathroom, toilet, or whatever else until I was 17. The swinging door faced away from the house. A well-worn path from the kitchen door pointed like an arrow to one of the most important buildings on our farm.

Our holes had no lids and were ready for use upon arrival. *Sear Roebuck* and *Montgomery Ward Catalogs* provided the paperwork. I don't recall when I first heard about those flimsy white rolled up thingees which town folks bought in a store. But why bother – catalogs came twice a year, and

The two-holer

and pop back under the several blankets of the double bed. What was quite novel in the morning was to tend to clean up duties and find the contents of the pitiful potty frozen solid.

The other, more time consuming process so gurglingly flushed down an invisible drain today required greater adaptations. The object behind the bedroom door was variously called a pot, a slop jar, or more euphemistically, a thunder bucket. Then, after nighttime use, comes the dawn. As the oldest son, I was honored (by request) to trudge the path to yonder world of holes and catalogs before returning with empty vessel, sometimes vessels. How often did it happen: "As long as you're going out there, please take this other one, too." And the price was the same.

Tedious? You bet your boots. Repugnant? And then some. Necessary? Of course, but why, in all fairness, couldn't we take turns?

I've been told that careful observation can readily determine the nationality of users of the ancient outhouses. The one hurrying out yonder was Russian, while the country boy returning was Finnish. And so the memories linger, Sanborn County flavored, never to go to pot.

what's more, in those Depression times, we didn't waste anything. In 1935, Mother pasted a group picture of the Canadian Dionne Quintuplets on the south wall beside the door. On the west wall, two collies stoically kept silent vigil.

Now, come South Dakota winter, the business of the body involved different strategies. Snow covered the path. Night came early and it was no fun sitting out there alone when the wind howled and the flashlight batteries grew dim. And for all I knew, that noise outside might be the wolf from the bedtime story Mother read to us. With necessity being the mother of invention, voila, we had indoor facilities! For my brother and me upstairs in our unfinished bedroom (rafters, sheathing, and shingles exposed), the necessary receptacle was an empty and inexpensive tomato can. Oh joy! Oh delight! No more dreadful, dark, and dangerous forays to the distant outhouse world!

Winter toilet time was remarkably simple – hop out of bed, attend to tomato can business,

The Place Where I Grew Up
By Mathilda Nipper of Roscoe, South Dakota
Born 1953

The place where I grew up, when I think about it now, was a perfect place to raise children. Our place was surrounded by hills, with a river running through it. There were no close neighbors or towns nearby.

As kids, we were free to roam what we thought were long distances through the hills in the summer and on the frozen river in the winter. We were never idle. We took advantage of the short South Dakota summer days by roaming the hills and swimming in the James River in our long underclothes. There was no such thing as a swimsuit; we never heard of one. We went fishing for bullhead with just a string and a hook.

In the winter, we skated on the same frozen river. Even through the long winter months, we stayed busy with school, sledding,

The kids roaming free on the farm

and ice skating on homemade skates. These were made with an eight-inch piece of two by four, depending on our foot size, and two long pieces of iron for each skate, and a leather strap on the top to strap onto our feet.

My grandfather wove laundry baskets, so a lot of times when we were ice-skating, we would pick reeds along the riverbank for him that he used in his baskets.

I remember one time when one of our playmates broke through the ice and drowned. Besides this tragedy, there didn't seem to be any other major ones that I recall. We all got our scrapes and bruises, but never anything too serious. We were too busy staying busy to get hurt.

Our outside toilets served their purpose, but in winter in the middle of the night, it was no picnic. There was no running water in our homes. Our heat was a big wood and coal-burning stove, which thankfully heated the whole house. It had a big enough flat top to hold a large container of water to be heated for dishes and winter sponge baths. In the summer, we took a bath outside in the hen house, which was a storage shed with a bathtub. There were no hens, though. The water was heated in a twenty-gallon stainless tub that was fitted into the top of a barrel drum with a hole cut out of the bottom for wood to burn, made for that purpose. With so many in our family, we sometimes took turns in the same bath water.

We had a large garden and canned enough to last all winter. We had our milk cows, chickens for eggs and meat, and cattle and hogs for meat, also. We wore homemade

clothes and shoes. The shoe shop was always welcome and comforting and warm in the winter. We would sometimes hang out there during recess. We were self-sufficient in every way.

We were happy in that we didn't know much, if anything, about the outside world. We thought ourselves lucky if and when we went to town, because there was a Dairy Queen. The Dairy Queen had ice cream cones and malts, which was a rarity for us.

The place is still there, and it hasn't changed much. It's full of memories when I go back for a visit. If there is someone who reads this who was there with me, they will know it and maybe remember those times as I do.

From Electricity to None
By Larry L. Steele of Austin, Texas
Born 1938

I was born in Faulkton, South Dakota on January 14, 1938. We lived in a small house owned by my grandmother. It sat on half a city block, and included a tumbledown barn, a chicken coop, and another old shed. We had some chickens for the eggs they produced. I do remember that we ended up getting milk from a local farmer who milked cows and delivered milk. It came in glass bottles with heavy paper lids that fit into the top of the bottle.

We had electricity, running water, and an indoor bathroom. Our heat was a woodstove, and our cook stove was an old iron range that burned wood. I remember when Mom made lefse; she would cook it on that stove. She'd roll it up on a yardstick, turn it over, and brown it on the other side. We always had headcheese to put in it to eat. We had a summer kitchen attached to the house with a kerosene stove to cook on so that we didn't have to run the wood range. I remember going with my dad to pick up old railroad ties along the railroad tracks that had been replaced with new ones. We took them home, and when he had enough, he hired a guy with a circular saw to cut the ties up for firewood. We had no refrigeration; anything needing preservation was canned in mason jars, including meat. We had a root cellar we called "the cave" where things were kept cool. If we had company, Mom would make Kool-Aid and would have me go next door and "borrow" a tray of ice cubes.

I had a group of friends about my age that got into the normal amount of trouble. One spring day when I was about four, we went on a "runaway adventure" down to the local creek. We passed a couple of older boys (around 12) that we knew who were having a picnic. The ice had gone out of the creek, and we found a small dock that we decided would make a fine raft. We wanted to float down the creek like Tom Sawyer and Huck Finn. We tried to break it loose by rocking it back and forth. I leaned over the edge to see if we were making any progress, but it rocked toward me, and I fell in. I still remember the bubbles going up as I went down. My friends started yelling and the two older boys came running. I think I was up for the third time and they grabbed my cap (which of course came off), then they grabbed my hair to pull me out. It was a close call, but I was more scared of the paddling I might get for running away. The walk home in those wet clothes was extremely cold.

My sister and my mother passed away when I was seven years old. An aunt and uncle took me in since my dad had to work and couldn't care for me and a younger brother. That was a real transition, moving to a farm 26 miles from town. There was no electricity, no running water, and no indoor bathrooms. We used kerosene lamps and a Coleman lantern (the kind with wicks) for lighting. Our running water was for me to take a pail, run to the well, pump it full, and run back to the house. Actually, one of my chores was to take my little red wagon, put a ten gallon cream can in it, fill it, and then bring it back to the house. I always heard about picking up cow chips and storing them for fuel, but we didn't do that anymore. We burned coal in a big, heating stove. One of my evening chores was bringing in the coal. They had a kerosene stove to cook on. It had an oven for baking and roasting. I still remember that homemade bread and rolls with freshly churned butter! Yum!

We had a wooden wall phone with a receiver on the side and a mouthpiece on the front. It had two bells mounted at the top of the front and a hand crank on the side. It was a party line, one strand wire supported on short telephone poles along the section lines that went to every farm. No dial on that monster—each farm had a predetermined code sequence of long and short rings. To call an individual farm, you rang their sequence with the hand crank on your phone. Ours was two shorts and two longs. We always said it was "Ding, Ding, Daaaaling, Daaaaling." Everybody on the line could pick up and listen in anytime they wanted to. It was called "rubbering" when someone other than the calling and called party got on the line. It really wasn't considered nice or neighborly to listen in to others conversations then, but with Facebook, Twitter, and the other social networks now, that seems pretty tame.

There was no indoor toilet. At night, and especially during the winter, the men used a five-gallon "slop pail" in an entryway and the ladies used ceramic chamber pots or enameled slop pots. There was a two-seat outhouse, which was moved periodically whenever the hole got full, and a new one was dug. Nothing was ever bought that wasn't absolutely necessary, and that applied to toilet paper as well. You've probably heard the jokes about using corncobs, a brown one, then a white one to see if you needed another brown one. What we did use was the old "Monkey Wards" and Sears catalogs when new ones came out each quarter. The index pages were the softest, and by the time you got to the slick women's clothes section, you were hoping the new catalogs would be out soon so we could use the obsolete one.

Every spring they bought baby chicks from the hatchery. They were kept in a brooder house with a kerosene heater to keep them warm. They grew fast, and by early summer, they were big enough to butcher so we could have fried chicken. My uncle or cousin would chop off their head with a hatchet, and they would literally hop around like a chicken with their head cut off. Once they had drained out, we dipped them in boiling water, and then plucked the feathers off them. My aunt singed the fine hairs off and then butchered them, taking out the entrails and giblets, and cutting the carcass into the pieces ready to fry. Another of my chores was to feed and water the chickens, both the young ones and the older, laying hens.

Part of that chore was also collecting

the eggs daily. One day I had just finished collecting the eggs in a bucket and started for the house to put them away when my cousin came running out of the house yelling "The war's over, the war's over!" (World War II). I was so excited I threw the bucket of eggs straight up in the air!

When I was old enough, I was taught how to milk the cows. That occurred twice a day, morning and night. We milked by hand, no milking machines. We took the milk to the separator house and ran it through the machine that separated the cream from the milk. Of course, we kept eggs, milk, and cream that we needed to feed the family and farm workers. The rest of the cream was saved in a cream can and taken to town to sell as butterfat to the local produce station on Wednesday and Saturday nights along with the eggs, that had been collected. The "cream check" was then used to purchase food staples such as sugar, flour, vinegar, and spices.

Wintertime created extreme conditions. One time the roads were snowed shut for six straight weeks. The county managed to open the roads with contracted bulldozers. They stayed open three days, and then blew shut for another four weeks. During the worst periods, my uncle and cousin hooked up a team of horses to a bobsled and ventured to the nearest town, 13 miles away. We did need some food staples, but their main motivation was to buy cigarettes.

The grade school I went to was a one room building with a coal bin and cloak room. It was three miles from the farm. It had outhouses for boys and girls. We rode horseback to school. There was a barn at the school with stalls and room for hay. When we had heavy snow, it was too soft for the horse to stay on top of it; they would sink in and founder. For about a week, I would ski to school until the snow got a hard enough crust for the horse to stay on top of it.

There was no TV at that time. We had a battery-operated console AM radio. We mostly listened to WNAX from Yankton, SD. If my chores were done, I could listen to the Lone Ranger in the afternoon. The family always listened to Whitey Larson with the 6:00 news, and then the Bohemian Band. There were some dramas in the evening, I remember the Inner Sanctum, where they started out with a ghostly voice saying "Through the squeaking door," and then you'd hear this long squeak. My aunt never missed "The Neighbor Lady" on weekday mornings, and my uncle, who was a livestock buyer, never missed the noon market reports.

We played a lot of cards during the off seasons. Whist was the main game for the adults, and the kids learned how to play. The kids had "Fish" and "War," among others. The men played pinochle when we had family get-togethers. If the roads were open, Friday night was card party night. It rotated around the community, each family hosting. About half the families would bring card tables and chairs, which they stuffed in the back of the car with the kids. They kept track of scores, and the host always had a top prize for the high score and a booby prize for the low score. If they didn't have enough adults to fill the tables, kids were pressed into service as players. Otherwise, the kids would play with the host's kids as a group, doing whatever kids do when they get together.

Friday night or Saturday night was bath night. We took baths in a galvanized wash tub about three feet in diameter. My aunt heated water in a tea kettle on the kerosene stove then poured it into the tub. The man of the house, (my uncle) was first she was second, and on down the line by age. I was the last, and by that time, the water was cold, it was filthy and filled with soap scum and suspended dirt. I hear about the good old days, but this was not an experience I want to go back to. I guess that is why I always take showers rather than tub baths.

Saturday night was "go to town" night. I got a 25 cent allowance on town night. I'd go to the movie for 12 cents, spend five cents for a bag of Russian Peanuts (sunflower seeds) for the movie, and have eight cents left. I could get an ice cream cone for a nickel, and three pieces of penny candy to take home. Or I could save those eight cents until I came back to town next time and buy a bottle of pop (soda) for ten cents, and have six cents left to save or blow. Big time decisions!

As I look back on those days, I learned a lot and a lot of values were instilled in me. I've taken the lessons learned and moved forward. I am not ready to go back to "The Good Ole Days!"

My, How Prices Have Changed
By Emery Sippel of Groton, South Dakota
Born 1921

My name is Emery Sippel and I live in Groton, South Dakota. I served in the Navy during WWII. I grew up with three brothers (Lester, Arnold, and Ralph) and one sister (Edith). I have six living children (my oldest daughter Marcia passed away when she was 12): Meri Erickson, Marc Sippel, Monte Sippel, Marjae Schinkel, Mendy Jones, and Melissa Gilbert.

I was born in Riverside Township in November 1921 to Albert and Bertha (Johnson) Sippel. My grandpa Louis Johnson was one of the first county commissioners appointed at the Brown County courthouse in Aberdeen, South Dakota. His name is currently engraved on the front of the courthouse building.

In the 1920s and first part of the 1930s we did everything with horses. People came to church with their horses. That is how

Emery's family

people got around. I also worked on farms in my younger years. When I was eight years old, I drove a wagon and a team of horses to Claremont, South Dakota, with ninety bushels of grain. We got nine dollars for the load, which was only 10 cents a bushel.

Then there were the tractors, thrash machines, and the binders. The binder was pulled by three horses. The binder made bundles of straw. We had to pick the bundles up and make shocks out of them. The whole field was covered with bundles and it was hard work. After we made the shocks, a thrash machine would come in. We put the shocks in the hopper and it thrashed the grain. The straw came out the back with a long blower and it made a pile of straw 20 to 30 foot high. The grain was then hauled home by wagons pulled by two horses.

I remember dirt storms, which made four-foot high banks around the buildings. In one particular dirt storm, I was in grade school. We used kerosene lamps in school and it was so very dark outside. A man named Clarence Johnson and his son Lambert came across the road to the school to help us. All 12 of us students held hands and went across the road to his house and stayed the night.

In the '30s, Riverside Township had four schools. There was one school in each corner of the township. Three of these schools were built by the WPA. This was a program that all of the farmers could work at and the government paid them. During that time, there were no crops.

Emery Sippel in the Navy in WWII

When I was a young man in the '30s, I was a janitor at Augustine Lutheran Church. There was a motor in the basement that I had to start so we would have electricity for church that day. I would go to the church at three o'clock am to start the furnace. I also had to go up three stories to ring the bell to let people know that it was time for church. When the organist wanted to play, I had to crank the organ so the sound would come out. I had to crank the organ through the whole church service each Sunday.

When I was a young man, I used to attend what was called a "basket social." These were social events in which the ladies would bring baskets filled with snacks and goodies. Whichever young man was the highest bidder got to sit with the lady and eat the treats with her. I guess it could be considered buying a date. I met my wife at one of these dances.

I also used to listen to Amos and Andy and the Three Stooges on the radio after my chores were done. Our radio ran off of a car battery. We had a phone line and when you made a call, everyone that lived in the area could listen to your conversation. Every family had a different ring. Our ring was two long rings and a short.

You didn't want to get in trouble at school! I had a teacher that would make me put my hand on my desk and then she would hit it hard with a ruler for discipline. She hit really hard and it hurt. When I grew up parents didn't complain to the school. If you got in trouble at school, your punishment at home was worse.

For bathing, my mother had a big washtub that she placed in the middle of the kitchen floor. There was a tank on the end of the stove that heated the water. We brought in coal to heat the stove fire. Our wash machine had a gas motor in it. It had a double wringer on the back of it. That was two rollers that you ran the clothes through to get the water out. My mother used a washboard to scrub the clothes before she was washed them.

On Saturday nights, we would take the eggs and cream to town to sell. This was a big night for the family. The money we made would be all the money we had for groceries until the next week. My parents would let all five of us kids go to the movies. The movies cost 15 cents and if we got popcorn that was 5 cents. My parents never went to the movies because there were five kids to pay for.

My mother made lots of our clothes and she darned everything. I used to use her thread spools for toys.

We had a pond in our pasture that we swam in. Sometimes it had garden snakes and lizards that we had to throw out before we swam. Sometimes we would snap the snakes like a whip and their heads would just pop right off.

We had an icebox where we kept stuff cold. We had an icehouse that we filled with ice out of the pond in the winter. Then we packed straw around the ice so it would last all summer for the icebox.

Yes, things have changed over the past 92 years. When I was young, a new car sold for $700 to $1000 and now they sell anywhere up to $50,000. Land sold for around $10 an acre and now it goes for around $4,000 an acre. Many new things have been created to make farming more efficient and farmers can now farm much more land then when I was young. My son Marc now farms my land and more all by himself.

My wife passed away in 1994. I have lived with my daughter, Mendy and her family ever since. I have lived all of my life in Groton, South Dakota, except for a short time in Minneapolis and the time I spent in World War II. I raised all of my children here and they all live within 15 miles to this day. I have been able to watch my grandchildren growing up. I still go to their home ballgames to watch them play sports. I feel I have had a full life and have much to be thankful for.

Emery and his wife, Marlys

My Good Life
By Inola Weiland of Arlington, South Dakota
Born 1921

I was born June 7, 1921 on a farm near Canistota, South Dakota. The doctor came to the house to deliver the baby. I had three sisters and one brother. We lived in a five-room house, a main floor, two rooms upstairs, and a full basement with a furnace that burned wood, cobs, and coal. The toilet was outside, so we used the chamber pots in the cold winter.

We had an outside building where we washed clothes. We used the wringer washer and rinse tubs. We heated the water in a copper tub and carried it out to the washhouse. We hung the clothes on a clothesline outside and in the winter on a wooden clothes rack to dry them. We ironed with hot irons that were heated in ovens or on top of the stove. Everyone got a bath on Saturdays in a washtub. We all used the same water, starting with the youngest to the oldest.

We only had a radio to listen to. We always went to church on Sunday mornings. In winter with a lot of snow, it was by sled. We had horse blankets to cover up with and straw bales to sit on.

I went to a country school a mile and a half from home. I walked most of the time and carried my lunch in a syrup pail. There were 15 to 18 children in the school with one teacher teaching all eight grades in one room. There were two outside toilets. If a blizzard or bad storm came school was called off. In the Dirty '30s, we had bad dust storms that were like blizzards. It got real dark in the daytime, and I hung onto my sister's and brother's hands to walk home from school.

Farming was bad and was done by horse drawn machinery. Yes, I helped with farm chores, such as gathering eggs, feeding chickens, milking cows, and carrying wood from a woodpile that my dad and grandpa sawed up. We always had a dog and cats on the farm.

My parents didn't spank us. They just talked to us, teaching us right from wrong. My grandparents were very strict. One of my grandmothers made a lot of our clothes, and we wore second-hand clothes.

We always had to go to Grandma's and Grandpa's for Christmas. All the aunts, uncles, and cousins would go, too. We got one toy and after I moved from home, my folks gave us a box of groceries for our gift.

My dad built a dam at the farm to haul the water for the cattle to drink out of. We kids used it as a swimming hole.

After graduating from high school, I worked for several farmers. I worked one place for two weeks, and my pay was fifty cents in pennies. I did house work and some chores. The mother had a new baby, and I took care of a three-year-old little girl. My next job was for a farmer and the pay was $3.00 a week, but besides housework, I helped milk cows. I milked six and he milked seven. That was seven days, up at 5:30 a.m. While working for that family, my aunt in Checoga was having a baby, and she offered to buy my train ticket to Checoga and back. The pay was $5.00 a week so I took that. The farmer offered me $5.00 to stay but I would have many chores.

I met my husband while working in a café. The pay was $1.00 a day and I worked all seven days a week. We were married February 8, 1943, and he went to the service on March 3, 1943.

I remembered all these things to help write this book, too many things to write about. Children today don't have to work like I did, as times were tough and I'm not sorry for myself. I had a good life and was married 60 years and one day. I had a great family who are all doing well and in happy marriages. I have 15 great grandchildren. Be good to the old people, because someday you'll be old.

I learned to drive a Model T Ford at 14 years of age and still drive at 92. I get where I need to go. I raise a garden in summer and still mow my big yard with a riding mower. I have a good life.

The One-Room School
By Lois B. Carlson of Webster, South Dakota
Born 1932

I was born on a farm in northeastern South Dakota on May 23rd in 1932. I had a brother ten years older and later a sister a year younger than me.

The country school was one and a half miles from our farm. The school board came to visit my parents after my fifth birthday to see if they thought I was ready to start school, as there were few students. They said I could start, but if it was too stressful, they would take me out until the following year. It worked out, and I stayed, and so I finished high school by my 17th birthday.

Our school was one room with rows of desks and a slightly elevated area for the teacher's desk and the blackboards. There was a small coat closet by the door. The school was heated with a coal heater. The teacher had to know how to bank the fire so in the morning we could use a poker and stir up the embers and add more coal. Most of the time, we weren't very warm, as South Dakota winters can be brutal.

The school had six large windows for light. There was no electricity, only a kerosene lamp or two for the cloudy days. The teacher brought a covered pail of water every day to put in a water cooler for drinking and washing our hands. The toilets were outside, back of the building, so we really had to bundle up to go there. It made spring and fall welcome weather days.

Students were in all eight grades. The least students was five and the most was thirteen. We all used the blackboards and chalk for lessons. After school, we had to clap the erasers to get the dust out. The board was cleaned with a damp cloth. I never had a classmate in all eight years, but some classes were combined.

Teachers were often women from nearby farms or areas. If they were from a few miles away, they boarded with one of the families who lived closer to the school. Teacher salaries were $50.00 to $75.00 a month.

There were not a lot of books. There were ones for reading, writing, and "'rithmatic," and workbooks. There were County Superintendents of Schools, and they would bring boxes of books for reading and take the previous ones to another school. We all looked forward to their visit and were on our best behavior. Superintendents usually had their jobs for years. Their office was at the county seat.

We had two recesses and a noon hour for our lunch, which we brought from home each day. We probably packed it in an empty syrup pail or maybe a lunch bucket. Lunch was sandwiches, cookies or cake, and maybe a piece of fruit or a small jar of fruit sauce or jelly. Anything extra like a candy bar was great. I remember one boy always had grape jelly sandwiches. To this day, I don't like grape jelly because it looked revolting soaked into the bread. Most all of the bread, cookies, cake, doughnuts, or pies were homemade, not from a store.

We made our own fun, playing outside at recess and noon. We played Anti-over the School House with a ball (occasionally a window got broken), Fox and Goose in the Snow, baseball in the spring and fall, and dug snow forts in the snowbanks. Jumping rope was a favorite for me.

We always had a Christmas program for our parents and neighbors. Girls maybe got a new dress (probably homemade) and overalls for the boys, and sweaters and our good shoes. The kids had to wear long underwear, which we hated, and cotton or wool stockings. My, we must have been cute! The program was followed by a bountiful potluck lunch and gift exchange, bags of candy and nuts, and lighted real candles on the tree. At the end of the school year in May, there was a community potluck picnic. The men played softball, and we were given our yearly report cards.

We walked to school when it was nice enough, and we walked home at the end of the day. I'm sure we thought it was up hill both ways. We had strict orders not to get into a stranger's car if they stopped and offered us a ride. My dad sometimes had to take us in a sleigh with two horses hitched up to pull it. We covered up with heavy blankets and homemade quilts. In the spring, we liked to see the grass greening, listen to the song of the meadowlark, and see the red winged blackbirds. It was a good sign that the long winter were over. When we were out of sight of home, we would roll down our long stockings so we looked more stylish.

There is a lot to be said for country school. We were all friends, loved our teachers, and learned a lot. I don't believe today's kids would do so well. We had no modern conveniences or anything to work with, only tablets, pencils, Crayola's, and packed lunches. There was no water and poor heat, but many or most of us went on to attain a desirable life. Now I very rarely see an old building on the prairie that was a "one room school." It brings back many memories.

To See Momma and Norman Again!
By George M.C. Thompson of Garden City,
South Dakota
Born 1946

From my sixty-seven plus years, I could relate many stories, but this one is dear to my heart!

I had many jobs in my lifetime, one of them being a Motor Drome or Wall of Death rider on a carnival circuit. A Motor Drome is a structure consisting of twenty walls of boards, twenty-five feet high, along with cables, bolts, tarps, etc. to make a cylinder collar unit where riders on motorcycles ride on the sides of walls, and people are on the top side outer rails, watching the performers do their acts.

On one of the fair dates when we entertained, our starting time was a little later in the morning. At one point, I was walking on the Midway toward the Motor Drome. I noticed this gorgeous woman staring at the Drome from the Midway. I naturally introduced myself to her and eventually took her up to the top of the Drome. I began explaining to her

Pat

all about what we did at the Motor Drome. At one point of our conversation, this beautiful woman removed her sunglasses. I was immediately smitten. This lady had the most beautiful green eyes that I had seen in quite a while. Many years later, she admitted to me that she had known all about the Motor Drome and had been attracted to me.

Later that evening, she and I went to the bar and started drinking. She told me many years later that I had double shots put into her drinks. I got concerned when I went to drive her home, and she couldn't find her way back home except from the bar. She came to visit me at another fair date that we were playing down south. Eventually, she brought her three children, two boys and a girl, and came out on the road with me. We finished the year down in Florida and were offered a deal running joints at another major fair.

Because of my family being from the Philadelphia area, she, Pat, and I moved to Philadelphia, got jobs and became a family. Because of our ages, both being in our twenties, and me being stupid, Pat eventually left me and went back to her home in New York. Years later, I had also moved from the Philadelphia area to New York, unbeknownst to Pat. She was only living about one hundred

George and Pat in 1969

and fifty miles from me.

Twenty-five years later, with two failed marriages and one child, Pat and I got back together. I had inadvertently married two women, and Pat had also been married twice. After my last failed marriage, I was sitting in a truck stop one evening and I started to wonder how Pat was doing. I looked up her family using her maiden name and called the number. It was her mother. After she gave me Pat's work number, I called Pat. After all those years and failed marriages, Pat, later known as Momma and I got back together. Momma and I had six years together before she got cancer. She had lung cancer the first time and spinal cancer the last time. She eventually died in my arms the day after Labor Day.

In our time together, Momma and I acquired a Maine Coon cat from a garage sale. She named him Norman after seeing Henry Fonda as Norman in *On Golden Pond*, when Katherine Hepburn said, "Norman, you old poop," and "Norman was going bonkers."

I've since lost Momma, who died in 2002, and I had to have Norman put down in 2013, after sixteen years, due to heart problems. My life goes on, as it should, until the good Lord calls me to that other place. I miss Momma, and I also miss Norman. Life and death are part of living. Eventually, and I believe this wholeheartedly, I will be back with Momma and Norman. That's life and death! Nature is not human hearted.

Norman

Dolls, Spankings, and School Disasters
By Roger Hovey of Clear Lake, South Dakota
Born 1921

I and my twin brother, Rolf, were born on August 12th, 1921 in the hospital at Volga, South Dakota. My four-year-older brother, John Peter was born on August 19th in Sioux City, Iowa. My two-year younger brother, David, was born at the Hovey Homestead on May 1st, 1923. My grandfather, Peter John Hovey, was born at Washington Prairie, WS on May 25th, 1849.

In the spring of 1878, Grandpa homesteaded the southeast ¼ of Section 17 in Sterling Township, County of Brookings Territory of Dakota. In the spring of 1920, my father, Carl J. Hovey, moved from Sioux City, Iowa to this Hovey Homestead. Deer Creek runs through the western side of the school section. The pond in Deer Creek was across the road from the building on Hovey Homestead. It was 40 rods east.

The Drowning of the Dolls
My twin, Rolf, and I had a kid brother two years younger, David. David had two dolls. "Dave," we said, "It is sissy to have dolls. Boys don't have dolls." We told Dave there was a whistle inside those dolls and that we would butcher them and get those whistles.

Rolf and I were smart. We had watched Pa put unwanted puppies and stones in a sack, and then drown them in the creek. We found a sack and some stones. We trudged those 40 rods to the pond in the creek. We drowned the dolls and were well on our way to butchering them when the hired man, Pete Jensen came. "Boys," he said. "Your dad is looking for you."

We knew we had done a dastardly deed. We abandoned the whistle getting. We were fugitives from justice. We spent the rest of the afternoon avoiding Daddy. We were somewhat shocked at suppertime when Pa didn't seem to know about the drowning of the dolls. At bedtime prayers, we thanked the good Lord for sparing us from punishment.

The Schoolhouse Spanking
I was in the first grade in the springtime of 1928. Sterling #42 was a big one-room schoolhouse. There were 40 kids. The upper grades had man-sized kids. The entry was on the east side, with a cloakroom. Three or

four of these great big kids were teasing little Roger, the first grader. I was screaming and yelling at the top of my voice and flaying those big kids. Miss Viola Hexsom had red hair, came from Hendricks, Minnesota, and was the teacher. She picked me up and carried me down to the basement. All the while, I howled and howled. I had had spankings but always as instant punishments. Miss Hexsom took her sweet time. She went to the coal bin and got a stick. We then went to the east end of the basement where there was a big old chopping block. Miss Hexsom never let go of me. She sat down on the chopping block and took down my pants (disgrace of disgrace). I was given plenty of time to look around. On District 42's schoolhouse basement were windows on the north, south, and west sides. Every window was packed with kids seeing the "show." Miss Hexsom must not have laid that stick very heavy on my behind. I can't remember that it hurt.

Afterwards, Miss Hexsom wrote a note and gave it to John. I almost snatched it away. I would have eaten it up. John gave the note to my mother, and she in turn gave it to my dad. Only John told them about my spanking. Neither Mother nor Daddy ever said one word to me about the spanking. As far as I was concerned, I went about my merry way. I thought the spanking was par for the course.

The Burning of the Schoolhouse

In the spring of 1930, Sterling #42 had gotten a big load of pieces from a carpenter as kindling. Adjacent to the basement of that Brookings County schoolhouse was the coal bin. This kindling wood had been dumped in on top of the coal in the coal bin. Our teacher was now Mrs. Viola Hexsom Meester.

My brother, John wasn't in school that Friday afternoon. John had taken the Whippet and picked up Uncle Andrew at Bruce, S.D. John was 14, too young to drive, so he got Uncle Andrew to make it legal. John had a nasty infection in his leg, and they drove to Brooking to consult with Dr. Gulbranson. There were two reasons for seeing Dr. Gulbranson. One was his fee was reasonable. Secondly, he was Norwegian.

There was a stiff northwestern wind that early March Friday. As a TCL project, we removed the kindling from on top of the coal in the coal bin and stacked it behind the furnace. The big kids were too smart to work, but I took pride in the big arms full I would carry.

The furnace burned coal or wood. The outside chimney went way on down. It was some four feet from the furnace to the chimney. The stovepipe coming from the furnace to the chimney was twelve inches in diameter. It was scantily covered with asbestos. There was much more of this kindling than could reasonably be expected. We started piling wood around the stovepipe. We knew that wasn't right. Someone went up to ask Mrs. Meester if that was all right. I am sure instead of asking Mrs. Meester if it was okay to pile the kindling around the stovepipe, they said chimney. So the answer was, "Of course, that is where she wanted it."

Lawrence Thompson was a big eighth grader. He said, "I am a real handicap around here." The furnace had cooled off, and the chilly northwestern wind made the schoolhouse chilly. Lawrence built a fire in the furnace. He laid in a bunch of that dandy kindling, put coal on top, and tossed in a half-pint of kerosene. Fire roared up through the stovepipe and up the chimney.

We were doing what we did on Friday afternoons: art. It got very, very smoky. Windows were opened. It only got worse. Ralph Perso and Lloyd Thompson were sent to see what was going on down in the basement. It was too smoky for them to go down in the basement. They then opened the manhole cover to the coal bin. They reported seeing the woodpile packed beside the furnace was on fire. They whispered the news to Mrs. Meester. She then said, "Children, take your coats and dinner pails and go outside." By the grace of God, we did that and all got out.

I thought it to be wonderful. I was sick and tired of going to school. We ran as fast as we could, over a half a mile. We ran in the house and told Mother, "No more school!" Then we ran out and told Pa this wonderfully good news. He had a team of horses hitched to a bobsled. We stopped at the milk house and picked a quart sized sprayer type fire extinguisher and two scoop shovels and went back to the school.

The hired man, Pete Jensen and my dad opened the southwest window and scooped snow at the fire that hadn't broken through the schoolhouse floor. It soon did. We watched while the chimney fell to the west and when the school bell made its final bong as it fell into the basement.

The good people of Bruce emptied a downstairs room, supplied desks, and books, and Sterling #42 never missed a day. We were not only stuck with going to school, we had to deliver milk. We were most always tardy and always had dirty fingernails.

A Full and Busy Life
By Bonnie Kirchmeier of Waubay, South Dakota
Born 1931

I was born on Christmas Day, 1931, to Tony and Mable Soyland, in Waubay, South Dakota. Dr. Hawkins delivered me in my parents' home. Yes, I am 82 years old.

Recently at a party, we were asked to tell of a most memorable Christmas. My memory took me back to 1935 when my family lived in Holmquist. At that time, there was a church in Holmquist, denomination unknown. My Sunday school class was composed of five or six children, and we were asked to sing "Away in a Manger." My dad played the violin and sang, so he taught me the song. As the class stood before the congregation and sang, a certain boy in the class sang along, however one line behind the other class members. Those in the congregation began to laugh and giggle at his timing. I sang on until the song ended and then ran to my mother crying, because I thought they were laughing at me. Yes, I remember the boy's name but will not reveal it!

My first memories are of living on a farm three miles west of Holmquist. At age three, we sat on a blanket in the yard and my Aunt Doris Holosher taught me to tie my shoes! Our farmhouse was located south of Highway 12 and north of the railroad tracks. I remember many hobos coming to our door and asking for food. My mother asked them to sit on the back steps, and she would fry eggs for them. Then they would leave.

I attended first grade at Holmquist. The school was located one half mile north of town. We walked there, and I once froze my ears. In January, we moved to Webster. My first grade teacher was Miss Edith McDermot. In third grade, I remember winning the spelling bee.

The word that stumped my classmates was island. My teacher that year was Miss Mildred Packernig.

Music, singing, and dancing were a big part of my life. During my high school days at Webster in the 1940s, my friends and I attended dances in the area towns of Bristol, Roslyn, Grenville, Ortley, and Clark, We went to barn dances at the Darby Davis farm south of Waubay and at my favorite places, the Blue Dog Lake Pavilion, the Waubay Legion Club, and the Day County Fairgrounds at Webster. We even danced to the Lawrence Welk Orchestra at Lake Kampeska near Watertown.

The annual Day County Fair at Webster was also a highlight. I loved seeing 4-H projects, exhibits, demonstrations, the carnival, and bingo. I enjoyed riding the Ferris wheel, the merry-go-round, and the tilt-a-whirl.

My first love occurred when I was 15. Saturday nights were the highlights of small towns. All the farmers went to town, and the town people gathered to shop and socialize. On a Saturday night, I met a farm boy I adored. His name was John Albert Charles Kirchmeier. We called him Jack. I still have a golden heart pin Jack gave me the year I was 15.

Bonnie and Jack in 1995

115

Later, in 1950, I married Gordon J. Gramberg of Waubay. We were married 42 years when Gordon died. During my 42 year marriage to Gordon, he served as a rural mail carrier out of Waubay for 25 years. We made many friends among his postal patrons. We were active in the PTA, American Legion Post and its auxiliary, Sportsman's Club, Birthday Club, church choir, Sunday school, and Ladies Aid. I worked as a news correspondent to the *Waubay Clipper*, the *Webster Reporter and Farmer*, the *Aberdeen American News*, and the *Watertown Public Opinion* for many years.

Three years after Gordon passed away, my first love came to see me. I greeted him with a hug, and although I had not seen him in 42 years, when we embraced those years just melted away. We were suddenly those two teenagers so much in love with one another. We were married in 1995 and spent ten wonderful years together!

Now in my twilight years, I live in Waubay on property that once belonged to my maternal grandfather, William Holscher. My roots go deep. I have lived here since 1955. Waubay has changed drastically with the rise of Bitter Lake. Many houses were torn down or moved away. Waubay used to have five active churches but now only three remain. There are not many stores on Main Street however we have a grocery store, a bank, a post office, a medical clinic, a newspaper office, a bar, and a senior citizen center where I often go to play whist or pinochle. Life is never boring. I have family and friends and church activities to keep me busy.

Growing Up Near the Railroad Yard
By RuthAnn Major of Wessington, South Dakota
Born 1948

During my childhood, my friends, my sister, and I existed somewhere between the Sugar Creek Gang and the Little Rascals. We were "townies," with no chores or significant responsibilities. My sister, Margie and I lived amidst the sawmill, the railroad, Cimpl's Packing Plant, the box factory, and Marne Creek, and we explored it all.

Exploration at the railroad yards included the railroad round house, the railroad stockyards, the railroad bridge that crossed Marne Creek, and the rails themselves. Assisting in this exploration were our cousins, Billie Rae and Rusty. They lived all the way across town but often came to spend the day.

A Close Call
On this particular day, we had just finished playing at the roundhouse, where there were iron wrenches as big as we were and old abandoned Model T trucks with steering wheels but no seats. We would run up and down the long, slanting old wooden things that could be man-powered to position the turntable. On our way down the tracks, we'd jump from track to track. We'd balance on one rail while walking and then see who could get down the tracks the fastest.

Billie Rae and Rusty were well ahead of Margie and me when we felt the train coming. We yelled at Rusty and Billie Rae, but they were too far ahead and just kept running down the tracks, pushing and hooting. Margie and I had gotten off and were getting ready to wave at the engineer when he went by, like we always did. Then the conductor would toot his horn for us. Billie Rae had gotten off the tracks at the toot of the horn but Rusty just froze. The stock cars were already going by us when Billie Rae started running for Rusty, and then we couldn't see either of them anymore. That's when Margie and I started running alongside the tracks to the stockyards where we had last seen them. But they weren't there and the train just kept going.

When the caboose had finally gone by, there stood Billie Rae and Rusty. All the color had drained out of Rusty's face. I don't think Margie and I looked too good either, but Billie Rae was exhilarated and just bounced around with uncontrollable boyish energy. He was invincible for the rest of the day. He even walked around on the top of the corral fences at the stockyards, something the rest of us never felt confident enough to do.

Running Away from Home
Both Dad and Mom worked outside of the home, and because Margie was four years older, she was my summertime babysitter. Grandma lived right next door, and Margie knew she was there if anything was really needed. We ran in and out of her house most of the day for treats or a drink of nectar. There

wasn't such a thing as Kool-Aid, and nectar came in a bottle of concentrate sold by the Watkins man who sold his products from door to door.

One beautiful fall afternoon when Margie was in school, I announced to my mom that I was running away to be a hobo. My mom responded, "Let me help you." This was not at all what I expected. She got out Dad's green leather and canvas Army bag. She put in a sweater and some play clothes and said I'd sure need a clean pair of panties. Then she took the bag to the kitchen and made a peanut butter sandwich, which she wrapped up and put in the bag with a pint jar of nectar.

I hung the bag on the handlebars of my tricycle and headed out the driveway. Mom stood in the doorway and waved when I turned to see what she was doing. It was probably my first steps of independence. I had never gone anywhere without Margie or some adult leading the way.

I pedaled toward the railroad and Cimpl's Meat Packing Plant and then back between the stacks of lumber to the back road and the sawmill, which put me in my own back yard. Mom sure wasn't surprised when I walked in the door. I didn't see her watching, but maybe I hadn't been so independent.

A Helping Philosophy

Mom never wanted to see anyone go hungry and it was not unusual for Mom to feed the hobos when they came asking, which was nearly every day. "Hobos," Mom said, "were fathers, brothers, and men just down on their luck and trying to survive." I've since learned that our house was probably "marked" as a place that was known for her kindness.

When Margie was in charge, she had the same philosophy of caring but with a little variation. The stranger would knock on the door, and she'd talk to them from behind the screen door with the hook fastened. She had it hooked, because after all, she had the responsibility of me. She told them to come back later, and she'd have a sandwich and a cup for water waiting for them out by the pump.

She'd fix a sandwich and wrap it up in waxed paper, unhook the door, and take the cup and sandwich out to the well. I could never go with her, but I'd watch until she was back inside. It wouldn't be long and the sandwich would be gone and the cup hanging on the pump. Sometimes a coin would be left and sometimes not, but very likely the food was appreciated.

We knew some of the hobos by sight and name; they were regulars on this line. They'd gather under the railroad bridge and Margie and I would often go down to sit with them and hear their stories. Some of them would be sitting and others lounging on the ground. The stories were about family and distant places, and they listened to our childish tales as well. But when it got towards suppertime, one of those old regulars would say it was time for us to go home. I always thought that it was so nice of them to get us home on time for supper.

I didn't know then that they were looking out for us in more than one way. When darkness fell, out came the bottles of those who had been sleeping, and a lot of drinking occurred. These men were not hobos. Hobos traveled and worked. These men were bums. They'd drink all night and sleep all day and take the train when the notion would come. Another character who might ride the rail was the tramp, but he traveled by whatever means available and might stay a while, doing odd jobs or thieving.

The Circus Comes to Town

Semi-truck transportation was a new concept and the interstate highway system we have now was still a dream of President Eisenhower's. Trains were the major means of transporting freight across the country. Cattle, produce, and lumber all came by rail. If the animals had to be transported for any distance, then they'd have to be unloaded, watered, and fed at the railroad stockyards. It wasn't unusual to wake up and have the yards full. We'd sit on the fences and just watch them until they were loaded again and off to finish the trip.

One morning, it wasn't the usual stock. The circus had come to town and the pens were full of a lot of exotic animals, more like a zoo than what we now think of as circus animals. There were buffalo, camels, goats or sheep with big curly horns, zebra, and long necked animals that weren't giraffes, and a lot of fancy horses, and of course, elephants. Camels up close do not look any friendlier than they do in pictures. They always have a somewhat superior attitude, especially towards kids and wouldn't come near us. We had a healthy respect for the buffalo, but the long necked animals were very soft and liked to be petted. At least, we thought they liked it. The elephants were in the bigger pens in the middle of the yard, and we just watched them from the fences near the outside of the yards.

That night, Mom, Dad, Margie, and I went to the circus that had been set up along the bank of the Missouri River. The tent was big and white and had three large poles down the middle. Inside, the grandstand seating had been arranged around the center ring. I saw clowns, ladies in pretty dresses, and those same animals that I had seen earlier that day when watching from a vantage point much closer than the bleacher seats in the big tent that night. It was the last time the circus came to Yankton on our railroad tracks or set up on the riverbank.

Humble Beginnings to Business Owner
By George Schott of Britton, South Dakota
Born 1929

The question was asked, George, what do you remember about life in the Depression? Here is the answer. My name is George Schott. I was born in McPherson County, two miles south of Long Lake, South Dakota, in May of 1929. I had six sisters and one brother. We lived on a farm of about 300 acres. We cultivated about 100 acres and the other 200 were pasture. We raised Holstein and Hereford cattle.

My mother came from Russia on a ship called the *Kaiser Van William deGrosse*. She always told me how she was at Ellis Island when they brought the survivors from the *Titanic*. Her father was a Russian Army officer

George in front of one of his farming machines

who defected and fled to Germany with his family. She couldn't believe they had such a wonderful treat.

Our working time on the farm was from daylight until dark. In 1937, my dad and I hauled gravel with horses to build gravel roads.

My mother baked all the food. She raised turkeys and planted potatoes. We butchered our own cattle and hogs. We used a root cellar with ice and an old icebox, because we had no electricity. Our grain was delivered to a flourmill at Fairmont, North Dakota. We had it ground into flour. We had about twenty bags of wheat flour and rye flour. Our mother made all the bread.

I had an uncle in the Marine Corps who supplied me with .22 shells, because we were not supposed to buy shells during war times. My mother would send me to Slough Lake and Lori Lake to shoot ducks for dinner. I also shot several geese in the spring and pheasants year around. Mother would can them. I always rode Patty, my black pony. The birds were never scared of the pony. I got to be a very good shot. I could shoot pheasants on the fly.

In 1938, my dad and I planted 20 acres of squaw corn and five acres of popcorn. We had about 60 acres of rye and spring wheat. In June of the following year, we got up only to find the sky darkened at 9:30 a.m. The sky was covered with grasshoppers! Our fields were all eaten up by the grasshoppers and the Mormon crickets. This lasted for days. The people of North Dakota started to fill the ditches with water. This brought in the crickets. They then used arsenic and fuel oil to try to kill them. Our well water was not contaminated because we used hand pumps. Poison was only in the ditches. We lost the crop that year.

I took a job working for the Hutterite Colony picking rocks and working at the farm. I made twenty-five cents an hour. That was the best they could pay me. I made $74.00 for the whole season, and I gave the money to my mother. She had heard there was a store in Loyalton, South Dakota that sold material like coveralls and corduroy on rolls. My mother bought the material and made clothes for all of us for school. We walked the two and a half miles to school.

The next spring, 1939, started very dry. The dust storms went for days on end. They appeared like snowstorms. The sand got in

118

everywhere and was so heavy that when we woke up in the morning, there was as much as three inches on top of the covers. The sand left windrows and drifts on the highway.

We suffered with a lot of other problems, too. We had ringworm and bad rashes from the drought. My mother used anything she could to help us with the diseases. She made a poultice of lard and sulfur that finally worked.

In 1940, our cattle suffered from anthrax and TB. The government destroyed half of our herd. Others were shot in a pit to control the disease, and we received $11.00 per head.

The times got better in 1941. We again planted 30 acres of squaw corn and five acres of popcorn. That was all that would grow during the drought. I had the job of taking care of the corn. We had two small horses, Billy and Patty that I trained to pull the single row cultivator that now sits in my front yard. We did well that year, but our problems were so bad that we could not continue on the farm. We moved to Aberdeen, South Dakota. There, I took a job working a dragline that was moving the Lincoln Hospital to State Street, but they soon learned I was only 13, and I lost my job.

I hauled coal for Markavits Oil Company, and I delivered fuel. I also worked for Fairmont Foods. I was the youngest manager they had. For the next 19 years, I worked for Tiffany Laundry, and then moved to Britton in 1969, after purchasing Buhls of Britton. I bought the Wahpeton Plant in 1974. My son, Dan is Vice President of the corporation. My daughter, Donna is Secretary, and I have always been Corporate President. I am still working. I run the business quite successfully, with 26 employees, most of which have been with me on the average of 30 years.

In 1949, I met the love of my life, Dorothy Pfeiffer. We were married that same year and celebrated 58 wonderful years together. She passed away in January 2006. We had five children, of whom I am very proud.

A Letter to George

Dad,

Where do I begin? Well, first and foremost your children, siblings, and friends love and admire you more than words can say. You've always been a man with drive. We know you worked very hard as a child, being the oldest son in a family of many. You were always looking after your family, especially those lovely sisters. I've heard stories from men who grew up with you in Long Lake about how very protective you were with them. I'm pretty sure they didn't get many dates or at least any bad ones.

From the day you married Mom, your ambitions were limitless. You wanted many children and got them, too. You took great care of Mom and all of us, working from 5:00a.m. until sometimes 11:00p.m. We don't know how you did it all! Your work ranged from your job, the house, and yard work, to buying huge houses and moving them into our neighborhood and fixing them up and taking on renters and all. Always working, being a dad and husband, and still always dreaming of your next venture.

A new home was next and how exciting it was. What a fabulous treat for all of us. We loved it! Next was the move to Britton, buying your own business over a period of time, and tons more hard work.

Somehow, you still managed to find the time and the heart to hide Easter eggs and bring home Tootsie Pops, hiding them behind your back, and making us guess which hand they were in. You attended school conferences and took us to the dentist, fixed out boo boos, built us houses, bunted, fished, and somehow you found time to sleep in there somewhere.

Well, I could go on and on and still not touch the surface of all your life has been or will be in the future! Happy 80th birthday! You're the finest man I've ever known, and I'm so lucky you're my dad!

It All Began in Norway
By Chester Benson of Clear Lake, South Dakota
Born 1930

When 55 years of marriage have rolled by, there could be a long history of events to mull over, the sunshiny days, and the rainy ones, but the many blessings are most important. Iver and Martha Benson have traveled thousands of miles together in those years and are truly a gift of God. We are happy that Time led them, eventually, to our community. We are thankful to them for their kind, helpful ways, their friendliness, and the true enjoyment we have known, just having them as neighbors.

Iver was born in Redalen, Norway, on a little farm. One of eight children, he said he worked as soon as he was big enough to walk. There was no idleness there. Later, he worked on big farms near his home. Wages were poor, and as he labored, he dreamed of a land across the ocean where he could own his farm and no longer have to work for others.

Martha, one of six children, was born and raised in the town on Gjovik, a lovely scenic place beside the big lake, Mjosen. She, too, worked at various homes and learned much about cooking and baking delicious Norwegian delicacies.

Life has a strange way of bringing couples together. It was at a Luther League meeting on Easter evening when Martha and Iver first met. The place was a country schoolhouse. After the program, games were played and lunch was served. Neither of them had ever been at this particular place before, but Iver must have lost part of his heart when they looked over their coffee cups into each other's eyes. He didn't know it then, but he was never to forget the little Norwegian miss who was quick as a cricket and had smiles like sunshine. She thought he was better than any storybook hero, so handsome and tall, with broad shoulders to lean against and carry life's joys and burdens.

As men have a more adventurous spirit, Iver sailed to the New World first, in February 1915. His sister, Josie, living at Mission Hill in Yankton County, South Dakota had sent two tickets to Iver and his brother so that they could come to her home. The brother gave his ticket to a neighbor boy who accompanied Iver to America. Martha couldn't forget that young, adventurous fellow and having a brother at Alcester, South Dakota, she decided to follow him to the New World in November 1915. Iver kids her about coming after him, but he really was worth coming after.

Iver worked on farms for $30.00 a month in those days. It took three months' work, exactly $90.00, to pay for his horse and buggy. A young fellow needed that means of conveyance to go courting in those days. His little Norwegian girlfriend called the animal a crazy horse because it would always want to back up when it saw a car; and it was very easy to back up too far, as they found out!

Martha recalled the time, when working near Volin, when she had to drive a horse in to town to get groceries. Six or eight miles and never having driven one before, she somehow returned safely, but only because the horse knew the way, as she didn't.

Our honored couple spoke their marriage vows at Mission Hill, South Dakota fifty-five years ago. They lived on a farm two miles east of there until 1920. Their family circle then numbered four, with the addition of two husky sons, Barney and Melvin.

When Iver's brother-in-law, Knute Sletten received some printed material on Wisconsin, it sounded so like Norway that both families decided to migrate to the tree country and settled near Cushing, Wisconsin. It was there that Arnold was born. Now, with three sons, Martha thought she'd never be sewing dresses for a sweet baby daughter. Iver had gotten his help; now how about her.

They found Wisconsin a hard place in which to make a living unless one had a lot of dairy cattle. Then, too, Iver tried to do a little parachuting on the side, for he tumbled from the top of a 30-foot silo. He proved a big, healthy Norwegian could take that plunge and still live, although his foot was quite badly injured.

In 1925, South Dakota beckoned the families once more, but they settled near Rockham this time. Farming there was truly a disappointment. In five years, only one good crop was harvested. Iver remembers the one summer there when temperatures of 111 degrees for two days simply burned up their crops. Martha said the family eventually lived in the basement during the terrible heat.

In spite of their financial losses, they were overjoyed when at last a baby girl arrived. Dainty little Alice was the center of attention. Then Clifford and Norman were born while the Bensons were near Rockham.

By 1930, the Bensons and Slettens wanted no more of that part of South Dakota and moved farther east to Astoria and Toronto country. Home Sweet Home has been out on the little hill a couple of miles from town ever since. Chester and Esther made the family complete. Alice was so happy to have a baby sister at last, and there was another boy to roughhouse with his brothers.

Martha said her sons were hungry again before she could wash up the dinner dishes. The boys seemed hollow down to their toes, because they didn't ever seem to fill up! Twelve loaves of bread were baked every other day. How many would that make in a year? No wonder she now thinks, "How did I do all that work?"

There were a lot of other things to do, and no modern conveniences, but everyone helped. There was hard work and a lot of it. The old kitchen range needed wood and cobs to keep the fire roaring so the boys chopped and carried. There were water buckets to fill at the well for cooking and washing. There was no Laundromat for Iver to go to then in Astoria.

The youngsters attended school in Astoria. With the exception of Clifford and Barney, they all graduated from high school. Arnold received trophies for track and throwing shot put. He still holds the record for the longest throw.

Four of the boys served in foreign countries with the US Army: Arnold in Germany, and Clifford, Norman, and Chester in Korea. Martha has worked faithfully in the Auxiliary and helped with the very first Armistice Day Lutefisk Supper in Astoria.

Sioux Falls beckoned most of the family, so Iver and Martha have six families to visit in that city. Chester, Opal and family enjoy living in Astoria, while Norman is very well satisfied with Mom's cooking out on the farm.

Iver says, "We have to set a table for 51 now: 30 grandchildren, four great-grandchildren, five daughters-in-law, two sons-in-law, plus the family of eight, and Mom and Dad. No wonder we have to rent the Legion Hall!"

Martha has a brother and sister in Norway, one brother in Toronto, and one in Portland, Oregon. Iver's sister, Josie lives in Toronto and his youngest sister still resides in Norway. A granddaughter visited in Norway for three weeks this last summer. Perhaps, someday, Iver and Martha will also make the trip.

Martha holds quite an unbeatable record – 80 years of living and never once being hospitalized in all that time. How wonderful to have such good health.

The little Bethlehem Church, which the family attended, is gone and since the merger, Iver and Martha are faithful members of Bethel.

This little history would not be complete without this poem by Elaine Elmore:

Today we come to reminisce
Of bygone days of hers and his
Of changes you've witnessed
As years have gone by
Like radio, TV, and prices so high.

You've had happiness, you've had laughter
You've had trouble and lots of joy.
You've had washing, ironing, cooking and
sewing
And lots of places to be going.

Some days were cloudy,
Some days were sunny.
Through snow, wind, storm, or rain
As long as Iver called her honey,
Martha was always the same.

You've fed lots of chickens,
You've milked lots of cows.
You've baked lots of cookies,
You've cleaned lots of house.
You've cared for your children,
A gift from God above,
But the finest of all,
You've filled our home with Love.

And now Iver and Martha, as we
congratulate you on 55 years together, we
seek in prayerful words, dear ones,

Our hearts' true wish to send you
That you may know that, far or near
Our loving thoughts attend you.
We cannot find a truer word
Nor better to address you
No song or poem have we heard
Is sweeter than "God Bless You!"
God bless you! So we've wished you all
Of brightness life possesses
For can there any joy at all
Be yours unless God blesses?
And so "through all thy days
May shadows touch thee never
But this alone – God Bless Thee"
Then thou art safe forever.

Living on a Farm and Visiting Grandparents

By Joanne Brownell of Bellevue, Washington
Born 1933

I was born May 28, 1933 in South Dakota, where I lived until I graduated from high school. I had six siblings, four sisters, and three brothers.

I recall living on a farm three miles from Onida, South Dakota. Then my father felt the need for a bigger place and we moved. The new place had a house, barn, and a garage used for tools.

My father and brothers worked the fields, and I sometimes helped. They milked the cows and took care of a herd of sheep. There was plenty to do. Girls helped with the laundry, ironing, cooking, and cleaning. We sometimes helped in the fields.

For the first eight years, we attended a country school called South Buffalo. We walked three miles to school and back. It was very cold in winter. The school had grades one through eight. The school property had a barn for the students to keep their horses in if

Joanne's grandparents, Clara (Reiser) Yackley and Frank Yackley

they rode to school. The schoolhouse was two stories. But the basement had a large crack and was not usable, as the crack was very wide in the floor.

Parents of students took turns bringing water to school for drinking and washing hands. There was no running water at the school. We had another room used for hanging our coats and the main part of the school had a large potbelly stove. One day the stove emitted a large puff of smoke, and I fell over backwards. I did not get hurt and everyone had a good laugh.

Our desks were wooden and had drawers under the seat. Teacher had a large desk in the front of the room. Blackboards lined the walls.

We had outdoor toilets, one for the girls and one for the boys. There was no playground equipment so we played hide and seek and anti-I-over with a ball. We also played ballgames.

The weather was very cold in the winter. I remember hanging clothes on the line at home and bringing them in frozen to hang on a clothes rack to dry. It was my job to do the ironing. I did all the ironing for the family.

We had an iron cook stove in the kitchen, and my mother would bake eight loaves of bread three times a week.

I loved to visit the grandparents. My father's parents lived about 13 miles from us. Grandma was a good housekeeper and the floors were very slippery. We would run and slide across them. Their basement floor was dirt. It had been swept so often that it was hard.

Joanne's parents, Viola (May) Yackley ad Benno Yackley in 1928

My mother's parents lived outside of Watertown, South Dakota on a farm. It had three rows of lilac bushes and a wonderful big house. My mother was one of nine children, so there was a good time had when we went to visit. My aunts would sing, "Hail, hail the gang's all here" when we arrived. I loved visiting my grandparents and have wonderful memories of those times.

Joanne's family

Washday Preparation
By Kenneth Wherry of Faulkton, South Dakota
Born 1928

In the 1930s and early 1940s, there was preparation for washday made the night before. Wood, cobs, and or dried cow chips were gathered for the fire in the kitchen range the next day. The next morning the wood washing machine was pulled from the pantry and sat in the middle of the kitchen. Then a copper boiler was placed on the stove. My mother would carry buckets of water from the well after she pumped them unless the wind was blowing. The stove filled and when the water was hot, it was transferred by pans and buckets to the washer and tubs. Then the clothes were washed by pushing and pulling on the washer handle until clean. Then the clothes were rinsed and run through the wringer. When the last load was finished, the clothes were hung on the line outside and the washer put away. The water was then used to wash the kitchen floor and when dry newspapers we relayed down to walk on. The balance of the water was used to scrub down the outhouse for the next week. In the winter, the clothes came in stiff as a board and were frozen dry.

Brrr!
By Clara Hegg of Brookings, South Dakota
Born 1912

It's 2014 and everyone is talking about the "polar vortex," a cold spell here in January with the jet stream bringing very, very cold air from Canada. I'm a 101-year woman living at the Unite Living Community here in Brookings, South Dakota. My name is Clara Hegg, born and raised in South Dakota. To say the least, I've had many experiences with very cold weather here in South Dakota.

The year was 1936 and it had been a very cold year so far. I was a young teacher of 24 years of age. I taught in a one-room schoolhouse located between Estelline and Toronto called Longman School. I had about 30 children in my charge. The day I remember most started overcast and cold. I bundled up in my heavy coat, cap, and overshoes because I had to walk a mile to the schoolhouse in this harsh weather. When I arrived at the school to my surprise, the thermometer read -32°. I had to quickly build a fire in the pot-bellied stove or we would all freeze. It was a challenge to get it started. It sputtered and finally got started. It was beginning to get warm when the children arrived at Longman School to begin another day of classes. We all had to endure the freezing trip home that day. My feet got frostbite and I had to doctor a long time before they healed!

Scared to Death
By Eileen Hoover of Mobridge, South Dakota
Born 1939

When we were in the 8th grade, we went to the Perrocio School. My girlfriend and I took in a movie at the Mascot Theatre, called the War of the Worlds. Alice was afraid to walk home alone after the scary movie. I told her to come and stay with me. My home was closer to walking. On the way, we got to 3rd Ave. East. The streetlights were all out. The city was digging a sewer ditch on that street. The kids from that street threw dirt over the lanterns that were on the dirt piles.

We were walking along talking about the movie. I was a few steps ahead of her, when suddenly I fell in the sewer ditch that was being dug. It was pretty deep, concerning we were just kids. Alice tried to pull me out. She couldn't reach my hand. She went to Pat Huber's place, but found she was not home. Pat lived just a couple of houses down the street. While Alice was gone, I dug some steps on the side of the hole, so she could reach my hand. It was so dark we couldn't see. She finally got a hold of my hand and pulled me out. I was filled with dirt from head to toe. My hair was full of dirt. We got to my house and when we walked into the living room; my mom was sitting on the davenport watching TV. She was shocked when she looked at me and asked what had happened. I was scared and out of breath. I finally said to her, "I was buried alive!"

I Miss the Farm
By Verna E. Schutt of Rancho Cordova, California
Born 1929

I was born at Artas, South Dakota. I remember the old radio program with Jack, Benny. I still have a wind up record player with the records. That brings me to Saturday night baths, which were in a metal tub. Everyone used the same water that were heated in kettles on a wood stove and sometimes cow manure was used instead of coal, which were expensive. We had a wringer washing machine that I ever brought along to California, but wash boards were also used before wringer machines arrived.

I had nothing but homemade clothes, as my mom was a seamstress. The first bought clothes that I had was after I got a job at age 16 and worked in a grocery store for $80 a month, farmers shopped on Wednesday and Saturday evening until 1:00 a.m. and I worked at 9:00 p.m. until the store closed. My brother took me to school in the buggy, storm, or no storm that was our transportation. We had snakes all over and lots of big lizards in the basement and potato cellar. I had to go out in the field and call the cows to come home to be milked and I had to feed the chickens and gather the eggs. The only trip to town was Wednesday evenings and sat Saturday evenings. When cream and eggs were sold and we took cream and eggs to grandpa and grandma's house. The only telephones were rotary phones, which I still have as an ornament. Sometimes when I see cows and horses on TV, I miss the farm because we had a Shetland pony, which later got too old and had to be put to sleep.

Harvesting Before the Combine
By Donald G. Steward of Chelsea, South Dakota
Born 1933

I was born at home on a farm one mile south of Chelsea, South Dakota in 1933. My story is about harvesting in the good old days before the combine. The war was on and the hired man was drafted so the harvest crew was my dad, my brother, and I. Dad had an eight-foot grain binder that was ground driven with a large bull wheel to make it work. We pulled it with a McCormick Derring 1020 International tractor. My brother drove the tractor and I rode the binder. He was about nine or ten years old and I was two years younger. My job was to dump the bundles in windows, make sure the knotter was tying each bundle and adjusting the reel and platform height. Dad would help make the first outside rounds around the field, and then we would take over while he shocked in the same field. If we had trouble, he would be there to help us. When the binding was finished we'd all help finishing the shocking.

Now it was time for threshing. Dad bought a hay bucker and we mounted it on the front of a regular Farmall tractor. My brother ran the bucker and pushed the shocks up to the thrashing machine. Dad pitched the bundles into the thrashing machine with a pitchfork all day long. My job was to watch that all the thrashing machine belts stayed on and the grain wagon didn't run over. The grain wagon held only about 50 bushels; so we'd have to go home and shovel the grain into a bin, then go back to thrashing. The work was hard and days were long, but that's the way it was because combines were unavailable for several years after the war. God was good to us and we would finally get it all done.

Getting Into Mischief
By Mark Kisely of Volga, South Dakota
Born 1956

I grew up on a farm north of Lake Andes, South Dakota until I was 10 years old and attended a one-room country school called Pleasant View for grades 1-3. From our farm, it was one and a half miles to the school. The road we walked to get to school crossed a small valley. Because of the small valley, we had to walk up hill both ways. Sometimes my brother and I had to help the neighbor kids carry the water can so we had water to drink at the school. A guy in my 2nd grade class brought matches to school one day and started the boys outhouse on fire by lighting the toilet paper. It was fun watching the fire truck come down the road and put it out.

One Halloween night, the high school kids from town came out and tipped over the outhouses. The next morning when everyone made it to school, the teacher made us all help set them upright. On our way home from school one day, my brother, the neighbor kids, and I decided to have a dirt clod fight. I was the youngest one and got pelted a lot. One of the neighbor kids was hiding behind a tree, I threw a dirt clod toward the tree, just then he stuck his head out from behind the tree. I broke his glasses. All of us knew we were in trouble. We all found out trouble makes your butt hurt.

I was raised catholic and had to go to Catechism classes on Saturday afternoon. We had to learn certain prayers for those classes. I learned my prayers from my mom. She taught them to me when we walked out to get the cows. She would say a sentence of the prayer, then me. It went that way until I could say the whole prayer by myself.

Saturday night was a big night for farm kids; we got to go to town. Mom would go have coffee with the women at the bowling alley, dad would go play cards at the pool hall, my brother and I would run up and down Main Street raising cane. The stores on Main Street would stay open until the last customer walked out. Sometimes it was 10 or 11 at night. My uncle would have his popcorn machine set up. If we didn't get into too much trouble, we would get to buy a five-cent bag of popcorn from him.

If We Saw Smoke, We Knew the Teacher Made It
By JoEllen D. Johnson of Brookings, South Dakota
Born 1943

When I was eight years old, my father and mother moved from Clear Lake, South Dakota to my great-grandfather's homestead. My great-grandfather was a pioneer that came to America from Denmark with his new bride also from Denmark. He acquired the land by running a Land Race by horse. in Deuel County. So the farm was very special to us.

I left Clear Lake town school and went to a country school. It was very different. There were eight grades and you could hear and see it all. I learned about doing chores, carrying water, doing fieldwork, caring for animals, and herding sheep on the farm.

My most memorable happening was the first winter we lived there in 1951. It was a winter with an abundance of snow. The snowplows and equipment was small and slow at that time. My father would hitch up the team and wagon and take me to school. To keep his hands warm on the cold days he would keep one hand in his pocket and the other on the horse reins. We saw smoke coming out of the chimney. We knew the teacher had made it. If not we'd turn around and go back home. There were many days that we turned around.

The most memorable time was when my father and his friend decided to help a family move to Minnesota. He left on a beautiful sunny day in April. In fact, he'd taken me to school that morning. Around noon, a very bad snowstorm came up. My mother walked about a mile and half to get me from school. She'd tried to use my dad's friends Model A car but wasn't able to start it. It wasn't started with a key or crank in front of the car it was two wires together by the igniting place. We made it home but it was blowing snow and drifting across the road.

Our coal became low in the house during this blizzard. My mother walked the flat part of the roof of the house to the coal shed and returned the same way, as the visibility wasn't good. We managed to get to the barn to milk the cows and feed them hay. We couldn't let the cows out for water due to the bad weather. We gave them milk to drink after milking time.

Sometimes my great uncle and his children would pick me up with the team and bobsled. We'd put an animal tarp over us. It was lots of fun. It didn't take us long to ride over the hard snow banks. It was great when the snowplow came and got the roads open! We'd warm up the car and head to town for supplies. Most of our supplies were "laid in" in the fall. I remember my great aunt had many sacks of flour in her upstairs cold storeroom for the winter. Her basement shelves were full of canned cherries, peaches, pears, apricots, beans, peas, carrots, fish, and much more including corn on the cob in jars. It was a great place to play with my cousins in an old car we'd have club meetings. The food was so good I'd always stayed for supper too! Even if dad got mad. Canned cherries are delicious.

The electricity was off during the blizzard so everything was at a standstill. We did have a battery radio so tried to keep up on everything. We didn't have a telephone or any electronics like we do now. My father came home in three days. We were very glad to see him and that he was okay. They had made it back as far as Gary, South Dakota in the blizzard and stayed there.

I lived there until I was in the 7th grade. We moved to a larger place near Summit, South Dakota on a ranch. This was due to a shortage of water on my great-grandfather's homestead. There wasn't any rural water then. The homestead of today no longer stands except one large cottonwood tree and a rock pile. The rest is all farmland.

Riding a Horse to School
By Junior P. Bukaske of River Ridge,
Louisiana
Born 1921

I was born July 1921 at Loyalton, Edmunds County, South Dakota. My first home was two miles north of the old Loyalton School. Then

Junior in the Navy in 1944

my dad, Phil Bukaske, bought a farm from T.I. Oban four miles north of Loyalton.

My first grade in school I stayed with my grandparents, the T.I. Obans. I rode to school with my Aunt Vivian Oban on a very fast little horse. Sometimes I couldn't make the train to go home and went on for one mile before we could stop her to come back. It was quite a school year.

After that, I got my own pony and rode four miles to school every day, rain or shine.

I joined the Navy in December 1941 and spent four years there, most of the time in the Pacific. I came home in December 1945.

The horse that Junior rode to school with in the 1930s

A Flight in a Blizzard
By Ben Fowler of Bentonville, Arkansas
Born 1936

In the spring of 1959, I was hired by Montana Dakota Utilities Company to work in their engineering department. I was a draftsman in their branch office in Mobridge, South Dakota.

One of my side jobs was flying spotter of the company's high lines with a pilot named Warren Kelly. Kelly taught pilot training during World War II at Enid, Oklahoma, was a crop sprayer, and had a contract with the South Dakota State Fish and Game, along with a contract with MDU flying high line inspections. I always felt safe flying with Mr. Kelly.

In the early part of the '60s, we were in a raging blizzard. With high winds and heavy snow, one could not see across the street. My boss, Ervin Giese, called me into his office and told me that the towns of Herreid and Pollock, South Dakota were without power, and the line crew was out looking for the problem but at that time was stuck in a huge snow bank. They were attempting to dig their way out, and he asked if I was willing to fly with Kelly and try to find the trouble. I answered, "If Kelly will go, I will," and he said, "Well, get your warm clothes on because Kelly is on the way!"

My boss gave me a radio that only would let me talk to the office but not to the line crew. Kelly and I got the plane out of the hanger, started it, and sat there a few minutes, letting the engine warm up. When it became winter, Kelly always had snow skis on the plane. The airport at Mobridge was next to Highway 12. We took off and followed the highway east, flying no higher than fifty feet above the road. We flew eighteen miles until we got to the intersection of Highway 83 and headed north. All the time that we were heading east, the plane was almost flying sideways because of the strong north wind. Going north, we were bucking the strong north wind. We finally got to Herreid, found the high line, and headed east.

After about three miles, we found the trouble. It was a floater, which is when the line comes loose from the insulator and lays on the cross arm and grounds out the current. Two highline poles east was the line crew, stuck in

the bank, and the snow was so heavy that they could not see the problem. I wrote a note, tied it on a bolt that I had found behind the plane seat, and dropped it as close as we could get to the crew. I radioed the office and told them about the trouble, and we headed home again, following the highway.

We got back to Mobridge and put the plane in the hanger, and when we got back to the office my boss was standing in the door. He came out to the car and thanked us. The problem was fixed, and the towns had electric power restored.

That was a ride I have never forgotten some 50 years later!

A Great Mom and Teacher
By Nadine Matthews of Huron, South Dakota
Born 1941

I attended Harris School in Hand County. It was located approximately three miles southwest of Wessington, South Dakota. I had rather a unique situation from the second grade through the eighth. My mother, Gladys Major, was the teacher. I started the day calling her Mom, then to school calling her Mrs. Major, and then back home to Mom. I didn't always keep this straight. And no, I never saw a test paper early.

All grades were taught in one room. We all benefitted from listening to the other classes. Maybe we learned a little extra. We had the little blue spelling book and Dick and Jane readers. My mother always read to us in the mornings. I know that is the only way some of us would have gotten through Moby Dick.

We had field days when we would travel to the Bothwell School or the Rowen School or they would come to our school. We would have all sorts of contests: kitten ball throw, races, reading and spelling, etc. We didn't travel to events as much as they do today, so these days were really special.

The county nurse came directly to the school to check our eyes and make sure we were all healthy. The county superintendent, Mrs. Winifred Lorensen, came to make sure everything else was running smoothly. She was such a nice lady.

I remember the small school plays, which we put on every year. Every student was included. I remember falling down and dying in one scene and my glasses fell off and I reached over and put them back on and died again, but I was young.

Every student got to choose a special treat on their birthday. The big favorite was pulling taffy.

I remember the smell of potatoes baking on the old furnace while we patiently waited for lunchtime. To this day, I have never smelled a baked potato with such an aroma.

We played fun games at recess and noon, such as pump, pump pull away; steal sticks; and fox and goose. We would slide down the big hill behind the school. If the snow was just right, we could slide all the way to the road.

We knew when we came to school the day after Halloween that both outhouses would be tipped over. My father would always make them straight again.

My dad would take my mother and me in a tractor and trailer and pick up all the other students to get to school one winter when we had too much snow. There was no cab on the tractor and no heat in the trailer, but it seemed fun at the time.

I remember staying all night at the neighbor kids' home and getting to ride one of their horses to school the next morning. What a treat that was!

I remember the closeness we had with all the families. The schoolhouse is gone now. I think someone bought it to use as a garage. What stories it could tell. The big hill is still there to help bring back memories.

My mother passed away in 1998 at the age of 93. I will always be grateful for having a great mom and teacher, both at home and at school.

The Sound of Sleigh Bells
By Melba Gronau of Watertown, South Dakota
Born 1946

In early 1950, I grew up on a farm by South Shore, South Dakota. Like most farmers back then you needed to be a jack-of-all-trades: mechanic, blacksmith, and veterinarian, along with having a strong will and mind. Above and beyond the farming aspect, we raised stock cattle to butcher and sell, milk cows that we milked by hand then used an old crank separator for the cream to sell, horses to work the land and ride, pigs to butcher, sheep for wool and lambs, chickens for eggs, to sell, and to eat, cats to keep rodents down, and a dog to help with the livestock, be a companion, and be a watchdog.

When I was four and a half years old I stayed overnight with my aunt and uncle. I got homesick so, of course, they drove the 15 miles to bring me home. Letting me out of the car before checking for Mom and Dad was their first mistake. No one was home, and I wouldn't get back in the car. Spot, our dog Grandpa Yantzi gave us as a puppy and who was now full grown and the size of a St. Bernard, stood between me and them, not letting them touch me. They had to wait for Mom and Dad to get home before they could leave. My uncle was not happy!

My mom always had a very big garden. She raised all kinds of poultry: baby chicks, ducks, geese, and turkeys.

No running water meant hand-pumping bucketsful to carry clear across the yard to four different places two times a day.

In the fall, we would butcher, keeping some for ourselves and some Mom sold. The butchering of chickens carried over to our children's generation. Everyone from grandparents to grandchildren formed an assembly line during our "chicken pluckin'" weekend. No question about it, everyone knew their jobs. It was hard work, plucking by hand but we had fun, too. Family get-togethers sometimes bring back memories and stories of those "good old remember when" days of chicken pluckin'.

My first year of school I attended a one room schoolhouse with my three sisters. On nice days we would walk. "We know, uphill both ways!" our daughter would always say, having heard her dad and me talk of our school days when she was growing up. During the winter, Dad hooked the team, Duke and Minney, to the bobsled, put some hay in it, and an old robe to cover up with. We stayed as snug as a bug in a rug. If it was a blizzard before we got back home, Dad gave the horses their rein and got under the robe with us girls. He'd check a couple of times to see where we were but the horses knew their way home by themselves. The horses' harness had sleigh bells on them. What a beautiful and peaceful sound. To this day when I hear the jingle of sleigh bells I am taken back to the sound of horses' hooves crunching on the crisp white snow, and I smell the clean, fresh country air and also the scent of horses at work.

Thanks, Harry and Eunice Yantzi for teaching us the value of a dollar, how to work hard and respect others, and to live by the Golden Rule. Thanks so very much for being such good parents and role models. We love and miss you both very much.

The Sunday Outing
By Mary Flemmer Husman of Brookings, South Dakota

Heading out on that summer day in the 1950s toward a bright promise of a place at the lake, my family was a well-orchestrated combination of wild abandon and flurried, purposeful activity. My older sister and I rushed up the stairs of our big old house on the corner lot by campus, grabbing the curved wooden banister to take the stairs two at a time. We hustled toward our rooms to change clothes after church and grab our swimming suits and towels. Mom went to the kitchen to gather our melamine dishes to stuff in the wicker basket with the red-checkered tablecloth and beverages while Dad was already outside packing our 1952 green Chevy. He tossed tools in the trunk alongside our huge green aluminum cooler. That cooler was the mainstay for his Boy Scout troop camping trips and today it contained our meal of roast beef, onions, potatoes, and carrots wrapped in foil plus a jug of lemonade. He turned the radio to Wayne Pritchard's show or listened to Lawrence Welk's music as we traveled those country roads. When we got to our lot at the lake, he would bury our foil wrapped dinner in the sand on the beach and build a campfire over it, letting it bake there for hours while he mixed cement and started laying the foundation for our new cabin. It would be a delicious meal and one more thing to look forward to on this beautiful day.

As we piled into the car our feisty alley cat, Jingles, ran through the yard toward the car. Jingles was my pet, acquired from a visit to Grandma and Grandpa's farm. I'd set up such a ruckus about taking the striped kitten home with us that they relented, much to the dismay of the family and the neighborhood as time passed. He howled continually and escaped to wander the neighborhood, looking for a fight at every opportunity. But I loved him; determinedly ignoring the scratches sustained when I'd dress him and stick him in my doll buggy, and defending him whenever the option of returning him to the farm was presented. On this day, I jumped out of the car and grabbed him, wrapped him in my beach towel for protection since he clawed and scratched when I tried to hold him, and pulled him into the back seat. My mother looked concerned about including the wayward animal on our outing, but I got by with it since my dad distracted her with an issue toward the back of the car. He had locked his keys in the trunk.

With the help of an ax and some rope to mend the damage he'd inflicted on the trunk's lock (my dad was not the type to waste time deliberating the repercussions of a quick solution when we were on a mission), we headed out. First, a stop at the gas station, where Jingles tore around the interior of the car howling as soon as the car stopped. On his rotation round the backseat, he scratched my sister, who cried and screamed that my cat should've been left at home, which then set me to crying. My sister and I finally caught the cat with the towel while Dad filled the tank at the back of the car.

An hour later, we were at our vacant lot on the shores of Lake Madison. We all piled out and Dad headed back to the trunk

Jingles

to unpack. I heard him laughing as he untied his makeshift trunk latch and lifted out our day's provisions. Mom went over to lend a hand and heard the first edition of his story about the guy at the gas station next to him in town when he'd filled the tank, glaring at him warily and hurrying away. Apparently the ax was still lodged on the bumper where he'd absentmindedly set it after retrieving his keys. Combine that with the wild cat and crying children, and Dad surmised that the fellow hadn't thought of him as an ideal father on a grand outing with his family. "I think I'll buy my gas across town the rest of this month," Dad said.

Mom smiled and grabbed the beach towels and our colorful thongs, now called flip flops, and picked up a book to read as she lounged on the white wooden lawn chair Dad had built for her to relax in as she watched us frolic in the water while he constructed the cabin twenty feet behind her. We each carried whatever we could lift and ran to the beach.

The sun was shimmering on the water, miniscule curls of green floating in it, unlike the chlorine-saturated blue of the water at the local swimming pool that set your skin itching, bleached your hair, and made your eyes sting. This water was the natural temperature of a summer day, soft and unassuming with no illusion that it would be good enough for a fancy resort. It offered the comfort of a safe, personal gift from nature. It was the baptismal waters of our childhoods spent swimming, canoeing, and skiing at Lake Madison.

The structure was built and, as the years passed, connections with our gang of friends and family expanded, forming caring bonds that supported us for a lifetime. The stories multiplied, enriching memories, which would kindle a soft yearning in quiet moments of adulthood. The foundation for our characters, as well as the house, was laid in those Sunday outings of the 1950s.

How Big a Farmer Are You?
By Leroy Sauer of Roscoe, South Dakota
Born 1930

I was born in 1930 on a little farm near Java, South Dakota. I was born in a hospital; most babies at that time were born at home with the help of a mid-wife. It was the beginning of the Great Depression; crops were fair but commodity prices were at an all-time low. Wheat sold for as little as five cents per bushel. Was told of a farmer who shipped a carload of cattle by rail to Sioux Falls and they didn't cover the shipping.

Then the drought came in 1934, near nothing grew. Times were hard on the farm however, we were never hungry. With carryover from better years and the little crops that grew. We managed to feed a few milk cows, chickens, and enough hogs to feed the family. There were dust storms I remember it got dark one afternoon, we all went into the house. Mother put wet towels on the windowsills to keep some of the dust out. Then the grasshoppers came so thick that they blotted out the sun. They ate anything green.

I remember my father driving some of his cattle to Java where they dug a trench, shot them and covered them up. The government paid about $12 per head. Farm people could survive on very little money those days. They had no utility bills. They needed to buy a little kerosene for their lamps; a little coal they burned wood, cow chips we picked from the bare pastures in the summer and dried them. On Saturday nights, they all went to town with a few eggs and cream, enough to buy a few groceries and a little repair.

We had a telephone, it was called a farmers line. The farmers built it by stringing wires on fence posts and anything to keep it off the ground. They also maintained it. We had the old crank phones. We would crank out so many longs and shorts to identify each individual phone. There were 19 farmers on our party line, so it was a problem getting to use it at times and some people listened to all conversations. It was cheap, probably no more than $10 per year. Neighbors visited much more in those days. They could never leave without a meal. Mother would open a jar of canned beef, potatoes, gravy, home baked bread and some kind of canned fruit. It was a good meal and they enjoyed the fellowship.

The winters seemed harder those days and roads were not what they are today so if there was much snow they often parked their cars until spring. I remember going to my uncle's place with the horses and sleigh and us kids would hook our little sleighs behind. That was real fun for us.

I came from a family of four brothers and

one sister. We had this dog a real friend and playmate he loved to play ball with us. But he had a bad habit of chasing cars until one day he chased his last. Us kids mourned for days. It wouldn't have been much worse if it were one of us. We dug a grave in the trees and found a pretty red stone that looked like a real gravestone. My sister thought we should put a bible verse on it, but couldn't think of a proper verse so we turned to dad who was not a serious person. He thought a little and said, the wages of sin is death, and we didn't think it was funny, but I suppose old pups were sinning when he chased cars.

We attended country school though the 8th grade. They were one-room schools with one teacher teaching all eight grades. I wanted to stay home and help dad instead of going to high school, but dad insisted I go he wanted all his children to have an education. Dad was an easygoing man, short, didn't weigh more than 135 pounds soaking wet. He was sitting in the bar in Roscoe one afternoon when a stranger sat beside him. He happened to be one of the biggest and best farmers in South Dakota. He carried on and on about his operation. Dad didn't add anything to the conversation. He couldn't stand a bragger. He finally turned to dad and asked him how big a farmer he was and dad replied, "About five foot two." The stranger got up and went to the other end of the bar.

President Roosevelt took office in 1953. The depression had grown steadily worse. Thousands of unemployed workers men standing on bread lines to get food for their families, farmers, and city workers lost their homes because they couldn't pay their mortgages. Many banks closed and people lost their meager savings.

The administration introduced the new deal. There were many programs attached such as food assistance and various work projects, among those was the works progress administration. It employed an average of 2,000,000 workers annually between 1935 and 1941. They built and repaired country roads, dams, parks, etc. My father worked on WPA, they worked with small horse drawn scrapers and hauled gravel with their farm wagons.

The economy improved and rains came and people got back on their feet. Things went quite smooth until World War II. I was 11 years old and remember the sad news of Pearl Harbor. This changed the lives of everyone and all able-bodied young men were called to serve in the armed forces. Women served also and many women and older men went to work in Defense plants. The war lasted over four years. We can be ever so proud of the American people for how they worked together for the war effort. We can be especially grateful for those who served in the armed forces and those who gave their lives so we would be free.

I married the love of my life in 1950. I served in the Marine Corps during the Korean conflict. After being discharged, we came back to Roscoe and started farming. We have one son, Ron, who took over the farm and one daughter Sandra, working in Rapid City. They have families. We are retired and living in Roscoe. We have seen a lot of changes we went from horse and buggy days to where we are today. We celebrated our 63rd wedding anniversary and thankful for our good health.

Making Our Own Meat
By Arlowene Hitchcock of Conde, South
Dakota
Born 1926

I was born on a farm in South Dakota in 1926. In those days, the doctor came to your house to deliver a baby. I had two older brothers. I don't remember very much about my early years. The only toy we had had was the red wagon. We had to help with chores. We had cattle and we all learned to milk by hand on a tame white roan cow. We had horses, as that is how my dad farmed. There were no tractors. I remember him walking to the barn carrying a kerosene lantern to do the chores. You didn't put in long hours farming as they do now. The horses needed to be watered, fed, and rested. Our farm was diversified as we raised pigs, sheep, chickens, turkeys, and geese. Children had the job of feeding the poultry and gathering eggs. My mother had an incubator. It had a tray on which you put the eggs. The eggs had to be rolled every evening so you didn't have crippled chicks. The eggs had to be cooled at that time for a while. I remember holding a flashlight and my mother candled an egg over the light. If the egg was clear, it was not a fertilized and was discarded.

The incubator had a kerosene lamp, which had to be kept filled and regulated so it wouldn't get too hot or cold. We were excited to see the baby chicks peck their way out of the shell. We also had clucks (brooding hens) that were set on the goose or turkey eggs to hatch.

In those years people worked very hard. Water was carried from a well. Our well was brick lined, as it was also our drinking water. Water was pumped by hand into a tank for the animals. You carried it to the house for household use and washing clothes. My mother had a large copper boiler that was filled with water to wash clothes. The water was heated on a cook stove that was heated with corncobs, cow chips, wood, and coal. I remember my mother made soap for washing clothes from the tallow from butchering and lye. She washed clothes on a washboard. Then we had a washing machine that you pulled a handle back and forth to turn the dasher.

In those days, you didn't buy meat. You had a butchering day when relatives came and helped you butcher. Of course, you returned the favor when they butchered. When butchering they caught the blood from a stuck hog. The pan of blood was set on a tub of snow. We had to stir it until it was cold so it wouldn't clot. Then it was used to make blood sausage. Yes, it was very good. She also made liver sausage, scrapple, and wurst. With no refrigerator, she canned meat too. I remember the school lunch we carried to school was a plum jelly sandwich (a crate of plums cost 59 cents) and a piece of wurst. The wurst was made using hog intestines, which were drained, washed, scraped, and washed till they were clean. Then with a sausage maker, you filled lengths of them with the ground meat. You tied the ends together to form a ring. The rings of sausages were hung on a pipe in a smokehouse. The smokehouse was like an overgrown doghouse with a tunnel to the outside, which was lined with heavy tin to a fire pit. You kept this burning with wood, which smoked the meat.

The worst times were the dirty thirties. The dust was so thick that you couldn't see across the yard. Nothing grew except thistles so the livestock suffered and some died. The windowsills were thick with dust. Some people lost their farms, as they had no income. Times were very hard! There was no electricity; we used kerosene lamps, Aladdin lamps, and a pressure gas lantern for light. Men sawed ice from a lake, which they hauled home and packed between straw in an icehouse. The icehouse was like a roof built over a dug out. You had a metal lined icebox in which you put a chunk of ice to keep your foods cold.

We had no bathrooms. You had an outhouse. Ours had two large holes for adults and a small one for children. It was very chilling to set your bare butt on it in the wintertime. You used a washtub for bathing. The youngest was bathed first, then the next oldest, etc. Remember the water was all carried from a well and heated on the cook stove. The cook stove always had a teakettle on it so you always had some hot water.

We walked two and a half miles to a one-room country school. The teacher taught all eight grades. She had to board with a family, be the janitor, and build the fire to warm the school. During the '40s for high school, I lived in town in a boarding house during the week. There were no school buses. In 1946, I married a World War II veteran and I still live on the farm where we raised four children. We lost a daughter on icy roads in 1973. I lost my husband to cancer in 2009. I live five and a half miles from the place where I was born.

Life in Yale
By Delphine Decker of Yale, South Dakota
Born 1935

Yale was named after Yale University; someone was going to school there. I was born in Doland, South Dakota on December 30, 1935. I remember living north of Lake Byron before moving to Yale. Mom and Dad, Ernest and Anne Hofer, farmed and when moving to

West Side of Business Street in Yale, South Dakota

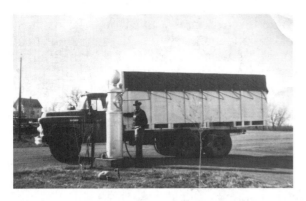

Delphine's dad, Ernest Hofer at his gas station

Yale he kept farming. When not farming he hauled gravel quite a few South Dakota places and to North Dakota. I remember Dad and Mom picking corn by hand and putting it in a wagon pulled by a horse, and I sat on the seat.

When Dad was graveling, he built a homemade trailer house with an icebox, cabinet, and camp stove on it. It had a table, chairs, sink, beds, and a small closet.

In those days was WPA days. If you had your own truck, somebody else had to be hired to drive it. Two people had jobs in them days, not one.

We had no bathroom; we had an outhouse and I hated it. I remember Mom washing clothes on a scrub board in a tub, rinsing them in another tub, and putting them in a hand wringer. Then she hung them out to dry. We had to haul all the water.

We didn't have a telephone. The only phone in town was at Bill Malon's house. They took the call and come to us. We had to use their phone for a small fee. Later we got a party line with six to a line. We had a box with a handle to make long and short rings.

In the early '40s, my dad bought the Duff McDonald stockyards and house, the whole two blocks. It was closed by then but all the buildings, scale, and tanks were still there, also a jail with two cells. As the years went by he sold lots and people built houses. The last to be built was my daughter's greenhouse and house. They sell plants wholesale.

Dad started a gas station later in the '40s. I remember standing on a stool and looking out the window to see if anyone drove up. Then Paul A. Hofer made gas stations two blocks south of us.

I started school in Yale in the fall of 1941. My grandparents lived by the school. They farmed and milked cows and sold milk and cream to the Footes Grocery Store. I remember going there after school. I would wash the glass jars and fill them and cap them. I used a separator to separate the cream from the milk. I even helped Grandma turn the handle on a butter churn to make butter. I still have it.

The main street has changed a lot. There were two elevators, Reese and Farmers. Reeses was managed by Paul Kienasser, Arlie Heater, Leon Shovland, and Melroy Hafee. Farmers was managed by Otto Zeigledrof for years. He also milked and sold his milk to the Musolf Store. They also had shoes and clothes.

Main Street from the south to the northwest side was Funk Lumber yard, later bought by Claude Green. Years later, it got sold. It's still there but not in use. Then was the Welch's Pool Hall, later owned by Oscar Carlson, Phil Harnig, and then Danny and Faye Gross. Then there was a storage building. At one time, there was an icehouse behind it owned by Otto Ziegledrof before our time here, then the Musolf Store with the Yale Gym upstairs. They had basketball games, bingo basket socials, programs, New Year with chili and oyster stew. Years later Yale Mission Church was up there. Next across the street was the bank building which closed in the early '30s. It had living quarters upstairs. High school girls stayed there; didn't drive in those days. Later Danny and Faye Gross bought and made living quarters out of it. Years later, it got torn down and there is a house there now. Next, was a small building; John and Anna Ross bought it and opened a café. School kids ate there. There was Foots Grocery Store later Fred and Joes Beck, John and Anna Ross, then Zachy Wepf had a fire it closed there

Fishing buddies
Otto, Phill, and Ernest

133

also was a living quarters upstairs. My dad bought it. Ernest Hafer tore it down and kept the good lumber and built the house I'm still living in since 1957. Then was a hardware store and the post office in it. It was run by Emil Dracek and later Eddie Hohm bought it and moved the stuff to the west side of the grocery store. Then there was a locker owned by Paul Hofer. It is gone now. Then the Kuehl building. Years ago, they built tractors with steel wheels. There were two in there yet, upstairs was living quarters. High school girls stayed on the west side and Luke and Anna Stohl lived on the east side. They moved and the Yale Mission Church started there. On the east side of the street was Maass Motor Repair and Gas Station, which later became Perry's Repair Shop. Now the elevator owns it and uses it for storage. They tore it down about a week ago. Then was Bill Gorham's gas station. It closed a few years later. Bill Malon bought it and moved his repair shop there. Later Danny and Faye Grass bought it and tore it down and built a new pool hall. It is still there and is now called the Red Line. Then there was a fire hall with a room in back for meetings and gatherings. Across the street was Eddie Stohl's gas and repair station. Later John and Anne Ross bought it and started a café again. Later Werner Hacder bought it and Cliff and Ruth Anderson. A few years later, it was torn down. Then there was an ice cream store, and then living quarters, then the post office, now living quarters again. A half a block in was Gross Creamery, later Herb and Renee Schultz bought it and it became a blacksmith shop. Now there's a trailer house there.

Before we ever moved here, there was a stable behind Maass Motors. When we moved here there was one church, a Presbyterian. Later Yale Mission and then they moved a Lutheran church here from the country.

Saturday Nights in Alpena in the 1940s
By Daniel P. Horn of Huron, South Dakota
Born 1940

I can remember World War II and ration books, with stamps in them, things like sugar, shoes, tires, and gas (not a complete list) was rationed. No new cars and parts were hard to come by. My family lived on a farm, three and a half miles west of Virgal and our mail route was Wolsey. Well we needed a different car and my dad (Erwin Horn) finally came up with a 1927 Chevy, with a four-cylinder engine. Gas was rationed, so this was a concern for my dad. If I recall right, the price of the car was $35.00. Today, I believe the vacuum operated fuel pump was a factor on the price of the car and painted on both front doors was Kellcy, which was the name for the car. Sort of an odd spelling but was a nice job of painting the letters.

The vacuum fuel pump, leaking vacuum was a never-ending problem. When the engine ran, the engine vibration worked on the fittings, the lines, and the vacuum tank and you had to fix the vacuum leaks, pretty regular. My dad drove Kellcy about 25 miles per hour on the road. He had a special repair kit, which was under the front seat and checked every time Kellcy went anywhere: a small bag of flour, a bottle of water, a snuff can, and a pop bottle of gas, with a cork in it, and usually a small stick. When we went to Alpena on Saturday nights, my job was to hold the snuff can for dad. Whenever Kellcy stopped running some flour and a little water was mixed up in the snuff can and this mix was used to seal up a vacuum leak. This wasn't a sure thing on fixing the vacuum leak, but a little shot of gas down in the carb and maybe we were off again. In the winter time the water was poured out when you got home and filled up with hot water and wrapped up to keep it from freezing when you left from home. This was what we did to get to town and back home on Saturday nights.

We went to Alpena almost every Saturday night. We sold cream to the creamery and shopping was a big thing. The grownups would visit with each other and had a network of friends and neighbors. In the war years this network was very important. If you needed something this network usually would come up with it to help out. Sometimes money would be exchanged on a deal but this was not always the case. Sometimes you returned a good deal to someone else and times you exchanged work. Kind of whatever was fair and helped someone. This seemed to work out one-way or other. And if you took advantage of the system you found yourself cut out of this network. I was just a young kid, but it was remarkable how this worked. I had a question or two a time or two and my mother (Lula Mae Horn) explained how this system worked.

Alpena was a busy place on Saturday night. There was a small outdoors movie theater set up in the summertime, for at least a couple of years. My first movie picture was in Alpena. Old yellow, a real classic and it was even in full color. Kind of wow was that a treat. And being the oldest, I had to watch over my younger brothers. I don't recall that we ever got into any real trouble. Most of the time we had to stay close to mother or dad, so we wouldn't get lost. I only remember one young lad getting lost for maybe 45 minutes. Seemed everyone was looking for him. He showed up all by himself. I had questions about him really being lost, but figured it was wise to keep quiet. Alpena is not a big city.

I'll never forget one night in early November, coming home from Alpena. This big old skunk was crossing the road in front of us. The skunk turned toward our car in the middle of the road and dad hit the skunk. There was a good thud and the smell was real strong. And seemed to get stronger as we drove home. By the time we got home we could hardly breathe. Well that dead skunk was lying on the front panel in front of the grill. Dad took the car down the road to get rid of the skunk. It took some time to get rid of the smell in the car. We were never sure just how that skunk ended up on the front of the car, but it did.

A Miracle for Brother Bud
By Rose Lamb of Willow Lake, South Dakota
Born 1926

My youngest brother always got to go along with Mom and Dad when they went to town to buy groceries. This one time I got into the back seat of our Model T Ford car. When we got almost to town, I sat up on the seat and started talking to my brother. I wasn't clean and did not have decent clothes on. Mom and Dad said they would leave me off at the school playground, so I played on the swing until my parents stopped and took me home. I learned my lesson not to sneak along in the back seat again.

When I was in grade school, we lived on a farm. We had a cook stove in our kitchen.

Every morning, my dad had boiled eggs for breakfast.

My mother had a setting hen on duck eggs and after 3 ½ to 4 weeks the eggs would hatch. Oh, the baby ducks were so cute! My mother had put a few ducks in a little container and kept them near the cook stove so they would stay warm.

This one morning, I took one ducky and put it on the back of the stove, and all at once, my ducky ran over on the stove and fell in the kettle of boiling water where my mom was boiling my dad's eggs for breakfast. I was so scared! I didn't know what to do. I was afraid of my dad, so I ran out of the door and ran down to our neighbors that lived a half of a mile away. I told them what had happened.

The neighbors gave me some breakfast and also some food at dinnertime. When it started to get dark at night, I ran home, scared to death about what would happen to me. Nobody said anything to me. I will never forget this.

My oldest brother, Bud, loved to hunt and trap skunks when he was 15 years old. He always put traps by places that he thought skunks would come to. It was cold in the wintertime so he asked my dad if he could go and check the traps. About a half an hour after he left home, a really bad snowstorm came up. My dad and mom and all of us were so worried, because it was so blinding with blowing snow that we couldn't even see our barn from our house.

My dad and mom said, "What shall we do?" We all were in the house and watching out of the windows for my brother, Bud. My dad and mother said a prayer that God would watch over Brother Bud. And guess what? All at once we heard someone opening the door. It was Brother Bud. My dad asked him how did he find his way home. Bud said he kept his hand on the fence by the field that was next to our farmyard. This was a miracle. We will never forget this day and how thankful we all were.

I grew up in South Dakota during the 1920s. Our big kitchen had a cook stove, a dry sink with a pump, and a bucket for drinking water. Most of our life centered around the cook stove. Mom prepared three meals a day, and all seven of us sat down at the big, round pedestal table to eat together. There was always warm water in the reservoir, a steaming kettle, and Dad's coffee pot. My dad, Emil, got up early every morning and started the fire. I thought he was so brave to get dressed in the cold and get the kitchen warm for all of us: my mom, Ida; my sister, Ruth; and my three brothers, Pepsi, Pete, and Sonny; and me.

Adventures with Cousin Jack
By Doreen Holmquist of Aberdeen, South Dakota
Born 1924

I always enjoyed spending my weekends out on Aunt Mae's farm with cousin, Jack, because most every morning, soon as breakfast was over, Jack would brief me on what way he had decided on for getting rid of his younger cousin, five year old Rodney. Rodney was Jack's other cousin, not mine. What nine and ten year old wants to have a five year old tagging along anyway? And we could get out of kid-sitting Rodney. Then we could play outside the fenced in yard; if Rodney was grounded, he would have to stay inside the fence.

One day, Jack asked me if I would like to see where Uncle Bill hid his beer. Those were Prohibition days. No one was allowed to brew their own liquor. Out we all went to an old well that was right in front of the barn. There was a large handle on the side of it attached to a rod that went completely across the top of the well. In the center of that rod was a large gear. Jack turned and turned; the handle and the rope wound into a big ball, and then up came a bucket made out of wood. Inside the bucket was a long handled cup. Jack took a drink of water out of the cup and then passed it to me. He pointed at two-quart bottles and winked at me. The plot was set to happen. One bottle was tan and the other was dark brown. Rodney was watching us, so Jack reached in and handed the brown bottle to me, then he grabbed the other bottle and yelled at me, "Come on, we'll hide with it." Naturally, Rodney ran out into the field where Uncle Bill was on the bailer to tattle on us.

We quickly ran back, putting the beer back into the bucket. We released the handle, and it spun as the beer lowered back into the cool water. We ran and rolled over the wooden fence and to the straw stack by the barn. We dug deep into the straw stack, covering ourselves with straw, and waited.

Uncle Bill stopped the bailer and ran to the grove of trees, following Rodney. When they came back out Bill walked to the well, pulled off the wire that held the handle in place, and turned the handle that brought the bucket up. The two bottles were still in place. He pulled out the cup and took a drink of water. Then he told Rodney, "You get in the house and stay there. I'll deal with you later!" Bill went back to the field. Jack laughed, "Freedom for the day!"

Another time Jack plotted to get Rodney in trouble. Aunt Mae always walked me upstairs each night to the master guest bedroom. She carried a kerosene lamp, which she held high while I undressed and put on my nightgown. Then she would set the lamp on the window seat, turning the wick way down to just a flicker, and smile at me cuddled up in the bed. Aunt Mae had no children of her own so she was delighted when I came to stay for the summer.

This room was huge, probably 30 feet by 30 feet. It had a window seat that extended the outside wall of the house. It was seven feet long with five windows surrounding it. So I could watch the moon from three sides. Between the window and the bed was what they called a washstand. It held a large clay ornamental pitcher inside a huge bowl. Draped on the side were a washcloth and a tiny towel. They were there to wash your face and hands before breakfast. The room had wallpaper with huge, six-inch red roses on a bright yellow background. This sets the scene for my next story.

Jack and Rodney followed Aunt Mae and me up the stairs and then ran on down the dark hallway to their bedroom. Theirs was three doors west of mine. I was lying there watching the moon while I said my thank you prayers when my door creaked open. It was Jack, still in his overalls but with stocking feet. He passed me and reached to raise the wick on the lamp higher. He whispered, "I pushed our door hard against the hinges so the creakin' would alert Rodney." Putting a finger to his lips in a 'shush' position, he crossed the room, sat down in a wicker rocker, placed one foot onto his other knee, and leaned the rocking chair way back. I knew he had something devious planned.

All was quiet and then Jack whispered, "Listen, that's him." I heard it, Rodney's slippers coming up the hall and then the creak of the steps on the circular staircase. I heard muffled voices in the kitchen below as Rodney tattled, and then came the sound of three sets of feet coming quietly up the stairs. Uncle Bill was in front as the three of them burst through the door. They glanced back and forth from the bed to the rocker silently. "Just visiting," Jack said. Rodney ran down the hall as the trio back out. Without a word to us, Bill and Mae backed through the doorway and closed the door. Jack snapped his fingers above his curly orange hair. With a crooked grin he stood, crossed the room, and said, "Freedom for tomorrow; he'll be grounded." And out the door he went. I thought mission accomplished!

To get an image my cousin, Jack, close your eyes and mentally picture orange, curly hair and a multitude of freckles from ear to ear. He had a Maverick-type persona that was kept in check only Uncle Bill's rule of "get it right" or Jack's own rule of staying one mere inch inside of those rules, mixed with the unconditional love of Aunt Mae. To describe poor Rodney's fate is like pushing on a rope with nothing on the other end.

Doreen Holmquist at seven years old

Shenanigans

Shenanigans was a common word in the '30s that meant *almost* wrong but if you get away with it, well…

The next morning Jack banged on my door, "Get up, breakfast time." "It's barely light, what's up?" I said. No answer came from the other side of the door. As soon as breakfast was over Jack said, "Doreen," and then his head and eyes motioned toward the back door.

"What's up?" I asked.

"I'll 'splain later," he replied.

"Later? What were the shenanigans last night for? Why'd ya' wanna get Rodney grounded?" I asked.

"Come on. I'll 'splain it later," he told me.

"Not 'til you tell me," I said.

"We're going watermelon stealin'," was the reply.

"Not me! That's dishonest"

"Not this way, it ain't. See, the neighbor plants watermelons between the rows in his corn. The leaves shade the ground so it don't dry out. And Uncle Bill's cornfield is next to his, so some of the watermelon vines are under the fence and over into Bill's corn, a long ways. Now I just think they ought to be nobody's. Right?" Jack explained.

When we got down to the creek, Jack said, "You stay here, and I'll bring one down to you, 'cause sometimes the neighbor shoots a shotgun filled with rock salt at me." So I waited while Jack jumped from one island to the next and then on over to the other side. Jack disappeared into the cornfield. I waited.

Then he came back with a big watermelon. At the edge of the creek he yelled to me, "Catch!" and he threw it like a football. It landed in the creek right in front of me. Mud and water flew up all over my blue dress and my long hair. Jack jumped the islands back over as I wiped mud off my face with the back of my dress, the only spot that wasn't muddy. Jack said, "Well, the damage is already done so we might as well eat it right here. The neighbor can't see us down here." He threw the watermelon against a big rock and handed me an eight-inch wedge. Well, my face couldn't get much

137

dirtier so I thought I may as well enjoy the spoils. Warm, muddy watermelon does taste great when you are only nine years old. So we feasted and then hid the evidence in the cornfield.

Back at the house, Aunt Mae was out gathering eggs and doing chores, so I washed my hair in the dishpan while Jack washed the mud out of my dress in the sink. I wore a pair of Jack's overalls while the dress dried on the clothesline. When Aunt Mae finished milking the cows and running the cream separator she came into the kitchen. She took one side glance at my clean but badly wrinkled dress, raised those all-knowing eyebrows, flashed me a tongue-in-cheek smile, and said nothing.

Greatest Achievement in Hunting
By Mary K. Frazier of Aberdeen, South Dakota
Born 1932

Seventy-eight years ago, when I was 3 years old and my brother was 4, I helped to capture a wild skunk from a culvert on our farm. I think the skunk died of pure fright when I crawled into the culvert to bring him out, and then I cradled him in my arms and carried him up the road to our parent's home. I cried and cried, and kept saying, poor kitty, poor kitty!

We were delighted with our day's catch. Our parents, however, were mortified and our clothes remained on the clothesline for a long time. Our local newspaper had an article in the paper and I still have that tattered and torn article in remembrance of our great achievement in hunting!

Blizzard of 1945
By Howard Roe of Manning, Iowa
Born 1936

In 1945, I was nine years old and in the third grade. I went to a country school, Oxford #7, located between Hazel & Thomas in Hamlin County. Classes from first grade to eighth grade were all in one room with one teacher. There were thirteen students in grades one through eight. My third grade class had two boys and one girl.

One afternoon a snowstorm developed with very strong winds. It was also very cold.

Some of the parents came to get their kids but others like my parents were snowed in and couldn't go anyplace. Our farm was two miles from the school.

John Mischke, a farmer who lived 1/4 mile from the school had just hired Albert Schamens, who had just gotten out of the Marines. Just a little before dark Albert came for the teacher and the seven of us students who were stranded at the school.

We all held hands with the smallest in the front holding the hand of the hired man and the biggest in the back with the teacher last. The hired man held on to the fence as his guide as we could not see where we were going.

We were so happy to arrive at the farm where it was warm and the farmer's wife had prepared warm food for us. We had a good time as we played board games until bedtime. My bed was an army cot right close to the parlor stove.

My parents did not know where I was or if I was safe because we had no telephones and they were snowbound. The next afternoon my dad got our township road shoveled out and found me and took me home.

The "Dirty Thirties" Made for Good Softball
By Donald Erickson of Hendricks, Minnesota
Born 1927

A Dry Lake: We had a lake two miles from our farm and with no rain; it gradually lost its water. Early settlers depended on this lake for its water for livestock and fish for food.

Good records were kept by the local residents.

The worst drought in the history of Lake Hendricks area and in South Dakota, and the surrounding states as well, occurred in 1933 and lasted about three years.

On June 1, 1934, Lake Hendricks was completely dry. It was the first time since the community was settled in 1873.

In the spring of 1936 the lake got about full again and has been full since.

Lake Hendricks covers approximately 1,015 acres of Lake Hendricks Township.

Softball Action: In the dirty '30s, young

men on the farm had excess time on their hands and one activity was softball.

Our neighbor boy played on two teams "Lakeside" and "Valley Cubs." They played a team from a larger town and they had a "Windmill" pitcher. Our neighbor was impressed with this type of delivery so he practiced by throwing balls against their barn. He became very good at this.

This family was one that went to Oregon. Work was scarce here also, so they scheduled a game with a team from a plywood mill and beat them with this "Windmill" delivery.

They were impressed with this pitcher and offered him a job if he would pitch for them. He said he would if they would hire his brother also. They agreed and he became an excellent pitcher and played softball for many years.

The Valley School: Our country school in South Dakota was located in a valley and therefore was commonly known as "The Valley School."

This school was located between two towns, one in South Dakota, and one in Minnesota. This created minor problems as location—"where are you from?" —was important.

I began school here in 1933. Times were tough, no rain, no crops, and families were moving out. One family left for Oregon during the school year. Two fathers died in a gravel pit accident. By spring, we were down to 4 students and 2 were 8th graders. Three were from our family and one neighbor boy.

His family followed others to the west coast as soon as school was out.

Two neighbor girls began school the next fall so things were improving.

The school was closed in 1973 and the students went to "town school" and the building stood empty for 35 years before it was removed.

The Plains Couple
By Ileen Groft-Tennyson of Kirksville, Missouri
Born 1939

Athol, SD, is in a small farming community in Spink County. In 1883, the town had a population of 1400. In past years, the town had many businesses.

By the 1940s, many of the businesses had closed. A young boy, Daryl, and a young girl, Ileen, were attending grade school in Athol. They didn't pay much attention to each other and neither of them was aware of the other's love of horses and riding. They both helped their dads with farm work, and they both could drive tractors, milk cows, and stack bales. Both of them had hopes of owning their own farms someday.

By 1954, more of Athol's businesses had closed. Daryl & Ileen went out on a few dates. Daryl's family moved away and Daryl had many experiences. He was in the USAF and at the time of his retirement, he was part owner of a shipyard. He is the father of one son and one daughter.

Ileen graduated from Athol High School and moved from the state. Through the years, she was a medical receptionist and then became a Licensed Practical Nurse. She is the mother of two daughters and one son. Her children found it hard to believe that Athol had been a thriving town, so in 1998, Ileen compiled and wrote a booklet about the history of her hometown.

In 2010, Ileen went back to South Dakota to visit relatives and to attend an Athol School reunion.

One day she received a phone call from Daryl, who was in the state of Washington. Daryl had been her first date and she had been his first date. Fifty-five years later, they made a date to meet and drive down memory lane. As they drove around the Athol area, they remembered the quietness of those flat plains and they heard a distant train whistle. They talked about their old friends and the businesses that were no longer there. They drove down dirt lanes and could smell the sweet smell of alfalfa fields and they watched buffalo in some of the pastures. They remembered pick-ups parked on Athol's main street, some with a dog in the back, waiting patiently for his owner to return. They laughed about being able to buy a Coca-Cola and a bag of peanuts to pour in it for about fifteen cents. They remembered Halloweens in Athol and how Main Street would be blocked with machinery, hay bales, tires, and outhouses. There was a place in the river called Goose Lake, where you could meet friends to swim in the summer and ice-skate in the winter. The ice was usually frozen a foot deep and we could have a bonfire going for warmth or toasting marshmallows. Many couples will remember the "lone tree" north and west of Athol. Over decades, young couples would go there to park. At a school reunion in 1971, someone cut down what was left of the old tree and brought it to the reunion so everyone could have a final look at it.

Daryl and Ileen went to the school reunion together in 2010. Neither of them have a farm of their own, but for now, they have each other. They will never forget their roots or their hometown of Athol, on the flat plains of SD.

Our Kool-Ade Enterprise
By Carol Shoup of Onida, South Dakota
Born 1943

The Cunningham Kids and the Kool-Ade Stand

We were a busy bunch and sometimes driven to earn money at an early age. There was not much extra money in Mom and Dad's budget in those days. In 1952, there was road construction near Onaka, SD. Many gravel trucks were driving past our house so we decided opportunity was knocking. We set up our stand with a sign, which read "KOOL-ADE 5 CENTS." We helped ourselves to the supplies in Mom's kitchen. She was at work at Deis' grocery store and could replace the supplies, right?

Our business took off like a rocket. Soon, we were making

Judy, Kathy, Carol, Arlene, and Richard Cunningham in about 1954

several pitchers of KOOL-ADE to keep up with the demand for our product. Then, trouble on the horizon. The Goetz boys soon noticed how well we were doing. Pretty quick, they had a stand directly across the street. We were forced to come up with some innovative idea to quell the competition. How about offering Mom's homemade cookies, one free with each cup of KOOL-ADE? It worked great, until the cookies ran out.

NOW WHAT? We checked Mom's refrigerator and found some bologna. How about a FREE bologna sandwich with each cup of 'Kool-Aid? Another successful strategy, right? Our enterprise was setting sales records. The Goetz's were about out of it until…

Someone must have tipped Mom off about what was going on. All of a sudden, there she was but, not to buy Kool-Ade. By the time Mom had taken enough of our nickels to replace the bologna, cookies, and bread, our venture was in serious financial distress. I believe we were forced into bankruptcy.

To this day I doubt I have ever seen Mom more angry. She worked very hard at the grocery for $75.00 per month, while us kids were at home giving away groceries.

DEPRESSION MEMORIES: Our parents were part of the "waste not, want not" generation. They were the original inventors of recycling; everything was used until it was either used up or worn out. No scrap of food was wasted. If we didn't eat it, it went to the chickens or pigs. Sunday's leftover mashed potatoes became Monday's potato patties. When bars of soap became so small they hardly seemed worth saving, they were pressed onto another, bigger, bar. Worn out T-shirts became dust rags. Nails pulled out of boards were hammered back into shape and stored in an empty coffee or tobacco can.

They seldom bought "paper products," instead outdated catalogs and tissue paper wrappers from seasonal fruits were the toilet paper. Cotton hankies or rags were used instead of Kleenex. Paper towels were unheard of. Homemade flannel diapers were washed and dried; disposable diapers didn't exist. Mom often said, "When they butchered a pig the only thing they didn't use was the oink." Fabric from worn out clothes became quilts. Outgrown clothes were handed down to siblings or cousins until they were worn out. Used grease from lard became soap used for washing clothes. Ice cream was made in a crank by hand ice cream freezer.

Patterned sacks from flour or chicken feed was used for everything from girl's dresses, boy's shirts, and underwear to dishtowels. Scraps from the sacks were used to make piece quilts. Today the old quilts that have sack fabric are prized quilts.

This generation was so conditioned by the Depression that they sometimes carried frugality to a fault. Later in their lives when they could afford a few luxuries they were reluctant to spend the money.

Instrumental in My Life
By Gail Anderson Winter of Borger, Texas
Born 1953

Some of my grandest South Dakota memories involve the Loyalton Public School, where I graduated from the eighth grade in 1967. Even though it was a very large building with three stories, all grades were split into three classrooms on the main level with three grades in each room.

I have fond memories of that grand ole building. Christmas plays and talent shows in the auditorium on the third floor inspire some of the most special memories. Students were forbidden to go on the third floor unless we were practicing for the plays, but sometimes we girls would sneak up there and explore the library and all those old musty, empty rooms. It was spooky and mysterious, and the allure was too much for us to resist. Of course, the boys would then sneak up behind us and scare us silly. And then we would get caught and would have to stay in from recesses and punishment. Evidently, it was worth it, because it happened several times over all the years.

I have wonderful memories of the lunchroom and helping Mrs. Nipp with dishes and memories of the teacher's lounge where we got to go when we were sick. I have warm memories of playing softball out in the field in the schoolyard; it didn't matter how big or how small, how old, or how young, everyone got to play.

I distinctly remember one winter when we had 18-foot snow banks after a fierce blizzard. Kids brought sleds and toboggans and got soaked to the gills playing in the snow and icy pond during recess. Every register in every room had coats and mittens, and boots and wool socks hung on them. To this day, I remember the distinct smell of the clothes drying on the registers. The next recess we would put on the nearly dry clothes and do it all over again! With cheeks and noses red, and our toes nearly frozen to the point of frostbite, the frigid temperatures of the South Dakota winters did not deter us. It was great fun. Today there are surely laws that prevent kids from having such dangerous escapades, especially with the blessing of the teachers.

Every year, the Loyalton School played host to spelling bees and track meets as several other area schools would come to compete. This was at a time when there were still two grocery stores, a lumberyard, a post office, and other businesses in Loyalton. We thought we were really something special when we'd get to walk to one of the stores after a track meet and get a Dr. Pepper out of the old-timey vending machines.

Every time I go home, it breaks my heart to no longer see that magnificent school building standing there. It was such an icon for the community, the place where many activities were held that bonded the community. Instead, in its place stands a small white building where township meetings and voting were held. Now even that building is rarely used. The yard is overgrown with weeds and parts of the old boiler from the original schoolhouse lay abandoned and rusty. As recently as two years ago, the maypole on which the older boys pushed us girls, and we'd fly through the air, stood there lonely with no hope of bringing joy to kids ever again.

My husband placed a geo cache in the schoolyard, so we always visit when we go to the farm. Our now adult kids always enjoy going there with us. Memories are stirred and stories retold and questions asked as I relay the nostalgia of the school and that special time in my life.

Our family attended the Loyalton Wesleyan Church where we obtained a great basis for our Christian faith. I loved Sunday school in the basement and particularly remember Anna Fredrickson as one of my teachers. The church never had indoor plumbing so we had to go outside to the biffy. That always meant a lot of squirming during the services as we resisted the urge as long as possible. Winter was pure torture, as we had to trek in the snow to the outhouse and hope we made it there in time.

Every summer we all looked forward to vacation Bible school. VBS was always held when the lilac bushes were in full bloom at the old parsonage down the street a ways. We'd walk back and forth several times a day between classes held in the church and lunches and crafts in the old parsonage. The parsonage no longer was the residence of the pastors so it served as the fellowship hall. Because the building was vacant most of the time, the basement was dark and creepy. We'd get in trouble for being down there, but who could blame us. We were fascinated by all the junk and old items left behind, such as an old phonograph player. We cranked and cranked on that old thing until we got music from the records left lying scattered. There was so much adventure to be had while exploring both inside and out during VBS and fellowship dinners. I don't believe we ever outgrew playing hide and seek on the property, which also included a dilapidated garage. Many times baby kittens were born there, and it was so exciting to find them.

I graduated from Ipswich High School in 1973 and went away to college. The summer after my freshman year in college, I came back home and helped my folks on the farm. My dad paid me to milk the cows and do field work. I remember keeping track of my hours on a calendar in the milk house. I had barely turned 19 when I returned to college in McPherson, Kansas and never returned home to live again.

I currently live in Borger, Texas with my husband, Raymond. I own Premiere Office Solutions and Raymond works at Chevron Phillips Chemical Plant. I am a relocation consultant and an ordained minister as well, so we travel and minister also. Raymond and I founded Speak His Word Ministries in 2009, and I authored a book, Spiritual Weapons Handbook, published by Whitaker House Publishing September 1, 2013.

I am firmly convinced that the work ethic I acquired while on the farm in South Dakota and my upbringing in a wonderful Christian family have been very instrumental in where I am today.

The Only Car in Front of the Grade School and High School
By Carleton Peters of Mesa, Arizona
Born 1918

I am 96 years old, the oldest of 6, born on a farm in northeast Clark County, South Dakota, in Mt. Pleasant township. My mother was Hazelle Mosey and my father George Fox. I have one brother, George D. Fox, still living at age 92.

Dad didn't want us to go to rural school so he bought a farm within the public school district. At 6 years old, I went to Clark Public School. My 1st grade teacher was Miss Ullyot.

Every Saturday night we went into town in a Dodge car. My folks sold cream and eggs and bought mostly flour and sugar.

Us kids got a nickel for an ice cream cone every week. One time 2 of my friends, Lucy Ann Coughlin and Norma Burns, went with me to get my five cents for an ice cream cone. On the way home my dad said, "When you come for your five cents, don't bring ALL your friends." This is because he passed out nickels to all of us.

The '20s and '30s there was a drought in South Dakota. Pastures were brown. My sister and I had to herd our milk cows in the ditches so they could eat grass. We had a nice pony, Peggy. One time she had four of us kids on her and she went into the plum thicket and we rolled off her behind.

In the '30s, FDR was president. If farmers buried their pigs, calves, and lambs, the government would send them checks. My dad did not want to bury his animals so he started a trucking business to Sioux Falls and let the two hired men run the farm. We never buried our animals. The hired men were Jimmy Patton and Leonard Everett.

In better times, Dad bought a Case tractor and had a threshing machine and threshed all the neighbor's grain. When I was 12 years old, Dad took me out in a stubble field and taught me how to drive a Ford truck with 3 pedals. Then he said I could drive our new Dodge to school every day. South Dakota did not require driver's licenses until the '40s.

My father wanted to treat his crewmen so in our basement he had a barrel and was making beer. One time my mom threw a gallon of vinegar in his beer.

When pheasant season opened, no limit,

our hired men and Dad would shoot two tin tubs full of pheasants. Mother canned lots of pheasants and we ate lots of pheasant.

There were 10 or 12 sitting around our dining room table for three meals every day. My dad needed meat and potatoes for each meal. He butchered one beef and five hogs every year.

I was an honor roll student most all the time. When I was a sophomore, I never had to write a test. I played my father's violin and played throughout grade school, high school, and college, and then bands took over.

Our new Dodge was the only car sitting in front of the grade school and high school.

I went to college at Minot State. Teachers with 2 years taught at Gardenia for $40 a month. They hired me back for $5 a month.

I married in '41 to Curtis R. Price. We had two children, James C. Price DDS, and Kimberly Price who lives in Dallas, TX. Curtis died in 1961 and I remarried in '73 to Howard Peters. We have traveled the world.

My Medicine Lake
By Dana Reeve of Sioux Falls, South Dakota
Born 1960

I grew up IN Medicine Lake! I'd wake up and put my swimming shorts on, waiting for the first swimmers to come to the resort. My name is Dana Reeve and I'm a fourth generation Reeve at Medicine Lake, Codington County.

My first memory is showing my grandmother Blanche Reeve that I could back float and swim at the age of four or five, while she was sitting in a chair soaking her feet in the lake. We lived at the lake from the end of May till the end of September, and during the swimming season I'm sure I swam 4 times a day! The water didn't taste good, hence the name Medicine Lake, heavy with minerals. You'd come out of the lake and the mineral would dry white & flaky on your skin and make your hair stiff. I was red haired and fair skinned and sunburned my shoulders, nose, and lips A LOT!

The lake water was crystal clear down 10 feet or more. You could walk straight into the lake right over your head, 20 or 30 feet deep all over! I remember swimming across the lake with my family (with someone in a boat

for safety). It was easy to swim because it was so buoyant. My grandfather, Clarence Reeve first built a pier for swimmers, and when I grew up, we had a diving raft chained to the shore. We played lots of games of 'king on the raft'! Once while standing on the diving board of the raft, I saw a dollar bill on the bottom of the lake 8 feet deep. So I dove off and got it. The top side of the bill was faded from the sun through the lake water.

The lake never turned green like most lakes do. It had a deep cold bottom. Ten or 12 feet down was a pink layer, 2 feet thick, and warm. Below that, it was cold and pitch black! Around the perimeter were many fresh hard water springs. The cows would stand in the lake to cool off but not drink the lake water. The ducks and geese would stop by and also not drink the water. The lake is called Minnepejuta (Medicine Lake) by the Indians because of the healing properties of the mineral water. It cures poison ivy, poison oak, and helps any open wound.

I grew up at Reeve's Resort, which my great grandfather, Howard Reeve started. He knew the lake was 'magical'. Ours, run by my parents, Devon and Marlys Reeve, was the only resort on the lake with a sandy beach. The resort had changing houses, a dance hall, and a confectionary. The confectionary had three covered porches. The steps to the porches were built from the big cement cylinders (10 in. by 30 in.); from the 30-year test of the University of MN, which ran from 1929 to 1959. The confectionary had big swing up doors over the counters.

My mother, Marlys, collected the 25 cents for swimming, sold candy, popcorn, pop, beer, etc. for 20+ years. It also had a horseshoe pit right off the porch. On busy days, the porch would be lined up with all kinds of people: swimmers, players, moms and dads, etc. It was the oldest building on the resort.

They held dances every weekend for a few years as I grew up. We had bands and sold set ups, beer, and snacks! One of my favorite memories was swimming late in the day with the local harvesters. They would come in the fall at sundown to get washed off and refreshed. The water and the minerals (dehydrated medicine lake water) has been sold nationwide and still continues to be desired. No one ever had a better youth than I, growing up IN Medicine Lake!

Chimney Fires were Very Scary
By Harold G. Thaden of Wilmot, South
Dakota
Born 1938

I have lots of fond memories of my youth growing up on the farm in Grant County and Kilborn Township, northwest of Twin Brooks, South Dakota. The winters were always worse than the summers.

My family consisted of Mom and Dad, my twin brother Gerald, and a younger brother and sister who were also twins, Ron and Ruth. Theodore and Grace were my parents.

Our country one room school was located on our farm about 200 yards from our house so I didn't miss much school during the school year.

One year the teacher was from Ortonville, Minnesota. It seemed whenever a teacher needed room and board, our home was selected. Our home wasn't large and having the teacher eating meals with us and sleeping one door away seemed a bit awkward. She was one year out of high school and had a summer of instruction at Aberdeen Teacher's college.

To begin with, we had no electricity to our place. The bathroom was a little house out back. And my chores consisted of hauling water to the house from the well. The cooking my mom did was on the cook stove. For fuel, we burned corncobs, which my brother and I had to pick up after the pigs ate the corn off the ears in the big lot.

I remember a number of times when the wind was strong and the weather was cold and the fire from the stove would catch the soot in the chimney on fire and the pipes would get red hot. Very scary.

In the winter whenever we had a fresh snow it was Gerald's and my job to shovel paths from the house door to the house out back, then to the barn and the well, and to the hog house and the chicken coop.

There were always the chores of milking the cows (10-20), feeding them, and separating the milk from the cream. By the way, we had to milk the cows by hand. The cream separator was a machine that had a hand crank, which had to be turned at a certain speed. Then the pigs had to be fed and the chickens had to be fed.

Then Mom would have a warm breakfast, mostly pancakes and bacon, waiting for us. And then we could get ready to go to school.

My life was so much changed on the farm when the day finally came when the Whetstone Valley rural electric brought electricity to our farm. It provided light, power to pump water, to power milking machines, heat in some instances, and numerous other conveniences.

I began life in the Milbank, South Dakota, hospital, weighing 4+ lbs. as well as my twin brother. We were very fragile. We were in the hospital 60 days and my mom too. She spent some of the days helping to do laundry. My dad's total hospital and doctor's bill was $60 in May of 1938. I found out later in life Gerald was born on the 22nd and I was born on the 23rd. We always celebrated on the 22nd. I am very grateful to be a twin. We played together as kids and farmed together as adults and I would want it no other way.

I will conclude my story by saying at a very early time in my life I wanted to make farming my lifelong work. I am now 75 years old and have not missed one year of my life doing what I love. The Lord has truly blessed me.

Harold, Gerald, Ruth, and Ron
Two sets of twins

Schoolhouse and Barn Memories
By Pat La Mee of Rapid City, South Dakota

My roots are in the northeastern corner of South Dakota, on a farm near Britton. My love of being outdoors can be traced back to that little farm, with its fresh air and hard work. Through the decades of my life, I have seen so many changes.

As I think back as a 70-year-old man, I have gone from a childhood of no telephones to every day carrying a cell phone. We had kerosene lamps dimly lighting our little house in the evenings in the 1940s and now there are lights, computers, and televisions that light up our nights. It is possible that my generation has seen some of the biggest technological and social changes during our lifetimes, in comparison to other generations.

A few years ago, we took a drive back to the site of my old one room country school. Pulling up, I shut off the engine and opened the door. I opened the door to a flood of memories as well. The tall weeds and grasses were standing tall, untouched by human footsteps in a very long time. We climbed over a fence that was not there the last time I walked this place. The little one room school was a pile of boards and shingles spread out across the ground scattered with odds and ends. Scattered in my mind, were memories of this place and the life I lived long ago. It seems like a separate chapter from a book, but it was my life.

Looking out across the field and hills, memories of childhood days crept back into my mind. My horse, Mankiller, used to bring me over these same hills every day to school. I struggle to think about putting my little granddaughter who is along this day, onto a big horse, and sending her across the prairie 4 miles to a little school in the middle of nowhere. Did my parents worry about me as a little child getting onto a 1,400-pound animal and being alone out here? I think today, I might worry about my granddaughter doing the same thing I did over 6 decades ago and doing it with no safety net like a cell phone.

The silence disrupts my thoughts for a moment, and I realize how extremely quiet it is in this moment. The silence almost seems "loud." In the background, only the crunch of my footsteps as I wander a few steps towards the south and squinting into the sun I recall 3rd grade and a rickety raft my friends and I constructed over the course of a few recesses out of some wood we found. The day we floated, it was perhaps one of my most memorable days of school. As an adult now, I look back thinking of the possibilities for disaster that little pond and raft could have caused that day, but as a boy, it was certainly all about the adventure.

Pushing off with a long branch from a tree, I felt like Tom Sawyer. However, my adventure ended when my long branch got stuck in the mud and the weight of my body combined with lack of movement started to sink our raft along with our adventure. After realizing there was no help on the horizon, I jumped into the cold spring water, walked to shore and ran back to the warm schoolhouse.

Entering the school with laughter and dripping clothes, our young teacher met my friends and I at the door with a stern look and maybe a bit of concern on her face. What a mess and what to do with these mischievous boys! We did not have extra clothes along, but because the teacher lived at the school, she had something dry for me to put on. My teacher loaned me a delicate pair of her pedal pushers (capri pants). To this day, I recall how awkward those felt and especially because they zipped up the side!

A memory comes to the surface of a day long ago. Mankiller and I were meandering along the dusty ground on our way home from school, when suddenly she stopped short for some unknown reason and I kept going right over her neck to the ground. Without anyone around to judge my tears, I sat there crying and my loyal horse just waited for me. She seemed like she tried to pretend she did not notice I was crying as if to say I was not being a crybaby. She stayed there politely nibbling at some grass while I decided what to do. After a few minutes, I decided nothing was broken and I would most likely live so I stood up and brushed myself off as I walked over to my huge companion who glanced at me with her huge brown almond-shaped eyes. I could not just put my foot into the stirrup and hoist myself up. I was small, even by second grade standards. Looking back, I recall with a silent chuckle that my family called me "Wormy" because I was small, thin and wiry (maybe working hard on the farm with my 3 older brothers and sister kept me that way).

I grabbed her reins that were dangling in front of her and led her over to the nearest fence. Up onto the fence and then easing myself onto my horse, we started off again. There was no time to evaluate the situation thoroughly or to develop any sort of fear or phobia of getting right back onto my horse. I just knew what I had to do, and quietly did it feeling pretty grateful that she was a patient, motherly sort of horse who didn't run off and leave me walking the rest of the way.

I had spent my first year of grade school perched behind my brother, Howard. During that year of sharing our horse, I had worn away some of the hair on the horse, sitting behind the saddle day after day hanging onto the waist of my brother. I was so small as a first grader, that I could not straddle the big horse. I had to sit with my legs pulled up a bit to accommodate this problem, and the miles of friction had worn away a spot of hair on the horse's back where my legs were positioned. At seven years my senior and my closest sibling in age, Howard went to school the next year in town at the high school. That left me and my horse to travel alone through the various weather conditions including snow and below zero temperatures.

My granddaughter's little squeaky voice breaks my train of thought. She is picking little purple and yellow wild flowers and the sun is glistening off of her little blonde curls. I wish the school and barn were still standing to show her where I spent my school days. It would seem so foreign to her reality of school with computers and big rooms with fancy furnishings.

Memories come back in little flashes as we find pieces of an old school desk. Suddenly, I think of the recess bell that used to clang a loud reminder to come back inside. I recall a few times, my friends and I took our horses over the hill at recess just far enough to be able to claim to the teacher we could not hear the bell. The end of the day would come and we would have to go back to the little school to grab our things and explain we did not hear the bell when it rang.

I learned at an extremely young age to work like a grown man. I have confirmed this memory with my older sister, Ione, because it really does seem so hard to believe, but she recalls it vividly as well. One month before my 4th birthday, my siblings and I were a mile from home fixing some fence with our father.

Somehow, there was one extra vehicle that needed to get home. It was a smaller tractor, not the biggest one we had, and my father plopped me on the seat and told me to drive it home. It was just how it was on the farm; everyone worked and everyone learned to drive early in life. My siblings were all much older and I had spent a lot of practice time steering the wheel of vehicles while sitting on their laps. I drove it up to the old barn that had a very, very severe lean to it, and the barn stopped my forward motion by the tractor running up the side of the building a tiny bit. After a few tries, I finally stomped hard enough on the clutch, which was difficult for my legs to reach at that size, and took it out of gear. In reality, this probably took seconds but felt like an eternity at the time. My mother came screaming from the house in a panic and I can't blame her! She was 43 when she gave birth to me and the sight of her "baby" driving completely scared her to death! Maybe Dad forgot that I was too small to drive, but my mother certainly did not!

We all worked constantly on the farm. When I was little, the thing I most wanted to do was help with the milking of our cows. When the day came that I could join everyone in milking, the illusion that it would be the time of my life faded quickly. Up at 5:00 a.m. to milk our 10 cows every day, 7 days a week, was not what I thought it would be. When my older brothers went into the military, it left my mother, Dad, and I to do this every day. To this day, I look back at those years and think about the heat, the cold, the long hours, and think about how different kids grow up today. Many times, I have thought about the fact that the bedroom I shared with my brothers upstairs in our house had one window near their beds, but nothing near mine. How hot it got up there during the summers without even a fan to circulate the hot air. Sometimes my brothers would flop their mattresses out the window and sleep on the roof of the porch of the house.

As the youngest child, it seemed that I fulfilled the usual role that the youngest child gets in the family, which is that of the "gopher" for the family (go for this, go for that). When we finally got electricity on the farm, which later led to television, I had the job of being the human remote control. We got 2 channels on the T.V. and anytime anyone wanted to switch channels, the antenna needed to also switch directions on the outside of the house. I got a lot of unneeded exercise at the end of the day, being the one delegated to move the antenna outside our house.

Life in rural South Dakota during the 1940s and early 1950s was so far removed from what life is today. Decades of changes have shaped my life and today I am grateful for a soft bed, air conditioning in the summer, microwaves, indoor plumbing, and showers: all of the things that make life easier. However, farm life gave me the gift of learning to work hard, to be resilient and strong, and also a great love of the outdoors. Maybe it was a simpler life in a lot of ways, but it was also more complex in some ways. Just thinking of the cold winter outhouse and no bathtub or shower reminds me of how complicated it could be back then just to do those simple things and how good a hot shower at the end of the day can feel.

I Remember When
By Edith M. Noeldner of Watertown, South Dakota
Born 1928

I remember a straw burner as our heat source. It was a big round barrel and would get red hot. One evening I remember a copper boiler with something cooking in it on the kitchen stove. It had a lot of copper tubing coming from it. A container at the end of the tubing caught the liquid. My dad was very cautious. He pulled the window shade and would peek out once in a while. One time he got a teaspoon of sugar and put a couple of drops of the liquid on it and gave it to me. He had made beer and wine before, but I hadn't yet seen this conglomeration.

I remember one afternoon about 3:30 we were in the yard trying to catch our chickens that were blowing away. The dirt felt like sleet when it hit my face. It got so dark that when we got in the house we lit a kerosene lamp. The dirt piled up along the fences like a snowbank. I remember one of our horses collapsing from the heat after too long a day in the field. It fell about ten to twelve feet from the stock tank and well. After pumping and pouring cold water on it for about three and a half hours, it

Edith's grandparents, Louis Ludwig Grewing and Johanna Leopoldine Pauline Nevendorf

got up on its feet.

I remember the first washing machine we had. The round tub looked like wood. There was a lever on the side. Your arm was the power of the agitator and a hand crank to work the wringer. The next washing machine was a square tub. It had a long hose like a vacuum cleaner now but it was metal. When the machine was working that hose was put in the ash pan of the kitchen stove.

I remember a hobo stopping by asking for something to eat. He had a long stick over his shoulder with a bag or sack attached to it. My mother fixed him a sandwich, and he went on his way.

There was no exchanging of Christmas gifts. One year I got a doll. It had been my sister's. They made a new dress for it.

When I was about seven years old, my dad worked for the WPA. I remember my dad fixing our shoes with a cobblers tool, a shoe last.

I remember quite well the house dances. Someone would play a violin or a fiddle. My dad would be the caller for square dances. The

147

little furniture that there was would be moved out of the way. I know the floor was swaying right along with the music and dancing.

I remember snowstorms when our mailman was delivering mail on horseback. Snow and cold didn't stop us from visiting the neighbors. A team of horses would be hitched to the sleigh and across the fields, we would go. I would lie on the bed of the sleigh covered up with a horse blanket.

In wintertime, we had homemade ice cream and homemade chocolate topping. Every time I eat ice cream, those memories

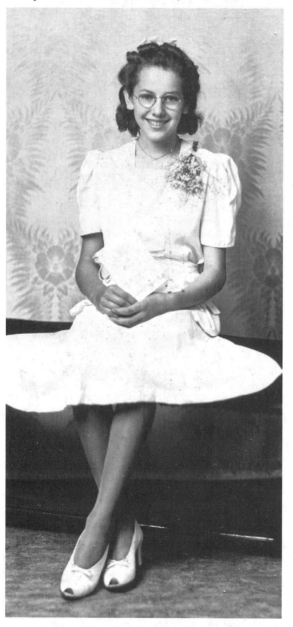

Edith M. Grewing Noeldner in 1942

come back. We were never out of popcorn. That was grown at home.

Mom and Dad had their favorite things to plant. Dad's favorites were long white radish, sweet potatoes, horseradish. Mom's favorite was ground cherries for pie. Peas were my favorite and still are. A big barrel with a screen over the top was used to smoke fish.

The men at our house usually played whist. I remember the kerosene lamp sometimes bounced on the card table.

I was told about someone in the neighborhood who was an excellent bread maker until she had a hex put on her. She could not bake bread after that.

One time my brothers were driving on a country road. Suddenly beside us in the ditch was a ball of fire about the size of a bushel basket. It rolled along for about 25 feet and disappeared.

For a short time, my grandpa, Mom's dad, stayed with us. I had several warts on my fingers. My grandpa told me to talk to the moon and they would go away. He said just to tell the moon you've got something he hasn't got and he can have it. I did that one night. The warts disappeared in a very short time and I never had them again.

Home remedies were fried onions in a cloth or towel put on your chest for a cold, warm milk for sore eyes, tobacco in a white cloth heated, and the juice squeezed out and put in your ear. One I was given but didn't use was skunk oil for whooping cough.

We went 16 miles into town one day to get twine for the grain binder. I was sitting on a bale of twine between the front and back seats of a Studebaker. There was a grate in the floorboard. When we were getting close to home, my parents noticed I wasn't moving. I had been asphyxiated. I don't remember if they took me back to the hospital or flagged somebody down. I think I came to about the time we got back there.

One time one of my brothers had undulant fever. They said he got it from drinking unpasteurized milk. He couldn't walk for a while. I would take him around in the wheelbarrow.

I remember the crank up Victrola and records of songs like "The Isle of Capri" and "On the Good Ship Lollipop."

Our outhouse was about a third of a block from the house. The windmill was in the

Edith M. Grewing and Ralph Noeldner in 1946

opposite direction about the same distance from the house.

The saying when a pig was butchered was they saved everything but the squeal. That is pretty much the truth.

Some cousins and a friend (who was later my bridesmaid) went swimming one day at a place called Mitchell Bridge. The boys were on one side of the bridge and my friend Jane Noelder Burt and I were on the other side. We were clinging on an inner tube. Suddenly all the air went out and down we went. One of the boys saw it. I don't know how he, Clifford Borns, got to us so fast and pulled both of us out. I went swimming with friends Eugeana Sherman Monahan and Shirley Monahan Sandager at another site called Monahan Bridge.

Some of my jobs were going in the pasture picking cow pies for heating the oven when my mother was baking, herding cattle with our dog by the creek, driving the tractor with my dad behind on the grain binder, and keeping a horse going around and around tethered to a piece of machinery called a power sweep. It was to run a grain elevator to auger the grain up into a grain bin. I also had to milk the cows. My mother and I milked 18 of them by hand during threshing season, then separated the milk and fed the calves. Threshing time was a lot of cooking and baking.

One time I was playing with the inside ring of an old tire. I would throw it up in the air and catch it coming down. Once it really smarted. About a week later, my hand was really puffed up like a balloon. The doctor pulled out a rusty wire about an inch and a half long. It didn't get me out of milking.

A few products were purchased from a Watkins sales person. Liniment was used for both humans and animals. Vanilla was in the bottle that was the same size and look. My sister was frosting a cake and took the wrong bottle.

We would take wheat to the mill. We got flour in nice sacks that made good dishtowels or aprons.

We had a lot of company.

We had canned meat of all kinds for meals, beef, pork, chicken, pheasant, and even pickled fish.

During first through seventh grades, I had a two and a quarter mile walk to and from school. Eighth grade was 3.25 miles away, and I rode my bicycle or walked.

My first job I was 13. I worked for an elderly couple. They were also raising a boy who was about 14. My job consisted of everything connected with the household. Besides that, I had to churn butter in a big barrel churn. My second job was all housework for a schoolteacher, including caring for three children, two were in school, and one was not. My third job was as a hostess for the doctor at our local hospital.

I was married at 17. My wedding dress cost $18.00. My husband had bought a small farm. The old house was a little chilly. The chamber pot froze under the bed. The dipper froze in the drinking water on the kitchen sink. I could write a book about this era.

My son and I happened to be in the yard and saw a snake a good seven feet long slither by. My hobbies are flowers, gardening, cutting news articles out of newspapers or magazines, local, statewide, or global. I have scrapbooks from about 75 years ago. They were my sister's. My niece had inherited them and didn't want them so she gave them to me.

I was within 25 to 30 feet of a UFO in 1963.

One thing that really irks me and reminds me of the good old days is some of our fruit. You buy peaches and they're hard as a potato, and then wait two days and they are rotten. Years ago you would buy a crate, put them in the cellar on a gravel or dirt floor, and they'd keep for weeks. When you ate one the juice would run down your chin.

Colored Plastic on the TV Set for "Color TV"
By Margaret Bradbury Jewell of Grand Junction, Colorado
Born 1932

I was born at home in Howard, SD, the 11th of 12 children. We didn't lack for entertainment as we made our own: baseball games, hide and seek, and anti I over the neighbor's biggest building. We went fishing and hunting with my dad and brothers.

In watching "The Walton's" I was reminded of the old permanent waves we got at the local beauty shop. It was a big machine with wires hanging down with clamps that went over the curlers. They got very hot and burned our neck, ears, and sometimes our hair.

Another thing we did was back when soda pop came in bottles with metal caps lined with cork, we would separate the caps and wear them on our shirts.

My dad always had a very big garden. He also had several surgeries so when it came time to plow the garden he would guide the hand plow and we kids would pull it. We had some good eating from those gardens and Mom canned many quarts of veggies.

One way we kids could earn money for the movies was to pick potato bugs. I think it was a penny a dozen, and it cost 10 or 12 cents for the movie!

Saturday night baths were quite an experience. In would come the round metal tub by the stove. We kids all used the same water. As my youngest sister was getting out of the tub, I threw a towel at her, and as she bent over to pick it up, she burned her bottom on the stove! I was in big trouble (again).

Another thing we liked to do was walk the wooden railing. I think it was used for tying horses, which was before my time. The depot agent watched from his window. I guess if we had fallen off, he would come and pick up the pieces. We also walked the railroad track for fun. It was also a good balance exercise except we didn't think of it as that.

Once when we were quarantined for scarlet fever, my dad was Sheriff at the time, Mom and us four youngest girls played card games while Dad and brother Tommy slept in the jail, so he could be available for whatever mischief might happen.

Living in a small town had both advantages and disadvantages. The good was that we knew most everyone. The not so good was "anything" you did everyone knew about it!

Mom rarely went to the grocery store but would send one of us girls. On one of these trips, I had both arms full and the elastic on my panties broke and of course, they fell down, right there on Main Street. There was nothing to do but pick them up and run home. (Now the elastic is sewn in.)

We were all pretty excited when the folks got a black and white TV set. To make it look colored they put a piece of colored plastic over the screen. My favorite programs were the hit parade and Lawrence Welk.

I worked at Rafferty Drug from the 8th grade through high school. The soda fountain was a popular spot, but it no longer exists. Two of my sisters worked across the street at Klein Drug Store.

Waiting for Santa and Walking in a Blizzard
By William F. Smith, Jr. of Huron, South Dakota
Born 1915

I sit back now, in this cozy warm room. It is about ten degrees above outside, and I am sitting in my comfortable easy chair, and I think about Christmas past. As my mind turns nostalgic, back to my much younger days, I think about my much younger days and Christmases that occurred in the old house at 1314 West Third Street SW. This old house is where my siblings and I were brought up. This one particular Christmas Mother had the house all decorated up with streamers running from the corners of the room and they crisscrossed the middle of the room. There was a Christmas tree, of course, with paper

150

chains and popcorn strings all around it. There were many ornaments, old-fashioned now. They were German oriented, as many of them were handed down from Mother's family. It crosses my mind, where are those ornaments now? Probably in some old, dusty cardboard box set aside and forgotten. Remember, too, the large coal heater with its nickel plating and fancy ironwork. The stove sat on a large stove board in the dining room. In the sitting room there was another sheet iron stove to use in real cold weather. I remember these stoves, because my brother Johnny and I had to haul out the ashes and to provide plenty of kindling wood and coal hauled in to feed them.

As I said, this one Christmas that I remember so well was the one that I sold out my little sister, Aletha, to Santa Claus in order to save myself. To this day, I'm not proud of what I did, because today Aletha makes great pies and occasionally I get some of those pies. I hope at this late date she has forgiven me. Our folks celebrated Christmas on the eve of Christmas instead of on Christmas Day. So this night we were all gathered in the dining room when we heard sleigh bells coming from our front lawn. There was about two feet of snow on the level at that time. We were all adither I can say, at least I was.

A knock came at the door. Hark! I wonder who's there. In comes old Santa, just abusting in. Now, this Santa didn't look like the pictures of Santa that I had seen. He had on a white beard all right and the red stocking cap. As I think back now, I think that this Santa looked kind of a little on the frowzy side, kind of scruffy as it were. I quickly took refuge behind the hard coal heater and squeezed in behind the heater and the north wall. I was quickly joined there by my little sister, Aletha. We hoped that Santa, if that he was, wouldn't see us. No such luck, because he came right over to us. Right away, he asked us if we had been good kids all year. This we confirmed by not saying anything. Frankly, I couldn't say a darned thing because I was so scared. But we both nodded our heads that we had been good all year long. Boy what a lie! Then he said to me, "Do you swear?" God, he had found me out! I almost swallowed my tongue. Finally, I sputtered and stammered out, "No, but my sister does." There, I had said it. I set the blame on my little sister. Shame! But I had to save myself didn't I. I think now that Santa

didn't believe me, because he kind of choked up. Then to smooth things over we gave old Santa a plug of tobacco and a roll of toilet paper. Santa made the rounds, shaking hands with everyone there. Suddenly he bolted out the door and we heard him shout, "Whoa! Whoa! Dammit, whoa!" I guess he was having trouble with his reindeer. But wait a minute; he forgot his sack of presents. He left them in his hurry. Mother took the sack and handed out the presents. We heard the sleigh bells fading out in the clear cold night. I think back now of those times. It was the best of times. I also think back fondly of the people who were there then and are not here now. It's sad, isn't it? A tear forms now and then and drops.

In March of 1948, I was working as a bill clerk in the old freight depot for the C&NW railroad. The freight depot was on the corner of Market Road and Dakota. I had gone to work that morning and was working on my typewriter when the wind came from the northwest and began blowing snow. By 10:00 that morning, you couldn't see across the street; it was a full western blizzard at its worst. There was no warning. There was snow on the ground, and it was being blown around so you couldn't see very far.

Some of the men in the building decided to go home before the roads became blocked. I stayed because if I had left, my pay would have been docked. I called home and told my wife to stay inside and keep the kids in also. I also told her that I didn't think I would be able to get home that night and would stay in the depot. We in the office were snugly warm because the freight depot, the passenger depot, and the central warehouse were heated by steam from three boilers at the east end of the freight depot. There were firemen around the clock so we were warm and safe from the storm. The only thing was we that stayed in the office were getting hungry.

Around 4:00 p.m., we were very hungry so we called the Service Café to see if they were open. Verne, the owner confirmed that they were, as no one wanted to try to get home. We told Verne that several of us were going to try and get to the café and to watch for us. John Marston came down from the yard office upstairs and asked if anyone was for trying to reach the café. John, Mike, and I elected to try. There were five of us.

I had on OD army pants, a heavy army shirt, and socks, all courtesy of Uncle Sam. I got some binder twine from the warehouse and tied down my pants legs army style. The others did also. I had a pair of zipper overshoes, and best of all, my large sheepskin coat with the fur collars. In my time on the railroad, most of the railroad men had sheepskin coats of this kind. Most all of the railroaders had a "Kromer" hat, too. This was a black hat with a bill and earlaps that went around your neck. It was felt and was the warmest winter hat I ever had. Most all "rails" in Huron bought their "Kromers" from the Geiger Clothing Store. I believe I got my sheepskin there also. I had large leather mitts with knitted liners. Most all railroaders had the leather mitts for winter wear. I had a knitted scarf that I wrapped around my face. It was decided that I would lead the five of us because I was the youngest and had Army training, I guess. At any rate, I was in good physical shape. I was to plow a furrow that they would follow. They decided this, I didn't, but on the railroad seniority, I was the low man on the totem pole.

We five went out west the door of the depot, and it was there that the full force of the wind hit us. Across the street to the south was the Cook Std. Oil filing station. We struggled past the station and by keeping close to the side of the buildings, we made the Service Café. Verne was waiting for us. Let me say this, I might have been the youngest, but I was out of breath. The wind drove the snow into us full blast. This was no cakewalk; I'm here to tell you. Verne knew what to feed us: mashed potatoes, gravy, chicken, and a lot of pie, plus a lot of strong coffee. We indulged, I tell you. There was no conversation, just eating. After resting some time and buying all the candy bars and snacks that Vere had we had to return back to the freight depot and the steam heat. The thing was if we were at work, we got paid for that day. That fact was uppermost in my mind. I had a family to feed.

We borrowed a length of clothesline rope from Verne and tied knots in the rope army style, about every five feet. Each man was to hang on to the rope in his place. If a man went down, we would know it and stop and find him. Going north, we had the wind full in the face. We would take a step forward and it seemed we were blown back two steps. We finally got there though, although we were bushed, to say the least.

We found out the railroad at Huron was tied up, all passenger trains were shunted to track near the passenger depot where they hooked up to steam pipes for heat to the coaches. At the west end of the large waiting room in the passenger depot was the Union News, a chain restaurant. This was open 24 hours a day. The passengers could get food there. Nothing moved in the train yard for some time. The yard was full of snow. Switches were frozen and blocked. This great railroad that operated 24 hours a day and seven days a week, couldn't operate, couldn't move a wheel. It was shut down by Mother Nature in the form of the hardest blizzard I had ever experienced. At the passenger depot, the first shift in the ticket office was Phil Peterson with Lawrence Rossman coming on at 3:00 p.m. Both men stayed there and had to answer the thousands of questions put to them by people from the trains.

At around noon the next day, the storm had abated somewhat, and we could hear plows working on Dakota Avenue. I decided to try and make my home. I borrowed a broom and shovel and went out to shovel my Ford. It seemed the snow had swung around the depot and deposited it on my car. I shoveled it all out and opened the doors, and there was more snow inside than out. I cleaned it out. I drove south to Third Street and then on west where it had been plowed. Through the fairgrounds was ticklish but the car had high clearance, and I made it home and drove into my yard driveway which had three feet of snow, but I was home. My wife and kids were glad to see me. She saw to it that I had a good dinner. After dinner, I got the kids out and we shoveled the driveway.

I never did tell my wife about the trip that we had made to the Service Café. She would not have approved. I have thought many times did we do the right thing walking to the Service Café during a blizzard. Perhaps we should have hunkered down and waited out the storm. Yes, that's what we should have done. But we didn't. Railroad men are a different breed. They are out in all kinds of weather doing a very dangerous job. You tell a railroad man that he can't have something, and he'll move heaven and earth to get it anyway. I myself in the course of my 40 years on the C&NW Railroad have had three different times that

I could have bought the farm. Someone was looking after me I guess.

A Sodden Holiday
By Shirley Reed of Holt, Michigan
Born 1935

We had ridden the train from our new home in Lake Andes, SD, to our former home in Hetland, SD, to stay with my grandmother, Ada Ballou, for the 1943 or '44 Christmas holiday. Grandma's tiny house seemed to explode in size once we arrived inside. We gave Grandma a hug, and greeted our cousins who were there for the big family meal.

The house had been the parsonage for the Congregational Church next door. Since the pastor lived in a neighboring town in a shared pastorate, the little house had not been modernized. My grandparents had lived in a larger house when they retired into town from their farm, but when Grandma was widowed during the Depression; she was forced to find less expensive housing.

The aroma of turkey and baked goods came from the kitchen. Grandma was turning out culinary

Charles Ballou, Shirley Anderson Reed, Caron Ballou, and Jim Anderson in 1948

wonders on her little kerosene stove and oven. Her water supply was a water pipe running up a wall with a faucet attached. A pail and dipper hung on the faucet, and provided Hetland's wonderful drinking water for the household. A flat sink stood across the kitchen with another pail and dipper holding water for washing hands and vegetables. The drain led to a pail beneath the sink. When it filled with wash water and potato peelings, it was carried out the back door, across the yard, and thrown into a pen that housed a farmer's pigs.

Everyone helped bring the food to the dining room. An oak table with four leaves stretched kitty-corner across the room, just skimming by the pot-bellied stove. We knew it was hot, so we were careful not to get burned. The grownups fed it chunks of coal to keep the house cozy. In warmer weather, corncobs were sufficient to provide heat. My aunts, uncles, and cousins all crowded around the table for good food and lively conversation.

When dinner was over, my brother Jim and my cousins Charles and Caron joined me in rousing games of War and Hearts as we took over the dining room table. Then the three boys decided that they needed more action. Warmly dressed for the cold day, they wandered down the street to the broad grassy area surrounding the railroad tracks, then beyond to the opposite end of town where my cousins' other grandparents lived. Hetland was so small that a journey of just three blocks was enough to go from the north end of town to the south end. It took only two blocks to span the town from east to west.

They were soon faced with the temptation of Lake Ole. This farm livestock watering pond on the outskirts of town was also used to cut ice for the town's ice house located in an alley behind Main Street. There it was packed in sawdust to insulate it from the heat of

153

Charles Ballou, Jim Anderson, Bill Ballou,
Shirley Anderson Reed and Caron Ballou in 1948

summer before it was delivered to ice boxes on back porches all over town.

The boys ventured out on the ice. Was it strong enough to hold them? They tip toed out, and then began sliding across it ever farther from the edge. Caron headed for the middle of the pond, but Charles warned him back. Suddenly there was a cracking sound and Caron slipped through the ice. The pond was shallow, but when Jim tried to pull him out, he plunged into the water also. Finally, Charles pulled them both out.

The sodden shivering boys made their way back to Grandma's house. Aunt Myrtle took up a station on Grandma's rocking chair behind the pot-bellied stove. She stripped the dripping clothes from the boys and hung them behind the stove. Mother went upstairs to search through our luggage for dry clothes. They were finally dressed warmly, ready to go outside again. It must have been easier to devise a new wardrobe for them than to listen to noisy children inside.

They proceeded once more across town. Certainly, there was a way to cross Lake Ole. It was frozen all around the edge. Maybe the middle was frozen by now. They ventured in ever larger circles toward the middle, taking runs and then sliding across the pond, careful to avoid the gaping hole. This time it was Jim who fell through, with Charles and Caron pulling him to safety. They trudged back to Grandma's with icicles dripping off their sodden snow suits.

The supply of dry snow suits was exhausted, so they had to be content joining me in another game of Hearts. Despite the dunking, it was another wonderful holiday time at Grandma's house.

A Snowstorm in 1975
By Mike Drooger of Edgerton, Minnesota
Born 1961

It seems like the snowstorms of my youth were far more powerful and longer lasting than the storms of today. When I was a kid, a doozy of a storm would knock out power for three or four days. Even an average size storm would force the cancellation of school for much of the week. Being a kid meant not worrying about the loss of electricity. That was for grownups to worry about. Being a kid also meant having many more important things to do other than school. A winter storm was welcomed with open arms.

Maybe the storms were bigger when I was a kid. Maybe we have better equipment to move the snow nowadays so we get back to regular life more quickly. Whatever the case, there was nothing quite as exciting as a good old-fashioned snowstorm in the 1960s and '70s.

One particular storm I remember was in the winter of 1975. Snowfall amounts measured more than a foot, up to two feet in some places. I've often wondered how the snowfall amount can be accurately measured when the snow is moving horizontally. The wind, with gusts measured at a peak of 80 miles per hour during that 1975 storm, blew nonstop for a 24-hour period. When the storm finally passed, there were snowdrifts higher than our house. We even had a snowdrift in our garage. The wind had forced snow through the garage door. We had to scoop snow out of the garage before we could scoop snow off the driveway. Once we had scooped our way outside, we had to dig down to get to the mailbox. Cows that had been left out in the open rather than the safety of the barn died standing up, which is the way they remained a few days later due to the frigid temperatures.

Unbeknownst to homeowners, the wind had blown snow through attic vents. The snow piled up and melted once the temperature in the attic rose above freezing. Water spots appeared on the ceiling. My dad volunteered me to clean snow out of neighbors' attics. It was then I learned what "volunteering" meant—don't take money even if it's offered to you. Can't say I'd be too excited about getting into attics in the present to haul snow out by the bucketful, but in 1975 it was an enjoyable adventure for a 13-year-old kid with nothing better to do.

My family was one of the lucky ones when the storm knocked out the electricity. We had a gas stove. We could eat a warm meal. Blankets were hung over the doorway of the kitchen in order to trap heat in part of the house. Neighbors came to our home with cans of soup. My mom gave them warmed soup in exchange for soup they brought.

Time indoors was spent playing games at the kitchen table. We hauled out of the closet games such as Monopoly, Yahtzee, and Aggravation—aggravation being the keyword that week as the days without power dragged on, taking its toll on everyone's nerves.

I worked out my cabin fever frustration by playing basketball in the kitchen on the Nerf hoop that was attached to the basement door. My boredom was relieved by a few games of one-on-one against an imaginary opponent, but family was less than pleased with my running and jumping in the house. "Don't you have something else to do?" I was asked more than once. There weren't a lot of options.

I had tried playing games. They accused me of cheating. Evidently I wasn't sneaky enough. I had tried playing basketball. They became annoyed. I decided to go to my frosty room and read a book under a half dozen blankets. A book report was overdue. The winter storm had helped me buy some time.

Finally, after the storm subsided and the electricity was restored, I headed outside to the winter wonderland. There really was no reason to stay in the house. There was no such thing as today's electronic gadgets to play with. On a good day, when the rotor on the antennae on the roof wasn't frozen, we could get maybe five TV stations. But the storm had knocked over the broadcast tower near Sioux Falls. That meant even fewer stations from which to choose. During the day the TV was tuned to some soap opera my mom and sisters were interested in. So, stricken with a severe case of cabin fever, I bundled up (including bread bags on my feet to keep the moisture that would seep through my boots away from my skin) and headed outside. The neighbors were beginning to come out as well to assess the damage and begin the daunting task of moving snow.

The snowdrifts, which were far higher than my head, were perfect for tunneling.

I spent the next few days hollowing out the mounds of snow throughout our yard. Large sheets of ice chiseled off frozen puddles made great windows.

Finally school resumed. I had to admit I was ready to go back. I had done all the tunneling, borrowing, and hollowing I could do in my yard. And it was great to see all my friends and swap snowstorm stories.

Were the storms of my youth bigger than the storms of today? I think so. Or are we better equipped to move snow after it has fallen. I think that's true as well. I also think it's true that as time passes, the stories of days gone by have grown bigger.

The Great Chicken Fly Away!
By James P. Kurkowski of Webster, South Dakota
Born 1942

Anyone that grows up in a small town in South Dakota knows chickens can't fly. At least they are not supposed to be able to fly. As a young boy, in the 1950s in South Dakota, I saw chickens fly! Well, they technically may not have been "flying," but they definitely were airborne.

Let me explain…

It was 1953. I lived on the edge of the small town of Webster, SD. In the 1950s, a small town in South Dakota was probably the very best place in the world a young boy could be growing up, especially if you lived on the edge of that small town. Your backyard was the doorway to the largest and grandest fantasyland in the world! From your backyard, you could see oceans waiting to be crossed. OK, it was just a large pond of water within a slough area below the hill, but with just a little imagination, it easily became an ocean. The reeds in the slough could be used to build the best western forts that ever were constructed and worked extremely well to keep out the arrows of the attacking Indians. On another day, about a hundred feet over, a hole could be dug in the soft dirt of the slough area, covered up with some old boards from your father's wood pile, and an amazing fox hole fort protected you during your battles with the Nazis. Yes, there was a whole world out there, down that hill. The world at that time did not yet include thoughts of exploring the moon as a future astronaut, but the moonscape could have been found in that wonderful world, I am sure, if we would have known at that time it would be made possible within our lifetime.

It is in this wonderful world of exciting possibilities that I and my older brother made chickens fly!

You see, he was older than me by enough years that he had owned an Indian brand motorcycle that he had driven back from San Antonio, TX, after he got out of the then-Army Air Corps, what was going to become the US Air Force. It is another long story as to how it all evolved into how that motorcycle became nothing more than a motorcycle engine mounted on an iron stand, with a wooden prop made to be mounted on the engine... but it did. And for a lack of another place to put it, this was set in a corner of our backyard, with the intention of becoming the engine to propel a future airboat that my brother intended to build. And there it stood, waiting for its future function, and in my mind to propel all manner of craft to take me into a vast number of new imagined adventures.

Then the day came. An older sister that had plans to be married that next fall season, thought it would be a grand idea for my dad to put up some fencing around an area of the backyard, and allow her to place about a hundred baby chicks in that area to grow up for her to be able to sell later in the summer to generate some extra money for her wedding plans. He agreed. As it turns out, a significant failure of this plan was that the fence he put up enclosed as part of its area the glistening, gleaming, ready for action, motorcycle engine on its stand! There it stood, in the "the chicken yard." What disgrace! For weeks, I had to look at that disgrace. That powerful engine that was taking me to wonderful places in the world, on glorious and powerful crafts of my imagination... was standing out there, among the chickens!

Then one day my brother, the designated genius of the family, announced to me that he had a thought. This thought was that he decided that he needed to "run up" the engine to give it a little exercise. I, of course, agreed that this was a grand idea, as I couldn't wait to refresh my memory as to the sound of that wonderful beast of an engine, so that I would be accurate in my imaginations of how powerful of a craft I could construct for further adventures. We mounted the propeller. We fueled it up. We attached the battery. We primed the carburetion. We were ready! We spun the prop; it sputtered and attempted to run. We spun it again... a few more sputtering strokes. We failed to notice that the wandering chickens behind us were getting quite nervous.

Then it fired! Wow, it was amazing! The power! The noise! The future adventures that it was empowering in my mind... it was totally grand... then the first chicken came by!

It seems that the noise of this wonderful beast had the effect of making the chickens start running around quite excitedly. Apparently, it seems it is a trait of chickens that when they run they have the unfortunate habit of lifting their wings in their enthusiasm of running. Lifted chicken wings, running in front of a whirling prop on a motorcycle engine had the dynamic effect of "lift" and flight capability!

It is my recollection that of the flock of about one hundred chickens, at least a hefty third of the flock made their great escape that afternoon. They made it in a rather abrupt and noisy manner as they exited over the top of the fence on lifted wing and a lot of clatter, landing perhaps thirty feet outside the fence, and running in blurs down the hill. If they ever did stop running, it was beyond my limit of vision, because my last recall of them was that they were still running at large, in many different directions. I had reports over the next couple of days from neighborhood buddies that relatives of theirs that lived up to two miles from our house saw chickens, still running, going past their places. I don't know if that was verifiable but seemed believable to me at the time.

Thus was the episode of the flying chickens. And yes, given the proper motivation and encouragement, they do fly!

Just Make Gravy and Set the Table
By Barbara Solsaa of Hayti, South Dakota
Born 1944

My good old days took place out in the country, near Estelline, South Dakota.

I remember the outhouse of years ago, that we had at home as a young child. We had one at country school, and for two years after we were married in 1965. It was cold and frosty in the winter. I was one of eight children in the family. In order to save money on toilet paper, I can remember using the pink tissues that were wrapped around peaches when my mother would buy a "lug" of peaches in the summer, for toilet paper. The old Sears catalogue pages were also used to save money on toilet paper.

I grew up going to a one-room country school. There were only 15 students at the school, which taught first grade through the eighth grade, and four to five of the students were always my siblings. I was the only student in my grade so when I went to town for high school my class size grew from one student to 16 students. It was a big change.

There was no running water at the country school, and since our farm had a good well, we hauled the drinking water to the country school in a three-gallon can. Our farm was a located a mile from the school, so we generally got a ride in the morning to school since we had to bring the water. We almost always had to walk home from school and carry the empty can for water home to refill for the next day. I can remember how cold I would get walking home from school in the winter.

Debbie, Susan, and a "True Finn" in the sauna

When Lee and I got married in 1965, we lived in an older house, with no running water and an outhouse. We had a pump in the kitchen that would bring up the water from a well, and a five-gallon pail under the sink to carry outside and empty out as it filled up with used water, as there was no drain plumbing.

I washed clothes with a conventional Maytag washing machine in the kitchen. We would pump water into a pail and fill the machine. We would then put an electric heater in the machine that would float on top of the water. It took all night to heat the water so I could wash clothes in the morning. This one filled machine of water would wash all clothes that needed to be cleaned for the week. You would start with the cleanest of clothes, such as your Sunday Bests, first and then you would keep reusing the water until all the clothes were cleaned for the week. Once the clothes were washed, I would hang all the diapers, bed sheets, and remaining clothes outside on the line to dry, even in the dead of winter, at which time they would freeze dry.

Once you were done with the washing, you would use a five-gallon pail to haul the water outside, as there were no drains in the home. I continued to use a conventional washing machine even when we got indoor plumbing up through most of the 1970s and 1980s. To this day, I know that when hanging clothes on the line outside in the middle of winter I froze my fingers. Now today when the temperatures drop to -20 to -30 degrees below zero wind chills during the winter and I am outside doing cattle chores, my fingers feel as though they could fall off, they are so damaged from those years of exposure.

In the early days, disposable diapers had just started to come out when we started to have children of our own around the end of the 1960s, and we could not afford them. I would use cloth diapers, and they had to be rinsed out a couple of times before going into the washing machine. You would rinse them out by scrubbing them in the modern day toilets once we got them, or prior to that in a pail of water.

Saturday nights were bath nights in my younger days. We would put water in a square tub that we would place in the middle of the kitchen floor in front of the wood stove, to keep you and the water warm while bathing. We would start off from the youngest to

157

oldest each taking a bath, all using the same bath water till everyone was done. Once we were done, the water would need to be carried outside to be disposed of.

I grew up in a Finnish family, and after years of taking a bath in the middle of the kitchen, we eventually built a sauna on our property. It was called a bath house. It was a small building that contained a wood burner stove with rocks on top, like you see currently in hotels. We would sit on benches with a basin of water and take a sponge bath. All the women would be together in the room and bathe together followed by all the men of the family. We would sit up on the top bench to take our bath. If you threw water on the rocks, you would get a warm steam. Anytime someone new would join us, we would tell them if it was too hot for them, to throw cold water on the rocks to cool them off. Little did they know that it got twice as hot once the water hit the rocks!

I was one of seven girls and one brother in my family. I was the chore girl as I enjoyed spending time with my dad. I can remember climbing up the silo (thirty feet in the air) and throwing silage down the chute for the milk cows. I also helped to fill the wheelbarrow with cow manure from the barn and my dad would push it out into a pile. The pile would grow through the winter and in the spring; the manure was spread out in the fields as fertilizer. We also had chickens and they had wire roosts for them to sit on at night. When it was time to clean under the roosts, Dad would stand the wire racks up and I would have to crawl up on the roosting area to fill his pitch fork with the chicken manure, as it was too high up for him to reach, and my dad would then throw it out the window of the chicken coop in a pile that was then also taken out and spread in the fields as fertilizer. The ammonia smell was very strong during this cleaning process.

As stated, there were eight children in my family. We were lucky if we each had five different outfits to last us a week of school and were worn over and over each week. We wore dresses and skirts most of the time and they were usually handmade. We did not have much money growing up. One Christmas one of my sisters received a partially made jumper for her one and only gift, as my mother had run out of time to get it made. That same Christmas, another sister just received three yards of material, that our mother would use to make an outfit for her to wear for the year, but she did not have time to make it prior to Christmas, so she just received a package with material as her one and only gift.

We milked maybe 20 cows a day back in the 1950s. We would use a cream separator and separate the cream from the milk and then sell the cream in town. We had chickens on the farm and we would also take the extra eggs to town and sell them for money. These two weekly sales gave us what money we had then for groceries. We grew a big garden and canned a lot of vegetables to last through the winter. We also planted a field of potatoes, which we would store, in our dirt cellar to keep them through the winter for eating. The cellar was located under our home and salamanders loved to live down there due to the cold and damp area. The salamanders would make it a place we did not like to go down to, but would have to in order to get the potatoes to eat. We did not have much, but there was always food on the table.

We drove 25 miles to a church each Sunday. It was a church that both of my parents grew up going to, and we continued to go to the same church. I do not remember missing many Sundays. My mother always planned for the noon meal prior to leaving for church. She would place a meal in the oven and leave the oven on low while we were at church, so that when we got home, dinner was done. We would just have to make gravy and set the table.

Johnny Cash Played "I Walk the Line" for Me
By Lyle L. Meyers of Huron, South Dakota
Born 1934

I am one of 8 boys and 3 girls in our family. I am the youngest. I will be 80 years old this May. There are only 4 left in our family: 2 brothers and 1 sister and I. We were all born at home in an old farmhouse by a doctor driving a horse and buggy. We never had electricity until we moved to Huron when the rural R-E-A went through in 1950. We had outside toilets and at night a pail by the bed. One cold day I crapped my pants. After 75 years, I can still remember Ma scrubbed my butt with cold water and a straw broom. I was 5 years old.

We had sawed-off tree logs to sit on as kids. I fell through an old glass window and cut my hand badly. I still look at the big scar I have and think about it. We had castor oil for stomachache and used skunk fat for rubbing on our chest for colds. We always trapped skunks and mink to sell for a few nickels. We had old kerosene lamps to see by at night. We were in the Dust Bowl, during what they called the Dirty Thirties, for 10 years.

We had a battery-powered radio. My ma was washing clothes one day and I was listening to it. I said to Ma, "Who is that funny talking man on the radio?" She said, "That's that damn crazy Hitler from Germany." It was only a few years later that 4 brothers got drafted; 3 of us were too young, and the oldest did not pass the Army exam. One got wounded in the Battle of the Bulge, 1 got hurt bad in a plane crash and the other 2 got home from Germany and Japan. When I got drafted, I went to Germany and it was still in a lot of ruins. I did not see combat but I was close to it when they sent me to rebuild Lebanon in the late '50s.

Our favorite radio program in "them days" was Fibber MacGee and Molly, Jack Benny, and later Gunsmoke and the Lone Ranger. At our old country school, we had kids from 1st to 8th grades. When I teased a girl one day I was in the 2nd grade, this old tough woman hit me in the butt and back with a rubber hose. Boy that hurt.

We never had running water in the house until the '50s. At Wessington town, 30 miles west of the town I live in now, we got water out of a spring running out of a hill. It was good water but we had to have a pet goat pull a small wagon with 2 pails, 5 gallons each, home about ½ a mile away. The only movie I saw in Wessington was a silent picture, no sound. It was a Western I think. It was named "Oxbow Innocence."

We made our toys out of empty spools of thread. You put a rubber band through it, had a piece of soap on the sides, and twisted it, then let it go. It used to travel across the floor. We used to burn wood in our stove but never had any heat at night. We had a big cover on us made of duck feathers. They called it a "feather tick." It kept us from freezing.

In those days, it never rained for months. A big black cloud would come up and it would all be dust. The grasshoppers didn't have any crops to eat. They were by the millions and when they came up in the daylight, it was just like a big shade got pulled over the sun.

If a jacket or piece of clothing was out on a fence, they would eat it, and also the wooden fence posts. The WPA workers would sit out and shake out a lot of poisoned saw dust to kill them. There were very few lakes in this country that had any water. I never got to go swimming until I was almost 18 years old.

I got my first kiss from a girl at school that liked me. We were 16 years old. My favorite pet was a sheep we had raised. I still remember how I cried when they sold it on the market. I also had a pet rooster chicken. I named him after Joe Lewis, the Negro boxer, who we listened to on the radio for fight night.

My favorite singers were Elvis Presley and Johnny Cash. Elvis got in the Army the same time I did. He was 50 miles from me but I didn't see him. When I was stationed at Fort Ord, California, in the Army, I paid $1 to go to a music dance. Johnny Cash was there. I walked up to him and we shook hands. He said to me, "What song do you like?" I said, "I Walk the Line." He played it for me and he also signed his name on the back of my girlfriend's picture.

I remember the first TV we got in 1951. We could get 3 stations on it, black and white picture only. We had an antenna we put on top of the house.

We had a cook stove and Mother did all her cooking and baking on it. She used corn cobs in the wood stove. I don't know how she cooked so good without burning things. I still remember when it would get red hot.

We had a big old wooden ice box out on the porch. Father would bring home a piece of ice from the ice house in town. Most of it would be melted as we lived 8 miles from town.

We had an old Model T car when we were still at Wessington. There was a big hill just south of town. The old Model T had bands in the transmission and they would not go up the hill forward so Pa would back it up in reverse. That used to scare me.

In those Dirty Thirties, there were no jobs and any job did not pay good. We got salted pork and flour and some clothing from the relief plan of the government.

I worked for the county highway

department for 42 years and served 2 years overseas in the Army. It was 4 years before I got an honorable discharge so I had 6 years total, and was in the Army reserve for 4 years. I was in Germany, France, Austria, Bavaria, Switzerland, Beirut, Lebanon, Adana, Turkey, Canada, Ireland, and Newfoundland.

I was in the Army Engineers yet I sailed on 3 different ships. I went through the English Channel 3 times on 3 different ships and flew from New York to Germany over England. I went fishing in the Pacific Ocean, sailed across the Atlantic, and sailed the Mediterranean Sea.

Tough Times, but Great Times, Too
By Ardis Dragsten of Buffalo, Minnesota
Born 1926

When my mother, Goldie Meisel Rovang, was about to give birth to me in 1926 she had to walk out to the barn and put the windmill in gear. This was a signal to my father, Martin Rovang, to come out of the field to bring the doctor to the farm.

I went to school through eighth grade in a one-room schoolhouse, which was located next to our farm. Because the school was next to our farm, the teacher would live with us. We had a 15-minute recess in the morning and afternoon. At lunch, we had an hour except in the coldest part of the winter when lunchtime was 30 minutes long. This allowed the children to get home before dark. Some of my classmates came by horse, and there was a barn provided for the horses. During recess

Martin Rovang, LaVayne (Rovang) Langan, and Ardis (Rovang) Dragsten

we would play Annie I over by throwing the ball over the horse barn. The schoolhouse was surrounded by fields and gophers were abundant. For fun, we would pour water down the gopher hole then snare them when they came out of the hole.

Our house was the equivalent of a city block form the school, but my sister, LaVayne Rovang Langan, and I would always bring our lunch to school. We did not want to miss out of the opportunity to play with the other kids. The schoolhouse was heated by a coal stove. We brought raw potatoes and placed them under the grate in the morning. By lunchtime, the school smelled wonderful, and we had warm baked potatoes.

One winter, just about every day, I wore the same dress to school. It was made from an old dress of my mother's. The dress was black with a red top, and my stockings were white. I tried to hide the fact that I was wearing long underwear and spent a lot of time pulling on my stockings so there would not be a big bulge showing.

I think I was 1934 that we had a particularly severe winter. Eleanor Kangas was the teacher and she stayed in the schoolhouse for six weeks with two students who otherwise would not have been able to attend school. Think of the dedication to one's job, just a cot to sleep on behind a curtain in front of the room. No running water, electricity, telephone, transportation, or comforts of home like a radio or easy chair. This along with the usual janitorial duties of keeping the school clean, carrying coal from the coal bin in back of the room to the stove in front, and then having to haul the ashes out.

The school was used for community club once a month. The adults and children would put on plays and talent shows. One time during a community club event, everyone could hear a pig squealing. My dad had dug a cistern and a pig fell into it. The pig interrupted the show because the men had to go save the pig. Everyone followed to watch the rescue. It turned out to be the highlight of the evening.

In the summertime, my sister and I would walk about a mile and a half to Garfield Lutheran Church for Bible school. The thirties were known as the Dirty Thirties or the Dust Bowl. It was a scary sight to see the dust come rolling in. It would blot out the sun, and it would be as dark as night, only it was caused

Martin Rovang, LaVayne (Rovang) Langan, and Ardis (Rovang) Dragsten

by the high winds and blowing dirt. One time during a dust storm, our father came and got us from Bible school. The car stalled from the blowing dirt. We could only see a few feet in front of us. We got home by walking along the fence line. During a dust storm, my mother would hang wet sheets over the doors to catch the dust that would shift through. The temperature would be over 100 degrees, so we would just lie down on the linoleum floor, which felt cool when we first lay down.

The grasshoppers liked the dry weather and were always around, but at times big swarms of grasshoppers would come. It can be best described as a cloud as it would block out the sun. There were so many grasshoppers the roads would be slippery. If you were fortunate enough to get a crop to grow, the grasshoppers would eat it up. Having food for your family was difficult.

We were lucky to always have enough to eat as we raised all our own meat. Every year we would buy 200 chickens through a mail order catalog. The mailman would deliver them to our door. We also had beef, pork, and lamb. In the winter, we ate fish that was delivered in a gunnysack. We had no refrigeration.

Growing up I saw two Shirley Temple movies. It cost ten cents to see a movie. I remember them both. We went to Bryant on Saturday night to sell our cream and eggs. A special treat for my sister, LaVayne, and I was to buy a Popsicle, which we divided. Our family treat was to buy ten cents worth of hamburger to take home. It would usually be 11:00 p.m. or later but we would fry it up and eat it. We had a 1928 Chevy. When it rained, the roof leaked, but if we sat in the middle of the seat, we could stay dry.

In the spring most of the hay was used up. My sister and I spent many summer days roller-skating around the perimeter of the haymow. I had two pets; a goat that had no name and a dog named Trixie. My dad made a harness for the goat, and it would pull us in the wagon. We would go to the neighbor's a half a mile away. Before we got home, the goat would get tired and start acting up.

We did not have running water. My dad set a barrel on the roof of the chicken coop and filled it with water. The sun would warm it up, and we would use it for a shower. It was just a trickle of water but it felt great. In the winter, we bathed once a week in a washtub that we set in the kitchen next to the cook stove. Everyone used the same water, the children first and then the parents. The house was not insulated; the water in the pan for washing our hands was always frozen in the morning.

At times during the winter, we were unable to get to town for six weeks or more because of the snowdrifts. To prepare for winter we would can chicken and beef, and we would buy flour in 100-pound sacks and stock up on other essentials. Our method of transportation was by horse drawn sleigh. My mother would heat the flat iron on the stove and wrap it in a piece of material for my sister and me to keep our feet warm. We had sleigh bells on the horses so the neighbors could hear us coming when we were going to visit.

The sacks the flour came in had nice floral designs. My mother taught me how to make dresses out of the sacks. My mother also would make a new coat out of someone else's old coat. Fabric was expensive at ten cents a yard.

Both of my parents had graduated from high school and business school and were determined that we get an education. The farm was seven and a half miles from Bryant, which was too far to travel every day. We were able to rent a room that I shared with two other girls. The room was small; just room enough for one double bed for the three of us. We brought our own food for the week and cooked, ate, and slept in the same room. I remember I ate a lot of fried potatoes, bread and butter, hamburger, and apples. We brought our own fuel for the small stove in our room. I would bring gunnysacks of corncobs from home to burn. The stove would get red

Ardis (Rovang) Dragsten

hot and would glow in the dark. It scared me at night, as the red glow would light up the room. There were no such things as fire extinguishers. We rented other rooms during high school. One of them was in a nice house with wonderful owners, but it was so cold we had to go to bed and do our schoolwork while covered with blankets.

I was 14 when we got a phone in the house. It was a party line and each party had a different ring. If there were two short rings, we knew the call was for us, but anyone could listen in on our conversation. Before we had a phone we communicated by going to our neighbor's for a visit or meeting them in church. Then there was the great time we had going to town on Saturday nights. Everyone we knew lived within a ten-mile radius.

Before we had electricity we had a battery radio that could receive a couple of stations, but we could get the news. Electricity became available sometime in the forties. The barn was the first to be wired.

Threshing required working with the neighbors. I would stay with a neighbor for a week helping to make lunches and dinner for 15 men. I was up at 5:00 a.m. and worked until 9:00 p.m. I was paid $2.50 for the week's work. The $2.50 was all relative. I bought my first box camera and it cost a little over $1.00. I still have that camera.

My mother played the piano and LaVayne and I took lessons. To get out of practicing the piano I would volunteer to help my dad milk the cows. I also helped cultivate corn. I was about ten years old and would drive the horses while riding on the cultivator. I shocked grain, which meant piling about five bundles in a teepee formation so they could dry out. I helped pick corn and this was all done by hand. I would ride in the wagon and pulled the ears of corn off. We always planted potatoes on Good Friday, with the belief that we would have a great potato crop. In the fall, I would help pick them, and this would be our winter supply.

After high school, I went to business school in Sioux Falls. I hated it but completed the course because my parents had paid the tuition. From there I went to the University of Minnesota and became an x-ray technician. I returned to Watertown and worked as an x-ray technician for Bartron Hospital and clinic and at the Medical Arts Clinic for Doctors Ruel, Larson, and Walters. My sister, LaVayne, graduated from Aberdeen Normal and began her teaching career at the Millet School in Watertown.

Even though life was difficult in those times, it was the same for everyone. I was fortunate to grow up in a loving home with parents who supported me and made the toughest times the best of times, too.

I've Seen Many Changes
By Lorraine Peickert of Browns Valley,
Minnesota
Born 1922

I was born in a farmhouse in New Effington, South Dakota on October 13, 1922. I was one of three siblings, an older brother, Leo, and a younger sister, Marion. My mom and dad were farmers and they worked very hard. It was tough times in those days. My dad never drove or owned a car or had a driver's license, or a checkbook.

I suppose you would have called us a poor family. We never thought we were. We had what we needed, and there was always a lot of family love.

There were plenty of home remedies for us when we were kids. My mom used to make a mustard plaster and rub it on our chest, cover it with a piece of flannel cloth, and it was supposed to cure a chest cold. We had to leave it on as long as we could stand it. There was always Vicks, and she would rub it all over us. When we were constipated, there was castor oil. It tasted terrible by took care of the problem.

The radio programs we listened to were *Ma Perkins* and *Amos and Andy* (the two black crows). We all gathered around the radio, and they would entertain us.

We lived on a party line of seven. Our ring was one long and two short. Our phone hung on the wall with bells on the front near the top, a mouthpiece, and a receiver, and a little crank on the side. Everyone would listen in on everybody's call. That's how the news got around; it was called rubbering.

I wasn't much for muscle cars or drag racing but I watch a lot of cars race side by side down the street in town.

We loved our phonograph. It stood quite high on four legs, had a big cover, and two doors on the bottom that held the big round records. We'd put the records on the turntable, lower the needle, and crank it up, turn it on, and we had music. We have it in our front room and now it is a valuable antique.

I don't remember a spanking at school or at home. We respected our teachers and knew they were there to help us. I know there was nothing more than a slap on the butt to get us going at home.

Saturday night was bath time. We'd fire up the cook stove; it had a reservoir on it that was filled with water. We took the water from it and also the teakettle of water on the stove we kept boiling. We'd open the oven door and get the big round tin tub and put water in it and take turns bathing all in the same water, we just kept adding hot water to it as needed. One time my aunt took her turn and the broom fell against the door, and she thought someone was coming and ran stark naked through the house.

I remember the wringer washing machine. We would take turns pulling the handle back and forth, and then wring the clothes through the wringer. It took two people, one to pull the handle and one to start and pull the clothes through the wringer. When we got a gas engine, we washed clothes and laughed all day doing it.

We went to silent movies in town on Saturday nights where they had a big screen outside. Charlie Chaplin was the actor. I remember he moved so fast. There was no voice; you had to read what they said in print on the screen.

In later years when the television came out, we were living in Minneapolis and we moved back to Browns Valley, Minnesota. We had the first colored TV in town.

Mom made all our clothes from flour sacks or old coats she would take apart or any material she could get her hands on.

We hardly had any toys, just a ball, a bat, and dolls made out of men's socks.

Ella Eddie was my favorite teacher and she roomed at our house. She walked to school every day with us. We had a one-room schoolhouse with a pot-belied stove and a blackboard that was across the front of the room. A map hung on the wall and a big crock for water, which we carried to school with us in jugs. A teacher's desk was up in front and student desks were in rows. Our teacher was also the janitor and cook. She would fire up the stove and put a potato, which we brought from home, down in top of the stove, and it was done at dinnertime so we ate it with our sack lunch. She taught all eight grades and subjects. I went through the first to eighth grade and never had a classmate. I was alone all eight years.

Sock hops were popular in our day. We went to New Effington to dances. It was a large hall. A lot of kids went, and it was fun dancing. My boyfriend, Garman Peikert, had a Chevy with a rumble seat. One time when we arrived at the dance, my sister, Marion, and a cousin were hiding in the rumble seat, as they wanted to go to the dance.

The winters were always cold. It was a blizzard almost every day. My mom and dad used to tie a twine from the house to the barn to find their way back. It was so cold we'd sleep under the feather ticks my mom made to keep us warm. Dirt storms were as bad in the Dirty Thirties. When the wind would blow, it was like a blizzard. The farmers in the field would just crawl in the wagon and rely on the horses to get them home. You couldn't see anything.

Our dog and cat were our pets on the farm. We had names for every horse and cow we had. We even hated to kill a chicken to eat because we had named them, too.

One terrible summer storm it was thundering and lightning and my dad said we should all go to the basement. The basement had a dirt floor and there were lizards crawling around. We didn't know if we were more scared of the storm or the lizards.

Our chores included the work on the

farm. We gathered and washed eggs, fed the chickens, milked the cows, curried the horses, shocked grain, hauled hay, and cleaned the barn and chicken coop. We all worked together.

The creek was our swimming hole. We had an artisan well that ran all the time. It ran down hill and made a creek. The water was cold but reasonably clean. We had a lot of fun.

My grandparents and parents came from Denmark, and they told us stories about their lives there and how beautiful the country was.

We got into a lot of mischief when we were kids. I remember my brother, Leo, and I put Marion in the baby buggy and let it go down the hill alone. We were laughing watching it, and Mom caught us. Leo ran up a tree to get away. Marion was all right, the buggy did not tip, lucky for us. One day my Grandpa had moved the outhouse. He was going to dig a new hole. The toilet had one big seat to sit on and one small one. My cousin crawled in the big seat with the big hole and hid from my grandma. When she found him, she pulled him right up through the little hole. His shoulders were all skinned up.

The games we played were anti eye over, tag, kick the can, pump pump pole away, captain may I, and kitten ball at school with our classmates. Post office was more fun when we got older.

We only went to town to sell our eggs and cream and to get groceries. Groceries were usually flour, sugar, coffee, and yeast. We always looked forward to the little bag of candy the grocer would put in the bottom of the egg case.

Before we had iceboxes, we would put our milk on the basement floor or put it down in the cistern in a pail with a rope on it so it would stay cool and not sour. After the icebox, we'd buy chunks of ice from the iceman. We still have our icebox in our front room, another nice antique.

We didn't get our milk in a bottle; it came straight from a cow. We'd milk and separate the cream from the milk by turning the separator. I remember my cousin came one day and would not drink milk because it came from the cows. Her milk came in bottles from the milkman.

When we got the rotary phones all we had to do was put our finger in the holes and dial a number, a change from turning a crank.

Telephones were much smaller, and they sat on a stand or hung on the wall.

I've had several boyfriends but when I met my husband, Garman Peickert, I never thought of them again. We were married 51 years, and he was my soul mate. After the war our son, Lannie, was born. He was our baby boomer, born in 1945.

I was married when Elvis, Bo Diddley, and Little Richard became popular. They were great entertainers, but Elvis made all the girls swoon. He was a great singer.

I remember when it came over the news that they were sending a man to the moon. Our kids had a storybook about Peg Leg Pete and Mickey Mouse going to the moon, but I never thought it possible. It did happen and in our day.

Lois Hansen and Arlene Dobbs are my closest friends. Lois and I have been friends for fifty years. Our husbands were good friends too so we were a foursome. We are both widows now, but we spent many winters together in Lake Havasu City, Arizona. Arlene and Lois have been my eyes and ears for me lately; they are there when I need help, although I have many other close friends who I love dearly.

Family time was most of the time. When we were working, it was together. At night when the work was done, supper was over, and the dishes were washed, we all would sit and listen to a play on the radio, play a game of cards, or some other game. Sometimes we'd have a songfest and all sing together. It was good times. Our grandchildren can't imagine being without electricity, bathrooms, cell phones, iPads, or computers. We have seen many changes in this world, but I still feel blessed to have had a loving family who kissed goodnight, tucked you in to bed, and heard your prayers. Those times will never change. What a blessing!

Wolsey of Yesterday and Today
By Florence Adermann of Wolsey, South Dakota
Born 1934

Hi! I'm Florence Lindhorst Adermann. I was asked to write a story of myself as I was growing up and my little town of Wolsey,

South Dakota that has 400 plus residents.

To begin with there were seven in our family. I'm that terrible middle child. I was born in the cold month of December in 1934. The years of the dust storms. I don't remember the storms, only what was passed down to me. We had two doctors in our town. The folks chose Dr. Cogswell. He delivered all five of us kids.

The house we moved to after I was born was a two-story house. The stairs going upstairs were very steep. But you know kids! We would roll down the steps. It would scare Mom half to death. But we thought it was fun. There was also a cave on the place. So whenever there was a storm we'd go to the cave.

When I was around three years of age, I came down with whopping cough. You'll never guess what Dr. Cogswell recommended to break the cough. It was kerosene and sugar. It worked. But I can still remember the taste of it. From the whopping cough, I got two ruptures. I had surgery when I was four and was in the hospital several days and had to stay in bed. When I came home, I still had to stay in bed. I don't remember how many days.

I went to kindergarten, but back then, we needed to have a blanket to rest. We didn't receive any training. It was kind of like daycare.

In first grade we were taught phonics, which really helped throughout my school years. I was five when I started school. We walked to school. My oldest sister was five years older than me so I guess I was her responsibility. Our school sat on top of a hill. In the wintertime, it was the town's place to go sledding. The school had all twelve grades. In grade school, there were two grades in one room. I went to Wolsey School all twelve years. We had a great school janitor. His name was Pug. He would watch for us and waited for us to get inside the school before he rang the bell for school to start. When any one of the students would go down the basement to clean erasers, he most generally had an orange or a small box of raisins as a treat. In high school, I participated in mixed chorus, girl's glee club, trio, and solo. I loved music. I was in two three act plays.

One time Dad walked a mile in a blizzard to pick us kids up. We walked home holding each other's hands.

One of my fondest memories is coming home from school and smelling the aroma of Mom's homemade bread. Of course, we'd have to have a slice while it was still warm. We kids would each try and get the crust piece first.

Throughout my childhood, we had the privilege of an outdoor john and chamber pots. For toilet paper, there were the good old *Sears and Roebuck Catalog* or peach wrappers when peaches were in season.

We didn't have a television until I was in high school. It was black and white, and we had to have an antenna to get the stations in. Even with an antenna, the stations weren't very clear. Most of the time we listened to the radio. Mom had her favorite soapies, which were *Ma Perkins* and *Young Widder Brown*. She also listened to *The Neighbor Lady*, which came over WNAX Yankton. Then in the evening, we'd listen to *The Lone Ranger* or *The Green Hornet*.

In the summer months, the neighbor kids would come over, and we'd play softball and hide and go seek. Sometimes in the summer, us three older kids would walk about two miles to our aunt's house and then spend the night. Winter months would find us playing games in the snow. Our favorites were run sheep run and fox and goose. One time there was a ten foot snow bank. We'd climb up and slide down. Our dog, Rover, would follow also.

Mom always hung the washing on the line, winter, or summer. She had to have the water hauled in and then she heated the wash water in a boiler.

We moved to Grandpa's house, which was also a two story house. They took care of Grandpa until he passed away. The house was heated with a coal stove. There was a register in the upstairs floor above the stove. This was the only way the upstairs was heated. So at night time we'd heat irons on the cook stove. We wrapped them in paper and took them to bed, which kept our feet warm. In the morning when we woke up there would be beautiful frost pictures on the windows.

We raised chickens, ducks, geese, guinea hens, turkeys, and goats. I was the outdoor girl. I fed the chickens and gathered eggs. Sometimes there would be clucks on the nest, and when I took the eggs away from them, they would peck my hands. Mom wasn't ready to have a hen set on eggs to raise chicks yet. Then there was the goats. Yep! I milked them and also staked them out.

I remember one Christmas when we had real candles on the tree. Of course, it was a real tree. Dad would light them. He was real careful not to let them burn too long.

I was in the sixth grade when Grandpa passed away. So we then moved into a basement house, which they bought. Water still had to be carried in for washing, 25 gallons down and when done 25 gallons up. We still had to heat wash water in the boiler. The house was then heated with an oil stove.

Ray E. and Florence Adermann and their children

One time when I was digging potatoes in the garden, a man came to the fence line and asked if he could have something to eat. It was breakfast time, and Mom was making pancakes. So I invited him in. Afterwards Mom gave me a scolding. She said that hobos mark a spot on a post so that other hobos would know that one was fed there. But no others ever came by.

In the seventh grade, I missed two weeks of school because of the intestinal flu. My teacher, Mrs. Schnetzer, wrote me a letter saying how much she missed me. As the years went by, we both belonged to the same extension club, and I had a chance to tell her how much that letter meant to me. Of course, she was my favorite teacher.

Wolsey in my younger years was a busy town. We had three filing stations, two grocery stores, a post office, N.W. Public Service, I.G. Drill Drug Store, a creamery, a jail, Friese Hardware Store, an elevator, two churches, Wolsey News, a barber shop, a swimming pool, a band shell, two cafes (Ma's Café and Carson's Café), and an opera house. The businesses changed from time to time. Oh yes, we did have a Kruegers Pool Hall and Sejnoha's. Mr. Sejnoha was a real good candy maker, and he sold his wares. One grocery store closed and a convenience store opened up. Ole's Service Station had a small diner. We had two railroad depots. Mr. Sears was station master in the Chicago Northwestern. He sold watches when he ran it. He later formed the Sears and Roebuck Company. There was even a passenger train, which I rode home from Huron when I worked late. The trains still come through town, but the depots are gone.

We no longer have the grocery stores, drug store, creamery, roller rink, hardware store, Ma's Café, barber shop, blacksmith shop, or band shell. The swimming pool has been modernized with slides. The café I worked at was Simons Café, run by John and Della Simons. Before it was Simons, Ethel Carson ran it. When she sold it, she opened a grocery store and lockers across the street. Simons then sold it to Hansens. The café was then sold to Ralph Brooks. He made it into a mortuary and also opened a furniture store across the street. The building that housed the furniture store used to be a blacksmith's shop. The blacksmith hung him and two high school students found the body. Those, too, are gone. The Wolsey Senior Center and Nutrition Site is now in the building where the furniture store was. Where N.W. Public Service office was is now a leather shop. The opera house still stands. In its time all the graduations, school music concerts, plays, and dances were held there. When they no longer used it for school functions, Mr. Miller made it into a movie theater. When that closed, it stood empty for several years. Then George McDonald bought it for his bee business. He also sold honey to

166

the community. That business is no longer there, and it stands empty. It is a landmark, and I would like to see it restored. The elevator, which was operated by Louie Christiansen, was torn down in 2013. The Wolsey News building has had several bars. It is still a bar called Shooters. The other bar started by Walt Krueger had several owners. The last person who owned it lost it due to a fire. I was told that years ago Wolsey had a terrible fire. Most of the buildings were wooden structures and were destroyed. The new buildings were made of bricks. I was also told that we had a flour mill.

US Highway 14 runs through Wolsey. Starting from the north end of town we have Frosty's Ice Cream Shop; Dean's Service, owned by Jim McGollvrey, which specializes in car and truck repair and St. John's Lutheran Church. Then uptown on the west side is the post office, Shooters, a craft shop that is no longer in operation, American Bank and Trust, and Auto Owner's Insurance, run by David Burnison. On the east side is Schumacher's Custom Boots, the senior center, and Pullman Drilling. Going south on the edge of town is 281 Truck Stop and Convenience Store and Rollen Wheel Restaurant, owned by Robert McGillvrey, and McGillvrey Oil, owned by Richard McGillvrey. Going out of town on the east side is East Star pipelines. Off a few blocks from the highway is Sandy's Beauty Shop, owned by Sandy Ehrk, the Baptist Church, and the Presbyterian Church. Along one of the railroads is Koch's Fertilizer Plant.

In 2006, we had a tornado. It was heading toward our little town, but it changed directions. It went east on the outskirts.it destroyed several houses and farm buildings. The roof of one barn landed on the Three Mile Corner Bridge of Highway 14.

Our school is now consolidated. It is the Wolsey/Wessington School and is fairly new. They've added a new gymnasium. They have open enrollment and students from different towns are attending. They are active in so many more activities than when I went to school.

Our town is active in different organizations, such as the American Legion and Auxiliary. They meet in the community hall. Then there are the Wolsey Business Association and Onward Wolsey, plus our church affiliated organizations.

Private Time and Flour Sack Fashion
By Kathryn Cole Quinones of Bronx, New York
Born 1942

Private Time
Mine was party dress pink. Just the size and roundness of my bottom.

In the winter, when my bedroom turned into a waxed skating rink and there were ice floes in the nightstand water glass, I did my best to avoid pulling that potty out from under the bed. I knew that if I had to get up in the night to sit on it, my feet wouldn't warm up until noon. I learned control very early in life.

In the morning, the nights' deposits were transferred to a bigger pot for some unlucky person to carry to the outhouse. The big pot was frost white enamel with a thin red stripe at the top and a domed lid that ballooned out. Very preppy.

My mom and her sister somehow thought the job of emptying the chamber pot was hilarious. They were young wives on their parents' farm waiting for their men to come back from a war. They had a long wait ahead of them.

Mom once snapped a picture with her Kodak of her sister, Mary, out of focus and way to the left (properties of all of Mom's snapshots) carrying the big pot across the gravel to the outhouse. Mary looked slender as a stalk of flax in a snappy flowered dress and fat tootsie roll hair.

They laughed and laughed over that snapshot. Chamber pots and outhouses were funny to them in ways that I've never understood.

That outhouse was something else, though. My mother's father, Sam, must have built it new after I was born. It was a two-holer—a big hole for grownups and a little hole just for me. The edges of the holes were sanded smooth, rounded and varnished to a shiny gloss. I was never to sit on the big hole because if I fell down in it would be just awful.

That outhouse was a private little getaway. It was my special place, and I was the only one who fit it. I liked it in that little outhouse even with the possibility of spiders or of being tipped over by rowdy teenagers. Mom had told hilarious (to her) stories of Halloween pranks and guys tipping over occupied outhouses just for the fun of it. We were far from town

167

and there were no rowdy teenagers anywhere near, but still, the possibility existed.

A Sears or Montgomery Ward's catalogue hung from a nail on the wall just within reach. A length of bailing twine threaded through the center page. I could sit and look at pictures of girdles and farm equipment, fancy dresses, canning supplies, liver pills, horse collars, trusses and other things that we never seemed to order.

The page to be used had to be carefully selected. I took the time to look for pages with boring pictures, but they were all so interesting. It was especially sad to come to the outhouse, pick up the catalogue and find a favorite page, one with dolls or dresses or grown up lady hats that looked like space ships, gone. Used by an unthinking big holer.

I still inwardly giggle at the sound of the word "pot."

Feed Sack/Flour Sack Dresses

Addie Barber was born in Tyndall, SD, I believe. She certainly lived on farms outside that town for most of her 93 years, raising children, chickens, hollyhocks, and pansies and baking the best bread to ever slide out of an oven. This is not a granddaughter's opinion. This is a scientific fact. I've taste tested a lot of bread, too much maybe, and none of it has come close to hers.

Maybe it was the high butterfat milk her cows produced. Or the eggs still warm from the nest with taxi cab yellow yolks that stood up high. Or maybe, the hand churned (by child power) butter? Or was it her obsessive, we called it persnickety, nature? Whatever the combination of devotion, attention, ingredients and yes, ego, she produced bread and rolls that were not from this world.

She measured by eyeball, as most did. Butter, eggs, milk, and yeast flew together in a flour dust tornado. Then came the poking: two fingers firmly into a soft balloon of kneaded dough. Then, the rolls—a precise dumpling of dough was extruded through that space that forms between your thumb and first knuckle when you make a strong fist. Each roll lined up next to its identical neighbor until the battered aluminum pan was populated by rows of fat little ghosts.

Then the newborn rolls were swaddled in a clean flour-sack towel and nestled in a warm spot to rise until they almost peeked over the edge of the pan. She put her hand in the wood-fueled oven to test the temperature. Counted to…who knows? She calibrated the temperature of the oven by the length of time she could hold her hand in the heat. Then she yanked her hand out and slipped the fat little rolls in. Then what? Clean the kitchen, listen in on the party line, and step out the screen door to shake off her flour-sack apron and admire the hollyhocks, always with part of her attention on those beautiful babies browning in the wood stove.

About that flour-sack apron, and the flour-sack kitchen towels, and the dress she wore that day: It was probably a well mended, once colorful housedress. Newer ones were saved for church and Home Extension Club meetings. There may have been some fancywork on it, too: embroidery or even lace around the collar or pockets. It was surely crafted as painstakingly as her dinner rolls were, by hand or on the treadle sewing machine operated at warp speed by the power of her feet.

She'd been sent to town as a youngster to learn dressmaking, and found that the apprenticeship suited her temperament. There she learned to sew quilts and bodices and christening dresses, night dresses, tailored suits, and fancy underwear. Her beautiful daughters, my mother and her sister, went to town dressed like models, although they didn't believe it. My mother, at least, said she had felt embarrassed to show up at high school in homemade dresses especially those created from flour or feed sacks. As soon as she had a job, she got herself a store bought dress. But snapshots don't lie. She's there in black and white; smiling for the camera. Stunning and stylish on her way to a picnic or a dance, or maybe to work wearing a dress her mother sewed from feed sacks.

The Pillsbury Flour Company figured out, even before the depression, that women were recycling the strong cotton fabric that flour and livestock feed were sewed into. Thrifty housewives made them into ordinary items like aprons, dishtowels, and nightshirts.

Each bag was printed with a dotted double ring the size of a barrel top (a nod to the times these commodities were sold in barrels) the circles made the words: Pillsbury's Best look as though it were the center of the sun and was printed in ink that was almost impossible to bleach out. When an innovative mill in

168

Tennessee started shipping feed and flour in bags of cheerful printed cotton with paper labels that could be easily removed their flour and livestock feed sales took off.

A woman's dress required about four feed sacks, one or two for a child. They look surprisingly modern in patterns and colors that are still beautiful to the modern eye: teals, minty greens and warm brick red with stylized flowers.

Addie no longer trusted her husband, Sam, to go to the feed store in Yankton by himself. She went along for the ride and spent, I am told, a "terrible amount of time" selecting and matching patterns. She was not a bit shy about asking the men move several 100 pound sacks to unearth the required number of matching sacks.

Making beautiful clothes from feed sacks was not merely a desperate measure in times of depression. The trend started in the early twenties and continued through WWII on to the late forties until paper bags became more practical for shippers.

My father told the story of a moonless night when he and his brothers were taking their dates, one of which was to be my mother, home from a dance in town. There was a problem with their Model T automobile and they were stalled on the road near my mom's family farm. He never admitted that they may have conveniently run out of gas or created some other opportune problem with the car in order to earn bonus time with the ladies.

Whatever plans they may have had were thwarted by the terrifying sight of a spectral white light and the word Pillsbury floating slowly towards them on the dark lonely road. Addie, in her feed sack nightdress— brand mark intact—had decided to take her flashlight and walk down the road to see what was going on.

Eleanore Rowan in 1929

Wholesome Fun
By Eleanore R. Moe of Rapid City, South
Dakota
Born 1921

As I reflect on my life, I am amazed at all that has taken place, not only in my own life but in the world at large. Encased in a rural area near Artesian, South Dakota, population about 600, my world was small. When I was born in 1921, the citizenry had not yet faced the dilemma of the 1929 Crash but were still reeling from WWI. My father Leo Rowan had been drafted but had not been called to serve; however, two of his brothers had served. One brother, Frank, had been gassed in France and another brother, Charles, had served at Omaha, Nebraska. In World War I, no married men were drafted so my Mother and Dad felt that it was unpatriotic to marry during the War. When WWI ended November 11, 1918, Bessie Smith and Leo set their marriage date for February 26, 1919. However, my mother Bessie Smith moved only 2 miles to her new home and Leo moved 3 miles. They paid a high price of $180 per acre for the land on which a $600 house ordered from the Sears

169

and Roebuck catalog had been built. Although the Model T Ford had been invented in 1908, my parents did not own one. They still drove a horse and buggy. After their marriage in the Methodist Parsonage in Mitchell, SD, they had no honeymoon as the auction sale of Bessie's father Edward Smith's possessions was scheduled two days after their marriage. Sarah Ann (Bessie's mother) had died July 1918 and so it was predestined that Grandpa Smith would live with the newlyweds, Bessie and Leo. In those days, retirement homes did not exist.

As a girl in the late 20s, I earned my spending money by drowning gophers; when they stuck their heads out of the holes, I killed them by stoning them, then cutting off their tails. Sanborn County where we lived paid 5 cents and then later 8 cents per tail. Also, I earned more money from my mother who would give me 5 cents for every basket of dried cow chips I gathered. The corners of the pastures where the cattle gathered were the most fruitful. Also, God gave me another easy source of income. He made me fast on my feet so I entered the races at all the summer celebrations and won every race I ever entered. Some of these netted over a dollar.

During the depression (1934-about 1941 for our area), what the folks sold did not bring in much revenue; however, neither did the products and services cost very much. We had no refrigeration until about 1933 when we acquired an icebox. Mother made my dresses from the material of bags, which held 50 pounds of flour. Teachers were paid $45 a month in warrants, which had to be cashed at a bank at a reduction. Sirloin steak cost 29 cents per pound; a quart of milk 10 cents; eggs 29 cents per dozen; bananas 7 cents per pound; shoes $3.50 or less; coke 5 cents (no cans yet); dental filling $1; vacuum cleaner $18.75 (these cents were used before the 99 cent idea hit the markets). No tax was collected on any items, large or small. My elocution lessons and also my piano lessons cost 50 cents each session. Hot dogs and hamburgers cost 5 cents; the movies cost 15 cents for me and a quarter for adults. I viewed my first movie upstairs over Quinn's Grocery where we sat on long wooden benches to watch Harriet Beecher Stowe's "Uncle Tom's Cabin." This film was a silent movie filmed in black and white with captions of the texts the actors were speaking. In about 1934, Gertrude and "Silky" Silkenson built a movie theater in Artesian but we still did not have audio. We read the captions and a pianist played the music to match whatever actions were being portrayed on the screen. Every summer we looked forward to the vaudeville show and the Barnum and Bailey circus. My future husband, George Moe, had a back stage view of the circus folks and animals since he helped his depot-agent father Nels when the circus arrived via the Milwaukee Railroad. Several times, some of the circus animals spent the night in the freight house. Sometimes this became very interesting such as the time the alligator kept trying to break out of its cage.

In spite of the dust storms that penetrated through the window sills, under doors and into every nook and corner and the grasshoppers that covered the fence posts and blackened the north side of houses and the anthrax that wrought extinction to some herds, life was not dull. We were among the few who had a radio to which 2 people could listen at a time using earphones. The country phone was part of our entertainment as everyone listened to everyone else's conversations. Music was a big part of my life where the church's unpaid music director, J.M. Best, formed a harmonica orchestra when I was about ten years old. As we learned to play instruments, about 20 players crowded onto the church stage where I played the clarinet.

Also, I attended the Congregational Church Camp at Lake Kampeska near Watertown for four years and one year I attended the camp at Yankton College. My mother thought it would be a good experience for me to live in a dorm, eat in a cafeteria, and see what a campus was like. The cost was $5 for the week. These experiences were available to me because Mother and I attended Glenview Congregational Church, 4 miles north of Fedora. Dad had been raised in the Catholic religion but when he married Mother, he gave up his denomination. Since Mother did not drive a car, Dad took us to and from church every Sunday and saw that we attended any activity at the church that we desired to be a part of.

During my high school years most of our parties were in the homes where we played Monopoly, spin the bottle, charades, post office, and fruit basket upset. Also, we played many volleyball games during the summer months and enjoyed ice-skating in the winter. Hot chocolate and cake were usually served. I don't know when Cocoa-Cola started, but I never had a bottled drink until the 1940s. We could get custom made soft drinks at the hotel where we would sit on the ice cream chairs to enjoy our ice cream or drink one of the soda fountain drinks prepared behind the marble counter. One of my friends and I would each order a dip of ice cream, then buy one small packet of Planters Peanuts to sprinkle on top—all for 10 cents each. Foot long hot dogs cost a dime. On Saturday evenings after we had played our band concert at the main street bandstand, a group of us would each buy a 5-cent sack of popcorn popped fresh from the popcorn machine on the corner; then we would walk around and around the 4 blocks of Artesian's main streets. When our popcorn sacks were about half empty, we would return to Mr. Gresbrink, our popcorn maker, and ask for more butter. He never refused—in those prohibition days everyone knew he was peddling liquor behind the popcorn stand.

Artesian was the only town in the area with a swimming pool, which had been built in 1929. Like hundreds of other young folks, I learned to swim in this gravel-covered pool, which the community still enjoys. Other entertainment was at my home on a pond where the water overflowed from the cattle tank; I pretended I was skating on Lake Placid. I also rode whatever horse happened to be in the barn. We had no dog, as a dog would chase the cattle, especially during sorting. However, we had several cats, which lived in the barn and earned their livelihood by devouring all the mice. Eight summers we had a hobo who lived in the hay loft. He had a long white beard, which he kept spotlessly clean. I can't imagine why, but we treated him as a guest. Probably we did this because he told stories of places we felt we would never visit. I can remember how we would sit on the grass after supper listening to tales of adventures created when he rode the empty cars of the freight trains that took him from one part of the USA to other parts. Usually these hobos cooked their meals and slept along the railroad tracks when they were not riding the rails.

Holidays with the Rowan family were special. We always gathered at the huge old homestead where about 20 members of the

The Girls Basketball team in Artesian, South Dakota in 1938

family would celebrate. Christmases were especially festive; the smorgasbord from all members of the Irish clan could have been a site for a cookbook cover. Aunt Jose, who lived her entire life in that home, would always have a huge evergreen tree in the second parlor. This decorated tree was magic for me as I would just sit and stare at it with all the packages piled under its branches. With so many aunts, uncles, and cousins gathered together, everyone fared well.

The huge pavilion at Ruskin Park near Forestburg, SD on the Jim River was another fun spot. This pavilion was built as a dance hall where orchestras such as Lawrence Welk played during the 30s and 40s. However, Sunday afternoons and other special times we rented clamp-on skates for a quarter so we could skate round and round holding hands or single file. Picnics were very popular here as folks could visit, fish, play games, and enjoy their neighbors and relatives. Ruskin Park was THE PLACE July 4th. Traditionally we ate the first fried chicken of the season and relished the first fresh peas from the garden.

Whenever my mother had an operation, I lived for weeks at the Rowan homestead with my Aunt Josephine and Uncles Bill, Charlie, and Tom. I never tired of the every-evening delicious meal of boiled eggs and diced potatoes, which Aunt Jose diced very thin with a soup can while she fried them in bacon drippings. Summer evenings we sat for hours on the back porch chatting about the local and world situations while we admired the sheep grazing on the distant hills.

During my Artesian High School years, I lived in town with my father's brother Jack and his wife Stella. I was very active in high school: played the clarinet in the

171

band, accompanied the glee club, starred as a basketball player (center), and took piano lessons. In the fall and spring, a group of us would play games under a street light. During the high school basketball season the girls played the first game and the fellows the second. We all rode on one bus to the out-of-town games: the boys in the front and the girls in the back with the coaches seated between us.

Dating was never a twosome affair; usually 4 were together but often it was 6 (a car full). Sometimes we would drive to Mitchell (30 miles) for a movie. One of the MUSTS was the Globetrotters basketball team, which visited the Corn Palace in Mitchell every year. Also, during Corn Palace Week, our high school band paraded—we then received free passes to the Corn Palace show, which always featured a well-known artist. A big deal was getting our pictures taken at one of those "do it yourself" booths.

Therefore, life was entirely different from the experiences of young folks today but when I look back, I have no regrets. I learned to save money, to value wholesome fun, to treat everyone as my equal, to be flexible in solving the situations as they arose. Little did I realize how much of the world I would have a chance to visit and what a different type of adult life I would experience.

Stories of Mischief
By Nadine Sievers of Rapid City, South Dakota
Born 1923

My name is Nadine Sievers and I recently celebrated my 90th birthday. I grew up on a farm near Gettysburg, South Dakota with four siblings—two boys and two girls. My stories are about mischief we got into when our folks weren't at home.

One time when our folks were in town, us kids made a devil's food cake. However, we didn't actually get to the baking part; we ate all of the batter! We all got sick. Boy did the folks laugh when they got home!

Another time we went to the corral and rode big calves. My mean brothers "sicked" the dog on my calf. He threw me so fast that I was on the ground. He stepped on my hip before he got past me. Now that was fast! I

don't know if the folks ever knew about that one!

A Drawing for...a Turkey?
By John Larson of Lake Norden, South Dakota
Born 1940

I have lived in Lake Norden, South Dakota for most of my life. The following story is about Christmas memories in "small town" South Dakota in the 1940s.

The local merchants in Lake Norden appreciated their customers. Each year right after Thanksgiving, the merchants gave their customers one small registration ticket for every dollar spent in their store. Our small town (under 500 people) had three grocery stores, two hardware stores (my parents were owners of one), three implement dealers, four gas stations, two pool halls, two grain elevators, one lumberyard, a blacksmith, and even a soda pop factory.

Every Saturday and Christmas Eve day, a drawing was held on Main Street. The unique thing about this drawing was that live turkeys were given to the persons whose names were drawn. Generally, the number of people in attendance was in the hundreds. At least ten live turkeys were given away at each drawing. My wife remembers bringing a live turkey home in the backseat of the car, along with the kids and groceries.

I have home movies of the occasion. It was a community experience that everyone loved. It provided Christmas turkeys for a number of families, and is a memory that I will never forget. It was probably unique to our community. I was not aware of similar activity in surrounding communities.

Rides Down Main Street
By Joyce R. Stanislzus Olson of Watertown, South Dakota
Born 1923

In the 1930s, many local farmers were still driving a team of horses and a bobsled to Wallace, South Dakota to buy coal, groceries, and other needs. Several of us younger children would take our small sleds and walk on Main Street to the east end of town. We would wait for a team to come along. When they did come, we'd wave and call, asking them to stop and let us hook on behind the bobsled and get a ride uptown. Most of the drivers would stop the horses and allow us time to "hook on" the back of the big sleds. Then they would cluck, "Giddy up," and away we were off for an exciting ride up Main Street. That went so well, and then we'd wait uptown and hook a ride back to the east! It was so much fun!

Joyce R. Stanislzus Olson in 1936

Sleeping in the Corncrib
By Peggy Westby of Aberdeen, South Dakota
Born 1950

One boring summer night in the late 1950s when I was about nine years old and my cousin was eleven, we decided we would like to camp out at her farm. I lived in a small town (Rosholt, South Dakota), and I liked to sleep over at her house and have some fun since we were close to the same age. We only lived about 14 miles apart. We didn't have tents or sleeping bags, but we used our brains. We figured, "Why not sleep in the corncrib?"

It was fairly empty, as the corn had not yet been harvested in July.

This was close to the barn, pigpen, and granary. We didn't think about the mice or rats that run around at night (especially in a place where they have food to eat). We also didn't think about the skunks, badgers, bats, raccoons, or foxes who also roamed around the countryside. We certainly didn't think about the mosquitoes biting us. This corncrib was not airtight, so many bugs and creatures were able to get in spaces in and under this old corncrib. After we decided to attempt this venture, we dared not to be scared. No, we were two brave, young girls.

We took a pillow and a blanket and went out with our flashlight around 10:00 PM. It had just gotten dark, as it was a warm, humid evening in July. The floor was very hard, but we were young and didn't seem to mind. We didn't have to worry about sore backs the next day at our age. We fell asleep with the moonlight coming in through the cracks in the corncrib's siding, and thought how much fun it would be to tell everyone about our big adventure the next day.

We awoke in the middle of the night, and our "being brave" was overshadowed by the darkness. We imagined someone, or something, coming and scaring us. We had just about enough! We both took our pillows, blankies, and flashlight and walked back to the house, trying not to awaken anyone inside. They did not have to know we didn't survive the night outside. We were through with this "camp out." I don't remember if we told them we slept there all night or they figured it out. My cousin's mom was a light sleeper, and I bet she heard us come in the door. I don't think we tried this adventure again. Once was great plenty!

A Town Full of Nicknames
By Helena Townsend of Willow Lake, South Dakota
Born 1917

My mother, Carolina Iverson, was born in 1887 in a sod shanty on a homestead that belonged to her uncle, John K. Saboe, in Section 34 of Richland Township, Clark County, Dakota Territory. She was the oldest of seven children of Tollef and Anna Bertha Iverson. The children were responsible for herding the cattle as they grazed on the open prairie. Mother told us stories of the Indian stone foundations that they played on while the cattle grazed. They were made of stones piled about two and a half feet high and probably were used by the Indians as a corral. The cows were milked, and when my mother became a little older, she helped haul the milk to the creamery.

John Opsahl had built a creamery on his homestead in 1884. Naturally, cool flowing springs were used to cool the milk. At one time, this creamery was the second largest creamery in South Dakota. This creamery also was the beginning of the little town of Carpenter, as businesses sprang up around it. My mother and her brothers would stop by the neighbors and pick up their milk, too, on their daily trips to the creamery. They waited while the milk was separated and then they took the skim milk and butter back home. Buttermilk was free! The trip had to be made every day while the milk was fresh and sweet. It was John Opsahl's that my mother met John's brother, Martin, in 1905. Martin had just come from Wisconsin to partner with his brother in a store. But a short time later, Martin bought a farm and built the home where he resided the rest of his life. Mother and Father were married a couple years later.

Mother began working out for neighbors when she was about 13. She did housekeeping duties but also cared for the sick and assisted the doctors with births. She quickly learned the skills of a practical nurse that she would use throughout the rest of her life. Flu epidemics hit often and hit hard; they were especially bad in the 1920s. People were told to stay at home and to avoid gatherings that might spread the disease. Quite a few people died; many were children. At times, even the funerals of those that died were not allowed. The dead were buried as quickly as possible. Many other pioneers of that time have told me that my mother was a "savior nurse" during those times. Many people were afraid to go into the homes of the sick. Doc Fleeger would go around and visit as many as he could, but Mother went into a lot of the homes and she stayed until they got better.

People around the Carpenter area loved nicknames. It seemed that everyone had one.

Scrawny, "T," Slivers, Spinny, Slats, Lefty, Porkey, Husky, Slick, and on. Sometimes when a visitor came to town and asked for someone by their proper name, the locals were left scratching their heads to remember who that was. And the mail wasn't a problem. A card addressed to "Scrawny Carpenter, South Dakota" would get delivered to the right person just fine.

Syrup Pail Lunches and Corncob Fuel
By Gladys Noack of Mitchell, South Dakota
Born 1933

My first memory was of living by the James River on a farm. There were hills to the south of us and the river was not very far from the house to the north. In the winter, we sledded down the hills and also played on the ice, but without skates. I was born in 1933 in the "dirty thirties," as it was called. We went barefooted in the summer as to save on shoes. I got a new pair when school started.

I didn't enjoy the hills come school time. We walked a mile and a half up the hill, and we crawled through the neighbor's field where he had cows with a bull and sheep with a buck sheep. We were afraid of both of them. I went to a one-room schoolhouse. Sometimes the teacher would have all eight grades. When it was windy and cold, we got to sit around the big stove that burned coal. I carried my lunch in a gallon syrup pail. We didn't have a lot to eat—usually just a sandwich and a cookie. At Christmastime, Dad would buy a box of apples. Then, we'd have them in our pail until they were gone. My mother baked bread from scratch once a week for eight people. The bread was good until the end of the week, and then maybe a little mold would show up. We'd just cut that off and eat the middle.

In the winter, my father would butcher a cow and pig for their beef and pork. Mother would can the meat, and that is what we ate until it was gone. She would also make headcheese. Yuck! That is what we got on our sandwiches for school. She would always bake a cake on Saturday in case we would have company on Sunday. But we school kids could never have any, as we had to save ours for our school lunch.

In the summertime, I helped in the garden,

174

pulling weeds. We played under the trees. We made a store out of orange crates and made mud pies that we pretended were cakes and cookies. Once in a while, we'd go to the chicken house and get an egg or two and put them in our mud pies. We played in the river when it was hot. None of us knew how to swim. The Lord must have watched over us. We had a plank bridge we had to go over to get to the other side of our land my dad farmed. We used to sit on the bridge with our feet hanging over, maybe doing a little fishing with a cane pole and a hook on the end of some string.

Then came the cold weather again. We had to pick cobs up out of the pigpen to last until the next night, and then we'd fill up the tubs again. Ma burned cobs in the range for cooking. It also burned wood and coal. We had to carry water for the next day. I wasn't very old, so I carried it in two syrup pails. When bedtime came, we went upstairs. It was so cold you could see your breath. We had feather ticks on the bed. They were warm with lots of covers.

When I was about eight years old, it was my turn to go and sleep with my grandma, as she had a great big house and she didn't like to sleep alone. Her house was about an eighth of a mile from our house. I had to walk through the barnyard where the cattle were to get to her house. It was dark and scary. No one walked with me. In the morning, we had oatmeal with no salt and a piece of what we called "water cake" with no frosting.

I don't ever remember getting punished in school. I don't think I'll ever forget the one time my mother sent me over to the neighbors to take some garden stuff over. It was a mile over there. I was told to come right home. They had three girls, and we got to playing. Well, it was about 5:00 when I got home, and I knew I was going to get it. I went upstairs and fell asleep. Mother came up and got me up out of the bed, got a chair, and told me to lay over it. She said that the longer I waited, the harder the spanking was going to be. And it was.

We lived on a farm, so we always had outhouses. I got to use the pot at night. When I was about nineteen, I went to town to work. That was the first bathroom that I had ever used. We had a wringer washer at home. The first one I remember had a gas motor. That was hard to start. When it did go, the exhaust was so stinky that Ma opened the door. The electric ones were really nice after we got electricity. I used one for a few years after I was married.

My mother made a lot of our clothes. She wasn't the best seamstress. We wore long socks in winter. She would patch the heels with the sewing machine. We were told as long as it didn't have holes, it was okay to wear. I remember when I was about 12 I got a hand-me-down fur coat from my cousin. I had to wear it for good. I often wondered how many people laughed at me.

One thing three of my siblings and I did was make candy. The folks went to town every Saturday, so we would make a batch of fudge and butterscotch candy. What we couldn't eat we hid and ate during the week. We never had a recipe, but I don't care for fudge now. I don't ever remember getting caught.

My siblings like to scare me with an old Santa mask. They would talk about "Bluebeard," ever who he was. When I was in the fourth grade, we moved from the river and walked two and a half miles to another one-room schoolhouse. That school closed due to lack of pupils.

I never got to go to high school. When I went to town, I worked as a nurse's aide at the hospital. I worked there three and a half years and ended up getting 99 cents per hour. I still saved a little. I left the hospital to get married and live on a farm again. I have four children, 12 grandchildren, and two great-grandchildren. I have been married for 57 years now.

Growing up Tough
By Doris Wenck Alberts of Britton, South Dakota
Born 1923

When I was growing up, walking a half of mile to a grove of trees was a special treat. It felt so good to play in the shade away from the hot and dusty farm where we lived. On one particular day, my brothers and I were headed to school with the horse and buggy. My older brother accidentally dropped one of the reins, and I was in charge of getting out of the buggy and retrieving it. About that time, the horse got spooked and took off. I hung onto the frame for dear life, but it didn't take long before I

Doris, Howard, Lloyd, Leonard, and Dileen Wenck

fell and the buggy ran over me. I escaped with a few scratches and a bruise that left a puffy lump on my cheek. Sometime later, I blew the blood clots out of my nose, and that was the final stage of my scary ordeal.

Our farm was close to the railroad track. Often we would see a small group of hobos walking down the road to our windmill in search of some cold water. Mother always gathered us up and headed us into the house. Years later, I learned the hobos knew just where to go to find food, shelter, and cold water.

The worst time in my life occurred during the "Dirty Thirties." Sometimes it was so dark during the day that we had to light a lamp to see. My mother tried to keep out some of the dirt by covering the windows with wet towels. When you woke up in the morning, the only white spot to be found on the bed sheet was where you had laid that night. Even worse, all we had to feed the livestock was thistles. There wasn't any harvest that year.

Things got better, and we moved to another farm. Now we walked to a country school with a total of 21 students in all eight grades. There were four sets of twins in the community. I didn't know that school could be so much fun! At recess, we all played games together and the older students always helped and took good care of the younger ones. During the winter, we spent recess time in the basement of the school. One time my brother fell and hit his head hard enough to knock himself out. We were all pretty scared, but sure enough, one of the older boys grabbed the ax and put the cold blade on his head for relief.

Our teacher was wonderful and so organized. When she was busy teaching another class, the older students knew their job was to quietly help out the younger ones. We often divided into two teams, and the teacher asked each student questions according to their grade level. It was a fun way to develop teamwork and learn at the same time. Our "hot" lunches consisted of the jar of food we brought to school, which was warmed in a pan of water on top of the stove. Discipline was never a problem. After walking home from school, we would immediately change out of our school clothes and begin our chores. Gathering corncobs, cleaning the lamp chimney, and milking cows before supper were some of our responsibilities.

Saturday night was a time we all looked forward to. It was the night we took our eggs and cream to town. If it had been a good week, we would receive a nickel. We could spend this nickel on ice cream, school supplies, or candy of our choice. Our little railroad town of Andover had an interesting history. Within a few years, the settlers had built it into a thriving place with all the necessities needed, including a doctor, dentist, pharmacist, churches, banks, and a school. Fires took their toll on the town over the years, burning first one side of the town and then the other. The finest hotel in the surrounding area, the Waldorf Hotel, was built in 1902 and became the hub of the community. This changed when transportation by automobile became popular. Imagine my delight when my classmate, who lived at the hotel, offered to show me around. Her grandfather was sitting at the big desk in the lobby where he could communicate with each and every room. I remember being impressed by the large cook stove and the massive staircase leading to the upper rooms.

Life seemed pretty good to us. Taking our horse and sled to visit the neighbors was always something we looked forward to doing. Whether it was going to church or just playing games around the kitchen table, it

Harvesting wheat after the Dirty Thirties
Howard and Leonard

was always a family affair. My 90 years have taught me that sometimes the simple life is the best life!

It Was So Dry
By Lucille (Foote) Green of Sioux Falls, South Dakota
Born 1926

My name is Lucille Green (Foote). I was born on the Foote Farm six and a half miles northeast of Langford, South Dakota. My grandfather, Chester, homesteaded the Foote farm. My father, Edwin, then farmed the land, followed by my brother, Ralph and his son, Neil. My mother, Anna, came from Germany in 1910. Throughout our grade school years, my two sisters, four brothers, and I traveled the two and a half miles to the Platte and/or Hamilton country schools via horse and buggy, horseback, or occasionally in winter via sled pulled by horses. Sometimes we just walked.

Times were hard often because of the weather, lack of moisture, very hot weather, hot windy days, and overall, because the land was so severely dry and parched and no grass or crops would grow. During several years (1932-36), the land was so dry that there was barely, if any, harvest. This produced little money for living expenses. We had a great family with a conservative lifestyle, but with seven children plus our parents, we needed a fair amount of food. However, somehow or another we always had enough to eat.

Potatoes and meat were our staple foods, and generally, we were able to raise enough potatoes for the family. There were a few times when they had to be purchased from elsewhere, and sometimes it was difficult to have livestock to butcher for our needs. My parents were great and always did the best they could for all of us.

It was so dry at times, that drastic measures had to be taken—such as the following. There was no feed available for the cattle, and water was scarce. Our windmill provided the water, if available, in the ground. So in order to keep the cattle, they had to be taken elsewhere where they could get food and water. One instance was where Ralph, my brother, had to ride our pony, Mac, to herd the cattle from the Foote Farm to West Britton (town name at that time), and from there to the train. From West Britton, they were shipped on the train to Fairmont, Minnesota (Rosenkranz farm) where there was grass and better pastureland for the cattle. The cattle remained there sometimes for long periods of time—many months, maybe even a year or two. When things improved, they were brought back to the farm. In exchange for this service, the keepers of the cattle received a cow or two and the milk from the cows. Often the cattle came back in a thin and bony condition and milk from them was scarce. Handling the cattle in this way allowed us to keep the cows for the future. It was not easy to provide for the family's needs during that time period.

It was so dry with no feed for the livestock available, that the men in the family had to mow the thistles. The thistles were rampant and wild. They continued to blow across the land. Then they harvested the mowed thistles by thrashing them on the main floor of the barn. This provided some feed to keep the livestock alive. The feed was not very good, but it was the best there was at the time.

It was so dry on the farm and area that my father rented land in Four-Mile Lake, which was located several miles northeast of the Foote farm. They then herded the cattle to that area which was one of the few places around where there was grass. This was a tough job and took many hours to get them to Four-Mile Lake and then, of course, return them to the farm when the situation improved. When there was some moisture in the ground, the windmill provided the water. At times, the milk from the cows had a poor taste, which they say came from the cows eating peppergrass. That is probably why most of the family members did not like milk.

It was so dry that in order to save dollars and have plenty of flour for cooking and baking, my Dad would take approximately 20 bushels of wheat to a plant in Frederick, South Dakota, approximately 50 miles from the farm, and have it made into flour. In this way, we were able to afford to have enough flour to make many food products for the family.

It was so dry that there was not enough work on the farm planting and harvesting. My brother, Herbert, joined the CCC (Civilian Conservation Corp) for a year or more. This camp was established by the government to give young men some work and do a service for their country. They were also able to make a little money and have a good job and place to be.

It was so dry that another brother, Ralph, joined the Army, not only because of the farming being so poor, but he was called and wanted to serve our country during World War II, as so many men/women did.

Even though times were tough, the war was on, and my parents believed that education was important. I attended high school during this time. Patriotism was high and very important, as was the feeling of personal responsibility. Looking ahead to a job after graduation led me to take all subjects that would prepare me for an office or secretarial job. (I had a great and helpful Commercial teacher who helped guide me in this area.) This resulted in my having a fine career as a secretary.

It was tough in those times to actually secure a high school education due to living on a farm six and a half miles from the school in Langford. The family had only one car, so it was necessary that my parents rent a housekeeping room in Langford for me so I could stay there during the week to attend school. I would return home on weekends. Rooming with my brother Kenneth and friend LaVaune, the first year and with my classmate Glenice the other years made life interesting, but not easy. She and I would take turns bringing food for the week on Mondays and cooked it together. A non-likable task was to build the fire (wood and coal) in a barrel stove for warmth. It was always cold by morning, so we would get up fast and depart as soon as possible for school. Other friends and classmates lived like we did—in housekeeping rooms during the week, so we used to visit back and forth and had fun together. (I was 13 years old when I first started this living arrangement.) Later, my sister Helen had a similar arrangement, and by the time the two youngest, Dorthy and Donald, went to high school, my parents had moved to town.

Going to sports games was hard since many games were held on Friday nights and we would be back on the farm. But for those games held in the week, my roommate and I would sell candy during the games, thus not having to pay for a ticket but still getting to see the games.

Many times snowstorms developed— sometimes on Fridays. Then the weather and roads would be very bad. We would have to stay in town all weekend, hoping we had enough food to cover. However, we always made it. Those weekends were not very enjoyable, but we tried to make the best of it.

All in all, my high school years were a lot of fun and very enjoyable, even though living this way was not always easy. It was important that our parents trusted us to be good and attend school regularly and behave, as we should. We would not let them down. I graduated in 1944 from Langford High School at 17 years of age.

After I graduated in May, my goal was to find a job. Having not been out in the work world, I hesitated to job hunt. My mother encouraged me to start searching for work, and soon I found a job. Many of my classmates married shortly after high school graduation, but that was not in my thinking at that time. I just wanted to get out into the world and into the workplace.

Since I lived on a farm about 50 miles from Aberdeen (our closest large town), it was not easy to search for and find a job from that distance. But jobs all across the country were quite plentiful, so I signed up at the employment office there for a secretarial job.

Several weeks later, I received a call offering me a job at an insurance company, which I accepted immediately for $80.00 per month. As my cousin Adelaide was already working and living in Aberdeen, I soon became her roommate and shared an apartment. After working there for about nine months, we decided to move to Sioux Falls and get good jobs there, which we did—she at John Morrell and me at Army Air Base with American Red Cross. Later I worked at John Morrell too, as a secretary and was employed there for nearly 35 years.

We went to Sioux Falls without jobs, a place to live, and very little money, but everything worked out fine. She and I lived together for about five years, at which time she got married. A few months later, I was married. We had a great time living together in both Aberdeen and Sioux Falls.

Unloading the Grief
By Roger Larsen of Huron, South Dakota
Born 1953

Tears rolled down her cheeks not long after I began talking—maybe "unloading" is a better word. That emotional day was nearly 40 years ago when we were on a lonely eastern South Dakota highway. It was just she and I in that 1951 panel truck—me quietly sharing, she tearfully listening. A deep sense of loss had been locked safely away inside me. Despite the years, the pain was still raw, and I had resolved to keep it far from the surface of my being, that is, until it all came spilling out of me on that day. It is a day I will never forget. It is also a day I wish I had allowed to come much earlier.

The miles had been flying by, the endless sky free of clouds, the wind unusually calm, and the highway dry and smooth. Our eyes looked out that windshield and saw a horizon that seemed impossibly clear, yet distant—a priceless prairie view as beautiful to me as one sees in the highest of mountains or near the bluest of oceans.

Roger's brother, Allen driving the panel truck he restored for Roger

Our conversation was light and easy at first. We were good friends, and several of us had just spent a lovely weekend away from town, from work, and from worries. When the subject was broached, there would be no turning back. She would want to hear it all. Even after so long a time, I remember that more than anything. She is a loving, caring lady, someone whose emotions, unlike my own, do run just below the surface and are quick to appear, who never hides her tears, who is there to help when needed, who is sensitive to the needs of others.

Oh, and one more thing. She's a nurse. Nurses are efficient and organized. They go about their work with a gentle touch, a kind word, a concerned look, and an easy laugh. They see pain and suffering every day, but take the time to listen.

Where do we find these people who embody the very spirit of South Dakota? Who are ingrained in its very fabric, who have lovingly cared for South Dakota families for generations? How can we ever begin to thank them for all that they do? I've had years to ponder these questions, and I'm not sure I'm closer to the answers today than on that day, on that lonely highway, with my friend in the mid-1970s.

She broached the subject and triggered an opening of the floodgates, not long after our conversation turned to our families. She knew I had grown up in California in an unincorporated neighborhood surrounded by hundreds of thousands of people in other Bay Area suburbs—a far cry from the wide-open spaces and huge star-filled skies of the plains. "Do your folks still live in California?" she asked. I didn't answer right away. I didn't know then how much would she want to know.

I plunged ahead. I didn't have a simple yes or no answer for her, and so how much she would want to know would depend on her reaction to this: "Mom is there…but dad died a few days before Christmas in 1970." I should have known before answering. I also should have known when she heard me say my father had died, probably, in her mind, at an early age. I should have known that the nurse riding with me in that panel truck would want to know more. She did, but she let me do this on my own terms.

First, though, I had answered her question

179

by stating a fact, without emotion, without a tug at my heart or a tear in my eye, just as I had done so many times since I had heard the phone ring one early morning, the call coming from someone at the hospital. I hadn't had to hear the words. Dad was in the hospital, it was six in the morning and Mom was crying in the predawn gloom. Dad had been granted his wish to go to his heavenly home for Christmas. His three-year battle with cancer was over. For the half-dozen years since then, when the question arose, that's where I had always left it. Dad had gotten sick, he fought it for three years, and he died. My emotions, for good or bad, and, of course, it was for bad, remained behind closed doors, sealed off from the world. That was not so on this day, about five years later. This day would be different. This day would change me.

I can still see the two of us riding in that restored Chevrolet panel truck, one of those some may remember that were workhorses in the 1950s as bread delivery vehicles. My clever younger brother, Allen, also now gone to heaven, also after fighting cancer, was still in his teens when he had poured his heart and soul into that restoration project for me. He and a buddy had exchanged the original engine with a 1967 Pontiac Slant-S model. Like its contemporaries, the truck had no side windows, so visibility for the driver was always a challenge, but that Slant-6 provided amazing and deceiving power for what, by all outward appearances, was just an old bread truck.

Now, living and working in Huron—and on this day, out on the open highways of South Dakota—I was driving one of the products of my brother's amazing handiwork—a beast of a performer he had painted dark blue. Generations earlier, mostly on rutted paths, our grandfather had been out in the wide, flat spaces of Hamlin County, South Dakota, enjoying life while maneuvering his simple, early version of a motorcycle—something he'd have to give up to satisfy the wish of his new bride—while trying hard to keep it upright on roads that were no more than trails.

My passenger's question had been simple enough. But the way she asked it, or the mood I was in, or the calm demeanor she exuded as a well-trained nurse, or all of that and maybe more, flipped a switch on that afternoon that had never been flipped. The floodgates did

open. The horses came running out of the barn. Toss in whatever cliché you like best. The point is, it all came pouring out. And, finally, I didn't hit the brakes. I didn't stop myself. I didn't stop the tears. I unloaded by telling her about that awful day, one of so many that would follow, when we were told dad was sick. Mom and dad tried to be positive, but they pulled no punches. This was going to be a rough ride.

I told her about his frequent hospitalizations. The horrible, frantic ambulance rides when he began hemorrhaging and the eventual loss of one leg. The incredible pain he endured, despite all of the pills. I told her about his burning desire to see and hold his little girl when she wasn't old enough to be up in his hospital room, and how the only alternative was for him to be wheeled down to the lobby, and the tears he shed, as strangers watched, as he hugged his precious only daughter Elaine and, I am sure, knew he would not live to see her grow up. Yes, I told my friend, he indeed must have known he would not beat this strong enemy, even though he was doing everything in his power to counter its every move. He had accepted the loss of his hair, the loss of a leg, and the loss of his dignity. The odds were against him, and yet he would not give up.

Still forever in my mind, I told her, was the agonized look on his face, caught by a camera when perhaps we didn't notice, one holiday when we were all gathered together, trying to make the best of things because it was a rare occasion; Dad was home from the hospital. Our two-vehicle caravan pulled over to the side of the road at one point on that trip back to Huron. There were no cell phones in those days, of course, and so we had stopped to ask each other if we wanted to exchange passengers for the rest of the way home.

The tears had already been streaming down my friend's face for miles. She'd wipe them away, but more would follow. "No," she said adamantly when the question was posed. "I want to hear more about your dad," she said, turning to me as the cars whizzed by on Highway 37.

Back behind that big steering wheel, I let the rest of it come pouring out. She continued to listen quietly, crying quietly. She never interrupted, even to ask a question. I was unloading pent-up emotions, and the caregiver in her let me do it on my own terms, in my own way, like a nurse always does.

She has long since moved away, but I still remember that special day and those special hours we shared in that wonderful old panel truck lovingly rebuilt by my brother, on those South Dakota roads and highways, the beautiful vistas all around us. When I was done talking and when my own tears had dried up, I took a big breath and relaxed, finally at peace with myself.

On an afternoon on a ribbon of a South Dakota highway—so long ago now—a friend and a nurse was there to help me accept my loss just by letting me talk about it. Where, indeed, do we find these people? And how can we ever thank them? I hope, Janene, that this is one way.

The Way it Was
By Bonnie Anderson of Roscoe, South Dakota
Born 1933

I was born in the early '30s, so I don't remember the dust bowl. However, I heard plenty of stories about it and wondered how many persons or animals could live through all that dust. Farming has changed a lot through the years, so pray there will never be such a blow again.

I was born and raised and have lived my life in a five mile area of Loyalton, South Dakota. My parents were Phil Bukaske and Zeldia (Oban) Bukaske. My dad was born in the state of New York and his family moved to Milwaukee, Wisconsin. My dad's parents both passed away in their thirties and left seven children behind. Dad was the second oldest, and there were no work laws, so he got a job in a stove factory, wrapping stove legs, at the age of 13. A land shark brought him to South Dakota, and that is where he stayed. My mom was born and raised and lived within a five-mile area of her birthplace at the farm. Her parents were T.I. and Lula (Barton) Oban— well-to-do farmers, but worked hard, as did the children. They were pioneer settlers in the county from the state of Vermont.

The town of Loyalton was started out as Vermont City. Later, the railroad tracks came and brought much to the country. However, Vermont City moved one mile east to be by the tracks and it became Loyalton. It had lumberyard, saloons, grocery and hardware stores, two depots, a stockyard (a place to load cattle to be sold), and coal bins along the railroad tracks. Before I was born, there was a hotel, a bank, and restaurant. It was great for the railroad town. Mrs. Hines owned the hotel, and my mom worked there while growing up. Of course, we all heard of railroad bums; they hopped the train for free and got food from whoever they could.

My parents were good farmers; they both worked the land. They used mostly tractors, as I remember. I can remember when we got the first tractor; it was an IHC F20. The folks had four of us kids. My brother Junior was a few years older than us three younger ones. He rode a horse four miles to school. He later joined the Navy for four years and married a girl from New Orleans. He ended up being a boilermaker. We three younger kids, Stella, Darrell, and I, were taken to school every day by car, in blizzards and muddy roads. There was no gravel, so deep ruts were common.

Vermont Township built a brick schoolhouse in 1921; we had three grades per teacher per room. I never went to a one-room schoolhouse. We had a high school upstairs along with bathrooms, and basketball court downstairs. So many games were played there. Kids from other towns came to high school in Loyalton. The teachers and some students boarded with families in town. By the time I got to high school, the school had lost ground, so we didn't have a high school. Because of this, I didn't attend high school. The Loyalton School closed in 1970; kids had to be bussed to bigger towns after that.

The first I remember, we didn't have electricity; we used kerosene lamps and gas lanterns for light, even for chores in the barn. In the late '30s, my parents put in a 32-volt light plant, which had many big batteries. We would then run an engine to charge the batteries. You could tell when the batteries were low because the lights would get dim. Afterwards, we got a 32-volt refrigerator. We were more fortunate than some in that respect; most people had iceboxes to store their food. To get ice for the iceboxes, my Uncle Ralph had an icehouse. It was a winter project to go to the Loyalton dam and use a big saw powered by a gas engine to cut blocks of ice. He would cut these blocks of ice in dimensions of 2x2x4 feet, and used big tongs to load it onto a truck. Then he drove to his home where he had an icehouse. There he unloaded the blocks and bed them with straw in between each layer. It would keep through the summer, and we even got to have ice cream that way.

We had an outside toilet and Sears & Roebuck catalogs for years. Later, my Uncle Stanley and Aunt Irene (around 1942) came from Milwaukee, Wisconsin to visit. He was a plumber and thought we should have better facilities, so he put a bathroom and running water in our house. How wonderful!

On washdays, we had to carry wood in to heat the water on the cook stove into a big boiler. Then we'd have to carry it to the washing machine, which we were fortunate to have. It had a wringer on it, also, and a gas engine that we hoped would start without going after my dad. Sometimes he would have to work on the engine before we started to wash. The clothes all got washed in the same water, starting with the whites and ending with the overalls. We thought the fancy washing machines nowadays wasted water.

In the late '40s, Harold Anderson, who lived in Wisconsin, had a car and asked two friends to head west with him to make some money. They headed into North Dakota to help harvest. The crops were green still, so they took off for South Dakota, arriving in Roscoe one rainy day. The bar was a good place for harvest information, and from there they headed for Onaka. However, the roads were muddy and slippery that way, so they turned east and made it to Loyalton. They then asked who needed help. They were sent to my Uncle Mike and Aunt Babe Lester's place.

Three guys in the field didn't take long to shock three quarters. They were making money. Uncle Mike sent them to my folks Phil and Zeldia Bukaske's, and there were two of us girls there. Anyway, they got the shocking done and my dad talked them into staying to thresh grain. By then, one of the guys, Floyd Hilden, had his eyes on my sister, Stella. They later married.

A few months went by, and one day I got a letter from Harold Anderson. So, I asked my dad if I could write back. He said that was okay, and we were married in the early '50s. He was my first sweetheart. There wasn't much work

in South Dakota at that time of year, so we went to Wisconsin and rented a house near his parents. Again, we had no running water or bathroom, but I was familiar with outhouses. Harold got a job with Swift Packing Plant, and a few guys from the area carpooled to South St. Paul to work. Some days I would walk through the woods to Harold's folk's house, and his mother and I would go to town for groceries. They had the crank telephone, which was new to me. In February, my folks found us a farm to rent, so we moved back to South Dakota. Again, we had no water or electricity. We lived there about two and half years, and then we moved to a farm south of Loyalton. It had electricity, running water, and a milking machine. Wonderful!

We got our start in Angus cows doing share cows. We had six milk cows and bought several more since we had a milk machine and five-gallon buckets that hung on the cows with straps. We separated the milk with a separator. We sold the cream and eggs to buy our groceries, clothes or anything else we needed at the store in Loyalton. We had sheep, pigs, chickens, and turkeys.

That farm was sold, and my folks had purchased a farm near town with better roads. They were remodeling the house when my dad had a stroke. He was in the hospital in Faulkton for 30 days and came home with no pills other than just aspirin. Three years later, he had another stroke and passed away. He was 58 year old. After that, Mom worked for Darrell (my brother) on the farm for a couple years. Then she got to work on a cook car for the construction of Highway 12 going through Roscoe. When that was finished, she worked as a cook in various cafes. She bought a mobile home and parked it at our farm, which we bought from my mom after renting for a year. At this time, we got a rotary telephone that was a party line phone. I think there were four families on a line, and you could hear all four rings and listen if you wanted to. Nothing was private then.

Mom passed away at almost 103 years old and was quite healthy. Harold and I had four children, Gary, Gail, Sandi and Rod; they all helped on the farm. We milked up to 55 cows and had sheep, pigs, and Angus cows. Gary is a DVM pathologist in research and has had many articles published. His wife Millie is an RN and has worked as a school nurse and with hospice. Gail is a licensed ordained minister. She also owns an independent office supplier and has authored a book. Her husband Raymond works for Chevron Phillips Chemical Plant. Sandi married Tom and they had three children. She passed away with cancer at the age of 36. Her husband did well raising their children. He later married a lovely wife and they have one son. Rod and his wife Coretta were brave enough to stay on the farm. They bought half of our land and raise Angus cows. Now they have around 400 cows to feed and have calves each year. Coretta helps on the farm and has worked different jobs off the farm, also.

We are so blessed our children all chose wonderful mates. We have a great family of blessing, ten grandchildren and 15 great-grandchildren. We worked hard and always went to church. If anyone didn't have a place to stay, our home was always open. We have kept several people for a few years 'til they found something better to do; we never charged a penny. After Harold and I retired from the farm, he worked for SD Statics and did crop adjusting.

Harold passed away suddenly in 2005. I still live in the home we were living in at the time, next to the farm. I worked hard all my life stacking hay, picking rocks, milking cows, running machinery, and butchering 200 chickens a year. I sold what we didn't need. We worked hard and enjoyed our family. It has been a good life and I know God has been with us and blessed us through the years.

I remember the rumble seat, the first moon landing, a president being assassinated, the twin towers being bombed, all kinds of phones (we now have cordless and cell phones), blizzards and huge snow banks as high as the barn (what fun), sledding, trips to Aberdeen and never eating 'til you got home. I remember our cousins coming for the evening and playing hide-and-seek outside in the dark. Yes, we three kids got into mischief. I am sure my kids never did, but who am I fooling?

Even though I never attended high school, I got my CNA license while working at a nursing home, and then earned a GED in the 1980s from Northern State College. My husband Harold was a great help to me preparing for the test. Harold and my Mom, Zeldia, were our living history books, and we miss their input so much. South Dakota has been a great place to live and raise a family with churches, Christian schools, and colleges.

Iceboxes and Home Remedies
By Juliana Malsom of Ipswich, South Dakota
Born 1934

I, Juliana (Baumstarck) Malsom, was born on a farm in Emmons county 18 miles east of Linton, North Dakota. I was the 12th child in a family of 14 children. We had no electricity, running water, or indoor bathroom. We had a crank, wooden-type phone with about 15 or 20 families that used the same line. The way you knew that the call was for you was that each household had a different ring. You heard everyone else's ring come in and you could listen in on everyone's conversations. Example of a ring would be that my parents ring had one short and two long rings.

Yes, everyone had an outhouse. It was very cold in the winter when we made those trips out there. We had a pot with a lid in the house to use at night or on very cold blizzard days. We had many big blizzards that lasted three or four days in a row. We had big hills all around the farm, and didn't have any snowplows. We would be snow bound for several months, so Dad would put his car by a neighbor's farm that was located next to a state highway. We would take the horses and sleigh about two miles to get to the car. We would then put the horses in the farmer's barn. From there, we would take the car and go into town. This happened only when really necessary.

I went to a country school with 30 some

Juliana is holding one horse by the reins

kids in grades one through eight. This was in a one-room school with one teacher. I had seven years of seven months of school per year. When I started school, I couldn't speak English; neither could the other students who were just starting school. English was our second language. We lived two miles from school, which was going across pastures and fields. This was a shortcut for us. We walked much of the time or went by horse and sleigh. Many times, I had to get up early enough so I could milk and then go to school. My favorite teacher was my sister, Kennegunda. She was my teacher for two years.

We had a battery-operated radio that was charged with some kind of a charger that was on the roof of the house. It needed wind to charge it, but of course, in the Dakotas we have lots of wind. Dad used the radio to listen to the news. We didn't have a record player.

For Saturday night baths, we used a big round washtub with everyone using the same water. The smallest kids were given the baths first and then on to the older ones. We did do sponge baths during the week. The washing machine I learned to wash with was a wooden machine that a wringer was attached to. First, we had to carry water into the house from the well with pails. Then, we had to heat it on the cook stove. When we were done washing all the clothes, we then had to carry out the dirty water.

I learned to sew my own clothes at a very young age on a foot pedal machine. Homemade toys were made of empty sewing machine thread spools. We would string the spools going through the hole in the center of them. We would also add empty spice cans to this. The string came from 50 or 100-pound flour sacks. We would also wash and sew the flour sacks together when they were empty and used these for blankets and dishtowels. People didn't have much money and didn't borrow money to buy these things.

We didn't go to movies or any kind of sporting events. We had lots of farm chores. We milked 18 cows by hand, and then we separated the cream off the milk as soon as we were done milking. We did this with a hand-crank handle. Much of the cream was used for cooking, baking, and making our own butter. The separated milk was fed to the pigs and our little chickens. We made our own cheese with the separated milk. The milk we drank

Juliana's dad in front by a smokehouse

was not separated. We just took it in the house the way it came from the cow.

We always hatched our own baby chicks by having a laying hen sit on a nest full of eggs for three weeks. We had these hens in our basement where we kept the coal for the stoves in a little room. We had two different kinds of stoves—a round one used just to heat the house and a flat rectangle-shaped one. The flat rectangle-shaped one had four shaped burner spots with a lid (round metal) on top to cook on. It had an oven with a gauge on the door to see when it was hot enough to bake. This stove also had a reservoir on one end were we kept water. The water in there would get warm enough to use to wash the dishes. When we got home from school with cold feet, we would sit by this stove and put our feet in the oven with our shoes on and then our feet would warm up real fast. We had to take the ashes out of both of these stoves every day. Under the stove burners, we would put dried cow chips or dry corncobs into the holes to heat up the stove so we could cook. During the summer, we would pick dry cow chips, (piles of manure) and save it to use later.

In the winter months, the milk cows were kept in the barn a lot of the time. Then when we cleaned the manure out of the barn, we would make a square bed with this manure. In the summer, you would use a shovel and make small squares of this manure and stack them to dry completely. These would be put in the basement to burn in the cook stove in the winter months.

Our icebox (refrigerator) was wooden box with one small corner lined with tin. The corner lined with tin was where the ice was placed. The ice was made in the winter. The men would chop the ice off the frozen stock dams or lakes. My parents built an ice cellar with clay, rock, and cement. That is where the ice was kept. They covered the ice chunks with straw so it would keep longer. This ice cellar is where we kept the ten-gallon cans of cream during the summer months. Once the cans were full, we would then sell the cream and eggs. This money was used to buy the little amount of groceries that we bought. We always had a big garden and a melon patch. We canned the vegetables and some meat. We butchered chickens and pigs for meat; because we raised meat, we hardly ever had to buy it.

Our playmates were our 66 first cousins and a few neighbor kids. The 66 cousins lived within a seven-mile radius. Some of the games we played were Fox and Goose, Ring Around the Rosie, and Hide and Seek. Some of the kids also went swimming in swimming holes or stock dams. I never did because I couldn't swim. We didn't get into too much mischief since we had to work or pray most of the time. We had many snakes and lizards. My favorite pet was our dog; he would always help me get the cows home from the pasture in the summer.

I worked in the grain, hay, and cornfields. I shocked grain bundles. When the grain was ready, I loaded the bundles on a big box on a four-wheel trailer that was hitched to two horses. I would put the bundles in the threshing machine. We also shocked corn and cleaned barns with a pitchfork.

We had many home remedies. One time when I was at the melon patch to pick some melons, a bug bit one of my fingers. It swelled up right away and really hurt. My mom butchered a big hen (chicken) and cut a hole in the chicken's butt. I had to put my finger in the warm guts, and I could feel it pulling out the poison. When the chicken got cold, we had a lot of barn pigeons, so one of my brothers would go and kill a pigeon, and I would put my finger in that bird until it got cold. We did this with several birds until my sore opened up and the poison came out. My finger healed nice and never left a scar. We used green drops for an upset stomach. Watkins liniment was used for sore muscles, etc. If you stepped on a rusty old nail, you would put black axle grease on and tie a rag around it. We never had gauze, band-aids, or first aid tape; you just used rags and string.

My parents never really told tales. They were both sick a lot when I was growing up. Mom told me when she was in labor giving birth to me the midwife told her that I was dead. She also said that if we didn't get a doctor and give him $32.00 cash, Mom would die, too. Dad didn't have a car or the money, but my Uncle Joe Vetter (Mom's brother) did. So Uncle Joe and Dad got a doctor. The least I can say is that we both lived. My dad and I would entertain at Farmers Union conventions by singing songs in four different languages.

My first and only love was my late husband, Valentine. I met my husband at my sister, Frances's wedding. I was the maid of honor, and my husband was one of the ushers for his Uncle Louis Baer, who was marrying my sister. It was love at first sight. In order to see each other, Valentine had to drive 105 miles one-way, all on gravel roads. There were no blacktop highways at that time. On almost every trip, Valentine made to North Dakota, one of his car headlights would get knocked out with gravel stoned from an oncoming car. We wrote a lot of letters at three cents a stamp. These were the good old days. We got married December 29, 1959 and I have lived in South Dakota ever since.

Life as a Resilient Farmer's Child
By Jane Curtis of Santa Fe, New Mexico
Born 1936

Farmer's children were resilient because their parents modeled resiliency. These children were relied on to carry part of the weight of the farm by doing "chores." Resiliency helped deal with the long, cold, and dark winters. Winters were very harsh when I was a child. I have been told how on the day I was born my father shoveled a mile and half of road so the doctor could get to the farm. Snow came as blizzards that piled snow too high for driving. When plowed, snow was as high as the windows of the school bus. One year when my sister and I attended a one-room school, my father came on foot to get us in a blizzard. He carried a rope and instructed us to hang on to the rope and never let go. She was behind him and I was behind her. We walked home that way, and the blizzard was so heavy I only remember seeing red the entire time.

Once I got a pair of wooden skis for Christmas with easy push-in footholds. Dad would pull me on the skis with the tractor, me being in the ditch holding a rope. When we lived on a different farm, it was not uncommon to hear of farmers who had gone out in a blizzard to take care of their animals (brought up to the barn for the storm) and never return to the house. They would be found in the barnyard or a few feet from the house, frozen, when the storm ended. Occasionally, someone's grandparent would die during the storm and the body would be put out on the porch to keep until the storm ended.

Mother hung blankets over the doors from the kitchen to other rooms during such a storm. She would cook to heat the kitchen. We rode out the storm in the kitchen during the day, but slept in our beds at night under a pile of covers. Mother must have worried when Dad left to feed the animals, but fortunately, he always came back.

After the storm, digging out began. After one long storm, I went out with my dad to shovel. We walked to the top of the snow that was piled in the yard. Dad walked around and said, "I think the car is here," and we dug down to the car. On top of this mound, I had to bend over to look into the attic window of a building we called the garage.

In the lower grades, my sister and I were close. We walked to school together and hurried home after school to be in time to listen to the Lone Ranger on the radio. Hi, Ho, Silver, Away! On Saturdays, if we cleaned our room in time we were allowed to listen to Let's Pretend before going to town.

Once we had new homemade bathing suits and Mother let us to go the creek east of the house with the admonishment to not get our suits muddy. She came frantically out to get us after a neighbor reported seeing us playing in the creek naked. Well, we were just minding Mother not to get our suits muddy! We took them off to assure they stayed clean. In the winter, I was persuaded by a playmate to go outside wearing my swimsuit hidden under my coat and take a dip in the hog cooler, a five-foot high barrel filled with water with an automatic water release at the bottom. It was very cold. I got caught as usual.

In the haymow, we made homes out of bales and paper dolls from Mother's discarded catalogs. We made corn babies out of immature corn from the field, with different colored hair (silk). We pretended to be tight ropewalkers on a wire that was in a grain bin, about eight to ten inches above the floor. We played with baby farm animals. We pretended to smoke by rolling up some brown weed seeds that looked like tobacco to us and lighting it. Sometimes we stole Mother's cigarette papers.

One year, an aunt built us a playhouse. The house was made of wood, approximately 8x10 in size, and situated in a large fenced-in gated yard. Trees boarded on the west, and the house was nestled there. Wire with vines covered the outside walls. The front door was a Dutch door. Inside there were cupboards, table and chairs, doll furniture, and a miniature cast iron wood-burning cook stove that actually worked like the full-sized ones. This had been a demonstration model used by wood stove salesmen. We had a sink and carried pails of water from the well like Mother did.

We had a baby brother, and used empty baby food jars to "can" small pea-shaped pods from a tree. Many hours were spent playing house. My doll was Baby Elaine; I loved her dearly. I left her out in the rain in her buggy and all of the paint peeled off of her face.

This was sad, but Mother pointed out that it was my fault for not bringing her inside. I still played with and loved her, the same. Once or twice, I played in town with our doctor's daughter who was also my age and had the same name as me. Her baby doll felt as soft as my baby brother's skin, but she would not let me hold her.

At one point, a playmate from a different neighborhood ran away from home. He came to our playhouse and I secretly sheltered him. I stole sparrow eggs from the nests and cooked them for him in the playhouse. He was only there for a day and a half before his parents took him home. He ran away because his mother had him on a diet and he was hungry. While the parents visited the day they took him home, my sister and I stole chicken eggs from the hen house to feed him.

My sister and I had seen the war movie Dr. Wassal, which had a beautiful nurse character. Acting out the movie as we interpreted it, we dug a foxhole by the sheep shed that was long and wide enough for us to get in and about three and a half feet deep. This was quite a feat for a couple of little girls! We stole Mother's best white sheets to make nurse outfits for ourselves. We talked about digging all the way to China. We played out the movie's war and romance.

That sheep shed offered hours of fun. Once we used the sparrow eggs, we stole from their nests to make our version of eggnog. We mixed the eggs with water from the stock tank and took it out to the neighboring field to offer some of that to Mr. Langner, who was plowing there. He was kind enough to keep a straight face as he pretend-sipped.

We usually stayed with our grandparents in Brookings for a week or two every summer. We were permitted to walk alone to the city swimming pool, and (importantly) carry the dime for our admission. At the pool, we learned to dog paddle and eventually to jump feet first off of the high dive. Occasionally, we went down the street to an older couple that we could visit with or without our grandmother. At night, we went to bed while it was still light and lay there listening to the unfamiliar sounds of cars driving by the house.

I began school in a large one-room school, which had students in every grade. I was the youngest in the school—the only first grader. I shared a desk with the one-second grader at the front of the room. We pretended to pull a bubble over us so the teacher could not hear us whispering. There I learned to read, add, and subtract. When the weather was bad, recess was inside the school building. We played Blind Man's Bluff. The older students would pick me up and carry me. When the 'blind man' came close to me, I would be handed to another student, so I never got caught.

This school served as a community hub. There would be occasional evening parties in the schoolhouse where the adults might put on a comedy skit, and/or dancing. The children accompanied their parents and had plenty of fun, too. We usually were carried to the car asleep because these parties ran late. Oil lamps lit the room and the toilet was outside.

The next year we moved, and my sister and I attended a smaller one-room school called Argo. The first years I possibly learned something, but don't remember learning anything academic. After a couple of years, our parents sent my older sister to a school in Brookings, leaving only six boys and one girl (me). I was a tomboy and played as hard

as the boys. World War II was the hot topic of the day, and since I had a German father, I had to be the Germans in our play. We had heard the term Guerilla Warfare mentioned by the adults, and we kids interpreted that to mean swinging in the trees. I fought like my version of a valiant German soldier. The rule was that the Germans always lost in the end. In the schoolyard was a pole that had chains hanging down. We would grab the handhold at the end of the chain and run a circle around the pole. The chain would swing us outward, lifting our feet off the ground. There was an outdoor toilet and a coal shed behind the school. The schoolroom was heated with a coal-burning stove in the middle of the room. We played Anti-Over over that shed, throwing a ball over the roof. The ball would roll back and forth down the roof and the team on the other side tried to catch the ball to win, and then they would throw it back. Come spring, we raked the schoolyard and had a picnic.

Our teachers were 16 years old, so we didn't do much except play. We would first recite the mandatory Pledge of Allegiance and the YCL pledge. Then our teacher would instruct us to open certain books on our desks in case the County Superintendent came to inspect. We took turns sitting at the window to watch for the county superintendent. If she drove in, we would all go to our desks and act like we were studying. One grade would be called up to the front of the room for a lesson while the superintendent was there.

The rest of our day was spent with games, recess, lunch, coloring chalk borders across the blackboards, and, for me, listening to the teacher talk about her boyfriend or complain about her acne—you know, girl talk. One of these teachers taught me how to play her saxophone.

The Ways of the Past
By Lois Hagemann of Madison, South
Dakota
Born 1935

My parents were Emil and Emma Beyer. Emil Beyer (1899-1987), son of Wilhelm and Augusta Beyer, was born on a farm five miles northwest of Ramona, South Dakota. He grew up in the Ramona area. Emma Schwartz

(1911-1969) was the daughter of Louise and Bernard Schwartz of Litchville, North Dakota. She came to Lake County from North Dakota when she was 18 years old. She worked for different families around the Ramona and Madison areas.

In those days, barn dances were popular for entertainment. Emil and his brothers played for barn dances. Emil and Emma met at a barn dance, and they were married in 1934. They lived on his dad's farm all their lives on the Beyer homestead. They had two children: me, born in 1935, and Roger, born in 1938. Roger lives on the family farm and is now retired.

On washday, they had a big old Maytag motor that run the washing machine. Boy was that loud! By the time that was roaring all day, you were about deaf.

Emil and his brother Oscar farmed with horses. That got pretty dangerous if the horses run away with the bundle wagon when they were threshing. Emil got an Avery tractor and a threshing machine in 1918 and had a threshing run. They would go and thresh a day for everyone in the crew so each one had feed, then go back and finish for everyone.

Emma and Virona, Oscar's wife, always cooked for the big threshing crew. Bright and early, you could hear them browning the chicken. They would bake fresh bread every day and pies, cakes, and cookies. Mom was a very good cook. Her raised doughnuts and bread would melt in your mouth. I can still smell that delicious aroma. We kids thought it was fun; of course, we weren't doing the work! Mom and Virona also helped in haying time and when they shocked oats.

In the "dirty thirties," the dust storms were so bad that it looked like midnight at noon. The dirt just piled up on the windowsills. The grasshoppers were so thick that if you stood in the shade of a building and looked up, it was like the whole sky was moving just like the clouds. Russian thistles were so thick in the ditches and fences that they had to burn them. They drifted across the road like snow, and one time a car got stuck in them. It was hard making a living

in those days. Emil worked for the WPA, as many other people did.

Emil and his brother Ted taught themselves how to cut hair. They were as good as any barber. They gave many haircuts. There were seven kids in my dad's family, and all of them were mischievous and got into a lot of trouble. However, they sure had a lot of fun. They made their own fun. One Sunday afternoon, a bunch of cousins were visiting. There was some new culverts sitting by the side of the road to be put in. Emil said the kids would stand in the culvert and run in it while the culvert rolled down the hill. One of the boys had a brand new suit on. It was his turn to run next, and (you guessed it!) he fell down and the culvert bolts just shredded his new suit. They all laughed when he crawled out of the culvert. My dad always said if they got to go along to town and his parents would buy them an orange that was really a treat.

Roger and I went to Smith School, which was a mile south of the farm. We walked most of the time, but one time Dad picked us up with the horse and buggy. Boy did the other kids look! We got a bicycle and were supposed to take turns riding home, but Roger would hop on it and ride all the way home. That made me angry. Another time walking home from school, Roger was teasing me again. I had the bad habit of throwing his cap when I got mad at him. I threw his new cap in water in the ditch. We just couldn't get it, so I said, "Let's get Dad's fishing pole." We took his new fishing poll and tried to reach it, but we couldn't. So they laid it across the road and

Lois's dad, Emil Beyer standing on a building almost covered with snow, with his sisters, Emma Bohlman and Erna Griebel

188

Lois's dad, Emil holding Lois and Roger

went to the other side. A car came along and ran over his new pole! Now we were really in trouble! We didn't get the cap either; it just sunk right into the water.

When Roger and I got home from school, our job was to go in the hog pen and pick up cobs for the cob box by the stove. But you'd better watch what you were picking up! Lots of times when I got home from school, I'd have to scrub the floor or whatever else needed to be done. My mom had rheumatoid arthritis, diabetes, and heart disease. She passed away when she was only 57 years old. My grandma made me a dress from a flour sack. It was a white dress with little red roses on it. I thought I looked pretty sharp!

Gordon's parents, Alfred (1891-1984) and Meta (1897-1959) Hagemann, had three girls and two boys. In the thirties, they got dried out and didn't get crops. They were hailed out three out of four years. In the early forties, it started raining again and a straight wind blew their barn down. They were having a big hailstorm, so Meta held a big pillow in front of a window. It sucked the pillow out and they never saw it again. They thought that there could have possibly been a tornado with the hailstorm that caused it to do this.

Gordon always told about his uncle taking a nap after dinner when they were threshing.

He would lean against a bale in his bib overalls with big, baggy pant legs. While he was sleeping, a mouse went up his pant leg, and a little while later, it came out of the other pant leg. Gordon's sister used to have him to nail blocks of wood onto her shoes to make "high heels" whenever they played house.

In the winter, they would take the horse and sleigh to the neighbors to play cards. They put straw on the floor, blankets over them, and a horse blanket over the top of them. (That very horse blanket is still in very good condition to this day.) They tipped over one time, and the oldest boy fell headfirst into the snow up to his waist. Thankfully, nobody got hurt.

Here is mine and Gordon's story: I went to a dance that I knew Gordon was going to. We had our first date there on May 21, 1954. We got engaged on July 4th, and married on October 28th, 1954. We will be married 60 years this fall, hopefully. We live on Gordon's parents' home place close to Winfred. We have five children, Connie Craig, Brenda, Barbara, and Jimmy. We have 15 grandchildren and 16 great-grandchildren. It is never boring. I always teased Gordon when he moved the outhouse. I said, "You didn't' have to move it a quarter mile west of the house in the trees!" It wasn't so bad going out there, but coming back was a swift trip with all the noises, etc. you could hear.

When our kids were little, that was trying

Craig and Connie Hagemann
Lois and Gordon's children

times. You never knew what they'd do next. Our two oldest kids, Connie and Craig, were out playing with the yard fence. They were three and two years old, respectively, at the time. They came in the house and Craig was all covered with dirt. All you could see was two little white eyeballs shining. I asked Connie, "Did you throw dirt on him?" "Yeah," she said, "He likes that." Another time they came in the house and said, "Mommy, we found some eggs for you!" They then dropped the container and they all cracked. We soon after realized that they were rotten eggs! Whew! One time it got pretty quiet, so I thought I'd better check on them. They were sitting on the floor in the entry with their feet together and had about 20 eggs busted. They were just playing around, smearing them with their hands. That's about in the same category as cleaning up a big bottle of Prell shampoo and a quart of liquid starch, which, by the way, I have also done! Temper, temper! I put a couple pies in the oven, and quickly dumped the trash in the barrel. When I came in, both pies were burning. The pre-heat button was on the front of the stove. I don't know which little angel hit that! I did a lot of crying in those days.

Every summer we'd load up the kids and go to the Black Hills and go camping and hiking. The kids really loved that. That made for a close-knit family. We got hailed out twice in 1976, and there was a drought. My dad was looking at our corn and said, "The corn didn't even look that bad in the thirties!" We had some close calls with tornadoes. One night one went over our place and tore tin off the hog barn, mangled the top of the windmill, threw bales into the trees, and blew shingles off the granary.

The winter of '68-'69 was a bad one. It snowed every day. If you went anywhere and was gone very long, your road would be blocked. The snow was so high it reached the high line. A pay loader worked on the road past us all day with snowplows and a Caterpillar. We took the kids on the snowmobile to a main road to catch the bus and went to Winfred to get the mail.

In 1997, we had a bad winter, too, with lots of snow. I remember our little granddaughter Mandi (age 5) being at our house. I was going to fold some laundry, and she asked if she could help. I told her that sure, she could help. We were talking, and I said, "You know our neighbors got stuck on our road in a snowstorm and walked to our farm. They stayed a couple days and slept in our bed." She paused and you could see that the wheels were turning in her mind. Then she said, "What side of the bed did you and Grandpa sleep on?" I told her, "No, Grandpa and I slept upstairs."

Our children, grandchildren, and great-grandchildren are so precious to us. We moved into Madison in 2006. Family—one of life's greatest blessings!

Just an Old Farmer
By Tom W. Jones of Webster, South Dakota
Born 1932

All the land in South Dakota that's farmable is the land now everyone buys and plants crops, mostly soybeans and corn. Not much wheat planted anymore. No pheasants anymore; all their habitat has been plowed up. Our land will be worn out from farming in a few more years.

I am just an old farmer, and don't know much. Just a farmer. But I know enough, that our land needs rebuilding, needs a rest also. That's my story. Just an old farmer.

Hearing the Call of God
By Erma Knutson of Webster, South Dakota

It was a Saturday morning and a day for cooking and cleaning. The husband and family still asleep, and I was hard at it. As I moved around the house working, I heard a faint voice saying, "Erma, Erma..."

Was it God trying to speak to me? I took good care of the family, was good to my folks and others, went to church every Sunday...

Then I heard it again. "Erma, Erma..." faintly toward the living room of our house. I thought it must be God. What could he want with me? I had paid my taxes, never cheated the milkman, was kind to my neighbors, and didn't swear.

Then I heard it again faintly, "Erma, Erma," as I followed it closely to our living room. And then I saw it: a phone slightly askew. When I got closer I picked up the receiver and it was my neighbor Minnie, as we had a party line together and the mystery was solved. She just wanted to use the phone. And that's my story of a party line phone.

Stepped on a Curled Up Snake
By Mae L. Palmer of Mansfield, South
Dakota
Born 1924

There were five of us South Dakota children. I was in the middle of four brothers. After a severe cold winter, we could hardly wait for warm weather so that we could go barefoot. Once I was in a pasture and climbed over the woven wire fence. I stepped down and landed on a curled up snake. It so scared me I ran all the way back home.

We walked to a one room school of all grades which was 1 ¾ miles away. Before and after school we had chores to do like feeding and milking the cows, gathering eggs, slopping the pigs with skim milk and ground feed, etc. We always had cows to milk. We turned the separator by hand to separate the cream from the milk. We sold the cream in town, which gave us money for flour, sugar, and other needs. Washing the separator was a dreaded job.

Dolly Never Knew the Saddle
By Edward A. Moeller of Redfield, South
Dakota
Born 1928

Back in 1934 when I was six years old, one of our mares had a colt. Because she had been tied up in the stall she was not able to clean the colt and she rejected her and would not care for her. I had to care for her and fed her with a bottle and cow's milk.

As she grew, I would ride her bareback without a bridle, but simply lead her with her mane. She never did have a saddle put on her. We lived a mile or so from school and each day I would ride her to school and then she would go back home. When school got out she would be there to take me home. She was a fine horse and her name was Dolly.

Another "good old days" story involved our family getting to town in the winter. My brothers and I would hook up the horses to the manure spreader and go down the mile and half road to the highway. My parents would follow in our tracks in the car. When we got to the highway and the neighbor's farm, we would put the horses in his barn and go

on to town. Upon our return, we'd hook up the horses and go home with our family car just following in the tracks that the manure spreader made. My dad didn't even have to steer!

Didn't Know Anyone Could Drive So Crooked
By Cheryl Vosburgh of Howard, South
Dakota
Born 1947

This is a story of me and my father. Back in the 1960s, I was a young girl going to high school at Ramona High School in Ramona, South Dakota. I was the oldest of four girls and one brother. Being the first born I was supposed to be "Douglas", but he came along three girls later and by then me and my dad had most of the work done!

I worked side by side with my dad doing fieldwork and farm chores. In high school in the spring, many boys got out early in the afternoon to go help their dads with the fieldwork, and many times I did too so I could help my dad.

I remember so clearly one day Dad and I were working in the fields side by side, he on the Farmall and me on my B John Deere. He was disking, I was dragging. He told me to first go back and forth till I had the whole field done, so I did. At the end of the day, he came over to my field and he was laughing pretty good: He said he didn't know anyone could drive so crooked!

I am so very glad I gave him that laugh as in the late 1970s my dad, at age 45, died of colon cancer. I will always be thankful that I spent all that time with him.

"9 Week Wonders"
By Jacqueline Lee of De Smet, South Dakota
Born 1934

I was born in a little town in eastern South Dakota during the Depression. My father worked for the WPA building roads and helped make a swimming pool. My grandfather operated a gas station. When the farmers came in for gas they had no money but he let them have gas. So it bankrupted him.

191

The dust storms were bad and mosquitoes so thick the trains couldn't move for the "slim" on the tracks. No rain so nothing grew. The government brought in stacks of hay for sale and the farmers would stand and cry, as they had no money!

When I was 2 we moved to California to find work. When I was 3 my parents divorced and Mom and I came back to SD. Mom worked out on several jobs and made about $1.50 a week. She had a chance to go to Chicago for work and I was left with Grandmother and Grandfather. My grandfather tried to farm for himself with horses and finally started to work for bigger farmers. I got to go to town a couple times during the summer. We had no car so I rode in a lumber wagon pulled by horses. There were steel tires on the wagon so it almost jolted you to death! Most of the farm houses were old and cold and of course with an outdoor privy. The holes were so big and I was a skinny little thing and always afraid I'd fall in.

We had a battery radio and I'd listen to Jack Armstrong and Lone Ranger. My grandfather was a prizefight fan so when a fight was scheduled we couldn't listen to the radio for a week for fear we'd run down the battery. We'd listen to Joe Lewis fight.

I went to country one-room schoolhouses. One had 3 students—me and 2 big boys. Next one had 16 boys and girls all in different grades and taught by the same teacher. My sister-in-law went to school to be a country schoolteacher. They went for 9 weeks. Everyone called them the "9 Week Wonders!"

We played Anti-I-Over, tag, and in the winter we went board riding pulled by a horse. I fell off a lot. We moved 5 times in my grade school years.

We always had a milk cow, chickens (for meat and eggs), and a lot of wild game. My gram made bread twice a week and everyone said it tasted like angel food cake.

I was married to a boy in my high school and he was drafted into the Korean War. I went to Chicago to find work. When he came home he had no desire to be a farmer so we stayed in Chicago and he worked for "Ma Bell." We lived 2 ½ blocks from Al Capone's "Old Hideout." Money was good and people were nice so we stayed for 5 years. But my husband couldn't hunt and fish whenever he wanted to, so we moved back to SD to the family farm and we raised sheep and calves. He had to work out so I learned to do a lot of farm chores, which I had never learned before: milking cows by hand, fixing a fence, putting up hay, and feeding stock, etc.

By this time we had 2 little girls who loved to ride horses and were a big help on the farm.

My husband died at 52 and I stayed on the farm and raised sheep for 27 years. I finally moved to the town where I was born.

I remember going to the movies for 12 cents and buying double dip ice cream cones for a nickel!

I'm glad I learned to do a lot of things. It makes life easier at my age of 79.

White Weasel in the Cow Line
By Lona Swanson of Gettysburg, South Dakota
Born 1941

I grew up northwest of Wessington Springs, SD, and rode my horses everywhere. One Saturday evening I went after the milk cows, and there was a white weasel in the cow line. It tried to climb up my horse's leg, but the horse finally stepped on it. I was going to get the cows home early, since it was a Saturday night, so I could go to town.

Lona riding Silver Belle in 1952

A Hospital Visit on New Year's Day
By Helen Gottsleben of Brookings, South Dakota
Born 1923

During World War II, I worked in the Personnel office of the FBI in Washington, DC. I lived in a large house on Rhode Island Avenue, with about 50 other women who were employed by different government agencies. It was New Year's Day. One of the girls said, "There is a guy from my home town that was wounded in action, and is now recuperating at Walter Reed Hospital. Let's go out and see him." We agreed it might be a good way to bring some cheer to the injured solider.

Entering the building, the medicinal odor, and the quietness gave me a dismal feeling. We whispered softly as we hurried down the vast corridors, trying to locate the ward where the young man was stationed. Finally, we found the right number, and looked in the large room.

There in the ward, we saw several men without arms, some without legs, several with bandages and casts covering their bodies. It was my first contact with the ravages of war, and the victims that had suffered severe injuries. My first instinct was to turn away and leave. I said a silent prayer that God would give me courage to at least smile at them, because strangely enough, they seemed to be smiling at us. Looking up from their beds, their faces seemed to radiate a happy greeting.

"Hello, where are you girls from? Nice of you to come visit us, we do not have many visitors." Instead of feeling sorry for them, we soon discovered they had a philosophy of their own. That was simply that they were alive. They would somehow work out their lives to again be productive citizens. Some of their comrades were not that lucky. They lay buried along with the rubble in Africa, Tunisia, Italy, and other battlefields in Europe. We lingered longer than we had planned, but they were so anxious to hear our chatter, about nothing really. Just being there seemed to brighten their day.

We went to bring cheer to the wounded soldiers, but in return, they helped cheer me. With a fiancé serving in the Army in Italy, and about 1600 miles from home in South Dakota, I was a lonely girl.

I will forever feel a debt of gratitude to those young men who helped cheer me on that New Year's Day in 1944. It was evident then, as it is today, if you extend your care and concern to your fellowman, it will somehow echo back to you.

Christmas Baby
By Shirley Kangas of Philip, South Dakota
Born 1940

I was working on Christmas Eve day at the hospital in Wessington Springs, South Dakota, as Director of Nurses, and was thinking of family members coming to our house that evening.

There would be 23 of us. I looked out my window and it was starting to snow, pretty fat flakes coming down so softly. The thought went through my mind, "I sure hope it doesn't turn into a blizzard." The snow began to come down faster and heavier. The phone rang and one of the nurses that was supposed to come for the 2 P.M. shift couldn't make it because of the weather. Found a replacement for her and then it was time to go home, get ready for Christmas with family.

The family arrived with packages and we were visiting, enjoying the occasion to be together. Our phone rang and I knew it was going to be the night nurse not being able to make it because of the weather. By now, the wind had come up and it was really nasty outside. No one else to call to come cover for her, so had to go in myself, even though I sure didn't want to.

Got to work, and after we had our report, the phone rang and it was a person that wanted an ambulance. He told us that a couple was on the way to the hospital because she was in labor. They got as far as his house and that is where they needed the ambulance to come get them. I called the ambulance and they started out in the blizzard. Soon they called me and said they couldn't make it the weather was just too bad. I told them I would call a snowplow to go in front of them, they consented to try. Wasn't long and the phone rang again and the ambulance said even with the snowplow in front of them, they just couldn't see and couldn't risk it.

I called the person back and told him that the ambulance wouldn't be coming and he said, "What do I do??" I gave him the name and phone number of the doctor and told him the doctor could tell them what to do and talk their way through the delivery. That was all we could do. I wished them "good luck" and said to call us when the baby was born, we would be praying for them.

We continued to do our regular work as the night wore on, but all we talked about and were wondering, what was happening at that house where a baby was going to be born on Christmas Eve or morning? About 5 A.M. or there about, the phone rang and they said they had a baby boy and everything went well. Mother and baby were doing fine. Those of us working were thinking what a miracle to have a baby born on Christmas morning in a blizzard!! I seemed so amazing to us that it worked out so well, didn't even want to think of what could have happened and the ending would have been much different.

Later we learned from the mother that she and her husband knew the storm was coming so they started for the hospital. But on the gravel roads the drifts were piling up faster and they got stuck. They could see a yard light in the distance and they decided it was the only thing for him to do was to walk there and get help. Of course this was in the late '70s or early '80s and no cell phones then. Her husband found a fence line and followed it to the farm and the farmer came to get her in his tractor. I asked her what she did while waiting, alone, in the car in labor. She said she just listened to the radio and kept praying the farmer would get there in time.

I went home that morning feeling blessed that I had known of the miracle and didn't feel badly about having to go to work on Christmas Eve and miss the family celebration. That family had a Christmas baby and what a story to tell him about his birth.

"If You Don't Want to Work, You Don't Eat"
By Jim Gloe of Estelline, South Dakota
Born 1933

I was born at Presho, SD, in 1933, one of 12 children. One of my sisters was a miscarriage. Dad's model T got stuck in a blizzard, and then he took horse and buggy to Presho with Mom in labor. When they got to Presho, she had a stillborn girl.

After the stock market crash in 1929 and grasshoppers ate everything, even Mom's clothing off the line, and livestock ate thistles; Mom and Dad had enough of drought and headed east to Sioux Falls, SD. Then when they got to Sioux Falls the model T caught on fire and burnt all the pictures and things they had saved from Germany. My oldest brother was born in the granary, converted into a house, in Presho, SD. He was a hefty 11 pounds.

When they arrived at Sioux Falls, Dad's cousin gave him a wagon for his horses that were towed behind the model T. They gave him a house to live in, and then Dad rented a farm and worked in the stone quarry by Rowena, SD. The stones are rare and shipped all over. The courthouse and post office were made out of that rock.

We never had electricity those days; we used kerosene and gas lamps. We never had modern conveniences like bathtubs, running water, or electric heat. We burned cow chips, coal, or cobs, in a Coleman heater. Mom had a cook stove that burned cobs or wood.

Us kids slept 3-4 in each bed. The girls had their own room. In the morning, the stove was only warm. Us kids upstairs in the un-insulated house kept each other warm. To warm up we had pillow fights or tag games.

We used to walk 3 miles to school in cold. Teachers came with horse and buggy. We never had sports or free meals in school. We did not date with girls. At graduation, you had to be with your parents. We had to be in bed by 10 pm.

We milked cows by hand. I cranked the separator to clean the milk to put in 5 and 10-gallon steel containers. The "wisk" we gave to the dog. That had cow hair, dirt, etc. in it. I and my brother used to squirt milk on each other from the cows. Cats would stand on their hind legs and we would squirt milk in their mouths. We used to put up hay by hand, and had a sling that pulled hay up into the loft, so cows had hay in winter. It was always a joy to go in the barn in winter with cows laying on the straw. We fed them hay before milking. It was my job to clean out manure from the gutter behind the cows after they were turned out.

Mom had a washer with a motor on it. One

time my little sister played with the gas and ended up in the hospital with severe burns.

Mom made all our clothes and canned meat and garden produce. Dad butchered our meat. We scalded the pig with hot water and skinned the hair off. Mom used to make headcheese. Pork hocks made good bean soup,

We didn't have fancy soap those days: lye, bicarbonate soda, and disinfectant did nice cleaning.

One time when I was young Mom had to get me away from a rattlesnake. They also killed a cow.

Us kids used to swim in the stone quarry where Dad worked. Once a horse fell in and it had to be rescued.

I remember when I was 6 years old; Dad and Mom had accordion music to dance to.

I remember one time when a doctor came to deliver my brother. When he left, he carried a briefcase and got some eggs or meat. Now you can't afford to have kids unless you have a lot of money.

I remember going to the grocery store when I was 7 years old. Bread was 9 cents a loaf, everything was cheap. We used to have a hand crank phone but we hardly ever used it.

We never used chemicals, only natural farming. We pulled weeds by hand. Corn was checked, so it could cross-cultivate. I used to walk behind a horse and drag until my legs got sore. I used a horse-drawn cultivator to cultivate corn. We picked corn by hand. Oats were cut with a binder and we shocked it. Then we had threshing crews and went to each other's farm. I remember my youth on the farm with pride and satisfaction.

My dad used to say, "If you don't want to work, you don't eat." Those were the days that made good people.

Teaching Pudwill School 1947-48
By Lorraine Kightlinger of Selby, South Dakota
Born 1928

This was my second year of teaching. I drove from Herreid, SD (living with my mother), and in the winter months I stayed at Julius & Rose Lang's, sharing a bed with Virginia, one of my students. What would people think about that today!

They were gracious hosts. I enjoyed my time there. There were 9 students from 4 families: Seibels, Pudwill, Lang & Lila Berreth, who came mid-term.

I heated the school with lignite coal and wood; it was the teacher's duty to have the school warm. A coal bin in the basement stored wood & coal, and ashes had to be carried outside each day. The school term was 8 months and my salary $140.00 a month. Students brought their own lunches, some in a syrup pail. I brought water to be put in a crock water cooler. There were a few cups! There were 2 outdoor toilets, but I can't remember toilet paper?

Recess & lunchtime were the highlights of the day: kittenball, anti-I-over, pump, pump pull away, hide & seek, tag, hopscotch, fox & goose, snow angels, etc. We had exercise and fun.

Also, we would drown out gophers by pouring water in their hole and waiting. The older boys had a bat or two and killed them while the rest stood by and watched—strange no one was hit on the head. Teachers wore dresses, but I was young and enjoyed all games. Playing kittenball, I hit the ball and running to 1st base I stumbled and my dress flew up way tooooo high!

There were Valentine & Halloween parties (students made their own boxes and costumes) and the Christmas Program at night was special. The lighting was gas/kerosene lanterns. We made the stage and dressing room by stringing wire and putting up white sheets. No piano or microphone. We had songs, poems, and skits (usually funny). Santa (Maynard Ackerman) came to hand out presents and goodies. Parents brought lunch; it was a fun & entertaining. Although getting props and outfits was a chore.

The YCL (Young Citizens League) was popular. There was competition in Declam, Math, and Spelling. Students made crafts, drawings, colored pictures, woodwork, etc. to be judged. They would receive a blue, red, or white ribbon. Marion Pudwill did well in Math, Virginia Lang in Declam (there may have been others). YCL duties for students included putting out the flag each day, cleaning erasers, washing blackboards, sweeping the floor (we used sweeping compound), straightening desks, sweeping toilets, hanging up clothes in the cloak room, and dusting. Friday afternoons we did Art & Penmanship.

Testing: every 6 weeks tests were sent to the school by the County Superintendent (Fred Renner). I had a Teacher's Manual to follow. Grade 8 was the BIG TEST; only the teacher and 8th graders were in school (1 day) to take tests, which had to be mailed to the County Superintendent to be corrected. Students waited patiently for results. The County Superintendent would visit schools twice a year, unannounced, and he would just walk into school. I don't remember an evaluation, maybe one was sent to the School Board.

Library: books were old and very limited. But there was a floating library, and 12 - 15 books would arrive and we could keep these books for 6 weeks, and then pass them to another school. Students enjoyed this very much.

On Rally Day schools were divided into districts which would meet and compete for 1st, 2nd, and 3rd in the high jump, sack race, running, relay race, 3-legged race, chinning, etc. We then would meet in Mound City for the county competition.

While at Reierson School (1949-50), which was 9 miles northwest of Herreid, it was bad winter and they blocked the roads. Four friends and myself hired a plan from Mobridge (pilot, Tom Kelly). He took each of us to our school, landing in a field close to the school. I do not remember the cost.

On the last day of school, we had a family picnic; potluck, wiener and marshmallow roast, and played games. Kittenball was the main event.

I started teaching December 1946 (teacher got sick), took a 6-week course at Aberdeen Normal (now NSC) and a few years later we were required to take a 2-year course to become certified. I decided not to and went to work for Fred Lang as Deputy County Auditor in Campbell County.

One of my students asked me to write memories of the school he attended. I wrote this in October 2010 and did not know that I would be submitting it to Hometown Memories,

Farm Girl, Farmer's Wife
By Ramona Kirkeby of Vienna, South Dakota
Born 1928

There is an old house, which has fallen down and is almost completely into the old cellar. The house is south and east of Conde, SD. That is where I was born 85 years ago, the 4th daughter of Pete and Gladys Bymers. One brother was born there and then Mom and Dad moved to a farm nearer to Turton where 2 more brothers were born and finally our baby sister was born in a delivery house in Conde. In 1941 Dad bought a farm, one section of land for $6,000, and all 10 of us moved into a 3 bedroom house—no running water, no bathroom, no basement.

While we lived near Turton we drove a horse and buggy, wagon, or cutter to a country school 2 miles away by road or about 1 ½ miles when we could cut across the school section. I went 7 years to that school and one year (my 8th grade) to the country school across the road from our new farm. Then four years at high school in Raymond, SD and then 12 weeks of college allowed me to get a 2nd grade teaching certificate, which qualified me to teach country school, all this by the age of 17. I attended college during summers and earned a 1st grade certificate and taught a total of 11 years.

I married Lee Kirkeby at age 21 and moved to the farm that he owned and I still own and operate with the help of my son and grandson. Thus I have been a farm girl, a farmer's wife, and indeed a farmer all of my life.

Ramona and her brothers and sisters

Country life, and living in this old country home, has been most satisfying for me. My family also consists of 2 daughters and 7 grandsons.

"Ah, But I Can Milk a Cow"
By Thelma Norris Hepper of Gettysburg,
South Dakota
Born 1927

I grew up in a large family on a farm 4 1/2 miles south of Lebanon, SD, during the '30s and '40s. Since the 5 girls were older than the 4 boys, we learned to work outdoors as well as do housework.

I was about 8 years old that pleasant summer evening when I went to the barn where my mother and sister were milking the cows. We had several farm cats who always showed up at milking time for their "treat." As I watched my sister aim an occasional stream of milk into the mouth of a waiting cat, it looked like such fun that I declared to my Mom, "I want to learn to milk."

To which she replied, "No you don't. You just think you do."

"I really do," I replied, "I want to learn how to milk."

"Alright," was her answer. "Go to the house and get a gallon Karo syrup pail. But you'll be sorry."

"No I won't," I replied. Soon I returned with the pail and my mother taught me to sit on a one-legged stool and the rudiments of milking. At first, I was only allowed to "strip" or finish milking the tamest cows but soon I was a regular member of the family milking team.

Of course, the novelty wore off. Milking cows happened twice daily—not just on pleasant summer evenings. I found out that Mom was right about "being sorry." On those COLD winter mornings when we went to the barn with no light but that of a kerosene lantern, we'd get a cow up on her feet and then try to position her so that our feet would be in the warm spot where she had been lying.

In the summer, there were swarms of flies although Watkins fly spray helped a lot with them. The flies didn't all die immediately so the buzzing continued and often a dying fly would land on you or in the pail of milk. It was hot sweaty work and there was that occasional ornery cow who tried to get her foot in the pail or swat you with her nasty tail.

Looking back, the thing I remember most about milking was the time I spent with my dad. My fondest memories are of singing. He taught me the songs of the World War I era and the simple songs from his boyhood in England. These memories become dearer as time goes by and I'm not sorry I learned how to milk.

Milking cows is like riding a bicycle or using a typewriter: You never really forget how to do it although you lose proficiency.

These days when I see young people doing seemingly impossible things on a computer or playing games, texting, or taking pictures with a small cell phone, I feel very inadequate. That's when I need to square my shoulders, take a deep breath, and remind myself, "Ah, but I can milk a cow!"

Our neighborhood was a miniature United Nations. My father had come to America as a young man from England. A mile to the south of our farm was the Carlson brothers, Albion and Gunner, only a few years out of Sweden. One mile east of the schoolhouse was the Allerdings family—the parents and 2 oldest children were born in Russia. One-half mile north of them lived Chris Erickson from Denmark. I can still hear him saying, "By Gott, Wick," as he did in each conversation with my dad, Victor Norris. A mile and a half north of the school were the Gus Schackels, both born in Germany. A mile west of our farm lived the Van Bockels, both parents were raised in Holland. Next to them were the Umikers from Switzerland. Just north of the schoolhouse lived Waldo Jones and family. He was a hillbilly from the Ozarks. About the only "true blue" Yankee was my Uncle Sam Crane whose ancestry on both sides had been in this country back to and before the Revolutionary War.

I only recall one incident and that was probably my fault as I was markedly proud of my English heritage. World War II was raging in Europe for some time and Hitler had overrun much of Europe.

England had been holding out almost alone for nearly 2 years and things were looking pretty bleak for them. One day at school, one of the Van Bockels teased me about the eminent downfall of England. It hurt my feelings and I repeated it at home.

I remember Dad saying, "You might remind him that Holland fell in 7 days."

There was a big party in the gym of Gettysburg High School where each one of us freshmen were told to come dressed as a particular character and had to perform in front of everyone. I had to impersonate Sonja Heini, a popular blond ice skater, and was feeling quite pleased with my short, chic red and white outfit and white boots—until they strapped roller skates on those white boots and gave me a push towards the center of the gym. I'd never been on skates before so it was just luck that kept me on my feet. They finally told me I could quit, but I couldn't get back to the bench!

My roommates were 2 sophomore girls, Alice Marie Lillibridge and Mary Lee Natchkee. They befriended me and took me with them everywhere.

I've always been sorry I didn't buckle down that first year and really concentrate on music, but I didn't. I'd wanted a trombone (there were a couple of cute boys in the trombone section) but Dad and Mr. Schuster decided I'd have a clarinet. I learned the very basics and discovered I could listen to the girl beside me and play by ear. I was the only one of my family who was given the opportunity to learn to play a band instrument and I blew it! No pun intended!' I've always regretted it.

In those days before Social Security, quite a few elderly people would rent out a room to country kids for something like $4 or $5 a month. Grandma Bramblee's house was located just south of a blacksmith shop, which was still operating in 1941. I used to see Mr. Stocker working at his forge as I walked past after school.

The window of our bedroom looked out on that shop (now museum). For some reason, the shade on the window was about a foot too short. One evening, I came home from band practice, reached up and pulled on the light, then unbuttoned my skirt, when I saw an eye—one single eye—looking in the window. I thought my friends were playing a joke, but there was something sinister about that eye! So I shut off the light. Soon I heard the rustling of leaves. From the light of the streetlight across the street, the silhouette of a boy was plainly visible as he ran from the alley. Only a few minutes later Alice and Mary Lee came in. After they heard my story, we stuffed a pillow in the window. That was my only experience with a "peeping Tom" but once was enough!

The most memorable event of my freshman year was Dec. 7—the bombing of Pearl Harbor.

The world forever changed on that day and it affected all of us profoundly. Immediately cousins and neighbor boys started leaving for service. Dad encouraged us to write to them as he'd been in the first World War and knew how nice it was to receive letters from home.

Early in March, we had a 3-day blizzard. It began on Wednesday and school was cancelled Thursday and Friday. There was about a 2-foot space next to the buildings where we could walk. Some of the business people had been marooned in their stores and they opened their doors and invited us in. There was a 2-bit bowling alley on the south side of the street. That proprietor let us bowl for free and when he did get a customer, we manually set pins for him. That was my only experience as a pinsetter. By Saturday, people started breaking out. We got word that a train with a snowplow was coming through on Sunday. I think half of the town's population made their way to the railroad tracks on the north side of town to see it. What a sight! It created a blizzard of its own for at least 1/2 block either side of the track as it broke through the big drifts.

My sophomore year was different. Dad found me a place where I could work for my room and board. It was with the Beulah and Tellof Hockesson family. Beulah had had surgery and needed help. My job was to get Tellof's breakfast and get him off to work by 7:00. Then I got Gerry, Norma, and Peggy off to school. Beulah and little Mary Lou were usually still in bed when we left. Norma, a 5th grader, quickly became my favorite.

I have fond memories of Beulah playing the piano and the girls, especially little Mary Lou, singing. But by Christmas time, Beulah was fully recovered and didn't need my help anymore. So Dad found me another place—with Frank and Myra Von Wald and their new baby Larry. One evening I didn't have time to do dishes before I had to leave for band. In the morning, I was shocked to see the supper dishes waiting for me. That was unheard of in my family. However, Frank was a good natured guy and he helped me do dishes and we got him to work on time.

One spring, a beautiful afternoon close to the end of the school year, I was walking to school with Alice Marie and Mary Lee when 3 guys from Agar came along. They were skipping school and talked us into going with them to spend the afternoon at the river. They had a coupe with a rumble seat, which looked like fun so off we went. The first couple of hours went by quickly and pleasantly. Then someone found an old rusty butcher knife stuck in the trunk of a tree. Mary Lee and her Agar friend, a smart-alecky kid named "Gabby" Merritt, weren't getting along too well by that time. They got to fooling around with the knife and jabbing at each other. Mary Lee got stuck in one thigh—enough to break the skin and bleed a bit. Soon after that, we went back to town. I think all of us were wishing we hadn't gone. I know I was. Without written excuses from our parents, we would need ADMITS from the principal for our afternoon classes the next day. That meant a certain percentage would be deducted from those grades. I was afraid it would keep me from the honor roll. The other two were afraid it would land them on the published failing list.

The next morning Alice Marie wasn't in school at all. Mary Lee and I concocted several stories to tell the principal but just before noon Mary came to me and said she was running a temperature and she'd better go to the doctor that afternoon. That left me to face Mr. Mogck alone. But Alice Marie came after lunch. She'd just overslept. We went to the office. Mr. Mogck (I can still see him) swiveled around in his chair and asked, "What can I do for you ladies?" All the excuses just evaporated and I said, "I guess we need ADMITS." He grinned and said he'd been expecting us! I can't remember if my friends showed up on the failing list or not, but I was greatly relieved to make the honor roll! That was the only time I ever skipped school. It definitely wasn't worth it!

Life in the Early Years: South Dakota
Ronald D. Cornell of Aberdeen, South
Dakota
Born 1928

I was born April 27, 1928 in Newark, South Dakota located on North Dakota border

Ronald's first car a 1930 Ford Model A Towing Coupe

(11 miles north of Britton, S.D.

I recall the dirty thirties—the dust bowl years. It was so bad that when the wind would blow, clouds of grasshoppers would cover the sky, thinking rain was coming.

I recall being in a screened outdoor building we used for spending times for relaxation. I was about 7 yrs. old (1935) and was in this building when a dust storm came up. My father had to tie a rope to our house and pull in along to reach the building to rescue me. The visibility was zero.

My grandparents lived on a farm about one mile south of town and 3 miles west. On occasions when we would drive out there, the sand would drift so bad along fence lines and across the dirt road, we would have stop and they would shovel sand so we could continue trip.

Newark had all the advantages needed, electricity, indoor water, and plumbing. We moved to Bath, S.D. (six miles east of Aberdeen, SD on Dec 22, 1937. My father was a Milwaukee Road station agent and telegrapher. They had closed the Newark station and Bath was available for transfer. Christmas was not very pleasant that year. Bath had no electricity and the depot we

Ronald's 1948 Chevy Coupe

199

moved into had no water. Living conditions were very hard. We had to haul water from neighbors across street. Saturday night baths were shared by we 3 kids but life was really homey. My family did lots of things together. We played cards and games made popcorn balls, etc. Finally, we got a radio in 1939 and listened to lots of music and suspense shows such as Hit Parade Weekly, Jack Benny, Burns Allen, Red Skelton, and others. War years 1941-1945 were tough. There was lots of rationing and it was hard to get certain items. (Cigarettes, coffee, sugar, and many more items.)

A tornado wiped out most of our small town on June 17, 1944 at 5:05 PM. Two people were killed (Mr. and Mrs. John Nelson) and two injured. Our living quarters were on second floor and most of it was ripped off and scattered. Thank God, we had just left town heading to Aberdeen. It rained so hard we had to stop at Bath Corner (1 mile away). When the rain stopped (all over in matter of minutes). We proceeded on to Aberdeen not knowing a tornado had hit our town. Somehow, word was gotten to us a couple hours later.

A farmstead just one-half north of Bath was completely wiped out. Every building on the place was gone. The Fritz family somehow got to the basement and the father, mother, and six kids all survived. The house blew away completely.

In 1945, electricity finally reached Bath and things started looking more alive again.

So Much for Revenge
By Norm Sparby of Napa, California
Born 1929

I grew up on a farm in eastern South Dakota. I was the youngest of eight children. My next oldest brother was 7-8 years older than I. We would have our arguments and disagreements as brother usually do. I think I was about 8-9 years old and we had a fight about something, I don't remember what it was about. Him being older and bigger than me, I didn't have much chance of winning the fight.

My devious little mind set in motion a plan to get even with him. He seemed to be the first one to the mailbox almost every day. Getting mail was always a big event back then in the late '30s, early '40s. We had to walk down to the road that ran passed our place to the mailbox. We had to cross a ditch, which was a couple of feet deep. As luck would have it this day, the ditch was about half-full of water, normally we could jump over. I found board long enough to reach across the ditch, and made sure the board was not the sturdiest. I put the board the across the ditch and went on my merry way, think, "I got him this time." Not so!

This day my Mother was the one to go for the mail, seeing the "nice" board someone had put across the ditch meant she wouldn't have to jump over the water! I wasn't there to see what happened but I sure heard about it. Seems Mom had got half way across when the board gave out and into the drink, she went. Needless to say, she was not happy about that. I fessed up to putting the board across the ditch. All I got was a scolding, while my brother stood there snickering. So much for revenge.

Making Hay before Modern Mechanization
By Margaret McPeek of Clark, South Dakota
Born 1917
Submitted by her daughter, Lois Peterson

Before hay was baled into large round bales, it was much more labor intensive to put up. My father cut hay with a horse-drawn mower, a 5 or 6-foot long sickle bar mounted between a set of wheels with the driver sitting on a seat above the bar. The sickle bar was lined with about 50 triangular shaped metal sickles, which needed frequent sharpening and sometimes replacement if they broke. Think about how many times you had to circle a field with a 5-foot mower to finish the job!

Once the hay was cut, it had to be rolled into rows with another horse-drawn machine, a rake, so that it could be picked up with a hay bucker and taken to the stacker where it was stacked into large stacks of hay. The rake had a row of metal tines that caught the cut hay as the rake was pulled over the ground. The driver sat on a seat above the tines and raised them at the appropriate time to create rows of hay across the field. After the hay "cured" for a day or two, it was ready to be stacked. First, the hay was picked up by a bucker pulled by a team of horses, one on either end of a low, 2-wheel frame with wooden teeth that picked up the hay. A full load of hay was taken to the stacker to make the actual haystack. The stacker was a wooden frame set on the spot where a stack was to be made. It had a platform of long wooden tines that the hay was put on, and then lifted to the top of the stack. The driver of the bucker had to carefully place the hay on the stacker, going between the wooden tines and keeping it level for easier lifting to the top. My mother, not being a very big person, could sure whip that bucker around. She had just enough weight to help control the bucker, and the horses knew to obey her commands. Well-trained horses were essential for this task. Once the bucker placed the hay on the stacker a team of horses pulled the platform to the top of the stack of hay where my father was waiting to make sure it was placed properly to keep snow and rain from the center of the stack so it would not rot.

In the 1930s during the drought, farmers cut and stacked Russian Thistles. They grew everywhere, were big, and were full of stickers. They did not have much food value but the cattle needed something to eat.

Saturday Night Baths and Daily Chores
By Julie Brinkman of Ramona, South Dakota
Born 1949

I know people of our generation, especially farm families, remember the Saturday night baths. We did not have indoor plumbing or running water like most of the farms around us. There were seven of us in the family, Mom, Dad, three boys, and two girls. We had a canvas bathtub that served all of us on Saturday night.

The copper boiler was filled by Dad and the boys and heated to almost boiling. In the summer, the tub was outside by the hand pump, in the winter we had to be more careful not to splash because the tub was in the living room by the furnace grate. Me being the youngest got to be first. I suppose Mom figured I was the least dirty. We then went up the line with Mom and Dad being the last to use the water. In the summer when the boys worked in the fields with Dad, the water was pretty dirty by the time it got to Dad. But at least you got some of the dirt washed off. We never thought anything of using the same water. We just thought it felt good to have a bath.

Mom had a routine that I pretty much stick to today. Monday was washday. The copper boiler was filled and put on to boil, the wringer wash machine and rinse tub were set up in the back porch and the first load was put in. The first load was always white clothes because you only got one washer full of water for all the clothes. Mom always put bluing in the rinse water to brighten the clothes. The work clothes were always the last load. Every load was hung on the line to dry. In the winter, they were still hung on the line to freeze dry then brought into the house to hang and finish drying.

Tuesday was always ironing day. If it was winter the clothes that you brought in from outside were just rolled up and put in a plastic bag ready for ironing. In the summer when they were dry, we had an old seven-up bottle that had a sprinkler head stuffed into the top to sprinkle the clothes so they were damp. No steam iron here.

Wednesday was house cleaning. We swept all the floors and did a "little" dusting. Because Saturday was the day we went from top to bottom.

Thursday was clean up the odd jobs, mow the yard tend the garden etc.

Friday was gearing up for the weekend. Mom started baking bread, making scones with fresh butter, yum. She made cakes and cookies, because from Saturday through Sunday we always had a houseful of company.

Saturday was the major cleaning day. It was always my job to dust the upstairs bannister. How I hated all those fancy carved spindles. Floors were scrubbed and waxed, furniture polished and a fresh tablecloth put on.

Sunday was a day of rest. But mom always wound up cooking for friends and relatives that came to visit. It was a day to enjoy family.

A Day of Excitement
By Thorine "Terry" Weiland of Madison,
South Dakota
Born 1928

When sorting my parent's belonging for auction, I found a box of old books in storage. What a surprise to discover an old book of mine. It was a diary of sorts—plans and times set for my daily routine. I was 13 years old and in the 8th grade at the Colton, SD School.

I opened the page to December 7, 1941. Written in my words—"Pearl Harbor was bombed by the Japanese. SNEAKING RATS! The Land of the Rising Sun will rise no more!" I was sad and angry that such a bad thing could happen. Growing up during the war years left an impression that has been with me all my life.

August 14, 1945, little did I realize what a great event that would take place that day! Looking forward to my senior year in high school, my sister Betty was also excited about her coming freshman year. We talked our mother into letting us go to Sioux Falls, SD to shop for school clothes. We promised our parents we would return home after shopping. My cousin Urma Sando drove a Blue Model T Ford and the three of us headed for the big city of Sioux Falls.

I remember we parked the car at a relative's home and then walked a few blocks to Phillips Avenue to shop. During that time breaking news came over the radio (August 14, 1945) President Truman announced, "Japan has surrendered unconditionally"—ending World War II.

Phillips Avenue turned into a parade of great celebration. The sights and sounds still linger in my memories. At the Sioux Falls Air Base, there were stationed 40,000 of the military we called, "G.I.'s" (Government Issue) and no one could have stopped them as they turned downtown Sioux Falls upside down! They packed the cars, sat on top, on the fenders driving down Phillips Avenue singing with great joy! Some climbed on top of buildings and danced. The streets were so crowded it was hard to move about.

We three young girls were taken in by all the excitement as the G.I.'s ran from the parade to the side streets and kissed the girls. We received a lot of hugs and kisses. Remember the old saying, "Sweet sixteen and never been kissed?" Well, on August 5th, I had just turned it, but every lady standing on the street received a big hug and kiss.

To our surprise, two military police with M.P. on their armbands came by and said, "We will be with you girls if you don't mind." "Sure," we said.

A bar was moved out of the Cataract Hotel and set up outside on the street. There was a lot of drinking on the parade route cheering and singing war songs! The G.I.'s exchanged their uniforms with the civilians with compliance.

The celebration lasted all day, into the night and early morning to the next day. We could not get to our car or to telephone our parents that we were safe. My grandfather, Peter Gran, worked at the military air base as a custodian. He later told us when the soldiers checked in at the early dawn the next day, they had to strip off all the civilian clothes they had worn, put in a pile, and report for duty. Grandpa Pete said in his Norwegian brog, "Ya, it sure vass funny to see the major running around naked!"

Thorine "Terry" Mellom, Urma Sando, and Doris Sandel

Grandpa Pete was a widower for many years. He married again even though his second wife would disagree on many subjects. Grandma did not hesitate to make known that she did not approve of all the celebration activities on V.J. Day! She said, "Instead of all that crazy stuff, everyone should have filled the churches and thanked God that the war was over."

I don't think anyone could have stopped the spontaneous energy that happen on V.J.

Day! I have no doubt there were plenty of heartfelt prayers of thanksgiving for the end of the war.

For me, I was so happy our uncles, brothers, boyfriends, sweethearts, husband, sons, and daughters were coming home.

As teenagers full of excitement of the day, we sang songs going home, songs like, *When the lights come on again all over the world* and *Rain and Snow is all that will Fall from the Sky Above*, and *A Kiss won't Mean Goodbye, but Hello TO LOVE*. Peace at last to a war weary world—V.J. DAY—August 15, 1945. Victory over Japan

P.S. We were given a lot of G.I. hats and neckties that V.J. Day after the hugs and kisses of course!

A High School Sweetheart and A '62 Chevy Nova
By Arlo Remmers of Watertown, South Dakota
Born 1953

I was raised on a farm in northeastern South Dakota. In high school, I was involved with athletics and I could not ride the school bus so my Dad bought me a car. To most fifteen-year-old boys getting your first car is a very huge deal. I was no different. When Dad told me that we would go car shopping on Saturday, I was ecstatic and couldn't wait for three days to pass. As my father and I pulled into the local used car dealership, I spotted a 1962 Chevy Nova instantly. Now I can't recall any of the other cars that were on that lot, as my eyes were fixed totally on that Nova. After what seemed an eternity of dickering over the price tag, my Dad and the salesman came to an agreement and we were on our way home with my most prized possession.

That car had bucket seats and four on the floor with an eight-track tape player under the dash. I couldn't wait to get over to my girlfriend's house to show her my pride and joy. Gas was 19 cents a gallon and we cruised until the tires fell off, or it would seem, usually with Hank Williams, Jr. or Elvis blaring out of those speakers.

I truly loved that machine, as I think that I washed it more than I ever washed my own hands. I was so proud of that Chevy that I often wondered if my high school sweetheart

stuck with me just because of the car. She was so pretty that I sometimes wondered if she was out of my league, but I didn't care as long as I had that '62 Nova. While the other kids in school were working on their cars by souping them up and so forth, I never changed a thing on it because I loved it just as it was. I babied that car with every spare moment of my time. I never raced it or abused it during the tough South Dakota winters. My girlfriend's parents never worried about their daughter while she was with me, as they knew that she would be safe as long as we were in that car.

The next spring I was driving down a country road with my girl at my side when she began tickling me. Now the spring thaw was over and there was water everywhere. We hit the ditch and as luck would have it, there was a dry spot about ten feet wide and we hit it just right. With water all around us we laughed until our sides hurt. When the laughter was over I carefully backed the car onto the road again and got to check my baby for any damage. Knowing my feelings for that car, my girlfriend thought that I would be very mad at her. So did I, but for some reason, anger never crossed my mind.

Later I found out that she didn't date me just because of that car, as I traded it for a 1966 Ford Galaxi 500 a couple of years later. I have often wondered just what ever happened to that Nova. We occasionally still laugh at that tickling incident, as that high school sweetheart and I are about to celebrate 42 years of wedded bliss. The lesson that I learned was that no possession that I ever had, or have or ever will have, can compare to that high school sweetheart.

Storm Clouds
By Lisa M. Droz of Rapid City, South Dakota
Born 1959

Barefoot Days! Sticky, Muggy, Dog Days of Summer! Twenty-five miles from the nearest public pool! However, only ten minutes away was true paradise wrapped up in a small, manmade dam called Rose Hill Lake in Hand County, South Dakota. This oasis provided the entire community a nightly respite from the daily chores, constant boredom, and above all the wretched heat of July out on the prairie.

A large family in a small, two-bedroom home with no air-conditioning, no running water, and no basement underneath for refuge set the stage for the worst storm this little 10 year-old girl ever witnessed. The fourth daughter born into a family of six children, she learned early on, that life can be a challenge and in order to be successful on the farm everyone needed to pitch in and do their part. She had previously witnessed many blizzards, hailstorms, and wicked storm clouds but nothing prepared her or her family for the famous Twister of 1967.

That particular workday in July involved stacking wagonloads of heavy, square alfalfa bales to feed the 150 sheep for the winter days ahead. It was a sticky, muggy, day that made a person sweat just standing still. The reward, of course, would be the evening spent at the swimming hole and was eagerly awaited by all of the children.

Rose Hill Dam became a spot for annual school picnics, family reunions, church gatherings, and 4-H activities. It had stellar cottonwood, ash, and poplar trees below the dam itself that shaded the perfect spot for picnics, complete with a large slide, swings, horseshoes, and a creek for exploring. Lots of hiking, horseback riding, fishing, and camping took place all summer as well. Out on the lake was a boat dock and not too far from shore was a sturdy, manmade square diving and sunbathing stand. Only the most qualified swimmers ever attempted to make it out that far, but when they did, it was heaven on earth. Never did the children wear lifejackets or flotation devices, which proved they had to be survivors of the fittest. Once in a while if they were lucky, they would find an old tire inter tube and use it for swimming pleasure. In most of their minds, this lake was so much better than the chlorine-filled public pool 30 minutes away in town. Even though it was a somewhat dangerous place to swim, with drop-offs and snakes, not to mention bloodsuckers, which on occasion, would stick to your legs or arms when you weren't looking. Did that keep anyone from dipping into the cool water? Not a chance.

That night the cool water in the lake made everyone forget about the long, hard strenuous day. The storm clouds were gaining momentum as the family finished their swim for the evening. Out on the prairie the horizon to the west, made it possible to observe the dark blue, threatening skies as they approached. But it was beginning to get dark and all that was witnessed was lightening in the far west. This was all before Doppler radar and less up to the minute weather reports that occurs in this decade.

By the time the family reached their home, it was pitch black and the wind was fierce. A mother home alone with her six frightened children didn't help the situation. The girl can still remember her mother calling out "Where is that man?" She could not realize that he was on his way home from town and only minutes away. Before he got there, the small house was shaking and rattling. Four of the children tried to remain calm as they sat on the sofa. A picture window was over their heads. Mother was trying to hold the west door shut, as the wind would not allow it to remain closed. Out of nowhere, the wind sucked the picture window out of its frame and the curtains went flying outside as well. That is the moment that they realized this wasn't just a normal windstorm, but a twister for sure. It was so dark, both inside and out, as the electricity had gone out almost simultaneously with the window. Trying to determine the best direction to take with her family, mother considered leaving the house and attempting to take shelter in the barn. But that idea was short-lived, as she could not remotely imagine going outside in this storm.

In minutes, the father appeared in the door. He stated, "I have never been in anything this bad in my entire life." He reported the big, old two-story red barn was ripped apart; the unattached garage was gone as well. The house, however, remained standing. Not sure how long this storm would last; it was decided to make the one-mile trip to his parent's farm, who at least had a basement for shelter. He told the children to hang on to each other and they would try to make it to the car. The children complied, but they were never more frightened of anything in their life.

What normally would have taken 5 minutes to drive, took about 15. It was slow going, but they made it to their grandma and grandpa's place and the long-sought shelter they needed. The wind finally went down later that evening and in the morning, the damage was evaluated. Unbelievable did not begin to describe the feelings as the family drove around the community assessing the losses. A metal tower that brought energy to rural America from the Missouri river was mangled and left in a heap in the family's pasture. The whole top floor of the prized barn was gone and sticks and boards were scattered for miles. A pet sheep had found its way into the house while the family was gone. He was asleep on the bed, not far from the wet, living room where the rain and wind had been the night before.

This whole event changed the lives of the children and most assuredly the parents and grandparents. Things can be replaced, but lives can never be brought back.

Ironically, just 30 years from the date of this famous twister, the Rose Hill Dam failed when over ten inches of rain fell and the creek rose too high. It destroyed the picnic area and the lake was empty. It is very hard to witness and see the devastation at this public lake area. It holds so many cherished memories of days of our youth.

Just One Happy Family
By Alice E. Buchheim of Highmore, South Dakota
Born 1926

I grew up in the "Good Old Days"— nothing modern. We went to the well, pumped the water by hand, carried it into the house, put it on the cook stove that was heated by coal, wood, and cow chips. After it got hot, put in washtub, and scrubbed the clothes on a scrub board. When we were done washing the clothes, we carried the water outside to dump it. Then we took the wet clothes to the clothesline to dry. When they were dry, took them in the house, those that had to be ironed was put to be ironed, when the iron on the stove was hot enough, we could iron them. The hot iron on the stove was fastened on to a handle, so we could use that to iron. When the iron got cold, we would unfasten the handle, so the iron could be on the stove and we would clip the handle on another iron that had been on the stove getting hot.

Yes, the babies diapers were cloth, had to be pinned on the baby, and each wet or dirty diaper, had to be washed, dried and used again. Nothing was thrown away.

We had an outdoor toilet, with a deep hole under it. Inside the toilet was a bench with 2 or 3 holes on it, for people to use, but no soft toilet tissue. There was always an old catalog or newspaper, and in later years the tissue that peaches were wrapped in, to use instead of the soft tissue.

We never let anything go to waste, even the cow chips. We took the trailer and baskets to the pasture; we filled the baskets with dry cow chips, then dumped the basket in the trailer and walked around picking up more cow chips, filling the basket again. When the trailer was full, we took it back home and unloaded the chips in the bin to use for burning in the cook stove.

Yes, we had fun times too. Our family would invite a neighbor family for a meal, and the neighbor would invite our family to a meal and we always played games. About every Sunday night, the Davis family and our family would get together for a homemade pancake supper.

We never missed a birthday. My mother always made each birthday an Angel food cake from scratch, beating those 13 egg whites, by hand, until they were white and fluffy.

By my time, in the 1920s, we did have a car, Model A. We lived 15 miles from the closest town, Highmore so we only went to town once a week to take a crate of eggs to sell for 20 cents a dozen and a 10 gallon can of cream. Yes, we had to work to get the eggs and cream. We milked about 20 cows, twice a day by hand. We set by the cow on a stool made of a short 2x4 for a flat board nailed to the top, with the pail between our legs. We stripped the milk into the pail. When the milking was done, we had to separate the cream from the milk, with the Separator. We had to crank by hand, the milk went out one spout of the Separator and the cream out the other spout. Of course when that was done we had to wash the Separator, each of the 25 discs were washed separately. Yes, quite a job. We didn't have radio or television. We did have a crank phonograph we could play music on. We had a party telephone line, about 12 families on the line. In the 1960s, 3 of our daughters were in a bad car accident. When I went to call for help, my line was busy. I politely asked if I could have the line and it was given up for me, but when I went to call my Mother, on another line, it was also busy, so I called a Special Friend that was on the same line as I. Even though she was making homemade bread, she called another special friend to go to her house to take care of the bread, so she could come to help me.

In the 1930s when I was going to school, my teacher was a neighbor and I could ride home from school, 2 1/2 miles with my teacher. She had a Model A Coupe, with a rumble seat. I could set in the rumble seat.

When I was growing up, there were 8 of us kids and Dad and Mother. We didn't have our own bedroom. I slept with my sister in the front room, in a bed that looked like a piano, when it was folded up. When we were ready for bed, we unfolded the piano to look like a bed. We laid the first part down on 2 legs, then lifted the other part up and laid it down on another 2 legs. Then it was ready for us to get into bed. The next morning, all we had to do was fold it up again to look like a piano. My Dad and Mother and 2 sisters slept in 1 bedroom, my other 2 sisters slept in 1 bedroom, and my 2 brothers slept in a bedroom upstairs. Just One Happy Family! When I went to school in a one-room school, with 15 pupils, and one teacher, we didn't have kindergarten. At 9 o'clock, the teacher would ring the bell. When the pupils were all in their seats, we would stand and say the flag pledge and the Y.C.L pledge. The teacher would read us story, or we'd sing a song, usually "God Bless America." Then we'd have our classes. If we want to ask the teacher a question, we would raise 3 fingers; to talk to someone, it would be 2 fingers; and to go outside to the toilet we would raise 1 finger. If it was 3 fingers, the teacher would usually answer the question, if 2 fingers, she would usually ask who we wanted to talk to and about what. If it was 1 finger, the teacher usually knew if we really had to go to the toilet, or if we just wanted to get outside to play. Then when it was recess time, we had 3 rows of desks - 1 - 2 - 3. The teacher would say, "In position"— we would put our hands on the desk and our feet flat on the floor, and then she would say, "Turn," we would turn so our feet was facing the aisle. Then she would say, "Rise," we would all stand. Then she would say, "Pass Row 1" would start walking towards the door, #2 would follow, and #3 would follow. That saved a mad rush for all of us to get to the door at the same time. The same ritual was used each time we were excused for recess or noon—Position—Turn—Rise—Pass.

We had no refrigerators. We kept the cream and butter in the cellar, a hole under the house, to keep it cool.

We didn't have electric buttons to push for everything. No electric lights. We used gas or kerosene lamps for lights. The lamps had to be filled every night and the chimney washed every morning.

Saturday night baths...yes, that was something. We had to go to the well, pump the water by hand, carry it to the house, and put it on the stove to heat. We put the washtub right by the stove where it was warm. Then we put the warm water in the tub. Then, the 1st one took a bath, when that one was done with the bath; more warm water was added in the tub, ready for the 2nd bath, and so on, until all were bathed. The tub could set there until the next day, when it would be daylight to carry the tub of water out to empty it.

Bethlehem Evangelical Lutheran Church
By Lois Peterson of Huron, South Dakota
Born 1946

After nearly 100 years of serving the community of Hague Township, Clark County, SD the country church my family had attended for as long as I can remember, has closed. The congregation organized and drew up a constitution during the summer of 1885, but the church building was not completed until 1908. My grandmother, Dora (Waldow) Bruns, was a member of the first class confirmed in the completed building in 1908. The church was organized by German Lutherans, and for many years Sunday services were conducted in German, but this practice was discontinued in 1914 when the United States was at war with Germany. Now, in 1993, the church has closed because of dwindling membership as older members pass away and fewer young people remain in the community.

I feel a very personal sense of loss, even though I moved away nearly 40 years ago. I was baptized and confirmed in this church and attended services nearly every Sunday of my childhood. When I was in high school, I was the pianist. I was paid a dollar a Sunday

Altar and baptismal font from Bethlehem Evangelical Lutheran Church

and I was very appreciative! These are my memories.

The church building with its many arched windows seemed quite impressive to me as a child. You entered through a small vestibule at the back of the church. The sanctuary was one large room with a very high ceiling, and the alter was at the far end of the building. The alter was wooden and quite tall—I think it may have been hand carved—and stairs behind it went up to the pulpit where the minister stood to deliver his sermon. A large wooden ornate baptismal font stood to the left of the alter. An aisle ran down the center of the building with unpadded pews on either side. A propane heater provided warmth (sort of) but it was never very warm in the winter and the pews were so cold that once you sat down and warmed a spot you didn't squirm around because you didn't want to warm another spot! Our family always sat together in one pew, but most of the men sat on one side of the aisle and the women sat on the other side.

After services, the adults gathered outside during the summer or at the back of the church in the winter and visit while the children attended Sunday school classes at the front. There were just two classes, older kids on one side of the room and younger ones on the other.

In the fall, we celebrated Mission Festival. This was both a social event after the fall harvest and a means to collect money to support mission work. We usually had a lot of visitors and everyone brought a dish to pass and a pie. Since our church did not have a basement, the festival was held in the local country school down the road.

As Christmas approached, we started preparing for the Christmas Eve service. Every child had a speaking part, some just a sentence, but as we grew older our speaking parts became longer and by the time we were confirmed we could recite by memory the entire Christmas story from the Bible. After the program, each child and adult received a brown paper bag containing hard rock candy, salted in the shell peanuts, and an apple or an orange. Some years there was also a single chocolate cream drop—that was my favorite.

Years later, one of my children's favorite memories was attending Christmas Eve services with their aunts, uncles, cousins, and grandparents. Our children were exuberant singers and the older members of the congregation enjoyed their enthusiasm! And of course, the highlight of the evening was receiving their bag of candy afterward!

Communion was served from a communal chalice. The offering was collected in a red velvet bag with yellow fringe that was suspended on the end of a long pole. The deacon would pass the pole in front of everyone down each pew and we would drop our coins in it. Each of my brothers and I had a nickel or dime to contribute.

In the churchyard is a cemetery. Most, if not all, of the people buried there are relatives of mine, and with their passing, we are losing a link to the past and the history they have lived. Perhaps that is why I feel so sad that the church is closed. It's the end of an era. The people, the heart of the church are mostly gone now, buried in that prairie cemetery, and the few left have scattered to other church homes. The church started by those early pioneers no longer exists, except in my heart with my memories.

Short-Sleeve-Play-Outside Day
By Mike Bezenek of Mobridge, South Dakota
Born 1940

I was riding my tricycle up and down the sidewalk in front of grandma and grandpa's old two story home, complete with its large open front roofed wooden porch. Mom and I lived there with Grandma and Grandpa because Dad had gone to war.

The "corner store" was only a few blocks south of our home and a quick run across the busy main street. We called it "The Greeks" because the folks who owned the mom and pop place were a Greek family named Skeezicks. Those were the days when we needed Ration Stamps to buy anything from gasoline to meat to cigarettes. The Skeezicks knew me and my family quite well. In those days, it was commonplace for Mom or Grandma or my aunt Betty who also lived with us to send me to "The Greeks" for whatever they might need. Often I'd be given the necessary Ration Stamps and money with instructions to bring home a cut of meat and one or two packs of Lucky Strikes. Luckies had changed the colors on their package then—from the green circle on the pack to a red one—because "green had gone to war." The green dye was needed for the war effort. But today would not be an errand day for me.

After Dad had shipped out to a California Army base, Mom took me on the train from Huron to California for a final visit before his departure to the South Pacific theatre. I don't remember much about the trip, but I do recall the conductor stopping by our seats to punch our tickets. He looked at my copper-red hair and asked jokingly, "Where did you get all that red hair?" I don't know why I responded as I did, but I blurted out, "From the milk man!" Mom recovered rather well as the conductor laughed and walked on to the next passengers. I think Mom could have strangled me that day. "from the milk man" was a common phrase in my family because the milkman came to the house every morning. The cream was always on top in the milk bottles, and we had to carefully spoon it off for cooking if we wanted the milk separated.

Well, as I said, it was a short-sleeve-play-outside day and I was happy riding my trike up and down the sidewalk. I stopped riding when I saw the Western Union messenger, complete with his uniform and Western Union hat, ride up on his bicycle, and stop in front of our house. He glanced my way and quickly moved his eyes away from me. He looked so serious and a bit afraid as he walked slowly but deliberately up the long walk to the front porch. He knocked firmly on the wooden screen door. Mom came to the door. The boy removed his hat and handed Mom the telegram he had come to deliver. Quickly he turned, went to his bike, not looking at me, and rode away. Before he was out of sight, I heard sudden wailing and crying coming from the house. I climbed off the trike and ran inside. I asked everyone what was wrong. None could talk. They just held on to one another as Mom clutched the telegram while they cried. Finally, Grandma came to me, held me on her lap, and gave me the news as gently as she could. Dad had been killed in action. We later learned he was killed by enemy machine gun fire on the island of New Guinea. I cried.

The memory of that short-sleeve-play-outside day will ever be mine. It still hurts.

The Blizzard of '49

The Blizzard of '49 sticks in my memory for a couple reasons. First, I was 9 years old and you can't keep a 9 year old indoors after a huge snowfall and this snowfall was huge. I was having a grand time wading up and down the backyard drifts of snow. Making snow angels was too tame for me. I had to run, jump, fall down, laugh, and do it all over again—until I went running through that huge backyard snowfall and tripped, falling on my face. What tripped me? It was Mom's clothesline! The snow was so deep it had buried the clothesline! Second, my uncle Keith Lyle worked on the Chicago and Northwestern Railroad as a fireman and brought home pictures of the huge locomotive snowplows on the tracks dwarfed by drifts of snow on both sides of the track. It took giant rotary plows on the front of the locomotives to clear the tracks. The rotary blades must have been at least six feet in diameter.

The Iceman, Icehouse, and the Icebox

Remember the iceman, the icehouse, and the icebox. All were important in our era. In our town, there was a huge barn-like structure about three blocks from our house where giant blocks of ice were stored. They had been cut from the river the previous winter. These were the blocks the iceman loaded on his truck for delivery to businesses and residential patrons. My pals and I, on hot summer days, would sneak into the icehouse where it was much, much cooler and play for hours—or until we got caught and shooed out of the place. The manager kept telling us, "You're gonna get hurt in here, so get out!" I really think he was genuinely worried about our getting hurt and not about any liability for injury falling on him. Not in those days, things are different now. The ice in that house was always covered with sawdust as an insulation to help keep it from melting. Of course, that meant our moms could always tell where we'd been when we got home! Our shoes and overalls would have sawdust in every crack and crevice.

When the iceman came, he drove a motorized vehicle. I think he came by every day, but we didn't need ice every day. Still, it was a chance for my pals and me to pester the iceman for chunks and slivers of ice to suck on. It was almost as good a treat as candy! Oh, there would be a little sawdust get past our lips, but that was no big deal. He would be dressed in overalls with a leather apron, a pocket for his icepick, and a leather shoulder patch. He was a real craftsman as he swung his pick penetrating the ice repeatedly in a straight line and then snapping the block into smaller cubic pieces. Using his large sharp metal tongs, he'd grab the chunk he needed for his customer, toss it on his shoulder, and carry it to a waiting icebox. THAT WAS THE TIME WE COULD SNEAK SOME MORE ICE FROM THE OPEN END OF THE TRUCK!

Then there's the icebox, I don't remember when we replaced ours with a refrigeration unit. Seems like we had that icebox for a long, long time. Two things about that icebox, first, the smell. It wasn't a bad smell, but it was a unique smell of moisture, coolness, and yes a hint of the sawdust. I can smell it now as I write. Second, there was always water in the butter dish! The ice compartment was in the upper right-hand compartment of the icebox so the coolness could settle into the lower compartment where the food was stored. I don't know why the butter was always at the top of the storage, but it was. That meant it was directly below the ice compartment and, when the ice inevitably began to melt, the drippings didn't stay in the catch-tray as they were supposed to. Somehow, they found their way into the butter dish. Yes, I can still see that butter dish with a pool of cool water surrounding the yellow spread.

We could talk about that "spread" too. We didn't have margarine then. We used BUTTER. When margarine came on the market, it was sold as "oleo-margarine." It came in a clear plastic sealed bag with a small red spot of food coloring, about the size of a dime, separately encased in a plastic bubble inside the sealed bag. After purchase, one would squeeze that plastic bubble to release the red dye and then knead the coloring throughout the "oleo" to produce the butter-like color of our new breed of "butter." When I was sent to the store to get "butter," I always had to be sure if Mom wanted BUTTER or OLEO!

Before Television, There Was. . .Radio.

It wasn't portable. It wasn't high fidelity. It was just. . . radio, and we depended on it.

Every night, the plastic box on top of a kitchen cupboard would bring us Whitey Larson and the news "from WNAX Yankton, studios also in Sioux City." Our family drove the hundreds of miles from Huron to Yankton one weekend just to see Whitey. That's how much we liked him.

Who knew Whitey broadcast his news from Sioux City! We never did get to see our news "hero." He was our source of local, regional, and national news, AND always gave us the forecast. Whenever he was the least unsure of that forecast, he would tell the housewives, "Ladies, it'll be a nice day to wash clothes tomorrow—if it doesn't rain."

After Whitey's show, "from out of the past come the thundering hoof beats of that great horse SILVER! The Lone Ranger rides again! Together with his faithful companion Tonto, they rode the western plains in the cause of justice."

I didn't have many of the family joining me as I listened to The Green Hornet or The Shadow, but Fibber Magee and Molly along with the Jack Benny show (and, of course Rochester—"Yeesss Boss"!) always brought the family next to the big console radio in the living room.

I would be sitting on the floor at Grandpa's feet right next to that big radio as we faithfully tuned in to the Friday Night fights, "with Don Dunfy at ringside. Brought to you by Gillette Blue Blades—the sharpest edges ever honed." The ten rounders were regular Friday night events for Grandpa and me, and the fifteen rounder title fights were really special.

And After Radio. . .

They started sending pictures through the air. In 3rd grade, our Weekly Reader announced the miracle of TV. After explaining its emergence into the broadcast business, the Reader told us "they call it Tele-Vision." I must have been in about 9th grade when we got our first TV. It was a DuPont console set and of course in black and white. With the rooftop antenna aimed just right, we could get one channel from a station 200 miles away on our tiny screen! Mostly we got test patterns, lots "snow" interference, and if lucky the evening news from KELO in Sioux Falls. Saturday morning I'd be sure to catch the adventures of Sky King.

Country Schools
By Dorene Nelson of Groton, South Dakota
Born 1945

I went to a country school (East Gem 24-1) from kindergarten through the 8th grade. At the time (1950), kindergarten was only for six weeks in the spring of the year. I was in the very first kindergarten class ever held at my school. Some of my friends have suggested that my being in that first class was due to my mother's request so that she could have some peace and quiet at home! I have no idea what they are insinuating by that comment; OK, maybe I do know.

The school building was about 2 miles north of our family farm, close enough to walk or ride bikes in good weather. However, due to the lack of indoor plumbing, water had to be hauled to school every day. My father either volunteered or was appointed to do this job; therefore, we benefitted by having a ride to school every day.

The water that Dad carried was used for a stone crock water fountain, located in the hall outside of the classroom. The remainder of the water was

Dorene Sager in 1951

poured down the two toilets, which we were lucky enough to have inside the building. Since there was no plumbing, the water served as the "flusher" each day. At the end of the school year, Dad poured a special mixture into each toilet, which was made to "clean" them out so they would be ready to use when the next school year started.

Although we had no indoor plumbing, our country school did have a full, finished basement. There was even a small kitchen in the basement along with furnace and storage rooms. We played in the basement whenever it was too cold or rainy to play outside. Potluck meals were also served down there for special occasions such as the Halloween and Christmas programs.

The only other building on the school grounds was sort of a garage. I believe that it was primarily used for protection of the horses in the days before automobiles were available. It is possible that the teachers parked their cars in the garage when the weather was bad. However, I remember the building as mainly being used during recess when we played anti-I-over.

The game anti-I-over is played by two sets of equal team members. We used a softball to throw over the roof. The ball was thrown over the roof with the team members hollering, "anti-I-over!" This was a warning that the ball had been successfully thrown over the roof.

The opposing team now had to try to catch the ball. If they were successful in this effort, all of the opposing team members would run around to the other side of the building, hiding and/or pretending to hide the ball behind their backs.

Once they were around the corner, the person who caught the ball would throw it and try to hit (gently, I'm sure) someone from the other team. If someone was hit, that individual became a member on the team who had caught the ball.

At the end of the game, the winning team was determined by which one ended up with the most members. We enjoyed playing this game so much that I taught it to my children and my grandchildren as well. They never got to play such exciting games when they went to school.

Even though I am a female, playing softball was probably my favorite recess activity. Once again, two equal teams were chosen with a "captain" being selected by a process I cannot remember (Perhaps the 8th graders were automatically chosen as the captains.).

To start the selection process for each team, one of the other students would drop a baseball bat, handle-end up, between the two captains. They would each grab the bat followed by the person whose hand was lowest on the bat moving his hand above the other captain's. This process of hand-over-hand would continue until the captains reached the top of the bat. The one with his/her hand closest to the end of the bat would start the selection process.

We had real bats and balls in the 1950s but no baseball gloves at school. Gloves were probably too expensive for us to be allowed to take them to school. My brother had a

Dorene Sager with her teacher, Myrna Wilke in 1958

baseball catcher's mitt at home and my sisters and I had softball gloves at home; I just don't remember any of that equipment being taken to school.

I remember playing anti-I-over and softball for recess practically all year long. Even when it was too cold to play, we would still do it. On several occasions, my hands would bleed from the cold and the ball playing, but I'd never give in! We did have swing sets and a merry-go-round that I also enjoyed, but softball and anti-I-over were my favorites.

We had assigned duties for cleaning our classroom every day. The wastepaper baskets had to be emptied; the blackboards had to be erased; the paper around our desks had to be picked up; the erasers had to be taken outside to bang against each other to get out the chalk dust (until an electric eraser vacuum was purchased); and the floors were mopped with a dust mop. There were probably other jobs that we did, but these were the important ones.

During the winter, we often brought potatoes from home to cook at school as part of our lunch. The school had a hot plate on which the teacher set a pot of water full of our unpeeled potatoes. We carved our initials in our potato so that no one got the wrong one! The smell of these cooking potatoes filled the classroom, making us extra hungry on those days. Even today, I love the smell of boiling potatoes "with their jackets on."

We had a variety of teachers over the years, but I don't remember if we ever had the same one for more than one year. My teachers were all female, and many of them lived near my family farm. The single ladies, who either didn't have a car or didn't want to drive to school from their homes, were boarded in my family home. We had a special room set aside for the teacher, a room that we were forbidden to go into! These young ladies would go home on weekends, some being picked up by their own parents, some by their boyfriends!

I was the only student in my grade throughout my entire elementary school years. I didn't have any classmates until I started high school in Groton. Then I had so many classmates (29 in 1959) that I thought I'd never remember all of their names! As it turned out, I didn't have any problem with that.

After I'd been in high school for a short time, I became aware of the fact that these "town kids" did not know anything more than I did. I was afraid that my having attended a country school meant that I'd been poorly educated. This was not the case at all!

Ruth Johnson was the Brown County Superintendent. She would periodically visit all of the country schools to check on how the students were doing. I remember her visits well. We had to demonstrate our reading and math skills for her every time. It seems to me as if our teacher knew ahead of time when the superintendent would be visiting because we never felt surprised, only a little worried that we wouldn't perform well.

Every fall close to Halloween our school had a carnival with a fishing pond, cakewalks, and other games after a program put on by the students. Our parents came to the school to help set up a stage consisting of large boards set on low saw horses. Then a wire was strung across one end of the classroom, and curtains were hung so that we could close and open them during the program.

In preparation for the carnival, we decorated the classroom with bright fall colors, carved jack-o-lanterns, and practiced for the program that had skits, musical numbers, and other events. We spent many hours, it seemed, cutting colored funnies into confetti. We bagged the confetti and sold the small bags for a dime. The confetti was used to throw on each other during the game section of the event. It was great fun even though it was a big mess to clean up.

A similar program, without the confetti, was held near Christmas. Everyone in the community attended these events, whether or not they had children in school at the time. Again the stage was set up, various Christmas skits were performed, and many musical selections were sung. At the end of the program, Santa usually visited the school and handed out small bags of candy.

Not only did our country school not have plumbing, but it also did not have a telephone. If there had been an emergency, a parent would drive over to the school with the information. We had electricity and a fuel oil furnace; of course, there was no air conditioning, in the school nor in the homes, at this time.

When we were ready to graduate from the 8th grade, all of the country school students met in Aberdeen where a graduation ceremony was held in the Civic Theatre. Our group picture was taken on the steps of the Brown County Court House.

Attending a country school may have actually fostered my idea of becoming a teacher someday. After I learned to read and became proficient at my grade level, I found myself listening as the teacher taught those students who were older than I was. I learned their material too, before I had reached that grade level myself. By the time I was in the 7th and 8th grades, I was actually helping the younger children with their schoolwork. I was sort of like a teacher's aide, I guess.

Even before getting into high school, I knew that I wanted to be a teacher. I would play school with my cousins, who were all older than I was. However, I was always allowed to be the teacher, either because I got really upset about not getting to be the teacher or because no one else really wanted that job anyway.

Therefore, it was no surprise to my parents when I went to Northern State University to major in education. Of course, it was called Northern State Teachers College at the time. I became a high school English teacher and, for nearly 40 years, had the distinct privilege of teaching hundreds of young people. My goals were many, but basically, I was trying to get my students to love learning as much as I did!

Even though teacher pay is still low in South Dakota, I believe that this is one of the best occupations in the world! You get to know so many young people who in turn keep you young even when you no longer really are. The challenges of teaching keep you on your toes, but it was a job I truly loved!

The Laughing Shetland Pony
By Virginia O'Connor of Redfield, South
Dakota
Born 1925

I am remembering the days of the Dirty Thirties. We lived on the McLain Farm, about seven miles south of Conde, South Dakota. My family was my parents, Elmer and Elsie; my sister, Irene; and my brother, Lloyd; and me, Midge. It was hard times and some good neighbors, Carl Morrell and his wife and their three children were kind to my family. About once a month, they would invite us all over for Sunday dinner. We kids would be so excited, as we didn't get to go places often. These would be the most exciting days of our lives.

They had a Shetland pony, and we knew we would get to take turns riding it in the yard. First the big kids would ride and then on down to the littlest kid riding last. We all rode in a circle in the yard.

All went well until my turn came up. Off I went on a walk. All at once, the pony got an idea; she must have thought, "This is enough of this." She took the straight bit in her teeth and started to trot. No way could I hold her in or turn that little Shetland, and I could only imagine her laughing to herself. She trotted right under the clothesline and wiped me right off her rump.

Cal caught the mischievous little pony and put a saddle on her. He said, "Okay that will fix her." But the same thing happened again. She went under the clothesline. The saddle horn caught on the wire and broke the line and the poles to the clothesline. I started bawling and screaming and off I went for whoever was around. We were wiped off the laughing pony over the rump. Out of the house came Mrs. Morrell and my mother to catch the pony and see if we were all right. Mrs. Morrell said, "Cal, you will have to fix my clothesline so I can wash clothes tomorrow."

But the next time we were invited over, we would do it all over again. What fun we had with that funny little Shetland pony.

Feeling the Effects of the War
By John F. Maciejewski of Blunt, South
Dakota
Born 1938

During early childhood, everyone including me was totally immersed in the world war. It controlled not only our everyday thoughts and concerns but economic needs as well. Vital commodities were rationed and purchases were accomplished with stamps or tokens accompanying the money. I still have one of my books. Sugar was one limited item, causing a civilian shortage of childhood wants, namely gum and candy. This driven desire caused me on one occasion to sneak a spoonful of this crystal white substance from its bowl and slowly savor its delicious texture in the dark beneath Dad's hallway desk.

The war caused such a knife-edge of feeling, to the point that virtually any activity an enemy may cause was accepted as possible. My elder brother exploited this as a small aircraft droned our area in a wide circle one afternoon. "That's a Jap!" he exclaimed. "He was closer, but I threw a rock and hit him in the head. That's why he's keeping out there and watching us!" This information caused my minds' eye to run rampant immediately. I could see the pilot's evil, grinning smile, and goggle-shrouded eyes staring out of the cockpit door, watching our every move, considering a dastardly revenge. I can't recall my brother, Jerome ever leveling with me.

Our farm was on the very edge of town, close enough so as to obey the blackout siren's wail. In the dark of an early nightfall, a winding up warning alarm came, and then followed by the increasing drone of heavy bombers in multitude. We had no concept of Japan's destructive range, but as there was an Army airbase close by that could be a likely target, Mother feared the worst. She would light a holy candle first, and then wedge my sister and me between a wall and refrigerator for safety until the all-clear call came.

This Pierre, South Dakota airbase did afford me a very close B-17 heavy bomber encounter some time later. At play between the workshop and henhouse, I heard the most impossible roar I'd ever heard heading my way. Coming out into the open directly in front a hundred yards and the same maybe in height was a full-fledged Army bomber, its four huge engine propellers thundering through my space, navigating the land contours. It was close enough so as I can still recall after seventy years the pilot glancing casually from his side window.

There Come the Sweethearts!
By Norman Barlund of Milbank, South Dakota
Born 1921

I was born in 1921, the youngest in a family of 12, so I do know about hand-me-downs. I started school one year early so I was 12 years old when I got out of the eighth grade. This was in the year of 1934, which in my mind was the year the farm economy took a dive. 1936 is the year that is always mentioned when talking about the drought, and I'll admit that was about the worst.

But in my memory, 1934 was the year when things on the farm started going downhill. So we didn't have the money for clothes or gas. So I did not go to high school. I did, however, read enough so that when I took A.G.C. test going in the Army I scored 132. You had to score 110 before you could go to Officer's Candidate School to become an officer. Since there was a five-year commitment involved, that didn't appeal to me.

My mother baked bread, as we didn't buy store bread back then. But if we did I thought that was really a treat. But things do change, and now just the memory of the smell of baking bread is pleasant to recall.

But getting back to the dry years, 1936 was the worst. We had to sell cattle, and we traded the horses for an F-12 International tractor. It would be hard for me to think of anything funny about that time.

As for love and romance, I didn't get serious about that until I was 33 years old and met my wife to be. She had been married but lost her husband to polio after two years of marriage. They had one son.

My wife passed away on the day of her 93rd birthday. That was January 9th one year ago. I really miss her. We had a very good life together, to the point that one time when we went to our usual coffee place one morning someone looked at us and said, "There come the sweethearts!" I took that as a compliment.

The drought was bad, but we lived through it, and I am now 93 years old. I can still drive and get around so I won't complain.

Sleeping on the Floor to Keep Cool
By Dorothy Bull of Watertown, South Dakota
Born 1928

In the Dirty Thirties, I remember it was so that hot that my dad put a quilt on the floor, and we slept there because that was cooler. In the morning, we took the dustpan and whisk broom to get the dust off the windowsills. Also, we had to wash the globes on the lamps and lanterns and fill them with kerosene so they were ready to light so we could see when needed.

On Sunday afternoons, we went to my grandma and grandpa's place, and several of my aunts and other people would come. We would walk the plowed fields and find arrowheads and other Indian artifacts. I can't remember what happened to them. I was only four years old then.

To keep milk, cream, and other things cool, they were put in pails and hung down in the cistern by the cool water.

To wash clothes, we had to draw water from the cistern, put it in the boiler on the stove to heat, and then put it in a wooden washer with a handle that we pushed back and forth to wash the clothes. White things were washed first, and then colored things, down to dirty coveralls and rugs. We had to run the clothes through a wringer to get the water out. They dropped into a tub full of water to rinse and then through the wringer again before we hung them on clotheslines outside to dry.

To take our weekly bath, it was the same. We had to draw the water from the cistern, heat it on the stove, and put it in a round washtub. We would start with the youngest and go on up to poor Dad. He was always the last one to take a bath. Otherwise, we would just take a sponge bath.

When the neighbors came over to visit, the adults would play cards, and we kids would go out in the barn and play hide and seek. Once in a while, we might fall through the hole in the haymow and land in a manger. It might scare a horse or a cow, but we had fun.

Our chickens had the run of being all over the farm. Once I was standing on the top of the cow stanchion trying to get eggs out of a pail hanging on a rafter. I slipped and fell down. I was lucky my pant leg got caught on a cow's horn. It made a good tear. I was glad it wasn't any worse.

One night, four of us went out to the outhouse. When one girl sat down, we heard a cat meow and we all hollered, "Oh, it's down in the hole." She got so scared she never finished her job and ran outside. She finished her job with her clothes half on. Yes, they were wet.

Ruthie and the Little Mouse
By Ruth Myrvold of Tucson, Arizona
Born 1930

When I was a young girl, our coats and jackets were hung on hooks in the basement stairwell. Unbeknownst to me, evidently a little mouse had crawled into my jacket sleeve.

I put on my jacket and went outside to the outhouse. While there, I felt a scratching and clawing on my arm. Something alive was crawling in there!

I ran yelling to the house, calling for mother. Calm and stoic as ever, Mother removed my jacket and showed me the little mouse.

"Why, Ruthie," she said. "You have squeezed it to death."

Ruth Haiwick Myrvold in 1934

We Had Electricity
By Clarice W. Kranz of Milbank, South Dakota
Born 1926

I was born September 9, 1926. In about 1930, my grandparents came from Goodwin, South Dakota to the farm where my mom, dad, and I lived. They were all worked up because, as they said, "The bank was broke!" A few days later, I rode to town in a 1928 Chevy and saw the bank building. I told Dad, Fred Wemmering, "Grandma is wrong; the bank isn't broke. It's still there!"

In 1932, I started school in Goodwin, SD. There were 12 grades, the baby room (one through four), the middle room (five through eight), and high school. We mostly played tag from the school building to the sidewalk. Our toilets were wooden outside ones, one for boys, and one for girls.

When Mom, Emily M. Johnson Wemmering was growing up, she told me they would have house parties. The rugs would be rolled back, and they would dance. My Grandpa Johnson played the accordion with no keys and when Mom got older, she corded on the piano for him. They would go to different homes every little while for their house dancing parties.

When I was in grade school, maybe third or fourth grade, my dad told me to walk across the road to Grandpa and Grandma W's home to see how they were. It was winter, and I recall how the teacher warned me to be real careful, as the snow was so high. The road was not plowed. We went to school with sleds and horses. I had to step over the electric high lines. To me as a little girl, it was sort of scary and when I visited those grandparents, they talked German when they didn't want me to know what they said.

Everyone and our school all had electricity and so did we on the farm. But more of our neighbors did. When Grandpa W put the buildings on the farm we lived on, he paid Northwestern Electric Power $100.00 a pole to bring electricity the 4/5th of a mile to the farm buildings we lived in.

During a blizzard in the '30s, it was so bad Dad put a rope from the house to the yard fence to the yard pole and then to the barn so he could find his way.

Also in the '30s, we would have to turn

our lights on in the summer because of the dirt storms. The dust would totally blot out the sunlight. Mom would have me stand on a chair by our front door, and I'd watch for Dad when he came from the field with the team of horses. I'd tell Mom when I saw him. Then she'd run out and open the big farm gate so he could drive right in, as the horses could not stand to work too long in the dirty conditions.

We never had a phone in our home or a refrigerator while I was living at home. We had a Home Comfort coal and wood cook stove with an oven. We did have a furnace and full cement basement. But Dad only ran the coal and wood furnace during the holidays when we had company.

Dad butchered hogs and beef for our meat, along with ducks, geese, turkeys, and chickens. The geese were hung on hooks in the part of the chicken house and then killed by stabbing a knife through their mouth and into the brain so the feathers would be easy to pull. The neighbors who had geese brought them there, too. The men treated them in hot water and pulled the rough feathers, and then they went to the house and the ladies pin feathered them. These geese only got water for a week before butchering, as they were not drawn. My folks left the heads and feet on and I had to wash the heads and clean out the mouths and scrub the feet when I got home from school. Usually this was all done in early November. Then the geese we didn't need were packed in 50-gallon barrels and shipped on the train to a Chicago buyer, because the price was better there.

Mom had a Maytag winger washer with an electric motor as long as I was home, and we washed every Monday. Clotheslines were outside for drying clothes. We were lucky; we had an electric iron. We had no running water or drains. The cistern pump was in the sink in the kitchen, and it seemed the pail from the drain was always getting full and had to be carried out.

When I attended high school from 1941 until 1945, it was wartime. Things were rationed, like coffee, gas, tires, other rubber, and more. We could only drive 35 miles per hour. That was the law.

When we high school girls went to dances, it was only our boys from high school and our parents. No one over 18 years old to maybe 25 years old was there as they had all been drafted.

Three other girls and I worked at picking potatoes by hand from August to November. High school started in October and was six days a week. We got out of school towards the end of April. This was all done so high school boys and girls could work on the farms, as young men were all in the services for the war.

That's part of my life from when I remember until I was 18 and I graduated from high school.

South Dakota Blizzards Can Be Hazardous
By Charles J. Hendricks of Lakewood, Colorado
Born 1932

It was early March 1950 when the Lake Preston High School senior class planned a trip to Huron, South Dakota to attend a special showing of Shakespeare's Hamlet. Mrs. Ida B. Alseth was the English class instructor and senior class advisor. It was with her planning and logistic efforts that this trip originated. Two and possibly three vehicles were employed to transport the group of about 14 students. Two of the vehicles were driven by Mrs. Alseth and class member Chuck Hendricks.

The vehicles left Lake Preston on a Tuesday morning when the weather was not noticeably threatening. Once we left De Smet, the weather quickly changed. By eleven o'clock snow was falling, and one of the worst blizzards in the history of the area had struck, riding in on a wind from the northeast with gusts sometimes reaching 60 to 80 miles per hour.

We got a few miles beyond Iroquois, and it became obvious that we should turn around and return to Iroquois. I remember asking passenger Gary Jensen to open the door to see if he could see the edge of the road. When he opened the car door, it hit a road signpost that was not visible from within the car. Moments later, I bumped into one of the other vehicles and made a small dent in my right front fender. At the moment, the damage was not inspected as my attention was focused on getting the vehicle turned around without going into a ditch or colliding with an oncoming vehicle. I was able to get the car headed back to Iroquois without incident and finally made it back to a small gas station along Highway 14 in Iroquois. The station owner welcomed our camping out for the duration of the storm, but we soon became aware that Mrs. Alseth's vehicle was not returning to our location.

Without much delay, the station owner or attendant called the local volunteer fire department for assistance. A volunteer fireman or two soon appeared to assist in attempting to find the lost vehicle. I accompanied the fireman in his fairly new Plymouth sedan to attempt to find Mrs. Alseth and her passengers. Luckily, we found her vehicle and the passengers stuck in a ditch at the location where I had turned my car around. Her car engine had stopped running because it had gotten wet from the driving snow, and they were becoming very cold and sleepy. Going to sleep in freezing temperatures is not a good sign.

We loaded everyone into the rescue vehicle and safely returned to the Iroquois gas station to spend the night. Obviously, there was not much comfort or sleep during that long, wintery night. Fourteen teenagers and their weary teacher were joined by two Lake Preston Co-op Creamery truckers, Al Baeder and Frank Winsor. In those days, nearly every farm had a flock of chickens and sold eggs. The 30 dozen cases were picked up with the trucks and then delivered to the creamery. Of course, these couldn't be allowed to freeze, so they were also unloaded into the station. The lady of the business got her hand eggbeater out, and we feasted on dozens of scrambled eggs; good stuff for hungry teenagers.

While all this was going on, another carload of students with Frank Kazmerzak as driver had taken cover at the Dave Paterson home but were able to return to Lake Preston the same evening.

The next morning, the storm had subsided and the sun was shining. I remember opening the hood of my 1936 Chevrolet to find the engine compartment completely packed with snow from the driving wind. Local folks helped us return to the location of Mrs. Alseth's car and rescue it from the ditch snow bank and return to Iroquois. With the help of the volunteer firemen and the local gas station owner, we eventually got everyone safely back to Lake Preston, but without the benefit of having attended the Shakespearian movie.

Several lessons were learned from this experience, and they have stayed with me for a lifetime. While traveling in South Dakota, be sure to pay attention to the weather and be prepared with adequate clothing and supplies, as even the weather forecast is not always accurate.

The Buick Sports Roadster Challenge
By Donald R. Bye of Midwest City,
Oklahoma
Born 1926

Most young lads growing up on a farm or in a farming community have a story to tell about their favorite vehicle: a tractor, a motorcycle, or an old jalopy. Mine was a 1926 Buick Sports Roadster. What a car it was.

The car belonged to my grandfather, Ole Hansen Bye. Ole was born in Aamot, Osterdalen, Norway on February 11, 1860. He immigrated to America in July 1881, spent four years in Alexandria, Minnesota, and in 1885, his family homesteaded in what is now Spring Valley Township near the town of Crocker. Ole died January 30, 1940.

I convinced my father, Oscar Bye who was a master mechanic working for Brown Brothers Ford in Bradley, that I needed the Buick to help out on the farm. It was 1942, and World War II was in full swing. My three cousins who lived on the farm and my two brothers were all on active duty in the military forces.

The car had been sitting in the machine shed for years. Chickens were nesting on the leather seats, and it was full of junk. It took a couple of days to get it cleaned and ready to start. But it would not start. Dad did a tune-up job, along with putting in a new battery. We pulled it with the old Farmall tractor, and to my amazement, it started.

I was 15 going on 16 years of age. I soon discovered that a couple of my high school classmates challenged my Buick against their Model A Fords to a hill climb. The hill was located just east of Bradley. It was formed by the railroad construction crew as they built the Minneapolis & St. Louis rail line coming into Bradley. It was approximately 50 feet tall and had an incline of about 50 degrees. My

1926 Buick Sports Roadster

mom, Alma Kleinschmidt Bye warned me not to race anybody with the car or do any smart aleck driving. The challenge was there, and I could not resist. I fearlessly charged ahead.

It was after school on a nice warm, sunny day. We met at the hill, one Model A and my Buick. The Model A went up the hill first and made it to the top next to the railroad tracks. Then it was my turn. I stepped on the gas and roared up the hill, but I only made it halfway up. The engine revved up but nothing happened; it would not move. The other team was jubilant. They towed me home, where the car sat for a couple of days.

I finally got up enough nerve to tell my dad what had happened. He spoke a few words in Norwegian, which I didn't understand. But it probably was a royal chewing out. Dad disassembled the rear axle and sure enough, it was broken. Dad obtained a used axle from the Wrexler Auto Salvage Yard in Watertown, assembled it, and the car was ready to go.

The fate of the Buick was this. While I was away at the University of South Dakota, Dad converted it into a pickup. It eventually ended back on the farm in 1952 and was later destined for the salvage yard.

Farm Life Recommended for All
By Dorothy E. Beam-Saddler of Dumfries, Virginia
Born 1939

Yes, we used outhouses and chamber pots until a year after I left home at age 18. I have a fondness for *Sears* and *Montgomery Ward*

catalogues. Very infrequently, we saw a snake or ground puppy (lizard) in the outhouse. My home was located two miles sought of Seneca, S.D. on the Beam Farm

Daddy blew smoke in my ears when I had an earache. We used Vicks and plastered it on our chests when we were sick. Then we made a tent with a towel over steaming water. When we had a stomachache, we mixed baking soda in warm water and drank it.

We enjoyed old radio shows such as *The Green Hornet*, *Inner Sanctum*, *The Lone Ranger*, *The Shadow*, *Sky King*, and Bobby Benton. They were good shows. On Sunday nights, we listened to opera that Texaco sponsored. We also listened to Hallmark Hall of Fame shows and plays. On Saturday afternoons when "skip" was running, we picked up the Spanish station out of Del Rio, Texas that played great music. We had a black and white television one year after I left home. We got to go to the movies on Wednesdays once in a great while.

We listened in on the party line phone if the conversations were interesting. We cranked an assigned number of rings to call someone. Each party had a certain number of rings. Our first phone was a crank type. We got a rotary phone in the late 1950s.

We took baths in a large, round tub. My family did that until after I left home.

To do laundry we used a wringer washer. The wringer washer and the rinse tub required carrying the water from the well. Who needed a gym?

My aunt made me some dresses and a couple had matching doll dresses from feed sacks. They were smart looking but at the time, I hated them. Daddy made toys for my brothers, button buzz saws, and an acrobatic monkey. Daddy made some china cabinets, tables, chairs, a little house, a barn, and a washhouse for me for Christmas gifts over the years.

I went to a one-room school for eight years. Between my folks and the school, I found out I was better educated than a lot of people. I found this out after I came to Washington, DC/Virginia.

We went to school in Daddy's homemade sled pulled by Fanny and Bess, the team. In the spring sometimes, Daddy took us on the tractor because of flooding. We walked to and from school sometimes, too. It was a two mile round trip. It was no big deal; I loved it.

While in school, I went to a couple of sock hops. I never got a spanking at school, and I don't think any of the other teachers spanked throughout my eight years.

I experienced many blizzards in South Dakota. One year when I was in first grade, a blizzard came up. It got worse while we were in school. The teacher and we pupils walked to the closest farm. I think it was about a half of a mile away. We got lost for a little while because it was a white out. The teacher ran into the house fence, which guided us to the house. It was like Laura Ingalls Wilder's The Long Winter.

My favorite pets were my cats. I once had a chicken named Lucy.

I churned butter sometimes. I pitched hay into and out of the hayrack. Daddy would take the team to the haystacks and then I would help him load. I shoveled grain into the bins. I fed chickens. I helped in the garden, weeding and picking. I helped herd the cattle form one pasture to another. After school, I saddled the horse and brought the milk cows home. I also milked the cows by hand, of course.

The biggest mischief I got into was running on the barn roof.

For entertainment, we worked jigsaw puzzles and played board games. We played dominoes, too. We played tag at school and at home. We played in the haymow. I learned to do front flips there. We went sledding and ice-skating. We ran on the rock piles and on empty oil barrels like loggers. We also rode bikes. We enjoyed riding our saddle horse. I took piano lessons and played the organ in grade school.

I loved reading. An uncle started bringing down a box of books to me. When I finished reading them, he would bring another box down. He did this many times. Also, when I was in grade school, the teacher got a box of books from the county library each six weeks.

We had family time at holiday dinners with relatives. We also got together at birthdays. My mother played the piano. She was very good.

My aunts, uncles, and paternal grandparents made sausage, headcheese, chittlings, and rendered lard. They made lye soap in the front yard.

I would recommend farm and ranch life for all, at least in the formative years. The quietness and privacy are needed much more today. What a place to dream, to hear the sounds of nature, whether it is the sounds of birds or the wind through the trees, the cattle lowing, etc. Chores are also a good relaxer. There is always something to do.

We also had the fortune of choice to experience social life; neighbors stopping in, visiting back and forth; church later in life; MYF Church Camp; community club; women's club; 4-H; school plays; singing in high school and church; and piano lessons.

I learned patience, as I had to wait many times for many things. There was no instant gratification! I learned frugality and ingenuity.

Stand Off with a Coyote
By D. Ransom of Huron, South Dakota
Born 1933

In the spring of 1958, my husband, three children, and I bought a 160-acre farm 25 miles west of Huron, South Dakota in Sand Creek Township. Sand Creek flows through a pasture a half of mile south of our land on its way to the James River. This creek goes along through a meadow lined with big old cottonwood trees. Under these trees are many, many wild plum and chokecherry bushes. Milkweed grows abundantly throughout this area.

In the fall, thousands of Monarch butterflies migrate through here on their way south, feasting on milkweed and resting in the cottonwood trees. What an awesome sight!

Soon on our farm, we had a few cows, a flock of sheep, and a couple of horses for the kids to ride. Our two daughters and the neighbor kids would get together for trail rides and would have a horse race or two to see who had the fastest horse. Our son preferred to ride his Moped. He could round up the cows in a short time with that!

To supplement our income, my husband worked during the day at Armour & Company in Huron, a 50 mile round trip. So keeping track of the kids and livestock kept me busy.

As was my routine early in the morning, I would walk out to the gate leading to the pasture and see where all the animals were. One morning, I noticed in the corner of the pasture and the alfalfa field there was a dog attacking one of our sheep. Although this was

¼ of a mile from where I was standing, I went on the run, waving my arms and screaming like a wild animal, hoping he would leave her. When I got there, I saw that what I had thought was a dog was actually a coyote!

The sheep was shaking violently, with blood running down her face caused by big scratches from the coyote's claws. He had tried to get her to run out of the corner so he could bite her in the jugular vein, and then the fight for her life would have been over for her. Due to my loud screaming and the waving of my arms, he had run a few feet away from us and then stopped and turned around. He stood and stared at me with his yellow eyes. I was between him and his breakfast and he wasn't leaving!

I pushed the sheep along the pasture fence, while I tried to watch behind us. I wondered if the coyote was going to attack. The sheep was extremely disoriented and weak, so trying to keep her going for home was a challenge. I looked around for a stick, a rock, or anything I could use to protect us if the coyote did make his move. We finally made it to the barnyard and the sheep survived! The coyote ran the other way.

I called the state trapper about the coyote, and he said he would come out early the next morning and cull him in. He would use a calling device that could make a sound like a wounded coyote. If there was a coyote within hearing distance, it would come in and check this sound out. I had mentioned to Glen, the trapper that the coyote had a slight limp in his right leg. When he drove in the next morning, he showed us the dead coyote's right leg. The leg wasn't deformed just deformed front toes where most likely it had been either caught in a trap or shot at. He was an eight or nine year old male.

Glen told me never to do this type of thing again! He said there may have been other coyotes close by, and this story might have had a different ending!

I Don't Know What Bored Means
By Laura M. Jones of Huron, South Dakota
Born 1927

My first memories of the good old days were when I was four years old. We were rushed over to an aunt's house. When we came home, there was this baby. Where in the world did he come from? Then two years later, the same thing happened. This time a girl was there in the baby bed. We didn't question it. I guess we thought the stork brought them.

I remember the dust storms. My dad worked with the WPA. It was dark and the lamps were on all day. My mother put rags around the windows to keep the dust out. My dad went to work with a wagon and team of horses. He'd stop at the house to pick up his lunch. We could not see him going down the driveway. He helped when the WPA built Carthage Lake.

My first day of school was awful. I was so scared. Of course, we walked to school. My folks didn't bother to take me. I just went with my brothers and sisters. We went to town. So the kids went to their rooms and left me at my room alone. What did I do except cry. I cried that whole year, so of course I failed first grade. I did better the next year.

We didn't learn to read in the first grade. We only had big charts with sounds and pictures. We walked to school in all kinds of weather. We had a lot of chores before we went to school and after we came home.

Most of my grade school years were spent living close to the James River. If we could get away from my mother and the endless chores, we would dig some worms and grab our cane poles and we'd be off fishing. If we were lucky enough to catch any bullheads, we'd have a feast for supper. None of us could swim. I am amazed that we didn't drown. I guess the Lord was watching over us.

Of course, we had no electricity, so when it was hot, and the summers in South Dakota were very hot, day after day of over 100 degrees, my mother would make a great treat.

D. Ransom and an old wagon frame

She'd make lemonade in the morning and put it in the well. At dinnertime, we thought it was ice cold. In the wintertime, we'd make ice cream when company was coming. We had a lot of company. Neighbors visited back and forth.

My mother's homemade bread was so good. She always baked on Friday, so the house smelled really good when we came home from school.

I remember the first tractor I ever saw. We came over the hill from school and there sat that john Deere tractor. Thinking about it now, I realize how small it was. It had lugs on the wheels, no rubber tires.

We got into a lot of mischief. My grandma had an apple orchard. Of course, we weren't allowed to go in and pick an apple, so we'd steal them. We'd sneak along the river and into the orchard.

One of the things we loved to do was make candy. When my folks left us home to do Saturday chores, the first thing we would do was get out to the kettles and make a couple of batches of candy. If we had a failure, no problem, we dumped it in the James River. Sometimes we played so long the chores didn't get done. That was not a good thing.

My mother made all our clothes. She made my dress for eighth grade graduation. The skirt was circular but not round and it had two peaks on the side but it didn't matter. I didn't get to go to the graduation anyway.

The most excitement I had during my teen years was going to Alpena on Saturday nights and walking the streets with my girlfriends. We were hoping some of the obnoxious boys would look at us. It didn't work.

On December 7, 1941, we had company for dinner and supper. After they had left, my dad turned on our radio. It had a wet battery that had to be taken to town to get recharged, so we used it sparingly. When he turned it on and heard that Japan had attacked the United States, I'll never forget the look on my dad's face. He said, "We are at war." He had fought in World War I and now had three sons who were of draft age. He knew what that meant. I was just ready to go to high school.

Two of my brothers were drafted right away. The third one joined the Navy lying about his age. No high school for me. I shocked grain, picked corn, milked cows, and helped my mother raise and can vegetables and do whatever had to be done.

We made cakes with syrup if we could get it. Sugar was rationed. I wrote a lot of letters to servicemen. We sent boxes to them. Gas was also rationed but farmers got generous amounts to use to raise food.

Once in a while, a neighbor boy would get to use the family car. A load of us would go to Ruskin Park down by Forestburg to roller skate. They also had dances there, but I wasn't allowed to dance. We heard a lot of stories about the Rainbow Ballroom in Lane, but I wasn't allowed to go there.

When the war ended and the boys came home, I met the love of my life in November. We were married in June. The house we moved into should have been condemned. It's a wonder we didn't freeze to death. There was a floor furnace to heat it, but we couldn't afford to buy coal so we used cobs. The next winter we had a baby so we had to keep warm. We put in a propane heater in the living room. The rest of the house was still freezing. That summer, we bought a propane refrigerator to keep the baby's milk. What a thing to have real ice cubes. I would hang the clothes out on the line, bring them in frozen, and dry them over the furnace. We didn't have a problem with dry air in those days.

Through the years, I raised geese and a lot of chickens. At one time, we had 800 laying hens and sold eggs. A truck would stop once a week and pick them up. They all had to be washed and sprayed with oil. We did that until there wasn't a market for them with all the government regulations. When boilers came, I raised a lot of them. The kids and I dressed them and sold them in town.

I could write a book about the Good Old Days: the winters when we kids woke up to frost on the quilts and dressed in the cold; the hot summers when we pushed our beds to the window hoping for a breeze; taking a bath on Saturday nights, the little ones to the older ones just adding water to keep it warm; and many, many more things. If that's the Good Old Days, then I guess I would not trade my warm home in the winter and cool air in the summer for what I lived through. But I have to say I still don't know what bored means. We kids could always find something to keep us busy. Our life was simple, but I'd have to say it was a good life.

Amazing Medicine Lake
By Devon M. Reeve of Watertown, South
Dakota
Born 1926

I am writing about a very different body of water, which is 16 miles northwest of Watertown. My grandfather, Howard Reeve came here from Wisconsin in 1900 and farmed a few miles from this lake called Medicine Lake. The Indians had named it. Because it cures many open skin diseases, they called it Minnepejuta Water. Howard had the University of Minnesota name the minerals that are in it and since then there have been a number of studies of the lake. It is heavy with these six minerals: magnesium sulphate, sodium sulphate, calcium sulphate, sodium chloride, calcium bicarbonate, and calcium carbonate.

The resort was operated for 84 years, and no one ever drowned in the lake. In the old days when people did not have bathrooms or bathtubs, there would be 400 to 500 swimmers on weekends. In harvest time, many came in the evening to wash away the grain dust from the harvest and take away the itch the minerals provided.

Howard built the resort with bathhouses that had lockers to lock guests' clothes in while they were swimming. There was also a confectionary for lunches, pop, and popcorn. There was a dance hall that was 40 feet wide and 50 feet long, and they held dances every Friday night with live bands in the summer time only. He had an icehouse, and he put up ice for use in the summer.

The lake water has a bitter taste and livestock will not drink it. This is because of the magnesium in the water. But all around the shoreline of the lake there are several springs, and they run 24 hours a day, seven

Men swimming in Medicine Lake
No females went swimming in the 1920s

days a week. The spring water is very good to drink for both livestock and humans.

Another project that was started in 1929 was the Portland Cement Company's project. They were having problems with their cement not standing up in certain waters in the United States and foreign countries. The University of Minnesota told them if they could have a mixture of cement that would stand up in Medicine Lake, South Dakota; they could guarantee their cement for at least 25 years. So in 1929, they started a project and at one time had 300 crates of cement cylinders with about 24 cylinders in a crate put on a chain and put in the lake. Every summer, two engineers and one or two students would come to Medicine Lake. They would hire three or four people to bring all the crates to shore and remove the lids. They put the crates on a stand and took pictures of each one. Then they took them back to the University and studied them for damaged cylinders. In the early years, some of the crates would be dissolved. That went on for 30 summers, and the last six years the cylinders came out like new. The last six years of the cement test, they would have a field day and had engineers from foreign countries come and study the cylinders.

But today the resort is flooded and gone. In 1996, our lake came up 10 to 12 feet on the shore because eastern South Dakota was having a flood. The lake came up on the shoreline 150 feet. It took down our house and all the buildings were flooded, and our road was flooded. No person alive today has ever seen a flood like this. The school of mines in the Black Hills has had studies on it. They claim that the cause is the 100,000 tons of water the Ohio Dam in western South Dakota is holding. This has caused underground water in eastern South Dakota to build up pressure.

Medicine Lake

It has been flooded now for 16 years and many places in eastern South Dakota are still flooded. Medicine Lake has no inlet or outlet, only evaporation. It evaporates 3,000 gallons a day if it is 80 degrees and the sun shines.

Medicine Lake was studied on where the water comes from. They surveyed a 60-mile circle around Medicine Lake and said the lake is the lowest body of water in the circle. The lake is 440 acres in size.

I Fell Out of the Car!
By Sister Kevin Irwin of Yankton, South Dakota
Born 1929

I grew up on a farm about five miles south of the little town of Rockham in northeastern South Dakota. Our outhouse was quite a ways from the house. It was a two holer and always had a *Montgomery Ward* or *Sears Catalog* for toilet paper. When one of my sisters was with me, we would have fun by picking a page of pretty clothes and taking turns to choose which dress we would order if and when we had money to do so. We also had a chamber pot that we used at night.

My mother was a great seamstress and sewed all our clothes on a treadle machine. I was seven or eight years old, before I had a bought dress and 13 or 14 before I had a bought coat. Some people thought we girls were triplets because we dressed alike.

For fun, we played with our dolls and at least once every summer, we set up a playhouse under the trees or in a building that was no longer used. Other fun times were spent playing ring around the rosie, pump, pump pull away, hide and seek, and anti I over the wash house. In the evenings, we enjoyed playing cards like rummy, whist, and solitaire. But most of all, I loved to read, and my mother would order books that were on loan from the State Library in Pierre. She also subscribed to several magazines, which she would put on top of the refrigerator until we had finished doing our chores!

We spent many evenings playing cards like rummy, whist, and solitaire. In the wintertime, we almost always had a jigsaw puzzle in the making. Even my dad would put in a piece or so before he went out to do the chores.

Castor oil, cod liver oil (ick!), and a hot water bottle were home remedies for colds, measles, flus, and headaches.

Our icebox was a wooden chest, and Dad would store blocks of ice covered with hay in the barn. He would get more ice when we went to town. I remember emptying the pan of melted ice. We were very happy to get a bottled gas refrigerator and stove.

We were lucky to have a wringer washing machine, and I quickly learned how careful I needed to be as I put the various articles and not my fingers through the wringer. We kept the machine in the porch and moved it into the kitchen on Mondays in the winter. The water was heated in a big boiler on the kitchen stove. Because the exhaust form the motor was so strong, the kitchen door was left open, as well as a window. The motor was loud and noisy, and our beloved collie dog, Tony would go nuts and run around and around the house when the machine was running. I thought I was really special when I was big enough to hang the wash on the clothesline in the yard.

My godfather and great uncle, Bill lived with us, so we didn't have as many farm chores as some kids did. Gathering the eggs, washing the dishes, and working in the garden were the biggest chores. Our Victory Garden was big. One summer, I helped milk the cows, mainly so that I didn't have to help with the dishes. My dad always milked after supper. My little sister loved to ride her pony and would get the cows in the evening. Separating the milk and washing the separator was a big chore. We played with our favorite pet, Tony, a white collie. He saved the life of my youngest sister when she was lost in the cornfield. We had a lot of cats but none in the house. They were mousers in the barn and chicken coop.

My earliest memory of our party line phone was when my grandmother answered the phone and informed us at the dining room table that my sister and I had a baby sister born in the Redfield hospital. I was three years old. As we grew up, we would vie with one another to see who could get to the phone first to "rubber" when the neighbor's phone rang. They had teenage girls, and they might be getting calls from their boyfriends!

We looked forward to trips to town on Saturday night after taking a bath in the big tin washtub in the middle of the kitchen floor. Mom heated the water on the cook stove. She filled the tub and laid out the soap, washcloth, and towel. She also laid out good clothes if we were going to town or pajamas if we were going to bed.

The trip to town was great. When we were real little, we would hurry to be the one to sit on Uncle Bill's lap, because that would be the one who got the quarter for candy or ice cream or whatever we chose for a treat.

In later years, we girls went to the Legion Hall to dance and to meet our friends. The fee was ten cents out of our weekly allowance. After Mom did the grocery shopping and Dad and Uncle Bill went to the pool hall for a beer, they would join us at the dance. My mom loved to dance and had taught us girls as soon as we could walk!

If we didn't go to town, we gathered around the radio and prayed that the battery would last for the *Major Bowes Amateur Hour*, *Ma Perkins*, and *Fibber McGee & Molly* programs or a Joe Louis or Max Schmeling fight and a number of other programs, but I can't remember the names.

A couple of adventures come to mind. I was seven or eight years old when Dad took my sisters and me to town to buy a Mother's Day gift for our mom at Buss's Store. Being the oldest, I was chosen to carry the pretty little dish we chose, and I was chosen sit huddled up in the back seat of our four door green Whippet so I could be the first one out to present the gift. About three miles out of town, the door beside me flew open, and I fell to the ground with the dish tight in my hands. My dad never drove very fast, but it seemed to me that he was quite a way down the gravel road before he stopped. I presume my sister sitting beside me screamed, and he backed up to rescue me. The amazing thing was that I was not hurt, and the dish was still whole and clamped in my sweating hands when I presented it to our mother. One of my sisters still has the lovely little dish in her cupboard.

Sometime later, I fell down into a big bag of wool that was secured to a hole in the hayloft while the sheep were being sheared. I was lucky to have a soft landing.

I was in high school when I had another adventure I will never forget. I was driving our Farmall tractor to our uncle's place about three miles away. The road was muddy and rutted, and the tractor slid into the ditch. I did not fall off but continued to shake as I went on and finally could go up the side of the ditch and get on the road again. It was only later that I realized how lucky I was that the tractor did not tip over backwards as I climbed out of the ditch. By that time my uncle had moved, so we shocked grain and rode the corn planter so we could jump off and move the metal marker at the end of each row.

The first four years of grade school was in a one-room schoolhouse about a mile from our farm. Most days we walked to and from school. In the winter, Dad would take us with the sled and horses. I remember the teacher invited him in to warm up, and I thought that was so nice of her. There were only two of us in my grade, but I learned so much from listening to the upper grades read and recite. I think there were about 15 students enrolled in those years. The school was well built with a big furnace in the basement and a cloakroom. There was a barn for the horses and outdoor toilets, plus swings and a teeter-tooter, a slide and a baseball field for fun and games during recess.

We had various contests between the schools in our township. A boy from the other school and I came out even with the poem we recited so we were to do it again. The second time around he forgot some of it so I won! Santa Claus came to our Christmas program, and I remember he scared my little sister, who did not go to school yet and she cried. The teachers were women who boarded with a couple near the school. They were excellent teachers.

My Memories
By Darlene Konrad of Highmore, South Dakota
Born 1930

I was born on November 10, 1930 in Highmore, South Dakota at Mrs. Salmon's Maternity Home to Jess Naylor and Mary Larraine Joyner Fieldsend. I was their third child. My older brothers were Willis Eugene Fieldsend, born February 20, 1928 and Jess Neil Fieldsend, born October 11, 1929. Next after me, Katherine Eliza was born on February 12, 1932. Then Mary Lois was born on March 29, 1933 and Marlys May was born on September 8, 1934. A baby boy died at about 11 days. He was born a blue baby. Then

Darlene's parents, Jess and Mary Larraine Joyner Field-send Naylor and their children

Janice Fern was born on November 21, 1938 and named after Nellie's favorite teacher, Fern Ellerton. Then Laura Irene was born on January 19, 1939 and named after Dad's sister, Laura Rath, and Irene Williams, Mom's cousin. I guess after six kids they ran out of names so they started using used names. Oh, I forgot Katherine was named after both our grandmas, Eliza Joyner and Katherine Fieldsend.

I remember the baby boy was so cute, but I just remember he was in bed with Mom. When he died, they had a little white casket.

I was nine when Laura was born, I remember getting up in the morning, and Dad said we had a new baby sister. I was nine and never had a clue that Mom was going to have a baby. How things have changed.

When I was a baby, we went to visit Mom's Aunt Rella and Uncle Art. While we were gone, our house burned down. We lost everything except the clothes drying on the clothesline.

The first place I remember living was about 30 miles north of Highmore on Gordan Gadd's place. I remember playing in the yard with Katherine and Mary, making mud pies and playing house.

When Janice was born, she had a birthmark on her forehead. Willis and I had one on the back of our heads, but they didn't show. Janice's did show, so they had it removed.

We went to school about three miles away. Willis, Neil, and I drove a buggy pulled by a little Shetland pony named Billy. Every morning Dad would have to lead us out to the road or he wouldn't go. When we got to our nearest neighbor's there was a place in the road where the water ran across. Billy would stop and not go across it. So the neighbor would come out and lead him across, and we would be on our way. On the way home, he ran across the place in the road like it wasn't there.

As more kids started school, we got a four-wheeled buggy and a different horse. Billy had gotten into a fight and had to be put down. As bad as I hated that pony I cried and cried. The new pony was Bud and six of us went to school until I was in the third grade, I think.

After Laura was born in 1939, our house burned in August. I don't know for sure what caused it but we thought maybe an oily rag in the washing machine may have started it. It was in the middle of the night, and we all got out and sat in the garage in the car. The car windows got real hot. Neil got baby Laura and even took her bottle.

The next day, we all went to stay with

Darlene and her husband Howard visiting Darlene's grandparents

225

neighbors. Dad, Mom, Laura, and probably Janice went to a bachelor's who had a big house and lived a mile and a half away. As we got homesick, we would get to go home and then back again until they moved another house onto the home place. Then we all got to go home about the time school started. People gave us clothes and bedding and our auntie, Dad's sister made us a lot of new clothes.

Thanksgiving of that year, we went to Mom's sister Laurel and Joe Stransky's for dinner. I went to get somebody a cup of coffee, and Mary was running backwards into me. I poured the coffee down her back. She did get burned bad, but she also used it for quite a while. If she didn't get what she wanted, she'd lay on the floor and kick and scream.

I was always afraid of lightning storms, so whenever it stormed, I would go and tell Mom I didn't feel good so she'd say, "Crawl in with us."

Mom had real bad varicose veins in her legs. I knew she was sick for a couple of days, as she was in bed and had a bruise on her head. No one said but she must have fallen. Dad took her to the hospital in Pierre. A couple of days later, Auntie and Jay came and got us from school early. When Dad got home, he sat on the couch with his head in his hands, and said Mom had died, she was 32 years old. They called it septicemia. She died just before Christmas, 1939.

Our Grandma and Grandad Joyner had moved to Washington a couple of years before when they stopped at our place on their way. I think it was the first time and maybe the only time I saw Mom cry. It was the last time she saw them. They did come back for her funeral.

I thought Willis was so funny. I thought he would be another Bob Hope or Red Skelton. He also was a schemer. Once, he wanted to walk to some hills a couple of miles from us. He heard there were Indian graves, so he got a shovel and water pails in a little wagon. He led the way, and we carried things and pulled the wagon. I don't remember if we ever got clear up the hill, but I know we didn't find any graves or artifacts.

Once Auntie and Jay gave us each a turtle, and of course, they disappeared one at a time until there was just one left. Of course, it was Willis'. He had me and Mary watch it so it didn't get away but of course, it did. He was always saying he would pay us for things, but we never got anything unless it was something he found, like a pretty rock.

Neil was real serious. He was the one who did chores. We milked 15 or 20 cows. The worst thing I hated was the mosquitoes. If they didn't bite us, they made the cows swish those tails and hit us in the face or kick and spill the milk.

We lived in an area where there were rattlesnakes. When I walked out to bring the milk cows in I would see them. If my brothers and sisters saw me throwing rocks they would come out to help me. They knew I was so afraid of the snakes and would not get close enough to hit them with the rocks.

They would mow the hay and haul it in a hayrack with rope lying on the bottom and honk on to the roll it off. We also burned cow chips in our cook stove and heater.

We had a prairie fire. We could smell smoke but never saw the fire but spent a good part of the day wading in a creek in case it got close.

After Mom died, we moved to an empty house by Halebird and went to school there for the rest of the year. Uncle Jay drove a refrigerator truck with meat. We lived about a half mile off the road, so when he went by after he had delivered all his meat he would leave the ice at the road into our place. We'd walk down there with a wagon and haul it home and make ice cream. We had milk and eggs and sugar, so we ate a lot of ice cream. We had sugar because it was rationed but we had plenty with six kids. We didn't bake much.

Next we moved about 18 miles south of Highmore and went to Dewey School. We lived two miles from school. I went to school for sixth, seventh, and eighth grades. Dad had a heart attack, so Neil stayed home to help Dad for his freshman year. Dad died in October, so Neil started high school about a year and a month late. We four or five girls stayed with a neighbor, Mrs. Ginny Wilson, who took us in so we could finish the year. She was so good to us. We went to Aunties' on weekends, and Auntie would get us on Friday nights and take us back to Wilson's. When we'd get home from school on some days Mrs. Wilson had just baked bread, and we'd eat a whole loaf of warm bread for lunch. They had a dam by their house, so we did a lot of ice-skating that winter.

After school was out that year, we moved to town and lived in a little house close to Auntie and the school. That summer, I worked for a family with two kids for $4.00 a week. Some weeks, I'd iron 17 or 18 little girl's dresses and the husband's work shirts and pants. I made enough to buy some school clothes and shoes. Auntie made over a lot of our clothes that were given to us and made us almost all of our clothes. Willis worked in a men's clothing store. Auntie had made him a wool plaid shirt and when he wore it to school, one of the kids said, "It's not fair. You get first pick of the clothing because you work there." I don't know if he told them Auntie made it. When we went to school in Highmore one year all eight of us were in Highmore School at one time. Willis was a senior and Laura was in kindergarten.

After my junior year, Aunt Laurel, who was Mom's sister and Joe Stransky took Kay and me to Washington to see Grandma and Grandpa Joyner and Aunt Velma and Uncle Fred Pekarek. That was a big trip for us on the train. We met cousins we had not met before; Beverly, Linda, and Joyner; our uncle, Lee; Sandra and Claudette, Uncle Art's girls; plus some I can't remember their names. We got reacquainted with some we knew before they knew along with Grandpa and Grandma Joyner.

My husband passed away in 205. We had moved to Highmore, but he continued to farm. I remember walking in the cornfields and pulling weeds.

Darlene and Howard

Tales My Parents Told Me
By Darwin Jessen of Redfield, South Dakota
Born 1930

In January of 1932, my parents lived on a farm about twenty-five miles southwest of Redfield. My brother was three years old and I was one and a half.

My dad told me later about how he loaded us up in a bobsled, which was pulled by a team of horses. He heated up a bunch of rocks and put them in the bottom of the sleigh to keep us warm. We traveled to Redfield where our grandparents lived.

My mother was going to have a baby. She gave birth on January 23, 1932 at grandma's house. The roads were impassible for automobiles because of too much snow this was the reason for using the sleigh to get to Redfield.

Racing Home
By Donna Groskreutz of Watertown, South Dakota
Born 1947

When I was six years old, I started school in first grade. We had no kindergarten in those days. It was a one-room country school, with two teachers and she or he taught eight grades. I had three older brothers and one older sister, along with many neighbor kids. So in all there were about twenty of us.

We had no means of transportation; you could walk or ride with someone. We chose to all pile up in the old pickup truck along with gallon lunch pails and homework books. There were five of us and it was crowded. Boys sat on the seats and the girls on their laps. When the day was over, we piled back in the old truck again and headed for home.

Our neighbor always thought he could beat us home, so we usually raced home. He always took the long way home, which was about two and one fourth of a mile. We took the short way, which was as long as the way he took but we had a gravel corner, he didn't. My older brother had taken that corner may times, only this time he was going too fast, and we rolled that old truck. When the truck finally came to a rest, we could smell gas but we couldn't get the doors open. The neighbor took a tire iron and smashed the windshield out to try and save us. No one got hurt except a few cuts. We raced no more after that!

Choked up and Spitting Dirt
By Herbert Lokken of White, South Dakota
Born 1928

We moved from Hendricks, Minnesota to a farm in South Dakota in August of 1932 on the east shore of oak lake. During the summer of 1934, my brother Russell and I went down to where the lake used to be. We were not supposed to be there without permission. Down there we saw a black cloud rolling in from the North West. It scared us and we took off for home. It overtook us before we made it home. We were all choked up and spitting dirt when we made it to the house. It got so dark mom had to light lamps to see.

My uncle Orville has a 1929 model A Ford Convertible with a rumble seat. He was visiting us one time and wanted to go to White, South Dakota. So my brother and I were put in the rumble seat, dad and uncle took the front. The road we took was just newly built with no gravel yet. He always drove wide open. About five miles from home, dad looked back and there were no boys. We were on the floor choking and spitting up dirt.

We All Got the Same Education
By Lucille Ellenbecker of Gettysburg, South Dakota
Born 1918

I went to Herron School in Appomattox Township for eight years, and it is barely standing today. I walked to school. If there were storms, tornados, or blizzards, parents came after us. There were eight grades in our school. We studied arithmetic, reading, art, and geography. We brought lunch to school in a dinner pail, usually wild goose sandwiches. At recess, we played cricket, anti-I-over, and baseball. If you got in trouble at school, you stayed after school and did chores for the teacher. We were in school from 9:00 a.m. – 4:00 p.m. I had five different teachers. We had two outhouses. We had a container for drinking water at school that was filled when empty. A big heater with mostly coal heated our school. We had a big metal bookcase full of books for our library. We most all walked to school. Once in a while, we would ride a horse around and tickle her ribs so she would rear up and dump us off. Everyone got the same education. Went to high school and some to college.

My Little Hometown
By Shirley A. Neshiem of Brookings, South Dakota
Born 1935

My story is about my hometown. When I was 10 years old (1945), I can remember standing on the corner of 10th Street and Phillips Avenue and seeing three movie theaters: the State, Egyptian, and the Time. I remember mice running down the aisle at the Time. This theater was across the busy street from three dime stores (all with soda fountains or lunch counters): Kresges, Newberry's, and WoolWorths. Newberry's had the best hot turkey sandwiches with mashed spuds and gravy at $0.49. Also in this block was a Penny's with a new escalator, Mont Wards, Weatherwax, and two fantastic shoe stores (always with 30-60 pairs of shoes in front windows) Baker's and Kinney's.

Now if you moved down to 8th Street and Phillip, you could see four more theaters: the Hollywood, Orpheum, Dakota, and always a double feature for $0.12 at the Granada. We also had two outdoor movies, Starlight and Eastway! You could see three hotels, Catarac, Carpenter, and Albert; three hot dog joints, Frisco, Milwaukee, and Cone Island ($0.10 dogs and $0.07 chocolate milk); numerous department stores; jewelry stores; a food store; restaurants galore; banks; drug stores; and people all over, all the time. So now, my 49,000 little town is a 169,300 bigger city, with malls, malls, strip malls, and more strip malls. I guess they call this progress.

My folks owned three Mom and Pop type cafes and we lived across town, about 2 ½ miles from any of them. I would ride my bike, even across the river on a railroad trestle, or if it was cold, take a bus. My favorite bus driver would let my dog King on after he followed the bus three or four blocks. I

The Evolution of Farm Country
By Ronald E. Kangas of Lake Norden, South
Dakota
Born 1938

To grow up in Dakota Farm Country during the 20th century was to witness a rapid evolution of rural life. The evolution began as native prairies were homesteaded and tamed by Scandinavian settlers in the late 1890s and continued through the boom years of the early 1900s with rapid building of farmsteads and small railroad towns. Communities formed, schools and churches were built, and neighbors worked together to survive the harsh realities of pioneer life. The 1930s bought the drought and depression as dust storms raged, farms were lost for taxes, and desperate families left the land for the promise of a better life in California. The 1940s are remembered for World War II, when staples such as gas, tires, and sugar were rationed, young men went to war, and farm youth salvaged scrap iron, milk weed pods, even animal bones for the war effort. And times then got better, but the evolution continued.

Mechanization would wield a subtle, but powerful change. Oxen and horsepower was replaced by tractors with ever more power, and machines to replace human labor. Rural electricity was a welcome change and transportation made easier with better vehicles and improved roads. The change to increasingly bigger machines and larger farms continues, even as small town business give way to regional Wal-marts and Menards superstores.

The Ice Life
By Marvin Madsen of Corona, South Dakota
Born 1933

This is my story about my life on Madson Beach on Big Stone Lake. I lived there with my dad, mother, and 13 siblings. Martin Madsen was my dad's name and my mother's name was Anne Madsen. Every year in January, we had to put up ice in our old icehouse. It was dug in the side of a hill with a roof over it. We would have to go five miles down the lake on the ice and get Ed Schuher saw and cut the ice in 18"x36" chunks. We would only saw part

way through so the wall didn't get in the crack and freeze all the saw cuts up again. The ice was usually about two feet thick on the second day; we would take a handsaw and cut the rest of the way on a few pieces so we could get them hauled up to the ice house on the hill. We had to pull the first pieces out of the lake by hand so we could get two pieces together and my dad made us a carrier that would fit over two pieces of ice. We would pull them up the hill with my brother-in-laws we Allis Chalmers tractor and slide them down into the ice house and you had to get two pieces together and chunk in between them with flax straw. Then we would make layers until we had four layers chunked together. Then we would cover everything with flax straw. I would usually take about three or four days to get everything done. In the summertime, we would cut off the ice and put it in a sack and carry it ½ mile up to some of the cabins that had iceboxes and we would get $0.25 for all our work but my dad always got the $0.25, but we had a good life.

Radio Entertainment
By Katherine Deremo of Madison, South
Dakota
Born 1922

This information is taken from a diary that I started on January 1, 1936, when I was 13 years old. We lived in Iowa and my parents had lost their farm due to bank closures. They rented a farm in Lake County, South Dakota from Joseph Henkin, who was the owner of KSOO radio in Sioux Falls. We moved on March 30, 1936; 185 miles and we drove a 1930 Chevrolet car. We arrived at 4:30 p.m. A four-room house for my parents and four kids. My oldest sister stayed in Iowa to finish her senior year in high school. Farming was done with horses until a Farmall tractor was bought in March of 1938. I don't know the deal made to buy the tractor, but some horses with harnesses were taken to the dealer for pay.

We bought our first radio on June 15, 1936 and did not know that it had to have an aerial, so had to make another trip to town to purchase one. Radio was hooked up to a large battery and finally got everything working and could get WNAX-Yankton, South Dakota. On June 19, 1936, we listened to Max Schmelling versus Joe Louis fight; Max won. On July 2, 1937, we stayed up late and listened to the radio regarding the loss of Amelia Earhart's plane somewhere in the ocean. On July 10, 1938, we heard on the radio that Howard Hughes started his "Round the World Flight" and completed it in 3 days, 19 hours, and 30 minutes landing in New York on Thursday, July 14th. The radio was great entertainment for our family. The 1930s were hard years for the South Dakota farmers. Winters were bad and we missed many days of school because of the weather. My younger brother attended a one-room country school and in the fall of the year the teacher planned a box social for the neighborhood and it was a moneymaker for the school. Really a grand affair. That is how my sister met her future husband.

Redecorating the Car
By Elaine Ries of Watertown, South Dakota
Born 1941

When I was about six years old, I would try to find ways to amuse myself with activities I could do by myself. My siblings closest to my age were three years younger and seven years older, both of them were my brothers. Something I liked to do was to play in the family car, pressing every button and lever, pretending to drive. My dad could always tell when I was playing in the car because when he got in to drive the windshield wipers were on along with the heater and radio were turned on high. The most exciting for me was the cigarette lighter, which used to be standard equipment at that time. One day I decided to decorate the car, a 46' Chevy. Actually, this was a car that only a couple of years old at the time. I would press the lighter in, get it red, and then make some nice round designs in the upholstery of the seat and ceiling of the car.

Given more time, I probably could have had the whole car decorated, however I saw my dad coming from milking cows carrying a pail of milk toward the house. Some instinct told me to close the windows and get into a fetal position on the floor. As my dad got close to the car, he smelled something hot or

burning. He opened the door to look in. I'm not exaggerating when I say he wasn't a bit pleased with me. The decorating job never did get completed.

My playing in the car had been abandoned at the time. When I was about nine, my younger brother was able to be an accomplice, being six. Our mother had told us not to pick any watermelon from the garden yet, as they were not ripe. However, I was doubtful, as no one had cut one open to check. What if the melons were ripe and laying in the garden for days. I just needed proof.

I instructed my brother, Gene to sneak one from the garden. I told him I would meet him in the garage with a butcher knife. We got into the car trunk where no one could see us, leaving the trunk open about an inch to let in a little light. So in near darkness I cut into the watermelon. Moms usually do know best and of course, she was right, it was not ripe. We had to get rid of the melon. Moms,

Elaine Kelzer Ries and her brother, Gene in about 1946

230

Elaine Kelzer Ries

please warn your children about playing in trunks and with a butcher knife. Fortunately, to this date at age seventy-two I still have all my extremities. I guess I was just lucky.

Washing Clothes in the Winter in the 1950s
By Carol Joffer of Brooten, Minnesota
Born 1948

With the modern conveniences, and front load washers of today, women have come a long way from tedious work of washing clothes sixty years ago.

I grew up on a farm northwest of Wheaton, MN near the Minnesota, South Dakota border. If I had walked two miles west of our farm, I would have been in South Dakota. It was near the White Rock South Dakota Dam.

We did not have indoor plumbing, hence no running water, and the only heat in the house was one small fuel oil burner in the living room, and the old wood stove in our tiny kitchen.

Wash day was work for my mother. It took most of the day! This was a weekly or semi-weekly event. She would have to carry the water in big pails from the well over snow banks, about 100 feet from the house. Then she would put it on the wood stove in big kettles until it reached the boiling point. She would then get the wringer washer from the back porch and set it up in the middle of the kitchen. Then she had to wash the clothes, put them through the wringer, and do it several times if they were extremely dirty. She was very fussy and the white clothes had to be snow white especially the dishtowels.

Then the next step was to hang this clean wash outside, no matter what the temperature, to let the clothes drip. Her hands must have been extremely cold. After an hour it would be time to out and get the clothes and bring them in. they were as stiff as stiff could be. My dad's overalls could have walked in by themselves if there were feet attached.

The next procedure was to hang them up in the kitchen on the two clotheslines going from the north end of the house to the south end. Soon they would be limp. There was no need for a humidifier on clothes washing day. The air would have a wonderful aroma as they were drying. It made you want to breathe deeply and inhale that sweet scent of fresh air. They dried in an hour or two with the wood stove crackling below them.

It would be impossible to get to the refrigerator in the back of the kitchen to get a snack with all the clothes in the way.

The last step was to throw the dirty wash water outside and make sure it was far enough away from the house so we wouldn't fall on the ice the next day.

The next day was the process of ironing these clean, dry clothes. Even pillowcases and dishtowels were ironed. There was no end of work. No wonder my mother did not have to go to an exercise or workout room. She got all the exercise she needed on washday!

Blizzard of 1951
By Donald Schultz of Miller, South Dakota
Born 1934

It was tournament time when I was a high school sophomore in 1951 in Miller, South Dakota and we had won the District XV basketball tournament. That win established a record among class "B" schools as the Miller Rustlers has been victorious ten of the past sixteen years during the class "B" system. We were ready for the Regional tournament games.

The day we were to leave to drive the twenty-four miles west to Highmore it was a rather nice afternoon. In those days we traveled by cars to all athletic events having local men, who were sport enthusiast, be the drivers. One such man was Ted Jennings, a well know cattleman that had a heavy foot. So many of us liked riding with him knowing we would be the first ones to arrive back home in Miller after a game was over.

Another favorite driver was our basketball coach, Bob Schroeder, and this time I rode with him. When we got to the Armory in Highmore he parked by a tall tree close to the lumber yard which turned out to be a good thing as I will explain later in my story.

During the tournament games, we played Harold and Miller lost 51 to 36. Redfield won over DeSmet and later in the day we won over DeSmet giving us third place and Harold was the victor over Redfield for first place and they later went on to win the class "B" State Tournament.

Sometime during the evening games, the loudspeaker system came on to report that, no one from Redfield and DeSmet were to leave Highmore due to bad weather and road conditions. Later it came on to say Miller and Harold also were not to leave town and us kids all hollered and jumped for joy thinking what fun it would be to be snow bound in Highmore in the Armory. When the championship game was over all the boys from the four teams got out on the floor and started shooting baskets. A lady from Miller got on the stage and started playing the piano so kids and adults alike did some dancing and singing.

In one of the locker rooms there were men playing cards and I recall seeing more money on the table than I had ever seen in one pile. By 12:30, things had quieted down and a person couldn't find a place on the bleachers to sleep. A friend of mine and me decided we would go outside to just check on the weather planning on walking the block to Main Street. We did a half a block and turned around and were very glad to get back into the Armory.

The next morning the tree that Mr. Schroeder had parked by was the only way we found his car and we shoveled and shoveled to get his car out of the snow so we could get back home to Miller. Years later, I talked to a farmer friend, Gordon Strasburg, who told me that he had driven his pickup to the

tournament and when he parked, he didn't get his door shut tight and that morning he said he couldn't have gotten another shovel full of snow inside his pickup.

A Daily Journal of the Years
By Paul Erschens of Elkton, South Dakota
Born 1929

Frank Erschens of Drammen Township kept a daily in which he listed income and expenses, a daily weather report, comments on crops, and much more. It is fascinating to read, you also realize that life was slower paced in those years (1914-1955) so that a man had time to record such items daily. You get glimpses of our changing methods of agriculture as you note that in the early years, he farmed with 15 horses.

1919. March 11, first robin, blackbirds, ducks, and geese are here. April 21, started to plow corn ground. April 23, first barley sowed and dragged. April 26, sowed wheat. April 28, sowed oats and bought a David Bradley cultivator for $45. July 1, last corn planted.

1920. March 14, all the robins and ducks were here, and on the 23rd, he began breaking pasture. April 9, he helped Vicks thresh.

1921. March 5, was again an early spring with meadowlarks and geese were here. March 16, the first mosquito appeared and the weather was dry and dusty. November, he sold cattle for four cents and five cents a pound.

1926. March, traded for a new Ford touring car for $395. April, May, and early June there were dust storms. June 13, early frost appeared.

1927. Middle of March, early spring was common and the first robins were seen.

1928. A windmill was purchased for $110 and gas for automobiles was 18 cents per gallon.

1930. March, dust storms were common. July 3, hogs weighing 1,010 pounds brought $8.25 per cwt, netting $83.32. Early June, temperatures were commonly near 100 degrees for daily highs. June 27, culminating in a hot Sunday when the heat reached 114 degrees.

1931. February 19, found 160 people were poisoned at a farm auction sale. Freshly slaughtered pork and beef had been cooked the day it was butchered and made into sandwiches. Stored warm in tightly covered kettles until the sale the next day. They created much havoc though no fatalities. February and March, there was extremely warm weather and dust storms. Late March, was blizzardy and rainy. April, brought dust storms and very warm weather again. May, turned very cold with a blizzard and more dust storms. Summer started cool and damp, and then turned hot and dry. November 1, started the killing frost that was a poor year for crops, with poor yields.

1932. January was stormy. July was hot but dry and windy. October 15, Mr. Erschens sold 13 hogs (4,310 pounds each $2.86 cwt) for $122.83. December 15, was 35 degrees below zero.

1933. A terrible blizzard killed most pheasants. Temperatures were below 33 degrees and 41 degrees for a short time. May, a great dust storm happened. June was a hot and dry month with temperatures in the 100-degree range. June had hot dry south winds, which began to burn the grain. July, corn was burned by the temperatures. August 10, hot dry spell, corn tassels have dried up, much corn is dried up with no ears. There was no moisture on the ground. August 11, Lake Benton is now completely dry and has no more water in it.

1934. January, brought dust storms but little snow. February 17, barnyards were all dry with no frost in the dry grounds. Dust storms, a little light rain then day after day of dust storms. March and April had 12 dust storms. Big dust storm began after dinner. In the afternoon, the wind changed to North West. Greatest dust storm ever seen here. The sun disappeared in the dust clouds with a great wind. It was so dark, like about midnight. It was a blinding storm and was so dusty it was hard to breath. May 15, Lake Shaokatan is dry. May 29, 104 degrees with an east wind and a dry clear sky, you can almost taste the dust as you read this.

1935. There was more rain than the past several years with only one dust storm in March. February, there were seven blizzard days, and some other snowy days, but mostly clear and cold. February 23 and 24 must have seemed unbelievable after all this cold weather as sunny days reached 42 to 50 degrees during the day, but the 26th brought the worst blizzard of the season.

1936. That was a year of terrible contrasts in temperatures, which brought the most frigid January in many a year. January 1 through the first through the seventh was a consistent 30 below. Not until after February 10 did the thermometers register above zero.

The Wind of the Storm
By John Zilverberg of Highmore, South Dakota
Born 1913

About the first moon landing, there had been some version of it in comics but I thought some people sure have a good imagination. I was surprised when it really happened. We, like everybody else, had the out houses in those days. They were really cold places to visit when the weather was cold and of course we had chamber pots under the bed to use at night or if the weather was bad. I can remember when dad brought home the first radio and the first program we got to listen to was Amos and Andy. When we first moved to Holabird, South Dakota, they had some party lines. When you cranked someone's number, everybody on the lines phone rang so everybody on the line could listen in on our conversations and find out what was going on in the community. We had wind up record players for entertainment. As for school spankings, they didn't happen very often. The teacher usually had a ruler handy as a deterrent. We were always warned that if we got a spanking at school we would get another one when we got home.

As for the Saturday night, baths they were taken in a round steel tub and the water had to be warmed up on the kitchen stove. We used the wringer washer for years when we kids got big enough we had to pump the wash machine till my older brother, who was a kind of a mechanical genius, figured out how to hook up our one cylinder gas engine onto it.

As for movies, we never went to one till dad bought a Ford touring car for $400. Then we got to go once in a while but they were silent black and white. Mother was a good seamstress she made some of our clothes but mostly they bought them at local stores or ordered them from Sears Roebuck or Montgomery ward.

The first bad storm I remember was at Wessington Springs on a Sunday. We had been on a fishing trip with a couple of neighbors and had just gotten home. I noticed the sky was an awful dark gray. We were in the barn and the folks were milking the cows. I was standing in the barn door when the wind hit mother said the barn lifted a foot off the foundation. Then there was a big crash. It was the cupola off of the top of the barn and it had blown off and crashed through the roof of a shed attached to the barn. I saw the hogs come running out of the hog house and when the wind hit them, they went rolling across the yard. After the storm, we got to looking around and saw a neighbor that lives about a quarter of a mile from us that had a big new barn that was no longer there. Another one our neighbors that had been fishing with us had also been milking his cows when the wind lifted the barn right off of him and left him and the cows just standing there.

As kids, we usually had pets of some kind. Once we had a badger, we had him on a chain staked out in the yard. Sometimes a young unwary chicken would get too close to him and he would have a chicken dinner. Sometimes we would take him out and find him a gofer hole to let him dig out the gofer. We would take the tail that we needed to collect our bounty and let him have the gofer.

As for swimming holes at Wessington Springs, we had a dam in our pasture where we kids went swimming. Once my younger brother got in trouble and would have drowned if I hadn't managed to get him out. Later we had a big rain and the dam washed out and it was never rebuilt.

As for sports, we didn't do much except what we did at school, unless you call fishing a sport. Dad liked to fish and he liked baseball, so shortly after we moved to Holabird we laid out a ball diamond in our pasture and formed a baseball team including my three brothers and myself along with some neighbor boys. After that, we had a ball game every Sunday and most holidays until December of 41 when the japs bombed Pearl Harper and I enlisted in the U.S. Marines.

I spent the next four years in the South Pacific. After the war, I returned to the ranch and got into the business of raising and selling purebred registered cattle.

The Infamous Car Ride
By Cheris St. John of Fort Collins, Colorado
Born 1930

Henry Bohnhoff was born in Germany in 1863. His family was butchers and lived above their shop in Hoxter, Germany. Henry migrated to the United States about 1890 where he followed the only trade he knew by working in the stockyards in Chicago. He moved to Gladbrook, Iowa where he met and married Hannah Renner Glandt, a divorced mother of five children. Hannah and Henry had two sons, Carl and Heine, after they moved to Gettysburg, South Dakota in 1904. He bought a butcher shop and continued with his trade. Heine died of the flu in 1916, but Carl became a butcher and worked with his father.

Henry would buy cattle and hogs from local farmers and butchered them in a slaughterhouse north of Gettysburg. Once they were ready, he would transport them into town on a wagon drawn by his horse named Kate. How he loved that horse, and they became a familiar sight around town, as Henry never trusted motorized transportation even when it became available. The meat hung on hooks in the shop ready for shoppers to choose the cut they wanted.

Henry would only ride in a car if his daughter-in-law drove and then only if he could sit with his door ajar and his leg on the running board. The door opened forward, which meant he got a lot of dust and flying insects in his face on occasion. The day came when his son Carl decided that it was time for his father to learn to drive a car. They went out to an open field near the slaughterhouse for the first attempt. Henry sat in the driver's seat of the Model A with his one leg hanging

Henry Bohnhoff in his market

234

out and Carl beside him. That was when the excitement began. Henry pushed the gas to the floor and around the field, they went. Henry with his leg dragging in the dirt and shouting over and over, "Whoa, Kate. Whoa! Carl finally managed to turn the truck off and they stopped. Henry never drove a car again. When his horse, Kate, died he rode very reluctantly with others. The store became a full grocery and meat market and was operated by the family for over 60 years in Gettysburg as Bohnhoff's Market.

Henry passed away in 1936. Carl and his wife Lillian passed away and are buried beside Henry and Hannah in the Gettysburg Cemetery. Their daughter Cheris and her husband John St. John and their two sons Mark and Kent are the only family left to remember the infamous ride of 1918.

Waiting For the Next Blizzard
By Suzanne Unzen of Milbank, South Dakota
Born 1948

Growing up on a farm in western Grant County in the '50s and '60s proved to be a major challenge in the winter. The first snowfall sent our family outside to rescue all the chickens that had found shelter under the granary where they could find food. This project needed a long pole with a hook on the end to pull the chickens out and deposit them back in the chicken coop. With this process completed, we would retreat back to the safety and warmth of the house.

Our heat source was a warm morning potbellied stove for our living room and kitchen range for the kitchen. As the snow increased and the winds blew, a favored spot was the oven door on the range. Sitting there, getting our back toasty warm and eventually grabbing a chair for sitting on to warm our feet, led to disagreements as to who got the oven door next. The colder and windier it got led to putting more coal in the stoves, which produced a blazing chimney fire. My dad would retrieve a ladder and bucket of water. He would rush to the chimney and pour water on the fire, which would extinguish the fires inside. Therefore, there was no heat in the house for some time. This is where our long

legged union suits came in handy.

Our farmyard had snow banks at least 10 feet high so dad would tie a rope around his waist in order to get to the barn to care for the animals. We had no inside plumbing, so getting to the outhouse proved to be useless. The chamber pot and slop pail were used very often during blizzards. We were on a party telephone line, which was usually out because of lines going down. We could pick up the phone and listen to see if anyone else was on the line. Our bachelor neighbor often listened on the phone during a blizzard, wondering if anyone else would pick up. We knew who was on the line because he had false teeth and we'd hear them clicking. This was our connection to the outside world.

Our township road would be blocked for days at a time. Eventually the neighbor would appear with his big snow blower and open roads. We were often taken to our one-room school with a team of horses and a wagon. During a blizzard, the electricity would often be off so we relied on hurricane lamps and candles for light and many blankets for heat. Eventually the blizzard would stop and we could drive to town, replenish our supply of food, visit with others, and see the outside world while waiting for the next storm to appear. Winters were hard but spring would arrive eventually and we'd be back to the world with green grass, beautiful May flowers, and planting the fields.

Party Lines
By Raeburn Moore of Mitchell, South Dakota
Born 1934

My earliest memory of the telephone is the use of party lines. Several people would be on one line, each given a series of short or long rings to notify the house that they had a call to answer. The telephone itself hung on the wall, with the receiver hung on the side and the mouthpiece somewhat adjustable for the person answering the telephone. Every person on the line would hear the ring coming in so one of the favorite pastimes for other parties on the line would be listening in or rubbernecking. If too many parties picked up their telephone receiver, it became more difficult to hear the party calling.

A general ring was a series of staccato short rings, which would relay a message from the operator, referred to as the central. This message usually concerned a fire, a bad storm coming, or perhaps a special meeting of all. If you wished to talk to anyone not on your line, you had to call the operator who would connect you with the party you wished to talk to. You would then be charged for a long distance call. It cost about four dollars per year to be on the party line.

Our Saturday night bath would begin by bringing in the round washtub, which doubled as a rinse tub for washing clothes. Water would be heated in a boiler on the kitchen stove. The youngest ones got to be first, with the older children taking their turns according to age. Water was not wasted. It was warmed up as each one took their turn. The kitchen was closed off as the official bathroom for the evening.

Clothes were washed in a Maytag wringer washer, with rinse tubs for getting the soap out of the clothes before they were hung outside on a clothesline. They were suspended between wooden poles, and clothes were secured with wooden clothespins. In the winter, they had to be dried inside on wooden racks. Ironing was a big chore in those days with no automatic dryer to take the wrinkles out! Everything that had to be ironed went in a basket to await their turn at the iron. The iron had to be heated on the kitchen stove, and before using, had to be tested for correct temperature with a dampened finger, very quickly touched to the bottom of the iron. We had to have two or three irons so the one in use could be replaced as it cooled off.

The other use for an iron was to keep warm with as we went to school, riding in the back of a horse-drawn buggy, with a blanket over our heads and the iron close to our feet. My sister was the teacher at our one room school. She had to drive the horse and bring the water from home for the children to drink and wash with. She also had to start a fire in the wood-burning stove after getting to school when cold weather arrived. All for fifty dollars a month! (Afton school #2, Sanborn County, SD)

We didn't have an icebox so keeping meat fresh in the summer was usually a matter of dressing chickens in the morning for the noon meal. Pork would be kept in the basement in a large crock filled with brine to preserve it. Our basement had a dirt floor and was very deep so it stayed quite cool even in the summer. We saved milk each morning to use that day so it would be fresh. Most of the milk had to be separated using a hand cranked cream separator. Cream that wasn't needed for butter would be kept in the basement too, in ten-gallon cans. Once a week, a truck would come to the farm and pick up the cream cans and thirty dozen-egg cases, which provided the only extra grocery money available for many people.

I was born during one of the worst dust storms of the Dirty Thirties according to my older family members. Dust clouds obliterated all sun light and our kerosene lamps had to be lit in order to see at all. It was May 31, 1934. The day also holds the record of the highest temperature for that date, well over 100 degrees. Shortly after I arrived, my face, (and my mother's) was covered with dirty sweat streaks. My crib was covered with a wet cloth to keep some of the dirt off, which infiltrated all cracks and crevices. Mothers had to stay in bed for at least ten days after having a baby in those days. Three days after I was born, our twelve milk cows broke open a shed door where some poisoned grain was being held before being put out to kill grasshoppers. They ate the grain and all died, taking our only source of income with them. My dad had to go to work for the WPA, a government program to help farmers survive in those days. But we did survive.

Outside Was Frozen Up
By Jean Hansen of South Shore, South Dakota
Born 1934

I was born in 1934 and do indeed remember events growing up. Old radio programs; we didn't listen to the radio much, only for news and occasionally *Amos and Andy* because otherwise it would run the battery down. We didn't have electricity until I was 12 years old because my parents couldn't afford it before then. It was very cold in the winter. We had feather ticks on our beds to keep warm. The windows were frozen up so you couldn't see outside. We had a warm morning stove in the living room and a cook stove in the kitchen for heat.

My parents had enough food in the house to last most of the winter, potatoes in the basement. Mother did a lot of canning in late summer; she canned meat, homemade soups, vegetables, and sauce, and always baked bread. We had no indoor plumbing, the pumps outside were frozen up, so my parents would boil hot water to take it outside to pour on the pumps so we could have drinking water and also for cooking and washing.

Saturday night baths. I was the youngest of three children, so I was fortunate to receive my bath first in a round galvanized tub. We all used the same water for my sister, brother, and my parents. Washday was every Monday. We washed with boiling hot water, a rinse tub with cold water. Clothes were always hung outside and in the winter throughout the house. Tuesdays were for ironing, Wednesdays for mending, and Thursday's mother would do sewing. Fridays and Saturdays were for weekly cleaning and baking. Sundays were always for church, weather permitting. We had company for dinner often on Sunday because mother was a good cook. Mother sewed my dresses when I attended school. I was made fun of and laughed at because I didn't have up to date clothing.

I attended school in a one-room schoolhouse all my grade school years. I remember walking to school for two miles. One time when I walked, it was below zero. I was dressed warm. When I got there, the teacher wasn't there because the roads were either blocked or she couldn't get her car started, so I walked two miles back home. I froze my hands and feet. My favorite teacher

The one-room school that Jean attended

was when I was in the 5th and 6th grade. My mother was born in 1905 and didn't speak English until she was in 3rd grade. The one-room schoolhouse where she attended is still standing.

We went to the bathroom outside, which was very cold. One winter my dad built a wooden frame with a pail inside and put it in the basement; we thought we had it made that we didn't have to go outside. I wasn't allowed in the barn that much because I would get ringworm from the animals. Growing up I had two pet dog terriers; one would sleep in my doll buggy. I would cover her up like a doll. Another one was dad's farm dog, Rover. In the winter, he would sleep in the barn, in the summer he would sleep on the ground outside my parents' bedroom window. Dad passed away at age 55 from a heart attack. Rover howled every night and two weeks later, he also died.

We couldn't afford a telephone. I remember when we would visit an aunt and uncle. They had one. When they would use it, they had a party line and many of the neighbors would listen to the conversation. Memorable people in my life were my beloved parents who were very special. I didn't get a lot of spankings, but I do remember one I got from my dad because I was pouting and didn't want to participate with the rest of the family, it made me realize what was important.

We played a lot of pinochle growing up. I've been playing since 10 years old and still do every day. I got married for the first time in 1954, which lasted 51 years. Never had TV to watch until that time. Family time is still very important to me to get together with my three sons, their wives, and seven grandchildren.

Musings of a Country Gal
By Beverly Kluess of Clark, South Dakota
Born 1929

One cold, wintry day I popped into the world! Dad, although we had not been formally introduced, had gone to town with the bobsled to get supplies. When he told the doctor that mom, whom I had grown quite attached to by that time, was quite nervous that morning, he decided to return with dad. They found me already on the scene, calmly sucking my thumb! I was lucky to have been born and raised on a farm. Looking back, I now realize how most of my adventures involved some type of work, some I really enjoyed, and some I really disliked.

Shearing time was an exciting experience. I had to tie wool when I got big enough, but there were a few fleeces that were so huge I needed help with the wool box. It was an oily, smelly, eye-burning job in the heat, but I liked it and received two-cents for every fleece I tied! But of course, threshing was the highlight of the year. How I loved to ride the bundle racks and tend the grain wagon! All of our grain bins were bulging and there was even an improvised bin in the sheep shed. We found that small melons and muskmelons kept for months in the oat bin, until the rats found out they were quite tasty. We were not allowed to play on the huge, golden straw pile until it had settled. After about two weeks, it made a great slide and hiding place. What a thrill it was each fall to get a new pair of shoes, a pair of striped, overalls, and a pair of flannel pajamas. Those overalls were my prized possession!

It seems as if I was cold so much of the time. Even the drinking water froze in the kitchen. One day we tied our sleds to the hayrack when dad went after a load of hay. We got so wet and cold we could hardly stand it before we got home, and usually we'd have to go to the pot so bad we almost didn't make in time, and pot it was in the bedroom closet!

Speaking of such indelicate things reminds me of our outhouse games. My sister and I would take turns seeing who could read the most paint names on the chart in the back of the Sears catalog. We spent a lot of time picking out our families and their furnishings. When it got cold, we would rip out pages and burn them in a coffee can for heat and light. Occasionally there was a burnt finger and some scorched bangs, but nothing serious, fortunately!

Our old battery radio kept getting fainter and fainter until I had to put my ear right on the speak to hear *Jack Armstrong, the All American Boy* and *Hi Ho! Silver, Away*. He would be without for about a week while the battery was being charged at a filling station in town. Mom liked Major Bowl Amateur Hour and dad enjoyed *Fibber McGee and Molly*. The 20-person party line was a sport for many. Often when you were hanging up you would hear 10-12 receivers clunk down! I still remember 4960 was our number, and one long and three shorts was our ring.

One of my least favorite chores was empting the water pan under the old icebox. Of course, it was always full to the brim and with my agility, I managed to spill about half of the water in the process! The neighborhood men cut huge blocks of ice at Antelope Lake and covered it with flax straw in an old dugout. It was hard work, but we were assured of ice all summer.

Our stubborn old Maytag washer was very unpredictable. Sometimes it would start after a few steps and other times it took all of us to conquer it. Once it got the right mixture of gas and oil, it performed well. But then there would be the carrying out and dumping the wash and rinse water. Often it would be nice soft water from the tubs of melted snow.

Speaking of chores, one I disliked was herding sheep, even with the wide, front-end Alice Chalmers tractor. Those brilliant sheep could spot the slightest opening to get into a grain field, but the dumb beasts couldn't find a neon-lit exit! I even admit to getting so immersed in *Little Shepherd of Kingdom Come* that about 1/3 of the flocks was munching grain before I noticed!

One job I did like was driving the tractor cutting grain, although I didn't always do too well at it. Sometimes late in the sultry afternoon sun I would get drowsy and start driving into the grain. A yell would alert me and I managed to stay awake by singing at the top of my lungs! Yes, even way back then I fell asleep at the wheel!

The "Dirty Thirties" were part of my childhood also. Being born in 1929, I was young, but old enough to realize the seriousness of the condition to a farmer. I remember the wavy, fine, black sand rippling over the fence lines, thistles piling up in the fence corners, and cows having lockjaw from eating those thistles and hot scorching sun, winds, and a few clouds, but no rain!

And now at 85 in retrospect, I recall so many little unimportant experiences that made for a happy childhood and a rewarding life. I never had a bike, a pony, roller skates, ice skates, or a car, but I had a wealth of experiences only a farm gal could appreciate. I hoed weeds in shelterbelts and picked potatoes and did many other unfeminine jobs. After graduating from high school, I went right into teaching. A husband and 3 children later, after 22 years, I finally obtained my B.A. It comes pretty slow a few hours at a time. I've put the education and love of kids and learning to good use, teaching for 38 years and then subbing for 17 more. I retired in 1991 and still miss the students and the camaraderie of the teachers. Looking back, I realize what a happy, useful, amazing life I had had!

Basket Socials
By Delores Henning of Veblen, South Dakota
Born 1935

My first memory was when my sister was born. My dad lifted me up and told me that I wasn't the baby anymore. I was overjoyed, as I hated being the baby. The year was 1937, I was two years old.

In those days, doctors made house calls and my sister was born at home in my parent's bedroom. My older sister took my four-year-old brother and me outside until the ordeal was over.

We lived in an old farmhouse that was rumored to be haunted. Every night at the same time, the stairs creaked one by one all the way to the top step. It was said to be the woman who was supposedly poisoned there. She would rattle the spoon in her glass of poison. We shivered and believed every word.

When my baby sister was a toddler, she tipped over a pan of hot lard over her face and chest. The crying was incessant, and was terrible to hear. She still has the scars to this day.

When I was six years old, we moved to a farm two miles away. We chased our cattle on foot to the new farm. The house was small. It was only three rooms and there were eight family members. There was my mom, dad, and six other children. Later my twin sisters were born but one died at 2 and half months old.

I started school that year in September of 1941. Two of my older brothers and sisters walked with me to the one room schoolhouse over a mile away. There was only one other first grader and he was a great playmate. We were allowed many privileges the other students were not.

One teacher taught all eight grades. There were about twenty pupils most of the time. The winter months were very difficult, as everyone walked to and from school. The snow became very deep and the ravine filled with snow too. We had to walk around the road, which was a half a mile further. We girls all wore long underwear and long brown cotton stockings held up by a garter belt. We also wore snow pants, long coat, mittens, caps, and overshoes with snaps on the side.

We carried our lunch in Syrup pails. Our lunch consisted of jelly sandwiches, an orange or an apple, a cookie or a cake. My

Delores Jacobson Henning and Dean Hofland in 1941

Stanley Hill School class of 1941

mother baked breads twice a week and a cake or cookie that day as well. The first one that arrived at school carried out the ashes and started the fire. Can you imagine entrusting a child with that responsibility today?

Although those were very difficult times, we also had fun. The games we played were red rover, anti and over, fox and goose, and softball. Many parties were held at the schoolhouse especially Valentine's Day, Christmas programs, and basket socials. My sister and her friend, who were eighth graders, made a basket for me also, although I was only a first grader. The basket was made from shoeboxes and decorated with crepe paper. The basket was filled with a delicious lunch. They were auctioned off to the highest bidder. You had to share your lunch with whoever got your basket. A younger man bought my basket, and I was scared to death of him as he was a rough looking fellow. I cried all the way through that delicious lunch, but I choked it down with tears rolling down my face. I was so disappointed as I thought my little classmate would buy my basket.

We had outdoor toilets, one for the girls and one for the boys. The boys liked to catch a snake and put it through the windows of the girl's toilet. We had a water cooler for drinking and washing your hands, a basin, and a towel. All the boys carried a pocketknife with them, even the little ones.

The older boys loved to ski and were very good at it. The younger kids brought their sled to school. We had a wonderful hill to slide down. You could go almost a half a mile and hardly have time to return before the noon bell. The hill became very slippery and the farmer who used that road chased us off it many times.

One day it was cold and stormy when we arrived at school and the teacher was not there yet. We waited awhile and then when the teacher never showed we started for home. As we went into the trees, we saw the teacher coming up the hill. But, we hid in the trees until she left. We can tell it today as that teacher is no longer living

All the children were friends and played together. I never witnessed any bullies until the county school closed and we had to attend school in town. There I quickly found out what mean kids there was in our community. Now that they are adults, they would not admit to it, I'm sure.

Teaching in Country Schools
By Luella Schultz of Miller, South Dakota
Born 1933

Do you ever reflect on how your life evolved and why it happened that way or how? In the fall of 1954, I decided not to go back to college because I just wasn't happy with the history degree I had been working toward and I felt sort of in limbo. I went on vacation with my parents. It was great to see relatives and all the views from the vehicle from SD to CA and then back. However, when we got home I thought to myself, now what?

One day in December, a telephone call came from our Hand County School Superintendent. That call put me on a path that controlled my life for the next thirty-six years. She was looking for someone to teach a country school some twenty-eight miles southwest of my home town of Miller, South Dakota. There were eleven students ranging in grades one through eight.

Looking back, I cannot imagine myself agreeing to go, but it became the very best life experience with the students and parents that I could ever have hoped and wished for. They became lifelong friends that I dearly love to this day. Roads back in the 1950s were gravel at best. There were no cell phones and in fact, the telephone in the schoolhouse was one that still used the rings of the long and short version.

Driving in the country was one scary time after another for me. The first Monday I left Miller I wished I was anywhere but where I was headed. However, today I wouldn't trade those years for anything. That January morning it was cold and the road leading from Ree Heights, which was eleven miles west of Miller and then turned south another eighteen miles to the school, was snow packed. There was no trace of another vehicle tire tracks plus I wasn't real sure of the turn off from the Ree Heights road to go west three miles to where the school was located. I had only been there one time with the superintendent. That was the first scary drive.

I had several others over the course of two winters going to that school. I would drive out Monday morning and I roomed with one of the families, during the week, who lived the closest to the school and drove home after school was over on Friday. The family I lived with had an old two-story home with one central kitchen heating stove. There was no indoor bathroom but the people inside that house made up double time for any inconveniences inside of the house. Plus, a double blessing was that the farm wife had been a country school teacher so she helped me enormously about how to arrange times for classes and other things. I had no instruction from the country office since I had missed all the August teacher meetings. Can you imagine going in blind plus then hearing how the students had run the previous teacher off, a wonder; I didn't back off and run away myself?

I was not aware that there were regulations about days when a teacher could not possibly make it to the school so one snowy bad Monday morning I called the local airport man and hired him to fly me out to the school. I had never flown before plus if I even turn around quickly, my stomach can turn over and go upside down. Anyway, the pilot took off and before we had reached the Ree Heights road, it became so foggy he couldn't see the ground. Between a few swear words he turned around and started back toward Miller but before we got there (and that was when I should have told the pilot to just land and let me go home) he decided to turn around and try it again. How he had any idea what was below us I have no idea. All at once, he flew down to the ground and there we were not far from the farm house where I boarded. I don't recall but I'm sure my legs were like rubber. Now as I write this I'm wondering how I got back to town come Friday afternoon without my car?

Then another Friday afternoon looking out the window it appeared to be rather windy but it was Friday and I was going home. When I went to the farm house to collect my suitcase the farmer man said he was going to go ahead of me with his tractor the three miles to the Ree Heights road to make sure I got there safely. Sometime later I learned that the wife had told her husband to tell me that I couldn't go to town and he told her that he wasn't telling me that I couldn't go but that he would show me that it was not safe. By the time we got to the main road, I knew I wasn't going anywhere. I stood on the back of the tractor bar with my arms around the middle of the farmer and prayed that we would make it back home to the house safely.

Other Friday nights I was happy to find Ivan Hancock on the Ree Heights road in his county snow patrol and if it was iffy at all I would just drive slowly behind him and smile when I saw the small town of Ree Heights as I knew then I would arrive safely to my bed in Miller.

I have another story about an airplane ride I took. I had one male first cousin, six foot six and a good Miller Rustler basketball player. Since I had been in college one hundred and twenty miles away for his first three years in high school, I had missed most of his playing time. So one Friday night came and the team was playing in Miller but the roads were blocked. I called a farmer I knew from north of Miller that had a small airplane and he agreed to come get me. I hated flying, and still do, but I so wanted to see him play that game. I felt a lot safer flying with this man and so happy to land in Miller and go home for two days and two nights in my own bed and get to go to the game. This was in 1957 and some thirty five years later, that farmer pilot told me that when he landed his plane near the farm house he noticed gas dripping out of the plane's fuel tank. He said he didn't know what to do but he was chewing gum so he took that gum and pushed it into the hole. He plugged the hole hoping it would hold until we landed at the Miller Airport.

After two winters at that school, I went back to college to get my four year elementary degree and then taught four years at another country school just eight miles southwest of Miller. I was home in my own bed with the exception of a few nights when I had to go home with one of the farm families without pajamas or a toothbrush. Then my high school superintendent talked me into signing a contract to teach sixth grade in Miller town school. There I remained in the same sixth grade classroom for the next thirty years. What a blessing to have had that time with students who I still get hugs from and reminders of why people spend time teaching young people.

An Unusual Marriage and Honeymoon
By Loran Perry of Brookings, South Dakota
Born 1936

It was a sultry Saturday night in July 1954. My girlfriend, Carol, and I were cruising the streets of Bruce, South Dakota. All three of them, in my light blue 1937 Chevy coupe! Carol saw her two cousins, Joyce and Naomi on the sidewalk, so we stopped to talk to them. Joyce wanted us to go to Toronto for the dance. Her reason was obvious, her boyfriend was there. So I told her yes and to hop in. Four people in a single seat, was real cozy.

Out on the road the girls were laughing and having a good time, everything was funny. As we approached the county line, a car came up behind intending to pass. Joyce reached over and jerked the steering wheel back and forth swerving us all over the road so the person behind

Loran and Carol Perry in 1954

couldn't pass. He kept honking and trying to get by. Finally, I pulled over and let him pass. The girls laughed and waved, but it was a sobering moment when we came to the next intersection and he was standing in the road trying to flag us down. We sped on by and went on to the dance but when we started home, we were stopped by a highway patrol and given a ticket for reckless driving. The man we irritated just happened to be the state's attorney for that County.

The next morning, with great apprehension, I approached my dad in the milking barn and showed him the ticket. His face turned white with anger and he told me that I would have to face the judge alone because he wasn't going with me. I had to sell my pet sheep to get the seventy-five dollars for the fine. That was a lot of money back then! My license was suspended for thirty days and I was forbidden to leave the farm. I was also forbidden to see Carol again.

We had a bunkhouse in the back yard where I slept in the summertime. I was surprised a few nights later to see Carol and Joyce at the door with flashlights. They parked on the road and walked across the alfalfa field. We made plans to meet at night by signaling with flashlights and I would come out to the road across the alfalfa field and we would spend time together. It was then that we made plans to elope.

When I got my license back, I left the farm under the pretense of going to a youth meeting at the church. From there we headed for Pipestone Minnesota where the next morning we were married by the Pastor of the Lutheran church. I'm sure he wondered why we had our eye on the door during the whole service. By that time, my parents had the highway patrol looking for us. With fifty dollars in my pocket, we pulled out of Pipestone taking all of the back roads and headed for Stanley, North Dakota.

Carol had an uncle in Stanley who we knew we could stay with until we got established. When we found them they were living in a moved in house that had not yet been set on a foundation. When we walked in the living room, we saw grass growing up through the furnace grate in the middle of the floor.

The Tioga oil fields were close by and I thought I could get a job there. I soon found out you had to be twenty-one to even get on the oil rigs. I had lied my age to get my marriage license but it wouldn't work here. It was fall and they were laying people off of the oil rigs. The foreman told me I would never be able to find a job in this town. So I hit the street and before nightfall I had a job. It wasn't much it was just bagging groceries in the local market, but I worked my way up to butcher's helper.

A meat market was a little different in those days. We would hitch a trailer behind the butcher's car and drive out into the pasture. I would hold the knife while he shot the critter, then I would hold the gun while he bled it out. We would dress it out and drag it up on the trailer and haul it into town where we would skin it, quarter it, and hang it in the cooler. One day out in the pasture the bull smelled the blood and came after us. We almost had to leave the critter and go back to town without it, but we finally got away.

I got a second job working for the local TV repairman. Stanley was located down in a valley, and everyone who had a TV had to have a tower to get there antenna up high enough to get reception. So I spent my evenings climbing TV towers to repair the lead in wires. Our first apartment was above the Oldsmobile dealership on Main Street. We had nothing to set up housekeeping with, so the TV repairman's wife gave us a kettle and Carol used it for everything. She would cook the potatoes and set them aside, then fry the hamburger in the same kettle and then make the gravy. We enjoyed it, however, because we were making memories. My parents, trying to get us back to South Dakota, put out a stolen car report on my car. So we bought another car and snuck back and left the stolen car at the sheriff's office in the middle of the night.

After six months we decided to return to South Dakota. After all who else gets to have a six-month honeymoon? By that time we had purchased a trailer house, which was a big mistake. They call them a mobile home today but ours was a trailer house. We hitched it to our car and we pulled out of Stanley at midnight Saturday night after I got off work. It was Sunday afternoon by the time we got to the South Dakota border. There we blew a tire on the trailer and were unable to get a new one on Sunday so we abandoned the trailer on and approach and headed for Bruce. Carol was in the back seat sick and I had to get her to a hospital.

We had intended to not have children right away but my mom was determined to annul the marriage so we changed our plans. We arrived in Bruce at midnight and I took Carol right on to the hospital in Brookings because she was severely dehydrated. The next morning her brother LaValle and I headed back to get the trailer house. We got as far as Millette, South Dakota and a rod went out of my car so we were stranded there. We found a lady in town that took in boarders so we had a bed for the night. In the morning we had to walk a mile out to the highway to flag down a bus so we could get back home. The bus dropped us off on the highway ten miles from Bruce and we had to thumb a ride from there to town. The next morning we left again in LaValle's car to get the trailer house. It was so heavy that I would get out and bounce it to get clearance to get across railroad tracks. It was Thursday morning when we finally pulled into Bruce with the trailer house. I had to use my dad's cattle truck for transportation for the next few weeks until I could pull my car home and get it repaired.

You might think a marriage with such an unusual beginning might not have a very good chance of surviving, but we stayed together for fifty-nine years and raised twelve children. We had Carol's funeral on our fifty ninth wedding anniversary.

My Mother
By Diann Dauwen of Milbank, South Dakota
Born 1945

My mother was energetic, strong, hardworking, and determined person. She was born in 1923 and in maturity only reached the stature of five feet two inches. She never let that stop her from enduring many setbacks in her short life, dying at the age of 69 from pancreatic cancer.

I was probably about 10 years old when she started telling me stories of her youth. We would be in our farm kitchen sharing the task of doing the dishes in a completely non-modern setting, in which there was no running water, no bathroom, and few electrical appliances. The house had been my paternal grandmother's house, having been wired for electricity only a couple years prior, when we moved there from a farm my Dad had been renting.

As we worked, her mind would wander back to that long ago time when she wasn't much older than I was at that time. Already at birth, her life was not to be the normal life of a baby growing up with both her parents, as her mother died when she was only five days old. My grandfather decided he could not take care of her and made the decision to put her in the care of his own parents. His family was large, 12 children, and so there were many aunts at home to care for my mother. She loved the attention and the spoiling that naturally was showered upon her.

At the age of seven, my mother went to live again with her father and new stepmother and her brother who was two years older than her. She had not been to school yet, and so that

Diann in 1949

was the first priority. However, she had one big problem. She spoke only German, as that was the language spoken in her grandparent's home, where she had lived all this time. She had a big struggle to overcome the language barrier, but she knew she had to do it! Then there was the problem when the boys of the neighbors hid along the route where she walked to school and beat her up. She usually had to stay behind and finish all of her chores before leaving for school. By that time, her brothers had gone ahead of her, so she had no one to help her. She not only got in trouble at school for being late, but also at home if she came home with torn clothes.

By the time, she was 12, she had seven brothers, and it was her assignment to do all the dishes every day after school. That being the case, she was busily going about her work one day while her parents were attending a funeral. One of her brothers brought a gun in the house to clean it. Another of her brothers warned him to be careful and to make sure it was not loaded. The one with the gun assured him it wasn't and went about his business, until the gun went off and hit my mother! The oldest brother was 14. The others were younger than my mother. One of the younger ones jumped on a horse and rode to a neighbor's house to get help. This neighbor had a car and came and took my mother to town to the doctor. The doctor who operated on her happened to be an old army doctor and knew how to deal with this type of injury, which had made a mess of her intestines. It was nip and tuck as he opened her up and placed her intestines on the table beside her. He had to painstakingly clean out all the blood and waste, fix the damage, and sew her back together, which he did! She lived to tell about it.

It was one of those bad South Dakota winters not so long after this when her Dad's car became stuck in the snow. My mother had to get out and push, as Grandpa would go forward and then back, trying to rock the old car out of the snow bank. One time he backed up farther than she expected, knocking her over and running over her shoulder and breaking her collarbone. She could have been killed, but apparently God was watching over her! As time went on, her shoulder hung and was not normal. She was then taken to the doctor and learned that the collarbone had grown together, but not correctly. The doctor

Farmall Tractor in about 1950

said "wild meat" had grown in the crack where it was broken. He then had to re-break it. It took both my grandfather and the doctor to do this, each pulling in opposite directions. The pain must have been excruciating!

She told about the dirty thirties and the rationing of gas and sugar. Being her family lived on the farm they had enough eat, as Grandpa was a butcher. He would use every bit of the hog or cow he butchered in some way. He used the blood to make blood sausage. He even used the brains of the animal. The intestines were cleaned out and used for skins for the sausages. My mother would get only one pair of shoes per year to wear and would go barefoot all summer. She had two sets of clothes to wear. She told how sometimes the days were dark and how the wind filled the air with dirt from the fields. When they set the table, they placed the plates face down because by the time they were ready to eat the plates would already have a dusting of fine dirt on them.

My mother finally met my Dad, and after some courting they were married. My parents were both very good dancers, and my paternal grandfather played the violin in a band. In those days, they had house parties, and the old porch/dining room in the house where I grew up was the dance floor. My dad and mother lived with my paternal grandparents during the early years of their marriage, as they were very poor and had no money to start farming on their own. During that time, they farmed Grandpa's land. (My paternal grandmother told me years later this land had been homesteaded by my great grandparents who lived in a dugout in the side of the hill. Two dugouts were there, each facing the other.

One was occupied by my great grandparents and the other by some relatives of my great grandparents.)

Then I came into the world and gave my mother some more trouble! I was born breech and a large baby, weighing eight pounds and two ounces. We both survived the ordeal, and mom recorded it in my baby book! Now it was my turn to be spoiled rotten, and I was told grandpa did a good job of it. We lived with them until I was two years old, and then my Dad rented some land and struck out on his own.

The farm became one big adventure to me. I loved all the animals. Dad farmed with big black farm horses, and they were my favorite! Pictures document how my dad would let me hold the reins while he went in the house for a break. I was so proud. Whenever I could, I would steal a ride on the hay wagon out to the field.

I wasn't afraid of anything, so I became a real nightmare to my parents. When they took me along to the barn to do the milking, I fell in the gutter or got stepped on by the calves.

The solution to the whole problem seemed to be to leave me in the house while they did the milking chores. That was also a potential danger, as the lights in those days were kerosene lamps placed on our kitchen table. What if it got knocked over? My usual position, however, was to sit next to the window and sing. Even though the barn and the house were a good distance apart, my mother could check on me by listening for my singing at the window. However, one evening she didn't hear me and knew instantly that something was wrong. She soon learned that I had seen a mouse run across the woodwork at the top of the door across from me. I guess that was one animal of which I was afraid!

Eventually my Dad decided it was time to get rid of those beautiful horses. That was the final straw for me! I begged and begged him to keep the horses, but technology even then was improving. He had bought a used Farmall tractor to work the fields and wouldn't have to put all that feed in those big horses, but I just couldn't understand why he had to let them go. I loved them so much!

Us Three Boys
By Leland Olson of Arlington, South Dakota
Born 1940

The outhouse or little house out back was usually some distance from the house, specially in town. The distance in the country was dictated mostly by the climate. You didn't want to put snowshoes on for that emergency trip to the toilet. A good policy was to keep a path shoveled, less chance for a fall in the snow to interrupt your business trip.

Large families might have had a three or four hole luxury type biff with a kerosene lantern even. Two hole facilities were most common. A wooden duct system was built into some toilets that served as a backrest and for ventilation that vent created an updraft below your seat; best to cover the outside vent holes when temp was below zero. Fly spray found its way from the barn to the toilet in the summer months, so did the flies.

It was best to secure the toilet to anchors in the ground, in spite of wanting to move it to a new hole location someday. Halloween tricksters liked to tip toilets over, "usually while they were occupied." In bear country, you didn't want to become a boxed lunch. In the upper Great Plains the wind might turn your toilet into a Porta Potty if it wasn't anchored down.

Those quiet little outhouses were perfect for thinkers. If you listen closely while nature calls, you have real power to shape your destiny. You could read the Sears or Wards catalog and dream or bring a paperback book for enlightenment or entertainment, preferably with soft pages. Thinking about your walk on this earth was usually the best spent time. There have probably been more good ideas incubated in the old outhouse than in Washington D.C.

When I was maybe three years old, I dropped a Kitten down the toilet hole. My dad put his belt around me and lowered me down the hole to get the kitten. I handed the kitten up to my dad and he left me down there for a while. There was lots of poop, kittens are born in the spring, there must've been about nine months of poop piled up down there. He turned me around a few times while I was hanging in midair so I got a real good view on the way up. I didn't do it again.

Water parks are the thing in this new age. In the past, livestock water tanks attracted little kids on a hot summer day. Rule one at our farm, "all kids stay away from the water tank." My brother and I must have been a little slow. One day we walked into the house still a little damp, mom asks, "you kids been in the water tank?" We both say, "noooo." My brother still had some moss in his hair. Mom told us, "dad will deal with you two tonight." Oh, what a long day!" We didn't have any attention deficit problem when dad was there."

City kids had little red wagons for playing. Country kids used them for some of their first chores. The load and speed wasn't as important as learning to help. We hauled coal or firewood to the house a little at a time. The old kitchen cook stove loved corncobs. They made a quick hot fire. The hogs ate the corn off the cobs and we kids would gather the cobs in our little bucket and then dump them into our wagons and bring them to the house. Going after those cobs was scary at first, some of those old hogs looked just plain ornery. Guess they knew not to eat kids though. Grandma had a Rhode Island red rooster that would stand in

Frank, Francis, Carlton, Harland, and Leland Olson in 1947

front of little kids looking them straight in the eye, biggest old rooster I ever saw.

We started helping around the farm at a young age. As we got older, we graduated from turning the milk separator to jobs like carrying water into the house and to the milk cows during a snowstorm. Pitchforks and shovels fit fairly small hands. If the arms and back were strong enough you could stack hay or haul in hay, and shovel grain. Cleaning a chicken house also cleaned your nose with the ammonia smell. Even if you're not real good with a fork you can help clean the barn. When you clean the hog house you have to marvel at their clean beds. When the hay baler came along you learned to handle and stack hay bales that weighed as much as you did.

There were very few snowplows in the War Years, hardly any for townships. Several people could shovel all day and still not get the road open. The wind would blow at night and drift everything shut by morning. Those who kept a team of horses and bobsled were busy. Most couples on the farm had kids but those who didn't could easily find people to work for room and board and a few dollars for wages. There were no welfare programs.

Our little country school was two miles away. After my first day, I told mom that I was not going anymore. She told me that it doesn't work that way. My education had started and I hardly realized it! There was at least one child for each grade, one through eight. The teacher's pay was small and she boarded at the students homes. My uncle came home on furlough in 1945, he thought she was real cute, but no romance there. We usually walked to school, until my dad got us a two-wheel cart and a pony. The first day the pony walked out into the slough on the way to school and just stood in the water. Three boys stranded on a cart, my older brother waded in, and led Shorty the pony back up on the road.

My folks sold the farm and moved to Bryant in 1947. They got divorced in 1950 and mom moved us boys to Watertown. I went to seven different schools in two years. When we started junior high, we had to walk as far as we did on the farm, no more pony, and cart. There was no TV or electronic games in those days. Mom worked at a dress shop. We three boys became latch key kids and were expected to hold up our end of the bargain. We raised a big garden for vegetables, cleaned house, and

Leland, Carlton, and Harlan Olson in 1944

learned to use the old ringer wash machine. We lived in town then but still pumped water, heated it in a tub with cut soap on the gas stove. We washed clothes and hung them on the line. My brother, Harlan was the only one to run an arm past the elbow in the old ringers. Our free time was spent at the golf course. We caddied every spare minute for our spending money.

Watertown was a big railroad town until the 1960s. There was a hobo camp down by the river not far from where we lived. My brothers and I got started visiting them; some of their stories had our minds traveling the rails everywhere. They even shared their hobo stew with us. We bought a few ingredients once in a while. We took short rides on trains while they were switching cars in town. We learned to be real careful crawling under any trains. I was intrigued by the activity in the roundhouse building and snuck in there a lot, hiding down below while they turned those big steam engines around. I suppose I would have gone directly to reform school if they had caught me. Another favorite cool hangout was the big old icehouse. Ice was cut into big blocks and harvested on Lake Kampeska most of the winter. There were two icehouses at the lake and one in town. The ice blocks were covered with sawdust and piled about thirty feet high in those buildings.

We continued to expand our rail travel by hopping on a train in town and going out to the edge of town before jumping off, then walk back if no inbound train was coming. We rode farther out and jumped off later as the speed increased. Those old steam engines were very fascinating, one of the best times in history. If my mom had known all the stuff we were doing, she would have had a full-blown conniption. Our stepdad didn't seem real concerned as he suggested we bring some coal home from time to time. I don't know why we quit riding the trains, afraid of getting hurt or not old enough to go to California probably because the hobos were mostly gone. We must have stuck out like three sore thumbs.

Starting in the twenties, all through the depression years and World War II people were dancing up a storm. The big band era gave the people a feeling of hope while looking to the future. Every little town and wide spot on the road had a dance hall, the bigger towns had more dance halls. There were many local bands and orchestras and big name bands traveling through. Some of those same folks are still dancing today. They outlived the dance halls, not many dance halls are left. The saying "dance and stay young" still rings true. Maybe not with some new dances though.

It wasn't all dancing and fun, my dad seemed to get into a fight no matter where we went. The War was still raging in Europe. I wonder if that is why there were so many fistfights breaking out here. Those who didn't get drafted were in a delicate situation, I think that brought on many fights. My uncle was home on leave and staying at our house. He was maybe eighteen at the time, just a kid. A big dance hall bully beat him up real bad because he was my dad's brother –in-law. This guy must have been both big and dumb. When my dad took one look at my uncle, he loaded us in the car and went to find this guy. We went to three different towns before we found him. My dad called this guy out of a beer joint and proceeded to beat some of the orneriness out of him. That was the bloodiest mess I ever saw, thought my dad was going to kill him. The big bully guy laid pretty low for a long time after that.

My dad was exempt from the draft being an only son and his folks needed him on the farm. I don't think that set real well with him. There is a song called "War is Hell on the Home Front too." This song rings true because it is hell for the whole population one way or another. War brought the people together at one time now it is driving them apart.

Hunting, fishing, and trapping have always been a part of life in N.E. South Dakota. It is big time reaction today. They were mostly done for survival in 1868 when my great grandfather arrived. A second cousin told a story of him leaving over a trapping dispute in 1905. It was probably getting too crowded here then. People fortunate enough to have grown up here have a love for nature and their fellow man that few others can comprehend. I hope we can always hang on to that.

Let's Talk About the Important Things
By John "Matt" Sutton of Sioux Falls, South Dakota
Born 1931

People my age talk about the old days and the new things they have come to appreciate like: television, computers, internet, interstate highways, microwave, air conditioned autos, heck, just heated automobiles. Those things have benefitted mankind significantly, but personally none come anywhere near the top. Let's talk about something really important, indoor plumbing and thermostat controlled central heat. You say, "Why not electricity?" For one thing, we had some form of electricity quite early in my life. Another thing, kerosene lamps and iceboxes were much better alternatives than anything we had available to replace running water and central heat. No indoor plumbing meant hurried trips in 20 below weather, often with a flashlight, to that little house 40 yards away that had a bench with 2 large holes in it. Why two holes? I don't know. I don't ever remember sitting there visiting with someone else.

The relief was an important part of the trip, but only half of the adventure. Of course, the cleanup had to follow. The most common cleanup aids were Sears and Roebuck and Montgomery Ward catalogs. One advantage of a mail order catalog was that if you saw something you liked you could order it out of a newer catalog when you got back to the house. The big disadvantage was the large number of slick pages with colored pictures. If I remember correctly, Sears and Roebuck had the most black and white pages. A high point in late summer was when crates of peaches became available. Not only did we enjoy fresh peaches to eat, but also each peach came wrapped in tissue paper. What a great alternative to even Sears and Roebuck. I've seen Dad use a corncob when nothing else was available. I tried it once, but it never gained favor at our place. The story in the neighborhood was that some neighbors had boxes of corncobs in their outhouse. Some even claimed that in 1936 the corn crop was so poor some had one cob on a string.

The primary alternative to the outhouse was the pot, mainly for the very old and the very young. Also, it was somewhat common for the young males to simply open an upstairs window. You had to be sure from what direction the wind was blowing. Not only were the toilet facilities inconvenient, the mere availability of water was a problem. We had a well with a hand pump on it close to the house. We'd fill buckets and bring them in as needed. We always kept a pail of relatively clean water with a dipper in it for drinking. Of course, there was the ubiquitous slop pail where all the wastewater and garbage were deposited. When it became full, it was carried out and dumped on a side hill a short distance from the house. It attracted scavengers of all kinds, but

Matt's father, John Sutton

we were careful not to throw anything there that was not biodegradable or would smell bad. That sort of waste went into the burning barrel or got carried off to the fields.

Another ritual that was a necessity of course was the Saturday night bath. We had the conventional round tub that was big enough for the kids to get into. Big kids and adults had to sit on the edge and use a washcloth. A very enjoyable exception to all this water problem came about in the summer time. After supper, following a hard day's work, we'd go to a nearby stock pond that was generally full of clean, fresh water to have a swim and a bath. Floating soap like Ivory and Swan may be a convenience in a bathtub, but they are an absolute necessity in a stock pond.

I imagine one of the concerns of our caveman ancestors was how to keep the fire burning all night and how to spread the heat to all corners of the cave. It seemed to me as I turned 12 that civilization had not made much progress in that area. We did have a stovepipe that got the smoke out of the house. We had a heating stove that held a substantial amount of wood. If you put in enough wood late enough at night and reduced the air supply to the fire there should still be hot coals in the morning. This wasn't so bad for my parents and sisters on the first floor, but my little brother and I slept on the second floor. Ken and I slept between blankets rather than sheets. Have you ever crawled between two sheets when the temperature was below freezing? We also slept with our winter caps on and the earflaps down. Our top cover was a full sized, tanned buffalo hide with all the fur still on it. An adjoining bedroom was cold enough that a buffalo carcass would keep all winter. We would cut off what we needed to eat each day.

Coal was available then and most people burned it. We didn't. We had an ample supply of top quality firewood within a mile of the house. Gathering it was an adventure in itself. My cousin, Neil Hanson, and I often did this when we came home from high school on weekends. We'd harness one of the draft horses and head for the timber by the river. We'd go through the woods looking for dead ash trees either standing or fallen. We'd cut them down if necessary and trim them enough so we could drag them through the standing timber to a central location outside the tree stand. We'd hook the horse to the trimmed log and lead him rather than drive him. It was kind of fun to dodge the standing trees and fallen logs at a half trot because that was the only speed the horse knew. The regular ranch crew would set up the buzz saw and cut everything into 15 to 20 inch lengths. It would then be hauled home and piled near the house. It was usually my job to haul it into the house. There were no power driven log splitters at that time and I remember a sense of pride when I got big enough to split the larger logs with an ax into sections that would fit into the kitchen cooking stove.

I started high school in 1944 and began to enjoy the luxuries of city life. The first significant change at the ranch was central heat from a propane furnace. Shortly after that, a propane space heater was installed upstairs. REA didn't come to the ranch until 1951. That gave us enough dependable electric power to provide a pressurized water system and a resulting sewer system. We could now dispose of the proverbial two-holer.

My Eddy School Saga
By Lois B. Warfield of Fairfax, Virginia
Born 1932

This tan sheet of paper that came to me with the Wessington Springs paper has been laying here on my table waiting for me to pick up a pen. Now that I'm housebound from falling on ice and entertaining nine staples and eight stitches in my head well, here goes. My name is Lois Warfield. I was born in 1932 on a farm west of Wessington Springs, South Dakota. I am now 81 years of age.

Our one-room schoolhouse was Eddy School. The schoolhouse had a basement below, which was nice when the weather was blowing and snowing and very cold. The toilets at the school were small wooden structures, often upset by high school kids at Halloween. That year we had seven students attending. The year of this incident was 1940. Our teacher was a single gal who rode her horse two miles to school. There was a small barn for her to tie her horse there. Our problem with Ms. Weiss began when weather turned extremely cold after Christmas. In the fall it was kind of fun hanging out around the school, playing ball, waiting for the teacher to come let us in. I must admit some of the boys found a way to climb up and go thru the window to place a tack on Ms. Weiss's chair or put a frog in her desk drawer. I think someone's uncle put us up to this kind of prank. Alas, when the cold-cold winter weather arrived after Christmas, it was not fun to be outside.

One morning, we decided to build a huge snowman, rolling the snow around toilet chemical cans. Certainly, we did not intend to cause the resulting chaos! About 10:15, when the teacher came galloping her horse up the lane, neither she nor the horse saw our magnificent snow structure. The horse hit our snowman, and flew one way and the teacher another way. Our teacher wasn't badly hurt, thank God, but we decided one of the boys would run home to get our dad since he was on the school board and she was crying. Oh my, we were in for some stern discipline! Finally, our dad realized we had been waiting around for our teacher to arrive nearly all year. Between the school superintendent and our dad, they decided we needed a different teacher. They assured us she would be a very stern teacher who would expect us to do our very best. How happy we were! She was always on time! We were learning, we loved our teacher, and wished we could have her back the next year.

Teachers were hard to come by out there on the prairie in rural Dakota. My dad was still on the school board for Eddy School and was frantically searching for someone to step up to take the position for the school year of 1945. Dr. Fite said, "Rudy, your daughter, Doris, was an excellent student and has just finished a year at the local college, would she be available to teach this year?" And so she stepped up to fill the position. By that time, other people with children had moved to farms nearby and we had 16 students! Our Aunt Tressie was a teacher and she coached Doris and shared materials and lesson plans, and we had a teacher! It was not long before Sister Doris (Miss Kurkowski) realized it was impossible for her to teach all those children! And suddenly, guess who became her teacher's aide for the 1st thru 4th graders?

That year we put on the most wonderful Christmas program for the parents and grandparents. Parents and friends helped us decorate and I was appointed to go into town to sell tickets for our show. We had a huge crowd, raffled off a turkey, getting enough money to buy some curtains for the windows. We invited a couple boys back who were excellent in doing plays, had lots of music, and guess who sang "White Christmas," wearing my pretty red dress. All went well for the year and Miss Kurkowski was on for another year. I will have to say she was one excellent teacher, very organized, and got rave reviews from the county administrator on her performance.

A small highlight, however. While I taught the youngsters, I was not being taught 7th and 8th grade material. My test scores were excellent as I was coached on the test material. I don't suppose this had a major effect on me, but when I got to high school, believe me I came to realize what I had missed. Still haven't figured out Algebra. But thankfully haven't really needed it.

Just a little note to finish up on my Eddy School Saga. At the end of my 2nd year at Huron College, that fall, once again my dad was short a teacher. He came to me pleading for me to come home to teach Eddy School. I was to have only six students and dad pleaded with me because my mom was very ill, my grandmother had recently passed away, and frankly, he just needed me to come home. And so I did. What a delightful year, weather relatively pleasant and wonderful young students. I was challenged by one student who had a learning disability and I worked ever so hard to teach him all that I could. It seems he has found his niche and is doing just fine in life.

My challenges at teaching old Eddy had nothing to do with the children. We had a wonderful year. I was always concerned about banking the fire when it got cold. How many times did I walk back or get my dad to let me use his car while I went back to see that the dampers were properly set. It turned out to be a wonderful year with my grandfather living at home with us. I would help with chores and cooking, and washing the dishes while Grandpa dried. What wonderful stories he had to tell. I married a military officer and became a military wife. We moved 28 times in 30 years. Our children were born in California, North Carolina, and Texas. They graduated from high school in Hawaii; Newport, Rhode Island; and Virginia. And I did substitute teaching along the way.

Lesson from Chickens
By Joyce Yexley of West Fargo, North Dakota
Born 1953

Introduction—I loved summer days on the farm. Each day was adventurous! My memories are collected from our family farm and my grandparent's farm located along the James River, in Columbia, South Dakota. My favorite days were spent with my grandma Mae and her chickens. These are a few of my lessons from raising chickens.

Grandma Mae, dad's mother was a master in raising chickens. She had four chicken coops on her farm. She named them the Swen Coop, Big Coop, Winter Coop, and the East Coop. Grandma was Swedish. When I stayed with Grandma, she let me gather the eggs, clean eggs and feed the chickens. She was smiley and positive like dad. Collecting eggs looked easy, but I soon learned that some of those chickens didn't like me. Grandma kept most of the laying hens in the big chicken coop. On the north side of the coop, grandpa built two rows of wooden boxes 15 inches by 18 inches. These boxes were called nesting boxes for brooding chickens to incubate their fertile eggs. I loved watching baby chickens emerge from their white oval shells.

The incubation period lasted three weeks. When the chickens weren't brooding, the

Joyce's family in 1949

baby chick died. On day four, Ray's chick died. Now, I was feeling very confident. On day seven, my baby chicken was strong and chirping. Halleluiah! I named her little chick.

The next morning, a disgusting odor radiated from the cardboard box. It was brown and white poop! I didn't understand how such a sweet cute chicken could create such an odor. It was time for a bath for little chick.

I found an old metal mixing bowl and filled it with warm water. I poured in a tablespoon of liquid soap and stirred the water until it became sudsy. Who wouldn't like a bubble bath? In the water, went little chick. I think she enjoyed her bath. She chirped the whole time. After I removed the brown smelly poop, she looked clean. Just to make sure she smelled better, I drabbed some of mom's Evening in Paris perfume on her wings. I dried her off her body with a soft cotton towel. However, the fuzzy feathers remained matted against her small body. Little chick started shaking. I

Joyce Larson Yexley in 1958-59

boxes were used and filled with yellow straw to protect the eggs from breaking. It was fascinating to watch hens exhibit their theatrical dance moves as they strutted towards the nesting boxes and shuffled their body into a comfortable position. You could tell some of them had a mean spirit. When I tried to fetch an egg under a hen's warm body, they were quick to bite my hand. It hurt.

Grandma knew which hens would bite. When the chickens bit grandma's hand, they drew blood. Grandma didn't flinch. She was tough. Grandma would wipe her bloody hand with her apron and continue her chores. Grandma was short and petite. She was tough like dad. I wanted to be like her.

One spring grandma Mae gave us three yellow fuzzy baby chickens one for my brother Ray, one for my sister Vonne, and one for me. Grandma challenged us to raise the chicks to determine who could raise the best chicken. Ray located a cardboard box and placed a small round tin pan of water inside the box for the three baby chickens. After 3 days, Vonne's

Grandma Ida Buntrock with Louise and Lloyd in 1929

needed to get her dry and warm. (Electric hand hair dryers were not invented as a household item.)

An idea. Dad just purchased mom a new clothes dryer. I loved this new machine. The last time I hung three loads of bedding on the clothesline, flies deposited little brown specks all over the clothes. It was fly poop. The sheets also smelled like the new feedlot dad just built. Mom made me rewash all the clothes. It took all afternoon scrubbing out the flyspecks by hand. Would mom's new dryer warm little chick? I took little chick and placed her inside the large clothes dryer. Hopefully, the warm heat would dry the fuzzy yellow feathers and warm her body temperature.

Gently, I placed little chick inside the huge round dryer drum. "Don't be afraid little chick. I will get you all nice and dry in a minute." I said. I turned the temperature control on warm and closed the dryer door. The heater started. The dryer drum started turning. Then I heard, clank, clank, clank. What was that noise? I quickly opened the dryer door and retrieved my chick. Oh, gosh! What was I thinking? I thought little chick would ride around on the outside of the round dryer drum. Instead, little chick's body fell as the drum rotated around

and around. Clank, Clank, Clank was her little body hitting the walls inside the dryer.

As I held little chick in my hand, I noticed her yellow fuzzy feathers had started to puff out again. The bad news, little chick could not stand. She could not hold up her head. Little chick was limp and lifeless. I tried shaking her to wake up. I pushed my finger on her breast to resuscitate her. It did not work. I killed little chick. A tear rolled down each of my cheeks. How could I tell grandma? She would be so disappointed in me.

Grandma Mae didn't give us anymore baby chickens.

In the fall, Grandma Mae called to inform us that she would be butchering chickens on Saturday. Wow! I loved my Grandma's fried chicken. This would be the perfect time to learn how to make grandma's fried chicken. I told mom, Doris, I wanted to help.

She agreed. When Saturday came, mom told me to wear my old clothes and a hooded sweatshirt. No problem. I didn't think I would get too dirty frying chicken. I put on my old jeans and a torn ugly t-shirt.

When we drove into grandma's farmyard, I saw Grandpa Carl standing between the big chicken coop and the east coop with an ax. My aunt Janice had already arrived. She was carrying a bucket towards the shed. Grandma was following Janice with a large black cast iron kettle. Mom parked the car next to the east chicken coop and we got out. When Grandpa Carl saw me, he said," So, you want to help today?" "Sure" I said. "Well, just stay away from me, the ax, and the tree stump." Grandpa said. Mmmmm, I wondered what that was all about.

Janice poured a bucket of water into the black kettle sitting over the fire pit. Grandpa said, "When water begins to boil, we will start." Next, grandpa picked up a chicken tying its two feet together with brown twine string. The water started boiling. Grandpa said, "We are ready. Stand back Jo (Joyce's nickname)," Grandpa picked up one of the tied chicken with one hand and the ax in his other hand. He draped the chicken's head over the tree stump and quickly raised the ax with his right hand slamming it down across the neck of the chicken lying on the tree trunk. Bang! The chicken's head remained on the tree stump. When grandpa let go of the headless chicken, blood squirted from the remaining

253

neck as it flapped its' wings around in circles. Yuk! I jumped out of the way, as the chicken flew over my foot leaving a bloody trail on my pants and shoes. I was glad I wore my old clothes. Yuk!

Grandma picked up the headless chicken by its feet and dunked it into the hot boiling water neck first. Whooooo! It was a terrible smell. Wet dirty chicken feathers in boiling water are another odor I don't like. Grandma held the chicken in the boiling water for a few seconds. Then, she pulled it out of the kettle and handed the chicken to Aunt Janice. Janice started plucking the chicken feathers off of its body until it was bare. Before Janice was finished, grandpa had already axed (de-headed) two more chickens. Mom was handed the second chicken to pluck. I watched Janice and mom pluck a few feathers before I tried to help. My hands were only half the size of mom's hand. It was too hard for me to grasp the large feathers and pull them out. Besides, the feathers stunk! I turned my head away to gasp some breaths of fresh air. I pulled out a few tiny pinfeathers. I discovered I would rather watch instead. My clothes were bloody with feathers stuck to my jeans and t-shirt. I was tired.

It was a long stinky day of de-heading and plucking chickens. Grandma's recipe for fried chicken was the best! Someday, I will buy my chicken meat from the grocery store.

The Understanding
By Barbara Booton of Brookings, South
Dakota
Born 1954

1968. I was 14 years old and had outgrown the Chincoteague pony that served as my steed for 7 years. My little sister Suse had been riding him more and more, leaving me just wishing for a bigger horse. My family lived in town, and the pony "Tony" was boarded at the Circle K ranch about two miles down the highway. It was a time when we would ride our bikes safely to the barn to spend time with the horse riding, brushing, braiding, feeding, and comparing him to the other kid's horses.

One Sunday Dad said he would give us a ride to the barn after he made a quick stop at the other end of town. The place was the Rocking Chair Ranch and in the big arena stood one of the most beautiful, spirited animals, I had ever seen. He had the body of a quarter horse, the head of an Arabian and the markings of an Appaloosa. His name was Tomco. And my Dad was there to buy him. For ME!

Suse and I stood on the lower rung of the corral's fence and listened while the men talked. Dad held onto the reins of the bridle while the man fastened the saddle. Tomco appeared to be skittish. "Don't break this animal's spirit. He needs to be taught. Not disciplined. He will run till he drops if you let him. Treat him kindly."

My dad stepped into the stirrup and swung up and over till he sat tall in the saddle. Tomco took off on a trot to the other end of the corral. Suse and I giggled as we watched dad bounce away. Tomco made a sharp turn and went in a circle as if my dad commanded him to do it. Boy! Were we wrong!

Suddenly Tomco reared upon hind legs and pawed the air like (Hi HO) Silver did before coming down and breaking into a full run straight towards us. We heard dad yelling what we thought was "GO! GO! GO!" Soon we understood he was yelling "WHOA! WHOA! WHOA!" The horse did stop until he reached the fence. That is when Tomco and I had intense eye contact. Dad got down and stomped the ground yelling about how he had no more control of that horse than the man in the moon, and some other colorful language. Tomco held my eye as he strutted quickly back and forth. I reached out for the reins and took them when he was close enough. He snorted a few times, even reared up a bit, but I crawled through the fence unafraid and easily settled him down. I stroked his face and scratched his forelock. I spoke gently to him and we bonded. Right then, right there. We developed an understanding of each other.

Dad tried to tell me he was too much horse for me. The horse was only "green broke." No one had ever ridden the horse outside of the corral. Dad feared I would not be able to handle him. But the man told dad to let me try to ride him and see how it goes. He thought I had an effect on Tomco that seemed to settle him down. It went beautifully. It was like I had been riding him all my life. The deal was made. The pastureland with a building was cheaper rent at the Rocking Chair so Tony left the Circle K and moved in with Tomco. They became fast friends. I would ride Tomco with Tony and Suse always behind us. Never ahead. Like an unspoken rule. Tomco ALWAYS led the way. I never called him my horse. He was my friend. Companion. Fellow adventurer… but I could not and would not own him. I would take care of him like he was royalty, but never felt that I, or anyone, ever "owned" Tomco. He was a free spirit and always would be.

Now Suse and I were in a new land…new horses, new kids, new unexplored territory for us. It wasn't long though before we were invited to go on a trail ride that would begin early on a Saturday morning and end just before dusk. Our folks were a little nervous about letting us go for the whole Saturday with kids we didn't know well and all the other things folks worry about. But they relented and helped us pack bologna sandwiches, beef jerky, potato chips, Oreos and a couple of canteens with water to stuff into our saddlebags.

Oh yeah…my new saddle! I saved babysitting and corn detasseling money for 2 years so I would have enough to buy a nice saddle for a big horse. The leather was still stiff and squeaky even after a few days of oil and rubbing. I was excited and proud to saddle up the handsome Tomco and show off my new tack. We had gotten to know one another pretty well in the big arena and the pastureland he grazed in. I rode bareback often. We both liked it when I would stand him on the hillside to jump and swing onto his bare back. I used leg muscles to hold on. He never ran wild with me. He had a smooth cantering lope and a thrilling run when we both wanted to. In fact, he became a one-girl horse. He would not behave for anyone but me. Grown men, owners of other horses that boarded at the Rocking Chair, asked to ride him. After a spirited lap or two around the corral, he would sometimes slam them into the fence while they tried to rein him in. Suse and I had some pretty good laughs at seeing Tomco make others think he was a wild animal. Once he jumped a six-foot gate with a terrified passenger. That was the last time I ever allowed anyone else to ride him. We had another understanding.

The trail ride began with nine riders at 6:00 am. We walked along the highway about half a mile and went behind an old abandoned greenhouse to the beginning of the trail. The vegetation we rode through was wet with morning dew. We all got wet with morning dew. We went single file at the beginning because the path was pretty narrow. Tomco was not happy that he was 4th in line, but I think he behaved himself because he knew neither of us knew where we were going… and I kept stroking his neck and talking low to him to keep him calm. To be honest, I was a little afraid that he would act up and I would be embarrassed because I couldn't make him behave. A railroad track ran parallel with the trail about 50 feet away. The chatter amongst the boys was all about bull riding and calf roping. The girls talked of barrel racing and pole bending. I had watched a few of them practice their skills in the arena secretly wishing I could train Tomco to perform like that. When we neared the end of the trail, the talk turned to racing. Who had the fastest horse, who won the last time, and "remember that time the train came through and Joey tried to beat it?"

Suse and Tony were right behind us as we emerged from the trail out onto a grassy flat stretch of land. We lined up side by side waiting to hear the word "GO." Tomco was antsy and eager to run. I was a little scared but tried to act cool. The GO was shouted and we were off.

Tomco lurched ahead of the others. The sound of all those horse's hooves hitting the ground was thrilling. I tried to hold him back a little because I had never been on such a fast horse. The wind was blinding me. I heard shouts behind me but couldn't tell what they were yelling. Up ahead I could tell we were nearing a gravel road. I saw a truck go by. They must be trying to tell me there is a road ahead. I squinted left and right and did not see any traffic so decided I would just let him have his head while I held on to his mane with both hands. Up ahead, past the road we would cross, was a small hill. I figured he would slow and let us catch our breath and let me take the reins and have some control again.

Nope. I yelled at him to slow down, I had the reins and pulled back but he kept going to the top of the hill. Then all I could see was sky. The sound of his running stopped. Not because he decided to mind me, but because we were airborne! We were falling down about 25 feet of nothingness into a body of water known as a sand pit/swimming hole.

Tomco's legs pawed the air with fury. The closer to the water we fell, the more perpendicular we became. I could not stop what was happening. And neither could he. My main concern became trying to stay on him because if he kicked my head under water trying to swim up, it would kill me. I twisted mane hair tight in my left hand and grabbed the saddle horn with my right. I squeezed his body with my legs as tight as I could. I jammed my boots deep into the stirrups but, after impact, in the cold water my body forcefully floated away from him. Yet I hung on for dear life as we descended. I wondered how far we would sink. We both needed air. And soon.

Before too long Tomco's powerful legs reversed our direction and we began to surface. I could see the blurry sunshine getting closer. When we broke the surface I saw my fellow racers had arrived. Not the way Tomco and I had. They rode around that small hill and now gathered at the edge of the water to help us out. The mane I had held was missing quite a few strands of hair, but we were alive! Wet and quite muddy by the time we emerged from the deep pit, but alive.

Suse was crying as she hugged me. The others told me they tried to warn me what was beyond that hill. I hugged Suse, then hugged the mighty Tomco and scolded him for not slowing when I wanted him to. He kept snorting and sneezing but he did put his head low and nudged me gently. We had another understanding.

The rest of the afternoon was spent drying myself, Tomco, and the saddle in the warm sunlight. Some of the other riders decided to swim in their clothes and laze about letting the sun dry them, too. The kids I did not know well at the beginning of this ride shared their lunches. Tomco and I had given them a memory and a friendship that would last for many years.

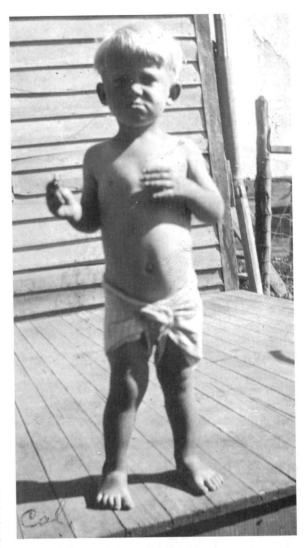

Cal Huber

Recording My Memories
By Calvin C. Huber of Hoven, South Dakota
Born 1930

Thank you for the invitation to write about the "good old days." They may not have been easy days, but they were always good. I am 83 years old, born in 1930 on a century plus farm. In 2007, when I was 77 years old, I was diagnosed with Lymphoma cancer. Seven years later, after 16 chemo treatments, I am doing fine. The 3-hour treatments gave me an excellent opportunity to pass the time by writing my memoir. After running out of memories I had someone put it in a book form.

My grandparents were German, living in Russia. When I was born the language was German, we then learned English in a one-room country schoolhouse. The number of students attending school at any given time was probably between 10 and 20. A girl and myself were the only two in my grade. We usually walked the 1-½ miles, sometimes rode the pony. Sometimes in the winter with snow on the ground, our neighbor and dad would take turns hauling us with a bobsled pulled by horses. Sometimes mother would heat up some rocks and wrap them in blankets to keep our feet warn. Some of the games we played were Anty-I-Over, kick the bucket, pump, pump, pull-a-way, last couple out, steal sticks, and fox and the goose in the winter.

Many times the school had a skunky smell. They lived under the schoolhouse; sometimes our dog would accompany us to school and tangle with a skunk in a culvert and then come and rub on us. I must have liked the smell because I am still trapping them now. I never had a spanking in school or when I got home, but I definitely remember the time I should have. My brother and I backed up our horse very quietly to the northwest corner of the school after school was out where the window was open and the man teacher was sitting at his desk close to it. Our horse was an old horse and loaded with gas and we were riding bareback and we both kicked him in the flanks at the same time. Need I say more? I can't believe we did that! We gave up our recesses the next day. One other time that same teacher was giving us a spelling contest and in the middle of the test, all went quiet. He had fallen asleep. Sometimes there would be a pie social get together where the students would bring a pie that would be auctioned off to make a little money for the school. As I remember it, the highest bidder would then eat the pie with the student that brought the pie. If it was a pie that a female, single teacher brought, it brought the most money because there were a lot of young single men around.

After school when we came home we sometimes got to listen to the radio programs. *The Lone Ranger, Jack Armstrong*, and *Captain Midnight* come to mind. Sometimes we would walk kitty corner to school through a pasture. We would pick wild onions and chew on them, they had a very strong smell, and everybody could smell them in the room. This smell also showed up in the milk after the milk cows ate it. Milking cows morning and evening was one of the biggest chores. We usually milked about five or seven. It was kind of a nasty job for a young boy, especially when the flies were biting the cows on their legs. The tail would always be slapping ones head and they would be kicking. I thought I was pretty smart when I tied the tail to my leg. I just split the long hairs at the end of her tail and brought it up the sides of my leg and tied it with a common slipknot. But it kept coming

off, so I decided a square knot would solve that problem. But she didn't like the idea of not being able to switch her tail so she took off with me hobbling along behind with one leg trying to untie that knot. As I hobbled along behind her, she thought I was chasing her. I thought I was going to die. Lucky for me she pulled it off of my leg. That was a good knot! I will "knot" do that again.

Sometimes we would milk early or late when it was dark so we had to use kerosene lanterns for light. The cows were usually in a pasture during the day and when we brought them home they pretty well learned the routine and let us jump on their backs and ride them home. We weaned the calves off of their mothers as soon as we could. We trained them to drink separate milk from cream out of a bucket until they probably weighed about 250lbs. And this is where we learned to be cowboys. While one of the brothers let the calf drink out of the bucket the other one snuck a rope around his belly and quick jumped on him before it knew what happened. The bucket was removed and the bucking started. Oh, did we take some bad spills! But we were young and healed up fast.

The windmill in the middle of the yard served many purposes. We covered about 2/3 of the tank with wood in the wintertime and put manure on top of it for insulation so it wouldn't freeze so hard. The cattle needed water. There was always a pile of ice from which we would fill up a burlap sack and crush it for around the ice cream freezer and

Cavin's grandmother, Mrs. Karl Huber and his aunt, Christine

257

Calvin and Keith Keltger in about 1946

add some salt, crank by hand, and oh what a treat that was! In the summertime the well was our refrigerator. A long rope with a big bucket filled with anything that needed to be cool.

Saturday nights was "go to town" night. Can of cream and a case of eggs to sell to buy the basics such as sugar, flour, etc. Dad would head for the garage or pool hall, mother would go to the store and visit with the ladies, the kids would go and do what kids do. We would take our sleds to town and see who could go the longest distance on a steep hill right behind Main Street. At that time people parked in the middle of Main Street and when some left to go home we would sneak up behind, grab the bumper, and get a free ride on our sleds. In the summertime we would sometimes crawl up the ladder of the train depot water tank and swim in it and in the winter breaking the long icicles hanging down the tank. One of the town people wanted to do something for the kids, so he built a diving board by an old stock dam that was pretty shallow. Many times we ended up with mud in our hair.

On the farm when we had some free time there was always something to do. Hunt jackrabbits, fish for bullheads in local ponds with bamboo poles, make slingshots to hit something, lie up on the windmill boards and throw rocks at birds below, and on and on. To sum it up, just a wonderful life growing up. Times of blizzards, snowed in for weeks, walking five miles to town to get some groceries, walking over to the neighbors by moonlight to play cards, eat ice cream and fudge. Great times!

Our first phone was a big box with a crank on the wall, I think it was sometime in the '40s. A friend of mine and me were hired by

the county to put the blue colored insulators on the posts (probably about 14' tall). A party line consisted of maybe about 8-10 farms. Each farm had its own ring with the crank such as 1 short and 1 long, or 2 shorts or 2 longs, etc. We had a wind up tubular record player, or phonograph with a megaphone to amplify the sound. I believe the music was from the 1910-1920 era. The first lights were kerosene lamps, and then the 2-mantle kerosene or Hi-Test with a tank at the base, which had a pump on it that you pumped air into to build up pressure. This was a big improvement. From there we went to the light bulbs turned into sockets with wires leading to the big glass batteries in the basement that were charged up by a wind charger, or Hippro, that was as tall as a windmill with a propeller on it that charged up the batteries to store the power when the wind wasn't blowing. I was able to see a couple of silent movies in our small town in the early '30s.

In closing, I would like to say that memories mean so much to me. In my memoirs I list the memories that I have from the time I spent with my parents and grandparents while they were alive. So I know that part of their lives, but what I am missing is what their lives were like before I was born. When it's not on paper we have a tendency to forget. So I guess I could say if it weren't for cancer I probably wouldn't have recorded mine either.

What Will They Think of Next?
By David G. Anderson of Champlin, Minnesota
Born 1939

I was born in Webster, South Dakota on November 11, 1939. My home was in Summit, a community of about 500 that was located 26 miles east of Webster on Highway 12. Summit is located at the southern end of Roberts County. Summit became a town in 1892 and grew to more than 600 people in 1908. It became a railroad hub but rejected accepting a roundhouse station for environmental reasons. The town's primary employer was the Milwaukee Road for dozens of years. My grandfather was a section foreman who worked for them for 50 years.

My father died in October of 1947 of a heart attack. He had heart problems for most of his adult life after contracting rheumatic fever while he was serving in the Army at a North Carolina training camp. He owned a Whippet, but after he passed away, we never had an automobile in our household. While he was living, I can recall making car trips to visit his brother and family who lived eight miles north of Summit, just west of Highway 81.

A highlight of every summer was when a traveling carnival would come to Summit and spend the better part of the week there. It was great fun for the kids and the adults in the community to watch the rides being constructed and assembled and my friends and I spent long hours watching the carnival spring to life. The rides included a Ferris wheel, a tilt-a-whirl, an octopus, a merry-go-round, and a number of smaller rides for the younger children. My favorite was the merry-go-round and I can remember how thrilling it was to ride on the beautiful white horse that was my favorite.

Our refrigerator at home had a very small freezing compartment and many of the people in town had a similar situation. The solution was to rent a locker at the local creamery to keep their frozen meat. On Wednesday and Saturday nights, the people from surrounding farms would come to town to shop, sell their cream, and fraternize with their friends in town. The kids would walk up and down the two blocks that included most of the town's businesses. I met a lot of the boys and girls who lived on farms and made some very good friends. Outdoor movies were shown in the large lot immediately south of the opera house. At the end of the night, I would meet my mom and we would go together to the creamery to get a chicken or whatever meat she intended to prepare for Sunday dinner. I didn't look forward to going into the freezing locker with my mother. I lived in fear that the freezer door would lock and we would freeze to death.

Summit had more than their share of snowy winters and the people living there had to wait for the county snowplows to take care of the roads. The north-south road just west of our house was left unplowed for a good portion of one winter when I was about 10 years old. A block north of our house, the road had drifted shut and become a very sizeable hill of snow. Kids from all over Summit brought their sleds to slide down the new hill. I can remember that at the top of the hill, the top two or three feet of a telephone pole poked through the snow, which meant that the hill of snow in the middle of the road was about 25 feet high!

In the early '50s, my mother and I had ridden with good friends to Sisseton to watch the Summit Eagles play in the District 1 boys' basketball tournament. Sisseton, the Roberts County seat, was located about 26 miles north of Summit and that stretch of road had a history of seeing a lot of bad weather during the winter. After Summit had played their game, many of the Eagles' fans had congregated just outside the auditorium. It had started to snow heavily and it was decided that they would form a caravan of cars for the trip back to Summit. I sat in the backseat with a good friend and his sister and my mother sat in the front passenger seat. Visibility was very poor from the beginning and the caravan moved along at a little less than 20 miles per hour. When the caravan had gotten within two miles from Summit, it had become impossible to see the road, so the standard oilman in town, Dick Hansen, began walking in front of the lead car to point out where the right side of the road was! He continued to lead the group into Summit, but the roads were so bad that the cars had to be left on the road leading into town from the north. That night my mother, our three friends, and I spent the night at the Summit Hotel, which was located on the north end of Main Street. It was the only time that any of us had ever stayed at the hotel. In the early 1900s, there were three hotels in town.

We didn't have running water or an indoor bathroom until my senior year of high school. I never did like having to use the chamber pot and would usually opt for the outhouse, which was located about 50 or 60 feet from the backdoor of our home. We had to carry water every day and the pump we used to fill our pail was less than 100 yards from our house near Alfield and Rungvold Binde's barn. We had a fuel-oil heater in our living room and a cook stove in the kitchen in which we burned wood and coal. We stored a little coal in the building that served as our outhouse. Several times every winter, I would take my sled to the lumberyard to bring back a gunnysack of coal.

There were school and community functions held in the opera house, which also had the only indoor basketball court in town. I can remember the "box socials" that were held at school functions until the mid '50s when for whatever reason they were discontinued. Junior and senior girls would prepare a lunch that was then packed into a larger box that was heavily decorated. These boxes were auctioned off to the highest bidder. The winning bidder would then eat the lunch with the girl who had prepared it. I got the impression that it wasn't a secret who had prepared each lunch, so the surprise element wasn't always there, but it was still an interesting event that was very well received.

When I was in the 1st grade, there was a mass-inoculation of all the students' grades 1 through 12, in the opera house. I believe that the shots that were given would protect one from diphtheria, smallpox, and whooping cough. The nurses and doctors who were giving the shots were in the middle of the stage on the east side of the opera house. There was a line of students leading up to the north side of the stage and when your turn came, you marched across the stage to take your medicine. There were numerous cases of people fainting and the tension of having to watch the students take their shots probably added considerably to the emotional anxiety. I got through it all right but a few minutes later after getting my shots, I was sitting on the running board of our Whippet when my mother had to make a brief trip back to the opera house. When she returned, she found that I had fainted face down in the sand.

When I was seven or eight, I was ill and my mother took me to a doctor in Watertown. I remember that the doctor asked my mother what she had done to help me so far. She said that she had warmed some Vicks Vapo Rub and had massaged my body and kept me in warm pajamas. The doctor told her that she could have rubbed the Vicks on the walls for all the good it would have done. My mother didn't say anything, but we never went to that doctor again!

Catching frogs was an activity that many of the kids in town engaged in. A gentleman named H.O. Utne bought frogs for many years. The smaller ones were sold as fishing bait and the larger ones would be shipped to the east coast, where they were served at restaurants. One year when I was 10 or 11, I had a nice meal. I don't believe that my mother had ever prepared frog legs, and it was the only time in my life that I ate them. I do remember that we had a great meal and it is interesting that we never had frog legs again.

My brother, Bob, graduated in 1946 and was one of the best players ever to play at Summit. In his senior year, the Eagles lost to Sisseton 31 to 28 after trailing 21 to 8 at the half. When the conversation was focused around basketball, Bob would explain to anyone who would listen how Summit would have won the game if they had pressed Sisseton for the entire game. When people reflect at length about games from the past, you will often hear from someone that, "It's just a game." Bob passed away in 2007 and I heard him talk about that game dozens of times. I would be surprised if he hadn't told the story a number of times in his final year on earth. It was "just a game," but it could still be important to people who were there.

Less than a half-mile east of our home was a substantial slough that was about 100 feet wide and 400 feet long. It was known as Godfrey's slough. Godfrey Hansvold had been a muskrat trapper from the past who supposedly could skin and stretch a muskrat in a minute. Pieces of Godfrey's cabin were still found near the slough when I was last there in 1957. His skinning cabin measured approximately four by seven feet.

I didn't have a lot of training as a trapper and had only average results. I generally caught about 10 muskrats a week and caught only 2 mink in my 3 years as a trapper. My dog, Rufus, accompanied me on my trap line and that didn't make catching mink any easier, because they can smell the dog and would find a way to avoid being around. I would skin the muskrats and stretch them on wooden frames to dry. I would then dry them and mail them to Sears and Roebuck in Minneapolis. I could expect a check in about a week. For average-size quality furs, I would receive $2.25-$3.00 for the muskrats and $25.00-$30.00 for a prime mink.

In a storeroom that covered half of the upstairs area of our home, I found a huge stretcher that had obviously been built to stretch a mink. I never envisioned catching a mink that could be legitimately stretched on that frame, but in the winter of 1956-1957, a friend of mine and I caught a mink that fit that frame like a glove. We received $36.00 for that

David's trapping partner, Rufus

pelt. I'm not sure of the date but I believe that it was in 1951 or 1952 when our neighbors to the west built a steel tower that was at least 50 feet tall to get television reception. I can recall sitting with my friends on numerous occasions to watch the test pattern on the television. Television, what would they think of next?

Life at a Country School
By Earl Randall of Aberdeen, South Dakota
Born 1928

One morning, I was walking a mile to the schoolhouse down a country trail, as there were no improved roads at that time. I came across a rattlesnake, coiled and ready to spring at whatever might come by. As I approached, he did strike at me, but I was young and able to jump and land at a safe distance.

I hunted up a few rocks and proceeded to throw them at the rattler until I was lucky to strike a killing blow. After I was sure the snake was dead, I took my trusty knife and cut off his nine rattles. We discussed this in school for a few minutes. Nowadays knives in school are no longer allowed.

Another time during recess, an old porcupine had come into the entry in the school and was sitting in the exit. We had to use a window so as not to bother the porcupine. Bull snakes were spotted as well occasionally. This was life at a country school!

The Saturday Night Bath
By Arlene Randall of Aberdeen, South Dakota
Born 1930

Saturday night supper was generally served a bit earlier than usual in order to get through the ritual of Saturday night baths.

First, the round, galvanized washtub was set up in the kitchen. The door was closed for privacy and warmth. The kettles of water were heated on the coal-burning cook stove. I, being the only girl, got to go first. The youngest child followed me and up the line, until all six brothers were scrubbed from up to bottom. More hot water was added after each bath.

When spring arrived and temperatures warmed, we all put on bathing suits, towels in hand, and down to the gravel pit for the Saturday night bath we went. Consequently, we were all clean for church attendance on Sunday morning!

The Hard Times
By Lawrence L. Peterson of Watertown, South Dakota
Born 1929

When I was born in September 1929, my family lost their farm because of the Great Depression. Due to no crops, they couldn't make the farm payments.

My folks moved to a farm on the Henry Wallace Road on shares from the crops. I was only about one and a half or two years old and can vividly remember opening the back farmhouse door and looking up at the sun that was completely blocked out by the swarms of grasshoppers flying in the air.

I can also remember my mother lighting a lamp in the middle of the day because strong winds were blowing dust and dirt so thick that it blotted out the light. The other thing I remember is the tumbleweeds lodging in the fence lines so high that the wind blowing the dust around filled them. Then the fences turned into big dust mounds.

It was so dry that the crops wouldn't grow. Corn making any height was cut for silage for the animals.

My sisters and I walked to the country grade school every day. It was about a mile and a half from our farm. In the winter, when the temperature dropped to 20 degrees below zero, it was quite a chore.

I remember that when my family drove to Watertown, we could get a hamburger at the café across from the courthouse for five cents each. Gas for the car was ten cents a gallon.

They say it was the good old days, but for many it was the hard times.

Egg on Me
By Twila Sanborn Ruden of Groton, South Dakota
Born 1930

It was a weekday afternoon in the summer, which my mother chose for grocery shopping. We were farmers in the Ipswich, South Dakota area. I was about age 11, being the oldest of four children. I had two brothers and a little sister. Mother asked me to go to the hen house to gather the eggs. Usually, they were gathered only in the evening. However, we needed a few more to fill the 24 dozen-egg crate, which we would take to town to trade for groceries. My dad also milked cows, so we had a can of cream to take to the local cream station.

As Mother had asked, I promptly took the egg basket, which was an old kettle with a newspaper pad in the bottom, and went off across the yard. Our chickens were white leghorns. We also had young chickens, the roosters being fresh fryer age.

Inside the hen house, I collected a fair amount of eggs. Some of the hens were "setting" and on the nests. Of course, they didn't like my robbing their eggs.

I promptly started back to the house. One of the roosters decided he didn't like me, so he started to chase me, flying up and pecking at me. I turned around and was walking backward so I could watch him. Of course, I tripped and fell backward. The egg basket went up over my head and all the eggs broke. The yolk went all over my freshly ironed white blouse and in my hair. I'm sorry to say, our egg crate was not quite full that day.

After I had a total wash job and put on an entirely clean outfit, we were off to town. Needless to say, I was glad when all those roosters were canned for our enjoyment during the winter.

Memories of the Good Old Days
By Blaine Hoff of Volga, South Dakota
Born 1944

I was born in November of 1944 in Volga, South Dakota. Our town's population was about 800.

I attended a one-room schoolhouse with 12 to 15 other students. I went there for grades one through eight. When it was nice weather, we rode our bicycles to school. The distance was about one mile each way. A few times in the winter, our dad would bring us to school with the sleigh and horses. Otherwise, the neighbors would take turns driving us to school and coming to get us home.

We would bring our lunches to school in dinner pails. The pails usually had logos on them, like The Lone Ranger.

The older students had chores to do, like getting water from the well, cleaning the blackboard erasers, keeping the outdoor toilets clean, organizing library books, and sweeping the floor in the school.

During recess in nice weather, we would

Blaine at age 2

262

play tag, softball, basketball, and run races. In the winter, we would build snow forts and throw snowballs at one another.

Other school highlights were playing ball against other schools. Boys and girls played together. In December, there would be a school program and then a school picnic when school was out for the summer.

Sumer activities included playing baseball, helping Mother with the garden and going to town on Saturday nights. While in town, we would listen to the local band and eat ice cream.

We also enjoyed a church picnic in the summer, playing softball while our fathers pitched horseshoes and our mothers visited and fixed the food for the picnic. I remember the pastor bringing pop, which was quite a treat. I always took a bottle of grape pop.

We would help our dad with chores, feeding cattle, hogs, sheep, and chickens. When we got to be about 11 years old, Dad would show us how to drive the tractor, a John Deere. Another chore was herding livestock along township roads. When we hauled hay for our dad or neighbors, we would get paid 50 cents per hour. Also, at that time, the girls did many chores outside to help their dads.

Feeding Dillinger
By Danna Garber Mercer of Blunt, South Dakota
Born 1936

John Herbert Dillinger was born June 22, 1903 and died July 22, 1934. He was a bank robber. He robbed two dozen banks and four police stations.

In 1934, Dan B. Garber and his wife and three children homesteaded on land deeded by the government near old Highway 14 north of Pierre, South Dakota. One day, a black car drove in their yard with steam coming out of the cap. Dan helped the driver get water to cool off the car.

In those days, if it was noon you invited people to eat a bite. So Essie put a meal on the table and fed the four men from the car. While they ate, Mrs. Garber recognized that the leader was John Dillinger by the boots he wore. He was known to wear that kind of boots. The men ate, thanked her for the meal, and went on their way.

They took the back roads to Sioux Falls, where they held up the Security National Bank and Trust. During this robbery, they gunned down a traffic cop named Hale Keith. He was shot through a plate glass window of the bank. After the robbery, the men proceeded on to Mason City, Iowa.

In the Depression, Dan Garber lived one mile north of Highway 14 and ten miles east of Pierre, South Dakota with his wife, Essie and three children. He heard that wheat was up in price at Blunt, South Dakota. So he loaded a wagon with wheat and started for Blunt with his team of horses and the buggy.

When he got to Blunt the wheat had dropped in price. It wasn't worth anything. He didn't know how he would feed his family for the winter, so he went to the Dakota State Bank and borrowed $500.00 from S.F. McDaniel.

Mr. Garber started the twelve miles for home. He kept thinking about that money he had borrowed. He was halfway home when he decided he could never pay it back. He turned his team around and took the money back to the bank.

That's How It Was
By Ervin Spitzer of Silverdale, Washington
Born 1922

My name is Ervin Spitzer, and I was born at Long Lake, South Dakota. I don't know much about the moon landing but my parents used to say they went out here to a mountain. Haha. They put houses out behind the house a little ways away, a two holer. It was cold in the wintertime. My mother used to say castor oil manure spreader works while you sleep. And that's how it was.

Home remedies were, if you remember, liniment from the Watkins dealer. He used to come to the house. He used to visit with our parents an always had a box on the rear of his car. He took chickens in trade for Petro Carbo Salve. We would pull around the corner of the house.

The first radio we had they talked our dad to buy a raffle ticket and he won it. If I remember, it had about them dry batteries in it. We used to listen to WHAX Younton, South

Dakota to Happy Jack and the Fiddlers. We had a wind up record player. It was a cabinet type. We had it for years.

The old phones were a wooden box on the wall. They had to have batteries. There was a line to the neighbor, and we would call and hear all the clicks. All the neighbors would listen in on the same line. The top wire on the fence was the telephone line.

I went to a one-room school in my uncle's pasture. We had to go about 3/4 of a mile to go to school in those days. The kids were seven to eighteen years old. Before they ever got the eighth grade, most kids had to stay home and work to make a living.

We had Saturday night baths. We had a big, round wash tub. We heated the water on the kitchen stove and carried it to the granary. There were nine of us in the family. About four or five of us would take a bath, and then the water would be kind of cloudy. That was the way life was then. There were no indoor baths or toilets.

Yes, we had a wooden washing machine. We took it behind the house in the summer time and put it in the shade. There we had to pump water by hand. We had no electricity until years later after most of us six boys and three girls were gone from home.

There were no Saturday night movies around where I lived. I don't remember when we got the first colored television.

Our mother made all of our clothes or she went to the Salvation Army to find old suits and jackets.

One room school had a potbelly stove in the middle. There was one teacher for all eight grades. Most kids only went to the fourth grade.

During the old Dust Bowl, there were days with no rain or very little of it. Nothing grew for the cattle. All the farmers had to cut down their herds because they were starving to death. The government had an inspector at the stockyard and if the cattle did not pass inspection, they shot them and buried them.

I tell the young people that I am telling the truth. I was ten years old at the time. After the rain came again about seven years later, there was hardly no measuring the rain. That is in the Dakotas where I grew up on the farm. I hope them years will never come back!

Our pets were our ponies. It was walk or ride the ponies.

We had no car until 1927 when Dad bought a Model T Ford. What a time it was.

There were no such things as swimming holes where we grew up.

My grandparents told me how they had to live and get started here. They came from Germany then to Russia then to the United States. They came to about eight miles east of where I grew up. They had to report to a separation center and were given land. They had to dig their own well and have a building in a year, so they built a sod house. I remember it real well. So they took a wagon box, tipped it upside down, crawled under it to sleep for a year. They told me they had the house done. What a life! I was born on this home place. The farm is still going. One of my nephews is farming it.

Love Was Plentiful
By Betty Walker Schinkel of Ferney, South Dakota
Born 1947

My father married my mother on December 31, 1945 after serving three and a half years in the Medical Corp during World War II. He took his basic training on the island of Hawaii and had been stationed in Maui and the Philippine Islands. I was born on August 1, 1947 in the Ipswich Hospital. It was originally someone's home.

Life on the farm was primitive compared to our lifestyles today. There was no indoor plumbing or running water.

Dad built our home on the farm. He also built two chicken coops and the barn. The first chicken coop was destroyed by a spring storm. I am not sure, if he built the granary or if it was a building that was moved onto the farm. Then of course, there was the outhouse.

As a child, I was the one who carried the water to the house. Being the oldest, this was one of my first responsibilities. Every Sunday, I had to bring in extra buckets of water for Mother's washday on Monday.

Saturday night was bath time. A metal tub was set up next to the oil-burning stove. Each of us took our turn. Only hot water was added as each family member took his or her turn. There was no disposing of the water until that last person bathed.

Betty Walker Schinkel, Joyce Walker Hammrich, and Shirley Walker Fisher

Growing up with just two younger sisters, a father, and a mother, our family life was very close. Dad was so happy to have only daughters; he did not want us to serve in the military. When I graduated from high school, our country was involved in the Vietnam War.

Our income was from the cream and eggs Mom and Dad sold at the little town of Beebe. Dad also had sold grain to buy other farm items. The cream and egg checks bought our groceries.

Mom always had her garden and chickens to help feed us. Dad raised hogs as well as cattle. Of course, there were the milk cows for milk.

As a child, there were many things to enjoy. Dad rebuilt an old car body for our playhouse. Mom taught us how to make mud pies. There was the old swing Dad made. There were the two boys' bikes we had to take turns riding. In the spring, there was always the annual gopher trapping to look forward to. We always loved discovering that first crocus, too.

Farm life was simple, but love was plentiful.

I Don't Regret the Hard Times
By James W. Geditz of Selah, Washington
Born 1938

We lived on a farm about three miles from town. One winter, the snowdrifts were so high that we could not get to town. Roads were totally blocked, plus it was so cold the car would not start. Dad finally hitched a team of horses to the car. We all got bundled up good and went to town right over the top of all those snowdrifts with the horses pulling the car.

I started first grade in 1944. We lived over two miles from a one-room schoolhouse. The school had a pot-bellied stove. We had to put our lunch pails close to the stove or our lunches would freeze. Most of the time, we had to wear gloves while we did our lessons. That wasn't the only drawback; the outhouse was 50 feet or more from the schoolhouse.

Weather permitting, I had to walk to school, and I hated that walk. Once in a while if a car should happen along, they would give me a ride. Highway 45 was a gravel road at that time and had little to no traffic.

Spring came and the snow began to melt. I had by this time found a faster route to and from school. I would cut across country through the fields, and it saved me some walking. One of those really nice days, I was taking my shortcut and to my surprise, the normally dry creek bed that was about 200 feet from the house had become a river. I knew I could not cross it, so I had to walk all the way back to the highway and cross over the bridge. Needless to say, I was an upset kid.

In 1946, Dad sold out and moved to town. He had farmed for seven years and had not had a crop, so he gave up that spring. It is unbelievable, but in the fall of '46, everyone had a crop.

When we moved to town, housing was hard to come by. We ended up in a very small house. It had one tiny bedroom, a living-dining room, and an attached porch for a kitchen. The outside had a siding made of material like asphalt shingles with a brick pattern. I think that was what the insulation amounted to. While living in this tarpaper shack, as I like to refer to it, one night all we had for food was one loaf of bread and nothing to put on it. I remember chewing my two slices for a long time to make them last longer.

While living in this shack I got into trouble, and my mother was going to spank me. I decided to run. That way I figured if she couldn't catch me, she couldn't spank me. Boy was I wrong. I ran, and she was in hot pursuit. There were some straw bales on the backside of a shed that looked like it was ready to fall down, so onto the bales and across the roof I went. I jumped off the opposite side. That would ditch her for sure, I thought. I was wrong again. I hit the ground, and she was right behind me, madder than a wet hen. Now I was panicky to get away, so I made another run over the top of the building. She was breathing fire by now. I jumped again with her right on top of me. I was out of wind by now and took the whipping. I never tried that again, as I had learned the hard way. Old ladies of 26 can run fast and long!

Just when things appeared that there could not be any worse living conditions, we had to move out of that shack. Dad had no work and couldn't pay the rent. The County had a small homemade trailer-type of building mounted on steel wheels that they sometimes used for a cook car when the crew was working at the far end of the county. I think it was about eight feet wide and maybe 20 feet long and had bare walls, just the framework showing and tarpaper for siding, but this time without the brick pattern. It had a small room in the rear that was the kitchen; the rest was the dining area. It was not much for five kids and two grownups.

We were able to park this little mansion on a vacant lot across the street from my grandmother's house. How we did not freeze to death that winter still amazes me. There was no skirting, just some straw bales all around the building. I think the mice enjoyed the straw more than we did, and there were plenty of those creepy little guys that tried to take up residence inside. We did not have an outhouse. No, this high-class little mansion had no inside plumbing. We were allowed to use Grandmother's outhouse, which was a good 200 feet from us. That is a long way away when one is desperate.

Dad's mother passed away during our stay in the cook car, and Dad's share of the estate was $1,600.00. It just so happened that a house was for sale just two blocks away for $1,600.00, so we finally got a bigger house. Yes, it had the brick siding attached to the outside and no insulation to speak of. Ten feet away from the stove was too far away to be comfortable. This house was really modern; it had city water piped into it but no other plumbing. A five-gallon bucket sat under the sink to catch the water and in the winter that bucket would freeze every night. We also had our own outhouse again and only 50 feet to get to it. We had really moved up in the world, almost high class compared to what the previous two years had been. This house did work out fine for us, and all six of us kids grew up in it.

There were many times Dad would be out of work and have no money for food. Dad had two wonderful half-brothers who kept a close eye on us. When we were down to the last crumb of bread, they always showed up with a load of groceries and saved us. I will always be grateful to these two wonderful uncles, and I think of them quite often, even to this day at 75 years old.

I survived growing up in South Dakota and have no regrets about any of the hard times. Would I like to try it again? Really, what kind of question is that? The answer is no way in hell.

The Night the Church Burned to the Ground
By Nancy Stakke Bauer of Mandeville, Louisiana
Born 1931

It was February of 1941, and I was ten years old. My parents, Margaret and Harry Stakke, were out of town, and I was staying with my grandmother. She lived next door to my home and one block down from the Methodist Church in Woonsocket, South Dakota. Dad had a large five or six room chicken house at the south side of the lot and a couple of hay stacks in the yard.

The church sanctuary was raised above the ground. It had gorgeous stained glass windows that impressed me, even at that young age. The east window was of Christ carrying the lamb; the south window was Christ kneeling in the garden. I think the west window was of Christ standing, and there was another smaller, more plain window on the north side of the choir.

On this night, the District Superintendent of the Methodist Church was there for a meeting with the pastor and the governing board of the church. Of course, the women served dinner in the basement dining room.

It was a terrible night, extremely cold and windy, and in an effort to keep the basement warm, someone put a fan in the furnace room with the intention of it blowing the hot air out into the dining room. This was a big mistake. The building caught fire. The local fire department came, but it soon was a devastation that could not be stopped.

My grandmother was terrified that the wind was blowing bits of burning wood and would ignite the haystacks. She kept running from the window facing the church and then to the back porch to be sure one of the haystacks hadn't caught fire. My house was in the way, so we really couldn't see anything except flames shooting up into the sky.

For my friends and me, a huge fire like that frightened us and our reactions were different. My friends both lived three blocks away. Connie (Webster) Burrill had never seen her mother cry, but this night Con saw her looking out the window with tears streaming down her face. Janet (Padmore) Armajani heard the sound when the church bell dropped to the ground and gave its final gong and asked her mother what that noise was. For me, I was worried about the fire getting started on my home, which was even closer to the church than Gram's house.

The next day when I could see the site, empty but full of glass, concrete, charred tables, chairs, and books, realization hit. It was over and that church would never be the same again. Strangely enough, I have no recollection of my parents' reaction when they returned home, much sadness, I'm sure, but still relief that Gram and I and our houses were okay.

We had services and all other activities for several years at a church on the other side of town. When the new building was completed at the old site, it felt like we were finally coming home. I grew up, went to college, married in the new church (which was old by that time), and moved around the country

Connie Burrill, Nancy Bauer, and Janet Armajani

with my family.

We lived in New Orleans for 30 years, during which time I learned to work with stained glass, and often I would think of that night and wonder what had happened to the broken stained glass in those three huge, beautiful windows in the sanctuary. I remember asking someone long ago when we were visiting in Woonsocket. She didn't know but guessed that it was probably hauled away to the dump ground northwest of town. What a shame! It could have been cleaned up and the pieces, big or little, used in new projects; not windows probably, just smaller things that hang in a window and spread their beauty just the same but in a different way.

Things from the Past
By Jeann Bevers of Watertown, South Dakota
Born 1924

The Icebox

We had an icebox. The first one I remember was a big oak box, about 30 inches wide by 56 inches long and maybe 40 inches high. To a little kid, it seemed a lot higher. We lifted the lid or top up to open it. The ice was put in from the top and the foods were put in from the top, too. It was a heavy lid with about four inches of insulation, and it was lined with tin. As a kid, I could not open it until my brother installed a pulley and weight, so that when the lid was lifted the weight would pull it open and hold it open until a slight pressure to close it was applied. The ice compartment was on the bottom, and the entire box was insulated like the lid and lined with tin. There were wooden slatted shelves over the ice, which had to be lifted or removed to put in a new cake of ice or if something had been stored against the ice in that lower compartment. It had a drain pan, which had to be emptied regularly; otherwise, the floor would be flooded. Eventually, about 1946, after the war, it was replaced with an electric refrigerator.

While we were living in Iowa in the 1920s, Dad harvested ice from a flooded pond in the front yard of the farm. He stored it in icehouses and sold it around the area. Ice was packed in layers covered with sawdust for use

267

during the summer. The ice house was a great place to spend a hot, dusty afternoon with a good book to read while sitting on a layer of sawdust covered ice and leaning against another layer.

When I was first married, we had a small upright icebox in our apartment. It was a beautiful honey oak, although I didn't appreciate that fact at the time. It was much easier to use than the first icebox that had been part of our furnishings as a child. This one was insulated and lined with tin like the older one, but the ice compartment was on top of the box, with a lid, which lifted up. The food storage was in a lower compartment, which had shelves beneath the ice compartment. It had a door, which opened outward, much handier than a lid, which opened from the top. As the ice melted, it too would drain down into a drip pan beneath the icebox, to be emptied at least once a day depending on the weather.

In the winter, we hung some kind of a wooden box out the window of that first apartment and kept our "needs to be refrigerated" items in that box. We had to open and close the window to place and remove food. Bottles of milk would often freeze if left overnight in that makeshift icebox.

The Iceman
In town, we got ice from the iceman. He made deliveries about three times a week, less often in colder weather, of course. Each household had a large, circular card with each quarter marked with a different number, ten, fifteen, twenty, and twenty-five. This card was placed in the window with the amount we needed on the top side so the iceman could read it from the street and know how big an ice cake he had to deliver to us. He carried the ice using ice tongs, which were sort of gigantic pinchers made of steel or wrought iron. He wore a leather apron-like thing; it went over his shoulders to cover his back and protect him from the frigid ice. For our apartment, he brought the ice upstairs, into the kitchen, and put it into the top of the icebox. For that, he was paid the amount of the cake, 25 cents for a 25 pounder on down to 10 cents for a 10-pound cake. He chipped cakes to size on the back of his truck, and the neighborhood kids loved to catch the ice chips to suck on as they played in the hot sun.

The Milkman
The milkman was another door-to-door deliveryman. We got milk in glass bottles with little cardboard caps to seal the bottles. There was no homogenized milk in the 1940s, so the cream would rise to the top of the bottles. Deliveries were made three times a week, the same as the iceman's. The clean bottles were left in the metal rack on the front step and would be replaced with another rack of fresh milk, etc. We left a note in one of the clean bottles with a list of our needs for his next delivery, cream, butter, eggs, and sometimes cheese. At the end of the month, he brought a bill for the total of our dairy needs that month, and we were expected to put a check or cash in the bottle on his next visit.

We would listen for the rattle of the milk rack on delivery day to make sure we got it before the milk froze. If it froze, it expanded, of course, and the round cardboard caps would be pushed up by the frozen milk about an inch out of the top of the bottle. It was just the reverse in the summer; we wanted to get it refrigerated before the sun got to it.

Party Lines and Old Phones
Party line telephones were another convenience, or at least we thought they were convenient. Often the instrument was mounted on the wall. It was an oak box about eight inches by sixteen inches with two bells mounted on the front. The mouthpiece was a trumpet-shaped metal device mounted below the bells, and the speaker hung from the side of the instrument from an oarlock-shaped hook on a cord containing the wire connected to the innards of the phone and the speaker. When our number rang, it was a matter of removing the hearing device and speaking into the mouthpiece. There was a hand crank on the opposite side from the speaker, which was manually operated to call anyone on our party line or to call the Operator to place a call on another party line.

Every party on every line had a different ring. For example, the number 3-2 would be three short rings and two long rings; 4-1 would be four short rings and one long ring; and 3-3 would be three short rings and three long rings. There were several combinations like that, one assigned to each household. There would be seven or eight telephones on a party line. If I recall correctly our number was 27-F-31, three short rings and one long ring. If there was a fire or other event that everyone would need to learn about, the phone would ring one very long, continuous ring, alerting everyone on the line to pick up immediately. By the same token, if the number of rings was not yours, but you were curious regarding the call, it was often other listeners who picked up their phone, covered the mouthpiece, and listened to a conversation not meant for them.

After World War II, those crude old telephones were replaced with black Bakelite instruments. These were often a cradle-type desk model or an upright instrument with a hook for the speaker as in the old wall boxes. There would be a rotary dial at the base of the instrument and each telephone was assigned a different number. There was no longer a code for the number of rings. A call was answered when the telephone rang, and no one could listen to a private conversation. We used those old rotary telephones for several years.

Sometime in the 1950s, the black Bakelite rotary phones were replaced with plastic telephones, which eventually could be ordered in different colors. We could have more than one phone in a household, one in the kitchen and one in the living room perhaps, but we were charged two or three dollars by the telephone company for each additional phone we used. The phone company was Bell Telephone back then, and they owned all the instruments. They would furnish one telephone or more if we wanted to pay extra for another phone. This is a far cry from our telephone service today. Cordless instruments were the next communication miracles, followed in the 1990s by cell phones.

It Didn't Take Much to Make Us Happy
By Lena Schornack Holgerson of Aberdeen, South Dakota
Born 1926

The little town of Crandon, where I spent most of my childhood through fourth grade is history, just a memory. Crandon was a small, rural town located east between Tulare and Redfield in South Dakota. Memories of the little town are still vivid with the churches, school, grocery store, etc. It was a neat little town until the second elevator burned to the ground. Everything disappeared gradually. My father came to the U.S. as a young legal immigrant from Germany. He worked on

Lena's parents, Lillie (Petersmeyer) and Fred Quitsch with Erma and Emma

WPA projects and helped build the viaduct by Tulare on Highway 281.

Living near the railroad tracks, we frequently had a hobo or two come to the house for lunch. I remember when I was very small I would sit with a hobo outside on the front steps while Mother prepared a lunch for him. They would always eat outside on the steps. Back then, everybody trusted each other. People didn't carry weapons for greed. They seemed more appreciative. Many men hopped a slow-moving freight train for a free ride to the next destination.

One of my first recollections, which still makes me smile when I think of it, was my mother having me deliver an Easter basket to an elderly gentleman named Frank. When I arrived there, the basket was a lot lighter, as I loved candy, too.

Reminiscing about my childhood days brings back fond memories of the Christmas

269

The Quitsch family in 1943

Eve services at our church that we children participated in each year. To me there is probably nothing more beautiful with a pleasant aroma than a freshly cut evergreen tree at Christmas time. Each year the men of the church would cut and set up a tall evergreen tree in the front of the sanctuary shortly before the Christmas Eve program, which was traditional and special. The huge tree would be decorated with candleholders clamped to branches holding four-inch candles. To celebrate the birth of Jesus, each of the children would feel important and walk to the front of the church on the stage facing the congregation and recite his or her memorized portion of the Christmas story. For Children's Day during the summer and for Christmas Eve, I remember getting a new dress and shoes, which made it special. Maybe the dresses were hand-me-downs, but they were new to me.

At the end of the program, each child would receive a brand new little sack of treats. We knew year after year, what would be in the little sack: a shiny red apple, a chocolate candy drop, a stick of gum, assorted hard candies, a variety of nuts in the shell, and a big piece of ribbon candy. The sacks were neatly folded over at the top and were a special treat for us.

The close of the service was what was so special. The candles on the tree were each lit, and the congregation stood and sang "Silent Night, Holy Night." This was indeed beautiful and never once did a tree go up in flames. Of course, the men had a five-gallon bucket of water beside the tree!

Afterwards, it was traditional to have family time at home by opening the presents, which probably didn't take long, as we received little and shared our toys with our siblings, such as a little red wagon. Santa came during the night. My only doll had a cloth body with a tin head with painted curly hair and face.

Although in those days, we made a lot of our own entertainment. I especially remember in the Dirty Thirties the dirt was so fine it made great mud pie cookies; just add a little water and pat the dirt into a form of a cookie and let it dry on the steps in the sunshine. With three girls and two boys, we also had a lot of fun making and flying kites. The brothers were real good with their own plans made from scratch. I remember helping to tear little strips of cloth to form the tail. Playing anti-I-over was also a popular game.

To this day, my younger sister still laughs about how she used to chase me around the yard with a feather. She, of course, knew I hated feathers!

For special occasions, I would curl her blonde hair. Today, the hand held curler is

Lena Schornack Holgerson

270

heated with electricity. Back then, I heated the gadget with the flame from the kerosene lamp. We kids all had dark hair, so I tried to convince her that, being as she was blonde, she was adopted. I don't think I ever really succeeded with my scheme.

As I mentioned before, we lived near the railroad tracks in a small town. The engineer, all decked out in his gray and white striped cap and uniform adorned with a red kerchief around his neck, would always wave and blow steam. How I loved that smell of the engine steam back then. When some train cars were sidetracked by the elevator, my brothers and I would climb the steps on the side of the boxcar. They would make it to the top and walk around, but I made it to the top step and that was it. I hated heights and if I had ever made it to the top, I would probably still be there! Nowadays, I really miss the caboose at the end of the train. It completed the train, and I think of it every time I see a train. After all, the man in the caboose had an important job too, and he also waved to us.

Out father unexpectedly passed away when I was ten and my younger sister was only six. I had three other siblings. Shortly afterwards, our family moved to Redfield.

I remember the large, black coal-burning stove in the kitchen. Often we would come home from school to the aroma of freshly baked bread. What a treat! In the winter, the stove kept the flatirons warm and ready to be wrapped in towels as foot warmers between the flannel sheets at bedtime.

My younger sister and I loved to walk every Sunday afternoon about eight blocks to Main Street to buy the Minneapolis paper, regardless of the weather. Even in a blizzard, we would be seen walking home eating a double dip ice cream cone. I wonder to this day, what the drugstore owner thought of us. At that time, the paper had one complete page of paper dolls and cut out clothes, which consumed a lot of playtime.

Sunday afternoons we always made candy, sometimes taffy, but mainly chocolate, panocha, or divinity. To stay healthy, we had to take a teaspoon of cod liver oil each day. I can still taste it!

Once I was sent to the store to get a can refilled with kerosene, as we had a small kerosene stove in the kitchen that we sometimes used. Instead of asking for kerosene, I asked for gasoline. Luckily, my older sister noticed the smell or I wouldn't be here today to write this.

I am now 88 and my younger sister is 84. So, you can tell it didn't take much to make us happy as kids. I don't recall anyone using the word bored.

The Best Childhood
By Milton Wolff of Tukwila, Washington
Born 1938

My name is Milton Wolff. I was born and raised on a 1050-acre farm 18 miles southeast of Eureka, South Dakota. I had a sister who was seven years older named Florence and a brother eight years older than me named Christ.

On the farm, we raised wheat, corn, barley, and oats. We also had around 125 head of cattle, 50 hogs, and 65 sheep. Much of the work was aided with around 25 workhorses. There were always three or four young colts around, and these became my playmates. They were so cute. We had some ten cats, so we never had a mouse or rat problem.

My favorite was a big, orange tomcat. When I used to milk cows, he always came around and stood next to me. I sprayed him with a squirt of milk. He would run off and take a half hour to clean himself, only to return a little while later for another dose. We played this game for years; it was a lot of fun.

I had a pony named Gallant and spent many hours riding on the open prairie. Many times our sheep or turkeys would run away. My father then instructed me to ride over the entire neighborhood to look for these creatures with my dog and pony. It sometimes took all day. When I finally found them, my dog helped me herd them home.

We milked 20 cows each morning and night. The fresh milk was separated from the cream and was stored in ten-gallon cans and sold in town. We also had about 500 chickens. Their eggs were collected and placed in cartons to be later sold in town. There was a small lake next to our house. We raised a large number of ducks and geese. The lake also attracted a large variety of wild fowl.

Over the years, we had many dogs and I named them all Rex. Most died young by getting run over by visiting cars. Our neighbors many times had new pups born every year. I would then be allowed to choose the pick of the litter. I spent many hours training these dogs to do a lot of tricks and to herd the cattle and sheep.

Inside our home, we had no electricity, indoor plumbing, or running water. Water had to be brought in from a well nearby. Our home was heated with a coal stove and radiators. My mother could perform miracles on this stove. Her specialties were German-Russian dishes, such as knoeple, strudels, dumplings, and buttons. She also baked an assortment of pies and kuchen.

A favorite memory of mine took place on Christmas Eve, 1943. My parents were devout Lutherans and had plans to attend Christmas Eve service at our country church. This was a three and a half mile trip from our farm. It was forty degrees below zero and there was a blizzard. The road was blocked with snow. In those days, when the thermometer read forty degrees below zero it was really forty below not including a wind chill factor. Our 1937 Ford would not start in the cold weather, so my father hooked up a one horse open sleigh, and we were off to church. We all wore several layers of clothing and used a lot of blankets to stay warm. My part of the evening was to sing a few songs in the German language solo. After the church service, there was always a lot of socializing, and I was able to play with my friends. We then made the long trip home and spent the evening opening gifts. We also ate my mother's homemade ice cream with hot fudge.

My siblings and I attended a one-room schoolhouse a fourth of a mile from the farm.

Milton Wolff in 1944

All grades were taught in this room by a teacher who only had a high school education. The school closed down when I finished second grade, and we all attended school in Eureka. My brother, Chris drove us to school daily in the spring and fall. During the cold, snowy winter months, we stayed in Eureka with my grandmother. Many times a blizzard would start over the weekend and it would take a week to get back to school.

After graduating, my sister left home to work in Aberdeen. My brother worked on the farm for another year and then was drafted into the Army. I personally graduated in 1956 and then joined the Navy with six boys from my graduating class. After my release from the Navy, I embarked in a career in sales that allowed me to travel and work in all 50 states and 157 foreign countries. In all my travels, I dined in some of the finest restaurants in the world. None ever measured up to my mother's home cooking.

My parents were hard working people and there were many difficult times. My father often told a story of when he and my mother spent the week gathering hay for the bales to sell. He would drive a load of bailed hay by the wagon with a team of horse to Eureka. For all this work, he would receive $1.00 per load. This took place during the Great Depression of the 1930s. During this time, they planted crops five years in a row to no avail. They were ruined because of drought, grasshoppers, and dust storms. They survived by selling cream, eggs, and farm animals. My father often bought small calves for $5.00. He would bring them home and raise them to be part of his herd.

Another favorite memory goes back to the

years of the threshing machine. All our grains were harvested by a machine called a binder. This machine cut the grain and formed them into bundles. They were dropped into piles in a row. They soon were stood upright with the grains toward the sun. This was also called shocking. After about a week, these shocks would be hauled to a central location and fed into a threshing machine. This machine would separate the grain from the straw. The grain was then sold to a grain elevator in Eureka. This went on every year and was very labor intensive. All our neighbors would help us and then we would return the favor with their crops. Typically, this took three days at our farm. My mother and my sister, Florence would cook for around twenty hungry farmers. They did all this work with a small coal stove in a small kitchen. The farmers all raved about their skills as cooks.

Until 1948, all our machines were pulled by teams of horses. After a hard day, my father would feed them a pail of oats and give them a rubdown. Even after acquiring a tractor, he always kept some horses and would have them do various farm chores. When my father died, he still had four horses. The horses were all over 30 years old.

As a kid, one of my most dreaded chores was picking rocks. This had to be done every summer by hand. The rocks had to be hauled to the rock pile. A new crop of rocks always came up every year, and they had to be cleared to protect our machines.

Growing up, I also became a good hunter. My uncle, Albert, my mother's brother always visited our farm at the beginning of hunting season. He was an avid hunter and sportsman from the old school. He taught me all aspects of hunting and safety. We would rise early to hunt ducks and geese. We usually had our limit in an hour or less. In the afternoon, we would hunt pheasant. My mother knew special ways to cook wild game to make it taste delicious.

Our local game warden often visited our farm. We trapped many live ducks in a cage. We then placed a tag on one of their legs and released them again. These tags contained information about where they were trapped. One of the ducks we trapped was later shot in New Zealand. I used to plant wild rice around the edges of all our small lakes. This was quite an attraction for wild fowl.

My father often stated that he was the luckiest man in the world. My father's greatest disappointment was that none of his children wanted to take over the family farm. He loved his family, all the animals, and the land. The only thing we needed to buy was salt, sugar, and spices. My mother made most of our clothes. I was also a good trapper. There were a lot of muskrats and mink on our lakes. They lived in little huts made from sticks and brush. They brought me a lot of spending money when I sold their furs in town.

Every year we trimmed the wool from the sheep. There were always contests to see who the fastest sheep shearers were. It was quite an art, and we were judged by how little the sheep were hurt and how quickly they were sheared. The wool was sold in town to a local dealer.

About twice a year, we had butchering day. We slaughtered two hogs and two steers and turned them into roasts and steaks. We also made the best sausage and salami, which was smoke. My parents won many awards for their sausage. My father used to try to bribe my teacher with a sausage, hoping to improve my poor grade. This is probably why I graduated from high school.

On the farm, we also had a big vegetable garden. Many of the vegetables were canned to be used in the long winter months. All foods we raised on our farm were natural. We used no pesticides, hormones, or growth-enhancing drugs. They were all organic. Today, organic products cost two or three times more than regular foods.

All during my growing years, I sold many products door to door. Among these were greeting cards, magazine subscriptions, and Rosebud Salve. This salve was my best seller. It sold for 50 cents per jar. During this time, I also sold nylon stockings that were guaranteed not to run. These, of course, ran like crazy and I received many complaints. This experience taught me all about selling for my future career. During my last two years of high school during the winter months, I boarded at the Dakota Hotel. As part of my rent, I worked as a bartender serving beer. I was 15 to 16 years old but never had problems or had complaints. The owners were never around.

My father encouraged me to sing songs, especially "You Are My Sunshine." However, my personal favorite was a song called "Cool

Water," Which was written and sung by Sons of the Pioneers. In my second year of high school, some classmates and I formed a musical band. I became the sole singer. We became popular enough to perform at many weddings and dance halls. In my senior year, we even had a half hour variety program on KABR radio station in Aberdeen. When I visited my hometown after all these years, there are still people who come up to me and ask if I was the guy who sang "Cool Water." At the time, it was the beginning of Elvis's career and many other fine country singers. Who knows what might have been if I'd had the proper training?

I think of my farm experiences every day. Even though we all worked hard, it was the best childhood we could have. My South Dakota upbringing gave me an understanding of how to manage my whole life.

I lost my sister and my brother late last year within three weeks of each other. Over the years, we always lived far apart. We exchanged thousands of letters and phone calls. I will miss them forever.

World War II Family Code
By Dorothy Van Kempen of Bloomington, Minnesota
Born 1936

Today communication for our military and their families is a modern miracle. In this small town of Bradley, South Dakota, my parents, Oscar and Alma Bye, were aware that they're two oldest sons, Warren and Leslie, were of the age to be called to military service in World War II.

Knowing that letters to home were censored, my parents devised a code using a world map. They renamed continents with family names and in those newly named areas, they made several zones. So if my brothers wrote home (as an example): "Mary wrote that she fell roller skating and broke her arm in two places." Mom would search the map for "Mary, "Zone 2" and know about where they were stationed.

Families in America at that time were given ration coupons to use for butter, sugar, and other necessities. The war effort also

called for scrap metal to be salvaged and used for the military. My brothers were discharged and returned home safe and sound. After that, our lives came back to a normal routine.

My First Love, Dyson
By Kristin Gedstad of Sioux Falls, South Dakota
Born 1954

The year was 1968 when my parents enrolled me in Augustana Academy, a Lutheran boarding school in the tiny town of Canton on the plains of Eastern, South Dakota. A new administrator had been hired, Robert, "Bob" Nervig, who shared Martin Luther King Jr.'s belief that the tensions between the races could be mended in an atmosphere of Christian love, education, and equality. Students came from all over the United States to live out the dream of Pastor Bob and Martin Luther King Jr.

His name is Dyson and it was no ordinary friendship. In fact, I do not recall its beginning. He was just there, tall, dark and cute, a smiley young man with a fondness for me. What I do recall is we were instantly the best of friends and confidants. Both of us naive, innocent, and fun loving, we were sweet and mischievous in our flirtations with one another. I loved to say things that would shock him, for when I did, his entire face would open to his emotions, and I found great pleasure watching his deep brown eyes flash and sparkle with his astonishment of me.

Our times together were spent in the school library among literary giants such as Tolstoy, Jane Austin, and books declaring rights and liberty that all people, regardless of race, shall be free and equal under the law. With the library table between us, we spent two years talking as we looked into each other's eyes and searched one another's soul as we smiled, dreamed, shared, and laughed. We felt afraid as we watched on television the uproar over racial riots, injustices, the Klu Klux Klan and horrific murders throughout the country against black people because I loved him, and because Dyson was black and I was white.

Dyson lived his life in a Christ-centered manner unlike anyone I'd ever known; he had respect and love for all people, and he was my safe haven. Dyson was going to become a Pastor, following in the footsteps of his grandmother, who had started one of the first integrated churches in a large metropolitan city. Dyson told me God had spoken to him when he was eight years old and he knew following where his grandmother tread, was his path.

Dyson was different. He responded to hate with love, anger with understanding, and fear with sensitivity. He focused on hope for every tomorrow and on forgiveness rather than personal success. While our peers experimented with drugs and sex, he honored me. His character was uncommon for someone his age. Although he identified with no specific clique, everyone liked him and he fit in everywhere. He was the best part of everyday. We never kissed or held hands, but we had a profound affection for one another and we prayed for a more tolerant world.

Somehow, I knew Dyson would be one of the most significant people in my entire life. I am now 60 years old and have never forgotten the dream or that dear young man who is now a Bishop in a major metropolitan city. For 46 years, I have held these memories within my heart, and I always will.

Living with Dust Storms
By Eugene McMillan of Huron, South Dakota
Born 1926

I was born May 24, 1926 on a farm a ½-mile north and 1 mile west of Carpenter, South Dakota. I was the third one in the family, one older sister, Florence, one old brother, Charles "Bud," on the Dueer Farm. In 1929, we moved ¼ mile west to the Baker Farm. In the '30s, the dust storms were real bad. One bad storm caught us out in the field. Dad and Bud were picking rocks. Dad let me and Irwin ride on the team. When dad seen the storm coming, him and Bud jumped on the wagon, hollered for us to hang on the hames and we headed for the barn. The horses on the dead run, Irwin and I were crying and hanging on for dear life. We made it to the barn; I think we had to stay in the barn 'til the storm was over. We didn't get much for crops as we didn't get much rain and a lot of the topsoil blew away and then the grasshoppers moved in real thick and ate most everything that did grow. They even ate on the fence posts and trees.

Florence, Bud, and me went to Bunker Hill school one mile west. We had to walk when it was nice; dad took us with horses when it was cold. We never had a car 'til about 1931. Dad bought a 1926 Model T. Bud got his arm broken in school by some of the bigger kids, so some of our relation took him to Huron, South Dakota. The doctor couldn't fix it good, so he ended up with a stiff left arm all his life. In 1934, we moved to my mother's folks farm, six miles west. The crops weren't very good until later in the '30s. We always had something to eat. We got some relief food and some clothes. We always had to milk two cows, morning and night, and chores. Dad worked hauling gravel for roads with horses in the '30s. They hauled the gravel on wooden wheeled wagons. Dad got a 1928 car in 1935, as there were more kids by then, eight altogether; the last girl in 1940. Only went eight years then worked for dad and relatives and other farmers 'til 1944. Went to the Army 'til 1946. The rest of my life has been pretty good.

What One Pig Can Buy
By Roy Heintzman of Onaka, South Dakota
Born 1923

My name is Roy. I married my wife Philipina (Phil) on September 30 in 1947 in Onaka, South Dakota. We settled on a farm that belonged to my parents. My dad gave me two horses, a set of harnesses, and two little pigs. They were both female pigs. My mother left us some spring chicken fryers. After those were eaten, we got hungry. The pigs had grown up. I borrowed my neighbor's male pig and had it bred with my females. We had to butcher one pig to eat, but both were pregnant. The one we butchered had eight little pigs inside her. I thought I should have butchered the other one, but luck was with me and the one we kept had 13 little pigs. There were five female pigs and eight male. I kept the female pigs and the next year I got 35 pigs. I kept 15 female pigs the following year and

Phil and Roy in 1948

I got 135 little pigs. When they were grown, they weighed about 200 pounds.

My dad came to the farm and said, "Roy, if you sell your pigs, you will have a nice bunch. I will sell you my farm and two quarters of land for $12,800. I will let you pay the balance in ten years." I sold 60 pigs and paid the down payment of $2,800. I even had $200 left over. Each pig brought me $50.00. All I fed them was wheat screenings. I would go to town six miles with a tractor and wagon and buy a load for one cent per pound. I had to grind it with a hammer mill grinder. I soaked it in water and they liked it.

I paid off the farm in six years. So, with one little pig I bought the farm. Now I have 11 quarters of land and still live here. This is a true story.

A Storm Not Forgotten
By Cynthia Bartels of Charlotte, Iowa
Born 1958

It was summer and the events of one day will forever remain etched in my mind. I was ten and living on a 750-acre farm, 10 miles from Hosmer, South Dakota. That morning my mom and her classmates were busy decorating the high school gym for their class reunion in Hosmer. Dad took my three-year-old sister and me to a small carnival in Hosmer later in the afternoon; mom decided to stay home with my one-year-old brother.

When evening set in, the weather took a drastic turn for the worst. The gentle summer breeze abruptly stopped, making it eerily quiet and almost impossible to breathe. Lights were flickering; the Ferris wheel lost power, stranding riders. Suddenly, a gust of wind hit us. My dad, in an urgent tone, said, "We need to go now." On our way home, the wind was violently gusting pushing the car all over the road. Dad dropped my sister and me off at the house and proceeded to put the car in the garage. Our garage was not attached and located a few yards down from the house. Meanwhile, I struggled against the wind to open the door; my feet were no longer touching the steps. I was hanging onto the screen door while keeping my sister tucked under my arm. Suddenly, mom grabbed the back of my shirt pulling us both into the house. We anxiously awaited dad's return. He finally came through the door; his face was covered with dirt and tiny cuts. He managed to park the car in the garage, but as he was closing the door, the storm took it from his hand. Immediately, he dropped to his hands and knees slowly crawling to the house. After assuring us he was unhurt, dad and mom needed to decide what part of the house was the safest. We had just recently moved the house onto a newly constructed basement. Unfortunately, the stairs were not built yet or a ladder readily available to the basement. Dad feared if we managed to get to the basement, there would be no way to get back out if the storm collapsed the house on top of us. The five of us huddled together, in the dark, waiting out the weather. Our two-story farmhouse was being pelted with debris and shaking on the foundation. The tornado roared like a train that was going to come through the door at any moment. It seemed to go on forever but probably only lasted seconds. Then at last, the noise was gone and rain gently began to fall. I had trouble falling asleep that night mentally questioning every sound I heard.

We awoke the next morning to see the aftermath of the tornado. The garage was scattered, board by board across the yard, luckily leaving our brand new 1969 Oldsmobile without a scratch on it. One barn was partially collapsed and another shed leaning sideways. A huge tree was pulled out of the dirt and laying on the ground; all its roots still intact. The top floor of the house had shifted leaving the doors hard to open and close. Later that morning, mom cried when she received news that the high school gym's roof was damaged, ruining their decorations. She went to help clean up the gym later that day. I still have a vision of her hands blackened from the crepe paper. I have not lived in South Dakota since 1970, but to this day, I am still occasionally traumatized by dark rolling storm clouds, strong winds, and memories of that one storm.

The Years of Muskrat Trapping
By Martha Mehlhaff of Mina, South Dakota
Born 1934

The one-room country schoolhouse in Jackson Township, 12 miles southwest of Eureka had a lake less than ¼ miles away. In the winter, one could see muskrat houses being built by eager and ambitious furry muskrats. I was in the 7th grade. Our teacher got the idea that maybe she could trap some. The dollar signs were in her eyes. During lunch hour and beyond, she took us students with her, along with traps and axe that she brought from home, and we walked back to the lake. The axe was to chop a square block about 8"x8" in the igloo-shaped house.

Many times, we did not get back to the schoolhouse until 3 o'clock. Classes fell by the wayside and I missed yet another day of history and arithmetic class, and other students missed out on their classes too. I knew that in high school I would have to take algebra. I was worried that I would not be prepared for it. Our teacher was not too interested in educating her students, but I probably would have gotten an A in muskrat trapping. The teacher promised to share the profits from the furs with her students, but that never happened. As I recall there might have only been two or three muskrats that were trapped. After some time, the school board had been informed of the "goings on" and the muskrat trapping came to a stop. Needless to say, she was not rehired for the next year.

The farm I grew up on had a lake near the northwest side, not far from the house.

The lake was an ideal haven for muskrats as it had reeds and rushes in it, and of course, that is what they used to build their houses. In the winter as the lake iced over, muskrats swam and worked hard to prepare for the cold season. Their houses were somewhat rounded and igloo-shaped.

My brother, Allen became a muskrat trapper. He bought about a dozen traps, took an axe with him, and walked back to the lake. He chopped a square block out of the house and then set the traps near the opening in the water where the muskrats came up, and pounded the stake into the frozen part of the house. He made daily trips (morning and evening) to the lake.

Those days a license was not required to trap and besides it was on our land. Allen "set up shop" in one room in the basement of our house. He became an expert in skinning muskrats, turning the skin inside, and carefully sliding the fur skin on a thin, flat shingle to dry. He hung them up and nailed them to the beams. It was a profitable two winters for him. I liked tagging along after Allen when he checked the traps. By watching him I learned how to carefully remove the "door" to the house, open the traps, take the muskrat out of the trap, and then resetting it. Sometimes, they had to be rapped on the head with the axe. Other times, they dragged the trap partly down into the water in their struggle to get away if the chain and stake were not secure enough. One time when Allen had to go somewhere for a couple of days, he put me in charge of checking the traps with the promise of getting paid for the price of one muskrat. It was fun opening each house hoping for a surprise that I had caught a muskrat. As I recall there were several fur hides to be had in those two days and Allen carried through on his promise.

We Learned to Listen to Our Parents
By Luella Miller of Selby, South Dakota
Born 1929

George Haux brought his family to the United States from South Russia in 1899 after his oldest son had come over and informed him that land was available here. He brought his wife and children (Jacob age 21, Katherine age 17, Caroline age 15, and Christian age 11) to a farm near Java in north central South Dakota.

In 1900 Gottlieb Bamesberger, age 19, also of South Russia, came to the Java area with his friend, George Reuer. Having worked in the carpenter business he built many of the early homes in Java. Soon after his arrival, he met Katherine Haux, whom he married in 1904. Soon her sister Caroline married a young man named Ferdinand Beitelspacher.

At that time a man named Joseph Weisz owned land two miles south of Lowry, a town south and west of Java. He donated land to the Zion Lutheran Church in Lowry for a cemetery. Later Ralph Tanner bought the land. However he died or was killed, leaving a wife and children who could not make the land payment. George Haux heard about this and he helped his two sons-in-law acquire the land out of that foreclosure in 1909. The two farmed together for about two years, but did not get along, so they decided to separate. To decide who would move they drew straws and Mr. Beitelspacher got the short straw. His family then located on land about two and one half miles east of the original farm. Each one thought the other had the better land, but the first farm had a lot of gumbo on it. So perhaps the one who moved did better. They both raised nice families and my dad, Christian Bamesberger, and his wife, Matilda, took over the farm when Gottlieb and Katherine retired and I was born there in 1929.

Our family was always active in our local church and we never missed a Sunday service. There were also prayer meetings on Sunday afternoons. However the service that got us all involved was the Christian Endeavor service, which attracted all younger families on Sunday evenings. Many times the groups met in churches in the surrounding area for hymn singing and readings and many young families attended.

One rainy Sunday, I think in June, which is our wettest month; all of my family of eight loaded up in our car and attended a Christian Endeavor in a church some distance away. It was getting late on our return trip and the roads in those days were not great and got even worse in rainy weather. Our farm had a long hill coming down and a creek, which caused problems getting in and out of the place in winter or during rainy spells. Dad

Luella's father, Chris Bamesberger with her sisters, Colleen, and Judy

drove to the top of the hill and even in the late evening we could see that the creek running wide with water. "I'll try to drive on the side where the water is not so high," he said, "and I hope we can make it."

Things were okay for a while, but when we got to the middle of the creek, the car either got wet or stuck in the mud. This meant we would have to walk through the creek and up to the house. My youngest sister was on the front seat and mom told her to stay put. "Just wait and dad or I will carry you," she said. We all climbed out, but Judy did not wait and suddenly she flopped in the water and was yelling. Mom screamed and reached for her and caught her by her skirt and quickly pulled her up from the dirty water. She lifted her up and was able to carry her. We finally all made it, soaking wet, to the house in our Sunday clothes. The most important thing was we were all safe.

The road down the hill to our farm, south of Lowry, was always a challenge, but winter snow and summer rains made things worse. One year my grandfather and my dad built a kind of cabin, which fit on a wagon. It had some windows, two benches, one in front and one in back, and a door on the side. There was a slit in front where the reins of the horses fit through when hitched up to the wagon. It was very good on snowy days to get my sister, Colleen and I to school.

One day when we were returning home from school with the three of us riding inside the cab, my sister was not sitting on the bench, but leaning against the door. Suddenly the door opened and out she went into the deep snow along the way. Instant panic! My dad got the horses stopped and got out and picked up a crying sister all covered with snow. Luckily the wheels on the wagon missed her and she was not hurt. Needless to say when dad told us to sit on the bench while we were riding home, we really listened after that.

Party Lines and Milking Cows
By Philipina (Phil) Heintzman of Onaka,
South Dakota
Born 1926

My name is Philipina (Phil). I married my husband Roy on September 30, 1947. We were both raised on a farm and knew how to work hard. In 66 years, we have seen many changes. We had no electricity, telephones, or running water. The only "running" water we had was to take two pails to the windmill and pump water to fill the pails and then *run* back to the house.

In later years, we got telephones. There were 10 families on the same line so you had to take turns using it. There was no privacy and anyone could listen in. My sister lived one mile from me, so we would borrow from each other. One day I called my aunt for her good cookie recipe. I ran out of sugar, so I went to borrow some from my sister. She had already baked them! She had listened to the call. So you see; nothing was private.

The first morning we were married my husband helped me milk the cows by hand and then went into the fields. So in the evening

Phil in 1947

I had to milk all the cows myself. When he came home he said, "How did you make out?" I was so proud of myself. I said, "I milked all 13 cows!" He said, "We only have 12 to milk!" Whoops! I had milked a cow that had not had a calf yet! She ended up giving milk the next day after she had her calf. He will never let me forget that. We had to separate the milk from the cream. You had to crank a handle and the cream came out of one spout and the separated milk came out of another spout. We would sell the cream and used the money for groceries or other things we needed. We were poor but didn't really know it. It did not bother us; we were happy.

We had three children—one boy and two girls. We now have 12 grandchildren and 12 great grandchildren. Last year we celebrated our 65th wedding anniversary at the town hall. We had a free polka party dance. There were free drinks all night and supper for us all. We had ever 200 guests and they all still talk about the good time they had. We are still in our own home and taking care of ourselves.

Philipina's sisters in 1951

Memories of Main Street
By Catherine Hausman Ching of Brookings,
South Dakota
Born 1951

When people that grew up in small towns hear the words "Main Street," images of local barbershops, grocery stores, gas stations and implement dealers come to mind. Those memories of the small town in eastern South Dakota that I grew up in are just a small part of the collection of memories I think of when I hear those words.

We moved to Estelline, South Dakota when I was 4 years old. Our family at that time consisted of my mom, my dad, my older sister, Pam, and younger brother, Mike. My parents purchased the local journal office and we moved from Pierre, South Dakota to what seemed like an awful long way away from my cousins and my grandma. The business was located on Main Street, nestled between the bank and the local hardware store, smack dab in the middle of the two-block long business district. We lived above the "shop," our name for the newspaper office, in a small two-bedroom apartment. My sister and I had trundle beds. As the floor in the bedroom kind of sloped, we would ride the bed from one end to the other. It didn't take much to entertain us because I think the room was only 9 feet wide, so it was a short ride.

The narrow wooden stairs leading to the small two-bedroom apartment were at times scary, but well worth the trip down as we reached the bottom to go out the front door, our front yard, otherwise known as Main Street. Our backyard consisted of a tarred fenced roof with more steps leading down to a graveled area that turned into the alley. Needless to say, our playground area was quite limited, but that didn't stop three creative, curious children.

Boring was a word not in our vocabulary as we always found something to do. One morning my sister and I decided to dress up our brother, Mike, in one of my old dresses. Oh, the smiles we received as we walked up and down the two blocks that housed the business area of the street. Thankfully, he was too young to remember, so never did get revenge, at least not for that. Every weekday in the summer, we patiently waited for 6:00 pm. That is when the stores closed and we were able to play ball in the front yard. The middle stripes served as home plate, pitcher's mound, and second base, while first and third bases were provided by the street light posts.

Saturday night was the highlight of the week. All the businesses remained open and Main Street turned into a huge parking lot with cars lining both sides of the street and one strip of cars down the middle. The sidewalks were filled with residents of the town and the surrounding farms. Young people entertained themselves by traveling up one side of the sidewalk across the street and down the other. The band was playing in the gazebo located at the end of Main Street. The smell of fresh popcorn filled the air as you approached the popcorn stand, owned and operated by our neighbors. We remained friends with their two daughters throughout high school and spent many hours together. But that's another story as shortly after we built a house one block off Main Street; they followed suit and built one right next door. As I said, the popcorn stand was my favorite thing and at times, we were privileged to help them run the stand. There were movies in the local theatre playing every night and we received free passes many times, as my father practiced the barter system with the owner. Free tickets for free advertising in the newspaper and popcorn was a nickel!

There were some not so happy memories of living right on Main Street as well. One that I particularly remember included the grocery store located right across the street and a bottle of ketchup. It was close to 6:00 pm and mom sent me across the street to get a bottle of ketchup. I grabbed the ketchup from the shelf, went to the counter, and said, "Charge this please," as was common then, and started to cross the street swinging that bottle of ketchup. I felt so grown up and proud that mom trusted me to venture to the store on my own, after all, I was only 5 years old. Anyway, I guess my hands were a little sweaty and the bottle slipped right out of my hand and crashed and broke all over the middle of Main Street. Climbing those scary stairs was not a pleasant experience that time, knowing I had to tell my mom I broke the bottle of ketchup and the store was closed. I don't remember getting yelled at, but do remember dad going out on the street to clean up the mess so no cars would run over the glass and get a flat tire.

Another not so pleasant memory included

my sister and that tar roof I talked about earlier. Although the roof, which served as our backyard, had a fence so, we wouldn't fall off; it didn't fence us away from the adjoining hardware store and other buildings to the south. My sister and I would run across the roof playing tag and eventually the lady who worked at the hardware store would come out the backdoor and yell at the top of her lungs, "Who is on this roof?" You would think she was scared that we may fall off or something but no, she screamed at us to get off the roof and said that every place we stepped, the roof leaked when it rained. I don't remember that it stopped us from going on the roof again; however, we tiptoed across that roof to get to the next one after that.

Okay, so it sounds like we were just running wild as children, however that wasn't the case. We also had to help get the newspaper out every week. Every Thursday I spent catching the paper as it rolled off the huge press and sliding each one in the corner so that they could be folded. The papers went from the catching bin to the folding table where my sister had to slide each one into place so the folder could make the paper ready to mail. Then we rolled each paper and placed a label on it to get it ready to sort for the post office. It was a family business and it took all of us to get the weekly newspaper out.

One memory serves as a source of embarrassment to this day for my mom. Remember how I said that on Saturday the stores were open in the evening? The people who owned the hardware store next to the shop asked my mom and dad to go out to their cabin at Lake Poinsett after they closed for a couple drinks. As all three children were snuggled in bed, sound asleep, they decided to go for an hour. Guess you can't count on kids staying asleep. I don't remember who woke up, but it wasn't long before the three of us were standing by the screened window that faced Main Street asking those who were still walking up and down Main if anyone knew where our mommy and daddy were. Oops! Of course, if that happened now days, child protective services would be called; we probably would have been removed from the home. Needless to say, they never did that again and we were fine. I'm not sure how mom and dad found out that we were awake, but someone called the owners of the hardware store and they were home shortly after that.

We always seemed to find something to do on our Main Street front yard. Our building bordered the local bank on the south. The bank had just recently enhanced the front of their building by adding brick facade. One morning Mike, who now owns his own concrete/ construction company, was found practicing his hammering skills. Unfortunately, he was pounding off the brick facade that the bank had so recently added to their building. At that point, in time you would have thought mom and dad would have hidden the hammer. But no, Sister Pam decided to try her skills in front of another Main Street building. She wasn't destroying property however; she was trying to figure out what was inside that turtle's house. She is still embarrassed about that incident, feeling bad for the turtle. Needless to say, I think the hammer disappeared after that.

Okay, I can't just pretend to be the innocent, always perfect, angel. One day in the backyard, that patch of gravel before you got to the alley, I must have thought the back of the bank needed a little something added. I really don't know what possessed me, but I was caught breaking a pop bottle on the bank, so maybe we had too much curiosity as children. Again, I was in the backyard getting yelled at by another business employee.

Now that I think about it, I bet Main Street had a party when we finally vacated the apartment and moved into our home. That home had an actual yard for a playground. Although we moved to a new location, Main Street continued to provide entertainment to all the children in town. The north end of Main Street is a wonderful hill that leads to the cemetery. Many hours were spent in the summer riding down that hill on our bikes, often "no handed," or with a passenger on the handlebars. I don't ever remember any vehicle/bike accidents, as I am quite sure the adults in town knew to watch for bikes flying down that hill. When the season changed and the snow fell, the hill served as an excellent pathway for sleds and toboggans. It was the place to be after school well after dark, and Saturdays and Sundays there was a constant stream of children traveling up and down that hill as well as adults.

Every August the shops would set their goods out on the street for the annual "stinker days." I'm not sure where the theme originated but do remember the black and white skunk logo displayed in advertisements and flyers all over town. Again the street would be full for two days with activities for the children, and opportunities for the local stores to deplete their inventory and get ready for new things.

Eventually I would work on Main Street again helping my dad put out the weekly newspaper while raising my five children in the town I grew up in. Main Street changed over the years, many businesses closing, no more Saturday night adventures, no movie theatres, no popcorn stands and fewer and fewer residents. Many attempted to start facilities aimed at providing entertainment to young people, but they never lasted. What we considered fun seems boring to kids now. They built a nursing home on the end of Main, which took half the hill that so many had enjoyed sliding down. They still slide down the hill, but it's not the same.

My brother and his family still live in Estelline and my mom lives there in the summer. I still visit occasionally and at times my entire family will be home. However, Main Street has changed. When you turn that corner going north and enter Main Street, many times there are no vehicles to be seen, no children riding their bikes down the hill and many empty spots where thriving businesses used to stand. But no one can take away the memories; they continue to live in our family and many others who grew up in that small, eastern South Dakota Community.

The Life of My Mother
By Janet Keenan-Hauck of Watertown, South Dakota
Born 1938

I feel like I could almost write a whole book about my mother. Yet there are tons of times in her life that I never learned about. She was born on May 7, 1912 to a large family. She was born when her mother was 42 and she was the youngest. Her father, Lars Stensland, had come to this country at the age of 16 from Norway all by himself. He wanted to farm so he helped a farmer near Canton, South Dakota. Living conditions were deplorable with rats running around the building where he slept. The last name "Stensland" means

Janet's parents, Roy and Veronica Lorenzen

"stoney land" in Norwegian.

Lars was able to buy a farm near Garretson, South Dakota. He married Lavina and they had 11 children, one son died in childbirth and another in his late teens. Veronica, my mom, was the baby in the family. Her sister, Luella, at age 6, thought the doctor brought her in his black medical bag. The oldest sister, Emma, spit on my mom because she knew that she would have to help with the baby care and also sew her clothes. She sewed for the whole, entire family.

Veronica was the only child to be confirmed in English. All the others were confirmed in Norwegian. The older sisters helped in the house, but mom did all the outdoor jobs. The one job that I remember was shoveling manure to clean out the barn. Company would come and she would run and hide. No way, as a teenager, did she want to be caught smelling of manure!

Mom's school was a one-room type with all eight grades there. Her teacher was her sister, Lorenza. Mom did so well that she skipped a grade. However, she didn't complete high school due to just one subject, physics. It was a required subject back then and she didn't believe that she could pass it. However, as bright as she was, I'm sure she could have.

As teenagers, the girls and boys in the family loved to go to dances. Remember there was no TV! Their father would sit on the front porch waiting for them to come home at daybreak. He was cheerful and didn't reprimand them for being out late. Mom always said that she would much rather dance than eat! Mom married young at 17 and my father was 23. I'm pretty sure that she met him dancing. He played the banjo and sang in a band. They were even on the radio.

I guess that I will never get over how hard times were for my folks starting out in the depression. Mom had to learn to cook, which meant using an old cook stove. The heat source was to burn corncobs. Of course, everything she cooked or baked was from scratch, bread, cakes, pies, puddings, and whole meals. When threshers would come to the farm, it would mean feeding several men. The men threshed grain by hauling bundles to the threshing machine. Grain came out into the grain wagon and straw out the back. This meant preparing huge morning lunches, noon meals, and afternoon lunches, and sometimes suppers.

The blizzards were probably the worst. Mom said that she would go stir crazy so she would walk outside around the perimeter of the house. They would go to town for groceries and have to shovel out a very, very long driveway (I think it was almost ½ mile). When they got back home, it was blown shut with snow. Out came the shovels again!

One-room school

My mother became pregnant and said that she bought 10 cents worth of meat for my dad to eat. In retrospect, she thought that she probably should have had some of the meat for protein during pregnancy. My sister was born and barely weighed five pounds. She had to sleep between mom and dad for warmth. I know that they slept fitfully so as not to roll over on her.

The folks had terrible luck with their horses. One hung himself in the manger. Another one a neighbor borrowed and drove it so hard that it had blinding staggers. He tried to run through a barbed wire fence and had to be put down. There were other horses with problems too. When the folks were picking corn, my sister, Bev, was in the wagon. The horses ran away with her. Poor dad had to chase them forever to get her back.

One exciting time for my folks was during prohibition. The federal revenuers burst into their house one night when they were asleep. They thought that they were trafficking alcohol. Guns were drawn and they checked under the beds and all over. Mom was terrified! At any rate, the folks were found to be in the clear. However, they actually did know the man that they were after.

When the depression became too hard they had to give up farming. Mom's first job in Sioux Falls was plucking chickens. She came home splattered with blood and had to quit after the first day. Mom just didn't have the stomach for it. I certainly can't blame her!

Her next job was at Manchester Biscuit Company where she packed cookies. Being a diligent employee after working on the farm, she quickly became their fastest packer. When she finally saw that the other ladies worked slower and got paid the same, she slowed down. Then her boss said, "What's the matter, Veronica? Are you sick?" Manchester closed their plant five years after she started. Next she tried packing Walnut Crush candy bars at Fenn Bros. My dad already worked there in the ice cream department. He delivered ice cream to all the stores on the east side of the city. Mom packed 114 bars a minute into boxes. She then threw the boxes over her right shoulder to a conveyor belt. Fenn's closed their plant after she worked there for 28 years. She was beginning to think that she was a jinx for closing two plants!

I would like to write more about my mother's work ethic. On Saturday mornings, after working at her fast-paced job, she would wash clothes with the wringer type washer, hang them out to dry, clean the house, iron, and bake two apple pies from scratch. She still found time to go shopping with me and my girlfriend, Sylvia. Mom always let me sleep late (I'm now ashamed of myself) and never enlisted my help with any chores. I think that she felt that she had worked so hard on the farm as a youth that she wanted me to have it easier. I was probably 11 or 12 at the time and my sister, Bev, was already married.

As for any lessons on cooking she was sorely afraid that I'd set my braids on fire. We had a gas stove so there were flames, of course. Therefore, when I got married my husband did not get a bargain. I was really lucky. Denny's mother let her five sons shift for themselves. They subsided on peanut butter sandwiches and cold cereal. Then progressed to learning how to fry eggs! Anything that I cooked was so appreciated. His favorite food was the mashed potatoes that mom fixed when we were going together. He called them "slip easies" because they did slip down very easy. Was he ever happy with mom's cooking!

My Beautiful Blue Dress and Petticoat
By Rose Grothe of De Smet, South Dakota
Born 1933

For Christmas in 1940, I received, from our minister and his wife, my first boughten dress. It was a beautiful blue color with little white flowers all over. It had a Peter Pan collar, puffed sleeves, and a quite full gathered skirt. There was rose pink piping around the collar, the puffed sleeves, and the waist. Also included in the gift was a light pink taffeta "petticoat."

We didn't go to church the Sunday after Christmas, but we did go the next Sunday, and I of course wore my wonderful Christmas gift. When we got home from church, I was very reluctant to take off my finery. But finally, my mom persuaded me to change so I didn't get it dirty. Our "closet" was just a wooden pole held up on both ends by a wooden frame. My dress was on the end closest to the window where I could see it very well every time I went in to my parent's bedroom, which I did very often all day long.

That evening my dad, my brother, and I were playing cards when I said, "I smell smoke!" The cards flew every which way as dad (who was crippled) quickly made his way to the bedroom. The curtains, my dress, and petticoat were on fire! Dad grabbed the burning material and carried it to the living room (only a few steps away), hollering for someone to open the door to the wood-burning stove. He thrust the mess in, slammed the door, and went back to the bedroom. I'm sure he must've gotten burnt, but I don't remember for sure.

By some miracle, what he had grabbed had been the only things that were burning, but the fire had scorched the window casing, and in a few minutes more, our house would have been aflame. The heat from the burning curtains and dress had been so intense that the teeth of a comb lying on the dresser next to my dress had melted together in a solid mass. Dad had saved our house from burning to the ground, but all I could think about at the time was my absolutely, wonderfully beautiful new dress and petticoat that had gone up in flames. I cried and cried and cried.

Dad later determined that when my brother had gone into the bedroom to light the kerosene lamp, the lighted head of the match flew off when he struck it on the sandpaper on the side of the box of matches. There were quite a few of the matches in that box that did that, but that was the only time it started a fire. But whenever anyone used those matches, they always watched to see that the head didn't fly off into combustible material and start a fire.

After the WPA workers finished making

Lake Osceola and Lake Agnew at Bancroft, not only was Lake Osceola area used for swimming, fishing, picnicking, baseball games, etc., but the water was also used as the source of ice to fill the icehouse. This building was just west of the grocery in Osceola and had been an auditorium at one time. It had sat unused for some time, until someone got the bright idea to use it for an icehouse because there was a basement, which was ideal for storing the ice.

When the Osceola Lake had frozen to a depth of maybe three or four feet, neighbors and friends set a day to "cut ice." The men would make several cuts, probably to the middle of the lake, approximately 18-24" apart, then make crosscuts and end up with 18-24 inch cubes of ice. The blocks would be hauled to the icehouse where other men were waiting to unload them into the basement. A thick layer of straw had been spread on the floor in preparation for this very thing. The ice blocks were packed with straw between them so they wouldn't freeze together. After the blocks were all deposited in the basement, the team drivers would go back to the lake for another load, and the "straw guys" would cover the blocks with more straw and be ready for more ice to come in. Layer after layer of blocks were put in the basement in this manner, each layer covered with straw until the basement was filled. Sometimes it took some waiting for the lake to freeze some more after ice had been harvested, but the basement eventually got filled.

Some people had "ice boxes" to keep food cold. These were made of wood with a small compartment for the ice, and shelves in the rest of the area for the food. Sometimes the block of ice would have to be broken in half to fit into the compartment. The rest would be broken into smaller pieces, which would go into the drink of the day, mostly water, as lemons for lemonade was hard to come by. Sometimes it was iced tea, but I never cared for that. There would be a pan underneath the box to catch the water as the ice melted, and the chilled air, cooled the foods. This pan had to be emptied quite often, but sometimes the pan ran would be filled to overflowing before it was emptied, and when this happened, it really made a mess.

The men who helped with the cutting, hauling, straw covering, or anyway pertaining to the ice was allowed to get ice from the icehouse. It was sure a great treat to get a block of ice and make homemade ice cream. One of the neighbors had a huge freezer and would make it full, then ask the neighbors to come for a great evening of cards for the adults and games for the children, topping off the evening with the homemade delicious treat.

Usually enough ice had been harvested to last into spring and at least part of the summer. When the ice was gone, the straw was cleaned out of the basement so fresh straw could be put in the next year. It was heavenly to go down into that cool basement with dad when he went to get ice. He always took old rugs, quilts, gunnysacks, etc. to wrap the ice in so it wouldn't melt before he got it home. Newspapers also made a great insulation to keep the ice frozen. Some years, after cutting the first layers of ice, the men had to wait for the water to freeze deeper before they could harvest more ice before it got too dangerous to be out on it.

My father, Roy Currier, was only one of the group of men around Osceola, South Dakota who were "employed" by the works progress administration (WPA) in the late '30s. This was a government program that hired jobless men to do public works, like making lakes, building dams and spillways, etc. The project that dad was working on was making man-made lakes at Osceola and Bancroft. He had a team of horses and the government hired dad, his team and wagon. At one time, I believe he had two teams and wagons, and his brother, Iral, drove the other one. But a lot of the time, dad worked with a hoe, grubbing out the weeds and tree stumps to clear the area for the lake.

The teams and wagons were used to haul rocks from wherever they were found to the site where they were used to build a bathhouse so the lake could be a swimming place as well as picnic grounds. Some of the teams were used with scrapers to dig out and pack the dirt for the bottom of the lake. The rocks were also used to build "fireplaces" with a chimney and a covered grate for outdoor cooking in the picnic area. Rocks were also used to line the turnarounds at the picnic area and the baseball field at the Osceola area. The Bancroft area, named for Frank Agnew a local businessman, was never developed like the Osceola area was. I believe the rocks were also used to make the spillways at both of the lakes.

The bathhouse constructed at Osceola was quite large with a center room with rock walls on the four sides. There was a wood burning stove for heating and an area for tables for eating in, in case of inclement weather. There were no windows or doors, just the openings. On either side of the large room there was a row of partially partitioned off, no doors, small changing rooms for the swimmers. Each one had a wooden bench and was maybe two to three feet wide. The east side was for the girls and the west for the boys. There was no roof over these spaces, but it had a cement floor with a drain for the rain to drain away.

The area to the south sloped down to the edge of the lake. It was a good many yards away so there was no danger of flooding if the lake got too high. At either side of the area a cement trough carried the rain from the level land behind the bathhouse down to the lake so it wouldn't wash away the gravel beach.

Incidentally the hoe dad used had been sharpened so often that it was only about 1 or 1-½ inches deep. The body had been worn away to sharp corners and made an excellent hoe for gardening in later years. One time the hoe was lost and as dad had used it last he was very upset because he couldn't remember where he put it. One of my parents had a dream in which the vision of the hoe hanging on the fence was seen. An investigation of the fences the next day revealed the hoe just as in the dream. It was used by my mom into the '60s. I will always be grateful for this government program, which enabled my dad to support our family for a few years.

Prairie Pasture
By Sharon L. Hansen of Aberdeen, South Dakota
Born 1939

The time was the 1950s. A young girl was growing up on a farm in eastern South Dakota. Life was lonely at times, but the loneliness was the impetus for her wonderings into the section of the farm that was and still is native pasture—virgin sod. She wandered winter, spring, summer, and fall, sometimes on foot and sometimes on her trusty steed, Trixie.

Riding the prairie pasture

Winter brought a walk through the drifted snow, huge drifts along the shelterbelt with beautiful big lips of snow curled over the edge of the drift. Sometimes she would jump on the curls and then feel guilty for ruining the beauty of the snow banks. She then returned to the warmth of the farmhouse, cold and damp, but happy.

Spring was exciting, sparked by the snowmelt and words, "The creek is running." The creek was a small waterway. When the weather warmed and it thawed, spring was in the air—grand, glorious spring! Soon the snow would be gone and the native prairie grasses would sprout and flourish along with pasque flowers, thistles, buffalo grass. The cows would be turned out to graze on this bounty. In the late afternoon, the girl would saddle up Trixie and lope out to herd them back to the barn to be milked.

Summer was a feast. Most of the farm was under till, planted to wheat, oats, and rye. However, the most endearing part of the farm was the virgin sod of the prairie pasture. The grasses turned slightly grey and the creek was no longer running, but the water hole, which it fed, was filled. This was all natural and still is, with no man made stock dams.

Summer was a time to ride horseback, with or without a saddle. The girl could ride through the rows of the shelter belt, which is now too overgrown to even walk through. Sometimes branches would slap her in the face or Trixie would stumble in a hole. She always regained her footing and the small rider didn't tumble off.

Fall brought harvest. The young girl had to drive a tractor pulling a trailer to unload grain from the combine. Fall also brought

286

school and the curtailing of wondering about the prairie pasture.

As you may have guessed, this young girl was me. I didn't know it at the time and had never heard the phrase, "communing with nature," but that was what I was doing. The prairie pasture left an indelible stamp in my mind. Years and years later my love of nature lives deep in my soul.

Thank you, prairie pasture.

School Days and Grasshopper Swarms
By Joseph Nuhsbaumer of Zell, South Dakota
Born 1930

As I write this article, I'm reminiscing my early childhood. It all started when my father came here in the turn of the century from Switzerland. He homesteaded on the southeast quarter of section 29- 116- 66 in Plato Township. In 1996, my wife, Rose Mary Bush and I built a new home on the same hill.

I think about the times we went through, but also the times our parents went through. I think of my mother getting up in the morning and walking 60 feet to the outhouse in below zero weather. The only seat warmer was from human heat. I remember my mother lighting the kerosene lamp in the middle of the day when the dust storms hit. Dust sifted everywhere. I got a preschool education early. I would stand by the low windowsills covered with a very fine dust. I could write some numbers and spell my name—Joe. I didn't need a pencil and paper—only my index finger on my left hand. I recall going to the barn early in the morning to milk cows. We carried a lantern, and sometimes the wind would blow it out. Dad would not allow us to carry matches because he was afraid we would burn the barn down, so we didn't have any light.

I got my education in a little one-room schoolhouse. The pupils varied from four to ten students, depending on the year. My first day of school was quite a day. My teacher was Merrill Miller. I was strictly left handed. I picked up my pencil in my left hand and Miss Miller said, "Joe, we do not write with our left hand in this school." What choice did I have?

To complete my eight years of education, Ms. Miller was followed by Miss Sawler, Miss Mullens, Miss Becker, Miss Benning, and my eighth grade teacher, Miss Bush. Looking back I think the education system was pretty good. The teacher taught all subjects to all eight grades. When your lesson was called, you sat on a bench by the teacher. I tried to remember the lessons in the class ahead of me so when I was asked those questions the next year it was easy. Multiplication tables were drilled into us day after day. When a teacher flashed that card, you had better know the answer real fast! I thought the teacher had a big advantage. When she held the card up, the correct answer was on the back of the card facing her! Not fair! We had no calculators and didn't even know what they were.

1936 was a very hot and dry year. We had grasshoppers and grasshoppers and more grasshoppers. They came in swarms. They would hang on a wooden post always on the shady side. As the shade moved, they would too. In a few days the bark would be are eaten off and the post would look like new lumber.

This is a short glimpse of my early childhood in Hand County, South Dakota-- the best place on earth! Hope you enjoyed it!

Reminiscing Past Years
By Kathy Scharn of Watertown, South Dakota
Born 1933

The "Good Old Days" surely brings back a variety of memories from the '30s, '40s, and '50s. I so remember when many of the schools in those days had a metal tunnel fire escape that extended from the top story of the school. This got to be used as a "fun" activity of the schoolyard. Climb up, slide down, climb up, slide down, always hoping the principal wasn't in his office to stop the fun, Saturdays seemed best. A popular game at recess and at noon hour was Pump Pump Pull Away, running between the outhouses and school property line. The people in the middle would yell, "Pump pump pull away! Come out or I'll pull you away!" as we were all lined up on one side or other of the boundary lines, ready

The Country School

to run and not get caught. I haven't heard of that game in many a year.

I remember when I first got inside a country schoolhouse, which still stands on Hwy 15 north of Altamont. Of special interest was that "stove" in the corner of the large one room. Our school in town had a janitor that took care of the big furnace. I remember thinking; they even have their own stove! I found out the teacher had to keep it fired up and wood on hand.

We had fun evenings sitting in the living room to listen to the radio programs. A big favorite was "Fibber McGee and Molly" when somebody invariably would open the "closet" and the sound of everything falling out would come through the speakers. The "Great Gildersleeve" would often say in his low scary voice, "Only the shadow knows." A daytime goodie was "Old Ma Perkins" and the ad of Rinso White and a whistle.

The outhouses were part of our daily life, but the worst day was when my cat fell down one of the holes. My Dad knew just what to do. He got a noose, brought the cat up, and my mother had a pail of water ready to use. Our sewing machine was a busy part of the house. My mom was an excellent seamstress and I remember being 13 years old and begging to have a coat that was bought from the store.

Hunting pheasants was a big activity at our house in the fall. When my dad got done working at his shop, he and I would go road hunting. I helped look for birds and run after them after he shot. He rarely missed. The limit was many more than today, and we could have hens, too. We never tried to get the limit, as we didn't have freezers to preserve them for any length of time. You went out and got what you could use and came home with what you wanted. There was no question "if" you got enough.

Oh yes; castor oil was a hated word by a kid, but we sure lived to talk about it. Also disliked was when you had to hang your head over a pot of hot Vicks with a dishtowel over your head to be "steamed" for a bad cold. Then you had to go to bed with the Vicks rubbed on your neck and a wool sock wrapped around it for the night.

The icebox had to be watched constantly. When a small piece of ice was left, Dad would go to the "ice man's place" and get a new chunk, bring it home, and chip away until it fit just right for the size of our box. A treat was to go down town (three blocks away) just before supper with 25¢ for a pint of ice cream. We would bring it home and put it in the icebox until we finished eating. Then we would eat it immediately.

As to school discipline, I do not recall spankings. However, when the student was unruly, the teacher would say, "If you don't behave I will send you to the principal's office," and sometimes it might be the "superintendent's." Those were threatening words, and most of the time that is all it took for discipline.

In remembering the first man to go around the world, my friend and I watched every minute from takeoff to the landing. When he landed, I remember her saying, "Well, he's been around the world and I haven't done a darn thing yet today!" I have truly enjoyed reminiscing those past years.

Being a Wartime Teacher
By Ruth Nelson Beitelspacher of Aberdeen,
South Dakota
Born 1926

I was a teacher during World War II. I graduated from Veblen SD High School in 1944. That summer I went to five weeks of summer school. This was at Northern Teacher's College in Aberdeen, and now it is Northern State University.

I took classes on how to teach first grade reading and an arithmetic class on teaching the basics of math. I still have those report cards. Then all of us who were wanting to be teachers had to go to our county seat towns; I went to Sisseton, South Dakota and took tests in all subjects pertaining to the first to the eighth grades taught in country schools. My certificate was a second-class certificate and good for 2 years. I had to get a permit to teach, as I wasn't 18 until October and schools started in September. I had a small school: one seventh grader, three third graders, and a second grader. This was a neighborhood school about three miles east of my home school. I boarded with the parents of the second grader. They charged me ¼ of my wages or $25.00.

The second year I took a school further from home and not in our township. This school was closer to the Coteau de Prairie range of hills. I heard this strange noise and the children knew it was the echo from Sica Hollow. Sica Hollow was a beautiful limited park. Its creek was fed by natural springs from the hills. My school took our lunch pails and hiked there one noon for "skip" time. It was beautiful. Sica Hollow has been a state park for years. The roads are improved and the trees stay so well groomed. It is a fantastic excursion in the fall to view the fall colors.

I had to return to summer school that summer and take another test for a first grade teacher's certificate that was good for five years. I taught three more years and got married.

My teaching years helped me to teach my own children in preparation for school days. My daughter studied to be a teacher. She has been a math teacher her entire career. She taught one year at the Bowdle SD High School, and following her marriage, she moved to Oregon. She can start to make plans for retirement, as she will be 64 this September I like to say that I should be classed as a veteran after being a wartime teacher for five years!

The Twins' Birth

I was born October 7, 1926. That is a long time ago. My mother had twins, a girl, and a boy, on April 30, 1930. We were eating breakfast when a man came in carrying a black bag. My sister, Jane, just a year older than me, said that he brought the babies in his bag. They were placed each at one end of a funny looking bed with a gate on the side. So our family now had six kids. My mother told my brother to take his shoes off and run to Grandpa Nelson's farm and tell him that we have two babies. It was raining that morning and throughout the day. The twins were named

Cornar John and Helen Joy. My brothers were Sherman and Cecil and my sister was Jane. I am Ruth. My mother changed the boy twin's name when the boy was so naughty, so they became John and Joy. He was always Johnny to us, but all through school, army, and marriage he was John.

Our winter here at Aberdeen has been long and very cold this year of 2014. It reminds me of many snowy winters at the Veblen SD Flats, which are just below, or east of the Coteau de Prairie range of hills stretched across eastern South Dakota. There were no roads in the area, just prairie trails made by wagon wheels or buggies. Our farm was in Roberts County and Norway Township. Just one mile from our farm, but across the road in Marshall County was a big knoll. It was a perfect place for adventurous boys and girls to hike with sleds, scoop shovels, and other stuff to get speedy rides down the slope in the clean white snow.

I mentioned that there were no roads, just trails back then. The drought years came in the '30s, so the government hired the farmers with their equipment and horses to build up the main roads that went east and west along section lines. I remember my dad being so tired after a day of work. He would steer the team of horses and press the bucket into the ground to fill and pull it to the top of the new road. He would then dump it. He did all of this work only by his own hand power.

The higher roads were necessary, as everyone was getting automobiles. I was surprised when I returned one summer to find that the road didn't go around that knoll anymore. It had been cut down and the road right where it should be. That happened when country schools were closed and busses drove around the districts to pick up the school kids.

Oh! I was such a good babysitter for the twins. I would feed them their meals with a little spoon and blow on each spoonful so it wouldn't burn them. My mother made little cloths filled with soft bread, cream, and sugar. She tied it together with a string. They sucked on when they shouldn't have more to eat.

Fast forward to now: I am now 87 and all my family have passed away. I have 3 sister-in-laws, one daughter, three sons, three grandsons, and two great grandsons. My husband Rueben passed away in 2006 and I miss his companionship so much.

My Siblings and Me
By Sharon Gill of Watertown, South Dakota
Born 1942

Well, hello there! My name is Sharon Gill and I was born in April of 1942, the second to the last of six children on the family farm in Bristol, South Dakota. I could write about our first John Deere tractor bought after the war ended or our first combine—a beautiful orange case with a six-foot pickup and that eagle emblem on the hopper, but I guess I will write about my growing up years and the relationship I had with my siblings. My brother and two older sisters I didn't mix with much, for they were far too old to be playing with us little ones. Besides, they were out in the fields working with horses or busy stacking hay. Of course, there was an endless list of things to do: the dozen cows that were milked by hand twice a day, calves, hogs, and stock cattle to be fed and watered, the chickens to be taken care of, eggs to be gathered, garden to be weeded, fences to be fixed, and you name it. It went on endlessly. When the weather cooperated, they were out plowing and disking, dragging behind a team of horses from sunup to sundown, so I didn't see them much. Anyway, the girls went to high school in Bristol three miles away. So they work on most of the time, too.

Also, I should explain that we did not have running water at our fingertips. The only running water we had was when we had it in a pail and ran with it! We didn't have the bathroom; a two hole outhouse got us by. In the wintertime, us little ones used the pot in the basement. We had a form of electricity in our house that came from a wind charger and a storage battery that was underneath the cellar steps. We burned wood, corncobs, and coal in our kitchen cook stove and "warm morning" house heater. Mostly Mom carried the water to the house in two milk pails from the deep well that was our water source on the farm for everything. I still remember seeing her lugging those heavy pails of water, her dress whipping in the wind, for isn't it just about every day that the wind blows in Dakota land? We had a cistern by the house that caught rainwater and a kitchen sink with a hand pump that was used for doing dishes, bathing, laundry, etc. Poor Mother! Baths only came on Saturdays when we cleaned up to go to town. Imagine the field dust on the bedding and clothing come wash day!

But what I was going to tell you about was us three little outlaw sisters and our naughty ways! We had our playhouses and stole eggs to mix with dirt for baking cookies and cakes. We always had a worthless dog that my little sister and I would cover with mud in the summer to keep it cool. When Dad wasn't around, the three of us would strip off our clothes and swim in the stock water tank, riling up the waters so bad that the cattle wouldn't drink it. Then there was our sneaking into the garden to pick fresh peas and baby carrots to eat. We were always throwing rocks at the pigs, cats, dog, and chickens, and sometimes at each other.

My older sister and I would ride the pigs until we got our first pony. We attached a long rope to it and my older sister would ski behind us as we pulled her through the pastures and cornfields. My little sister would ride in our little red wagon behind the pony. One day the rear wheels dropped into a badger hole and we pulled the front wheels and handle right off the wagon. She cried and cried. Then there was the pig pasture that had huge rocks in the center of it hidden by sunflowers taller than us kids. It was there that we would sit and smoke, or tried to; the cigarettes we stole from our brother. I was about 12 when Mom caught me smoking the first time. She planted the toe of her shoe firmly in my behind and warned me she would tell Dad if she caught me again!

Saturday night had us cleaned up and going into town for necessary foods and

Sharon with her siblings

supplies. We would also sell the cream and eggs. Us three girls would get our quarter spending money to go to the show, which we usually did. Tickets were 12¢ each and popcorn was 10¢ a bag. Sometimes we would skip the movie and go to the grocery store and buy a jar of olives. Oh, how we loved olives! I hope you enjoyed my story.

Home of Edith and Emil Bunting

The Illinois Hunter Visitors
By Marion (Bunting) Nordquist of
Watertown, South Dakota
Born 1925

My South Dakota story is about my parents, Emil and Edith Bunting, who lived in Albee, South Dakota. I was born in Albee in January of 1925. When I was seven years old, there was a fire that destroyed the hotel and a grocery store. I do not remember much about it, but there must have been an eating establishment in the hotel because soon after the fire, our home became the place where traveling salesmen could get lunch or supper

Edith and Emil Bunting in 1948

or if needed a place to stay the night. Those days it was called "Room and Board." Now they are known as a "Bed and Breakfast." Over the years as I was growing up, many people came through our doors for a meal and a night's stay. My mother loved to cook; she could fix a meal for one or many. On one occasion, there was a train derailment west of town. She was asked if she could feed a large crew. She said "Yes, but they will have to come in shifts!" She could accommodate 12 to 20 at one sitting. My father had several large gardens, plus chickens and cows, so the basement shelves were always filled with plenty of canned foods plus the eggs, milk, cream and butter.

In the later '30s or early '40s, my father's nephew who lived in Belvidere, Illinois had been asked if he knew of a place to stay in South Dakota if they were to come out for pheasant hunting. Of course, he told them about my parents. In August of one year, my mother received a phone call inquiring if she would be available to have a group of hunters come for the opening week of pheasant season. She explained to them that our home was not modern and if that was acceptable to them, she had the room and would gladly welcome them. That was the beginning of a long relationship with those Belvidere, Illinois fellows. There was always at least four who came—sometimes six or seven and as many as eight. Two of them, Andy Whiting and Floyd Houth, were the ones who always came and they became our family and we became theirs.

I married in 1945, and after my husband came back from World War II, we moved to Watertown, South Dakota. Mother and Dad continued having the hunters come and I would take the week to go home and help her with them. My father died in 1948. They continued coming to her home for a few years, but when she could no longer do it, Andy called me to see if my husband and I would consider having them come to our home. By that time, we had three children. I explained that our home was a very small three-bedroom home, but if they didn't mind, we would certainly find room and would love to have them come.

That year there were four fellows who graced our home for a week. They were such a great bunch of guys. The following year we had bought a larger home, as my mother had come to live with us. In August, the phone call came once again. "Are you willing to have us come again?" They came for a few more years. By that time I had had my fourth child, I had known them from before I graduated from high school in 1942 and they had known our children and saw them grow. Our son's birthday was in October and it always fell during that first week of pheasant hunting. They never forgot to bring him a birthday gift. My parents and our family always received a Christmas gift over the years.

They invited us many times to come visit them, so the year our fourth baby was born, we drove to Belvidere to visit them. They were so gracious. Andy and Floyd had summer homes on Lake Delavan, Wisconsin. They had made arrangements to take us and our three older children to Chicago to the zoo. Mother stayed at their place to babysit the baby. In 1965, my husband was transferred with his job to Omaha, Nebraska. For several years, they continued to come out the first week of hunting but stayed with a relative at Clark, South Dakota.

In 1967, we were transferred to Wausau, Wisconsin where we resided for 13 years. On one occasion, Andy and Floyd came through Wausau on their way to Canada to fish. Andy passed away after that, but my husband and I drove to Belvidere one weekend to visit Floyd who was then in an assisted living home. In 1984, we moved back to Watertown. A few years later, Floyd called to ask if we would be home, as he and a friend had come back on a short vacation and would like to stop and visit. We of course spent the afternoon reminiscing about our many years of that "one week in October." There was always one night out of that week when they came to Watertown that

they announced when they arrived not to plan to feed them, as it was "our" night out. Yes, the week they were here was lots of work—early mornings, a big breakfast to prepare, a lunch to make that they could take with them wherever they hunted, and then a late "after sunset" supper when they returned from their day's hunt. They would clean up because they never came to the table in their hunting clothes. After supper, they played some cards and many times, we were included in their evening's conversations. It was a joy to have them come each year. We have many cherished memories of our Illinois hunters in our Albee and Watertown, South Dakota homes. They became a part of our hearts and lives.

Party Lines and Radio Programs
By Orville Hilbrands of Milbank, South Dakota
Born 1924

In the "Good Old Days" in the wintertime, a lot of times we had to cross over a snow bank just to get to the outhouse. After we did our business, we finished the job with one of the softer pages of the Sears & Roebuck catalog or peach wrappers when available. When one of us was constipated, there was one teaspoon of castor oil waiting for us once a day, or as long as we needed. If one of us had a chest cold, Mom would warm some goose oil and warm a flannel cloth. She would then put it on our chest.

Orvill Hilbrands and Marvin Hilbrands

Evelyn coming through the snowbanks from the outhouse

On Saturdays, we took our bath in a regular sized galvanized tub. Each kid got clean water. The tub was by the cook stove in the wintertime. On Saturday nights, we also got to go to the movie at the Chateau Theater. Before the movie started, they showed previews for the next week's movie. Admission was 25 cents.

We had a Maytag wringer washer with a gas engine on it. Our telephone was on a five party line. Sometimes it was hard to get the line. You would have to tell your neighbor it was an emergency so they would give up the line for you to make your call. When we went to visit Grandpa and Grandma, we got to listen to their windup record player. We weren't allowed to wind it, though.

I went to a country school and walked ¾ of a mile there and ¾ of a mile back. My favorite teacher was Esther Jenson in the fourth grade at a one-room schoolhouse. If there was a blizzard, we didn't go to school. In the spring, we had a dust storm. It was so bad walking home; we followed the fence line for the ¾-mile walk.

When I got home from school, I had chores to do. I milked cows by hand, fed chickens, and picked eggs. After the chores were done, I got to listen to my favorite program on the radio, "Jack Armstrong." About that time, Wheaties offered box top promotion to get a "Jack Armstrong Dragon's Eye" ring. My favorite toy was a racecar and tinker toys. We played with marbles outside, making a circle with them in the dirt. Using a larger marble in the center for the shooter, we'd shoot the marble with our thumb to see who could get the most marbles out of the circle. One time my buddies and I got into mischief on Halloween and tipped over an outhouse. We didn't get caught.

Looking Back
By Darlene Carlson of Sioux City, Iowa
Born 1928

I was raised in the small town of Jefferson, South Dakota. Main Street had the Catholic Church, a grade school, Feinberg's Grocery, Fox and Mose's Tap, a gas station, a barbershop, Gary's Café, and Kent Drug Store where you could buy almost anything. My dad was a smoker, and I remember him sending me there with 25 cents to get him a pack of either Old Gold or Camel cigarettes. They were put to use if I had an earache, too, as Dad would blow smoke in my ear and Mom would quickly put cotton in it. It seemed to work, but I doubt that would be legal today.

My dad raised cattle and had a trucking business. One of our favorite things was riding along to the Sioux City stockyards and stopping at Young's Dairy for ice cream on the way home. With friends close by, there was always something going on. I remember watching a free outdoor movie on Friday nights in summer. Dad would park the car early for a good view. With no TV, the radio was our entertainment. Though I doubt my parents were big sports fans, we did listen to the World Series. I remember my mom saying, "No use hearing the ball game, the Yankees always win anyway."

I was an only child until I was six. Then my sister was born, and two years later, a baby brother. I thought they were the cutest kids ever. We lived in a small two-story house and the bathroom was only accessible through my parents' bedroom. It was also, where my baby brother slept. Seems we always had to use it when he napped. So, one day when my friend and I were playing upstairs, we had to use the bathroom. Knowing it would make Mom unhappy, we peed out the upstairs window! I have no memory of how we accomplished this, but distinctly remember the two yellow streaks on the outside of the house.

My friends and I bought the magazine called Hit Parade with all the latest songs and would sit on our front porch singing for hours. There were usually four or five of us together. One friend kept house for her grandfather after her grandmother died, so we were there a lot. He wore hearing aids, so one of our tricks was to sneak his car keys after he was asleep. Another friend did the driving, as she was the

293

bravest. We never got caught, but couldn't go very far in the town of Jefferson. She was also the one who would sneak cigarettes from her mom's and sister's purses. We all tried smoking, but other than laughs, we didn't get anything out of it. One girl singed her hair trying to act sophisticated with her hand in the air. No damage, but she didn't try that again!

Shopping in Sioux City was a big deal to us. We would get the bus in front of Kent's Drug Store at 10:00 AM. At 3:15 PM, we would go to the Milwaukee Train Station for a ride home. I remember shopping for school shoes and bought pair of Huaraches. They were not exactly what my mom considered as school shoes, but it was too late, as I had worn them home.

The war was on during my high school years, so I only got to go to out-of-town activities in my freshman year due to gas rationing. The summer of my junior year, my friend and I got jobs at Fairmont's in Sioux City breaking eggs to go to men in the service. I never did figure out what they did with them. It was an assembly line along a trough for the shells with pails overhead to fill. There were pails for the bad eggs too, but once in a while, they got "accidentally" dropped in the trough. We thought it was great fun and even made 45 cents per hour. Many years later when walking along the street where we live now, a lady remembered me, as she was working there at the same time. Guess they didn't like us very well, as we were always acting silly and they only made five cents more than we did!

I met my husband Bob in high school and have a picture of me with my foot on the running board of his car. Years later, my

Darlene Carlson in 1945

daughter-in-law showed me a picture of her mom in exactly the same pose! We were married in 1946 in St. Peter's Church on Wednesday morning at 9:00 AM. The church law at that time was no food or drink before Communion, hence the early hour. My mom made food for the wedding party and relatives, but the big celebration was the dance in the city hall that night. We hired a band and my uncles "passed the hat" during the evening. We made enough to pay the band and some left over. I still have the list of "givers." My friends and I always thought it was so funny, as most of the "old ladies" (probably not as old as I am now) came to the dance and sat along the wall to watch. I don't remember if they ever danced.

We rented a farmhouse for $12.00 a month. It didn't have plumbing, but we did have lights for a while, as there was some type of windmill in the backyard called a Windcharger that made electricity. It didn't work for long, so we went to kerosene lamps. Often I wonder if they were anything like what they have today. After two years, we rented a farm with an old house. Bob farmed and worked part-time at the Sinclair gas station. That was back when they filled the gas tank for you and even washed the windshield. We had electricity, but no plumbing of any kind. We had a bucket and dipper for water by the sink. I remember the time I had shampooed my hair and realized the pail of water was empty! Out to the yard to the pump I went! It was so cold that when I came in my hair was frozen in strands! It probably was not so funny at the time.

I saved rainwater for laundry or got it at

the pump and heated it on the woodstove. We did get a gas stove later and then clothes dryer! One of the businesses had used appliances for sale. It was great because by then we had two little ones. It was good for diapers, etc. And, no kidding, it played "How Dry I Am" when the clothes were dry. It was a Westinghouse and I have never heard of another like it. The party line phone was fun, too. Our number was 59, and if it rang three long rings and two short, it was for us. Of course, we listened in on the others and thought it was hilarious. Most of the women talked in French, but as they said some words in English, you could sometimes get the gist of the conversation.

I wanted a family soon, but it wasn't meant to be until our first baby was born nearly 5 years later. I worked for Gary's Café until a branch bank of Union County opened in Jefferson. My cousin was manager and new to that position. He hired me to help and we sort of learned together. I remember we did double 'postings' so we could check each other for mistakes. I loved the job and knowing all the people was great. I stopped working when our first daughter was born.

In 1961, we gave up farming and moved to Sioux City where Bob went to work for Swift Pkg. Co. Riverside has always felt like another small town to us. All in all, I have had a good life and the times without modern conveniences didn't seem bad at the time. I still wonder how we had time for company, played cards, and nearly always had something "baked" if anyone stopped by. We now have seven children (yes, all my prayers for a family have been answered), 14 grandchildren, and soon 22 great-grandchildren.

Dust Storms
By Barbara Behrend of Brookings, South Dakota
Born 1923

Growing up in the dust storm era was probably the best lesson in economizing, thriftiness, and surviving that a child could have. Getting through those years, with absolutely nothing but hope and faith and perseverance was an accomplishment that we all experienced. We survived with the barest of necessities. One of those necessities was

Barbara and Dale Baker

not having a toothbrush, for instance. This accounts for my having to have a complete set of dentures by age 32! In later years, my Uncle Bob Baker was a dentist in Blue Earth, Minnesota. He tried to save Dad (Ray,) Mother (Eleanor,) and Dale's teeth as much as he could, but it was too late for me!

We had a small stone building with a roof that we called a smokehouse. It was here that the butchering was done and where the hams were cured. Mother canned most of the beef, and to this day, I have never tasted any beef that equaled the taste of that meat. It was delicious. The folks also made headcheese from the pigs, but never "blood sausage" as some of the neighbors made.

It is behind the smokehouse that I received one spanking that I never forgot. This particular spanking was memorable because I was wearing a pair of silk panties and was embarrassed when my dad took me across his knee and saw my pink pants! The spanking was necessary because Dale and I wouldn't stop fighting in the back seat of the car coming home from town. We had been warned many times, but did not heed his warning!

When the smokehouse wasn't being used for processing the meat, Dad would make dandelion or chokecherry wine and home brewed beer. This was a treat we experienced when we had company. When professionally made beer was first made legal in Minnesota, we took a trip across the border and brought a few bottles home. Oh, what a disgusting taste! It was no comparison to our own home-brewed beer.

We missed a lot of school days during the winter months because of the blizzards, but we also had no school on the really bad dust storm days in the summer. Because of no lights in the school building, school would be called off because it was too dark to see! The farm wives gave up trying to keep the houses clean because they could not keep ahead of the dust that filtered in the cracks and windows. Road ditches filled with dust level with the roads just as they did in the winter when we had several feet of snow at a time. And of course, there were no crops, although the seeds were planted in the ground in the spring. However, with no rain and just dust and wind, nothing would grow, only thistles.

One of the saddest memories I have was the day the government loaded all our cattle in trucks to be hauled away for slaughtering because we couldn't pay the loans and taxes, nor could we get any money to buy feed for them. We had names for all our cows, so it was almost like losing part of our family.

Dad was a staunch Democrat, so, obviously, Franklin D. Roosevelt was his hero. He was so fed up with President Hoover, and so were a lot of others in the nation, which proved he wasn't alone in his feelings. The W.P.A. provided a meager income for the families and the government also gave

Barbara, Dale, Earl Somsen, and June Loats in 1928

food commodities consisting of flour, sugar, butter, cornmeal and powdered milk that supplemented our garden products.

Entertainment

In spite of the fact that money was somewhat of a premium in the 1920s and 1930s, we went to shows (movies) at least once a week. My favorite stars were Janet Gaynor and Charles Farrell in the '20s and Bing Crosby, Fred Astaire and Ginger Rogers in the '30s. It was my "secret ambition" to be a dancer!

We had a large barn, and when the haymow was empty, we would have barn dances occasionally. I wondered why Mother had to have a good supply of sugar and hot water in the house on dance nights, but now I know it was the ingredients the dancers needed to mix with the "beverages" they brought with them. Klatts also had barn dances, and these were special because Dale and I could go along and play with Bob and Doris Klatt.

Sometimes we would take in the Deuel County Fair at Clear Lake. One time when Dad didn't have the money needed for all four of us to get through the gate, Dale and I had to sit floor in the back seat of the car with a blanket over us. Dad only paid for the two people in the front seat!

Saturday night was the time for all the farmers to take their cream and eggs to town to trade them for the week's supply of groceries. It was important to get there early so we could park on Main Street. It was a good place to sit and "watch the people go by." But first, Mother would go into the grocery store and read the list of groceries she wanted to the clerk who would write down all the items on a little ticket. He would then proceed to gather the items and pack them into the egg crate so they would be ready for Dad to take out to the car when we were ready to go home. The groceries were paid for with the eggs that were brought in the crate, thus trading them for groceries.

Dale and I would each get a nickel to spend, and what a hard decision I had to make! Did I want an ice cream cone, bar of candy, box of popcorn, or something to drink? Mother's cousin, Monroe Simons, who was blind, had a popcorn wagon, which he parked on the street in Castlewood every Saturday night. He and his wife, Mary, who was also blind, made their meager living this way. They had several children and I have often wondered how they survived. I guess we didn't have it so bad.

Neighbors

Neighbors were so important to the farmers during the depression days. Of course, there was no television and only a few subscribed to newspapers or magazines. Most everyone had a radio, though. When I think back, I realize how stupid it must have looked when we would sit around the room, staring at the radio, while listening to Amos and Andy, or Fibber Magee and Molly! For some reason, it was more fun to be at the neighbors listening to these programs with someone other than with your own family. But the highlight of the evening would be getting together in the neighborhood to play cards. Pinochle or Whist seemed to be the favorite. And the ladies would conclude the evening with a bountiful lunch of cake, sandwiches, and nectar made from good old Watkins Nectar mix!

Every farm had a telephone, too, which was an important necessity. The phones were a big box that hung on the wall with a crank on one side, which was "cranked" to make the call. Our "ring" was "a long and a short and a long and a short. The ring would be heard in every house and even though it wasn't your ring, you usually listened anyway to hear what was going on in the neighborhood. This was called "rubbering." Mother was one of the worst on our "line" for "rubbering." She was fit to be tied one time when she received an anonymous funny Valentine depicting a lady "rubbering on the telephone."

It was common practice for neighbors to help each other at threshing time. Dad had a threshing rig, which he moved from farm to farm to assist with harvesting the crops. As soon as I was old enough, I would "hire-out" to the ladies who needed help at this time to cook for the threshers. A large meal was always prepared in the house at noon, also a mid-morning and mid-afternoon lunch, which would be taken right out to the threshing site.

A new family moved into our neighborhood which excitement and anticipation because they were a family from Holland. The predominating German families soon found out that the Verhoeks weren't much different than we were and we got along just fine. It was a little odd to see them buy onions in the hundred-pound bag like potatoes and eat them like apples!

Dale and Barbara Baker in 1926

Our Health

I don't recall many visits to a doctor while I was a child. Of course, we experienced all the childhood diseases, including scarlet fever when I was two! I would never want to go through a siege of whooping cough again! Picking up the "itch" in school seemed to be the norm. Every night, for many days we would be bathed in s solution of sulfur and lard then dressed in our "long underwear" and put to bed. We bathed in the washtub beside the kitchen stove in the morning before going to school. If I remember correctly, we missed several days of school before we were finally cured. I suppose we had head lice, too, but I don't remember that.

One of the most hazardous tasks we kids were responsible for was the shelling of the corn with a little hand sheller. The sheller was mounted on a board and one of us turned the crank while the other fed the ear of corn into

297

the cogs of the sheller. Well, one day Dale was attempting to put a short, nubby ear into the mouth of the machine but neglected to get his hand back out in time. His finger was injured, but he was not taken to the doctor. As a result, he always had a crooked middle finger on his left hand.

While walking home from school, I fell while attempting to walk on a corrugated culvert that was in the ditch, waiting for a road to be repaired. I scraped my left knee, but continued to walk home (three and a half miles) with my coat rubbing the wound, thus allowing the knee to become infected. After a few days, it was evident that the knee was not going to heal in spite of Mother's home remedies. By the time Dr. Watson saw the wound, it had developed an abscess. What a painful experience that was! Every time I look at the scar on my knee I remember how really stupid we were about good health habits. Probably the most obvious of this was the fact that we did not have a toothbrush in our house until I really don't know when.

The Unsolved Mystery
By Hazel L. Eilers of Aberdeen, South Dakota
Born 1919

Welcome to eastern and northeastern South Dakota, the "Sunshine State," and the "Land of Infinite Variety." There are many untold tales of yesteryear in our state.

There were winter blizzards when we were cooped up for weeks. Sometimes we could hear the coyotes howling at the moon at night. I remember big threshing crews and the cook cars, party line telephones, and iceboxes. The ice was cut by hand and stored in an icehouse. There were coupe cars for two and cars with running boards and side curtains. We used kerosene lamps and lanterns, because we had no electricity. There was a wood walk leading to our outhouse. We took baths in the laundry tub. Salt and soda were used for toothpaste, and we chewed wax to whiten our teeth. Castor oil was the cure all. We used tokens and food stamps to buy our groceries. Gas was ten cents a gallon, and we could get candy for a penny. The Dirty Thirties were really rough. I remember the grasshoppers that ate the crops.

I went to a one-room school with one teacher for all eight grades. Mr. Mike Guhin was a great teacher. We had foot races during recess. We also had spelling bees. Teachers went to Northern State Teachers College of Aberdeen, South Dakota for one year to get a teacher's certificate.

Excitement was caused by a late night knock on our door. Dad opened the door. A stranger barged in. He insisted he stay all night. Dad and Mom gave up their bed. So we all went upstairs. The next morning, Mom fixed breakfast. The stranger ate heartily, thanked them, and on the way he went. It remains an unsolved mystery.

Glass Chamber Pots and Tumbleweed Ball Gowns
By Judy Miles of Colman, South Dakota
Born 1943

All of the years that I lived at home we had no running water or indoor plumbing. We learned not to waste water, as whatever we carried in we also carried out.

Our outhouse was in the backyard. One of our chickens, an old tough rooster, would watch us go out to the outhouse, no problem. The problem was getting back to the house with him tight on our heels. After a while, Dad took care of the problem, and we had chicken soup.

Of course, we had chamber pots. The one for my little sister's potty chair was clear glass. My great-uncle always seemed to drive by when one of us was on the way to the outhouse to empty it. He always said he could see what was in it from the road. So embarrassing!

We always washed clothes on Monday. On Sunday evening, we would pull up water from the cistern with a pail and rope and put it in the washing machine. Early Monday morning, Mom would put an electric heater in the water, and by 7:00 a.m., we were ready to start. The first load was whites, followed by light colors, dark colors, jeans, and rugs.

Everything got hung on clotheslines. Everything had to go together on the lines. Sheets were on the outside line with underclothes on an inside line, so people who drove by couldn't see them. Towels had to be together, and then washcloths, etc. It had to look neat, even on the lines. In the winter, they froze dry. They always smelled so good and fresh.

We didn't have many toys, but we had a playhouse with Mom's old dishes, pans, and soup cans. We made mud pies in all shapes and sizes and decorated them with different types of weed seeds. Then we baked them in the sun.

We used to tie tumbleweeds around our waists with twine. Then we would wrap a blanket around them. We would walk down the lane like we were princesses in our ball gowns.

Thanks for getting my memory jolted back to the "good life." What a wonderful life!

The Attraction to Teaching
By Phyllis Meseberg of Watertown, South Dakota
Born 1927

I'm looking back and wondering what it was that made me want to teach for 38 years. The attraction must have been that first year in 1945.

It was World War II time, and I turned 18 years old three days after school started in the one room country schoolhouse too far from home to drive to every day, and besides the roads were poor from the main gravel between Henry and Wallace, South Dakota. The schoolhouse was within walking distance from where I stayed. Maybe the attraction was the beauty of my classroom with a pot-bellied stove in the back, an old piano, teacher's desk, and of course, blackboards, and desks. The teacher's job was to teach all grades or as many as were needed for the children enrolled, do janitor work, which consisted of putting that pink sweeping compound on the floor every night to sweep, clean, etc., check papers, and to prepare for tomorrow. Oh yes, playground duty and disciplining was also part of the job. That consisted of playing ball with the kids, which seemed to take care of both sometimes. There were other times, such as when my eighth grade boy wondered what would happen if he took the ivory off the piano keys and put it on the warm stove. That took some airing out!

If you remember the winter of 1945, you will understand why I didn't get home for a month and then I had a wagon ride for a number of miles to meet my dad on the gravel road. That storm came very fast and unexpectedly. Two of the fathers brought blankets to school and, holding them in front of the children and me, we walked home. I wonder why they didn't bring a car. Maybe it was the visibility. I don't remember.

Maybe the attraction to teaching was the wages. At the end of the month, I stopped at the neighboring farm and picked up a warrant, which was to be cashed at the bank for $150.00. The wages were considered very good compared to other teachers in the county.

Maybe it was the good people, the great kids, or because each year got better. Guess I'm too old to do it all over.

Hay Making Days
By Louise E. Beld of Big Horn, Wyoming
Born 1945

I remember hay making days in Hamlin County, South Dakota when I was young. The hay was cut with a sickle mower converted to tractor mower from horsepower and left to dry for a short time. The amount of time depended on the humidity. We all hoped for no rain until the hay was put up. I rode the dump rake pulled by a "B" John Deere driven by my brother, Laverne. It was a challenge to kick the dump lever at the right time to make a decent windrow so Dad could push it with a hay bucker on an "A" John Deer. Dad built the bucker. He would push the hay onto the stacker tines then the "B" would be hooked with a clevis onto a rope that would pull the tines up in the air over the haystack.

Then I would be up on the stack with my sister, Carol. When the load would come up on the stack and be dumped, it was our job to pull it to the corner and make a nice square stack and tramped down tight. When the hay came down we wanted to be far enough out of the way, because if we weren't it would be down our backs and in our hair and noses and eyes and mouths. The foxtail grass and Indian needles were pretty sharp and would poke through our clothes. It was a hot day, and we would be all sticky and itchy and sweaty.

To make a good stack that would shed rain

was a challenge. We had to drag forkfuls of hay and build the corners up but not too fast, because we could put more hay in a stack if it was built right. But if we drug the hay out too far, the whole corner would slide down and it wouldn't last, as the stack would slide apart.

Mom would come out and bring a hot dinner with dishes and oh so good flat bread, fresh out of the oven. A picnic out in the hay land! Also, she said if we got the hay put up, we'd get to go to the lake and go swimming. After swimming, we'd get ice cream floats at the lakeside drive-in. So at the end of the day, we got cooled off and our tummies were full of a delicious treat!

Learning the Hard Way
By James A. Schmidt of Huron, South
Dakota
Born 1950

Living in the country by Crow Lake, we grew up with just the basics, but we did have one thing, a television. Our first TV set was a black and white set with tubes. It seemed to take forever to warm up before we could see a

James A. Schmidt
A Christmas to remember

James and his dad ready for church

picture. One of the household rules was no TV until the school homework and family chores were done. I remember watching *Gunsmoke*, *Howdy Doody*, and *The Ed Sullivan Show*.

For chores, it was my job to go get the water. We had no indoor plumbing. The pump was up the hill some distance from the house. As a small framed little guy, I learned how to time my steps so the bucket would swing between my legs on every other step. That gave me balance. Then I poured the water into a big crock next to the washbasin. In the crock was a dipper we all used to get a drink.

One night I broke the rule. A program came on called *One Step Beyond*. It was a spooky show that would give me goose bumps. So I put off getting water until after the show. Big mistake! It was now dark and windy. I was all creeped out with my knees knocking. I hated the thought of going up that hill into the darkness by myself. So I mustered the courage for the journey. With a deep breath, I started up the hill. Oh, what could be my fate? I just wanted to get this over with. Halfway there, so far so good. I hated this wind. I couldn't hear if anything was sneaking up on me. All of a sudden, a big white thing came out of the darkness right at me! The bucket went flying and it was back to the house as fast as my legs

300

could carry me. There was no way I was going back out there tonight. They could send me to prison or feed me to a pack of hungry wolves, but that was not going to happen.

Early the next morning, I went to find my bucket. There it was, up against the fence with a blown apart newspaper right next to it. After that, I was very faithful about getting the water before it got dark.

Stuck on the Train Tracks
By Hazel Erickson of Langford, South Dakota
Born 1920

I grew up on a farm a mile and a half from Langford. But if we walked on the railroad tracks that ran beside our farm, it was only a mile to town. In the spring when the snow was melting, a creek ran under a bridge on the tracks. We had to walk across the bridge, because we couldn't walk in the creek. When I was in the fourth grade, my older sister, Carol, and I were walking to school that spring. My sister was ahead of me on the tracks. When we came to the bridge, I started across and my foot slipped in between the spaces of the tracks. My galoshes got stuck, and I could not get out. I called to Carol, but she didn't hear me and went on to school. I tried and tried to get my foot out. I knew the train would come by eventually and I would die. What I didn't know was that when Carol got to school, she realized that I was not there. The school let her call Dad and she told him something must have happened to me on the tracks. He came along beside the tracks with the wagon and horses. I didn't hear him coming and suddenly he was jerking on me. My boot came off and fell into the creek, but I was loose. Dad put me in the wagon and held the horses so they wouldn't be spooked by the train. It was a close call!

During the 1930s, my dad didn't really have many good crops. But he always had milk cows and my mother had chickens, so we had milk, butter, and eggs. My mother sold the extra butter and eggs in town to buy other groceries. She always had flour and would bake six loaves of bread twice a week. What a lot of work! We had bread, butter, eggs, and milk to eat, so I never thought we were poor. She had a good sewing machine and made all of our clothes. There were six kids in the family. Carol and I were the oldest and helped out with washing dishes and putting up lunches for those of us in school.

It seemed like the winters were endless with a lot of blizzards. During the winter, Dad would take us to school in a sled pulled by horses. We would cover our heads with blankets, and he would wear a horsehair coat. When school was out for the day, he would be there to meet us and take us home.

All of us kids attended school in town, so I never attended a country school. I only taught there one year and that was enough! My next job was at Barnard, South Dakota, and that's where I met my husband, Morton Erickson. World War II had started, and he was going to be drafted. We married in 1943, and he was in Europe during the war. He returned after the war and settled into teaching.

Both of us taught for many years with the Langford School. We had two boys and two girls. After retirement, we went on many bus trips to 48 different states. It was a lot of fun. Morton died in 2011. I am now 94 years old and still live in my own home.

August on the Farm
By H. Lynette Olson of Brookings, South Dakota
Born 1934

My dad worked as a pharmacist at the Kress Drug Store in Mitchell, South Dakota when Pearl Harbor was bombed December 7, 1941. Within a week, he enlisted in the Navy. He attended Great Lakes Naval School, becoming a Navy recruiter. Next, he rented our house and sold our 1937 black Ford. My mother and I, his eight-year-old daughter, spent the next fifteen months following him to Navy stations in Sioux Falls, South Dakota, Omaha, Nebraska, and Buffalo, New York. He then attended Officer's School and was sent to San Diego, California to ship out on an LST for the South Pacific. At that time, my mother and I returned to South Dakota and lived with various relatives while waiting for our home in Mitchell to be vacated.

The month of August we lived on a farm near Salem with my mother's sister, my Aunt Dorothy, her husband, my Uncle Ed, and my three cousins, J.C. eighteen, needed to help work on the farm, Dale, twelve, and Mary, ten, the same age as I.

Monday through Saturday, Dale, Mary, and I walked a mile to get the mail and a day old *Argus Leader* newspaper. We sang and skipped along the way, listening to meadowlarks' flute-like calls, and watching their bright yellow breasts and outer tail feathers flashing white in flight. When we arrived home with the mail and newspaper, Dale hurried to the kitchen table to read the war news. He specialized in the European Theater articles. After reading the news, he cut out the maps and drew them larger on paper. Then he placed his maps on the west wall behind the kitchen table.

Another activity Dale enjoyed was buying World War II balsam wood kits and making them into model planes. One of the planes he constructed was the B-17 Flying Fortress that had begun operations in 1941 with the Royal Air Force. The B-17 was noted for its ability to absorb battle damage, still reach its target, and bring its crew home safely. Dale made many other World War II model planes, which his mother allowed him to suspend by cords from the living room ceiling.

I didn't share Dale's enthusiasm for model airplanes and didn't pay too much attention to the war news, even though my father was preparing to leave for the South Pacific. Perhaps my mother shielded me from the reality. I did make dull gray plastic punch out models of ships: aircraft carriers, battleships, and submarines. I was often miffed there were no LST kits, as that was the ship my dad commanded. I made no attempt to display my model ships but kept them under the bed.

Shortly after getting to the farm, threshing season began. Uncle Ed owned a threshing machine. Eight of his neighbors helped him thresh, and then he took his machine to the other neighbors to help them thresh their grain. This summer threshing began on a typically hot, sultry day. The work was backbreaking, with much dust and noise from the machine. Uncle Ed, J.C., and their neighbors picked up bundles of shocks with pitchforks and hurled them into hay wagons pulled by horses. The men parked the wagons near the threshing machine and tossed the bundles on to a slatted feeder that pulled the bundles into the machine. The machine beat the grain out of straw heads into a wagon or truck bed. Dale's work was to keep pushing the grain toward the back of the wagon or truck. The grain was then transported to a nearby elevator or stored in a granary on the farm for winter livestock feeding.

Hard as the labor was for the men, neither was it a free time for the women or children. Aunt Dorothy and Mother spent hours over that hot cook stove baking and cooking large quantities of food: breads, fried chicken, fresh green beans with bacon, pickles, cakes, pies, cookies, and whipped cream canned fruit salad. Mary and my jobs were to set tables, to serve food, to wash and dry dishes, and to haul water for drinking, cooking, and dishes. In addition, Mary and I took sandwiches, cookies, and orange nectar to the threshers in mid-afternoon. It was hard work, but everyone joked and had fun – a great gathering time.

At first, I wondered where my aunt found rationing coupons for sugar to bake all those goodies, but I soon learned farmers were given extra coupons. I also discovered they were given as much gas as needed to plant, to harvest, and to get their products to town. Of course, they needed to feed the home front and military. In addition to gas, farmers were given coupons to re-tread tires. They had few coupons for new tires as they were needed for the military.

The day before my father shipped out for the South Pacific, he called my mother. The farm phone was the old-fashioned party line and most neighbors listened in on calls. This day the reception was especially static. Mother was in tears. Aunt Dorothy grabbed the phone and gave a number for my dad to call back in fifteen minutes. She quickly took Mother in the 1930 Chevy the seven miles to the Salem phone office where Mother and Dad had a long, private good-bye.

At the end of August, our home in Mitchell was vacated. It was time for school to begin. Aunt Dorothy, Uncle Ed, and my cousins took Mother and me back to Mitchell where the Navy had delivered what was left of our furniture from Buffalo. When my relatives left, I suddenly realized the stark emptiness of Mother and me alone.

The Car That Stole My Heart
By Violet Nelson of Hendricks, Minnesota
Born 1945

Looking back at my childhood years, I think about the 1947 dark green Chevrolet my parent drove. How many times would I find myself jumping around in the back seat of the two-door sedan. Seat belts didn't exist.

Life back then was simple. We lived on a farm in eastern South Dakota, just a few miles from the Minnesota border. Besides going to school and church, life pretty much included a weekly five mile trip into town and several trips to Grandma's, just three miles east of our farm.

Going to town was a big thing in the middle 1950s. Me and my sister would each take a corner in the back seat. We would peek out the windows and breathe in the smell of my dad's cigar. To this day when I run into somebody smoking a cigar, I immediately think of my dad. My dad, mother, sister, and I enjoyed each other. Life was fun. We were not wealthy, but we were making great memories together.

While going to Grandma's house one afternoon, I saw the front wheel of our car spin out into a field. I don't remember much about the event other than ending up walking to Grandma's.

Weeks later, my mom picked up our neighbor lady on the way to the ladies group at our country church. The front seat of a 1947 Chevy was six feet wide, so they sat pretty close together. The neighbor lady braced her feet on the floor so that she could pull her coat out from underneath her. The cars were not made for speed, but she had braced her left foot right on top of my mom's foot on the gas pedal. Our car sped across a gravel road and down a driveway. Lucky for us no oncoming cars were in sight.

There were no interstates and probably very few paved roads of any distance. People didn't drive like they do today and the top speed was probably 45 miles per hour. One day when we were coming home from town, our Chevy didn't make it through the snow-blocked road. Dad put my sister on his back, and Mom put me on her back. They trotted through the cold and snow across the field to our home. I don't recall snow plows back then, so I suppose my dad had to take the tractor to

Violet (Sandro) Nelson and her sister, Juanita (Sandro) Noiz in 1952

pull the car out.

Mom was hospitalized for several days when I was five years old. My sister stayed with Grandma, and I stayed with Aunt Bernice. It is pretty hard for a child that age to be without her mother but it worked. When evening came, I watched for the old green Chevy to come down their driveway. When I saw Dad coming, I knew he would come in, visit, and play with me for a little while.

When me and my sister were attending school in Hendricks, on occasion my mother would park across the street from the school and pick us up. We considered that a rare treat. Even though some parents drove new cars, I wasn't ashamed of our car. To me it symbolized adventure and family togetherness.

Sadly, the day came when the car quit working. I was playing in the yard when I saw my dad coming from the shed driving his tractor. He had a log chain attached to the old green Chevy, pulling it across the road, and out of sight. I can still visualize it. Where was he taking the car, the one I had all the special rides in?

I've always been fascinated with the later 1940s and 1950s. It is the time when my parents were young, starting their life together and raising their daughters. It's also when my dad bought the used two-door 1947 Chevy I loved so much as a child.

Now, decades later, my sister and brother-in-law own my parents' farm. One summer evening while visiting them, I rode along with their grandson on his four-wheeler. My curiosity was piqued when he took me past the farm pit full of junk. "Caleb, stop!" I shouted. "Look! That's our old green Chevy," I said with tear-filled eyes. There it was, the most beautiful sight I'd seen since my young life, our old 1947 Chevy laying there on its top. For a few minutes, I was transported back in time. I shall cherish that night.

The Country School
By Myrle Sederstrom of Ramona, South Dakota
Born 1925

I was born on June 25, 1925. My memories of school start in the 1930s. When I was six years old, I started to go to country school. The school was three miles from our farm.

My brother drove a horse pulling a buggy to school. My sister and I were the passengers. If we got started early, we would pick up the teacher. She stayed at the home of her brother. He was the pastor at the church we attended.

In the winter when the roads were snow covered, my dad would take us to school on a sled pulled with a team of horses. Dad always stood on a rock slab called a flat stone. Mom kept it on the back of the cook stove so it was always warm. It would stay warm for a long time. There was a wagon box on the sled with straw on the bottom. We sat on the straw with a blanket over our heads. Our feet were cold by the time we got to school. Dad wore a long sheepskin coat, a warm cap with earflaps, and a muffler covering his face with just his eyes peeking out. He also wore huge mittens made of horsehide and sheepskin boots. Sometimes Dad picked up other pupils to ride to school with us.

There were two schools in our district. We lived three miles from either school. If there were more students in one school, we would attend the other. When there were less students in the whole district, they would have school one-half year in each school in order to be fair to all students. Dad was the clerk of the school board. I can remember that he wrote the teacher's check for $40.00 a month.

We had one teacher who taught all eight grades. I never had a male teacher. The teacher boarded at the home of the family that lived closest to the school. We never boarded the teacher, as we lived too far from the school. The teacher walked to school in nice weather. The people who she boarded with took her to school in bad weather. Sometimes Mom invited the teacher for supper. I was very nervous and afraid I would do something wrong.

We learned from the other grades, as we were all in one room. We would hear all that went on all of the time. I can remember once I had a reading lesson that was about a little girl who was going to jump across a little brook, but she fell in. I liked the story and possibly knew it too well. The story said she fell in the water and she was a sight to see. Well, I said she was a sight for "sore eyes." I can still remember my bottom lip quivering and finally many tears. All of the kids were laughing at me.

We really enjoyed recess and noon hour. Baseball was a favorite game of the older children. I did not like baseball. I think it was because I was small and a poor batter. I was usually a back fielder for both teams. So I stood way back and watched. We played anty-I-over. You would choose sides and had a ball like a basketball, which you would throw over the schoolhouse. If someone caught it on the other side, they would take the ball and run around and try to touch someone on the other side with the ball. Then you had to be on their side. When you had no one left on one side, the game was over. We also played pump, pump, pull away, and last couple out.

The boys liked to drown out gophers. It was quite exciting, especially if the gopher would come out of the hole and start running towards you.

At least twice a year, the county superintendent came to visit. We were all so nervous, including the teacher. The superintendent would sit in the back of the room in a "captain's chair" and observe. We really tried our best to recite well and behave well too. When she left, we all breathed a sigh of relief.

Some schools had cisterns for drinking water. We all drank from a pail of water, which had a tin dipper in it. Talk about passing germs around. If there was no water at the school, each person not only took a syrup pail with their lunch but also a pail of water. If your pail accidentally got tipped over and spilled, you were really thirsty by the time you got home, unless you had enough nerve to beg a drink from someone. If we had extra water, we all washed our hands in the same water in a little pan called a wash dish. If there was no water, no hands were washed.

Our heat in the winter came from a big round coal-burning stove in one corner of the room. We all had to use the outdoor toilet. If you wanted to go to the toilet during class time, you raised one finger. The teacher would nod her head and you could leave the room. Sometimes a kind teacher would even carry a little person (me) to the toilet when the snow was deep.

When we were getting ready for a program at school, it really disrupted our studies. We learned songs or recitations and plays. We strung wires across one end of the room and then put up sheets to make a stage. When the parents came in the evening, they brought lamps, lanterns, food, and coffee.

When it was warm, we walked home from school. We were always taken in the mornings, mostly by Dad but sometimes Mom took us.

Every year when school was dismissed for the summer, most pupils were very happy. I always left with a lump in my throat, especially if I knew that a dear teacher would not be coming back the next year.

We Finally Got a Bathroom!
By Nadine TeBeest of DeSmet, South Dakota
Born 1931

We lived on a farm by Vienna and were dried out like everyone else was in those days. My grandpa and grandma had some land in Washington with some trees that had to be cut down for some reason. My folks decided to go along and help them, because they had no work to do in South Dakota. I was four, one of my sisters was three, and the other was two.

My folks, along with us three girls and my grandma and grandpa, traveled in a truck that had no windows in it. We all had to eat and sleep in this truck. I am not sure if there were any hotels along the way, but we sure couldn't afford one if there was. We had to cross the Columbia River on a ferry called a barge. It looked like a big plank to me.

We found a house in Ardenvoir; that was where the trees were. While the guys were cutting down trees, one happened to fall on my dad's leg and broke it so he couldn't work for a while. I happened to get pneumonia again and always had to sleep with my parents to sweat it out. My sister stepped on a nail, and it went through the top of her foot, so my mom soaked it in Epsom salt like she did everything else, and it got better. I don't ever remember anyone ever going to a doctor, but Dad must have. We lived on two dollars that month.

Our very nice neighbors across the road had cows, and they gave us milk. While we were there, the guys shot a deer, which was illegal. Some inspectors came and looked all over and even smelled our cookware, trying to find out if we had shot one. If they found something, they didn't fine us or anything. Maybe they felt sorry for us and knew we needed something to eat.

When the trees were taken care of and there was no more work, all of us, including Grandma and Grandpa moved to Woodburn, Oregon to run a gas station. We all lived in the back of the garage until we found a house in the country. While we lived there, I started school. My parents picked hops and worked in a cannery until that was done. Dad eventually decided to go back to South Dakota, and Grandma and Grandpa stayed in Oregon. We had no bathrooms yet.

We came back to the same farm we lived on before we left. It was still very dry and dirty. Mom would hang wet towels in the windows to keep some of the dust out of the house. The wind blew so much that the fences were covered with dirt. My parents had another daughter. I had pneumonia again, and Mom still tried to get me to take cod liver oil, but I still couldn't keep it down. She made mustard plasters, which were very hot as I remember, but they must have worked. Now there was a baby boy. We also still had an outhouse. My sisters and I made playhouses under the apple tree and ate a lot of apples in the shelterbelt. We made one on the top floor of the dirt floor in the garage. It was very dirty. We made cookies out of mud and used rocks for chocolate chips and raisins.

We lived on the farm until 1942 when a tornado took everything but the house. All of the windows on the house had blown out. The chickens were dead all over the yard and fields. The cows were standing where the barn used to be and they were bleeding from the hail. They just stood where the barn used to be while we milked them; I think they were in shock. We had a team of horses in the barn tied to the manger facing west. After the storm, they were half a mile east of where the barn was, still tied to the manger facing west. We couldn't see the past porch because it was raining and hailing so hard, it was like someone had pulled the shade down. We had nothing left.

We lived with an aunt and uncle for a couple of weeks until we found an empty house by Thomas. Then Dad bought a farm a couple of miles away, closer to Thomas. This is where we started school, which we thought was so big, after coming from a country school. There were eight to twelve kids in one grade. I was scared to death with all those kids running around. We did get to go to Hayti on Saturday night to sell our eggs and buy groceries. Once in a while, we got eleven cents, which was probably left over from the shopping, to go to the show. We still had outhouses, even at school.

I started helping Dad cut grain. He was on the binder, and I was on the tractor. He had a big switch that he would hit the binder with if he thought I was getting tired. We had to shock the grain when we were done cutting it. We finally had some electricity from a wind charger that sat on top of the house. It charged batteries for one light bulb and a battery for

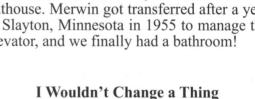

Babe, Nadine, and Darlene

the radio. Mom would listen to *The Romance of Helen Trent* and *Ma Perkins*; Dad listened to *Fibber McGee and Molly* and the news.

We had to keep our butter, milk, and whatever else that had to stay cool hanging in the cistern. We had an oil burner for heat in the living room and a cook stove in the kitchen for cooking and baking. Another one of my sisters was born about this time. I don't remember when we got electricity and a phone, but it was in the forties some time.

Dad bought a bucket loader so that was great, because we didn't have to pitch hay into the hayrack for stacking anymore. Dad also owned the threshing machine, so I had to go along with him to three different farmers to pitch bundles on a hayrack and then unload it into the threshing machine. When I got married, Dad bought a combine.

My husband and I farmed for four years and got hailed out or dried out every year. My husband got a job in the elevator in town, so we moved to Castlewood, and we still had an outhouse. Merwin got transferred after a year to Slayton, Minnesota in 1955 to manage the elevator, and we finally had a bathroom!

I Wouldn't Change a Thing
By Les Patton of Kenmore, Washington
Born 1931

My name is Les Patton. I was born October 1, 1931 at home on the farm, the last of nine children born to John and Eunice Anderson Patton in Hand County, Bates Township, 16 miles south of Wessington, 20 miles north of Wessington Springs on the edge of the Wessington hills. My parents' first child was delivered by a doctor who was called out from Wessington, and he botched the job so my sister, Eleanor, only lived five days. So my father said, "I have delivered all kinds of animals, and I can deliver children." So he delivered the next eight of us. Not too uncommon in those days in rural America. Our pastor, Omar Shantz's wife, Viola, was a nurse and only a few years ago she was in my home, and I asked her if she delivered me, and she said she assisted my dad. My father said he could always remember my birthday because the mortgage was due. In those days, the mortgage was paid in the fall after harvest, and we hoped we had enough left to tide us over for another year and for seed for the next year's planting.

The Down Side

We were two years into the worst draught and recession in the history of the nation. I recall the dust storms when the sun was dark red. Russian thistles would roll across the fields and catch on the barbed wire fence causing enough blockage to collect the dust and eventually a solid enough wall for cattle to walk over the fence and into the next field. I recall looking up at the sun at millions of grasshoppers flying so thick it would darken the daylight hours. When they landed, they walked military style, row upon row, all going the same direction and eating everything green in their path. We stuffed paper and cloth around the windows inside the house to keep the dust out to no avail.

My older brothers told of helping Dad drive the cattle down to a large trench that had been bulldozed out so the cattle could be shot and buried. There was not enough feed to keep them alive. The government paid $5.00 per head.

I read the anguish on the face of my parents when they had to take commodities provided by the government. They were proud people and hated to have to take welfare. The small red beans needed to be washed carefully to get the small red rocks out so we did not break a tooth while eating the beans. The meat on the prunes was almost as hard as the pit.

The Up Side

My parents were Christians, and we had a Bible preaching church just up the road. We all attended every Sunday, cold germs, and all. My parents were gentle, kind, hard-working people. They taught by example so the path to the cross of Christ was wide open to us, and we all learned how to work hard. Those are two awesome gifts.

Being the youngest, I got the menial tasks, like gathering eggs. If a hen was on the nest, I had to reach under her to remove the eggs, and she would peck my tender little hands. I cleaned the chicken roost, and lice were part of chicken raising. It makes me itch to think about it. I was given a quart size can with diesel fuel in it to pick the potato bugs off by hand and drop them in the container. It was boring, hot work but I was making a contribution to the family.

We raised a large garden and had a lot of chickens, so we had eggs to eat and young chickens to eat. We milked cows so we had a lot of milk and cream and eggs to sell to buy groceries with. We bought flour and sugar by the 100-pound sack and yes, Mother made clothes from the empty sacks. We had three changes of clothes, one for wearing, one for washing, and one for Sunday-go-to-meeting. Dad re-soled our shoes and cut the boys' hair and no, he did not use a bowl. He had hand clippers and did a pretty good job of keeping us from looking shaggy. We went without shoes all summer, and our feet got great calluses so when we put on shoes to go to church or to town they felt very uncomfortable. We hunted for wild game to eat, fished for bullhead,

Lester and his brothers and sisters in 1933

307

catfish, carp, and buffalo. Yes, there is a fish called by that name. None of them were very enjoyable to eat but filled the tummy.

In the winter, we would skate on the ponds that froze to the bottom. We had one small sled for all of us, and we would attempt as many as four at a time to ride down the hill. We never got all the way down. We used a scoop shovel for us little kids or a piece of cardboard. I don't think plastic had been invented yet. While standing on the hill waiting for the next available vehicle we would have to lean into the wind to stand up so if someone stepped behind us to block the wind, we would fall down. We wore long johns and two pair of pants, a heavy coat, and mittens, and kept moving to stay warm. We were outside a lot summer and winter because the house was small so outside was good.

I recall being tucked in behind older siblings as we walked north one mile to school to protect me from the bitter cold wind. I went to country school from first through seventh grade. We had hard-working, dedicated teachers, often not well trained, but they had a heart to teach and with not much pay. We learned respect for God, country, the Constitution, and each other. During the school year, we would have "literary meetings," where adults and children could sing a song, quote poetry, give a "declaim," or act out a play. We got to have pie and ice cream and do some folk dancing. It was a good social and cultural experience.

Once I was in the hayloft of the large barn and saw a spider web that spelled "silver" in perfect handwriting. When I told the family about it at dinner, they sort of snickered, and no one believed me or went to check it out. I got no respect down at the end of the line. I was the smallest of all the siblings, even as an adult and Dad said he guessed they ran out of building material. Only a few years ago I read that there is a spider called, would you believe, *silver spider*, so neaner, neaner, neaner, older siblings. You can Google that if interested.

In conclusion, we were dirt poor but so was everyone else and guess what, we all turned out good. All have been good business people and Godly people, so I can say with confidence, it was a GREAT childhood. If I could do it over, I wouldn't change a thing. Thanks, Mom and Dad and thank you, God.

A Blessed Life as a Farmer's Wife
By Shirley J. Dayton of Aberdeen, South Dakota
Born 1929

I feel so blessed to have lived for nearly 85 years as a farmer's daughter, a farmer's wife, and a "retired" farmer, able to spend 35 winters in Texas, California, and Arizona. I remember the Dirty Thirties, the W.P.A., and the C.C.C. Camps, which involved our neighborhood near Columbia, South Dakota, the first county seat in South Dakota, Brown County.

When I was in the first grade, I remember a November 11th snowstorm on Armistice Day. I also remember being transported to school in Columbia, nearly three miles away, by bobsled many times and often staying with friends in town for days at a time due to numerous snowstorms. I had three half-sisters older than I who worked for room and board during the winter while attending school, which I did also during my junior and senior years.

My four younger sisters, three younger brothers, and I shared the Saturday night bathtub in the middle of our kitchen, same water, and I, being the oldest, got the final bath.

My oldest brother and I milked cows morning and night, so we no doubt smelled like cattle each day at school!

During those formative years, we were blessed to receive food commodities and

Shirley without the hat and 3 sisters and 2 brothers

some articles of clothing sewed by ladies in Columbia. They were very much oversized as we were all quite small, but our talented mother remade them to fit. She also used patterned flour sacks and cut patterns from newspapers and designed frocks from the *Sears* or *Montgomery Ward Catalogs*. Mother also cut our hair and many of the neighbors, as no one had any extra money. However, we never had any idea we were poor.

We trapped and drowned gophers for a pastime and got two or three cents per tail from our township treasurer. We also had horses to ride for entertainment.

During the summer, the Columbia businesses furnished the community with free outdoor movies, shown on the side of the livery stable on Thursday evenings. The two grocery stores would remain open for shopping before and after the movie. Most Saturday nights farmers also took their families to town. On Saturday night, the Salvation Army Band came to town and stood in front of the pool hall, hoping to recruit "lost souls" to Jesus and also hoping for a few donations in a slotted coffee can.

Our outhouse toilet paper was last year's outdated *Sears* or *Montgomery Ward Catalog* with its many shiny pages, and the summer "treat" would be the softer tissue that came from the peach wrappings within the crates that were purchased for canning for winter's desserts.

We raised a garden, which gave us enough potatoes for the coming year, as well as vegetables, which we enjoyed and canned for the winter whenever God gave us enough moisture to bring them to harvest. We butchered a large cow and two or three hogs each fall and canned the meat, as we had no electricity or freezers at that time. We rendered the lard in a large kettle outside for frying, cooking, and baking pies. This gave us food for the coming year. We butchered and canned all of the chickens when they got too old to produce enough eggs, and we always had some hens that sat on a nest of eggs for three weeks and hatched babies for future laying hens and young roosters for summer frying for meals and picnics. My dad used to take wheat to a mill and have it ground for the flour we used. Most everyone baked their own bread, many loaves at a time.

Our water was deep well artesian, very

Shirley on a homemade tractor

soft, but very full of minerals, especially fluoride, which pretty much turned the soil if we used it for watering plants. It also had so much sodium that pickles would not be crisp when made, so we always borrowed hard well water from a neighbor who had a shallow water well for when we made pickles.

Our telephone was an eight party line, and often the neighbors listened in to our conversations and when a neighborhood crisis or event would happen, maybe a fire or a community event that had been planned, the "central" would give a general ring to alert everyone to listen. The farmers would often respond by helping contain a fire or attend the event.

I remember when my siblings were quite young our dad had emptied a pit silo of silage, which had been used to feed cattle during the winter, and he told us kids we could make a playhouse in it. Normally we made play houses in our grove of trees, which was north of our house and buildings. We'd had numerous rooms partitioned by tree limbs that were low to the ground. What an opportunity to have a big indoor playhouse. We used an old leaky washtub, turned upside down, for our cook stove and decided to build a fire in it. Not a good idea as we could have very well been asphyxiated, as there was a roof on the silo made of straw and chicken wire. Our dad saw the smoke and evacuated us immediately, and we got a spanking with a razor strap! Another time we took eggs from the hen house and made mud pies and threw the pies against the north side of our house. We were spanked again and had to wash the whole side of the house, plus the fact that the eggs were a source of income and food, which was very important.

When I graduated from high school in 1947, I borrowed $300.00 from my dad to go to Northern State Teachers College in Aberdeen for six weeks, as there was a severe teacher shortage, and I was able to teach in a rural school in September for $90.00 a month. I roomed with several families of my students and was able to pay my dad back and have enough money to go to six weeks of school the following summer and teach the following year at a larger, country school in Plana, South Dakota where I made $200.00 a month. I paid $30.00 per month for room and board to a lovely couple who lived a block or two from the school. I was the janitor, nurse, and cooked government supplied commodities for lunch at school, including a main dish contributed once a week by one of the families.

I was married on June 2, 1949 to Ben Dayton, whom I met while teaching the previous year in the Stratford, South Dakota area. We had 62 years together. I was offered $250.00 a month to return to Plana the following year, but Ben, being a farmer, didn't want me to work away. We had no money and lived with his parents and raised chickens and milked cows for income from eggs and cream. In two years, we found a farm to live on by ourselves and do our own thing. Our eggs and cream were able to support us, as we had no electric or phone bills to pay. Part of our crops the first two years were flooded out. My father had a heart attack and was advised to quit farming and asked us to take over his farm north of Columbia, where we farmed two quarters of land and were able to purchase that land and another quarter and rent several more as years went by. I was the hired man, and we had four children. The farm was good to us, as Ben was a good framer. He only had an eighth grade education but could fix, repair, or build anything. He often spent winters remodeling homes for neighbors, as he could even do the plumbing, electrical, and furnace work. He worked many winters for $2.50 per hour. We raised one son and three daughters. They blessed us with six grandchildren and at last count, I have eighteen great-grandchildren and one great, great-grandson! God has blessed us and continues to bless me and my family, as I lost my dear husband in an accident in 2011. In spite of that tragedy, God is good!

Ben and Shirley Dayton in 2006

A Truck that Goes "Burp-Burp"
By Donald Becht of Watertown, South Dakota
Born 1932

I was born on September 7, 1932 in the Peabody Hospital in Webster, South Dakota to Henry (Hank) and Gertrude (Gert Meuer) Becht. I had a sister, Patricia (Pat), who was five years older than me. This story is about my dad who was the area Hamm's Beer distributor located in Webster.

On a very stormy winter day, in the early 1950s, Dad was returning home from his beer route in the Britton area. Several miles north of Bristol, steam came rolling out from under the hood of his truck. He stopped and looked under the hood to find that the radiator hose had come loose. It was not broken, just loose, and he lost all of his antifreeze. There were no cell phones and it was storming so bad he couldn't see any farm to go to for help. He got a beer can opener from the truck (there were no pop tops in those days) to use as a screwdriver. He replaced the hose and used his screwdriver to tighten the hose clamp. He got cases of beer from the truck and filled the radiator. He then proceeded on to Webster.

His sister, Laura Koenig, heard the story and sent it to Arthur Godfrey who had a national radio program. He related the story on the air and finished it with, "Now Webster, South Dakota has a truck that when you press the horn it does not go 'beep-beep;' it goes 'burp-burp!'"

Some years later, I was told that the story was also in the *Reader's Digest* under the "Today's Chuckle" column. I do not know if this is true because my parents and relatives did not subscribe to that magazine and I was serving in the U.S. Navy at the time.

Pa's Icehouse
By Adeline Rumpza Tracy of Waubay, South Dakota
Born 1933

Even as a young child who was born in the '30s and just old enough to walk, I have always been able to remember the beautiful Pickrel Lake. I grew up on a farm adjacent to this wondrous lake, and always remember it being there. The icehouse was built into the ground on a hill behind the garage so that the roof was almost on the land. It had a door, albeit, a very old door that we could get in and out. There was a pathway dug into the ground to make it accessible.

Anyone who lived in South Dakota would know that there was no need to build an icehouse for the winter months. So why do it? These were the days before electricity, so we did not have the pleasure of a refrigerator. Instead, we had an icebox. It was a well-built contraption about five feet high with a right hand door that held a chunk of ice about a foot square. On the bottom was a bucket that held the water, which dripped into it as the ice melted. It was bad news for whoever had the job to empty it; sometimes it went all over the dining room floor. That person would just

have to enjoy the cleanup. On the left, there were several shelves that were reasonably cold for perishables.

Oh, but there were other things that were used for our special building. When the storm clouds gathered and it looked like there just might be a tornado in that cloud, our Dad led us there for safety. Remember, we had no radio, TV, or Phil Schreck. Still we kids found one more wondrous thing for the old icehouse. We would crawl in there when the temperature was 100 degrees to be in the shade. It was a cool heaven.

How did we get ice? I remember that clearly, it fascinated me. Every spring when the lakes were about ready to unthaw, my father would layer two feet of straw on the dirt floor just before the iceman would come. He would lay blocks and blocks of ice on the straw, then a layer of straw and another layer of ice. Then the last layer of straw was put down. This would happen several times during the summer.

The farm that we grew up on stayed in the family for over 100 years. The icehouse did not survive that long, but it lives in our most treasured memories.

Threshing Straw and Country Schools
By Devona J. Simonson of Chamberlain, South Dakota
Born 1931

We had no electricity or phones. We used what we called Aladdin lamps or kerosene lamps for light. In the living room, we had a big stove we called a coal stove. At night, my dad put a five-gallon pail of coal in the stove and it lasted 'til the next night. We had a range in the kitchen that used wood or corncobs. We would pick the cobs from the pigpen, but made sure we picked clean ones!

We did not have any indoor plumbing; we carried pails of water in. we had to use an outhouse. I walked in my sleep and would go outside. My dad would come out and take me back to bed. I never woke up when that would happen.

I went to a country school. At haying time after school, I would walk down to the hay field and drive the stacker team. It was a team of horses on a stacker thing, and I would put hay on the stack. The last day of school, we'd all pack picnic lunches and go to Ruskin Park to eat and roller skate. Years later, we went there to go to dances. When it was cold, our dad would take us to school in the car unless the snow was too deep. If that was the case, we would go in the wagon with the team of horses. We had one teacher that lived in part of the schoolhouse, so it was always warm.

Come wash day, we had a small shed with a wringer washer in it and a stove we heated the water on. It was run by a gas motor. If it was nice out, we would hang the clothes on a line to dry. When they were dry, we would take them in to fold and put them away. Some of the clothes had to be ironed. We heated the flat iron on the cook stove.

For meat, my dad killed a pig. He and Grandpa would skin it. My parents, with the help of my grandparents, would cut the meat up and can it. After trimming the fat off, the fat was rendered for lard to be used.

My sister and I were playing on the ice, and I fell through. I went under, but she grabbed a pail and told me to get a hold of it. She was able to get me out that way.

On Saturday nights, the whole family went to town. My mother and dad would get their groceries and visit around. They would sit in the car so us girls could walk around with our friends. My parents never went into a bar. We had a theater in town, and sometimes we'd go to the movies.

My job was to feed and water the chickens and collect the eggs. We'd clean the eggs and put them into a case. You could take them to the store or sell them to people that came around the country on a truck. When the corn got so tall, we would go up and down the row and either pull or cut off the cockle burrs and sunflowers.

After the ripe grain was cut and put into a bundle, I would help my Dad pick them up and put them in a shock. Later, neighbors all got together and thresh it with a threshing machine. The straw went in one big pile and grain went into the wagons. My dad took these to the granary and shoveled it into the bins. I would help him shovel grain. On the day of threshing, some of the ladies came to help my mother get dinner for all. My sister and I would put benches or a table outside with pails of water on them. The men would wash up in a basin with soap and water. We had towels out there for them as well. This was done at each place, as the men threshed and ladies gathered at the next place to cook.

Years went by, and I graduated from high school and was married. We had two girls. We worked and lived at different towns and places. My brother was killed, so we moved back closer to my folks to help farm the land, which my husband loved to do.

In 1969, we had a big snowstorm and the roads were all blocked. We milked cows, but had to dump the milk on the ground until a milk truck would get in. we were about a half mile from my folks and the weather was not that cold, so we would go down and check on them and visit. Snow banks were so high that we walked over them and could touch the highline wires.

We had a give-away dog that looked like Lassie. It was self-trained. In blizzards as Ken went to feed the stock, I'd go to another shed to bottle feed the calves. King would put his mouth around my hand and go to the shed. Same way he'd do that when we went to the house. When milking time and cows went out in the pasture, he'd run out and walk the cows back.

My family members have all passed away now. My husband has passed away also. His main family is all gone as well. I am the only one living as of yet. I have done many things and have worked hard, but I have enjoyed my life. I guess I can say that those were the olden days.

A Creek Runs Through It
By Gayle Charron of Faulkton, South Dakota
Born 1940

Growing up on a farm in the '50s, my brothers, and I provided our own entertainment. Usually we think of the barn as being a place of labor rather than amusement, but on rainy days or when the new hay was hoisted into the loft, it became our gym. Hours spent climbing the ladder to the rafters to leap out into the hay became a contest to be repeated to exhaustion. There always seemed to be a batch of kittens to cuddle as we rested before a climbing again to inspect a pigeon's nest.

312

Much of our free time was centered on the creek running through our land. As we would walk home from our one-room school in the spring, we would follow the rushing waters of melting snow. We would toss in sticks to watch them travel under bridges and over mini waterfalls. Arriving home wet and cold, we'd have a quick snack and then go back outside again to bring the milk cows in from the pasture, gather eggs, and feed pail calves and bottle lambs. Each spring, (before the anti-littering laws) as the snow melted, a treasure trove of glass bottles would be revealed in the roadside ditches. Much time was spent riding our bikes up and down the roads to gather bottles to be returned to the store for the penny or two deposit.

In the summer, without TV, handheld games, or even air conditioning, days could be hot and long. No farm child ever complained of boredom lest he find himself on his knees pulling weeds in the garden, or worse yet, cleaning the hen house. We turned to the creek to a spot with a sandy bottom. This place was too shallow to swim, but it was good for water fights or trying to catch crawdads.

Some days we went on "walks," or if we added a mason jar of water and some graham crackers, a "picnic." These outings took us along the creek through pastures and hayfields, just looking for adventure. Finding an arrowhead, bleached skull of a cow, or skeleton of a small animal made the walk worthwhile. Often we traveled with a length of twine in our pockets to make a snare for gophers. Dad would pay us a nickel for each gopher tail.

As the evenings grew longer in the fall, we often played hide and seek outdoors by the light of a big yellow moon. At the first good freeze, we were back at the creek with our ice skates. As winter came on and the ice was covered with snow, we turned to sledding on the hills that overlooked the creek. With only one sled for the four of us, we improvised with scoop shovels or cardboard boxes.

The farmhouse and outbuildings are long gone, with only a grove of trees to remind us of home. Even the creek no longer runs. Too many dry years and too many stock dams and dugouts have left only an occasional puddle. With the advent of factory farms, milk and eggs are purchased rather than produced. Chores are a thing of the past, and any children in the area are likely seated before a television set, with an electronic device in hand, and a can of soda and bag of chips nearby.

Only Two Years Old
By Verla Lindblad of Wolsey, South Dakota
Born 1928

I can remember one incident that happened to me when I was only two years old. My parents were moving from Iowa to South Dakota where my mother's parents lived. While they were building a new house, my mother left me with her sister. I was asleep, but when I woke up, I was scared because I knew no one. I can remember trying to pick up a chair to throw it at this strange lady. When I told this story to my aunt years later, she said. "Yes, it happened that way. I had to throw a blanket over you and take you screaming and crying to your mother about three blocks away!"

My Hidden Doll
One day, my mother went to town to shop. I was probably around twelve years old. She told me to dust the floors and to do a good job. She told me to dust under the beds real good. I did as she told me. When she came home, she asked me. "Did you do the dusting and dust under beds?" I told her I did, but I didn't dust under the bed too good because that was where she hid my Christmas present! It was the big doll I wanted for Christmas!

In Our Days
A few girls, including me, were walking home from grade school. All of a sudden, one girl was washing the face of another girl in the snow. I never knew what happened between these two girls. Every time I saw this friend of mine, I would think about what happened years ago. Finally, after many years, I got up the courage to ask. She told me, "She called me fat!" Wouldn't it be better, if today, all disagreements could be settled by getting one's face washed in the snow?

Where Were You?
In 1963, my father-in-law and brother-in-law went to Sweden where my father-in-law was born. My husband and I ran his gas station while they were gone. It was a busy station, being situated on two federal highways. My husband put the gas in the cars and I washed

313

the windows of the cars. We were paid $10.00 a day while they were gone. That was where we were when we heard the sad news that President Kennedy was shot!

Santa's Sleigh Bells

I was getting to the age that I was thinking that there wasn't a real Santa. I told my older brother this, and of course, he disagreed with me. He told me to go outside and listen and he bet I would hear Santa's sleigh bells. I did as he told me, and I listened real good. In the distance, I could hear sleigh bells. Later on in years, I think he found some bells and shook them so I would believe there really was a Santa!

A Player Piano

When I was around twelve or thirteen, I had, in those days, what they called "Bright's Disease." I wasn't really sick, but I couldn't go to school. One day the Truant Officer came to see me, checking up on me. She heard a piano playing and told my mother, "Well, she can't be too sick; she's playing the piano!" She didn't know that we had a player piano!

Earl Perry holding Murvin in 1922

Swede Gets Wet
By Murvin H. Perry of Johnson City,
Tennessee
Born 1922

Some years ago in response to a request to help preserve memories of Bruce High School, I wrote accounts of several incidents that occurred during my days of attendance. There are many memories of the old school

The Earl Perry Family in 1932

that I would like to see preserved, and some that I am afraid will be preserved whether those of us involved want them to be or not. Elder "Swede" Anderson was the central figure in this particular escapade.

The school was located on a flat plain at the edge of town, less than a quarter mile from the banks of the Big Sioux River. (Everything in Eastern South Dakota is located on a flat plain.) The "Big" in Big Sioux River bears no relationship to the size of the stream. It serves merely to distinguish the river from another trickle that joins it further south as it meanders toward the Missouri. In summer, its turgid pools of muddy water provided cooling swimming holes where abrupt changes in the course caused the current to scour the muddy silt from the sandy bottom. In early spring, melting snow turned it into a rushing flow that prepared the swimming holes for the coming summer.

The river was spanned at the edge of town by a steel bridge, suspended from overhead girders, (manufactured incidentally by the Tennessee Iron and Bridge Works of Johnson City, TN, where I have lived for the past 34

314

years) until an erring motorist slammed into one of the supporting girders on frosty night in the late 1930s and caused the whole structure to fall into the water below.

On summer days, boys, eager to prove themselves, would inch their way hand-over-hand on the truss rods that crisscrossed the underside of the bridge to give it lateral stability. Only the strongest could make it beyond the pier that supported the first span. For the more determined, there were two more spans to negotiate.

During lunch hour one spring day, I was with a gaggle of fifth and sixth grade boys who had gone to the river to watch the ice floes carried on the flooded stream. One of the older follows dropped from the bridge onto a large chuck of ice and rode it downstream until, in a bend in the channel, the current brought it close enough to the bank for him to leap ashore. He dared the rest of us to follow. Three or four of us accepted the challenge and managed to negotiate the maneuver without incident. Not Swede. The floe he selected stayed in midstream all the way around the bend. We raced along the bank shouting instructions and encouragement to him as he became more and more apprehensive about his plight.

At about the third bend, when it began to appear he might be permanently stranded, he made a running leap from the floe he was riding to a smaller piece of ice halfway to the shore, intending to jump from it to the bank. He came down hard—too hard for the chunk of ice. It split beneath him and he belly flopped into the icy water.

We dragged him ashore and pondered how to warm him up and dry his clothes. One of the boys had some matches. (He probably had tobacco, too.) We gathered a pile of Russian thistles (tumbleweeds with stickers on them) and soon had a blazing fire, which we fed with more thistles, cornstalks, and scrub branches. We wrapped Swede in a couple of coats near the fire. Four of us held his overalls and underwear in front of the fire to dry them quickly, with only minor singes, while the rest gathered material for the fire.

Since we had drifted a least a half-mile downstream, and the drying out had taken more time than we anticipated, we were late getting back to school. As we filed sheepishly back into our classroom, our teacher, Miss Velma Klock, who always seemed to be sniffing disdainfully, sniffed Swede's clothing and asked accusingly, "Have you boys been smoking?" We assured her we had not been!

Murvin Perry stradling tier poles putting tobacco in the barn

Memories of the Year 1880 and After
By Mary Hymans of Lake Norden, South Dakota
Born 1944

I am the fourth generation from the farm my great-grandfather purchased in 1898 for my grandfather, Henry Lehtola. He was born in Finland on January 8, 1876. This truly makes me a South Dakotan. The following story was written by in 1950 by my grandfather:

Father Henry Sylvester Lehtola was a winter hired hand for Efraim Palavalehto. The father (Palavalehto) left for America in the fall, and from there, sent a letter to his wife instructing her to sell their house and belongings by auction and come to America. He also told her that if Lehtola wanted to come, that she was to give him money for travel and help so that he could do so. This is how Father came to be in America.

It was springtime when we left by ship

from Oulu and came to Stockholm, Sweden. Then they got on another ship, which went around the land of Sweden to Copenhagen, Denmark. This was cheaper than going by train. We went by ship to England and then by train cross-country to Liverpool Then we were off onto the Atlantic Ocean via a ship.

The weather was real pleasant during the entire three-week trip. To me, it was a pleasant trip as all were so good to me, especially the Negro cook. Each day he gave me something good to eat and also sweets. I thought the blacks were the best people. The ship came to New York City. We then went by train to Buffalo NY. From there we went to Hancock, Michigan on a charter ship. No food was furnished on the fare ticket. Some became hungry; Father had prepared lunches, so we fared well.

When we arrived at Hancock, Efraim Palavalehto and Kalle Jynkala were there to meet us. They had come earlier and decided to leave for Dakota to file a homestead. All that was required was to break the sod and plant it, build a home. A portion of that land was required to be field. After five years, they would become full owners.

We spent three days at Hancock. We went by ship to Duluth and then by train to St. Paul, Minnesota. At St. Paul, there was a translator when tickets to Owatonna, Minnesota were purchased. At Owatonna, we got tickets to Volga, South Dakota. At Owatonna, it became somewhat difficult for us, as we couldn't speak the English language. The depot master just shook his head when Father showed him Volga on the map and said, "Ticket." The agent got a pushcart from outside and motioned for them to put their belongings on the cart and follow him. The cart and belongings were brought to another depot and the tickets to Volga were purchased.

Not knowing when the train would arrive, we went to sleep on the depot floor. The train came early while some were still sleeping. We were hurried to board the train and our belongings got left in the Owatonna depot. We arrived in Volga. Then came the puzzle of explaining to the depot agent that our belongings were left in Owatonna. Father showed the agent Owatonna on the map and pointed to some trunks and boxes on the floor, not knowing whether he understood or not.

We knew that word must be sent to Poinsett.

We decided to draw lots, and the lot fell on Jacob Paso and Kalle Jynkala. They were told it was 25 or 30 miles to the northwest. They arrived early in the morning and could see the lake. The first place they came to was a Finnish man, Lainonen. Then, Lainonen, T. Estensen, S. Houl, and Matti Rautio left for Volga to meet and get the newcomers, and stay there for the night.

The first night, the depot man gave Father a broom and showed him a coal room that he could sweep out and sleep in. We stayed there for two nights. The second day, a train came with a baggage car behind. It was put on a sidetrack. The depot man motioned for Father to come see, and when they opened the door, all their belongings were there.

In this group were six families, namely: Efraim Palavalehto and wife Briita Kaisa, son Efraim and daughter Maria; John Efraimson and wife Liisa with daughter Maria; Henry Matson (Havilainen) and wife Maria Liisa and daughter Kaisa; Jacob Tofferson (Paso) and Wife Anna mid son Adolph; Kalle Jynkala and wife with one daughter, whose names I do not remember. There was also my father, Henry S. Hendrickson (Lehtola), wife Walbor, and two sons Henry and John.

John died two weeks after arriving here. We were first at Matti Routio's where son John died. He was buried on the southwest side, of Lake Poinsett, where one other was buried before. Now it is called the Poinsett Cemetery.

It was the 14th day of August when we arrived at Poinsett during harvest time, so work was available at once tying grain into bundles. The work was done with a machine that was pulled by three oxen or horses that cut five feet wide and laid the grain in rows.

We then moved to August Kinnunen's on the east side of Lake John where we stayed in the winter of 1880-81. This was closer to where we started to build a home on a hillside. It was dug in the ground with two steps to the floor, a few boards on the roof with hay on top, and sod on the hay. There were two small windows—one on each side of the door. We didn't move there 'til the following spring after the water had somewhat settled.

There was so much snow; they said there was ten feet on the level and a lot higher in drifts. The snow came early in the fall and blew till the 10th of May. There was no travel, even to get the neighbors. The only way possible was by skis. Kinnunen's barn got covered by snow, so they had to dig a hole from the top to feed and water the oxen and cows, with the manure taken out by the same hole. The hay was next to the barn.

The flour supply was getting short so Kinnunen said, "Let's make a mill," as they had wheat. So, they went to the shore of Lake Albert and dug down 'til they found suitable mill stones. They fitted one stone on top of the other to be turned by hand. The mill was in use both day and night, as everyone's flour had run out. They all helped one another to turn the stone since everyone was in a hurry to get a little flour.

In 1880, all the lakes had been dry, but in the spring after the big snowmelt, all the lakes filled up and the fish came. Father bought a cow from T. Estensen and we planned to move to our own sod house. Mother started to lead the cow and Father helped her to get past the water between Lake Mary and Lake Norden. When Mother arrived at the dugout, there was already someone there. Jacob Paso had come a few days before and stayed at our house 'til he got his roof over his head on his own land. Father came the next day along with Kinnunen with his oxen.

Father traveled from place to place doing carpenter work and also making shoes, so he wasn't home much the first year. He got a neighbor, Peter Thue, to break ten acres of sod where we planted a little barley, corn, turnips, and potatoes. A good portion was not planted that year. The barley did not grow well, as the ground was raw. It was cut with a scythe and put up "Finnish fashion" for chicken feed.

One evening, Mother asked me to go tell Mrs. Efraimson to come and keep her company, which she did. She brought a lamp along that we didn't have. In the morning when we got up, we had new company. John Efraimson had come to see what had happened. A little boy had appeared in the night. John went to bring the news to Father, who was working for Alex Huikka. Father asked Huikka for a dollar, but he didn't have any money. So, he went to the next place, Solomon Salmonson (Korpi) and got $1.50. He then walked to a store on the shore of Lake Badger, and bought what might be needed, as well as a little lamp. By the time he reached home, he had walked his feet raw in the hot weather.

Father worked one summer for the Great Northern Western Railroad when it was built between Brookings and Watertown. He also worked at threshing in the fall around Watertown. When the cow had a calf, he realized that it was a bull. Father decided to raise it as an ox. She next had a heifer calf, and a neighbor wanted to trade for a bull calf that was somewhat larger. Therefore, we had two oxen to raise. When they were two years old, lines were made and we started to train them for drawing.

One evening, we left for Castlewood intending to stay the night. We slept in the wagon box on the west side of the bridge. This was my first time in town after moving to the dugout. We couldn't buy flour on time, so we had to go to the bank to borrow $5.00. They said they didn't loan less than $10.00, so we had to mortgage one cow and calf and the oxen at 12% interest. This brought us $8.00 and we were able to buy flour.

With the oxen, we were able to start farming and breaking more land. Until this time, the land had been farmed on shares, but now we had to buy a plow, drag, and planter. The harvesting had to be hired, but we could not hire a binder since everyone's crops ripened at the same time: Father went to Estelline and bought a binder to be paid in three yearly payments. The first year he couldn't make the payment, but the following year he paid it all off.

All went well and when the land was proved, we took a loan on the land for $400, paid off the small debts, and bought another team of oxen. We rented more land from others and repaid the land debt on time. A pasture was fenced. We built a new 14x18 foot sod house where we lived for many years. The new house was built, then a barn. And then horses were purchased and another 160 acres of land.

There were four boys and four girls. One girl died in Finland and one boy here—John, of whom I have already mentioned. Another son, JaImer, died in 1947. The later years have gone, so there isn't much to relate. As from the beginning, things have gone well. We have not had to go to bed hungry. Mother Walbor died in Minneapolis, Minnesota on June 15, 1931 at the age of 79 years from a blood clot during eye surgery. Father died at home from a stroke on New Year's Day, 1940 at the age of 87 years. Father left 360 acres of land, debt-free, which is in the care of us children and it remains debt free, as he left it.

The Blizzard
By Joan I. Oster of Eureka, South Dakota
Born 1949

As I was getting off of the school bus in the afternoon one day in March of 1966, I noticed a strong, steady wind, which was a rather common phenomenon in North-central South Dakota. "You kids stay in your beds as long as you can," Dad said the next day, climbing the stairs to our bedrooms. Of course, as our curious minds were we kids had to see why he would say that! Soon we found the reason. Looking out our porch window downstairs, we saw only white! It was a raging, old-fashioned blizzard!

There were no warnings and no electricity. That was the reason that Dad wanted us to stay in bed as long as we possibly could. Because it was March, lives of people and cattle were saved. Whole trains were buried. We made *Life* magazine! Cooking and heating came from our old kerosene stove. Our old, antique kerosene lanterns were used for light. Our stove had to be off at night, so we all slept together with half our bodies on the couch and then boxes or chairs!

On day three, we decided to all face the 70 mph blizzard by heading out to the barn to our milk cows. I thought it would be a lot of fun. We roped ourselves together so we wouldn't be separated. As soon as I stepped outside,

Feeding the lambs

what was expected to be a fun and exciting new adventure, turned out to be a tough struggle to look ahead and keep my eyes from freezing shut! We had to climb over two 5-7 foot drifts. After we lost Mom when she tried to retrieve more kerosene, we finally found her.

We had to dig open the barn door. A sow pig with her little ones was in a snowdrift in the first stall. Our thirsty cows ran to the tank outside. After milking the cows, I wanted to stay and sleep in the hayloft rather than face the blizzard again! But, of course, that alternative was short-lived. All of us made it back to the house safely. The storm blew another two days.

Even though this town of Eureka, is a "gem" on Hwy 10 and was once the wheat capital of the world, it can have very inclement weather. In the fall of 1965, we had a horrific ice storm, where we kids had to stay in town with our aunt in order to go to school! I guess these hardy German Russian immigrants (Black Sea Germans) had just once again found what felt a lot like their home in Russia!

Joan, her twin sister, and brother riding their tricycles

Debbie

Awaiting the arrival of our two uncles, we three kids became anxiously excited to see three little lambs in one big box. These would be our pets until school time. As the youngest of three, I usually got the weaker lamb. I would always give it a little extra TLC. They eagerly drank their bottles of milk! One time we gave them "Beatle" names. I named mine Ringo.

However, I'll never forget Debbie, a healthy, black-faced lamb. She ran all over the barnyard and even played hide-n-seek with me! She was one of my many pets that created wonderful blessings to my childhood farm life!

Joan's twin sister and her brother with their pets

Fun in High Places
By Mike Jurgens of Aberdeen, South Dakota
Born 1947

One pleasant summer evening in the late '50s, my friend and grade school classmate Jim and I decided to have some fun in downtown Milbank, South Dakota. We thought it would be exciting to climb the water towers and enjoy the view. I had a part-time job with a local TV storeowner helping him install TV antennas on rooftops, so I figured that was good training for conquering something higher.

We first climbed the shorter of the two towers, which was at the north end of Main Street close to Jim's house by the railroad tracks. We climbed to the very top and sat on the big iron ball. After our descent, we walked across the tracks and snuck into the Old Dutch

Grist Mill, a popular area landmark. Once inside, we climbed the stairs to the top and scared off a few pigeons that were roosting up there. We found an opening that allowed us to walk out onto one of the windmill arms. Nothing eventful happened on those first two climbing adventures.

Next, we decided to climb the tallest water tower, which was on the south end of Main Street next to the city auditorium. About halfway up the iron rung steps, we encountered a large cable secured to a rung right in the middle of the ladder. We had to swing our bodies out to get around that cable, wanting to avoid contact as we thought it might be electrical.

When we got up to the landing, we encountered many roosting pigeons that were quite noisy as they all took flight. Their noise and our talking and laughing were our downfall, as we notified someone below. They had come out to take out their garbage to the cans in the alley, and were directly below us. They obviously heard us and called the police because shortly thereafter, we heard someone hollering at us to come down. We looked way down there to see a police car at the base of the tower and an officer looking at us. At that time, Jim was at the very top and I was just ready to take the short ladder up to join him. I immediately thought of how much trouble I

Mike Jurgens in 1971

319

was in, as my parents were quite strict.

We started the long descent, once again being careful to avoid the big cable. When we reached the bottom, we were scolded and asked our names and addresses. When the officer took me home, we went up to the front door and the officer knocked. My dad answered, and didn't look too pleased to see me standing there with a police officer. The officer asked him if I was his son, and he replied, "Yes." Then the officer told him what I had done. My mom's brother and his wife just happened to be visiting my folks that evening, so that only added to the embarrassment for my parents. The officer left and then I really got it from my dad.

At that time, I also worked part-time at my dad's Mobil gas station doing grease and oil and wash jobs. The next day while working at the station, I overheard customers kidding my dad and asking if he was raising a steeplejack. Word spreads fast in a small town! I don't remember his reply, but his face showed that he wasn't too amused about the whole event. The climbs were exhilarating and we sure had a great view of the lights of Milbank, the surrounding Grant County, and a little further to the east of Ortonville, Minnesota.

Later on in high school, I worked at the local weekly newspaper, the *Grant County Review*. Some years after I had moved away, I was back visiting my former employers who still owned the paper. They gave me a picture of that tallest tower. It was featured in a newspaper article about the dismantling of both water towers, as the city had opted for a better water supply distribution system.

My friend Jim is gone now, but I know he would still agree with me that it was one of the most exciting evenings we ever had!

The Moving Playrooms
By Carol Langner Dusharm of Brookings,
South Dakota
Born 1949

I grew up on a farm with three other siblings in South Dakota during the 1950s. Growing up on a farm at this period of time meant no television or telephone for many years—and definitely no battery-operated toys. You used your imagination and the things you had at hand for play.

Carol with her grandfather

Building a playhouse or forts consumed many hours throughout the year. What you built depended on what Dad did and didn't need and where you built it depended on where Dad did and didn't need space at the time. I had three places to make a playhouse for me and my dolls. Our house was not that big, so as soon as the weather allowed, outside I would go with my dolls in a baby buggy (the one used for us as babies), little folding table and two chairs, dishes, and boxes to make furniture for my house. The first place was the brooder house. This was the little building that the baby chicks were kept in until they were big enough to lay eggs and move to the henhouse. I would sweep the floors and walls and wash the windows that were on the south side of the building. I would find something to make curtains and then I would proceed to set up my kitchen and other rooms of my house.

The second place for a playhouse was the steel corncrib. It was circular and had a cement floor. It was cool in here, as the sides were open steel cribbing. However, it did not keep the South Dakota breeze out. This was always a temporary house until the grain bin in the granary was empty. The granary was a building that Dad stored his grains in until time to sell at market. It was about 50 feet long and 40 feet wide. There were three bins on each side with an open space in the middle. The car was parked in this open spot on one end and a tractor on the other end. The one bin had an eight-foot opening; this is where I would set up my house. The floors in here were smooth from all the years of use. Again, it would have to be swept out and cleaned before moving in my things.

In between all of these playhouses, we had a big sandbox, swing and a merry-go-round. Dad had taken an axle and an old wooden wheel to make it. He put the axle in the ground, re-attached the wheel, and round and round we could go!

As I got older, my siblings and I would make forts in the lilac bushes. We would trim the bottom braches and rake and sweep the ground under them until all debris was gone. Then we would move in the toys, blankets, or whatever the fort of the day called for.

Our favorite place to play, though, was the haymow. It depended on the time of year as to what we did in the haymow. In the winter, the mow would be full of hay for making forts in the loose hay or the straw bales. The haymow was the length and width of the barn. At one end there was a 12 foot by 12 foot opening for throwing hay down for the cows. In the case of us kids, that is where we did our jumping from the haymow to the bottom floor. It was about eight feet from floor to floor, but if we added on another ten feet of hay, we had some good jumping! You would go and fluff the hay to keep it soft to land in. No one ever broke a bone or injured themselves doing this.

As the haymow emptied, the big wooden beams that held up the barn started to show up. That was the time for us to walk those big beams and pretend we were in the circus. The beams were about 12 square inches. One of the beams was near the opening. If you were really brave, you could try walking the beam near the opening. Again, no one ever fell into the opening. This would have easily been a 20-foot drop.

In the spring and early summer, the haymow would be completely empty and it turned into our roller skating rink. The wooden floor was as smooth as glass from all the years of hay being on it. We could build up quite the speed as we spun in circles on our skates. We never skated off and into the opening either.

Carol and Sharon (in the swing)

The haymow was very hot in the summer and a warm place to play all winter. That haymow was our winter playground.

We never lacked for something to do or someplace to play as we grew up. Most of our time was spent outside, on our own, with Mother every hour or so yelling to see where we were. Then, she would go about her business and we would continue on with ours!

Old Days in Waubay
By Wilferd (Buzz) Greening of Waubay,
South Dakota
Born 1932

We moved to Waubay in 1935. I was three and a half years old at the time. My dad bought the Corner Drug Store. It was located on the corner in the middle of Main Street. It was a long, narrow building, and we lived in an apartment in the back. We had an icebox, and an iceman would come and put ice in it twice a week. I always ran out and got myself a sliver of ice from his truck to suck on. When I was about five years old, we moved into a house and got a Frigidaire refrigerator.

We also had a hand pump by our sink to pump water out of a cistern. Up front, we had a cigar counter, which I would sit behind on a tall stool, and watch the customers come and go. We handled a lot of out of town newspapers at that time. The *Chicago Tribune, New York Times, Denver Post, Minneapolis Triune,* and the *Sioux Falls Argus Leader* were all newspapers that we had.

When I was real small, we had a telephone in our house. I would pick up the phone and tell the operator that I wanted to talk to my dad. She would connect me with my dad's store phone!

There was a man who came in once in a while that I called the "fire eater." He would put a lighted wooden match in his mouth, flip it over into his mouth, close it for about a second, and then flip it out of his mouth again. He really fascinated me. We had a fountain and a booth room. After school, we would meet a lot of school kids at the fountain.

We had an Atwater Kent radio. We could get WCCO in Minneapolis and WNAX in Yenton. On Saturday nights, I would listen to

321

the Grand Ole Opry and Minnie Pearl. When we got a new radio, I would listen to The Lone Ranger, Abbott and Costello, The Shadow, Lum and Abner, Fibber McGee and Molly, and the Green Hornet. Sunday December 7th, 1941 when the Japanese bombed Pearl Harbor, I was sitting on the stool at the back of the cigar counter. I'll never forget that day. Everybody was talking loud and fast.

When I was sitting on my stool, some out-of-state fishermen came in to buy a newspaper. They were talking among themselves about a special screw that one man had lost off of his expensive fishing reel. He had called some place in Aberdeen, Sioux Falls, and even Minneapolis, but couldn't find this special screw. My dad overheard them, and said, "Why don't you try the secondhand store next door?" They sort of laughed, but went over anyway. The secondhand store used to be a jewelry store, and the man running it was a little old man who was by trade a watchmaker.

Well, anyway, in a little while, the men came back. The man that needed the special screw was walking about a foot off the ground. He was amazed. He told my dad, "I went over to that store and showed my fishing reel to the little man. He took it and put this little eyeglass in his eye and looked at my reel for a long time. He put it down and went to a stack of cigar boxes about eight feet tall and about ten feet long. None of them seemed to have writing on them. He pulled out a box from the stack and brought it back to his workbench. He opened the box and looked around in it with his eyepiece. He got some tweezers out and pulled out a screw and stuck it in my reel. He handed the reel back to me and charged me 25 cents. I couldn't believe it!"

When we were little, I and four friends would talk Reverend Nowell into taking us out to the swimming beach at the lake north of town in his Model A Ford. He had a two-seater. When he wasn't available, we would go across the street and talk Father Stencel into taking us. He had a Model A Coupe, but it had a rumble seat; we could all squeeze into it.

When we were older, we would ride our bikes out to the swimming beach. There was a pasture next to the beach with an electric fence around it. One day, a bunch of us were sitting around next to the fence when another guy came walking up out of the lake. Somebody

The Cream Station after the cyclone in 1937

had the idea for us all to hold hands, and when the guy got close to the last guy in the group, the guy next to the fence grabbed the wire. At the same time, the guy closest to the guy coming out of the lake (all wet) grabbed his hand all wet. He got a nice shock!

On Halloween, the older boys would sneak around own at night and tip over all of the outhouses they could find. We little guys would tag along and watch. We would daringly tip over a few trashcans. One time the big boys were tipping over an outhouse and one of the boys slipped and fell into the hole right up to his belt! Boy did he ever stink!

On Saturday nights, my dad would give me a quarter. I would go uptown to buy a ticket to the move for ten cents. I'd buy a bag of popcorn for five cents. After the show, I would go down the street and get myself an ice cream cone for five cents and a bottle of pop. A quarter bought me a great Saturday night.

When we were growing up, the county paid a bounty of three cents a tail for gophers, so we trapped a lot of gophers in the city pasture. One morning I was upstairs in our house. My mother was in the basement

Aftermath of the cyclone in 1937

washing clothes. All of a sudden, I heard this terrible scream coming from the basement. I thought that Mother had probably gotten her hand stuck in the wringer. I went flying down the basement stairs. When I got to the bottom, I saw my mother standing there with this very angry look on her face. I didn't know why, but I knew I must be in big trouble. Apparently, I had forgotten to clean out my jean pockets of my accumulation of gopher tails. As she was going through my pockets, she felt the gopher tails!

The house we lived in had a coal furnace. My dad would bank up the coal in the furnace at night in the winter. By morning, the fire would be almost out. He would stir it up and put more coal on it in the morning, but it would take a while to warm up the bedrooms. My sister and I would rundown to the kitchen and get dressed sitting on the open oven door. My mother insisted we take our cod liver oil as a vitamin. It tasted terrible!

In about 1937, a cyclone hit our town just after dark. It entered Waubay on the west side of town. It came down east to the street north of our house. There was a barn at the back of the house next door to the north. It took that barn completely away. No one has ever seen it since or found any part of it as far as I know. It kept going east about half a block and blew apart the front part of a brick garage. It took the bricks up in the air and scattered them in a large area in front of Dilly's Garage It then kept on east right past the north side of my Dad's Corner Drug Store. When it got to Main Street, it made a square corner and went north, up Main Street and took the front off of the Red Owl Grocery Store, a wood building, and laid it down on the street. There

18 foot snowbank

was some furniture sitting only inches from the edge of the floor that was not disturbed at all. It kept going north to the end of the block, then made another square corner to the east and flattened the wood cream station building on the northwest corner of the at block. It kept going east out of town. It was a very strong storm!

When I was about ten or eleven years old, my buddy, and I would hang around the railroad depot and watch the switch engines form Milbank move the boxcars around the elevators and stockyards. One day we were very close to one of the engines, looking it over, when the engineer said, "Hi." We asked if we could come up and look at the engine cab. He said that we could, so up we went. We had a good conversation and he let us ride along while they switched rail cars around the elevator and stockyards. Also, we backed down to the sand pit east of town and picked up a couple of cars full of washed sand.

In the spring of 1940, it started to snow in the afternoon and evening. The next morning there was a bank of snow 18 feet high in the middle of our Main Street. It started as nothing at the northwest end of Main Street and grew to 18 feet high in front of Dilly's Garage at the south end of the street. Two other boys and myself dug out a tunnel through it so people could get from one side of the street to the other. All the kids in town had a good time sliding and running up and down the snow bank!

The summer I was 13, a friend and I worked for a dairy farmer on the southwest of Waubay. We helped put up hay for him. We mowed the hay and raked it into piles and then bucked it up to a stacker to make haystacks. We did all of this with horses. You got to see a lot of nature, especially when you were mowing. You would encounter rabbits, gophers, fox, deer, and a lot of birds. Later on in summer during harvest time, we would hire out together as a one man operated bundle team and wagon, then throw the bundler onto the thrashing machine. We would get to the machine early so we could set around and talk and eat. One of the guys started doing a dance, slapping his overalls, and jumping up and down, trying to get his overalls off. A field mouse had run up his pant leg and was running around his waist inside his overalls. We all about died laughing!

Wringer Washers and One-room Schools
By Margaret L. Grottke of Chili, Wisconsin
Born 1943

I am Margaret L. (Holzberger) Grottke, adopted daughter of Arthur and Melva (Rawstern) Witthoeft. At 15 months, I came to South Dakota in a baby buggy to the Ernest and Mathilda (Maas) Witthoeft family farm six miles northwest of Wolsey, South Dakota. One of my earliest memories is Mom pushing me in the buggy to the wheat field. A blanket on the hood protected me from the sun and an old lace curtain draped over the opening kept out mosquitoes and flies. It was hot! Somehow, I slept while Mom and Dad set up the eight bundles into each shock.

Threshing was a very busy day! Mom butchered several chickens for frying and had a huge kettle of mashed potatoes, garden vegetables, fresh bread and pies, coffee, and lemonade. The men washed up outside with a pail of water, dipper, basin, soap and towel

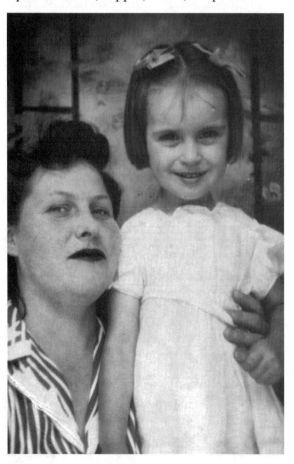

Margaret with her mom, Melva Witthoeft

before being seated at the extended table. Horses also had been watered and feedbags had been looped from their bridles over their muzzles at noon. Hayrack loads of bundles were forked head first into the threshing machine. The grain, separated from the straw, came pouring from one spout into a grain wagon. The straw spewed from a long pipe to create a huge straw pile, for which we used for winter bedding. Grain wagons were off loaded by hand into the granary or sold at the grain elevator in Wolsey.

We had no electricity until 1949. We used Aladdin lamps—one in the kitchen and one in the dining room. As a baby, Mom tucked me into my crib and turned the lamp down to a soft glow before going milking. The lamps cast flickering shadows in the corners of the room. When I leaned too close to the hot lamp globe, there was an awful stench of burning hair. Mom always set a kerosene lamp on top of the icebox when she used the mirror on the wall behind it to pin curl her hair. We had cold running water from our artesian well, but all water was heated on the cook stove for laundry and our Saturday evening sponge baths at the kitchen sink.

Mother washed clothes with the same wringer washer for more than 15 years. At first, it had a gasoline engine. I still remember the exhaust hose tucked out the kitchen door. Later, Dad replaced it with an electric motor, which was much quieter. Once the clothes were washed, they were put through the wringer into a tub of rinse water, sloshed up and down by hand, and then wrung into the laundry basket to be hung on the clothesline. On very windy days, the first clothes were dry by the time the last load was hung.

Our telephone was installed sometime in the mid-1940s. It was square and black and hung on the dining room wall. The mouthpiece protruded below the rotary dial and could be adjusted up for tall or down for short people. The receiver rested between two prongs on the left side. It could be lifted to check if anyone was talking before pressing a button at the base of the prong to achieve dial tone. It was a party line among our neighbors. Each had a specific ring combination. Our number was 3861 and our ring was one short and one long ring. Others had two shorts, two longs, two shorts and a long, one long, etc. To call Huron we had to dial the operator and tell her the

Margaret with her dad, Art Witthoeft

number. How often I remember Dad saying, "2453 please." It was the phone of August Lemke, our gas delivery truck driver. People who listened in to others' conversations were said to be "rubbering," therefore were given the nickname "Rubberneck." We had an Edison phonograph in our living room with many thick 78-rpm records that we played over and over. My favorite was a whistler that sounded like a bird. I played it so often, I nearly wore it out.

I remember the sacks that held flour, sugar, and livestock feed. The white cotton flour sacks had narrow rainbow stripes, perfect for dishtowels. Chicken feed bags had colorful patterns we used for sewing aprons, dresses, blouses, skirts, and quilts. Pity the poor proprietor who had to move heavy bags to satisfy the customer whose heart was set on a pattern at the bottom of the heap!

My grandfather, Ernest Witthoeft, donated the land on Highway 281 on which Weeks School, Allen Township, stood. Both my Dad

and I attended there. My favorite teacher was Jessie Gordon who taught my first, third, fifth and sixth grades. In my primary grades, she began the day with scripture, prayer, the flag pledge, and then she read Nancy Drew or the Hardy Boys. All eight grades were in one room. Our classes were held on the recitation bench at the front of the room. Large maps were lowered like window shades over the blackboards. A globe was suspended in the corner with the weight painted half-black and half-white to resemble the moon. Once a week we sang with the "Music Lady" on the radio. Once or twice a year our county superintendent, Margaret Long, visited. At recess, we enjoyed the swings and slide. We played "pump pump pull away," "New Orleans," "freeze tag," besides softball in fall. Winter brought a rousing chase of "fox and geese," sliding on the ice in the road ditch, and snowball fights (until the teacher caught us). In bad weather, we played indoor games like "fruit basket upset," "musical chairs," and "clap in and clap out."

I remember one Christmas program when a colored cardboard "sleigh" was tacked to the ends of benches. A cardboard horse was suspended from the ceiling and moved with the "reins." A bright winter mural was displayed on the wall. We students sat in the "sleigh" to recite our pieces and sing our songs. Oh! The butterflies in the tummy and uncontrollable nervous giggles! How proud we were of our new plaid taffeta dresses and our parents smiling in the crowd!

Sometimes my calf, Whistler, would meet me at the corner of the pasture and we'd walk home together. After school were the radio dramas: Sky King with his plane Songbird, and sidekick Penny, The Lone Ranger starring Brace Beemer, with Tonto, Silver and Scout, Johnny Dollar, Our Miss Brooks, My Little Margie, Gunsmoke, Straight Arrow, Bobby Benson, Big John and Sparky, Storybook Lady and Space Cadet.

I slept upstairs with only a six-inch heat register in the floor from the dining room. I slept under a feather bed and five quilts in winter. The window at the end of the hall was not weather tight. Snow sifted into a small pile at the head of the stairs. I usually dressed beside the heater in the dining room. We burned coal or wood, whatever was available. It was my job to pick up four laundry tubs of corncobs from the hog lot after school. Mom fed the cook stove with them every fifteen to thirty minutes. Somehow, she regulated the heat to bake bread, pies, cookies, and even angel food cakes with great success. Such tantalizing aromas! I especially remember fried potatoes and onions, fried chicken, and those work-intensive black nightshade pies, which we relished (and I still do).

A winter trip to the outhouse was a real adventure! Because the door was askew, we carried a shovel to clear the path and a broom to sweep the snow from the seat. Little time was spent reading the comics or perusing the catalog, which served as toilet tissue!

The winter of 1952-1953, my Dad was hospitalized with a heart attack. Mom barely reached home from the hospital when a blizzard began. Our hired man picked me up from school in the heavy snow. The wind blew with such force, it was whiteout conditions. He wanted to get home to Huron, but got stranded at Holforty's gas station until it subsided the next day. Only once was our half-mile driveway plowed that winter. Mom

Margaret on top of the plowed snowbank

took a picture of me atop a snow bank higher than our car.

We milked cows by hand for many years. The milk was carried to the house. The cream separator sat in the northeast corner of the kitchen. The handle was turned at a certain rate of speed while milk descended from the tank on top into the disks. Cream came from one spout, skim milk from the other. The skim milk was fed to the weaned calves, and hogs. The cream was stored in five and ten-gallon cans until Saturday when it joined 30 dozen-egg cases to be sold at Earl Long's Cream Station located behind Newberry's store in Huron.

Sometimes eggs were only 13 or 15 cents a dozen. That produce check was the sum total of our weekly budget to be divided for clothing, groceries, lamp wicks, mantles, and farm supplies. Bargains were eagerly sought at Montgomery Ward's (who gave free Rudolph books at Christmas, of which I still have one in possession), Woolworth's, Sears, Penny's, Coast to Coast, Gambles, Humphrey Drugs, Dry goods, Council Oaks, Ed and Ebs, and if there were a few cents left, a stop at the Double H ice cream store for a ten cent double dip cone for each of us. A large box of groceries was about $5.00; hickory striped overalls were $2.50 for men, $1.50 for children. These overalls often comprised the school wardrobe of the farm boys in country school. On rare occasions, we even ate out at the Colonial Bakery where a hot beef sandwich with mashed potatoes and gravy cost 55 cents.

One treasured memory is Christmas shopping in Huron. Christmas carols played from loud speakers on the Marvin Hughett Hotel, snow drifting down, the blue of dusk settling over the town as we completed our grocery shopping at O. P. Skaggs, loaded the car, and headed home for chores. Christmas at church on Christmas Eve was special. Chimes rang out, bubble lights shone in rainbow colors on the tree, and children's recitations and carols were sung with the congregation. Then we drove home to discover Santa had been to our house!

A tornado that took place on July 3, 1957 destroyed our barn. A thoughtful neighbor helped my Dad construct a corral where we tied the cows to planks nailed between a couple of trees for milking. The first snowfall came just as the new barn was completed.

My Dad tried his hand at raising sheep. The baby cheviots looked like cute bunnies with long legs. Orphans were brought into the house in a tub by the stove with a heat lamp dangling from a yardstick laid across the backs of two dining chairs. When the lambs got warm and perky, we'd hear the clicking of tiny hooves headed for the kitchen to see if we had their bottle warm yet. Dad made a pet of one. As a ram, he still begged to be petted at a time when Dad was carrying two five-gallon pails of water. Because he felt ignored, the ram knocked Dad flat in the ice and snow. He was in the next truckload to the sales barn!

Those long, gray winter days provided ample time for many checker games, Sorry, Rummy, and Whist. I entertained my folks and guests with guitar and song, and read many books. My favorite high school teacher was Arlys Delvaux. She patiently read all my descriptions and stories, instilling a deep love for writing. She always urged me to "write what you know." I hope you have enjoyed reading it!

Times in the "Dirty Thirties"
By Margaret Schmidt of Lane, South Dakota
Born 1927

Having been born on Feb. 21, 1927 in a farmhouse in Eastern South Dakota, I have many vivid memories of the "Dirty Thirties." Our farm was located about 15 miles southwest of Wessington Springs, in Crow Lake Township.

The wind blew hard and often. The air became so full of dust you could hardly breathe outside, so we all stayed in the house. Many times, it was so dark in the middle of the day that we needed to have kerosene lamps lit. Mom would tear strips of cloth and poke in around the windows and doors to keep the dust out. However, it was a losing battle, as everything inside got covered with fine silt.

Outside, the dirt would pile up wherever it could find a stopping place, and fencerows full of tumbleweeds were a prime spot. After the storm was over, my dad and two brothers had to go out and scoop away the dirt from the fences to keep the cattle from walking right over them.

There were eight of us in the family, and we lived in a house with a kitchen and living room on the ground floor and two bedrooms upstairs. We were always pretty compact. Winters were harsh, and it took a lot of fuel to keep the house warm. Many times when fuel grew short, I remember my dad sawing logs in the kitchen to keep the wood burner going. The door was closed between the two rooms, and the rest of us were all in the living room trying to keep warm. Another source of fuel for us was cow chips! In the summer and fall my brother Lawrence and I used to play a game we called "cowpokes." We would take our little wagon to the pasture, and armed with a couple sharpened sticks; we "poked" the chips and put them in the wagon. We hauled them home to pile up for the cold weather. They burned very fast and hot, but soon you were hauling out about as many ashes as you hauled in chips.

I remember one year while we were in the house the sky just turned red. It was pretty scary, so we ran out to see what was going on. The sky was red from horizon to horizon. While we stood there, a few yellow two-striped grasshoppers fell from the sky! They were so thick they blotted out the sun. We knew there were millions of grasshoppers moving over us from north to south trying to find food. They would clean up all in sight, even eating the paint from the buildings and chew on fence posts. In order for Dad to try to save a few crops, he, like many of the farmers, used to plow a deep furlough around the field and pour a mash, which was laced with the deadly poison, Paris Green, into them. It didn't do much good, as the hoppers flew over the trenches. However, this did more damage than good; it killed the birds! I'm sure all that poison is still in the ground, as it doesn't deteriorate.

One summer day I remember my Mom and I walking over to visit a neighbor. Mom noticed a dress wrapped around a hub of their wagon to keep the grease in. Mom asked the neighbor lady to see it. It was very greasy, but mom thought it would fit me, so she took it home and boiled it out. Then I had a "new" brown and white checked dress to wear to school in the fall. I was proud of it, too!

We walked to school across country for over a mile. Sometimes when it was very cold we would freeze our noses or fingers or something. When we got to school the teacher

Evelyn, Josephine (mom), Mary, Margaret, Helen, Joseph, Jr. and Lawrence

them. We walked on top of them to press them down with our bare feet! Speaking of shoes, I once had a pair of tan sandals. Lawrence and I were down by the creek, which was nearly dry, with deep cow tracks all around the water in the sticky mud. Of course as a young child I did not worry about my shoes. One of them got stuck in the bottom of a cow track and neither Lawrence nor I could find it again. We went back to the house and never uttered a word about it. Well, when Sunday came and we were heading for church they looked all over for my sandal; it was nowhere to be found. I went to church barefoot, which at the time was quite normal anyway. I can't ever remember telling Mom where I lost the shoe.

Things that helped us survive were the WPA and NYA. The government hired men to make roads, dams, bridges, and even some buildings. The money was a Godsend. Dad used a Fresno, a bucket scraper, pulled by two horses. It had two handles and was used to load and unload dirt to make roads. He also learned how to split rocks for dams and bridges and learned how to help build the rock field house in Wessington Springs Park. He even made some money by housing the horses of workers from further away in our barn when they were working on roads near our place. In fact, some of the men slept in our haymow. The NYA was for young women to make some money, and help by sewing clothing to give to people in need. Two of my older sisters worked there. The NYA also took in donated shoes, etc. for people, and I remember once my sister brought me a pair of high-top tennis shoes. They were too big; but what the heck, I wore them proudly. Mom also made some clothes for us from flour

would hold snow on them to thaw them out slowly. It must have worked because I still have my nose! If a bad blizzard hit during the day we would sometimes have to stay in the school overnight. We had a large coal-burning stove with a jacket around it. We'd all huddle around it on the floor with our coats on. The schools had kerosene lamps, so they were lit all night. If we got a nature call we needed to go outside to the "biffy!" Also, the boys had to make trips to the coal shed for fuel. Times like these we never went out alone, so we never got lost. On very harsh occasions my dad would take us, or come to get us with a team and bobsled. What fun that was to huddle in the hay, wrapped under a heavy quilt and listen to the harnesses jangling as we went. Sometimes the snow was so deep that even the horses got stuck with the bobsled!

One government program that we never understood was, when it was so dry that only part of the corn sprouted, the government paid the farmers to chop it off! So my brother Lawrence and I got paid a few cents from Dad or a neighbor to go hoe it off. Thus the soil was free to blow, as well it did, and we could walk out in the fields and find arrowheads, which were exposed.

We were so poor that many times we did not own a pair of shoes. Thus, in the summer our feet got very tough soles; walking outside was no problem. One year I remember that feed for the cattle was so short that Dad cut tumbleweeds that were green, but already were thick with stickers, and we helped stack

Rural Sefrna School's class of 1934-35

sacks that had printed designs on them.

In a different vein, we had some pretty illustrious neighbors. One of them had a whiskey still and made some pretty potent booze. He and his father both used to walk over to our place pretty lit up. One time the "Old Man McCormick" came and knocked at the door. When Mom opened it, he fell straight into her bed of pansies that she was so proud of. When he staggered up, he said "My, but it is windy, Mary." In truth, it was a very nice, calm day!

Another time when he came down Mom was wanting to put muresco onto the ceiling. (This was a powder mixed in water and was very messy to apply.) The ceiling was very high and McCormick said he would paint it for Mom, but he wanted something over his clothes, as it was so messy. Mom found an old overcoat in the storeroom and he put it on and crawled up on a table to begin painting. All of a sudden, he was hollering and dancing around hitting himself all over! There was a mouse in the lining of the coat! It took a little while to get the mouse out and for Mr. McCormick to settle down to resume his job.

He, and another old neighbor, Mr. Mohr, gave us a lot of entertainment! One day the two of them came over and they were hungry. They asked Mom to fry them some eggs. Before they began to eat, they thought they should say grace. Mr. McCormick said, "Oh Lord, we thank thee for these eggs which we have not forgotten. Oh Lord, these eggs are rotten." Mom was just shaking, trying to muffle a laugh!

Then, of course, there was the music. As no one had radios yet and TV was not even in anyone's wildest imagination, most of the folks took up playing some kind of instrument. My dad used to play the cello. Laying on its side, it could be imagined to be a horse and saddle. While Mom and Dad were out milking the cows, my older sisters used to pull it around while one rode it! You can understand how mad Dad got when they wrecked it for him! So then, he settled for a "fiddle." Mom played the piano and other neighbors played drums, accordions, horns, etc., so when they got together they had a pretty neat band. They played in each other's homes and danced. When they played at our home I remember Lawrence and I crawling under the table and watching their feet as they whirled to the music. They even played for barn dances, and the countryside rang with music and laughter. Sometimes the folks took us kids along. One square dance they did was "Swing Them Like Thunder." The square formed of four men and four women formed a circle. The men circled so fast that the ladies feet flew off the floor and into the air! Strangely enough, I never saw them fall. I remember one time a fellow, who was pretty juiced up, fell down one of the feeding areas for a stall. Everyone was worried he killed himself, but soon he came back up the stairs, no worse for wear!

I expect those reading this think: Wow! She sure had an awful childhood! But on the contrary, I truly enjoyed my life! I just didn't realize we were so poor. We were a close-knit and supportive family who always seemed to have a lot of good times and laughter in our home. I do refer to them as the "Good Old Days." Crime was unheard of, neighbors all helped each other, and you could go anywhere without locking your doors! We didn't have much money, but no one else did either; we knew how to make do. We didn't have huge bills for fuel, electricity, insurance, food, health, communications, etc. that we get hit with today, and we didn't have to be on the lookout for those wanting to take advantage of us. People truly cared about each other, not just themselves and making the almighty dollar. I loved the "Good Old Days," but now it would be impossible to go back.

A Letter from Mother
By Clarice Logan of Lake Norden, South
Dakota
Born 1925

The following was written by my mother, Palmena Hansen Iverson, telling of her parents' move from Vermillion, South Dakota to the homestead in Hamlin County, South Dakota.

The homestead was northwest on banks of Poinsett.

Great-grandparents came and homesteaded in the late 1870s. Their names were Trine Brunick. She homesteaded and filed on a tree claim and her husband was Jacob Hansen. They were married at Oakwood in 1880. They had many trials, a lot of snow, and no conveniences. Travel was done mostly on foot. The nearest post office was about 20 miles away. Later Jacob Hansen became the first master in Norden Township. Provisions were meager and hard to get at. One sack of wheat was bought down south in Kingsbury County. They had it milled and divided it among their neighbors.

The water was drawn in buckets from the well. Hay was outside in stacks and had to be carried in by the forkful to the barn for the stock. Fieldwork was done with oxen and a walking plow. Oxen obeyed when they were trained. You would say gee and haw.

There were no churches. Families who had faith in God met in homes and sang praises to their Savior.

Great-grandmother was left alone by the drowning of her husband, with four small children ages six to three months. She had very few provisions. She braved her tacks courageously through the years. Fuel was mostly twisted straw and pasture cow chips. Wood was not available as there were very few trees.

People lived in sod shanties.

They had frame houses.

Slept in hay stacks when coming from Vermillion

Walked two miles to school.

Goodbye, Old Lady
By Francis Parsey of Watertown, South Dakota
Born 1939

Things I remember from growing up as a child:

We took a Ford tractor over to Naples to have a tire fixed. On the way home, I was driving and for some reason I ran in the ditch near Naples. And lucky we had a guard bumper on the front. That saved the radiator.

I remember I attended Brantford School. I had a teacher I didn't like. She was crabby. As I left one day I said, "Goodbye, old lady." She made me stay after school for half a day for four days. I stayed for two days, and then the last two days there was no more school.

Winter Adventures
By Susan Hines of Carpenter, South Dakota
Born 1952

When I was young, maybe ten or eleven, we had a lot of snow. I think it was the winter of 1962 to 1963. It snowed and blew over and over, and after the snowplow went down the road, the snow would be heaped up on the edges. The snowplows were not equipped with winging capabilities, so they just cut straight through drifts. When it snowed again, it filled in twice as deep as before. The roads got really bad. Our driveway, my dad gave up on. We played and ran sleds on the large drifts since the drive sloped down from house to road. Dad managed to bulldoze out a less congested area out back around the trees and to the road through a field. He couldn't trust the car on that route, so he put the cattle rack in the back of the pickup, covered it with a tarp, and put hay bales inside for us to sit on. Then he loaded us six kids in the back and that is how we went to church, over six miles through bitter cold. We had a large old buffalo blanket that we covered up with plus quilts.

We lived at the end of a half mile of gravel that was narrow and not often plowed out, except by my dad with the Farmhand, for Sunday mainly. So the school bus driver hesitated to come down the road, knowing there was no way to turn around. So we bundled up, crawled in the Farmhand scoop on the tractor, and Dad drove us the half a mile to meet the bus. For a kid, it was quite an adventure, even if it was bone chillingly cold. We had to hold on tight so we couldn't get bounced out. If the weather was not too bad for wind chill, we sometimes walked the half of a mile home in the afternoon when we got off the school bus.

Picking Cobs and Going to Town
By Beverly Langner of Madison, South Dakota
Born 1932

I lived in the country in Lake County. I attended country school for eight years. All eight grades were in one room with a coal heater. I walked one and a half miles to school. It was very cold. In the spring when it was getting warmer, I would roll up my long underwear and roll down my long cotton stockings.

I walked two miles to meet the school bus. I went to Beadle High School in Madison, South Dakota. No one went to high school in my area at that time.

My home was heated by an oil burner heater in the dining room. I slept upstairs with no heat. I slept on a feather bed.

I picked up cobs out of the pigpen and chicken house for burning in the cook stove. Pigs were fed corn on the cob. The cobs cooked our food and baked bread in the oven.

In the summer, Mom had a kerosene stove. I helped with preparing the food for threshers. The men would help all the neighbors to thresh the oats, and they made a big straw pile. I helped Mom make the forenoon lunch and dinner and afternoon lunch. We had hot weather and a lot of flies. There was no fly spray and not good screen doors.

I would go to town every Saturday night to get groceries. The stores would stay open until 10:00 p.m. I would walk the streets with my friends. We would get a five-cent ice cream cone.

On Sunday, my folks and I went to our country church, and I went to Sunday school and youth group.

We had a big wooden phone on the wall. Our ring was one long and one short. All the neighbors could hear our phone ring, and they would all listen to our conversation.

Sloughs and Gravel Pits
By Donna Lewandowski of Grenville, South Dakota
Born 1944

As a small child, my family and I lived on a farm about a quarter of a mile from the main road. I started school at the age of six. My brother and I had to walk to school, and it was a mile to school. It was a one-room school. My brother would always walk ahead of me, and sometimes he would leave me behind. So in the winter it was so cold, so by the time I got to school I would be crying. We didn't have very warm clothes to wear. Our lunch bucket was a syrup pail with only a piece of bread with syrup on it, so by the time it was noon, the bread would be soggy.

My dad had a car but never drove it in the wintertime. He would park it in a gravel pit, so when we would have to go to town, Dad had a team of horses and a wagon. He would put in straw and a few blankets to try to keep us warm.

In the spring, we had a slough to cross to get to the main road, so we had to wade across it. There was a gravel pit on the way to school, so there was a few times when my brother and I would not go to school. We played in the gravel pit all day long. So when school was out we would go home. Then one day my parents had to go to town, so on the way home they stopped at the school to pick us up. The teacher told them we weren't in school all day. So we never got to do that again.

We lived in a two-story house and us kids had to sleep upstairs. There was no heat. When it snowed, there would be snow and frost on the bed. When we got up in the morning, we would grab our clothes, go downstairs, and put them in the oven to get them warm.

In the summer time, the older kids got to ride horses. I was so scared of horses, and they would chase me. I thought if I would go into the slough, the horses wouldn't come after me, but they did. My older sister got bucked off one day and fell on a rock, so they could not ride anymore.

After a few years, we moved to town and that was much better. We lived in a two-room house, and then it was closer to school. But we still didn't have electricity or running water. The well was right by the house and that is where we put the milk and butter to keep them cold. We had a wringer washing machine with a gas engine.

Main Street, Arlington
By Jerry Peters of Owatonna, Minnesota
Born 1934

Hi. My name is Jerry Otis Peters. I was born in Sioux City, Iowa in 1934 and raised in Arlington, South Dakota in the 1930s, 1940s, and 1950s by my parents, Otis James Peters and Gladys Augusta (Blackstone) Peters. I would like to tell the story of businesses and their owners during that period of time on Main Street in Arlington, South Dakota.

Let's start with the farmer's elevator, which was operated by Albert Ecklein and Glenn Lohman; two railroad depots, operated by Mr. Rasmussen and Ben Roske; the creamery, operated by Jim Holt; and the locker, operated by Cliff Mohror.

Moving south across Highway 14, we now go to Smitty's Bowling Parlor and then John Deere, operated by Leon Dill. This later became Kneip Implement, owned by Frank Kneip, which later became Council Oak Grocery and was managed by Jack and Ann Mulholland. Larry Mulholland was their son. The next business on the same side of the street (east) was Ella Brooksmith's Niffiwear shop. Next came the City Café, owned by Otis James Peters (my father), then by Sonny and Gladys Papineau, then Hart Erickson and his son. Other businesses along the street were The Gamble Store, owned by Jack Walters; Ingvalson Drug, owned by Mr. Ingvaldson; the pool hall owned by Art Ackerman; a small grocery store where Hart Erickson worked; Friess Grocery Store, owned by Jack Friess; Arlington Post Office with Postmaster Mrs. Ingvalson; Nelson Barber Shop, owned by Oscar Nelson; an insurance agency owned by Ben Hook and Blake Williams; Super Value Grocery Store, owned by Vance Larson; Miller Pharmacy, which is now Nelson Pharmacy, owned by John Nelson; Nelson Barber and Guns, owned by Tilford Nelson; the popcorn stand owned by Raymond Nelson; New Lunch, owned by Sis Morman; and The Corner Café, owned by Haddie Sederstrom.

Move across the street that leads to Arlington Lake and you find the AT&T Telephone Company with Leah Kruse as the manager and the "concrete" auditorium, managed by Mr. Ness. Going south, you find Kruse Plumbing. The K-12 Arlington High School is on the west side of Main Street. Going north/northwest, you find Stram's Church; the Masonic Temple, which is now the Arlington Museum; and the home of Ben Kruse, the town police officer. Next is the *Arlington Sun* newspaper, owned by Jerry Sturgis; Dr. Failing's office; the Cardinal Café, operated by Cal Burns, then Violet Buchanan, and finally Lila Larson. It became Tuttle Plumbing, owned by Max Tuttle. Next is the Big Chevrolet Garage, owned by Martin Kjellsen and Arnold Eide.

Across the street is Bonde's Grocery and Dry Goods; Sis Herrick's Beauty Salon; Louie Mohror's Shoe Repair; Jack Mohor's shoe shine stand, Dr. Hopkins' office; Dr. Jensen's dental office; and the two stores,

Arlington Auditorium

Glendenning's Dry Goods and Grocery and then My Popcorn Machine. The popcorn space was just a "hole in the wall" and was originally owned by Ben Hook, Jr. and Monte Shanks. Later my brother, Donald, owned the popcorn business. Next came Crandall's Electronics (radio and TV), owned by Ray and Cecil Crandall; a jewelry story (owner's name unknown); Wally Ecklein's bakery, which earlier was Joe Engle's; the Hetland Café, owned by Clarence and Cora Hetland; a vacant space with no building which later became the new post office; the Citizen's Bank with a big clock by Ray Tande; and the Arlington Movie Theater, owned by Guy and Lydia Abbott. Lastly are C.C. Maxwell's Drug and Jewelry Store, where I bought many comic books; and Hugh and John Maxwell's store, Maxwell's Furniture and Sporting Goods which sold hardware, paint, furniture, and I think, Case tractors.

I hope you have enjoyed this trip down memory lane on Main Street in Arlington, South Dakota in the 1930s through the 1950s. Arlington, South Dakota is located on US Highway 14, eighteen miles west of Brookings, South Dakota.

A Date from the Party Line
By Helen Johnson of Rosholt, South Dakota
Born 1928

I went to a business college in Fargo, North Dakota and to work at Allis Chalmers. I had a ride home, only 70 miles, on the weekends.

I came home to my mother and father's farm home. It turned out there was a dance at a nightclub five miles away, so I called my cousin and he said he was not going.

We had an old wooden telephone on the

Helen going to high school in 1946

wall with a crank on the side. I didn't hear her, but a lady on another farm heard my call so she told her son to take me to the dance. No one called to tell me, and he drove in the yard. So it was a surprise. Then a few minutes later, my cousin drove into the yard, too. So I had two rides to the dance. I decided to go with the first one who had shown up to drive me to the dance.

I had no idea someone was listening to my call. My neighbor lady lived to be 100 plus years old.

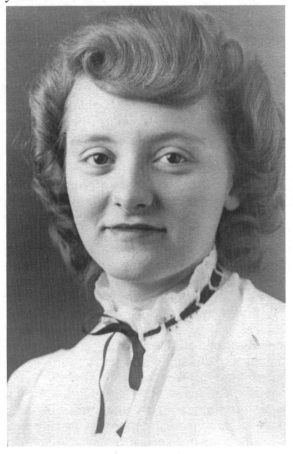
Helen Johnson in 1946

Education, Country Style
By Grace Wangberg of Sinai, South Dakota
Born 1927

At age six, my parents took me to our one room school, District 22, to begin my education. I carried my lunch pail, a tablet, a pencil, and a clean handkerchief, and a lot of excitement for this new chapter in my life. My parents already knew Miss Evenson, the teacher of all eight grades in that room, but I needed to learn to say her name correctly and to understand the rules of daily routine. When I needed lesson help, I was to raise my hand. To go to the library in the back corner of the room, I would raise one finger high above my head, and if I needed to go to the restroom, the sign was two fingers high in the air. I learned that we would have a fifteen-minute recess each forenoon and afternoon. During our noon hours, we would get our lunch pails from the coatroom and join the other children in the basement near the water cooler to eat our peanut butter sandwiches, cookies, and apples before going outside to play.

Ours was one of the newer country schools in our county, and we were proud to have a full basement with a hot air furnace in the furnace room. This brought the heated air through a large floor vent at the front of our big schoolroom, and kept us quite comfortable all winter. The front entry on the east side of the building opened to a cement landing from which we could take the half flight of wooden stairs up to the classroom or the half flight of cement stairs down to the basement. The basement became an indoor play space during inclement weather.

Going up the stairs, we entered the well-lighted classroom with a western wall of windows bringing in the afternoon sun. Of course, the single panes of glass also let in the cold temperatures during the 30 below zero South Dakota winter days. On the east side, near the back of the main classroom was the girl's cloakroom where we hung our coats and warm scarves and placed our lunch pails on the shelf. And there was the door to the private chemical toilet room. The large opening of the toilet seat above its large chemical tank was often very scary to the younger smaller children. I don't remember hearing of anyone falling in, but it certainly made all the children extra cautious! The boy's cloakroom was similar and located toward the front of the classroom.

The entire front wall of the classroom held a slate blackboard used by teachers to write out daily schedules and assignments or whatever information she (or he) wished us to see and remember. We used a portion of that blackboard for working out our arithmetic problems, and to practice our spelling. Screechy chalk on the blackboard really got to some teachers as well as some students, and of course, that encouraged certain of the students to continue making the chalk screech, until Teacher said, "That's enough! Go sit down at your desk!"

After the younger grades finished their recitation or reading class for the teacher, they often were sent to sit beside an upper grader for help with a reading word or simple assist in adding or subtracting their numbers. Thus, older kids learned to be patient helpers, and younger ones learned to relate to children older than themselves.

Walking to school during the winter and swinging our lunch pails served to turn our chocolate milk into a milkshake – a special treat. Of course, it also froze the canned fruit or the fresh apple we carried that day. We learned from the older students that we could bring a freshly scrubbed potato wrapped in foil. This we carefully placed in the ash pit in the furnace. By noon, we had our baked potato (sometimes a much over baked, hard, inedible potato). But that challenged us to figure out the timing and positioning of the next potato we brought.

Recess time on a beautiful fall or spring day gave time for the older kids to play softball, while the younger ones played pump, pump, pull away; captain may I, or some other game. When there was fresh snow on the ground we loved to make snow angels by lying on the clean snow, spreading our arms to make the shape of angels wings, and then carefully getting up and away so as not to leave any human footprints nearby.

Fox and goose was another snow game we enjoyed. First, we carefully stepped out a large circle in the fresh snow, then we divided it into pie shaped sections, and if the circle was large enough we liked to make a second circle about halfway inside the larger one. The very center became the safe home, and the appointed fox chased the geese on the pathways until he or she caught one and turned that one into a fox and then headed for the safe home.

When our county superintendent came for a spring visit we were pleased that she, Miss VanMaanen, wanted to play our recess games with us. Leaning on her crutches, Miss VanMaanen said, "Captain, may I?" and proceeded with the game just as each of us did. By her actions she taught all of us a lesson in acceptance of someone who may be a bit different than ourselves.

Springtime brought pleasantly warm days, even before the ice was gone from the roadside ditches. In fact, that rubbery ice surface over weedy ditches with about a foot of water under the ice was always a challenge to adventurous middle schoolers. The challenge was to safely scoot across the two or three feet of open ice between the tall weedy fence line to the graded up gravel road. Yes, there often was at least one of the boys sloshing his way back to the schoolhouse, and spending the next portion of the day seated by the edge of the large floor register, drying his pant legs as his socks and shoes lay drying on the edge of the register nearby. Every student paid close attention when alongside one of the boys sat our young man teacher, drying his shoes and socks, too.

Yes, we worked hard at our play and we worked hard at our lessons too. We practiced our penmanship, following the teacher's instructions and carefully modeling our letters after the green handwriting cards hung above the blackboard. The beautiful cursive capital A was followed by a small a right on to the big and little Z, z. These were always there to be followed in any handwritten papers we were to turn in. Yes, our handwriting was on display in every subject we put on paper. We used our best handwriting as we prepared gift tags to go with the crafted gifts we made for our parents for Christmas, as well as for Mother's Day, Valentine's Day, and Easter.

The school basement became our shop as we used our handsaws, coping saws, sandpaper, and paintbrushes to turn peach crates into bookends, wall shelves, letter openers, and many other unique gifts for our parents or other family members. Together with the handmade cards, we wrapped our gifts with love for our special people. Sometimes our teachers helped us do embroidery or other needlework to make dishtowels, table runners, or other decorative pieces for our mothers. These were also wrapped with our own designed and handwritten gift tags or cards. Often we decorated plain paper to make special wrapping paper for these gifts. I guess you might say we were recycling long before that became the modern promotion.

The Christmas program was the big social event of the year. As students we helped pick out our Christmas play, our choice of songs, and our individual poems or other pieces to add to the program. Some of us were able to bring a bed sheet or two, which the teacher and the taller boys hung on a long wire stretched near the front of the classroom to make our stage. The nearest cloakroom became the costume room, and each prop was prepared by the teacher and students to bring out the theme of the play we were to present. Yes, there were parts to learn, but memory work was not unusual, so we just expected to learn our parts, sometime more eagerly and sometimes more reluctantly. But we wanted our parents and others who came to be impressed, so we did our best. Yes, again we were learning: stage presence, accepting responsibility, being creative, and sometimes inventiveness as we prepared for our big performance.

We could be stage decorators, costume makers, musicians, speakers, or whatever was needed. Would you call this being a "jack of all trades?" For some students this led to their later choice of career or hobby as an adult. A country schoolteacher had to be able to improvise and share his or her enthusiasm in many ways to deal with all ages within the same setting. Learning to think things through, determine likely outcomes, and build self-confidence in each student was a worthy goal for both student and teacher. All of this took place while learning the basic education to prepare for high school and college for most of these young people. Yes, many of these students went on to excel in adult careers in our modern world. As I think back over my 85 plus years, I can give much credit for my enjoyable life to those eight years spent in School District 22, Brookings County, South Dakota.

Grandpa's Tales
By Frances Carmody of Wessington, South Dakota
Born 1935

Here is my remembering "Sundays in the good ole days!"

My grandfather and my two uncles came for a visit, and we enjoyed a big feast of homemade food and sometimes pie and ice cream. After our meal, we gathered around Grandfather to listen to his stories of his past. He told such interesting stories we felt we were there.

My favorite was about when he came to South Dakota in a covered wagon with his father, four brothers, and one sister. His father was very ill and couldn't make the long, hard trip from Sedalia, Missouri to 30 miles from Fort Randall and the little town of Pickstown. They made land claims close together, so they could work together and help each other. They had to measure and mark each claim, build a house, and dig a well by hand. They also had to live on each claim a certain amount of months to prove up their claim.

After four years, my grandfather sold his claim and moved to near Armour, South Dakota. He broke his new sod with oxen. He said oxen worked good until they got ready to rest, and then you were done plowing for the day. He thought they were very funny, so he got horses as soon as he could afford some. He hauled his grain to market down at Fort Randall, where the soldiers were stationed. Grandfather drove 30 miles down, sold his grain, and bought supplies, and then went back with a load of wheat, which he got ground into flour, bran, and middlings, which he used on his farm. While around Fort Randall, he

Grandpa and Sons

335

learned to talk to the Lakota natives who were stationed around there. He taught us how to count in Dakota. It was fun to talk in another language.

In the fall, Grandfather hauled a hayrack load of watermelon, squash, pumpkins, and vegetables into Armour, which he sold. The townspeople were really happy to buy fresh produce. They always waited to get Fred Fersuson watermelons.

Grandfather told a funny story about the time he caught somebody out in the watermelon patch late at night. He loaded his shotgun with buckshot and went out firing in the air. They went running, jumping melons, and flying. Every time he told this story he laughed so hard he couldn't hardly talk. He didn't care if they took some watermelons, but they were going and breaking them and leaving them lay.

Memories of Madison's Theaters
By Nadine Mikel of Madison, South Dakota
Born 1934

Back in the '40s and '50s, our town of Madison, South Dakota had three theaters: the State Theater on the east side of the street on Main Street, the Lyric Theater on the west side of the street a block north of the State Theater, and the drive-in west of town. The State Theater was nicer than the Lyric, a little more expensive, and it showed the better movies. The Lyric had mostly westerns and kid shows. The drive-in was outside of town about a half of a mile on Highway 34.

My brother, Ron, and I, and sometimes the neighbor boy, Dennis, would go to a western quite often on Saturdays. One time I had an errand to run first, and I told them I would meet them at the front of the Lyric Theater. When I got there, they weren't there, so I waited a while and then decided to go in. I sat down and when my eyes adjusted to the dark, I looked around and discovered I was sitting next to Ron, of course!

We lived about six blocks east of Main Street and usually walked downtown. But one time Mom and Dad were going to go to a movie at the State Theater and took us down. When we got out of the movie and started home, we saw the car was still parked in back of the courthouse so we got in it. When we

saw the folks coming, we hid; two of us got between the seats and one laid down on the back seat. We got about a block away and Mom said, "I wonder if the kids are home yet?" We didn't say anything. About a half a block from home, we straightened up and said, "Thank you for the ride." The folks really got startled. They didn't say anything, and we were never punished for it. I don't know why they didn't realize we were there as Dennis was giggling most of the time.

When we were in high school one of the homecoming events was a free movie at the State Theater. So one year my sister, Evelyn, Ron, and I and a friend, Mable, went to the movie. It was "The Thing" and was really scary. Mable lived one and a half blocks away from us. So as the four of us walked home we walked fast and stayed close together. When we got to Mable's house, Evelyn and I waited for Ron as he escorted Mable to her door and ran back to us. We ran the rest of the way home. I'm glad it was only a movie.

Another time my sisters, Marie and Nina, Marie's friend, Diane, and I went out to the drive-in. It was a Bette Davis movie and very scary. Nina had a sore toe, and she and I were in the back seat, and I kept wiggling around and would bump her toe, making it even sorer. The movie held everybody's attention, and a few minutes before the show ended, and as a head rolled down the stairs, they stopped the show and ran across the screen something about "anybody wanting to leave, do it now." Not one car left the theater. I think everybody else was as engrossed as we were.

Now there is only one theater, and it is a short way out of town on Highway 34. What a change the town is. And what memories these are of the theaters.

Catching Slimy Critters and Climbing Doors
By Gail Torrence of Webster, South Dakota
Born 1940

In the 1940s and early 1950s, before television, video games, cell phones, and playing with the neighbors, the nearest being two miles away, my brothers, James, Mike, and Louie, and my sister, Kae, and I entertained ourselves with whatever we could think of on the farm where we grew up.

Mom didn't indulge us kids with toys since survival and necessities were more important. I was the oldest of the five of us. My three brothers were younger by one and a half, four, and nine years. My sister was ten years younger. We were rough and tumble kids and found our entertainment in the most unusual ways.

On our farm, located between Brentford and Conde, in northeastern South Dakota, we got our water from an artesian well. That meant, in those days, that after the well was dug it had to keep flowing or it would stop. So we had a cattle tank that the water would constantly trickle into and it overflowed into a 40 x 60 foot pond. The pond was about one foot deep and muddy. You couldn't see to the bottom of it. It smelled in the later summer and moss grew in spots. It was not something we played in, but we would race around the edge of it.

However, when we got really bored we would venture in it and collect salamanders or mud puppies out of it. I was never sure what the slimy little things were called. They were between three and four inches long, blackish-gray, and looked like lizards. In order to get them, we would have to wade in the pond. Our bare feet would sink into the smelly mud and since we couldn't see through the pond water, we had to paw around on the bottom of the pond for the slippery, slimy, wiggly things.

One time we took our bucket, the bottom full of them, down into the basement of the house. The house had a coal door on the outside and steps leading down into the basement. We took our salamanders down that way so Mom wouldn't see us. No harm though, as the basement was full of coal dust, cobwebs, ashes, and coal. The next day when we went to get them, they had all crawled out of the bucket somehow and we couldn't find them anywhere. There were a lot of places for them to hide down there, behind the furnace, under the coal, and in the dark nooks and crannies. We always hoped that they had crawled up the coal steps. Every once in a while, though, we would hear Mom squeal when she went down into the basement. She said she had been frightened by a lizard. We just looked at each other and smiled.

But probably the most entertaining thing James, Mike, and I did was shinny up the sides of the door between the kitchen and the living room. Kae and Louie were enough younger that their arms and legs weren't long enough to span the door. You have to visualize the doorjamb as being about a foot wide with no door hanging on it. This in itself was quite unusual. We were told that the house had originally been two claim shanties pushed together. Maybe that accounted for the size of the door.

To shinny up we would put our left hand and our bare left foot on one side and the right hand and bare foot on the other side of the door. Then we would "walk" up the doorjamb. There we were, hanging at the top of the door while the other kids could walk under. What fun! We would like to show this stunt off to Grandpa and anyone else who would come over. To this day, I know of very few people who could do that.

It was simple things like that that kept us entertained.

The Father's Day Flood
By Ed Buck of Flandreau, South Dakota
Born 1942

The first 18 years of my life were spent growing up on our family farm located 1 ¼ miles west of Egan, South Dakota on Highway 34. The Big Sioux River ran through our farm (SE ¼ 14-106-49) with approximately 40+ acres of pasture on the south side of the river and the remainder of the quarter on the north side of the river.

In addition to providing water for the cattle when they were in the pasture, the river provided both entertainment and recreation opportunities for our family. After the ice was gone off the river in the spring, it was time to go fishing in our favorite spots. In the summer, we would go swimming in the river and boat riding on the river. The fall season would provide hunting opportunities along the river. The fall was also the time to cut wood along the river for winter heat. In the winter months, the river provided opportunity for ice skating and sledding.

The river wasn't always kind and friendly all of the time, and an example of this was the Father's Day Flood of 1957. I had just completed my freshman year at Egan High

School in the spring of 1957. I don't recall the exact time of day that it started raining on the Sunday of the Father's Day flood, but I do remember that it rained very hard during the afternoon and into the evening. My dad had been taking a nap on the living room floor Sunday afternoon. I went in and woke him, and suggested that we go down to the river (between 300 to 400 yards) and open the gate that led from the pasture to a lane that led up to the barn so the cattle could get out of the pasture and up to the barn and be safe in the event that the river could flood in the continuing heavy rain. My dad didn't think this was necessary. My horse, Flica, was tied up in the barn and I can remember thinking that if the heavy rain continued and the river flooded and got to the barn I didn't want my horse to drown because she was tied up, so I went to the barn and untied her. It continued to rain very hard, so I went down to the river by myself and opened the gate from the pasture to the lane that led up to the barn.

Our farm is in a valley with hills to both the north and south. As evening approached, we could hear the water running out of the hills and it was likened to a low roar. About midnight our telephone rang and it was a member of the Egan Fire Department informing us that the river was indeed flooding and they were coming out to get us because of the danger from the flood. Our driveway from the highway was already under two to three feet of water. The firemen who came to get us tied themselves together with a long rope when they walked up the driveway so they wouldn't be swept away by the water that was rushing over the driveway.

When the firemen reached our yard, we hooked a wagon to our M Farmall. My dad had a severe vision problem, so I was the tractor driver with my dad, mom, and younger brother and sister riding in the wagon pulled behind the tractor with the firemen leading the way down the water covered driveway. To say that I was very scared being in the tractor's driver seat following the firemen up the driveway would be a vast understatement! When we got out of the driveway and onto the highway, it was on to Egan to spend the night with our friends, the Francis Delay family.

About mid-morning the next day, the water had receded to the point that we were able to go back out to the farm and assess our damages. We found that a lot of both our crops and fences were gone. We also found every single head of our cattle that had been in the pasture standing safely beside our barn after escaping the roaring river through "The Open Gate."

I would explain that our farm site sits on a little rise and during this flood and all other high water events during the lifetime of our farmstead, water has never got into the farm buildings, as during the high water events the water flows around the building site instead of through the building site.

Our family was fortunate, as we didn't get harmed from the flood and all of our livestock survived the Father's Day Flood of 1957. Others were not so fortunate, as the flood caused loss of life of some young men from the community and there were many head of livestock lost up and down the river.

The events of the Father's Day Flood of 1957 happened just a couple of months short of 57 years ago, but they still remain firmly fixed in my mind.

Good Water and Fresh Food
By Dorothy Goodspeed O'Neill of Portland, Oregon
Born 1917

I was born December 28, 1917 at my parents' farm. The roads to Ipswich were blocked from a heavy snowstorm. The doctor was driven 18 miles by horse and sleigh to our farmhouse. In those days, there were no snowplows to clear the roads.

I went to a one-room country school with one teacher for all eight grades. There

Dorothy in 1918
On the farm

338

Dorothy in 1922

were twenty kids. Classes were Monday through Friday from 9:00 a.m. to 4:00 p.m. I think back of how hard it must have been for one teacher with all grades and how we all managed to study and learn our lessons in one room. We lived about a mile from the school. If the weather was bad, my dad took me on his horse. I never wanted to miss even one day of school.

My parents had a large farm with a lot of livestock: cows, horses, sheep, pigs, chicken, ducks, and geese. I liked to work outside. After school, I had chores to do. I would feed the chickens, gather the eggs, and help milk the cows. I was in 4-H Club and had my own chickens. My dad built a shed for them.

I went to high school in Mina, which was five miles from our farm. It was a three-year school. I was thirteen years old when I started. Back then, I was allowed to drive the car to school. You did not have to have a driver's license. Mina now has a beautiful lake. I recently read that it is one of the nicest lakes in South Dakota. The lake was funded by the Roosevelt Administration.

I believe it was in 1933 that we had a very bad year. It was hot and windy with dust storms. There was no moisture, and we had no crops. It was so dusty in the daytime that we had to light our lamps in order to see. There was no electricity in those days. We were thankful to have kerosene lanterns.

The summer before my senior year in high school, I went to a picnic where I met a nice,

handsome young man. A short time later, he and a couple of his friends came to see me. He asked if he could have a date sometime. Of course, the answer was yes. That was the beginning. Jim and I went to Ipswich High School for our senior year. We did break up a couple of times since I had a previous boyfriend who was still interested in me, but I was faithful to Jim.

Money was scarce in those years so we could not go to college, so we decided to get married. It was 1937; we married and decided to come to Oregon. Jim and I and our best friend drove to Oregon. What an adventure!

Jim and I went back to Ipswich every fall for many years to visit our relatives. He also loved pheasant hunting. We drove at first with our three boys and later were glad we could fly to and from South Dakota. I lost my husband, Jim, in 1999 after 63 wonderful years. He has been missed very much.

A couple of weeks ago I went to my dentist. While walking up some steps (I was

Dorothy Goodspeed O'Neill in 1935

going a little slow) I said to the young man beside me, "I can't walk so fast anymore; I am 96 years old." He stopped and said, "You are 96 and you have your teeth and you can walk!" "Yes," I said, "and it's because I grew up on a farm in South Dakota. We had good water and lots of good, fresh food!"

I have been receiving *The Ipswich Tribune* every week since 1942. I feel like I am still a part of South Dakota. By reading this, I can keep up with friends and family that I knew while growing up.

Mother Left Us Music
By Evelyn Paulson of De Smet, South Dakota
Born 1926

My dad, Ephriam J. Lee was from a family of ten children. He had eight brothers and one sister. They lived on a farm just north of Oldham, South Dakota, located by the railroad tracks. His father, my Grandpa, Halvor A. Lee, came from Norway when he was twelve years old. After he married, he and Grandma lived in a sod house. As soon as he was able, he built a nice wood frame house that is still in the family today. My grandma would tell us of how Grandpa fed all the bums who jumped off the train. She was sure that they had their place marked. When their boys got a little older, my grandparents started a dairy and delivered milk to people in Oldham.

In 1918, dad's oldest brother enlisted in the Army to serve in the First World War. My dad wanted to enlist also but they wouldn't take him as he was only 17 years old. About this time, he and another older brother decided to go to Montana, where if they stayed for seven years on the land they would then own it. They moved the cattle to Aberdeen, where they loaded two immigrant cars and rode with the cattle on the rail to Winnett, Montana.

Dad met my mother, Olive D. Bridger, a girl from England, who worked in a bank in Lewistown, Montana. In 1923, they got married and had a very nice wedding.

My oldest brother and sister were born on the ranch there. My dad tells of riding his best saddle horse to death when he had to try to reach a medical doctor 23 miles away when my sister was being born.

In the summer of 1926 after he proved up his land, they moved back to South Dakota. I was born in September on a farm that my grandfather owned. It was by Lake Henry in Kingsbury County. I believed that we only lived there little more than a year when we moved to a rental farm between Oldham and Ramona closer to my grandfather's home. My sister, Betty, was born there in 1928. A set of twin girls were born in 1930. One of the girls lived only a few days and the other was crippled from cerebral palsy. Another set of twins were born in 1933. They were healthy, but it was very difficult for people to make a living now, as we were in the Great Depression. No rain to speak of, dust storms prevailed, and the grasshoppers moved in and could eat a crop to the ground overnight.

After seven years at that place, we moved to another farm that Grandpa built on the banks of Lake Henry. It seems that in those years that many, many farmers were renters. Each year on March 1st it would be moving time. Our move this time in 1934 would take us to a farm place just a mile west and one-half south from De Smet, still in Kingsbury County. I remember that my mother was so thrilled with a house large enough to accommodate her family and very nice varnished woodwork all through the house. The land wasn't as fertile in this location and with terrible heat, no rain, and the creeping jenny weed and thistles to deal with it was hard to have food for both livestock and the family. I remember having many meals over and over of corn, potatoes, and eggs. These were things that we could raise along with having some milk cows so we had plenty of milk and made our butter. With no way of refrigeration we hung or milk and cream down in a cistern to keep it from turning sour.

In the fall if there was a little extra money my dad would buy a battery pack for an old radio, and we would have that to listen to during the winter until the battery went dead. My parents liked *Amos and Andy* and we kids liked western music.

Two more babies were born to our family in 1936 and in 1937 my mother died in childbirth and the two babies did not survive. She was 37 years old. This left my dad with seven children with one being crippled. Relatives and friends wanted to take some of the children to raise, but my dad just couldn't do it so we all stayed together. My older sister just turned twelve and I was almost eleven. We had charge of the house and family while my dad worked with the animals and crops at making a living. In the wintertime he worked with the WPA, a program that was started under Roosevelt's Administration. We were in the country and didn't even realize how much we didn't have.

We made our own fun and there were enough of us to play games and cards when we did have time. When my older brother was about fourteen he had made and saved $10.00 and bought a chrome bicycle from a friend. We were all so thrilled. Another time we were pushing an empty four wheeled hay wagon down our long driveway and it got going too fast and one sister fell under one of the wheels and got hurt.

Another thing that we did have were musical instruments that my dad purchased for us after my mother died. I am sure that he had to borrow the money. This was a wish of hers because she loved music and had played piano growing up. Of course, during those times we couldn't afford a piano, but I remember as a very small child that she would mark the piano keys off on the oilcloth that was on the kitchen table and teach us the proper fingering. We all grew up playing an instrument or two, and music became a part of our family then and continued through the generations.

My dad remarried in 1943 and he and my stepmother had two more sons to add to the family, making a total of twelve children for my dad.

My Family was Richly Blessed
By Phyllis DeJong of Hitchcock, South Dakota
Born 1923

I, Phyllis DeJong, was born November 6, 1923 on a farm in Eldorado Township, Buffalo County, South Dakota, near the town of Gann Valley, the youngest daughter of Frank and Mae Marshall Henrichsen. Dr. Tandy, a doctor back from World War I, delivered me. He did not get his 25 cents for registering my birth, as my mother found out several years later.

I, too, found this out after they required passports for travel. I have made several trips into Canada without a passport, but I wanted to take a trip with my son, Gary, his wife, Vivian, and my daughter, Vivian, but I needed a passport. They wouldn't accept the birth certificate from the state because of the late date. They wouldn't accept my older sister's word or my grade school report cards. They finally did give me a temporary passport for one trip. I wanted to go again but stayed home, as I did not want the hassle. My grandson, Jon, wanted to know if I'm not a citizen, were they going to export me. It has been quite a conversation piece for a woman who is 90 and has lived her life in or near the same community for all those years. We chuckle now that "Grandma isn't a citizen of anywhere."

I have many memories of my childhood, but as I grew up during the Dirty Thirties, I will write about things I remember from those years. We had a lot of dust storms. Mom would have us put wet towels on the windowsills to help keep the dust out. She would put wet sheets on the screen doors.

The grasshoppers were so bad the posts would be covered on the shady part. As the sun moved, the grasshoppers would move, staying in the shade.

We had a very good well. Neighbors who just had an artesian well would haul drinking and wash water in barrels from our well. The land sloped just south of the well, so Mom made her garden there. She had a pipe from the bottom of the tank into a ditch that ran across the top of the garden, then as she wanted to water, she had small ditches down the slope beside the rows and she'd let the water run down them. Of course, the garden was a sight, with every kind of old rag, as the plants were covered to keep grasshoppers off. She lost a lot of produce, but managed to salvage enough to eat and vegetables to can.

My dad lived in the same area when he was a kid, and he always told of picking cow chips to burn for fuel. A neighbor girl who was later his teacher always accused him of stealing her pile of chips. I heard this discussion between them every time we were together.

We lived near the Sioux Indian Reservation, and we had Native Americans who would come in their wagons to trade plums, chokecherries, and wood. We had cattle, hogs, sheep, chickens, and turkeys. They especially liked the poultry. Mom had a chokecherry pitter, so she could can sauce as well as jam and jelly. She canned a lot of meat, too.

I remember after I was married, my sister and I, along with several others, were setting in the courthouse visiting and the conversation about the Dirty Thirties came up. Some told about how hungry they were. One fellow claimed that he, as a kid, picked sheep showers. They were very small sour plants that grew in the gumbo soil and you could cook them as greens. I liked them raw, but I couldn't imagine a family ever picking enough to fill them up. Another lady said she couldn't eat pumpkin because they were so poor and the owner of the grocery store had a bunch of pumpkins at the end of the season. He sold her all of them for 25 cents and she canned them. That winter they practically lived on that pumpkin, and that made her sick of it. My sister and I decided we were very lucky that our mother canned a lot of meat and vegetables.

My husband, Richard DeJong's cousin, Harry, was going to get married in Chamberlain, South Dakota and his wife said the grasshoppers ate a hole in her slip she had washed and put on the line to dry before they left. Then on the way to Chamberlain, they ran into dust blowing across the road. It killed the motor on the car. Harry and his brother had to push the car through the dust. Their white shirts were black from dust and sweat. Later, there was dust blowing across the road when we were going to Miller and the same thing happened to us.

When I was in Pierre, South Dakota and my cousin's boyfriend took us for a ride up in the hills, it was so dry there were big cracks in the road. One of the tires on the car fell into a crack and we were stuck, so we had to jack the car up, push it over so the tire wouldn't fall back into the crack. Tires were narrower then than those we have now.

Tires reminded me of my cousin taking us to Grey Goose to a dance. Coming home, we had three flat tires. Back then, you had to jack up the car, take off the wheel and take the tire apart, find the hole in the tube, scratch it so it was rough, and put glue and a patch over it. Then you had to put it all back together, pump air into it, and put it back on the car.

I worked cleaning houses for two dollars a week. When I received three dollars, I felt so lucky. I also worked at the hotel. I cleaned, waited tables, cooked, made beds, and emptied chamber pots, and I got $3.00.

We did not have running water or electricity, but we did have a telephone. During the Depression, neighbors gave up their phones and the poles blew down. There were phone wires lying in the pastures around the country.

We rode horseback to school 3 ¼ miles. My mother thought I needed warmer clothes so she sent for some long legged underwear, and you could see it under my long stockings. I cried. I did not want to wear them. On the way to school, we got off the horse under an old bridge, and my sister, Irene, cut the legs off with her school scissors. I did not have to wear them. Mom sent the other back.

We were poor, but we always had plenty to eat. Through my eyes, I believe my family was richly blessed.

We Grew Up in a Good Era
By Claraa Waldman of Aberdeen, South Dakota
Born 1928

My father, Philip Steppler, emigrated from Russia with his parents in 1888 at age 12. They lived in Colorado and Kansas and settled in North Dakota. He worked in the railroad and as a young adult ended up in South Dakota. My mother, Katherine Binfet emigrated from Russia with her parents in 1894 at age six. I don't know how they met, but they got married in 1912 in South Dakota and moved to Devils Lake, North Dakota. My mother was so homesick and cried a lot. So her three brothers arranged for them to move back to Onaka, South Dakota on a small farm. A son and seven girls were born to their union. I am the youngest of the seven girls.

The first house that I remember that we lived in had one square upstairs bedroom. Each of the four corners had a bed. My brother slept in one, and the rest of us slept two or three in one bed.

We had chamber pots to use for nighttime. Otherwise, it was the outhouse. There was no toilet paper so we used the sheets in the Sears and Montgomery catalogs. In the fall when the peaches came in for canning, they were wrapped in nice pink tissue paper and sure

Senior class of 1945 Onaka High School

worked good in the toilet! It was spooky to go to the outhouse at night and very cold in the winter. Each spring a new hole was dug by hand, and the outhouse was moved there.

Later we moved to another location and had a bigger home. We had a large family but were never hungry, as we had all our own food: beef, hogs, chickens, milk, cream, and eggs. My mother had a big garden each year.

We had no electricity, running water, radio, or telephone. When the wind didn't blow to pump water, we had to pump by hand for house use.

I was the youngest of three girls, so I always got the first bath in the washtub half-full of cold water!

We had no furnace so had space heaters and cook stove downstairs but no heat in the upstairs bedrooms. We would pull our clothes under the covers to warm them up so we could get dressed.

My brother was drafted during World War II so we had to shock the grain in the summer months. We didn't have much cropland in those days. Also in order to get our crop threshed someone had to work the threshing rig. So I hauled bundles, loaded them with a pitchfork and a horse-drawn wagon, and loaded them off into the threshing machine. My sister and I did that for six weeks. I was 15 years old.

During World War II, coffee and sugar were rationed, and we got only a few stamps a month. My older sisters walked to town, five miles, on a Saturday. Gas and tires were hard to get, but they always found a friend to bring them home in time for chores. Our parents became citizens in 1945 for fear of being deported.

In 1940, a baby brother joined our family. I was almost 12 years old and didn't know my mother was pregnant. We enjoyed him and spoiled him!

Those days we ordered from the catalogs. I was so hard on shoes, so my mother sent them back to Sears Roebuck and my sisters had to write for her, telling them that the shoes didn't last long enough for the money she paid for them, fifty cents. So I always got a new pair for free! Our address was Onaka, South Dakota all those years. We had enough businesses to be able to get all the supplies we needed.

We got to go to a movie once in a while on Saturday night. It was 25 cents. If the movie film didn't come in the mail, we roller-skated.

We appreciated what little we had, and we realized we grew up in a good era, comparing the lifestyle of our grandkids and great-grandkids!

Mr. and Mrs. Waldman in 1949

343

Party Lines to Cell Phones
By Lewayne M. Erickson of Brookings,
South Dakota
Born 1938

As a young boy in the 1940s and 1950s living on a farm in Miner County in eastern South Dakota, I remember the existence of one lone black rotary dial telephone in our home. In those days, as far as I knew, all telephones were on party lines; that is, a telephone line that was shared with six to eight of our neighbors. All of our neighbors also had only one telephone in their homes except the telephone of some of our neighbors were affixed to the wall, and they had to talk into a cone-shaped receiver while they listened over a similarly shaped device next to their ear. I believe all of the neighbors sharing the party line also owned the line. Our number was 416 but I do not remember the number of any neighbors. When the telephone rang, it rang in all of the homes on the party line. The ring for our telephone was one long while some were two longs or two shorts and one long and so forth. If we wanted to talk to a person via telephone not on our party line, we had to dial O to call the operator to make a long distance call.

Even though a telephone call may have been for somebody in my family, it was common practice for neighbors to "rubber" or listen in on telephone calls to our house, and I know that it was not unusual for somebody in our house to "rubber" or listen to telephone calls to our neighbors. Some neighbors reportedly listened in on every telephone conversation; and some seemed to dominate the party line, which deterred the use of the telephone by others. Most neighbors were considerate of others and would relinquish the use of the line for somebody with a presumed emergency or other urgency. I remember however the time my dad lost his patience and told a couple of people engaged in a long conversation to "get off the phone as I need to call the vet (veterinarian)."

In the summer of 1959, I attended six weeks of Army ROTC summer camp in Fort Riley, Kansas. There were only six weeks remaining between ROTC camp and the beginning of the fall term of college. I had been dating Nancy Tobin for several months and we planned to get married on December 30 that year. Nancy's parents formed Citizens Telephone Company in 1948 and acquired the telephone rights to provide telephone service to Plankinton, South Dakota and the surrounding farm area. Over the years of their ownership, there were several party lines and calls had to be placed through an operator. Sometimes the operator was Nancy during her teenage years. In 1957, the telephone system in the Plankinton area was totally converted to dial telephones, but there were frequent problems with the overhead wires, especially following ice storms and related weather problems.

Due to these problems, in the summer of 1959 all overhead bare telephone wires were being replaced with overhead telephone cable. Apparently, since I was marrying their daughter in a few months and needed the income, I worked for the telephone company the remaining weeks of the summer of 1959. I learned how to put on the "climbers," which were hooks strapped to my boots, and how to ascend wooden telephone poles, "belt in," and perform the work that needed to be done at the top, and then descend the poles safely. Actually, it was interesting work. We switched the lines from the bare wires to the cable wires, which contained a number of very small lines separated by a thin paper coating inside the cable. I carried a test phone and after switching lines over, called into the office to test and insure the connection was made properly. Test phones were very magnetic and at the end of summer, my wristwatch gained 15 to 20 minutes every 24 hours.

On the very last day of the summer, I made the last scheduled switch over, called in on the test phone, released my belt to begin the climb back down to the ground, and promptly hit the ground in one-step. That incident was called "burning the pole," and I had just experienced the only fall I had all summer. I realized I was falling so I apparently automatically pushed myself away from the pole to avoid what could be brutal slivers and, as a result, tore the skin off of two fingers of my left hand. I immediately pulled a handkerchief out of my pocket and wrapped it around my bleeding fingers, and then I climbed up the very same pole, belted in, released my belt, and climbed down the way I had intended to all the time. I thought that if I did not do that right away I would be too scared to climb a pole again if it ever became necessary. Thankfully, I never had to climb another telephone pole.

Nancy and I did get married on December 30, 1959 but unfortunately her mother died on December 15, 1966 and her father died one week short of a year later. Before my father-in-law passed away, however, in the six years prior to his passing, he had converted the entire telephone system from overhead cable to underground cable, further eliminating problems caused by weather and other natural causes.

Many times I have thought about my late father-in-law with his knowledge of electronics and the workings of a telephone system, and how I wonder and think he would react to the almost unbelievable and extraordinary advancement of telephone usage from party lines to cell phones; cell phones that we can use to converse with persons almost any place in the world; cell phones that we can put on "speaker" and not even hold in our hand; cell phones that can send and receive text messages, photographs and videos worldwide; cell phones upon which we may watch movies or current events; and cell phones which, on a daily or more often basis, invade the privacy of our lives.

In my lifetime, the use of a telephone has emerged from a single rotary-dial telephone attached to a party line at home to a cell phone, smaller than a deck of cards that I can carry with me in the palm of my hand or in a shirt or pants pocket, and use almost any place in the world.

Homemade Root Beer and Saturday Trips to Town

By Gracene E. Petersen of Aberdeen, South Dakota
Born 1923

I am 90 years old now and recall very little until I started school. We three sisters and three brothers walked two miles to school every day until it got too cold. Then Dad drove us in the very first car that we had. It was a 1911 Buick with some kind of material for the body. The windows were isinglass. On the right side running board was a sedaline tank that was attached to the headlights. The headlights were lit with a match and did not give off much light. The only time we went out at night that I remember was to go to the Christmas program and our school program. I will never forget a school Christmas program. The teacher asked me to learn a reading instead of a poem. I have always liked poetry, but I learned the reading. The night of the program, I went out on the stage, stood there, and my mind went blank. So I looked down and said, "I guess I don't know it," and left the stage. How embarrassing that was!

When spring came, Mom would put eggs in a couple of incubators to hatch chicks. It was so much fun to hear the first peeps after weeks of waiting.

Summers were hot and dry. Some days the wind blew the dust so hard it blocked out the sun. The wind blew thistles into the fences, so Dad and the boys had to pull them out to burn them. That left mounds of dirt. There was always dust in the house.

One of the most difficult times was not having running water. We had to carry it for everything from the well.

Dad used horses to plow the fields to plant wheat, corn, and oats. When fall came, he took a binder that made bales and cut the oats and wheat. Then we kids put the bales in stacks to keep the bales off the ground to dry. That was such a hot job. Dad and his three brothers owned a big threshing machine. So they helped each other. When they did ours, Mom always had a big meal for them. I still can't see how she did it on that stove, and the kitchen was so hot. The chickens had a feast too when the men brought their hayracks in the yard, because the bottoms were full of crickets and grasshoppers.

In winters we took baths beside the cook stove in a galvanized washtub. First we three girls bathed, and then Mom put more hot water in for the three boys. Mom washed all our clothes with a scrub board in a big tub. The first washing machine was one that had a handle you had to pull back and forth. Even in the winter she always hung the clothes outside on the clothesline. They were always so frozen when she brought them in and put them on the clothes rack to dry. They always smelled so fresh.

One summer when we were older Dad made a shower out of a large barrel. It was near the well. So every morning he filled it so that the sun heated it. A tarp was put around it, and a shower really felt good after a hot day.

Crops were scarce. Corn liked hot weather, so usually there was enough to feed the pigs and for seed to plant the next spring. Dad had nailed headless nails on the granary wall. He'd pick out the best ear and push the end of the cob on the nail. When spring came, the corn was shelled and ready to plant.

Grasshoppers and flies were plentiful. One summer Dad took a wagon, put a top on it, and loaded a bunch of chickens and took them out to a wheat field. It was hard loading them in the morning and catching them at night.

Flies were so hard on the cattle. I remember we three girls took dishtowels and chased the flies from room to room out the kitchen door.

Every farm had a little outhouse in the backyard. Ours had two holes with a box in the

Doris, Grace, and Gracene

middle for the *Sears Catalog*. It was really a treat when Mom bought a crate of peaches. She canned the peaches, and we smoothed out the wrappers and used them. It was so cold in the winter to run out there. Summers it was so hot and the flied and spiders were terrible.

A birthday gift was a new dress made by Mom. I remember our aunt took my twin sister and me to a Shirley Temple movie when we were twelve, and she thought she could get us in for ten cents, but the ticket taker asked how old we were and she had to pay 25 cents each. The only Christmas gifts I remember was a doll, a flat iron, and also a cupboard my dad made, which I still have.

Grandma had the first radio. We used to walk across the field and listen with her. She liked to listen to George B. German. Years later we got one and liked *The Hit Parade*. We did have a phonograph. The records were ¼ inch thick and so scratchy.

Grandma could not see very well, so we three girls helped her a lot. She paid us each time a quarter. The three boys caught gophers, and she gave them a penny a tail. That's the way we made our spending money.

We never went hungry those years. We always had milk, cream to churn into butter, chicken, eggs, and potatoes. Dad butchered in the fall. Mom canned the meat. She made the best sweet and sour pork and rendered the lard for baking and making soap. Ice cream was always a treat, especially taking turns licking the dasher.

Every winter Dad and his brothers would take the horses and wagon to the lake east of our farm and bring a load of ice. Grandma had an icehouse but Dad had dug a deep hole and put the ice in it. He covered it with straw and put some planks on top. We would have ice until the 4th of July.

Every few months, the Watkins man would stop at our farm. Mom would order spices, yeast, and root beer extract. She would make root beer and bottle it. Dad would use the yeast to make beer. He bottled it and capped it. The root beer and beer were put on a shelf in the basement. I remember our pastor was visiting and a bottle of beer exploded, and we kids looked at each other and laughed.

Saturday night was always a big deal for us. We got to go to town. Britton was about four miles west of our farm. The folks always took a crate of eggs and a large can of cream to buy groceries. We kids took our pennies or nickels to buy an ice cream cone or candy.

Church was very important. I never did understand why Mom and we three girls sat in the pew on the left side and Dad and the three boys sat on the right side.

Also during those early years I don't remember ever seeing an overweight child or person, which are so numerous today because of the lifestyle today that leads to so many health problems. The world is changing so fast, and I think too much focus is put on looking for the "road to riches."

A Rural Utopia
By Sharon Cole of Gillette, Wyoming
Born 1944

Growing up on a farm in rural central South Dakota during the later 1940s and the 1950s was pretty close to heaven as I look back. Facebook and e-mail often show pictures of appliance, ideas, and attitudes of those nostalgic bygone decades, bringing to mind a life that was peaceful and carefree during my youth. My mom, Marian Thomas Lehmkuhl, married my stepdad, Elmer Lehmkuhl, when I was about two years old. Dad had just returned from his service in World War II where he was injured at the Battle of the Bulge.

Dad purchased a farm south of Onida, South Dakota in Lincoln Township where the three of us began to make our home. I remember the farmhouse having tarpaper siding, no lights, no running water, and no indoor bathrooms. The house was really unattractive before many changes took place, but to us it was home. I also remember the kerosene lamps we used until we got rural electric power. Soon I had a baby sister, then a brother, and another sister; three babies three years in a row! I was nine when my baby brother arrived, the last member to make our family of seven complete.

Living on the farm with my two brothers and two sisters was a great life. Mom would always make Christmas special by crocheting or sewing clothes for the girls' new dolls. She would also make pajamas for all of us as part of our Christmas. We three girls had the two upstairs bedrooms; there was a round hole in the floor of the one bedroom where a stovepipe had been when we first had coal-burning heat. After floor furnaces were installed, the hole remained to allow heat to escape upstairs. Well, we especially enjoyed that at Christmastime as we could peak down to see what Santa was leaving us (but never succeeded in seeing him!).

Other entertainment we enjoyed during our younger years included riding our bikes up and down the gravel road between the school one mile north and our neighbors one mile south. We girls also loved to play with our toy dish sets, making mud pies to serve to our brothers. I also loved to play with paper dolls, often designing clothes for them or using hollyhock flowers as their skirts. As I grew to a teenager, I became a sun worshipper, spending many hours by our propane tank to lie in the blazing sun on summer days. Can you believe I even used a concoction of baby oil and iodine for my tanning lotion! Saturday evenings we would often go to town as a family to watch a show at the Onida Theater. Roy Rogers and Gene Autry were my heroes when I was a kid. Another town event that I enjoyed was roller-skating, which I usually did every Sunday evening at the Onida Auditorium.

With five children, Mom and Dad established a chore routine for all of us. When we still had the old wringer washing machine, we girls would help Mom sort the laundry, wash it, and get it on the clothesline before we left for school. On Saturdays, we cleaned the house, dividing it into three sections and rotating the three areas each week. During harvest, we had to help Dad outside, so my job was to milk the cows. We only had two so it never seemed much of a chore.

Sundays were always a family time, attending church followed by gathering at one of our cousin's homes or ours for a big dinner and then playing cards. Canasta or pinochle was the standard fare. As I grew older and would go to dances on Saturday nights, I would be up later, but it never mattered to Mom and Dad. We always had to be in church on Sunday mornings!

In the summertime, we had many picnics at the park in Pierre with cousins also, and we especially looked forward to swimming in the Pierre Municipal Pool. Birthdays were always a big event in our family, so that was always a reason for a family gathering. Several family members' birthdays, including mine and my baby brother's, were in August, so I enjoyed wonderful birthday celebrations as I was growing up.

Now to back up to the year I started school. There was no kindergarten so I began first grade in September 1950 at North Lincoln School. The school was only one mile north of our farm so in nice weather I would walk, carrying my little tin lunch pail and listening to the meadowlarks sing. I was the only one in my grade for all eight years, eventually becoming the teacher's helper as I advanced in grades. I had taught my younger sister to read before she started school, so even at this early age my future career was already decided

– a language arts teacher. There are many favorite events that I remember participating in during my elementary school days: pie social, box socials, "Blaine Days," which was our field day at another larger elementary school, spelling bees, and Declamation Days, the forerunner of speech competition. We participated in everything from flannel boards as first graders to reading poetry to dramatic/humorous pieces as we grew older.

Weather events are fresh in my memory, as they always seem to cause extra problems to rural living. An event that I clearly remember occurred during a blizzard in 1956. Our mom and dad had gone to be with our grandma in Huron, South Dakota, as she was very ill with pneumonia. My teacher heard on the radio that the winter storm was going to get extremely bad, so she closed school and sent us walking home in the snowstorm. I was staying at George and Josephine Fanger's who lived just a mile south of us, so Earl, their son, who was slightly older than me, and I started walking. Reports soon were out on the radio that Earl Fanger and Sharon Lehmkuhl were lost in the blizzard. I don't remember the details, but George eventually picked us up on his tractor.

Another weather-related even that I remember involved Mom. She would contract pneumonia quite often. One spring she was feeling extremely sick and the only way she could get to the hospital was for Dad to take her in the back of a wagon pulled by a tractor so he could cross a flood-swollen creek to meet the ambulance on the other side. The snow we received that winter had washed out many of the rural roads and bridges.

Dad continued to lovingly and painstakingly remodel and modernize our farm. The biggest renovation was when he added on a huge living room, and our former living room became a dining room. I remember watching our first black and white television in the new living room. Our favorite show, of course, was *The Ed Sullivan Show*, and once Elvis appeared on there he became my "first love." I collected all of his 45s, bought teen fan magazines containing his pictures, and made an Elvis scrapbook.

Our farm now belongs to a huge wheat growing operation. Mom sold the farm in the mid-1980s after Dad died in 1978. We often drive by it when we get back to central South Dakota. It is wonderful and refreshing to see

that the farming tradition has remained, but I can still picture our farmhouse, as it was when we were living the good old days back in the '40s and '50s.

Raising Big Gardens and Fowl
By Alice M. (Stegeman) Mentzel of Huron, South Dakota
Born 1939

Gardens
It began in the spring of 1922 after my parents, Arthur and Mahela Stegeman, were married on February 22, 1922 northeast of Wolsey, South Dakota. There were no greenhouses in those days where one could buy their plants. My mother sowed tomato seeds in a wooden box in March, placed in front of a window. After they grew some inches in height, they were transplanted into a "hot bed" in the garden, which was a plot with wooden sides the size of a glass storm window, 30 x 66 inches. The window would be placed over the plants at night until the danger of frost was past, well into May. Then the plants were set out in the garden, usually near a hundred. After tomatoes ripened in late July, they were canned, either whole or made into juice to drink, mostly in two-quart size

Canned goods in 1955

348

Alice's parents, Mahela and Arthur Stegeman in 1922

jars. No one bought fruit juices in stores. Were they even available back then?

A garden consisted of all the usual vegetables as well as some uncommon ones. We had huckleberries and ground cherries that made the best pies. The ground cherries were husked after they ripened in the fall and were also canned for use as sauce.

Pickles were made from string beans, beets, and cucumbers – sweet, bread 'n butter, dill. Dill clusters grew plentifully in most gardens.

We had a strawberry bed and raspberry patch at times, as well as eggplants, Swiss chard, citron, and other not-too-common things. And there was always rhubarb, too. Everything was canned and filled an entire wall in our basement in rows of shelves.

Potatoes were planted, usually the custom on Good Friday afternoon unless there was still snow on the ground. In the fall we borrowed a "digger" from the only neighbor who had one, and my, what a delightful sight – to see all those big potatoes which would fill a good-size bin in the basement. They would begin to grow sprouts in late winter which then had to be picked off at least several times before the potatoes were used up. And some were saved for seed the following spring to be planted.

In the fall, we had squash to harvest, mostly the large Hubbard variety that kept well through the winter. We also had pumpkins, melons, large heads of cabbage (made into sauerkraut), and carrots to be dug and stored in a large crock filled with sand to store over the winter.

Think of all the hoeing that had to be done throughout the summer. There were no tillers like we have now. And the watering was done from an artesian well, not with hoses but with galvanized pipes.

I must say that women took care not to let their arms become tanned from the sun. After the cotton long stockings they wore would become worn out in the foot part, it was cut off and the leg part would be pinned onto the shoulder of one's dress. It was a disgrace to have browned arms and legs. A wide-brimmed straw hat was always worn to shade the face.

After cold weather had set in, there was the task of butchering a beef and one or two hogs. All this was cut up and taken care of at home, until in later years when locker plants became available. Most of the meat was canned; hams and bacon was smoked in a small outdoor building, fed by corncobs in a cauldron that had a pipe going into the building. Rings of smoked sausage and liver sausage were made. That liver sausage, fried and served for breakfast with pancakes or cornbread, was oh so good.

Lard was rendered from the fat cut off the pork meat and no better piecrust could be made. I still bake with it and have never made a piecrust with Crisco! Soap was also made from the tallow, using lye and borax, set in a large porcelain dishpan to firm, and then cut into chunks. It was used to wash clothes and what a delightful odor that had!

Saturdays

Saturdays were baking days. This was the day when bread, cookies, a cake, a pie or two, and sometimes cinnamon rolls or doughnuts, either fried or baked, were made. Then later in the afternoon, my mother began house

349

cleaning. She often ended up scrubbing the floors at 11:00 at night. My father and my brother who was born in 1924 sometimes went into Wolsey and visited with other neighbors and maybe played a game of pool. My mother never went along as some women did. Most women also helped hand-milk the cows and after separating the cream from the milk had the morning chore of washing the separator machine.

Company

Seldom was there a Sunday when we were without company or went visiting. People did not call to say that they were coming; they just came. If it was in the afternoon and those folks had no evening chores, you would keep them for supper. You had plenty of canned meats, vegetables, and sauce to serve and usually left-over "jacket" potatoes (cooked with skins on for dinner) you could fry, and of course, plenty of baked things.

The "front room" (living room) as it was then called, was not used except for company so was not heated in wintertime. The door was kept closed and children were not allowed to play in it. We had a small kerosene heater in our room, and my mother would light it well before I came home from country school so I could practice my piano lessons, but it was still pretty cold on my fingers.

Fowls

My mother had ducks, geese, and turkeys, as well as chickens and would set those eggs under clucks (broody hens). When grown by fall, she'd butcher and sell those, all to help earn some money to recover from the Dirty Thirties' Depression Days. My parents had lost their farm in 1936 and lived in Wolsey for one year with my grandparents until the spring of 1937 when they rented another farm southwest of town. That farm appealed to my mother most because it had running water into the house and into the two chicken houses. Oh, how I enjoyed looking for and bringing in those eggs that the fowls had laid around the farm, sometimes on top of the straw stack. After the goslings hatched, they would follow me around the farmyard as if I was their mother. Even now when I see them for sale in farm stores, they warm my heart and I sometimes pick up one to hold.

Town Trips

Fridays were always town days when we'd go to Huron. We took along pints and quarts of cream to deliver to regular customers and also eggs. My father usually went to the lumberyard, the hardware store, and the bank, and once a month he paid the phone and REA bills. He never kept record of business (checks). It was all stored in his mind. My mother went to grocery stores to buy specials that each had and to the dime stores. The last stop was at Mike Gibbs' gas station for gas, and there I would get a nickel bottle of orange pop (always orange). Once in a while I would be allowed to get a hot dog at the Red Owl Grocery Store's lunch counter for a dime. It was 15 ½ miles from our farm to Huron but my, that seemed like such a long trip to a child, especially in the hot summer.

I must relate that at one time when my parents had butchered spring fryers and taken them along to sell at a restaurant in town, they said they were too busy to pay us and to come back later for our money. It was in hot weather and when we went back, they said the chickens were spoiled; they had left them setting out. So what a blow that was of losing the money they had worked so hard for as part of making a living.

One last memory: once a year in summer, the dining room floor, a good-sized floor at 16 x 16 feet, was repainted. It was just wood so Mom would paint the floor a light grey at night after the rest of us had gone to bed. It would be dry by morning. The next night she took a sponge and stippled it with green paint. My, how glossy and pretty it looked for quite a spell!

A Slower, Rewarding Pace of Life
By Barbara A. Kallstrom of Sisseton, South
Dakota
Born 1945

I was born February 13, 1945 at Tekakwitha Hospital in Sisseton, South Dakota, the first child of Ingvald and Ruth Running Langager. This former hospital is now the site of a nursing home going by the name of Tekakwitha Living Center. I was not technically quite considered a Baby Boomer, but close enough! My sister, Beverly, was born on February 23, 1946, and my brother, Douglas, was born on June 30, 1949. I guess that makes them true Boomers. We also had a baby brother, Donald, who

Barbara with her dad, Ingvald Langager in 1950-51

was born on August 26, 1952, who only lived for an hour after birth due to prematurity by approximately six to eight weeks due to placenta previa. His lungs were not yet fully developed, but in this day, he would surely have survived, as he weighed about seven pounds and was perfect otherwise. I was only seven years old, but vividly remember the little funeral service at Hustad Funeral Home, and the beautiful, perfect little baby lying there in the little white casket.

Tekakwitha Hospital was also, where I had an appendectomy at age four and a tonsillectomy at age five. What would now be just a same day surgery involved several days stay in the hospital. It seemed like it always smelled like ether at the hospital, which was the choice anesthetic at that time.

Like many others, my folks did not own a home; they rented. As a young child from birth to about age four, our house was located on a hill east of the main street, now called Veterans Avenue. This hill was removed many years ago and new buildings were built. There are many buildings still standing in that area. One of those is the old Powell Hospital, which was across the street to the north, along with a building now called Aden Apartments and the old Community Hospital building, which is now Social Services. To the east there are houses still standing and being lived in, plus a new post office at the south end of the block.

The DeCoteau family lived next door to the south of us, and we kids all played together every day. I do recall some things we did get into, which now as a grandmother make me shudder. One thing that stands out in my mind (maybe it only happened once) was going down to the nearby railroad tracks in town. I still recall being carried home by my dad along Main Street, crying (perhaps I had gotten a spanking), but even at that tender age I recall being embarrassed that people were seeing me cry and that I had gotten into trouble!

To the south of our houses, there was also an apartment building called LaSalles, which is also gone, along with our houses, but the Sisseton Courier Building next to that still stands, and remains *The Courier*, our local newspaper on the corner of that block. To the west of us across the alley in the apartment building, which also still stands and is occupied, was the McDonald family, Johnny and Barbie, who also joined us in play.

My dad was employed by the local dairy as a milkman during those early years. Milk was delivered in glass bottles with paper caps, right to the person's doorstep. No one ever thought to tamper with them, so there was no fancy method of bottle top security. The fact that someone may steal the bottles if they we on the porch for a short time never occurred either.

I also recall as a small child something that looked like lard, and there was a little packet or capsule of red coloring my mom would mix into it to make it yellow. An older friend tells me that was oleo.

In that era, there was also the threat of polio and the iron lung, a type of respirator for the more serious cases. There was no preventative vaccine at that time. I recall my mom talking about it in later years, how scary it was, as her sister's kids in Minnesota had come down with it, but were fortunate to not have serious and lasting effects from it. We also had whooping cough, measles, mumps, chicken pox, and the usual childhood diseases

Barbara's mom, Ruth Langager with her children in 1952

351

Douglas, Beverly, and Barbara with her doll in 1953

at that time, before all the current vaccinations were developed and used. The only one I ever recall being vaccinated for, as a schoolchild was small pox, which left an everlasting scar. We all lined up and got our shot at school!

By the time my brother was born in 1949 my dad was then employed as a city policeman for many years. We also had moved to a new location to the east side of town. As a small child while we were moving to that location, I was chasing a kitty and ended up in some tall hollyhock flowers and started crying, as I was lost. The lady living there assumed I was the "new kid on the block" and got me safely to Mom and Dad right next door! When we became school age, a big treat was to once in a while get to ride to school in the police car. I am sure that would be against all rules now. One of the kids would always call us "copper kids," which of course, irritated us!

At some point in time, we moved to another location for housing on the west side of town for a short period one summer. I remember my dad rocking and singing to me in the evenings. One of the favorite songs was "On Top of Old Smokey." I also remember Dad reading the Sunday funnies to me. We also had neighbors, the Rice family across the street, who had a relative who would play the accordion in the evenings for all to enjoy! We kids all enjoyed Popsicles together! That house is now gone and the Westside Elementary School takes up that whole block.

We mainly lived on the east side of town until I began high school and then moved to the west side, west of where now the new police department is located. Those houses also are now gone and others take their place. During our early growing up years on the east side, we had so much good, old fashioned fun growing up along with many neighborhood kids, always outdoors: barefoot summers, new shoes when school started! We played hide and seek, anti I over, jumped rope, and swung on a simple board swing that was hung from a rope on a big old sturdy tree, not a fancy store bought gym like it would be now. We played cowboys and Indians; some of our playmates were actually Native Americans and we all took turns as to who was going to be what, no discrimination there. We rode bikes, played marbles, red rover, jacks, kick the can, and hopscotch. I don't recall any obese kids in that day; we were all too busy running outdoors all day!

In the winter months we played indoor games such as I spy, coloring (a real treat at Christmas was a big, fat coloring book and a box of 48 crayons), paper dolls, baby dolls, and board games. We were always busy. A lot of time was spent outdoors in winter, sledding, building snowmen, snowball fighting, playing until our hands, feet, and faces felt numb. Then we would come in to warm up, dry things off on the oil burner stove, and then go back out for more!

Also, there were no locked doors. Most moms were home and moms and kids visited each other's homes without having to make a planned appointment to do so. Most of us didn't have phones, but in an emergency, there would always be someone who did and would gladly help another. We had a black lab named Pal who played alongside us. Dogs, cats, and kids all ran around freely with no fear of abductions at that time.

We did not have television until I was a freshman in high school and then it was black and white. Thankfully, we did get to see Elvis and the Beatles on *The Ed Sullivan Show*!

Saturday nights were bath nights in a big old washtub, and we went to Sunday school the next morning. As we grew older, my sister and I helped Mom with the family laundry on Saturday, using the wringer washer machine. Clothes were hung outdoors on lines, not only in summer but also winter. They were "freeze dried" and later carried back into the house to finish drying. Those that needed to be ironed were either ironed while still damp or sprinkled with water and rolled up to be ironed at a later time. Who irons anymore? Another Saturday job was scrubbing and waxing the floors. In the spring and again in the fall, windows were washed. This included taking off or putting on "storm" windows!

Our trips usually were to Summit or Claire City to visit the grandmas on a Sunday, or the whole family going fishing with Dad, usually on Lake Traverse. We also did a lot of chokecherry picking as a family around that area in those years. Mom made yummy jelly and syrup from that labor. My dad's sister, Marie, lived just up the hill from the fishing site, so usually we stopped to see her and her family, including cousins Darlene and Donald. She always graciously welcomed the company of many people. The first time I had a homemade Rice Krispie bar was at her home, what a treat! Mom had to get that recipe! I have had and made many since that time.

Holidays were usually spent at home where grandmas and single relatives came to our house for the meal and visiting. I recall standing at the window wondering if they would make it during stormy winter holidays. There were no cell phones to keep in touch!

There was no far away travel in our life. If desired, books could fill that need. I loved books and still do! I still recall the wonderful smell of the old Carnegie Library, where my sister and I walked many times to get another exciting book to read.

School was one building, where we were taught from first grade to graduation from high school, which we walked several blocks to and from. Although I was a shy, quiet girl, I loved school and all my teachers. After I graduated, I worked at the local community hospital as a nurse's aide before going away for nurse's training. That is another whole era of my life, which would take another story to tell.

Yes, life seemed much simpler in those days. No one was rich in wealth; in fact, many would now be considered at poverty level. It seemed like everyone was in the same situation as far as finances, etc. no matter who you were. If some did have more than others, certainly nothing was flaunted. Most lived "hand to mouth." There were no EBT cards, and I am sure if one had had that offer, most would have been too proud to take it. I don't recall credit cards either. Your word was good if something had to be bought on credit, until the next paycheck came along. Somehow,

we survived and a generation of good, caring people with good work ethics came from that generation. I have many memories and friends from those years. I am not saying life was easier then, but it was a much slower, rewarding pace of life. I truly miss that era at times.

Things I Remember
By Joyce Meyer of Miller, South Dakota
Born 1938

Here are some of the things I remember.

Pearl Harbor bombing: I was four years old. My folks made me sit in a chair quietly so they could hear the news on our car battery powered radio.

When World War II supplies were short and Mom got stamps to use for some groceries. We ate a lot of homemade bread, butter, syrup, or molasses. We always had milk, eggs, and butter, but not as much sugar.

Mom always had a big garden if the weather permitted. She canned all of our vegetables. We had a cave to store canned goods and potatoes.

Dad had a big team of horses, Fly and Fleet. He used them for farming until in the 1940s, and then he got a tractor.

Dad worked on a threshing crew for many years. They'd move the big machine from one farm to another to thrash out the grain.

We lived in a small three-bedroom house. There were five of us kids, so we had to sleep two or three per regular sized bed; what fun!

I learned to milk my first cow when I was

Joyce's dad with his horses, Fly and Fleet

Country School in 1957

six years old. We all had to help with chores. We had to feed and water the chickens, hogs, and sheep. We did a lot of walking, but we were healthy.

I attended first through eighth grades in a one-room school. My favorite teacher was Vera Collier. She was a large "grandma" who could really reach out to her students.

We did not have electricity or indoor plumbing until later. In the late 1940s, Dad set up a wind charger with glass batteries, and he wired one light and one plug-in in each room of the house. There was not enough juice for a refrigerator. We always hung a jar of milk and a jar of cream on ropes down into the well to keep them cool. Sour cream was kept down in the cave until the can was full and then taken to the little country store where they tested the fat content. Then it was exchanged, along with eggs, for groceries and staples.

Flour came in pretty printed cotton bags. Mom sewed them up to make dresses for us girls. We always had a new dress for Easter!

I remember Mom reading to us by kerosene lamp. It was not a very bright light.

We listened to *The Lone Ranger*, *Inner Sanctum* (the Squeaking Door) and *Dragnet* on the radio.

We lived about 30 miles from town so, of course, we never went. Mom and Dad went about once every one or two months, but they never stayed in town to visit.

We had a party line telephone that was a big box that hung on the wall. When you wanted to talk, you cranked the lever on the side. Everyone had a series of rings all their own. In case of an emergency, you just cranked one long ring. Everyone on line got on to find out where to go. Our news reporter listened in on every ring.

When Russia launched Sputnik, we would lay out in the yard at night to watch the satellite move across the sky. Rural Electric came out in the late '40s or early '50s. We got our first black and white television in the '50s. We watched the man walk on the moon. We watched spaceships being launched! We sat in the yard to "hear" the first super jet break the sound barrier. Wow!

Mom washed clothes on a wringer washer until the '60s. She didn't have a dryer either.

In 1961 my folks sold the farm and bought the little country store, Ames Store, 25 miles from town. They finally had indoor plumbing, electricity, and a modern telephone. No more Saturday night baths in the wash tub. We all used the same water heated on the stove before.

We were married in '59. I taught in country one-room schools for six years. We moved into a little town, St. Lawrence, South Dakota. We had five children and all attended town school.

The milkman delivered milk to our door all through the '60s. I sure missed that when it stopped.

There were many more memories but too much to write down.

Tough Times on the Family Homestead
By Dorothy Weinberger of Artesian, South Dakota
Born 1923

Remembering the Depression; yes, I have many memories of the Depression Era, better known as the Dirty Thirties in South Dakota. I was born in 1923 so I was quite young, but I recall very vividly the anguish my parents suffered because of the severe draught and Depression. Crops and livestock prices were at rock bottom, as the old expression goes. One of my first memories was at the time our local bank closed. I believe the year was 1929. Herbert Hoover was President of the United States. My paternal grandmother had opened a savings account for me in the amount of $10.00 – quite a sum for a small child. I still have the certificate dated May 4, 1924. When the bank closed, my money was gone. On March 10, 1936, I received a very small return – a check in the amount of 31

Dorothy with her parents Roy and Anna Edwards

cents.

My parents lost every penny they had in their savings and their checking account. They had written a check in the amount of $700.00 just a few days before the bank closed, but it had not cleared the bank. It was to pay for two pieces of new machinery Dad had purchased. Most farmers after that carried their savings in the upper pocket of their blue bib overalls. For many years after the bank closed, no one trusted depositing the little money they had in a bank. At that time, my dad and my uncle farmed together and had recently bought two new Farmall tractors. They farmed a total of 1,280 acres, including pastureland, which was considered a very large operation at that time. They hung kerosene lanterns on the front of the tractors so they could work in the field at night. No, tractors did not have lights at that time.

Many obstacles plagued farmers for a period of time of at least ten years, which included extreme drought, grasshoppers, intense heat, hot burning winds, and no crops or hay to feed the thin livestock, along with bitter cold winters and heavy snowfall.

For a number of years my father applied for feed and seed loans. Farmers never gave up thinking the next year would be better. The tractors he had purchased had been repossessed because he had no money to make the payments. He was again farming with horses. One year he did have hopes of a small oat crop, but almost overnight grasshoppers moved into the field and ate the crop into the ground. I recall driving to the field with my father. It was unbelievable to see the millions of grasshoppers devouring the grain.

At one time, possibly in 1933 or 1934, my parents had built their cattle herd to near 200 head. My father borrowed money from a neighbor who had some cattle for sale. As the terrible drought continued so, there was no feed. My dad was in poor health by that time. I'm sure his health conditions were brought on by the terrible drought and economic conditions, but no one had heard of word stress at that time. My dad saddled up his horse and drove the entire herd one mile into the yard of the man who held the mortgage. I'm sure that must have been a very depressing time for him, but as he rode home he was relieved of the terribly heavy burden of finding feed for his cattle.

My parents also raised hogs sheep and hundreds of chickens. My mother always sold hatching eggs to a hatchery in Mitchell in the spring. These eggs always brought a better price per dozen, but the time came when there was no feed as all the crops dried up because of extreme drought. My mother called a neighbor and asked if he would trade corn for some of our hogs. She asked him to trade one bushel of corn for one hog, but he was not willing to trade.

My parents were strong people. Each of their parents had come to South Dakota in the 1880s. My dad's parents came from Wales to New York and then on to South Dakota. My mother's parents came from Norway to Iowa and then to South Dakota. They too endured hardship so my parents had been through difficult times when they were children.

The Depression and drought did take its toll on my father's health. He developed ulcers and later he became ill with typhoid fever, yellow jaundice, and later pneumonia, which nearly took his life. My mother and I took care of him 24 hours a day and his health returned. He had weighed near 200 pounds but after his illness, he was down to 137 pounds. When the outdoor temperature was over 100 degrees, we did not have electricity yet so I poured cool water in a basin and dipped a towel in the water. Then I held the towel in front of the open window so a cool breeze blew across my father's bed. This coolness was very comforting to him.

After my father regained his health, a neighbor and friend asked my father if he would be able to be a timekeeper for our local Works Project Administration (WPA). He did this for quite some time, earning $20.00 a week. This was a godsend for our family. My uncle, who lived with us, worked on a local WPA project, using a team and a dump wagon helping to build a road. He earned $15.00 a week and used the money to buy groceries and other necessities.

My father's duties as a timekeeper were recording the hours of the workers, mailing weekly reports to the office at Woonsocket, known as our county seat. I was old enough to help him with the reports. We also delivered commodities to the families in our neighborhood. With the large sum of $20.00 coming in each week we were even able to take a three day trip to Minnesota, riding with my aunt and an uncle and their two children.

When I was 12 years old, we had no feed for our small herd of cattle. My father and my uncle drove the cattle 50 miles to an area where there was some feed, including stubble fields and cornstalks for grazing. They also stacked prairie hay for winter feed. For the trip, they loaded a small brooder house onto a wagon. This was used for cooking and sleeping, as it took several days to make the trip. My uncle returned home to our farm for the winter. He

Dorothy's father, Roy Edwards milking a cow

kept a team of horses to use to make the trip to town for supplies including coal for the stove to heat the house.

The farm consisted of 640 acres but sufficient feed hadn't been raised that year for one team of horses. It became necessary for my uncle to obtain hay from our local relief agency, which had been shipped in from other areas. My parents and I moved back home in the spring, and it was so wonderful to be back with all my former schoolmates and my teacher at our country school.

I recall some of the terrible dust storms. The clouds of dust would roll in and it would be as dark as night, making it necessary to light our kerosene lamps in the daytime. Furniture would be thick with dust. On one occasion, my dad and I took the car, using the headlights to attempt to locate our cattle to bring them in around the buildings. One could hardly breathe with all the dust in the air.

Another memory, which I recall very vividly, was the slaughtering of cattle that were slowly starving because of the terrible drought conditions. Some of the cattle were butchered and given to anyone who could preserve the meat. There was a cold spring nearby where the meat was thoroughly washed. This was many years before electricity was available to people in rural areas. My mother canned the meat on a cook stove as quickly as possible and saved every jar without spoilage for winter use. Many of the cattle that were too thin to butcher were killed and buried in the sand hills of an area known as John Brown's Mound north of Forestburg, South Dakota.

In this same sandy area, the winds made drifts of sand in the ditches and covered the fences completely. To this day, this area still shows the ravage of the sandstorms.

Our farm was heavily mortgaged after many years of drought. There were no crops to harvest and cattle, sheep, and hog prices were very low. It became evident that my parents would lose their farm that had been homesteaded by my great-grandparents in 1883. This was a heartbreaking experience for my parents and also for me. My father had to leave the farm where he was born and lived until he was 54 years old. I too was born there and was 17 years old when we left. My grandparents had built the house, nine rooms in all, so it was very special to all of us.

My parents were able to buy 160 acres

nearby for back taxes for the amount of $600.00. They also made a very small down payment on an adjoining 320 acres with buildings. The house we were leaving had running water and a furnace, but the place where we would be moving to had neither. I recall crying for days after we moved, as I was sure the new place would never be home. This was in 1939.

It became home to me, as we later purchased the land and moved the house where I was born to the new location. Both of my children, Lois and Don Weinberger, were raised there. My grandchildren, Kimberly, Krue, Kris, and Kyle Weinberger are the sixth generation to live in this community.

With some of the farm programs administered by Franklin D. Roosevelt through the Triple A Office, my parents received small payments for completing conservation practices. The income helped make the annual payments on the land.

As I recall, the drought and Depression was beginning to come to an end. My parents continued to work hard and as time went on conditions improved. Many judgments had been filed against my father at the courthouse in Woonsocket from past seed and feed loans. In time, my father was able to pay off all of the judgments, and he was once again free of debt. The terrible drought and Depression was over. I graduated from high school about the time, and then that winter on December 7 the World War II began.

At the present time, I recently celebrated my 90th birthday and have moved to an independent living apartment in Mitchell, South Dakota. I still own the farm where I lived as a child. My son farms the land and has a large herd of buffalo. He is the fifth generation of our family to live on and farm the land my ancestors homesteaded from 1881 to 1883.

Mom, the Entrepreneur
By Paul Bremmon of Britton, South Dakota
Born 1950

By the time World War II ended, my mother owned a small herd of dairy cows. Mom and Dad always planned to farm from the time they got together, so she was just planning ahead.

Paul's parents

After Mom and Dad were married, Dad shipped out to the North African Theater and Mom went to Chicago, Illinois to look for work. She found work at a factory that paid

Paul's mom's baby chicks

well enough so she could save a little money. Mom's brother contacted her and wanted to borrow $500.00 to buy five milk cows. For payment, she would receive one-half of the increase. By the time the war ended, she owned ten cows that were ready to start milking.

In 1947, my parents rented a farm south of Forman, North Dakota. They started farming here with a loan from the Farmer's Home Administration and their ten cows. They did well enough in North Dakota that they were able to buy their own farm south of Britton, South Dakota. The farm they bought was 320 acres with a good set of buildings.

In 1957, they were able to buy another 320 acres; in essence, this doubled the size of their farm. Then in 1958, they were hailed out on part of their land, and in 1959, there was a severe drought. All three things together put a strain on the family living budget, to say the least.

My mother was a small, quiet person, but she was a good leader and a tireless worker. Mom didn't like being so short of money for family living, so in 1960 she came up with a plan to make money that could be used for family living and not take away from money for land and equipment payments.

She decided to raise chickens, not just a few, but quite a few. During the winter, she saved a little money each week from the cream and egg check. By spring, she had enough to buy a thousand chicks and some chick starter. In 1960, chicks cost only $28.00 per 100.

The chicks came in the mail, so she picked them up at the post office at 7:00 a.m. When she got them home, she gave each one a drink as she removed them from the shipping box. She was so meticulous in caring for chickens that she lost very few. In those days, the hatchery would send a few extra birds in each box of 100. At the end of the summer, she usually had 1,060 live birds.

After the chicks were big, enough they were released to fend for themselves. They lived on crickets, grasshopper, weed seeds, worms, and whatever. They were truly range fed chickens.

By the first week of August, they were ready to start butchering. They biggest first, allowing the smaller ones time to grow. She could only do 30 each day because our freezer could only make enough ice to cool that many.

If the chickens weren't cooled fast, enough the bacteria started to grow.

Mom woke us kids at 7:00 a.m. By that, time breakfast was ready and the water for scalding was boiling on the stove. By the time we ate and carried the water out, Dad had several chickens ready to be picked.

Mom would scald them, and we three older kids would pluck the feathers. My brother was 15, my sister was 13, and I was 10. We were a pretty good crew, because by 9:00 a.m. we were usually done. My brother and I would usually help Dad service the combines and help with the harvest the rest of the day.

Mom and my sister still had to singe the hair, check for pinfeathers, and remove the legs and the entrails. Then they washed the chickens twice and put them in ice water to cool. Then they made the noon meal for seven. Not chicken.

After dinner, they would rinse them once more and package them for delivery. In the late afternoon, Mom would load the chickens in the car and deliver them. This went on almost every day in August. I was glad when school started so I could get a break.

Mom got $1.25 for each delivered chicken.

Paul's mom

358

This doesn't seem like much, but after she paid expenses, filled our freezer with chicken, and replenished her laying hen population, she had about $1,000.00 left. It still doesn't sound like much, but remember, you could buy a new car for $2,500.00 back then.

Those Were the Days
By Peggy Kasten of Hazel, South Dakota
Born 1943

You know when a person thinks back at things it's not all bad. Maybe it should go back some to slow things down.

First of all, we just had a small house, three bedrooms, and there were nine in the house. We had to share rooms, three in one bed. One bigger room had two beds in it, a small room with two boys, and then a room for Mom and Dad.

We would have to make sure we had enough wood in and enough water hauled in before nighttime. We had oil lamps to move around. We milked by hand, had chickens, a few pigs, and a few sheep. It was enough so that we had our milk and meat for us. We would have to haul milk to the house to separate the milk and cream. In that little room, we had a separator, a slop pail, our boots and chore clothes, eggs, and a washing machine out there.

When we would wash clothes, we put the washing in the kitchen. We would haul water to heat. We had double tubs so we could rinse two times. There was not a lot of water, as we hauled it in and hauled it out.

We would have to get up before school to do the chores, wash the separator, and

Peggy's mom, Dorothy on the party line

get things done. We didn't have a bathroom so we had to wash in the kitchen sink, brush our teeth, etc. out there, so we had to do the dishes on the table. Yes, it seemed like when the things had to get done, I would go to the outhouse. Sometimes I would waste time so I wouldn't have to do much.

Our Saturday night baths were something. We would hang a blanket up from the kitchen and living room. When it was cold in the living room the rest would stay in the kitchen. We always started with the small ones and kept adding hot water. I'll tell you, you got at it and out so the rest could get done. But when a person thinks of it, we had a lot of family time. We would listen to the radio, a lot of good programs and nice music. Also on Saturday night, we girls would put rubber

Peggy's family home after the storm of 1942

359

Getting together to play cards at the home place

rollers in our hair, and we would all polish our shoes and line them up in a row for Sunday morning.

When we went to school, we didn't have a lot of clothes or shoes. So when we got home, we would change clothes. We would hang up our school clothes and put our everyday clothes on. Also when school was on, if the teacher would get after us we would get it harder when we got home. None of us kids had a car so we would get up early to get things done outside, come in and clean up, and catch the bus. When we had ballgames, we couldn't stay after school. We had to come home, do our thing, and clean up. We would have pancakes or eggs and go to catch the bus. The kids could always tell what we had with frying or syrup; they could smell it.

On cold days when we washed clothes we always had to hang them on the line to freeze and then bring them in stiff and had lines to hang them on to finish in the house. But you know we never had any colds either. On blizzard days, we put a rope from the house to the barn to find one place to another.

If we did things pretty slow, they would say slower than molasses in January. Another saying about how slow you are was it gives me the seven-year itch. We had a lot of different sayings.

The party phones were something else. There were five or six parties, and then when you wanted to use the phone, never fear someone was on. You'd share the receiver or it sounds like somebody listening or want to use it.

When it rained, we had dirt roads so we had to take off our shoes and socks and run down in the mud. We would see how far it would fly. We never went swimming but in the cow tank to get cooled off. Also, if a lot of water was in the ditches we always got wet feet, and our boots got water in them.

We would do our own games. We would make mud pies and sometimes we got a few eggs to put in them. Then we put leaves on top to make them pretty. The cottonwood tree leaf would be ice cream cones, and the long thing bananas. But we would push our dolls around to get the leaves. We would play church on the stair steps with the dolls. We would sing and sometimes have to take them out. That was fun. More games were throwing the ball over the house, rolling on old barrels on the lawn, and hide and go seek.

We didn't have much, but we had more company than anyone. The house was plain, nothing fancy. Also, the best thing about every meal was we all sat down to pray, and we all ate together. When we had cake if you took the frosting off to eat it last, Dad would always try to get it away from you.

The memories we will have forever. I think there was more closeness than they have today.

The Good Old School Days
By Myla Johnson of Watertown, South Dakota
Born 1956

My mom wrote down how school was in the early days of South Dakota and how school days were for her children. She grew up on a farm near Corona, South Dakota. The country school that she went to was just a short walk up the hill from her home. Our great-grandfather, S.K. Johnston, had given two acres of his land to the Kilborn School District for the schoolhouse and outhouses. Her aunt, uncle, and father had all gone to that school. Then she and her sister went there for all eight years of grade school.

There is a bridge that runs across a creek on the farm. Mom told stories of how neighbor boys would walk across the top of the railings on the way to and from school. When highline wires came to the farm, these same neighbor boys would walk on the highline wires, too.

No fear there!

When country schools were closed, the land was deeded back to the Johnston farm.

Mom and her sister went to high school in Corona, South Dakota. In the winter, they stayed at their grandma's house with her and their two aunts. Usually they could get home by horse and buggy for the weekends then. She did tell of one winter when she and her sister didn't get home for two weeks due to the heavy snow. Then they caught a ride with a neighbor with horses and a sled and then back to town for school again.

My mom had memories of school supplies being a tablet, pencils, and pens. A crank type pencil sharpener was in every classroom. That worked better than a jackknife for sharpening the pencil. She had a fountain pen that was messy and needed to be blotted with a blotter so it was dry. In the 1940s, ballpoint pens were invented. BIC sold 20 million pens a day worldwide.

My sister, Kyleen, and my brothers, Richard and Mark, attended country school, too. It was about a mile from our home. They all had to take lunch to school. Mom told that in the early days she had to use empty syrup pails to take her lunch to school. My sister and brothers had metal lunch boxes. In the 1950s, the metal lunch boxes were marketed to children. The boxes featured bright colors, maybe an image of Hopalong Cassidy or the Lone Ranger on the sides. My brother, Mark, took peanut butter sandwiches to school every day.

My sister, Debbie, and I went to Corona to grade school and our brother, Mark, went to high school there for a couple of years. I was the only one in my family to go to kindergarten. It was held in the attic of the principal's house, and his wife taught it. We played on their swing set outside and played with homemade salt dough in their kitchen. Then it was back up to the attic for lessons of writing our letters and learning our numbers.

My sister, brother,

and I went to Corona School for a couple of years. Then there were too many students for that school anymore so we started riding the school bus to Milbank School. The ride from our house to school by bus took an hour and a half, a long ride every day.

The first year I went there, I was in third grade. My classes were held in a church basement that year while Milbank built a larger grade school. We had recess outside in a vacant lot, and when we were bad, we had to put our heads down on our desk covered by our hands. No peeking! Shame!

Junior high was in an old insurance office building in Milbank in the late 1960s. I remember the girls had to wear dresses or skirts and tops. The hem of our dresses could only be six inches from the floor when we kneeled. We had to do that test in the principal's office. If our skirts were too short, we had to change. Parents did not appreciate having to bring their daughters clothes to change into so that didn't happen often.

That was in the days when the Beatles were popular, so the boys wanted to have long hair. But that wasn't allowed at school. Any boy with hair that touched their shirt collar had to get a haircut. The next school day it had to be better.

I remember I had a speech class. For one of our speeches, we could bring a prop to talk about. I had gotten a colored baby chick for Easter that year. My chicken lived in our house in a shoebox with a door cut in so I could tuck him in at night. Each morning, I would call

Kilborn #5 Country School

361

him, and he would peck at the door to open it. He was so smart so why couldn't he go to school with me. He sat on my shoulder for most of the speech. The speech was a success, A+!

High school in Milbank went very well. I had classes of typing, algebra, English, and science. Study halls were held in the library, and we all had to be very quiet. My senior year, I went to one day of home economics. Some classes were just assigned, no choice. But I had been in 4-H since I was eight so I felt I knew more than the teacher. So off to the principal's office I went the next day. Since they didn't know what to do with me, I spent the morning sitting in the principal's chair. After that, I went to honors study hall. There was no teacher, just a lot of talking and treats to eat that we brought with us. That was fun.

My parents wanted each of their children to have a secondary education. We all went to college or vocational school. My mother had attended college in Aberdeen for a short time before she married. She and Dad were hard working farmers. They knew that they wanted their children to have choices in what they wanted to do with their lives.

I went to college in Marshall, Minnesota. In the middle '70s computers were just being developed. One of my college memories is of using a computer to put in results from a genetics class I took. I was supposed to breed fruit flies and then count which ones had a certain kind of wings. I had to enter my results into a computer in one room at a desk with just a keyboard. Then I went to another room where the printer put out the report. I never saw the hardware of the computer. Now we have home computers, cell phones, laptops, and iPads! And classes can be taken on line while you sit in your easy chair.

Trapping Animals
By Jack Kennedy of Watertown, South Dakota
Born 1940

Old Anderson died in the winter. In the early 1900s, the snow was deep, over the telegraph lines, and the temperature was near minus 36 degrees below zero in the land of South Dakota. Anderson had twin sons on their

Jack's father, Harry John Kennedy in the early 1900s

old homestead. They were grown men at the time. Blizzard conditions were daily and not easy to shovel and pick a hole in the ground. One of the sons came up with the idea that they had to do something with Dad, so they took him out to the old granary where they froze him standing in a corner with his arms bent and thumbs up! They hung grain sacks on his thumbs all winter when they bagged oats for the horses. When spring came, the old man began to thaw and sag, so they had to dig a hole to bury him. Old Anderson worked all winter and didn't say a word.

This account was told to me by my father, who was born in 1895 and lived to 88 years. Mother was born in 1898 and lived in three centuries. She passed away at 103 years of age. She was a strong Norwegian woman who worked hard her whole life and raised seven children.

Mother told me that when she was a young girl, the Sioux came one day to the old claim and were hungry. They held her family at gunpoint and seized a couple of their dogs and cooked them on the old stove and then left and went on their way. Some were walking and some were on horses.

Old Bill Macintire lived nearby in an old tarpaper shack. People who knew him called him Mac. He was a large man. The Indian people would raid his traps by a large slough. His shack overlooked the water. Old Mac would use an old Winchester .44 and shoot across the water to scare the trap thieves. They would scatter. No one heard of Mac shooting anyone.

This writer was born in 1940, the next to youngest of the Kennedy children. Many interesting things happened as I grew up.

362

We rode horseback to a one-room country school or walked a mile and a half. We staked the horses out to graze while we attended class. We baked potatoes on the furnace at school while we learned our three Rs (reading, writing, and 'rithmatic). We played games at recess or played tag and baseball. We played marbles in the dirt or kick the can or pump, pump, pull away. We played knives with our pocketknives, to stick them in the soil. Every country boy and some girls carried their pocketknives everywhere they went.

In the fall and winter, we would check our animal traps on the way home from school. Trapping was a way of life for country folks, for food and pelts. My younger brother and I caught a mink in a culvert in December before Christmas. It was alive in a small trap and jumping all over. We were so excited. This was in the 1940s. Brother and I had to figure out how to kill that mink. We wanted to buy Christmas presents for Dad and Mother. I had my brother hand rocks from a nearby rock pile, and I, being the oldest, threw them on the animal, eventually killing it. One problem was I broke the trap by hitting it with the rocks! Oh well, we had our Christmas mink. We took it to a local fur buyer with visions of big money. The old buyer, named Louie said, "Boys, you have a cotton female. It is not worth much." The hair was short and brownish, so they called it cotton. Well, Louie said, "Boys, I can only pay you $10.00." We were unhappy, but went to the store and bought the folks candy bars and Mom a flour sifter for Christmas.

My whole family trapped animals for sale to country buyers. Mink, weasel, muskrat, raccoons, skunk, fox, they were all fair game. The old kerosene lantern would be hung up on a nail in the basement and skinning would go on all night long, muskrats by the hundreds and all the others. We pounded nails in all the rafters in the granary and hung the stretched pelts in long rows for drying and so mice and rats couldn't chew on them and ruin the skins. After drying and when the prices seemed right, many skins would be bundled together with shipping tags attached and be shipped to out of state buyers who would send us their price lists. Those buyers would grade the furs pretty tough, but by and large, we got good prices. Some prime buck mink got $60.00; muskrats got $3.00, and $5.00 for large muskrats.

On Sundays in the summer, for fun and bounty, we would locate fox dens and dig out the pups and put them in cream cans that were ventilated with bullet holes. Often we would get six to ten fox pups out of a den. It took a lot of digging and a gloved hand to reach down and catch the rascals. We built wire pens at the homestead to hold and raise the fox. We dug a large, square hole in the ground and shot rabbits and gophers to feed the pups. The meat would stay cool in the ground and whenever we shot something, it would go in the hold for the fox. The whole idea was to collect the bounty someday and pelt the furs out when cold weather came along and the skins primed up. Bounties were $2.00, $4.00, and eventually $7.50.

Days gone by, we banked the old house with horse manure in the winter to stay warm. We ate ducks and geese and our mother made feather pillows and sold them. The poultry was shipped in barrels to Chicago. Mom bought new a 1929 Chevy for under $400.00.

Jack Kennedy

363

Spelling Bees and Baked Potato Feasts
By Ellen Dinger of Aberdeen, South Dakota
Born 1940

My dad was born in Denmark, but in 1914 during World War I, he came to the United States. He came over on the Lusitania amid all sorts of torpedo fire. The very next time the Lusitania sailed, it sunk. My dad did all sorts of odd jobs across the US and finally ended up in Badger, South Dakota working as a hired farm hand. While he was employed there, his employer hired a girl to help with the housework, but he didn't have any way to get the new hired girl. Since my dad had a car, his employer asked Dad to go pick up the hired girl. That is the way my mom and dad met. They eventually married and bought a farm of their own where they raised 13 children, of which I was number nine. They settled there on their farm near Badger, South

Ellen's mom, Elsie Marie Pedersen with her parents in 1903

Dakota where they remained until their deaths some 65 years later. Twelve of their thirteen children were born at home. Only the youngest was born in a hospital.

As a child growing up, we had few appliances or modern conveniences, as we know them today. We had no electricity for the first nine years of my life, and there was no indoor plumbing until 1963. One of the daily chores for the children was to collect corncobs and wood to burn in the cook stove. And we pumped water from the cistern for all our cooking and hygiene needs.

Going to school was considerably different when I was young than from what we know today. All thirteen children attended grade school in a one-room schoolhouse. A coal furnace heated our school, and we didn't have any running water. One of the special treats was when we brought a raw potato wrapped in tin foil. The teacher would place the potatoes on the furnace midway through the morning, and they would lie there and bake. We would bring some butter to school and have that on our potatoes. I don't remember any potato tasting better than that. Sometime if we were really being fancy, we would bring a can of corn and put that on the furnace, too. We thought we were really having a feast. The rest of the time, we carried our lunches of sandwiches and fruit in syrup pails and carried our own drinking water in a quart jar because the cistern at school had snakes and frogs in it.

We walked two miles to school every day,

Ellen's dad, Albeck Kjellsen in his coachman uniform

rain or shine. On rare occasions if the weather was minus degrees, Dad would break down and drive us to school with a team of horses pulling a bobsled. Some days as we would be trudging along to school, the cream truck would come along and stop and give us a ride to school. The driver would open the back of the truck, and we would sit back there on the cream cans. Then he would close the back truck door, and it would be pitch dark. But it sure beat walking. Sometime the school bus from a neighboring town would come along, but we usually tried to hide in the ditch so that the bus wouldn't stop and pick us up because the town kids thought we country kids were pretty funny in our big coats and boots and carrying our lunch pails.

Some of us kids were pretty curious about many things as we were walking to school. One day we noticed that someone was moving into the farm located just a half mile from our farm. We decided to go in and investigate the house since no one was home at the time. During the investigation the bathroom door inadvertently locked with us kids inside the bathroom. Not being accustomed to indoor bathrooms or locks, we thought we were locked in forever. After a few very scary moments, we were able to figure out the lock and escape without any problems. A very good lesson learned about entering other people's property uninvited.

Aside from learning and associating with our fellow students, some of the highlights of each year were the spelling bees, county chorus, and declam contests. If you got to represent your class in the spelling bee, then you got to go on to the spelling contest in Badger. If you were able to get a ribbon there, then you would get to go on to the county spelling bee in De Smet.

We would learn and practice music all

Judy, Squirt, Doris, George, Lloyd, Florence, Donnie, Harvey, Howard, and Helen

year long, and then near the end of the year all the little country schools in the county would join together and spend a day in De Smet putting all the voices together and then put on a concert. That was really thrilling and fun.

One of the most unique parts of either the spelling bee or the county chorus was that we would get to eat lunch in a restaurant, and that was really a novelty for us. Chicken noodle soup and orange pop was our special menu for that day.

Another highlight was when we would have school plays. We would have a stage, and then we would sting a wire and hang sheets on the wire so that we could open and close the curtain. Everyone in the community would come and watch us perform. We would be so nervous as we performed all sorts of acts. After the program we would have a variety of booths in the basement. One that comes to mind was the fortune telling booth. Prior to the program we would write fortunes on a paper with lemon juice, and it wouldn't show up. But when a customer came to the booth, we would hold the paper up to heat, and their fortune would magically appear.

Christmas was a special time for our family. Many years there was very little money to be spent on Christmas gifts, but we didn't care. We just enjoyed celebrating the season and being together. It was our tradition that we put up our Christmas tree the afternoon of Christmas Eve. Of course, since we didn't have electricity we put candles on our tree. Christmas Eve was the big celebration day for us and after a great dinner and getting the dishes done (this seemed to take forever), we would move into the living room to open gifts. As soon as the gifts were open and the wrapping mess cleaned up, we would pull the Christmas tree out, light the candles, and then join hands and dance around the Christmas tree singing Christmas carols.

Probably the most fun we had with music over the years was when everyone would come home with their families, and we would sit and sing all sorts of songs. I think the adults enjoyed this as much or more than the grandkids.

When I grew up and got married, I moved to Hecla, South Dakota where I taught school. I felt like a queen, as we had indoor plumbing, running water, and even a TV. My, how times change. I would never have imagined the computer age of today with all the modern technology.

Stressful Times
By Ray A. Johnson of Britton, South Dakota
Born 1930

I was born October 21, 1930 on a farm southeast of Britton. I was the youngest of seven children and had three sisters and three brothers. My father came from Sweden when he was 19 years old. My mother was born six miles south of Britton on a farm.

My father homesteaded near Ft. Pierre, sold that farm, and bought a farm north of Quarve Hill. It had a poor access in and out, so he sold it and bought a farm southeast of Britton. The big Depression hit and they lost everything. They rented a farm northeast of a golf course. In 1935 or 1936, everything blew away. I rode along with my dad to get seed at Kidder, six miles north of our place. We had to stop several times because we could not see for dust blowing.

Some days the grasshoppers blackened out the sun as they traveled in swarms. After eating the crops, they actually ate fence posts halfway up. My brother, Mike, and I came out of the theater one day and a swarm of hoppers had landed out in front of the theater. We squished them all over the sidewalk. The lights had attracted them.

My mother had a root cellar for all her canned food. My dad and older brothers would shoot as many pheasants in one day as possible, and Mother would can them for a couple of days.

My dad had milk cows and very little hay. He bought hay shipped in by rail. He started a dairy business in the late '30s and early '40s. He took my brother, Mike, and me into town to the hardware store. We bought us each a shiny milk pail. We really were happy with the pails and soon learned how to milk. Soon we were getting wages, 25 cents a week. My dad, my brother, and I milked 39 cows before school and after school.

From our wages, we could go to the show for twelve cents and get a box of popcorn for five cents. The rest we saved for stamps on war bond sheets. When we had $18.75, we bought a war bond.

We also had other income. We picked wool off the barbwire fence when the sheep crawled under the fence. When a sheep died, we would pick the wool off. It came off best if it would lie in the sun for about three days, if we could stand the smell. We also snared gophers with twine and the county paid a bounty of one cent for the tail. Then we took the body to the fox farm and received one cent more.

My parents lost everything when the banks closed and the stock market crashed and the crops blew away. My dad backed over my brother's head, and he lived through it. My mother was pregnant with me, and my oldest sister saw it happen from the outdoor toilet. I would call this stressful times.

At Christmas, we usually got fruit in our socks. The church gave us a sack of peanuts and candy. We saw pictures of Santa and his sleigh flying up in the air and losing toys out of the back. My brother and I went out early the next morning and looked at the hill where

Ray and his brother, Mike

366

we thought he would fly over but never found any toys. Our best toy was a top. You pushed it down and it would spin. We rolled rubber tires up and down the road. When I was real young, my older siblings went on sleigh rides at night when there was a full moon. I got in on the hot chocolate and marshmallows.

We had a fancy outhouse. It had two holes, one large, and one small. We had a chamber pot to use at night. One day my mother sent me upstairs to empty the pot, and I tripped at the top of the stairs and it spilled all down the stairs. It was time for the threshing crew to come in for dinner. Needless to say, my mother was very upset with me.

We had a party line phone. Our number was one long and two shorts tones. When my dad needed to use the phone, two neighbor ladies were always gossiping.

We walked three miles to school, uphill both ways. I still hate snakes. When I ran through the grass, bull snakes curled up and hissed.

There were many homeless men that rode the boxcars on the trains. Some walked through the countryside. They would steal eggs and suck them for food to survive.

Watching TV tonight, *The Voice*, I was reminded of listening to *Major Bowes' Amateur Hour* on the radio.

I had a pet dog named Brownie that we got from the neighbor boys in grade school. We knew our parents would say no to a second dog so after school we slipped him into the door so Mother would get attached to this tiny puppy and it worked. Brownie and I were real buddies. We took trips into the pasture. One time we had captured a gopher in a pipe, so I set a trap at one end of the pipe and hollered in the other end. Brownie got caught in the trap, and I couldn't get him out. So I ran the fourth of a mile home to get my big sister, Leona, to help me. One day I fell asleep in the middle of the road, and Brownie sat right beside me and would not move for cars. Brownie and the other dog started chasing the sheep and they had to get rid of Brownie.

My brother, Mike, and I packed raisins and water and went gopher snaring. We caught one and then saw she had two rows of teats and we knew she had babies in the hole. So we had a burial and put up a little cross. Mike said a little prayer and shed a few tears. We are both very emotional.

School Carnivals
By Mary Lynn James of Houghton, South Dakota
Born 1939

All the high schools in our area had school carnivals as fundraisers. Booths were made by using a framework of lumber and then dividing the booths with blankets.

Basketball free throws, fishponds, baseball and football tosses, cakewalks, dart/balloon throws, and bingo were some of the fun games.

It was fun to go to the neighboring towns, too. About four guys from Claremont High School went to the Hecla school carnival. One of their games was to guess the number of jellybeans in a jar. The Claremont boys figured out a plan. Two of the boys would flirt with the Hecla girls who were in charge of the jellybean game. The other two boys would grab the jellybean jar, take it outside, count the jellybeans, and then return the jar without the Hecla girls knowing anything. Guess who won the jellybean count!

Hunting Gophers and Playing War
By Lois (Kannegieter) Monahan of Watertown, South Dakota
Born 1936

I was the only girl in our country school with eight other boys, so at recess all the boys would want to hunt gophers and play 'War". So that's what I did, too. I went to the Anderson Country School, northeast of Willow Lake. The boys said I was supposed to be the nurse and fix everybody up. My mom even made me a nurse's cape I wore to school a couple times. Playing nurse was fun at home but not with all the rowdiness and noise. I got tired of that after a while. I never got to do girl's stuff.

My teacher in the early 1940s was Eunis (Pommer) Meester. She would let me stay in from recess at times and do art work. She could play the piano by ear, and that impressed me. That was how I liked to play the piano, too. When I got tired of artwork, I would play the piano, or we would play together. I was in the second grade at this time.

I remember one winter, my older brother Harold and I walked the mile to school, the day after a blizzard had hit. No one was there yet, so Harold took the coal chute door off and slid down the blackened coal chute into the coal pile. Then he let me in the locked school. The teacher and other kids all showed up later. It seemed we never did get a ride to school. It was only a mile away, so we always walked.

In the early 1940s, we had a phone at our school. One morning, my mom called shortly after we got there and wanted to send Harold down the road to see if my little three-year-old brother Clifford had followed us. She couldn't find him anywhere at home. Sure enough, he was lollygagging along down the road almost to the schoolhouse. One time I had to rescue him from out of the water tank under the windmill. He was reaching for something and fell in. I was right there, and thankfully saw him do it. He was sinking with his heavy wool coat on when I pulled him out and took him to the house. I was six years old at the time.

I had three brothers, Harold, Clifford, and Marlyn, and two sisters, Ruth and Nola.

My parents were Art and Olive Kannegieter. We moved into town when I was in the third grade, but my dad kept the farm and farmed along with my brothers for many years until he retired. We had a good life, being raised in and near Willow Lake, S.D., with a lot of good memories. Wednesday and Saturday nights were especially fun, when all the farm families would come to town to do shopping and trading.

Learning Right From Wrong
By Caroll Ann Whitman of Alpine,
California
Born 1942

This short story begins in my hometown of Lake Preston, South Dakota. It is just a few days before Mother's Day and I am six years old and in the first grade.

While I was sitting out on the front step of our old two story house, I sat there thinking of a plan on what I was going to buy Mama, but with no money... it takes some time to think.

Ah, ha—a brain storm idea. I walked down to the corner of our block to Mrs. Swanson's home. She was a sweet old widowed lady. Her yard had many lilac bushes, purple, white, and a soft pink. I helped myself and picked a whole bunch of them. I walked right up to her front door and knocked loudly on her door, standing tall waiting with a big smile on my face.

She answers the door, "Hello Carroll, what can I do for you?"

"Mrs. Swanson, would you like to buy some flowers? I am trying to make some money to buy my Mama a present for Mother's Day." She then asked me how much they were and I told her 25cents. At that moment, I thought I had really made the deal of the year, to sell a lady her own flowers.

I walked straight home, and when I reached the back door of the house, Mama was there to meet me. She had her hands on her hips and she was not smiling. She then asked me where I had been and what I had been doing. I gave her the best answer for a six year old.

"NOTHING."

Mama told me that Mrs. Swanson had called her and she thought I was so sweet to have been out selling flowers to make money for to buy a Mother's Day gift. Mama sat me down and explained to me that you cannot take... steal… flowers unless you ask; especially to sell them to the same person you took them from.

Mama said, "Carroll, you take this money back to Mrs. Swanson, and you apologize for stealing and then selling her flowers back to her."

The walk was the longest for me at six years old. I walked slowly down the alley, dragging my toes behind each step. Then the porch of her house was right in front of me. I stepped up two steps and hesitated at the door. Very slowly I knocked as softly as I could, hoping she would not hear me. NO CHANCE. She heard and she opened the door. I started to cry and hand her back the 25 cents. My voice trembled as I apologized and told her that I was sorry.

She said, "Carroll, all you had to do is ask me and I would have given you all the flowers you wanted." She then took me by the hand and we walked through her home and out the back door into her garden where she picked me the most beautiful bunch of irises, big ones, purple, white, and yellow. So beautiful.

She said, "Give these to your mother." She gave me a pat on my head and thanked me for coming back.

"Bye honey," were her goodbye words.

You would think that after being taught this lesson, I would have learned, but I had to have many more talks with my mama on what was right and what was wrong.

LESSONS LEARNED.

I loved my hometown. I grew up there and graduated from high school in 1960. My family had a grocery store.

Filling the School Hallway with Tumbleweeds
By Virginia Pulfrey of Claremont, South Dakota
Born 1928

My name is Virginia Pulfrey. I was born in 1928 on a farm south of Claremont. When I was three, I and my sisters went to live with our grandparents, Clint and Nellie Buffington. They lived 2 miles north of Claremont. The early years were uneventful until the dust storms started.

The farmers had a tough time. No rain, grasshoppers, and gophers eating the pasture grass and grain. The heat was terrible, and the wind would blow, the dark clouds bringing dust. It would become so dark we'd have to light the lights in the daytime.

We girls were to catch 100 gophers apiece during the summer. We'd take them to the township clerk, where we'd get 3 cents apiece ($3 each). We'd bring the money to our grandmother and she would keep $2.50 of it to buy cloth for dresses and new shoes. She'd give us the 50 cents to spend at the town's yearly field day. The main streets were full of rides and booths. Everything was a nickel: ice cream, pop, and rides.

When we weren't catching gophers, we would herd the milk cows in the ditches. The cream check and eggs was about all the farmers had to buy with. When we ran out of feed for the milk cows, my grandpa found a place to buy some feed. It turned into a tragedy. It was contaminated and killed all of our milk cows.

We went to a country school. We had to walk. The winter of 1936 was really cold. The mornings would be spent unfreezing all the kids. It was a great place to learn.

One time I got a spanking from the teacher for misbehaving and received more when I got home. Another time, the teacher was going to treat us to a peanut hunt. She sent us younger ones out while she and the older ones got prepared. We were indignant, so we filled the hallway with tumbleweeds. We almost didn't get that party.

In 1937, we moved to town. Grandpa wasn't able to make land payments, so my uncle took it over. Things started to change. The rains came, the WPA cleared the fences that were buried, the roads were redone, and they started planting the tree strips.

My grandpa kept some of the land for a garden. I was his helper. He'd sell produce in Aberdeen and take melons to the country fair. One time, we had rows of sorghum to clean. He rigged up a hand cultivator with disks, but we couldn't push it. I suggested using the pony harness and put it on me and hook me to the disc. It worked. We got done in a big hurry, and loaded up the tent and went fishing.

The town had about 350 people, lots of kids. We would play ball every evening, then play kick the can and Red Rover. Doc's Pond was a busy place in the winter. The sidewalks were great for skating.

Claremont was a great sports town. In the summer, there was a baseball game every Sunday. The team of 1938 won the state and again in 1984-1985. My son was a member of the last two.

In 1948, Bill Watch came to town. He started 6-man football. The school went 63 and 0 for 7 years and set a national record. They also had good basketball teams until the school closed.

I have always loved sports, and haven't missed many events. Now I go to Langford's games.

After living 63 years at the same place, 3 miles from Claremont, I moved back to town. It's different now, only around 100 people and not as many kids. The baseball field is still a busy place, though.

The kids now have 4 wheelers and snowmobiles. The sidewalks are shot, Doc's Pond has dried up, and most of the businesses have closed. The school is gone, but the church is still very active.

The community is a very caring community, and we have put on big fundraisers for families in need. Every summer a weekend of softball games is held with most of the proceeds going to a family, if there's a need.

I have lived here all my life. Now I am the oldest. I'm the one they come to, to remember events, and names, and who lived where.

Small Girls' Amazement
By Alice Mae Bjerke Miller of Sioux Falls,
South Dakota
Born 1942

We've all known the distress of the electricity going out and we can hardly wait for the power to be restored.

As a young child growing up in rural South Dakota in the late 1940s and '50s, we didn't have electricity or inside plumbing. In the winter when my parents would take my sisters and I upstairs to tuck us into bed, they would carry a kerosene lamp with them to light the way for us. After they left with the lamp, it was so dark in the room. There was no light unless the moon was shining bright.

Then REA (Rural Electric Association) came to the farm. Oh what a wonder to a small

Alice and her sister, Phyllis in 1947

little girl. Just a flip of a switch or pull of a string in the center of the room and "wa-la" light.

Then all the marvelous gadgets. Electric stove, refrigerator, iron, radio, vacuum cleaner, furnace, butter churn, ice cream makers, cream separators, washing machine, fans for cooling and heating. Lamps for beds, pianos, dressers, desks. Oh my goodness too many to name. The barn, pig barn, granary, chicken coop—all outside building had lights. There was a pump jack so we didn't have to pump water if there was no wind blowing to turn the windmill but oh how gorgeous was the light from the yard pole (which was a pole in the middle of the yard. It just lit up the whole yard.

You could look out over the landscape as you drove down the road and see all the little lights dotting the sky, letting you know here is a farm welcoming you to come if you needed a safe place.

The joy of electricity had come to our farm. Like Jesus the light of the world.

"Santa Tipped Over the Pot!"
By Karen Borgen of Veblen, South Dakota
Born 1937

Over fifty-five years ago, I came as a new bride to the farm. Having lived my whole life up to that point in small towns, surrounded by faucets that actually had running water, an indoor toilet that flushed, and an old claw foot bathtub, it was a rude awakening. It wasn't fancy by any means but it was handy. I immediately discovered that the most important activities of life revolved around water: the abundance of, the lack of, and availability of. I soon learned that the only running water was "you ran with pails."

We first made our home with my mother-in-law in her house. Now, she had a cistern with soft rainwater and a hand pump in the kitchen. This served for washing up, the daily ritual my husband referred to as a "spit bath." Washing up each morning and hand washing was carried out in a small basin on the washstand in the kitchen. I learned you could indeed keep clean daily in a couple quarts of water. Weekly baths were reserved for Saturday night in a large round tub on the kitchen floor. We used a teakettle to heat water for hand and dishwashing. For weekly baths, we heated water in a large covered copper boiler on a two-burner gas stove in the porch.

Then there was the matter of drinking and cooking water. This water came from the well in the middle of the yard. The well water was very hard, but tasted good and was very cold, even on hot summer days. We had two twelve-quart enamel pails to carry the water to the house (uphill). The pails sat on a metal stand in the kitchen with a tin dipper to drink from, or to dip out to make coffee or lemonade, or boil food. The well had at first a hand pump, and later on an electric one. This provided water for the household and also ran through a heavy metal tube outside the well house to water the milk cows in a large water tank. In winter, you constantly had to chip ice for the cows to drink. You had always to save enough water to prime the pump, pouring it slowly down into the well, and drawing the water up. Many a child lost skin from their tongue when they were enticed to stick it on a frozen pump.

For dishes, water was heated in the teakettle and poured into a large enamel dishpan to wash dishes, and the second one to scald dishes after washing them. One dishpan could be scoured out to make large batches of bread, carry lunch to the field, put buns in to take to the Ladies Aid, rinse out hand washables, and bathe the baby. A five-gallon pail called the slop pail held used water and smaller garbage. It had to be constantly carried out and dumped. It always seemed there was twice as much slop pail water as what you carried in.

Clothes washing was Monday morning's chore. Cistern water was heated in the copper boiler and poured into the wringer washer and two galvanized rinse tubs. Whites kept white with bleach, bluing, or boiling on the stovetop before washing. Clothes were carried to the clothesline in a basket and hung up where the sun and wind combined to dry them and make them smell fresh. In winter, you hung it all up outside, let it freeze dry, and brought it back to the house still partially frozen. Jeans, overalls, and long underwear stood by themselves in the corner. We hung small articles on a wooden clothes rack and draped sheets on top. Nothing ever smelled as good as towels and sheets dried in the breeze. Most things still needed ironing, so they were placed in a basket after sprinkling them with water, and ironed the next day.

Occasionally when there was little rain or snow, the cistern went dry. In spring, my mother-in-law and I would load as many 10-gallon cream cans as we could get our hands on and go down the road where there was a runoff in the ditch. We'd dip it out, strain it through an old dishtowel, haul it home, and pour it in the cistern. In winters of big snows, we'd go out and peel off the top layer, watching for dirt, and haul in huge chunks, then melt them down in the copper boiler. Then we'd heat it, and strain it into the washer and rinse tubs. The rest was stored in cream cans or dumped in the cistern. It was a real adventure and I liked doing it, plus the soft water was wonderful for washing clothes, bathing, and shampooing.

Of course there was the outhouse—two holes and a path. It was hot, smelly, and teeming with flies, spiders, and other bugs in summer and cold and drafty in winter. Old Sears Roebucks and Montgomery Wards catalogs served as toilet paper. When you bought fresh fruit in the crate, you got a bonus: the tissues they were wrapped in were as soft and tender as toilet paper and were a real treat. You had to sweep it out, scrub the seats and floor, occasionally whitewash (paint) it and pour lime in the holes to cut down the refuse and odor! An alternative was the covered enamel pot in the bedroom. It had to be emptied and cleaned each morning. A Halloween trick was older youth ran around tipping outhouses. My husband and a bunch of his friends once lifted an old WPA-built country school toilet, set in cement, and set it on the top step in front of the schoolhouse door. It took a tractor and loader to remove it so they could get in and have school. He also shared a story from his childhood about a chamber pot. His mother had arranged for Santa to come visit he and his sisters on Christmas Eve. Santa crawled through the window and tipped over the pot. What a mess! The kids stood around, shouting, "Santa tipped over the pot!"

I fondly remember those days while appreciating modern conveniences. The Cardinal Rule of Water was always to make sure the teakettle is full and if you are close to the last sip of water, you took the pails to the well and refilled them.

371

A Brief History of Onaka
By Rosalia Schmidt of Faulkton, South
Dakota

Our little village came about in the early
1900s when the M & S & L railroad came
through. The first elevator was built and is
still in operation. Two others were built later
and later burned down. The first elevator does
a big job of buying grain. The grain is hauled
out by semis to Ipswich.

At one time Onaka had about 200 people
living here and now maybe 13 remain,
including our home, the elevator, a bar (open
3 nights a week), the Legion Community Hall
with the roller skates left in it and a kitchen
attached, the post office, a garage for gas and
repair, and a good tire shop.

We had 3 churches at one time but the
Catholic Church is the only one left. The
church grounds and cemetery are always in
good shape and all the remaining houses are
always kept in trim shape, only one remains
a mess. But the trees in the weeds still have
fruit. Most of the newer homes were sold and
moved and my home is in Pierre now.

We had an Edison windup record player
and no phone in our home. We took Saturday
night baths in a laundry tub and had an
outhouse and chamber pots.

Most of Onaka was destroyed by fire and
a terrible windstorm that wrecked all the big
barns in the area, about 7 years ago.

Sundays started with Mass at the church,
then home for a chicken noodle soup dinner
and apple pie. Then after the dishes were
washed, we went to the baseball diamond for
a good ball game. Most all the little towns had
a ball team. We went home for supper, then up
town to meet our friends, load in a Model T,

A summer storm

and head out to the big barns for a barn dance.
The girls got in free and the boys had to pay
25 cents, but we all learned how to waltz.

The trains quit running in about 1939-
1940. The tracks and all railroad property was
taken out in 1941.

I married my first love. I had a beautiful
home and a better husband.

Onaka is on Highway 20, west of Cresbard
in Faulk County. I lived in Onaka nearly all of
my life. I lived on the west coast during World
War II. My husband, Andy, was in submarine
repair in the South Pacific during World War
II. I worked as an electric helper in X51 Puget
Sound in Bremerton, Washington. We were
both from Onaka as young kids. I moved into
an independent living center here in Faulkton
2 years ago.

Life on a Farm During the Dirty Thirties
By Dale D. Harpstead of East Lansing,
Michigan
Born 1926

THE DIRTY THIRTIES: Everyone who
lived through the so called "dirty thirties"
has a different story to tell; and so it should
be since the dust storms were not just
discrete events but a five year long series of
interrelated crises, each compounding the
effects of prior events. The collapse of land
values in the mid-1920s, the October 1929
crash of the stock market, and the subsequent
failure of the money and banking systems of
the entire nation all made the environmental
situation caused by a widespread, record
breaking drought practically unbearable. The

Rosalia's family's first car

billowing clouds of dust became the symbol of total depravation.

As an eight year old boy living on a farm in northeastern South Dakota the sight of a churning cloud of dust moving relentlessly across the landscape engulfing everything familiar left me with vivid impressions that are still as clear today as they were then. I remember many times when it was necessary to light the kerosene lamps by four in the afternoon just to be able to see around the house. On one occasion, school was dismissed early and we were told to go straight home since a major dust storm was on its way. Home was a mile south and a half mile west of the school by the road. My usual foot path was the diagonal crossing of weed and brush-covered untilled land. Before I was halfway home, I was totally enveloped in a blinding dust storm, which obscured all vision and sense of direction. Dad, anticipating the school would be let out, had driven to the school in our 1929 Chevy and failed to find me there or along the roadway. He realized that I must have taken my usual shortcut across some open fields and proceeded to drive cross-country to about the center of the route I would have taken. He stopped the car and sounded the horn, which enabled me to make my way to the car and the security of getting home.

Anyone who has not had firsthand experience living through a severe dust storm will have difficulty understanding what the environment was really like. Blown by wind, the larger soil and sand particles formed into drifts on the landscape, not unlike snow drifts after a blizzard. The finer particles were lofted high into the atmosphere and were carried far and wide by the prevailing winds. It was these particles that penetrated into even small air leaks in buildings and houses and it was not uncommon to find a quarter inch of dust on the window sill of your home after a severe dust storm. Also, some people would inhale enough of this dust to experience lung and other health problems. So far as I know, none of our family were afflicted by these health problems.

There were a number of years when we had practically no crop to harvest. Sometimes in the late summer or when fall rains came there would be a lush growth of what we called Pigeon Grass (or Foxtail), Kochia, and Russian Thistle. This forage was eagerly harvested as winter feed for livestock. Even stunted corn would be cut with the grain binder or sometimes a mowing machine to provide another winter feed source. As animal feed this was pure gold.

One fall I remember that Dad and the hired man had made three large "hay" stacks of Russian Thistle. Two of the stacks had been made when the plants were relatively succulent and were, under the circumstances, reasonable high quality feed. By the time the third stack was being made the plants had matured and become little more than stalks and branches the thickness of pencils. Dad made it known that the third stack was for sale and it was eagerly purchased in spite of its poorer quality.

During some of the worst drought years at the end of summer the Russian Thistles (or tumbleweeds) would be blown across the country side and became lodged in the fence rows. This became the perfect "snow fence" for the soil to be blown into drifts, which would completely cover a four foot fence. Thousands of cubic yards of soil were involved and these drifts became permanent features of the landscape and stark reminders of the devastating drought even long after the more normal rain patterns had returned.

When times are hard, people become very ingenious and find ways to stretch the food dollar. One fall we had harvested a small amount of wheat. Dad and two neighbors each took several bags of wheat to Watertown and had it ground into flour. That winter we had whole wheat bread, whole wheat pancakes, whole wheat gravy, and probably much more. Years were to pass before I could accept the idea that whole wheat flour was actually a valuable dietary component.

I don't think we actually ever went hungry. We always had something to eat. There were times when meat was in short supply and eggs may have been few and far between but there was always something. Quality and variety by today's standards may not have always been the best. But it didn't seem so bad because no one told us it was not the best.

As a rural poor family we were eligible to participate in a USDA sponsored commodity exchange program. Citrus from Texas was distributed in the Dakotas in exchange for something locally in surplus. On occasion we would receive a small bag of oranges or grapefruit. It was common in the evening for my younger brother and me to share one orange before going to bed. Another related event that has stuck in my memory was the time we received a bag of "red flesh" grapefruit. Our mother had never seen anything like that before and concluded that something was dreadfully wrong. After much wonderment, debate, and apprehension, the grapefruit were thrown out, i.e., no doubt fed to the chickens.

The Dirty Thirties and the Great Depression impacted not only individuals and families but also the community as a whole. From time to time we had our share of "far out" political activism. There was a Ku Klux Klan chapter in the area. There were people who were in the Farm Holiday Movement coming down from North Dakota as well as the Non-Partisan League Initiative from Minnesota. One such movement that I only became aware of later in the 1940s was a concerted and ongoing Communist Party organization. By the time I was in High School I was aware of local people that maintained some interest in the Communist Party. Later I found out that at least one person in town had routinely recorded the licenses of numbers from cars when certain meetings were held in the local community. By chance, years later I learned that during this same period a county official had been called in by the FBI to view film footage taken of people coming and going at a national Communist meeting in another State to identify people attending from Wilmot and the surrounding area. My home town was slowly but surely being forced into the national and indeed the world stage.

The "Dirty Thirties" left deep marks on all of us who experienced them first hand.

THE FARM: "The Farm" in Lee Township, Roberts County, became our home in 1928 when I was two years old. When Dad acquired the property it was a farm of 320 acres but after the collapse of land values in the 1920s the quarter section without buildings was used to offset a part of the indebtedness. It was always just "The Farm." There were neither classic names nor terms of endearment associated with it.

The buildings and other improvements had been built around 1900. They were constructed with great expectations for the future. The 320 foot drilled well was on a small man-made mound, which we called the "windmill hill." It was only five or six feet above the surrounding area but for my brother and me it was a dominant feature. Originally the well was designed so that water could be pumped into the house and other farm building. The expectations were great but good engineering expertise was lacking and the capacity to make the system work fell short. By the time our family arrived the system was nonfunctional. Only a pressure tank in the basement of the house remained. The drain at the kitchen sink actually worked from time to time but it probably only drained into a "dry well" which most likely had collapsed or simply filled up. An indoor bathroom was not even in the dream.

A large grain storage unit was a part of the great expectations. It was basically a large, three story granary surrounded on two sides by a lean-to type shed for cattle feeding. The granary had provisions for a bucket elevator powered by a stationary engine on a line shaft to carry the grain from a dump pit to the third level. There were grain chutes or ports to route the grain to various operations such as seed cleaning, feed grinding, and/or storage. There were even plans for a wagon scale. I don't think the grain elevator or the scale was ever actually installed. The beams and balances for the scale were around the farm but eventually were sold off as scrap metal. The building was a great place for boys to play. Our imaginations could run wild. We could isolate ourselves in the single room on the third floor, climb to an open window in the gable end, and see for miles across the landscape. To the best of my knowledge we never experienced a serious fall although we certainly tempted fate.

The farm shop was a special place for growing boys. There was a work bench along one side, a few hand tools, a hand-cranked grinder, and a vise, but not much more. There were boxes of used bolts, recycled nails, and Dad's carpenter chest with his tools inside. Despite its limitations my brother and I found it to be a wonderful place to be creative. We discovered it was easier to take things apart than to get them back together again. But we did let our imaginations flow as we built toys, bird houses, and personal treasures. Once I made a "hunting knife" shaping it from an old file with the hand-powered, five-inch, bench grinder and even made a belt sheath for it from an old boot top.

"The Farm" was not an easy place to live. Rural Electrification (REA) did not reach the property until after the end of World War II and I had left home. This left me to dream of wind chargers, battery systems, and an array of jerry-rigged alternatives but none of those achieved much success.

A reliable source of water was often a problem. There were long periods of time when it was necessary to haul water from a flowing stream about a half mile north for both household and animal needs. We did manage to keep a few head of feeder cattle and at times had 6 to 8 milk cows. Even then we had to rent pasture land to maintain them. More times than I care to remember it was my job after school to herd the cattle along the road side to supplement their nutrition. For me the only job worse than herding cattle was herding sheep.

Time took its toll on the original buildings. Sometime in the late '40s or early '50s the three story granary was dismantled. The last building to go was the house, which was torn down in the 1970s after our parents had moved into town. It is still possible to find pieces of broken china, parts of toys, and domestic items in the area where the house once stood. Vivid memories remain.

Aprons, Hats, and Overalls
By Marge Stewart of Milbank, South Dakota
Born 1932

Aprons, hats, and overalls were the dress code of my day. New aprons were gifts at Christmas, birthdays, and showers. A new hat was a must for Easter; new shoes and gloves were a plus.

Men wore either blue or striped overalls for average "going to town" and farm sales but a suit of course for church, as well as a hat, white shirt, and tie. They wore either kind of hat—flat or felt brim or straw.

I went to a one-room schoolhouse all eight years with four different good teachers. We had a pump and well for water to drink and wash hands and clean the blackboard and to drown gophers with.

Those ugly brown stockings were held up

by garter belts and the black bloomers were no prize.

We had our own hot lunch program. You brought your jar of soup or leftovers and put it in the water in a cake pan on top of the stove. In winter, frozen ice cream could go in the snowbank and hope it didn't drift over as then you couldn't find it at noon.

We had bees in the school entry. I got stung by the eye and it got all puffed up.

I'm nearly 82 and still have three of my grade school friends close by. Those were the days!

Marge's parents, Clara and Don

Time to Move the Lake Preston Times!
By Phyllis E. Nelson of Lake Preston, South Dakota
Born 1932

I have always enjoyed writing so it was a natural for me to be drawn to a newspaper office: the Lake Preston Times. During my junior and senior years (1949-50), it provided part time work during the school year and full time work during the summer months.

Kerm Sheimo and his wife Alice published the Times from '49-'56.

Like so many others trying to trim their budget while building a business, they established their home in the same building. This big brick building had as its original tenant the Merchant's Exchange Bank, which old timers told us went bust in the late 1920s. It had been built in 1885 and incorporated in 1888 with a capital of $20,000. The bank name was proudly proclaimed in stone on the northeast corner of the building. But this is getting to be the story of a structure so I will not dwell on it.

My job included lots of proofreading, writing, waiting on customers, keeping the mailing galley up to date, measuring ads and correspondent columns, etc., for bookkeeping purposes, sending out renewal notices, and whatever else needed to be done. On press day, I was given the job of doing single wraps and helping to drag mailbags to the post office.

Our printing method was called "hot metal letter press," an excellent description of a process that had its OWN sounds and smells. The odors of hot lead rose from two containers: one about a gallon capacity was on the Linotype and the other much larger casting box kept the metal at 550 degrees. It was recycled from week to week.

The Linotype, usually operated by Clayt Leonard, made a clattering yet tinkling sound as he set galley after galley of type. Each line dropped out as a separate lead slug.

These slugs were placed into galleys which were long shallow oblong trays used for holding the composed type. Then I would ink this type with a roller with a handle. I would roll it across an ink covered board and then across the lead type. After a clean strip of paper was laid on, another heavy roller was brought across to make a column all ready for proofreading.

After my corrections were made and noted in the margins, it went back to Clayt so he could re-set the slugs, which had errors. So you see there were not computers in those days. There were not typewriters with spell check either. We had to be able to search out our errors and correct them. We also needed to be able to read type on the slugs upside down and backwards!

Kerm and Alice were nice people to work with and they taught me many things about journalism and life in general. One bit of advice they gave me before my 1950 wedding was "When Sunday morning rolls around, just take for granted that you will be attending church and not that you will be staying home." Mr. Sheimo was the organist for our wedding.

Lake Preston Parade in 1950

I used to think that he chewed his wife out for lots of stuff that wasn't her fault. Sometimes it was even my fault! Once I mentioned this to her and she said "Oh, don't say anything to him. If he didn't have some way to let off steam, he'd have an ulcer! If it isn't my fault, I don't even listen to him." Many times in my own life, I have tried to adapt her technique, but it sure didn't work for me. It just gave me a headache!

Now once again my thoughts zero in on that building. It did have character. The bank vault came in handy because paper to be used for job printing was stored there. It also made a good darkroom for loading and unloading film in the press camera.

One of the biggest problems that this place had showed up when heating season came. Two rooms in the back on main floor as well as the upstairs were occupied by renters, but we were in charge of the heating system and thermostat!

It then became obvious that the steam heat distribution system had an advanced case of "arteriosclerosis." When enough steam got through the corroded pipes to keep the upstairs tenants warm, it was pushing 90 degrees in the newspaper office and print shop. That problem continued until living quarters were no longer rented in the upstairs. We just got used to it.

However, it was a big improvement when the theatre building on the east side of the street became available for lease. A move was made there in June 1977. The evening before the planned move, a fierce rain and hailstorm dumped 9 - 11 inches of rain in Lake Preston. The basement stairwell filled with water until the north door caved in and flooded the basement. Yes, it was time to move! Surprisingly, this old building stood until 1988 when it was cleared away for a new fire hall, community room, and library.

Bill and Em's Place
By Grace Wegleitner of Britton, South Dakota
Born 1943

When our parents, William and Emma Southmayd, decided to quit farming in North Dakota and wanted to try a new adventure in their life, they moved to Lake City, SD. a little town in the northeast part of South Dakota. The town had approximately 100 people. They purchased a little bar there in 1953.

Their son Bruce was already away from home at that time and the oldest daughter Gina had to go to high school in Britton and Grace and Dell were still in grade school. We remember going to the Lake City school building. The high school had been discontinued there and the building was in pretty bad shape, but 2 rooms were kept up for the grades 1-8 with 2 teachers. There was an outhouse out back, but eventually a bathroom was put in.

Fond memories of the school were when we had the oil burner going in the winter and we wrapped wieners in tin foil and put them on the stove when we got there in the morning. They were the most delicious hot dogs by noon. We also played basketball in the old gym with the badly warped floor and softball outside in the warmer months. We learned to dance to a record player that had

a very few records. We played waltzes and two steps during recess in the winter months when it was too cold to go outside. Another highlight was when the county superintendent came and brought a new box of library books about every 6 weeks.

Once a year we went to Britton for the YCL program. Gina stayed in Britton during the week to go to high school. Dell and I also "roomed" in Britton during our high school years. That is what we did back then, as it was 18 miles from Lake City to Britton. No driving back and forth each day. Our parents rented a room in a family home and would take us to Britton on Sunday night and come and get us on Friday night.

But back to Bill and Em's Place…

At the time, they purchased the place it was a bar that served beer and sold liquor (for the Town of Lake City). Later the bottle liquor was given up and the space was used for selling fishing tackle and even guns at one point. We girls used to go with Dad to empty the bait traps as he sold minnows along with night crawlers for the fishermen. We also tended bar, sold liquor, cigarettes, minnows, etc. besides doing the cooking and waiting tables. There were times when we "took care of the business" alone when our parents went somewhere. Some of the prices of items at the beginning of the business years were: glass of beer .10 cents, bottle of pop .10 cents, candy bars and gum were .05 cents, and coffee. 05 cents and free refills.

Mom added a little coffee bar in the back of the place and started making her famous oatmeal raisin cookies. Pretty soon, she was making hamburgers and before long, it was a whole meal that people could get. She was a wonderful cook and it was all made from scratch. Dad became a good cook over the years also. The dining business grew and they decided to try their hand at a Sunday smorgasbord as so many would come to drink beer, eat, and visit after church. This eventually led them to the fish fry on Friday nights. By then the business had turned into more of a cafe than bar. Lots of people were leery of "bullheads" but once they tried them, they were hooked. The cost of the fish fry was $1.10 and that included all you could eat of fish, french fries, bread, coleslaw and coffee.

As the fish fry's reputation grew so did the space needed to serve them. The bar was cut down to make a lunch counter. There were living quarters in the back of the cafe. First the living room was made into a dining area, then as each one of us girls left to go to high school our bedrooms were turned into dining rooms. Pretty soon the folks bought a schoolhouse and moved it in back of the place for living quarters so that their bedroom could be used for a dining room. Most every young girl in the area worked as waitresses and several of the women also worked in the kitchen at one time or another. Of course the dishes had to be washed and dried by hand back then.

I remember one evening when…

Dad always went to Browns Valley, MN, which was about 40 miles from Lake City on Friday afternoon to pick up the fresh bullheads for the Friday night fish fry and when he got there, the commercial fisherman that he purchased them from said they didn't have any yet. Dad said "What will I do??? I have to have them, it is Friday!" The supplier told him to go home and assured him that they would get the fish there somehow.

Mom had a few frozen from the past week and started the fish fry with them. About the time she was running out, a big truck pulled up behind the place. Out jumped several men and they started cleaning fish and bringing them in the back door. Another couple of men washed the fish and brought them to the kitchen for Mom to fry. I remember Mom saying the fish were still wiggling when she put them in the fryer. Needless to say someone went out back (probably to the outhouse) and saw the process. It didn't take long for the word to travel through to the customers.

No one could say the fish weren't fresh that night!

The most fish I remember serving was on one 4th of July Friday and we went through 13 30-gallon tubs of fish. I believe we served something like 360 people in that little old cafe that night. People came from a large area and would stand in line halfway down the block for a table just to eat these bullheads that Mom and Dad served. The "secret recipe" for the fish and coleslaw remains a secret held by Bill and Em's daughters, Gina, Grace, and Dell.

One thing we girls will never forget is having to scrub the floors and polish the tables and wash the ashtrays on a Saturday night after closing hours. Of course this was date night, but no matter how late we got in, that was our job to get the place all cleaned up for Sunday.

Bill and Em's Place also served as a place for many after church wedding receptions when free beer would be set up by the families. They also held community card parties there during the winter months on a Sunday evening. Our mother often became the barber for several bachelors in the area and could also be found doing some patching of overalls for someone if needed.

In the later years they would close the place during a couple of months in the winter and go to spend the time in the warmth of Texas. They would reopen the place when they returned. In 1977, they sold out the business and retired. They moved to Britton in the spring of 1982 and Dad died a couple of months later. Mother remained in Britton until her death in 2006.

These are just some of the memories of Bill and Em's Place, by their children, Regina Knebel, Grace Wegleitner, Dell Peters, and Bruce Southmayd.

"How Do You Want Your Eggs?"
By Arlyn "Butch" Smith of Oldham, South Dakota
Born 1942

If there could have been South Dakota's version of Tom Sawyer and Huck Finn, my cousin Dennis Smith and I may have been prime candidates.

My parent's farm was just 2 "easy bike riding" miles from Dennis' farm (Their house was sitting on the location of which is currently the "Spring Lake Lodge" site, 3 1/8 miles East of Oldham).

The year was 1954 and we were at the "adventurous" age of 12. This one particular fine summer morning I grabbed my BB gun, hopped on my bike, and headed out for Dennis' farm. This was one of those cherished days when loading hay bales or cultivating corn was caught up or it had just rained and was too wet for fieldwork.

We would usually start out the day sitting on the front house steps looking around the yard trying to decide what new and exciting

Arlyn "Butch" Smith in 1948

project would make our day worthwhile. It suddenly occurred to us that here we sat and how come 2 self-respecting, energetic, and able 12 year olds like us did NOT have a TREE HOUSE?

So we immediately began to seek out that "perfect" tree. It didn't take long to find one as right there 50 feet away stood this large old cottonwood with a perfect "tree house Y formation" in its trunk and located about 15 feet off the ground. Thus with the aid of a saw and about 20 boards, we proceeded to cut and attach steps up the tree trunk. It only took a minimum of around 20 nails to hold each step securely to the tree trunk. (We didn't want any faulty steps causing an interruption on our daily activities!) Thus as we climbed up to the "Y", one of us would sit there, lower a rope and pull up larger boards for the sides of this "dream home" in the air. There was enough room and supporting branches to be able to construct 2 sides about 4' high. The entrance area was simply left open and also we nailed boards down for the flooring so we could sit or lay on our bellies to look out over the countryside. Every tree house

needs a roof and it was just our luck to find a spare barn door (on a currently unused portion of the barn) that we pulled up and secured accordingly. The beauty of this was the roof was also basically waterproof.

We were literally in "tree house heaven" as we would take position and plink away with our BB guns at about anything and everything. This included the local various birds that shared the branches near us, or, just for practice, the rear end of an unsuspecting chicken feeding in the farmyard down below. We were spending many happy hours in our own special hideaway.

A couple weeks had gone by and one afternoon as we were sitting there reading comic books we saw an ad on "emergency survival" items. Now we certainly were interested in that as who knows what natural disaster might come along and we could be trapped up there for weeks.

One of the survival items was a makeshift camp stove. It showed how one could take a 2 gallon can, such as weed spray might come in, cut out an area about 4 x 5" on 3 sides of the can, leaving the bottom intact, thus having 3 open sides.

We could simply place branches or paper in the opening, light the fire, and today's menu could be laid on top of the can to be heated. It also showed where the lid of the can could be removed so smoke comes out, making the chimney opening, and there you were with this real cool little stove! We couldn't get ahold of one of those cans fast enough! A couple cuts here and there, a metal tube in the filler hole for a stovepipe and we were in business. We

Butch in 1950

379

had matches, paper, and sticks ready to go and now all we needed was something to heat up and eat. A glance over to a nearby branch and what do you suppose we see? A BIRD'S NEST and EGGS! Momma blackbird was not home, so we just "borrowed" a couple eggs. The fire was started; the eggs were frying on the top of the stove and smoke coming out of the chimney. All was going quite smoothly.

Dennis' mother Vi Smith had just stepped out of the front door to shake a rug. She happened to glance up at the tree house and became a bit concerned when she saw smoke coming from the chimney. She began yelling at us to "come down right away!" As no doubt, to her the tree seemed to be on fire. We calmly and coolly replied "no problem" and "by the way, how do you want your eggs"? It's a good thing she had a sense of humor, as she looked the situation over, shook her head, and went back in the house.

Needless to say, we had many more good memories in that tree house. On occasion, even in our high school years we would occasionally just climb up and spend a few moments reminiscing of days gone by.

As I drive by that old farmyard yet today, I look up the driveway and can see that big ol' tree still standing there, and, up in the branches still remain a couple boards from the floor of the tree house.

I might add that this was just one of MANY adventures we experienced in those days. Actually, we are lucky to be alive when I think back on some of them, but then THAT'S another story!

Sure Beats Television
By Cindy Neuharth Hofland of Veblen, South Dakota
Born 1954

As the Eureka School District bus pulled into the yard, Mom stood at the window counting heads as children piled off. One, two, three... six, seven, and eight. She smiled as she set a few more places at the supper table and plopped a few more potatoes in the pot. It was not unusual to have a few "city kid" visitors as guests since they seemed to love to come to the country to experience the good life, and the six Neuharth siblings were more than willing to share their farm life with their friends. There was no need for television or video games when the great outdoors beckoned my friends, neighbors, siblings, and me. Add a little imagination, and the entertainment opportunities were endless!

Whether it was with friends or siblings, we always found plenty of things to do to amuse ourselves outdoors and in the various farm buildings. I fondly remember the days my brother Mike and I would go gopher hunting. The county would pay a bounty of four to six cents for each gopher tail that was turned in, and we were determined to make more money than anyone else. We'd load the little Ford tractor with all the things we'd need for the afternoon's hunt: traps, the .22 rifle, .22 shells, tin snip, hammer, water, and lunch. The cattle pasture to the east of the farm was our destination as it was dotted with gopher mounds. Once the trap line was established, we'd try to shoot the gophers as they poked their heads up out of their holes; then we'd check the traps. If we had one in a trap, we'd pull the trap from the hole, and one of us would pop the gopher on the head with the hammer to kill it while the other would clip the tail off with the tin snip. With just a few breaks for water or a snack, we continued this routine until it was time to head home.

One day specifically stands out in my mind. Mike was feeling a little sorry for the gophers we had caught in the traps, so he decided that he would practice "catch and release." He'd clip the tails and send the gophers scurrying without their tails down their holes. I don't think that was quite what the county officials had in mind when they established the bounty!

On the days when we weren't hunting, we were happily engrossed in a variety of activities and not all of them were parent approved! We built forts in the massive bale stacks or in the hay in the hayloft, often taking a break from our toils to search for newborn kittens. We'd spend time swimming in the sandpit, jumping into grain bins, or riding horses or 3-wheelers. Even though we had horses, we often chose to try our rodeo skills by climbing on the back of a calf or pig just to see how long we could hang on. The birth of farm animals was a miracle we witnessed often as well as the fury of a new mother. It's amazing how fast kids can run and how high they can jump to clear a fence when an angry sow is hot on their trail! On cold winter days, we'd build snow forts, slide, or shoot hoops in the hayloft. The cold never seemed to bother us! There were so many diversions, some safe, and some not so much, for us on the farm, but a few of them are truly treasured memories for me.

One of my fondest memories is the sibling softball game. Since there were six of us, there would be three on each team. Sam, a three-legged German shepherd and a kid's best friend, played outfield. Teams weren't exactly evenly divided, but it didn't matter because Sam was always there to help the underdog. Jeff, who was probably three or four, could only hit the ball if he were pitched a grounder. He would squat and swing the bat on the ground with all his might as the ball bounced through the grass toward him. When he connected with the ball, the ball would roll about two feet, but he would run so hard, usually in the right direction, toward a base. The pitcher would scoop up the ball and race after him. Suddenly, there would be a streak of fur, and Sam, coming to the aid of Jeff, would trip the player chasing him. Jeff always made it to base! Sam was also the best as an outfielder. He would chase any ball, snatch it up, and head toward the infield. How quickly he gave up the ball to a player would depend on who was running the bases. If the runner were one of the younger kids, he gripped that ball in his mouth and often ran away from the infielders until the runner was safely on base or at the home plate. I can still clearly hear the cheers of the scoring player's teammates. Those resounding cheers are also part of a few other memories.

Sundays were days that could bring lots of excitement. Many Sunday afternoons involved a neighborhood softball game in our yard as we had the perfect field. Neighbors of all ages began arriving by various modes of transportation: cars, pickups, motorcycles, and even horses. We'd play softball for hours and then race around on whatever was available. If we were truly lucky, Sunday afternoon would bring a trip to Wolf's Dam for bullhead fishing with family and friends. We'd load up the bamboo poles, worms, bikes, softball equipment, pails, and even a 3-wheeler once in a while and head to the dam with our dads. Dad would bait the hooks

as some of the poles had multiple hooks, and we'd squeal with delight when we caught a bullhead. Dad would take the prickly fish off the hook, and the process would start all over again. When the pail was about half-full of bullheads, Dad would begin cleaning them. Some of us would fish all afternoon while others soon lost interest. That's when all that "non-fishing" stuff would be put to use. Mike found out that it wasn't really a stellar idea to try to drive a 3-wheeler up the spillway; it was a painful lesson for him to learn.

Dad would clean all the fish, and then everyone would head to a pre-designated farm for supper. The moms would have spent the afternoon preparing potato salad, beans, and bars, and they would be waiting for us to arrive with the main course. The bullheads would be fried, and we'd gorge ourselves on that amazing food. Afterwards, yup, there would be another softball game. Moms, dads, and children of all ages would play until it was too dark to see the ball. Then everyone would pile into their vehicles and head for home. I know that Dad had to carry several of us into the house as we dreamed about the adventures of that day.

If we weren't eating our catch of the day on a Sunday, we would quickly race through an early supper and wait for the phone to ring. Sunday night was visiting night; either we would go visiting, or we'd hope that friends, especially those with kids, would call to say they'd like to "come over for a while." Mom would quickly whip together some bars and sandwiches, and we kids would begin planning the night's activities. Two of my favorite activities were Starlight, Moonlight, Hope to See a Ghost Tonight and Corncrib War. Both took place under the cover of darkness.

When we played Starlight, Moonlight, one person would be it (the ghost), and the rest of us would stay at the place designated as goal and count. When we felt we had counted high enough, we'd venture away from goal and look for the ghost who was hiding. I can remember my heart beating so hard and being so scared because I knew the ghost was going to jump out and scare me practically to death. If the ghost appeared, the rest of the kids would have to race back to goal without being tagged. Anybody who was tagged then also became a ghost. The more ghosts there were the more exciting and scary the game became! When we tired of that game, we'd play Corncrib War. All the kids would be divided into two teams or armies. One army was stationed in the corncrib and had lots of ears of corn as ammunition. The other army's goal was to conquer the corncrib. To keep the attacking army at bay, the soldiers in the corncrib would hurl corncobs at the enemy. I can tell you that those corncobs could really cause some pain, and some of the soldiers had quite the arm because of all the softball games that had been played! Yes, there were a lot of bruises, but the pigs ate really well after those wars!

Now all six of us, Randy, Mike, Jodi, Karla, Jeff, and I, are all grown up with children and grandchildren of our own, who, in turn, love to go to Mike's or Jeff's farm to get tractor rides, pet newborn calves, or just experience the great and memorable moments that just seem to happen in the country. I only hope that the memories they make will be as vivid and endearing as the ones I hold close to my heart.

The 'Bum' Didn't Have to Drink Warm Wine!
By Gene Monahan of Watertown, South Dakota
Born 1927

In September of 1955, we were filling a silo at a neighbor's farm and had what could have been a disaster. My dad was up in a silo and with the gooseneck; you could fill the entire roof. We were shutting down and the silo tipped over with my dad still in the top of it. My dad, Thomas Monahan, was by the filler opening and the silo fell the opposite way. He was knocked unconscious. We went, called the ambulance, and when we came back, we were very relieved to see him on his feet! He ended up being in the hospital a couple days; he had a cracked vertebrae in his neck. None of those orange colored silos stood the test of time I think. They were made of baked brick to help eliminate freezing.

I was born in October 1927, on the third generation Monahan farm. It was 14 miles north of Lake Kampeska and 13 miles west of South Shore. The farm kids all went to country schools. One teacher taught all grades

and back then, after graduation you could go to three months of summer school and then teach in a country school. I remember at thirteen, I was big for my age. My eighth grade teacher was pretty and I developed a secret (I thought) crush on her. When I saw her years later, I 'fessed up and told her about the crush. She answered, "Yes... I knew that ".

It was a big deal for us when the Works Progress Administration (W P A) gave us a new outhouse. It had a nice cement floor, big and little thrones, windows, and ventilators. I think most of the schools got them. They also built a nice road by our farm, west to east, and some 80 years later, it is still a good road.

The Big Sioux River went through a couple quarters of our farm. We learned to swim, ice skate, and caught hundreds of fish, mostly bullheads. In later years, we rode snowmobiles on it when there was no snow. When we were younger, the twins Shirley and Sherman and I, 17 months apart, were skating on the river and our dad was there, and we had never seen him skate before. He put on my clamp-on skates and we thought, "This ought to be good." He got to his feet and skated like a pro... he could do anything on skates! Later shoe skates came into being, thank goodness.

My Grampa Doug (Bessie) Monahan, moved onto the homestead in 1905. I, like him, used to hunt waterfowl and trapped every animal there was to trap. He built a complete set of new buildings on the farm, including an icehouse. It always fascinated me when I was little to see where my dad and his hired man were pulling up ice down at the river by our house. They picked a place where it wasn't too deep. The wind had drifted snow over the north end of the hole, anyway. I fell in when I was five years old. I was promptly fished out and taken home right quick. No life is without some trauma it seems.

For those old enough to remember Stony Point on Lake Kampeska in its heyday, they were very lucky. They had a big round skating rink called The Spider Web. It was a round donut shaped rink built in 1948. I remember skating there after our eighth grade was done and it was our school picnic. I recall meeting new girls there. I would mosey over and say, as I saw them bending down getting all flushed in the face trying to tighten up their skates, "Would you like some help?" They would straighten up and say, "Oh gosh yes." Then later, I would see them out skating and would say, "Looks like they're staying on." Then they would extend a hand, and I made a new friend.

One of the highlights of summer on the farm was threshing, usually in August. Our very good friends and neighbors had a big steam engine and large threshing machine and a ten-bundle wagon. They would use grain straw and a supply of water. They'd pull a water tank and straw rack between the steamer and threshing machine for moving. There was a sleeping area behind the straw rack and the men would also sleep upstairs in the barn. It was like a circus was coming to town. When I was about 11 years old, they went to a smaller rig. I started pitching bundles when I was 14. In about 1947, everyone went to combines, and there was no more shocking or hauling bundles.

Gene's brother and sisters

My dad bought a new truck in 1925 and a new Chevy car in 1927. We outgrew the 1918 Model T Ford Coupe he earned from his dad for not smoking. In 1929, we got a new IH Regular Farmall tractor.

My life on the farm was like most farm boys. I learned early how beef and hogs became steak and bacon. When I later went deer hunting, dressing a deer or antelope was a piece of cake!

We had a big white hip-roofed barn that was built in 1918. They had barn dances in it till I was two years old. My older sister Leone remembers being held by my grampa, as he would walk around and sprinkle 'dance floor dust' on the wood floor of the haymow for the dances. The local church board frowned upon dancing and my folks later joined said church. My younger brother and the neighbor kids had the idea they wanted to have a circus upstairs on the old dance floor of the barn once. We had Welsh and Shetland ponies and they believed we could get the ponies up there.

I said they will probably go up the old stairs, but they won't come down. So we nixed that idea. That old barn burned down in 1966 on Father's Day. It was sad to see it go.

We had to make our own fun on the farm when we were younger and often times it would be constructing something. Once my little brother got in trouble when he was in the third grade doing just that. He was impressed with our older cousin's earmuffs he would wear in moderate weather instead of a cap. Our cousin was a town kid and town kids did not walk a mile and three fourths to school like we did. Anyway, my brother took some baling wire and cut in half one of our mom's sanitary pads, which we didn't know anything about at the time. He made his own earmuffs and wore them to school. The teacher sent a note home to our mom saying, "Please don't let Sherman wear his "ear muffs" to school."

In our family, it seemed 1941 was one sad time after another. My grampa Doug Monahan died in April at 68. My mom Lottie was in the hospital with a spell of rheumatoid arthritis. In July, my younger adventurous brother Sherman tried to build a fireplace out of rocks. To aid in getting a fire going, he got a can of what he thought was kerosene, which turned out to be gas. He was badly burned, a third degree on his chest and upper arm. My mom put him in water right away in the tub and called the neighbor, Glen Stadheim, and he took them both to the hospital in Watertown right away. My dad and I were in town at the time. He was in the hospital six weeks and kids couldn't visit back then. It was a real joy to finally have him home. We never had any disputes after that. We were best friends and often double dated when older. We kept close in touch all of our lives until he died last Easter in 2013.

My aunt Doris died and then after that Pearl Harbor happened, all in 1941.

Before the end of World War II, my mom's youngest sister Edna, and my Godmother, married a young minister, Herb Loddigs, and they decided to become missionaries to China. First, they went to the Philippines, to Manila, to study the Chinese language. The Japanese took over and they spent over three years in a concentration camp with 500 other people. We didn't hear from anyone for a year, then a letter finally saying they were okay. We never gave up hope and did a lot of praying. They came back and stayed in the states, S.D., C.A., and Minneapolis, Minnesota, and enjoyed well over 50 years of marriage together. While in California, they introduced my sister Eunice to her future husband, Jerry Dahl from Tracy, Minn. He was in the Army regiment that broke down the wall of the

Gene Monahan

Bilibid concentration camp when they freed my aunt and uncle.

My two older sisters went to the Augustana Academy in Canton for high school. I was supposed to do likewise, but due to a lot of expenses that year, it was decided I should stay home a year. Then World War II was upon us and it rained all fall and we didn't finish threshing until October. I guess I was too good a hired hand, so I stayed home to farm and my younger brother and sister went to school. To this day, I feel a tinge of sadness when I hear the graduation march.

We had a flowing artesian well and a cooling tank next to it. Once when an older teenager, I put a bottle of wine in there. There was not much gone, so it floated. My grandma discovered it when putting something in the cooler and they all thought for sure, there was a 'bum' in the hay loft. I retrieved my trusty Mogen David and went to the dance in South Shore as planned. My dad asked the next morning if I knew anything about a bottle of wine, so I told him the truth. He never did tell my mom, so it was soon forgotten. At least the 'bum' didn't have to drink warm wine!

My dad sold the last two horses when I was in Korea. I was drafted in June of 1951. After basic training at Fort Leonard Wood, Mo., I went to El Paso, Texas, for advanced training on anti- aircraft gunnery. Then I got Far East Command, which meant Korea. I was a Computer in a 105 Howitzer Firing Battery. I would figure the right data so the guns would hit their target. I rotated home and got home December 27, 1952. My family saved Christmas till I got home that year. Then I spent till 3-12-1953 in Camp Carson, Colo.

On a stormy night in January of 1955, a friend and I went to the Playhouse in Clark to a dance. Four girls were celebrating a very nice blonde girl's birthday. I started to see her around more. In April, we had our first date. It wasn't long and I gave my heart to her and she has handled it with care all these years. We became engaged in August and I married Lois Kannegieter in November. We'll be together 59 years this fall. We've got five grandsons, three granddaughters, and two great grandsons now.

We had a good life together raising our three kids, Kimberly, Ryan, and Julie, on the farm. I think a farm is a wonderful place to raise children. I also enjoyed being my own boss, and being able to come and go as you wish.

I've seen a lot of changes over my lifetime, especially in farming. Equipment and farms continue to get bigger. I thank the good Lord for the life we had. And I wish the young farmers of today the best.

The Schoolteacher
By Selma Lapp of Eureka, South Dakota
Born 1927

My father was born in America in 1899 to German immigrants who had settled in North Central, South Dakota. Their modest farmhouse was a two-story house with one large room on the second floor where dad and his two brothers slept.

When Dad was a very young boy, the school district hired a young female teacher and she boarded at my grandparents' house. The only available room for her to sleep was in the one large room where the three boys slept. There was no indoor plumbing, so the only recourse, was to go to the outhouse or use the chamber pot placed in the middle of the room.

At the time, dad could not understand why the teacher would not come back for the second half of the school year.

Imagine, if you can, the three boys kneeling around the chamber pot taking care of business and then the teacher having to use the same pot. Not until dad was older did he understand why she did not stay there after the Christmas vacation.

The New Ford and the Blizzard
By Delores Beckman of Marshall, Minnesota
Born 1952

It started on President Washington's birthday, February 22, 1964 when Uncle Herman bought a new tan 1964 Ford Galaxy 500 at the Ford dealership in Armour, South Dakota. He was so proud of his first new car. I am sure he gave us all a ride.

Then on March 4th and 5th 1964, we had a good old South Dakota blizzard with lots of snow and strong winds. On March sixth, a bright sunny morning we woke up to snowdrifts as high as the second story windows of our house. All morning long, we shoveled to get out. By that afternoon, we got to Grandma's house, a mile away. When we got there, Uncle Herman handed my brother and I each a shovel and said, "Find my New Car."

We dug one to two feet before we found the radio antenna, which was pulled all of the way up. It took us all afternoon to scoop that car out of the snowdrift. It started right up but we could not go anywhere for a while, it still had a huge snowdrift all around it.

Skunk Perfume
By Glenn Olsen of Alpena, South Dakota
Born 1936

During the mid-1940s, I was going to a country school in Northwest Aurora County South Dakota.

During the Noon hour, I and my friend was playing cowboys and Indians or cops and robbers. As I rode my bike across the yard, he would shoot at me with a homemade bow and arrow.

He hit me in the forehead with a tree arrow. It made a small cut and the blood was running down my face. As I got hit, the County Superintendent drove in the yard. She opened her trunk, and got a stick and caught him and spanked him. I still can remember him howling. Still when I see him and his wife today, he says there is the person who got me whipped by the County Superintendent and laughs.

We kids were scared of the County Superintendent It was said that she had a wooden leg, whether it was true or not.

Also, at the school around ten years of age, I had traps out for skunks and mink. I would walk to school, two and a half miles on nice days and check my traps. I got a skunk one morning and I got sprayed killing the skunk. The teacher put me in the far corner and moved the kids away from me.

At Noon, she sent me home, told me to go home, take a bath, and not come back until the next day. I was happy. I got the afternoon off.

Big Turkey
By Pat Herr of Watertown, South Dakota
Born 1954

Christmas Day was always my favorite. We would go to our grandparent's house, which was a one bedroom little shack next to the lake of Clear Lake up by Lake City, South Dakota.

Now this part might be nice to know. Twenty people stayed overnight in that house every year. I don't remember one year when the weather was good enough to drive home.

My grandparents made braided rugs for a living; that is what everyone of us covered up in to stay warm. We had people laying on people, but nobody ever complained.

My grandma always made a big turkey so we would have enough for supper too. So she put it in the garage to keep it cool.

The rest of us went out on the lake with shovels and made a skating rink and had a great time all day.

Well, by suppertime everyone was getting pretty hungry. So we got everything out for supper and grandma went out in the garage for the turkey and here the neighbor dog had just finished eating it and all that was left was the carcass. I don't remember what she said because most of it was German, but it was a good memory.

Lucky Listener
By Joanne Drenkow of Fargo, North Dakota
Born 1941

Party telephone lines, that's what everybody had, didn't they? In the case at our home there were three or four parties whose "ring" we could hear, and maybe that many more whose rings we couldn't hear. We could rubberneck the day away listening to the neighbors' conversations because in order to interrupt their call, or for them to hear us, you had to press the button on the telephone. Hold that thought.

KWAT radio, Watertown, a morning program on that station was called "Name that Tune!" A listener would call the station, whereupon the program host would play a blurb from a song, and the contestant who called in would win a whole slew of prizes from participating Watertown merchants if

they could name that tune! One day Ila Mae Luken, one of our party line people, was the lucky listener who called in to the station first, and the program host played the snippet from a tune. Ila Mae hemmed and hawed, it was on the tip of her tongue but she just couldn't quite spit it out, and time was running out, so my mother, Jennie Lakness, who was listening to the program, went ahead and pressed that button and answered "Home…'Going Home' is the name of that tune." Never the wiser, the radio announcer exclaimed "That's right, Mrs. Luken! Congratulations on successfully identifying the song! You are the lucky winner of (lots of prizes)!

Big Boys
By Marjorie Thoelke, Britton, South Dakota
Born 1929

This true story took place during the darkest days of World War II.

Patton's Army had been fighting fiercely through France. There was a lull in the fighting so the soldiers had a few hours to spend, cleaning their guns and various activities.

This soldier who had just turned nineteen years old decided to walk down to a stream nearby. He sat down on the bank, let the sunshine down on his face and thought of home!

Another chap from another outfit was also sitting nearby doing the same thing. Quietly thinking about home!

Finally, the other young soldier said "This creek reminds me of a creek we had back home, that we called Big Boys!"

This got the immediate attention of the other soldier, and he replied, yes, we had a creek at home also that we called Big Boys! Where are you from?

"Oh just a little town in South Dakota, White, you have probably never heard of it."

"That is my hometown as well!" They embraced and had an absolutely wonderful few hours remembering the "good times."

Both soldiers knew full well in a few hours they would again be in battle.

Big Boys was a retreat from the heat where a large group of boys swam and just had fun! These two soldiers were friends and part of that group since first grade. They remembered so much of the same things and people of that "little town."

It was such a special two hours to forget the war and remember the fun times in White, South Dakota.

That soldier is my husband of sixty-six years. He came back to the USA on a stretcher aboard the Queen Mary. He spent a year in Army Hospital where he recovered quite well.

Our Family Outing in October 1947
By Virgil Likness of Plattsmouth, Nebraska
Born 1936

My Dad had just purchased a slightly used beautiful, 1946, red and black half-ton pickup truck with only a regular cab. Our farm family consisted of five children, and Mom and Dad. At that point, in time, traveling was very limited as World War II was just recently over. Purchasing vehicles was a new experience to our family at that time. The kids ranged in age from sixteen to three years old and I was the number two child and eleven-years-old at the time. My big brother did not want to be seen in public but the rest of the family did want to be involved in our family outing.

This shiny, new pickup just seemed to create a sense of happiness for our entire family and we needed to try out this vehicle. We decided to make a major trip to our Uncle and Aunt's home, which meant a trip of nearly sixty miles from near Langford, South Dakota, to Summit, South Dakota. Our Mom even made a picnic lunch as a trip of this distance required extended sitting time, excitement, as well as endurance. After all, kids get hungry and eating in a restaurant was unheard of in our family.

Mom, Dad and the younger four children all climbed into this single seat with a stick shift and traveled to Summit on a Sunday, morning. We had a wonderful day meeting our cousins as well as playing with other new friends in Summit. After an exciting day, the sun began to lower and it was time to head for home. On our return home, we were traveling North of Webster, South Dakota, on a recently resurfaced road, which consisted of loose gravel. In 1947, driving regulations were non-existent in South Dakota. Piling six people,

two adult and four children, into a three-passenger vehicle was not a violation of any safety rule. We sat four abreast with Dad as the driver, seated close was nine year-old sister, with my Mom third abreast and me crowded between Mom and the passenger door. On my lap was seated my three year old sister and in mom's lap sat my seven year old sister. In addition, we had our lunch basket, a water jar, mom's purse, and some other incidentals. We all wanted to be safe, as we certainly did not want to wreck our new truck. About three miles North of Webster, my Mom looked at the speedometer and she said to my Dad, "Bennie, I have been told that if you drive over fifty miles per hour on the highways, the devil climbs in the seat next to you." My seven-year-old sister, Beverly quickly chimed in by making the following statement, "But Mom, there is no more room in the pickup."

Halloween from the Past
By LaJoy Thompsen of Esmond, South Dakota
Born 1930

I grew up in the Esmond Community, a small town in Kingsbury County, and Halloween has changed very much from that time.

One Halloween, a man found a cow in his house that lived a mile south of Esmond. Then there was the morning when the janitor got to school, he found a cow upstairs in the four-room schoolhouse. Can you imagine the mess he also found!

Upsetting the outdoor "back" house (as

Kids on a Merry-go-round in 1942-43

387

The threshing crew

outdoor toilets were called) was very popular. One time they were just pushing, them back a short ways. One woman must have had to go to the back house and she stepped into the hole in the dark.

The Halloweens that I remember were the get-togethers for everyone who lived in the area. They were held in the Township Hall. It was an evening of visiting, card playing for the men and women, and games for us kids. The one I remember was bobbing for apples in a wash tub filled half full of water. Have you ever tried it?

At one of these, get togethers someone went outside and came rushing back in with news that one of the stores was on fire. All the men became firemen and with the towns fire equipment got the fire out and in the days following, they became carpenters and helped with repairing the store. It was always thought by some that the guy that owned the other store set the fire.

Another activity at night was moving everything that they could move on to the streets of Esmond. I am sure this was a man activity.

Today's Halloween is far different than from I remember from the past. Of course, there isn't any back houses to tip over and many fewer people in the area. WE still get a knock for Trick or Treat by the young kids in the community to remind us of the date on the calendar.

Freight train with bums at harvest season

Corn Palace Week
By Donna O'Connell of Brookings, South Dakota
Born 1944

"Donna, Robert, Laurel, Mark, Greg, Jeff, Mary, Jane, and Brad-the ice cream buckets for your milk tabs are on the back porch. It's up to you how many free rides you earn. Try not to fight, and Mary, don't tear the tabs off the full cartons. Donna, you're in charge." Mom's words were music to our ears.

Growing up the oldest girl of nine children, my jobs were many, and probably not as time-consuming nor as taxing as I remember. But there was one job I assumed with pleasure. One I attacked with uncharacteristic organization and diplomacy. Each year I was in charge of Free Rides for the Corn Palace Week festivities. The first week every September, our small hometown of Mitchell, South Dakota, celebrates fall and its fruits by hosting a weeklong, Main Street carnival and nationally known entertainment which appeared nightly on the Corn Palace stage. Our local dairy, Culhanes, was cutting edge in the marketing department, and during the 1950s, 1960s, and 1970s their dairy exchanged a ticket for a free carnival ride for every fifty tabs torn from their milk carton sprouts. Because we had such a large family, we drank our way through many half gallons of milk and pints of half-and-half cream a week enough to qualify for Monday, Wednesday, and Saturday deliveries. Our grandmother and aunt hoarded their tabs for us too, and though we welcomed all donations. Robert and I secretly chuckled at their paltry monthly contribution.

For the next fifty-two weeks, we watched, vulture-like as milk cartons were emptied and disposed of. Not a single milk tab escaped our eagle eyes, (I liken this to the way my daughter, during her visits now, regulates my re-cycling efforts.) Pity the sibling who was negligent; he or she was instantly reprimanded and harassed throughout the remainder of the day. Mom would have rejoiced if we had approached any of our responsibilities with such dedication. But this particular endeavor resulted in a gigantic payoff; free carnival rides. Our priorities were indelibly set. So we assembled nightly at the kitchen counter, baby Brad in his highchair (drooling in what Mark and Greg decided was anticipation but what we experienced ones knew was teething,) and the other eight of us perched on stools, each with our own job; one week until Corn Palace Week and the rides. Our parents made plans with their friends to attend the shows, which throughout the years featured big names such as Bob Hope (he stopped at our house one year to get directions to the golf course and we enjoyed that notoriety for a full year) Andy Williams, Jack Benny, Red Skeleton, Jim Nabors, and of course the official house orchestra, Lawrence Welk. We frantically counted tabs into piles of fifty and then recounted Jane, Mary, and Jeff's bundles. Their counting skills were still developing, but if they wanted free rides, they had to put in their time. Robert and Laurel were deemed trustworthy enough to make the final rubber-banding or twisty-tie finishing touches. The overflowing ice cream buckets where the tabs had been stored slowly emptied.

September finally arrived. The excitement of returning to school on those warm, humid days was overshadowed by the impending arrival of Corn Palace Week. We had scoured the neighborhood, cajoled milk tabs from employees without children at Dad's store, and salivated as the free ride tickets accumulated. The carnival workers would arrive tomorrow.

And the recon began. The first or (in case of admirable restraint) second day after the carnival workers had overnight eerily transformed five solid blocks of Main Street into a fantasy land, we would prowl the streets in pairs, assessing each ride for thrill factor, length of lines, and actual time spent on the ride. Turning a deaf ear to the tempting offers of the hawkers (though a few of the boys silently entertained the possibility of winning one of those huge pink bears,) we maneuvered our way through huge electrical cords and hissing refrigeration, ignoring the saccharine smells of cotton candy and caramel sweetness of kettle corn. The Slim Jim, the Rock o Plane, the Octopus, and the Bullet boasted names exotic and tantalizing. As my sister Laurel and I aged, we based some of the ride's appeal on the cuteness and/or spiel of the forbidden carneys. But my brothers had no such biases. Their evaluations were weighted and spot on. Later in the day, we would come together. Information and opinions were shared and choices narrowed. Decisions were tentatively made, only to be revisited numerous times throughout the night in bed. Mom would talk to us all tomorrow when we were all together. It was finally time for dinner, dispersal, and deportment. We listened again as the rules were laid down.

You must have a sister or a brother with you at all times.

Don't eat the food on the midway. Use the money Mom gave us for caramel apples and such form Woolworth's Five and Dime.

If you get kicked off a ride, your week was finished. Come home immediately.

You only leave Main Street to walk home.

Be home before it gets dark.

Check Dad's store for messages.

Have fun and here are your eight (ten or eleven, depending upon the year) tickets to ride.

And every year, it was the "best carnival yet." No one got food poisoning or got lost or eloped. Mary and Jeff both threw up, but that just proved they chose the best bang for your buck ride. Mom and Dad praised the danceable music of Lawrence Welk and his orchestra and the piano prowess of JoAnne Castle. Amidst all the reliving of the week's events, all the discussions of which was actually the scariest ride, I was struck by the realization that I had orchestrated my last Free Ticket Assemblage. I was off to college next August and wouldn't return home until Thanksgiving. Fortunately, Robert had been primed and was anxious to take his turn at the helm.

Building a Car
By Harlow H. Rudolph, Dallas, Oregon
Born 1946

I have always loved cars, especially classics. Even as a kid, I wanted to create my own set of wheels. Well, one day I tried to do just that. I really don't remember what grade I was in but I will never forget this particular day in my life.

On this particular day, I decided to skip school and build my own car. I had the plans in my head and I started looking for things to build my car with. I found some wood pieces, nails, rope and some tools in the shed. I still needed wheels so I started searching for them. I found a lawn mower in the neighbor's yard

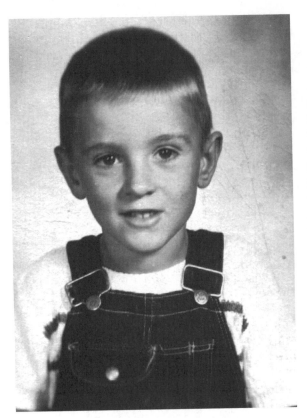

Harlow H. Rudolph

and the wheels were just the right size. I wrote a note, to the neighbors, and told them that I would bring back the wheels that evening.

While I was building my car, I had to go into our house and use the bathroom. Well, I did not know that my mother was having a ladies aid meeting and that there were quite a few ladies visiting with my mom. My mom asked me why I was not in school and I told her that I didn't want to go to school today and that I was building a car and went back outside. She did not say anything else and I thought I would be able to get by without any punishment, but I was wrong. Later on that evening, around suppertime, I found out that I was in big trouble. I ran around the kitchen table quite a few times to escape my spanking but knew that I would have to give in and receive my punishment. It didn't hurt too much, and life went back to normal.

Yes, I did take my car apart, took the wheels back to the neighbors, who just happened to be the Principal of the school, retrieved my note and went to school again the next day. I learned a good lesson that day; do not skip school and stay home to play.

Childhood Memories
By Doris Struckman Koisti, Hazel, South Dakota

During the summer when I was in high school, I would wash the clothes for our family of nine; of course, we only washed once a week, usually on Monday. First, the water would need to be heated in a big boiler on the cook stove; the fuel was corn cobs picked from the pigpen by my brothers. Then the wringer washer was wheeled out to the porch and filled with the hot water. All the clothes were washed in the same water, starting with the loads of sheets and ending with the loads of overalls. Mrs. Stewart's Bluing would be added to the rinse water to make the white clothes look whiter. The clothesline would all be filled with clothes so the overalls would be hung on the woven wire fences around the yard to dry.

Mother always had a large garden. We would pick peas by the "half tub" which was a metal container a little smaller than a bushel basket, with a wire bail for a handle. Then we would put the peas through a pea sheller to get the peas out of the shells. I thought that was a fun job and it always amazed me to see the peas come out.

We had a large yard to mow. The mowing was done with a reel mower, probably 18 inches or less wide, which had to be pushed. That must have been a big job.

I remember our first telephone on the wall. I remember it as being about 2 ½ feet long by 1 foot wide and being made out of wood. Then it was replaced by a black phone only about 1 foot long and 8 inches wide. There were several families on the line. We knew when it was our "ring" by one long and two short rings.

We had a pump in the entryway with a pail underneath where we got our water for cooking, bathing etc. There was always a metal dipper in the pail and we all drank from there. The water came from our cistern. The water supply was from the rain which fell on the roof and went into the eave troughs and then into the cistern. We had to be very conserving of the water in case there would be a dry spell.

I remember getting up very early in the morning and riding on the hayrack to our neighbors where my dad would help with the threshing. Several farmers would get together to thresh and then when they were at your place the farm wife would make a huge dinner, complete with pie for dessert. I also remember riding with the hired man to take a load of grain to the elevator in Grover. Horses were used for hauling the bundles and hauling the grain to the elevator.

We made our own entertainment. It was always lots of fun when the neighbors came over with their children. I know we made lots of noise so I wonder how the parents could stand it. When it was just our own family, we played tag etc. outside in the nice weather. In the winter, we listened to the radio. I especially remember Fibber McGee and Molly. I had a playhouse and made mud pies and cookies. I would go on "shopping trips" to get decorations for them, which consisted of leaves and weed seeds. Mother would get the outdated pattern catalogues from J.C. Penney's material department and I would cut out the people and have a family live on each step of our open stairway.

I lived with Mother's cousin in Hayti during the school year and only went home on the weekends. We had four teachers including the superintendent. Each class was responsible for a party during the year. Sometimes we went roller-skating at Lake Kampeska or just had a party at the school. Only the boys played basketball, no football, and we would ride the bus to games at area towns. That was always a fun time and we would sing songs to pass the time. Each town had their own school. At the end of the school year, we would have a picnic at Stony Point at Lake Kampeska and then go roller-skating in the round skating rink there. For the junior and senior years, we did not have a prom but there was a banquet where we got to wear formal dresses.

There was still a soda fountain at the drug store in Hayti. I remember all the stools to sit on, all the fancy dishes for ice cream, and all the machines to make malted milk. It was fun to have a treat once in a while.

In Memory of My Mother, Katy Myers
By Joyce Steinle, Alexandria, Minnesota

I'm going to tell you about my mom. She was a farmer's wife and mother of five children.

Katy Myers

Mother's Day will be the anniversary of her death. First, I would like to tell you how we all began. My eldest brother ran our farm and cared for her. At sixty years, he had a stroke, which ended up in having a leg amputated. We had to make his home in a nursing home. But what do we do with mom? Mom said, "I'm going with him and take care of him. She was ninety years old at the time. She never felt sorry for herself. And she made his time easier for him, and the staff found her a joy.

Sometime after they left the farm, my

391

eldest sister and I rode down to see how things were. But I had another reason to go. I wanted to say goodbye from the home I had lived until I married.

I felt emotions I dreaded to think about. Everything was dead, no farm cats, no birds crossing the skies. Summer storms had scattered limbs all over; my home was dead. I took a walk down our lane and there I saw an apple tree filled with fruit. It wasn't the time for an apple tree doing this I truly think it was a message meant for me to find. My first words; "there's still life here."

I couldn't wait to go home. Put my thoughts on paper.

I will have to ask you to use your imagination and remember I will speak first to the house and then in my mind takes over and speaks to me in the form of poetry and prose.

Today I came to say farewell and your silence said to me.

I will not care if you don't stay. I'm not missing you, you see I gave I gave then all the love I had and yet they gave me more. Now age and illness have crept in and made me close the door.

It isn't as quiet you think. Can't you hear them all? A baby's cry, a squeaking chair, a loving parent's call?

Close your eyes, concentrate, I know you will recall. I do! I remember! A windmill fan spinning in the breeze, the honking of the geese overhead coming home from their evening feeding.

I hear the rattle of harness and the clip-clop of Dick and Derby's hooves, trotting home in darkness from a long harvest run. There is the lowing of cattle waiting to be milked.

I see my mother bent over a tub rubbing clothes on a board, then ironing with a flat iron and mending children's clothing by the light of a kerosene lamp. I hear myself crying with an earache, while my mom rocks me and sings me to bye-bye to the tune of Rock of Ages.

Run, Run, that old mean goose is chasing me. Why does it do it? I'm smaller than him? Dad says he won't chase me after New Year's. I wondered what he meant.

I remember the awful blizzards that never seemed to stop. We had to wrap bricks and put them in the oven; then put them in our beds to keep our feet warm at night.

I hear music! Norma is sitting at the piano playing our favorite hymns. Our family loves to sing and nights we gather around to sing. We sing in harmony and our dad's bass makes it just the best!

We love popcorn and homemade fudge. We hear Fibber McGee and Molly and never miss President Roosevelt's fireside talks.

How fast time is passing. We have the happiness of marriage, the sorrow of our love one going to war, the death of our loving father.

Hard times; always a struggle but the will to survive.

House speaks.

Yes, I know all your secrets your sorrow and pain and joys. I've listened to some angry words and wept with each. In sorrow words won't harm for always comes tomorrow. I'll

Joyce Steinle

understand if you do not come for absence cannot part what we shared today.

Goodbye old house, our paths won't meet again. The weeds and cobwebs will be your "Shroud" and as all things end- AMEN.

I'd like to say one more bit about mom. She fought the fight; she finished the course, and never lost her faith.

Happy Mother's Day, Mother Norma, and I love you!

Fighting the Fire
By William E. Beastrom of Harrold, South Dakota
Born 1932

This is the story about my experience in the prairie fire North of Harrold and Highmore, on September 5, 1947, as I remember it, and from what was written about it in the papers of that time.

It was very dry and that day, there was a strong Southwest wind blowing. There were actually two fires, one was started North of Harrold about eleven a.m. by a tractor and the second fire started about one o'clock p.m. on Highway 14, a little East of Highmore, by a cigar or a cigarette thrown out of a vehicle. The fires burned north almost to 217 about 37. Then the wind changed and blew from the Northwest and turned the fire back towards Highway 14. This resulted in the West fire burning most of the area between the two fires.

About two years before the fires, we had moved from North of Highmore, to a place Northwest of Highmore. The fire got our place on the way back on that evening.

As I remember it, my brother, Boyd, and I were helping Dad around the place that morning. Boyd was thirteen and I was fifteen. We had just finished mowing the last of the hay a few days before. We did all of our work with horses at that time. Boyd drove a team on a mower with a five-foot bar and I drove a three-horse team on a mower with a six-foot bar. And we would both pull dump rakes; this left the hay in windrows. It took a long time to mow and 160-acres of hay with horses and we were glad to be done with it. It all burned that evening.

We had a big barn with the haymow full of hay and we had a large stack of hay on the North side of our corral, which was connected to the barn. We also had a rolled stack of hay about one third mile north of our place. By rolled I mean we had no tractor with a loader so we put up all of our hay with hay ropes, slings, and a long cable. We could roll the hay up onto the stack or into the barn with our horses.

About Noon on the day of the fire, we saw the fire west of us. We put two five-gallon pails of water and some burlap sacks into the trunk of our car. We then saw the fire North of Highmore, and Dad decided that since the fire to the West was already past us, that we would go over and help some of our old neighbors North of Highmore. About all we could do with water and sacks was to work around the buildings and yards by putting out the small fires that started up again. We worked most of the afternoon until the wind changed and it started getting very smoky. We knew that the west fire was probably coming back, so we headed for home. Dad stopped in Highmore and had the car filled with gas, which probably saved our lives. We hurried on home to find that my older sister, Beatrice, had taken her saddle horse, brought all the cattle, horses, and sheep in, and locked them in the corrals. My Mother and Beatrice also had a team of horses hooked up to the stone boat that had two fifty-gallon barrels on it. The stone boat was just two old posts with boards nailed across the top. You would hook the team to one end and the posts worked as runners like a sled. We used it to pick up rocks out of the field which is probably where it got its name from .The ladies had pulled it up to the water tank and used buckets to fill the barrels with water, and then they took it down along side of the big stack next to the corrals. There they would go up a ladder on the stack with buckets of water and sprinkled it on the stack so sparks wouldn't catch it on fire. They ended up saving that stack and thereby also saving the barn. You probably know that we had no running water, electricity, or telephones.

Dad left Boyd there to help the women and took me with him to see if we could save the stack north of the place. We took an old, regular farm tractor, which Dad had just bought, and hooked it onto a horse drawn plow. We tried to plow a fireguard around the stack but it was so dry, and hard that we couldn't get the plow to go into the ground. It was just scratching the top a little so we gave up on that and took the tractor and plow home. We then took the car back out so we could get a backfire started northwest of the stack, but we didn't have enough time. By now, it was dark, smoky, and very hard to see. I remember we could see the front of the fire coming through the smoke. When the fire was about one hundred yards away from us, we jumped into the car to go home only to find that a strip of the fire went between us and the place. There was a road that went east and west pass our place, so Dad decide to go east and get on that road. When we got to the road, Dad turned short to go through the ditch at an angle. The front tire must have just missed a big rock. The rock rolled under the running board and back to the rear wheel, lifting the rear wheel off the ground. There we sat. When the fire was less than fifty feet from us, Dad yelled at me to get back into the car. The fire roared past us. It was so very hard to breathe; we had handkerchiefs over our nose and faces which might have helped a little. The grass was quite tall where we were sitting along the ditch, so there was a very hot flame for a short time. It was just a few seconds until the worst of it was past and Dad yelled to me to get out. It was still burning but was burning down fast. We ran to the back of the car and got the five-gallon pails of water out of the trunk. We threw the water under the gas tank. The heat had expanded the gas and the pressure was forcing the gas out of the little vent hole in the gas cap. We got that put out then poured the rest of the water around the tires to stop them from burning. When we were sure that the car was safe, we went across the road and managed to break off an old fence post and used it to pry the car off of the rock. Then we went home. Everyone we told this story to, agreed that if we hadn't had a full tank of gas it would have exploded. Thinking back about it, after it was over, we thought that someone up above must have been looking out for us. All the paint on the 1937 Ford was blistered except for a spot on the roof. I should say here, that the car was very important to us because it was the only vehicle we had to get around in.

When we didn't get home ahead of the fire, my Mother and Sister thought we were gone, and they were really surprised when we came driving in. We were glad to see the barn and stack of hay were okay, but found that the horses had gotten spooked when the fire got close, and broke a gate down. All of the livestock went out ahead of the fire. There was a small dry lakebed South of the place where there wasn't much growth, the cattle might have been about there when the fire caught up to them, then they turned back and went back through the fire and returned home. The sheep we found on a hill that didn't burn and the horses we found on another hill that didn't burn. All we lost was two cows. They died a few weeks later from smoke in their lungs. The next morning, we found that the big stack north of the place didn't burn either. It remains a mystery because the fire went right up to it on all sides without igniting it.

There was a man by the name of George B. German who had a fifteen to twenty minute spot on the WNAX radio station. I think it was during the Noon news hours when he talked about things that had happened around the state. He told about flying up North and Northwest of Highmore to look over the damage done by the fire, He said that he saw a stack of hay Northwest of Highmore that didn't burn and the fire had burnt right up to it. We had seen a plane circle that stack two or three times so, we figured he was probably talking about our stack.

We had to put out small fires and smolders for about a week or ten days, and that was the end of our fire fighting for this fire.

Dad was able to rent another place about fourteen miles away and with the two places; we were able to keep all of our livestock. There were a lot of people that had to sell some of their livestock because they lost their feed, so overall we thought we came out fairly well.

Career Choice
By Bonnie Funk of Madison, South Dakota
Born 1933

After eight years in a one-room county school, my parents sent me to high school in Brookings. I was not allowed to attend high school in White, only seven miles away, as I would need to ride with the neighbor boys (no school busses at that time,) and it was too far to drive to Brookings, so I lived by town in an apartment by myself, and went to a school of over four hundred students. Being very shy, I made few friends there and felt lost most of the time. In the middle of my sophomore year, my parents moved to a farm near Madison, and I could then attend Orland Consolidated school, where there were only twenty-nine students in high school, only seven in my class, I learned for the first time to make friends, and to feel accepted. That experience kind of went to my head.

It was in the middle of my senior year at Orland High School, and Mother was asking me what I wanted to do when I grew up. My answers probably proved I was not grown up yet. I wanted Dad to buy me the car my friend's father had for sale for twenty-five dollars, and when he declined this wonderful opportunity, I chose to say, "I'll get a job working at the dime store and earn the money myself." What I really had in mind was finding a boyfriend, getting married, and becoming a housewife, after all, what does one do with four years of Home Economics, all I had really learned was how to do a bit of cooking and sewing.

In town, At Madison High School, they were holding career days, a chance for kids like myself to explore the options. Orland seniors were invited to attend, and my friend, who wanted to be an x-ray technician, asked me to go with her to the only choice close to that, nursing.

The director of Sioux Valley School of Nursing, Agnes B. Thompson was the presenter. She told us it only took three years to become a good nurse, and the cost of the school was only Seven hundred and fifty dollars, for the entire three years, and this included board, room, books, and uniforms. Mentally I compared this to the cost of any college I knew of, and decided it was a better deal by far, since it took less time than a college degree, and cost much less. But I did not send in an application, I was more interested in graduating and so, my Mother did it for me.

My head was filled with plans for the two vacation trips our class was entitled to upon graduation. One was our senior trip, for which we had been earning and saving money all through high school, selling lunches at basketball games and so on. The other was a trip with the Future Homemakers of America, to the Black Hills. My classmates and I sat down, counted up our money, and using a map, chose a city as far away as our funds would get us, and began to plan the trip to Saint Louis, Missouri

Sioux Valley's classes began in June, and so, the day after we returned from the Black Hills trip, Mother had my bags packed, had purchased matching curtains and bedspread for my dorm room, and she marched me off to Sioux Falls to begin school.

I shared the dorm room in the "nurses' home" with three other girls, all better prepared for the event than I was. The first three months, we walked from the hospital to Augustana College to take three classes, Anatomy/physiology, Chemistry, and Microbiology.

I squeaked through those with the help of my soon to be best friend, who was my lab partner. By the end of the summer, we were allowed to take classes at the hospital, learning how to do the hands on stuff like cleaning the rooms, making beds, backrubs and baths.

When we had mastered those skills, we began work on the floors, actually caring for patients. Classes continued, taught by Rn's or doctor's, about the science of medicine, disease, and nursing practices. We put in an eight-hour day. If we had four hours of classes, we worked four hours on the floor. Meals were served in the cafeteria, and we lived together, having moved into a room, which accommodated five students. Two of those were a year ahead of us, and could help us prepare ourselves for things to come.

The first three months or so of our hospital work, we were called, Probationers, or "Probies." Our uniforms were blue and white stripe dresses, with a white apron, and a big black tie around the neck of the detachable white (collar and cuffs.) At the end of the Probationary period, they held a capping ceremony, where the tie was replaced with a stiff white bib. It all had to go together with safety pins. The cap, bib, and cuffs were as stiff as cardboard, the cap needing to be folded and secured with a button, and pinned onto our heads. But, proudly, as we had proved ourselves as nursing students. The white shoes we wore had to be approved by Dr. Van. Demark, the leading orthopedic surgeon, and he made me buy size ten and a half. Up until that time, I had worn a size seven and half. Probably that is why I have foot problems to this day.

Doctors began to lecture in our classrooms, and we were rotated from one ward to another. I was lucky. When we were learning MED/SURG, I was working on the medical or surgical ward. We rotated through each ward: OR, OB, Pediatrics, and ER. This was at the height of the polio epidemic, and there was a special ward for those patients, some in iron lungs. Irene Fisher, RN, was in charge of this ward, and Dr. Van Demark was the doctor of record for most of those patients.

To my surprise, each ward I served on was more interesting than the last, and I realized that nursing was a good fit for me.

By the time we were in our second year, we were the staff of Sioux Valley Hospital. The only nursing personnel the hospital had to hire were the nurses who supervised us. Our working hours were varied to fit our class schedule; we would work seven a.m. to 9 a.m., go to class from ten to two, return to work from seven p.m. to ten p.m., so we were there to care for the patients when they woke up and when they were put to rest. Think of the money the hospital saved in cost by our work! After graduation, I married and had a baby, and the hospital costs for a five-day stay at a hospital at that time was only around Two hundred dollars. The charge for the MD's services was seventy-five dollars.

During our third year, we added a black stripe to our cap, and as our knowledge increased so did our responsibility. I'm sure malpractice occurred, but probably not more than it does today.

During our second year we went "on affiliation" to Yankton State Hospital, to learn about the care of mental patients. While we were there, we were housed in the dorm at Yankton College. We took two more college courses: Psychology, and Sociology, taught by Sioux Falls College professors, so we ended up with just five college credits, and on the completion of our schooling, we were awarded a diploma.

This allowed us to write the state board test to become Registered Nurses, but if I wanted to be a nurse today, I would have to begin at the beginning and take four years of college classes. My classmates and I agreed at a reunion, many years later, that we were possibly just as good nurses as the Colleges put out today. One of my classmates brought a "State Board Review" book to school with her at the beginning of school, and studied it every night after her regular work was completed. But I never crammed for State Boards, my theory was that if I did not know enough to pass that test after three years of school, I did not deserve to be a nurse, and I did well on the test.

I graduated in 1954, in June, and married in September. During most of my life, I have worked as a nurse; first on the Pediatric ward at Sioux Valley. While on duty there one evening; we admitted several patients who had respiratory illness, and put in orders for steam tents. Back then, one put the child into a crib, covered it with a draw sheet, and directed steam under the sheet to provide a moist environment. We soon had more patients than steamers, so I innovated a solution. WE put all those kids in the same room, removed the sheets, and just ran all the steamers into the room. Several years later, Sioux Valley created a "steam room," stainless steel walls, and several cribs or beds for the patients.

Later, I worked in a doctor's office in New Brighton, Minnesota, while my children were born and we moved back to farm in South Dakota. I began working at the Madison Community Hospital. When I retired, I was the "house supervisor." And I was still innovating! I shared this job with another RN, and I figured out that if we worked four ten hour shifts instead of five eight-hour shifts, there would only be about six days where we were both on duty. We worked from three p.m. to one thirty a.m., and so were able to cover the ER after the RN on duty came to work. This was the time when she was organizing her nights work, and also the time of day when parents were coming home from activities to find sick children, and so was a busy time in ER much of the time. It also allowed us to do evening tasks while the nursing staff took time to do their charting, and overtime dropped to nothing on our shift, while the day shift, supposedly ended at three thirty, often stayed until five or later to chart.

I've seen a lot of changes in nursing in my lifetime, but I cannot say they all have made progress happen. Of course, medicine is vastly different today from that time in the 1950s, but I will always be thankful for my career choice.

The Hopping Pickup
By Starla Fitzjarrell of Centennial, Colorado
Born 1949

So many stories about growing up in South Dakota! What wonderful memories, the adventures, the closeness of neighbors, and the imaginations that we cultivated because we had no Internet, electronic games, etc.

Families were large then. Our family was a family of eight, Mom, Dad, three girls, and three boys. One neighbor, had twelve children who we rode the school bus with each day. I still remember all of their names. We had to be at the top of the driveway early enough so we didn't miss the school bus.

I recall one day, at about eight-years-old, feeling like I was invisible, lost in the shuffle of my five siblings. I decided I needed to "test" them and one afternoon I hid in an abandoned wagon on our farm. It was like the old "covered wagon" in westerns but without the cover.

Well, I lay there a good part of the afternoon, waiting for them to miss me. Finally, I heard voices calling my name. It was music to my ears and I finally showed myself and pretended that I had fallen asleep. They did miss me! I was an important part of the family!

We lived in East Central South Dakota near Redfield. I remember lots of tornadoes and mom yelling at us to get in the house when we were outside playing. I remember being awakened night and told to get in the basement. We always "camped" in the southeast corner, which for some reason was deemed the safest. The winds howled and

Sheral, Starla, Gayle, and Greg Sievers

one time we lost our front porch and gathered up belongings in the pastures the following day. When there was really bad storms, the neighbors would all drive around in the aftermath to check on other neighbors, some who had lost farm buildings. It was both scary and adventurous.

We lived about a quarter of a mile from our grandparents and would often walk to their place in the summer. My Dad was an only child so we were very important to our

Nadine and Darrell Sievers with their children in 1957

Starla's brother, Greg and her sister, Gayle

397

grandparents and knew it. And we'd head right for the cookie tin. Grandma always had home-baked cookies and seemed always glad to see us.

As we got older, our parents would occasionally leave for a few hours to go to the nearest town to grocery shop, etc. We discovered that we could get into the old pickup and simply by hitting the clutch, we could make it move around the yard. We entertained ourselves for hours until one time Grandpa, (a quarter of a mile away) was watching us through his binoculars and said to us, "I think we need to tie that pickup truck up. When your parents leave, it hops all over the yard." We got the message and that fun was over. I recall Grandpa making us stilts out of some old pieces of wood. We were so impressed at his invention!

I recall watching Fury and Sky King on Saturday morning in our pajamas.

Our Mom taught my sister and I at eight-ten years old how to cook and bake. We would often do this when Mom was gone and have our "bakery" laid out for her when she came home. Usually she was impressed but we did have our failures, such as the cake with a cup of salt instead of a cup of sugar.

I remember taking a snack to Dad and Grandpa in the fields mid-afternoon, summers in the hammock, going to a nearby town for roller skating, helping Grandma and her sisters cutting and freezing sweet corn and so many other memories just too numerous to mention.

I remember the great always-home cooked meals, pheasant on Sunday, garden tomatoes, and corn pancakes with powdered sugar and always angel food cakes for our birthdays'. (No cake mixes and a dozen egg whites!)

I remember the chicken harvest to stock the freezer for winter. I was horrified watching my sweet Grandmother wring a chicken's neck and seeing the "headless chicken," run around the yard for a few seconds before it dropped.

What a world it was when we left our doors unlocked, lived off of the land, invented our own entertainment, and knew all of our neighbors!

Sock Hop
By Sheral (Sievers) Morrill of Chandler, Arizona
Born 1948

I remember our first "colored TV." It was a black and white TV with a clear plastic screen cover that was tinted blue on the top third, yellow-brown in the middle, and green on the bottom. It worked best for programs taking place outdoors.

Our telephone sat on a desk and had a big round dial on the front and a receiver on the top. You dialed the numbers to make the call. We lived on a farm and were on what was called a "party line." Several families were on the same line and each house had a different ring combination of long and short rings. I remember listening in on other peoples calls. You had to be very careful to keep the button under the receiver held down as you lifted the receiver so they wouldn't hear you. I also had to be careful that my Mother didn't catch me.

There was no such thing as video games or movies in the car when we traveled. We played games such as, "I see something…." And we'd say its color. The other passengers had to guess what you were looking at by the color. The winner was the next one to "see

Sheral, her brother, Greg, and their dog, Rusty

398

something." Another game was to find a word on a road sign or business starting with each letter of the alphabet from A-Z. We would also see how many different state license plates we could spot. A good memory game was where you would say your name, such as: "my name is Sheral and I went to Sioux Falls on a Scooter." The next person would repeat that, and added their name with information according to the first letter of their name. We would keep going from person to person. If you couldn't remember what everyone had said, you were eliminated from the game. The winner was the last one that could repeat everyone's travels. The most memorable travel was when my Mother said, "My name is Nadine and I went to Niagara in the Nude." What a laugh we had!

There were no seatbelts in cars, so if one of the children got tired they would crawl up in the back window and sleep. I now see how very dangerous this was.

When I was in the seventh grade our teacher, scheduled evening dances called Sock Hops. They were called sock hops because they were held in the school gymnasium and you had to dance in your socks so, you didn't scuff up the basketball floor. Our school was small so the seventh and eighth graders were in the same classroom. I had a crush on an eighth grade boy and he asked me to be his date to the dance. I was so excited as that meant I would eat with him at the refreshment break. He also told me he would pick me up at my farm and drive me to the dance. My Mother told me he would not be able to drive because he was only fourteen and could not drive after dark with his farm permit. I insisted he said he would drive. I was waiting for him to arrive but my Dad was in the car ready to take me to the dance. I kept stalling pretending to continue getting ready. Then my Dad was honking the horn and my Mother said, "If you want to go to that dance, you better go with your Dad because he is ready to leave." I slowly walked to the car and he drove me to the dance. My date arrived at my house five minutes after I left so when he got to the dance, he never spoke to me and I never got to dance with him. Thirty-five years later, our paths crossed in Arizona and we are celebrating our tenth wedding anniversary. We laugh about that first date and he still claims that I "stood him up." He also found

Raymond (Sheral's now husband) dancing with another classmate

out that his Aunt had followed him the seven miles to the dance in her car to make sure he arrived safely.

I look back at what we did for entertainment growing up without computers, video games, internet, and cell phones. After helping with chores like washing and drying dishes by hand, helping with the laundry using the wringer washing machine, gathering eggs, and working in the garden, we spent hours riding our bicycles all around the country on the graveled roads. Once we built a raft and floated it in the filthy shallow creek where the cows waded. We played many board games and had Monopoly games that went on for days.

My sister and I played a game outdoors called Orphanage. We pretended that we were in an orphanage and the staff were mean to us so we planned our escape. We had to escape thru the cattle pen past that big bull we were afraid of and under the electric fence. We went to what we called the forest, a shelterbelt of trees. My Dad had put an old brooder house (chicken house) out there for us to use as a playhouse. We would go to the farmhouse, which we called the "town" to look for work. We would do some small jobs for Mom, and get paid in food. We would take our snack back to our home in the woods. We had an old aluminum teakettle which we started a little fire in a couple of times. We also dug a hole in the ground outside and tried to cook a chunk of potato wrapped in foil. It is a wonder we did not burn the place down. I'm not sure we ever told Mom about our fires. One time we pretended it was Christmas and with no money for gifts, we made each other crowns of leaves.

I remember one time when I was very young making mud pies using REAL eggs. My Dad was a bit upset.

Our dog was a big collie and his name was Rusty. He was very smart and protective. I got off the school bus one day and no one was home. I was afraid and decided to walk to my grandparent's house, which was a half mile away and seemed very far. Rusty walked beside me and kept me to the very edge of the road. I had to walk past a pasture with all the cows and I was very afraid. They walked toward the fence and Rusty ran toward them scaring them away. Also, when we played in our yard, Rusty would nudge the little ones away from the road if they headed into the ditch.

Ruth Anne Moller in 1950

Weather Always Has the Upper Hand
By Ruth A. Moller, Miller, South Dakota
Born 1943

When I was a kid growing up in mid-South Dakota, nine miles southwest of Wessington, farms and farmhouses dotted the landscape. Today, much of the land has been purchased by larger farmers, and the houses either deteriorate or are taken down. I hate to drive in that area anymore.

But I still see all the homes in my mind,

Ruth and her dad, Rudy going to school in 1952

and I can walk from room to room in many of them, just by closing my eyes. They were the homes of neighbors, a sister's family, an aunt and uncle, and of course our own house. The "floor plans" are etched into my memory.

Our closest neighbors, "as the crow flies," were the O'Neal family. Our pasture was comprised of rolling hills, and I could easily get to the O'Neal place by just walking around a few hills. To drive by car, it was about three miles.

My dad's first wife had died of cancer, and my four half-sisters were several years older, so I was virtually an "only child." So for many years, my primary playmates were the six O'Neal kids. The two older boys were several years my senior, but once in a while they would play ball with us. An older girl was three years older than I was, her sister Margaret was my age, and then there were two younger boys. I was always thrilled with the activities at the O'Neal place, including riding a mean-tempered Shetland pony named Tony, who enjoyed racing to the water tank and coming to an abrupt halt, often dumping the rider into the water.

These kids climbed trees and went hand-over-hand on the beams in the old corncrib.

400

Ruth's driveway in 1952

I don't remember many shoes being worn during the summer. Sometimes we'd jump from the second story of the barn into the oats stored below. Surprisingly, nobody seemed to ever get hurt.

There was no store-bought anything, playground equipment, trikes, or bikes. But imagination reigned, and there were few dull moments.

The house had no running water, and a pot-bellied stove stood in the dining area. I don't remember, but I assume they got electricity when we did, when I was six or so.

In my earliest years, Dad used horses for much of the farm work, and he also had a team of mules. At this point, tractors were being utilized more and more, and I was embarrassed that Dad used the mules for hauling manure, or plowing up the garden patches. He kept them for many years, up until I entered high school, and of course, his "old-fashioned ideas" especially mortified me at that time.

But those horses (and mules) came to the rescue many times, too. The winters of both 1950 and 1951 were long and snowy. Three-day blizzards were often the norm. Both years, snow started in October and the last snowfall was in late April in 1951. The last snowfall in 1950 was on May 5. My birthday is May 6, and there is a picture of me seated on a big snow bank on my birthday that year.

Snowplows were a long time coming to clear out roads, and then it was only the county roads; many people lived on side roads. Our driveway was also long, and it would take a long time before a vehicle could be driven to a county road, when it finally was plowed. A horse came in handy, as it could be ridden to the end of the driveway, where the mailbox was, when mail was finally delivered.

When milking time came, my mom and dad would both trudge to the barn, carrying lanterns, walking over the fences, which were covered by snow. Of course being snowed in, days ticked away. The one-room school was about three miles away, and when roads are blocked solid, it might as well have been three hundred miles.

Dad decided it was important to get me to school and also the neighbor kids. He hitched up the horse team to an old hand-made wooden sled, and off we'd go "as the crow flies" to pick up the O'Neal kids, and then on to school. Of course, he'd have to do the same thing when school was out for the day.

The first few trips were highly exciting for me, but it was a cold ride, and the thrill of the situation wore off quickly. Still, thanks to Dad's tenacity, we kids made it to school during most of the long winters of '50, '51, and '52.

When we finally could get through to a plowed road, the folks were in need of groceries. Another photo of me is beside the huge plowed snow banks, much taller than I was, and a narrow path for the pickup to drive through.

Those bitter winters were hard on livestock as well as wildlife. Dad would pick up the frozen pheasants and take them home so the barn cats could have a feast. Of course, this was certainly before the days of television, although my parents did have a radio, fueled by a wind-charger, before REA arrived. But my dad also seemed to have a "nose" for impending bad weather, whatever the season. Over the many years that followed, I've seen my share of blizzards in South Dakota, as well as Minnesota, and I've been snowed in now and then, but only for short periods.

The hardy farmers of the mid-Twentieth Century certainly had more comforts than their parents or grandparents, but the winters were especially harsh, and they had no access to what we take so for granted today.

I still lament the demise of all the old houses, and I recall the strong people who lived in them. I'm grateful I was able to experience it, but I am also glad so much progress has been made when it comes to dealing with treacherous weather. However, one truth remains, in South Dakota, weather always has the upper hand.

Keepers

By Lois Marie Hubbard of Racine,
Wisconsin
Born 1938

The first farm that my family lived on was located one and one-half miles south of the town of Garden City. Along with the work of raising kids, crops, and animals, my parents operated the Davis Dairy farm from 1929 to 1942. The dairy was small and served only residents of the nearby town and a few farm families.

It was hard not only for my Dad and brothers but for our Mom as well. It was her job to wash and rinse the bottles in water that was boiled on a wood and coal burning stove. Our home was not equipped with electricity or plumbing until 1949.

She also bottled the milk and prepared it for delivery while her men did the remaining chores.

My older brothers were often late getting into school in the morning because of the dairy's daily chores and deliveries. Times were hard and the business was not profitable. In 1942, my brothers approached our Dad, and cut a deal with him to either "peddle milk" or attend high school. Trying to do both was not working! The dairy was abruptly ended and all of the children of John and Elinor Davis graduated from Garden City High School. With the sad exception of our oldest brother, LeVerne, who passed away March 2, 1942 from complications of pneumonia, he was nineteen years old.

Our area experienced an economic upswing after suffering through the dust bowl drought and years of the Great Depression of the 1930s. When the economy appeared to be improving, Dad decided to purchase a tractor to assist with the fieldwork. Before that, a faithful team of horses served us well. The horses, Joe and Daisy were sold when we moved in 1944.

Those good old horses were an important part of the Davis Farm history. I have several photos of brothers and cousins on the back of their favorite pet, Joe. He was not only a worker but a source of entertainment. When I was two-years-old, my Brother, Myron, found me sitting under one of those horses in the barnyard. I was in my own "little girl world," and the big horse stood there quietly protecting a tiny human who found refuge under him.

During World War II, immediate and extended family members served their country. Leroy was in the Army Air Force. His position in the airplane was a "ball turret gunner," My brother's unit was ready and waiting on a Pacific Island to go into battle when, in his words, "the BIG ONE was dropped," and the war with Japan was essentially over.

Lloyd was drafted for military service shortly after he graduated high school in 1945. He was in the U.S. Navy. Both of my brothers were discharged, and came home when the war ended. For a time, they continued farming with Dad until they moved on to marry, establish careers, and raise their families in other area.

Our cousin, Lyle Davis, was not as fortunate as my brothers were during his time in the military. He was captured and imprisoned in Germany for eighteen months. Lyle rarely talked about his days in the prison camp during WWII, but he did share the journal that he kept during those dark days, it was featured in a book published in Brookings, South Dakota. He was privileged to go to Washington, D. C. on an Honor Flight a few years before his health failed.

Another cousin, Wilton Davis, encountered a land mine and lost a leg during the war years. Those two brave men also came home, married, raised families, and had successful careers. An interesting side note about Wilton; he enjoyed, "showing off" his artificial leg; and he was a great dancer. Wilton, the Davis family historian, was an energetic, fun, but also humble, when engaged in conversation about his war injuries.

My handsome, fun, loving, Uncle, Hubert Blashill, was also in the army during World War II. He was stationed in the Pacific Islands where he contracted Malaria and almost died. He survived that war, came home, lived, and worked in South Dakota and Colorado. When the Korean conflict broke out, Hubert enlisted again. My Uncle, a medic, was killed in action in 1951 in Korea.

I have very few memories of the war. Of course, I missed my big brothers, and was thrilled when they came home on furlough and brought me teddy bears and pretty silk hankies or pillow tops with "SISTER,' embossed on them. I recall the "black out drills," ration stamps, and going without a few things for the war effort. A small sacrifice for the freedom of our country!

When WWII ended and our "boys," were safely home, another war was Unthinkable, yet in 1951, Lloyd was drafted again to serve his country during the Korean conflict. Fortunately, God answered Mom's prayers for her son. He was stationed in Germany, although he could have been shipped to Korea anytime; that never happened!

My parents had the opportunity to purchase a larger farm two miles south in Elrod Township. We moved in March of 1944. There was a country store, a schoolhouse, blacksmith shop, and a few homes in the village of Elrod. I spent my first two years of school there while my brother, Myron, completed eighth grade. I chased gophers with my friends in the field where we also played ball at recess. After school sometimes, I went with Myron and his buddies along the railroad tracks where we teased garter snakes. It was fun to watch them stick out their tongues and hiss at us. But it wasn't nice to tease them.

One stormy winter day, school was dismissed because of the bad storm. There wasn't a telephone in the building, so my brother and his friends walked two blocks to the store to call for rides home. All of the students lived on nearby farms. My teacher, Beth Lohr, kept the lower grades in our room until family came for us. While she was distracted, I "escaped," got my coat and boots and went into the storm to find my brother. The blinding snow confused and frightened me; I fell into a snowbank, lost a boot, and began to cry and scream. Lucky for me, I was near the home where the occupants, Mr. and Mrs. Bill Jones, heard a scared little girl's cries, rescued, warmed me, and notified the school, my brother, and parents that I was safe in their home.

Grades first through eighth were taught in two rooms. The school also housed areas for inside play and community gatherings. There was a spacious playground equipped with swings and a slide.

When Myron finished eighth grade and entered high school in Garden City. I started school there in third grade. I missed my friends from Elrod, but Miss Lohr also transferred to the same school and taught in the primary room, so I had her for my teacher for my first three years.

Through the years, I was required to help with chores and fieldwork. Gathering eggs was a hated task! The crabby old hens pecked at me and often I would get tiny insects called chicken mites on my arms. Oh, how I hated them! Finally, Mom found an ointment that repelled the pesky critters. During the summer, when the men worked late in the fields, it was up to Mom and me to do the evening chores. Chore duty included herding the cows in from the pasture and getting them in the barn to be delivered of their milk. The barn was hot, and smelly, and swarming with flies. The poor cows tried unsuccessfully to fight the pests. One evening the cow Mom was milking swished her tail and caught Mom's eyeglasses in the ropey tail hairs. Back and forth went the tail with Mother's spectacles precariously hanging in it. I stopped milking and collapsed in giggles. Mom yelled at me, "Get those glasses before they fall into the gutter." I finally rescued and returned them to a very unhappy Mommy!

I loved being a country girl and am proud of my heritage. Of course, there were times in the summer when "town" friends were going swimming and I had to work in the fields. Then I loudly complained! It didn't do me any good, but I grumbled anyway.

The last year that we lived on the farm, I realized how much I loved it. I took walks with my little dog, Bounce, along the shelterbelts that bordered our land and we enjoyed the sounds of birds, crickets, or frogs and farm animals settling in for the night. My friend, Sandy and I, ice-skated in our pasture on moonlit winter nights.

The last months before we moved, I helped my Dad stretch muskrat pelts on boards in an upstairs room that wasn't heated, but it was a warm bonding time for Dad and me. The furs also brought in much needed income for our family.

Sadly, we sold the farm, cattle and pigs in March of 1955 and moved to Garden City. The chickens moved with us and of course, my precious dog, Bounce. There was a barn on the property in town where the chickens were housed. Mom continued to raise her chickens, and vegetable and flower gardens. Dad was active in helping farmers with various jobs. He was an avid fisherman. Therefore, we ate a lot of fish! There has never been a fish dinner as delicious as the fresh bluegills, perch, and others that Dad caught in the Dakota glacial lakes. They were dredged in cornmeal and fried in bacon grease in Mom's cozy kitchen.

All of the homes where we lived are gone now. But the shelterbelt with trees that were planted by the WPA in the early 1930s and cared for by my brothers still thrives just north of where the house and out buildings stood.

One of my favorite memories is when my brothers, and husband, Ron and I came "home" to visit Mom in the summer. We crowded into a car with Ron driving and 'the Davis men' telling stories of people and happenings from the past, while we went for a "Garden City" ride. Our annual tour took us by farms where we lived so many years ago. Leroy bragged that the trees on the "home place" looked so good because of his hard work tending to the young plantings. After a few brief stops, to visit relatives we ended the day with a stop at the pretty little cemetery west of town where many of our loved ones are buried. The cemetery has lovely evergreens and other trees, and the surrounding countryside shows off with fields of corn, beans, and small grains.

The way of life that we grew up with is gone now. Schools, farms, stores, and homes are no more. Mom and Dad's sons and only daughter lived, worked, and raised families in other states. My parents and brothers have passed away. I am left with warm memories and the enduring love of family and those very special days of long ago.

Poems by my Mother, Margaret L. Grottke,
By Stephen J. Grottke, Chili, Wisconsin
Born 1969

Grandpa's Courting
I love to sit at Grandpa's knee
And hear him tell a story
When he was young and in his prime
And had no care or worry.
His tales of courtship are the best
'Twill fill you full of glee
He wrapped the reins around the whip
So that both hands were free.
He said in horse and buggy days
He still got home quite early,
He paused to smile and then he'd add

Joe E. Rawstern in 1916

"In the morning- bright and early."
But once he fell so sound asleep
Along his homeward way,
His horses turned to carry him back
To sweet, dear, lovable Ruby!
Grandpa learned in those hard days
No money grows like fruit,
The mother of his team he sold
To buy his wedding suit.
Frozen Time
Babies came and how they grew!
The years began to fly!
It wasn't long until they went
To country school close by.
Winter came and it was cold!
'Twas hard to rise and shine!
The house was cold; the fire was out,
The clock said half past nine.
Well, mother knew what Pa had done
And now their girls were late!
Soon warmly bundled by the door
One wondered at their fate.
"What shall I tell the teacher, Pa?"
Asked a daughter small and slight.
"Just tell her 'twas so cold last night,
The alarm clock froze up tight!"
They told the teacher what Pa said
Without a trace of guile.
The children could not understand
What made their teacher smile!
Grandma's Hands
I remember Grandma's hands
Never idle, always moving.
She showed her family greatest love
By all the work that they were doing.
They washed the clothes and hung to dry
They ironed the wrinkles without fail,
Always mending to catch up
Scrubbed the porch with mop and pail.
They planted garden, weeded, hoed,

404

Canned the beans and picked tomatoes,
Shelled the peas and cut off corn,
In the fall they dug potatoes.
Precious hands that made the bed,
Cooked the meals and milked the cow,
Fed the chickens, gathered eggs,
Touched a child's feverish brow.
I remember Grandma's hands
Smudged with dirt or caked with flour.
Loving, caring hands they were
Whate're the task, whate're the hour.
But best of all my memories
Was at the close of day.
Her gentle hands had combed her hair
And folded quietly to pray.

Father's Education

"I Got My Education
Out Behind The Barn"
Was an old, old song
That spun quite a yarn.
I never really had that chance
When I was just a kid
But Mother chuckled when she told
How Father surely did.
His Daddy smoked some Cuban Star
Tobacco- very strong.
For little boys like Dad to try
It was so-o-o wrong.
His parents went to town one day
And Father snitched the can.
Then out behind the barn he ran
To try his sneaky plan.
He rolled a fat old stogy there
In a handy comic strip.
If his old German Father knew
He'd surely get the whip!
He carefully lit the other end
And took a long, deep puff.

*Delpha Rawstern (Phillips) and
Melva Rawstern (Witthoeft)*

Say! This is really great, he thought,
So several more he'd huff!
Now at last he'd tell his friends
"See here, I'm no big sissy!"
But moments later, something's wrong!
Why, Father felt quite dizzy!
His sister came upon him there,
propped weakly 'gainst the wall.
His face was white, then sickly green,
She thought he'd surely fall!
But that's the lesson long ago
My Father had to l'arn
That day he "got his education
out behind the barn."

Mother's Fight

Did children fight long years ago?
Let's ask Mother, she would know.
Then Mother sat with twinkling eye
And told a tale of days gone by.
Two little girls, so naughty they,
Squabbling and quarreling most all the day.
Their Father and Mother could hardly allow
Their children should have such a terrible
row.
They screamed and they hollered, pulled
handfuls
of hair!
One threw a fork, and it stuck right there!
(breast)
Now Mother was angry and Father was mad!
Enough of this nonsense they both had had!
Father took them aside and bade them fight
And fight they did, and kick and bite!
Until at last, so tired and sore,
But Father bade them fight some more,
Until at last he said "tis done!"
The girls agreed it was no fun.

Art Witthoeft and Meta Witthoeft (Hiepler) in 1921

Such children! My! Who could they be?
Then with a smile and wink said she.
"Why child, 'twas my sister and me!"

Father's Flight
Our Father later grew to be
A very stalwart, handsome man.
The pretty girls for miles around
Plied tricks and wiles to hold his hand.
Pretty girls may come and go,
But one shy miss had caught his eye!
Willowy with freckled nose,
She did visit right close by.
It was there Dad courted Mom
Until one fateful summer night
When Mother's folks drove in the yard
Poor Father fled in quite a fright!
Through the house and out the door,
His feet just barely touched the floor!
He hit the porch—oops! Missed the door!
And through the screened in wall he tore!
The memory was slow to fade
For many years as they passed by,
They still could see that gaping hole
Daddy made like some huge "fly."

The Good Old Days
Ever wish the "good old days"
Would come again to stay?
Do you recall the bitter cold
Of that December day
When you two lovebirds drove to town
To get your marriage license?
You cuddled close to beat the cold
Which was a real nuisance.
But young in spirit, young in heart,
You felt it all was worth it.
Now after all these many years
Can you say "regret it?"
Early evening back at home,
Inviting supper's waiting.
Glad to share the meal there
The parting you were hating.
But fate was kind that wintery night,
Your car ceased operation.
Weren't you glad to spend the night?
Now that's cooperation!
The hose had broke. The antifreeze
Had leaked upon the ground;
And Christmas Day there was no help
In any shop around.
On Christmas Night when it was time
For you to "tie the knot,"
Your bride's dear Father went along
To keep the engine hot!
Don't you wish that once again

The world was tucked in white,
The Model T and just you three
Were chugging through the night?

Good Old Days
By Phyllis A. Bjerke Peterson of Polson,
Montana
Born 1941

I sit writing today having just turned seventy-three and my Dad will turn one hundred years old on April 28, 2014 so we both have many years of great memories. He is the lone survivor of fifteen children. We lost our mother a year ago at ninety-four and a half years old. She was the last of eight children. Both their parents and grandparents came to America from Norway and settled in South Dakota. My four siblings and I were raised by Christian parents on a farm in Clark County, which is in Eastern South Dakota. We went to a country church and a country one-room school. We had lots of Aunts, Uncles, and Cousins so holidays and birthdays were a lot of fun. I particularly remember one Christmas when we had a lot of snow and we were to go to Mother' parents so with the roads being so bad my Dad piled us all into a big potato truck and we then stopped and picked up his brother and wife (Mother's sister) and their seven children. We drove the twenty miles, which put us on a hill about a mile from the Grandparents farm home and could go no further. So Grandpa hitched up two of his horses to a sleigh and began hauling us all down the hill. He wrapped us up in a nice warm horse blanket. The horses' bells were so soothing to hear them ring. Our Christmas tree in the early years had real candles, which were only lit Christmas Eve for a few minutes. Our Mother always hung a red wreath in the living room window and it had an electric candle in the middle of it. On a cold crisp dark evening when we'd come from the barn that red light was very warm and peaceful to look at.

We had lots of chores; to do, milking cows, picking eggs, feeding the pigs, shearing the sheep, carrying water in the winter to all the sheep (who were in the barn out of the winter elements) watching for the ewe's to give birth and then penning them up with their lamb/lambs, picking up dried corn cobs (from the pig pens) to burn in the cook stove in the winter.

We had a very big garden so we helped with the canning by washing all the jars, snapping the beans, husking the corn, shucking the peas, picking chokecherries for making jam. We also canned peaches, apricots, pears, plums, Bing cherries, and apples. We butchered our own meat, and part of that was packaged and frozen and some of it was also canned. We also raised our own potatoes. We helped with fieldwork, like hauling grain to the town granaries where it was then put on trains to take to factories to make flour for baking. This was after we had first filled our own granary.

We raked hay and hauled hay bales (or straw bales,) picked rocks out of the fields (all farmers in the early years picked rocks to make the fields smooth for the machinery.)

Another chore was herding the cows and sheep up and down the ditches to eat the grass down. My younger sister, Alice, and I usually done this chore together. We'd take comic books with us to read and we also loved to lay and watch the clouds, and all the shapes they'd make. We kids always had pet lambs, calves, and pigs.

Clifford and Mildred Warwick Bjerke and their children Phyllis Peterson's parents

In the spring, when all the animals gave birth, if any were in trouble (some mothers would not take their young) our Mother would bring them in the house in a box and put them by or behind the cook stove. Sometimes we'd have five hundred chicks in boxes to keep them warm. (Very noisy!)

We did a lot of inside work, also. We cleaned house every Saturday, cooked meals, baked, washed, and dried dishes. We helped with spring-cleaning by washing curtains and then putting them on curtain stretches, washed windows, put quilts on the clothesline, and beat them with a broom. Our Mother sewed most of us three girls clothes, besides working in the field, helping with milking chores and running a household for seven people.

When we were young, she would curl our hair by putting a rod down into the kerosene chimney lamp and then wrapping our hair around it. Baths and hair washing was every Saturday night in a big galvanized round tub. When I was seventeen, we got T. V., indoor plumbing, and a bathroom. What a Blessing!

We worked hard but we also had a lot of fun times. We made mud pies, played with paper dolls, Tiddly-winks, anti-I-over(throwing a ball over the house for someone else to try and catch,) played house with our dolls, played school, hide-n-seek, red rover-red-rover, kick the can, softball, sledding, biking(we five kids shared one bike,) and making tunnels in the hay so we could slide down through them. Even rounding up the cows for evening milking was fun as my sister, Alice and I would pretend we were on a Safari or we'd pretend we were being chased by Indians or bank robbers.

The winter found us playing Monopoly, embroidery, putting puzzles together, reading, and eating popcorn, homemade ice cream and cocoa. But our favorite winter doing was sitting around our Dad and listening to him tell us about his childhood growing up the youngest of fifteen, he had lots of good stories. He would also tell us about a story he had just read in one of his hunting magazines. But his Bible stories were the best. He could make you feel like you were right there. He was never too busy for us kids. I have already noted being raised by Christian parents, which we are so thankful for. Dad at the end of a busy day while waiting for supper would pick up his Bible and read it before the Daily Paper.

We also came from a musical family so had many happy evenings singing around the piano. Dad also was a self-taught guitar player (think he got his music book from the Sears or Ward catalog) and Sister Joan played the accordion. Our Mother didn't sing but always sat and listened while darning socks or mending some piece of clothing. Sister Joan, Dad, and I done a lot of singing together at different events and sometimes it would be just we three girls. I played the piano for a couple years in the country church. Besides the country church and grade school, I also went to a country high school. Yes, we had an outhouse until I was seventeen. When times were tough we made good use of the Sears catalog and really enjoyed summer when the peaches came in as back then each peach was wrapped in pink tissue paper and we made good use of it.

We lived in a two-story house and our winter toilet was on the second floor and consisted of a five-gallon bucket with a handle and it sat inside a larger can with a pipe going outside. When the five-gallon was full, our Dad had to carry it down the stairs and outdoors. Our Mother always had a fear that he would trip and fall down the stairs with it or the bottom of the bucket would fall out! (This happened the very last time he carried it

Phyllis and her sister, Joan in 1959

out but it waited until he had gotten outdoors with it!) Our brothers were younger than we three girls but we had a lot of fun with them. Sister, Joan being the oldest took care of them when they were real young, as Mom had to help out in the field and do chores until we were old enough to help. She always seen to it we were cleaned up for church and Sunday school. The prettiest dresses I ever had were made by Mother (Some even out of flour sacks.) Sunday morning when we five kids would come down the stairs all dressed up, Dad would always whistle at us and our Mother and tell us how good we all looked.

We have seen a lot of changes come to the farm through the years-electricity, electric stove, freezer, fridge, phone, yard lights (a real blessing,) indoor plumbing, (but Mom always kept her wringer washing machine,) electric iron, (rather than one heated on the cook stove,) electric sewing machine with electric button hole maker, T. V., electric milking machines, gas lawn mower, (instead of push type,) electric Christmas tree lights, and coal burning furnace.

We had parent who were never too busy to talk to us, play with us, sing with us, and read to us. We always had our meals together and devotions were a part of our evening meal. When Dad was ninety-two, with the help of some of our cousins, we made a gospel CD. He and our Mother said the "Lord's Prayer" together every night for almost seventy-six years, so we ended the CD with them saying the "Lord's Prayer" together and then Dad saying it in Norwegian (which he still speaks very well.)

Our Mother also taught us the love of the star's, the moon, and the American Flag. They also told us we must keep up with modern things even if you weren't impressed because if you didn't you'd get left behind.

We would also all run outside when we'd hear an airplane as that was new to us and didn't happen that often. We were also tuned into the trains that ran across the South Dakota prairie. I always enjoyed the sound of the train whistle at night as it had an eerie but peaceful sound. We had lots of cool sounds, meadowlarks, mourning doves, pheasants, baby lambs, piglets, and calves, combines in the field, windmills pumping water, turkeys, geese, crickets, milking machines, pumping milk, cows mooing. We had cool smells also.

Smells of baking bread, newly mowed alfalfa fields, fresh straw being spread around for the animals, fresh sheets just in from hanging on the outdoor clothesline.

To sum things up, it was great being raised on the farm by wonderful parents and being close to grandparents, aunts, uncles, and cousins. We worked hard and played hard. The hard work has helped me my whole life. It's very satisfying to take pride in ones work. Life was more simple back then but each generation has something good to pass on. So we must strive to be good people, improving things for the better, and be kind and helpful to one another.

Hometown Memories
By Leo Robert Forsting of Aberdeen, South Dakota
Born 1921

Townships were formed to build schools and provide education in the community. My Dad gifted the township one acre of land in 1921 to build the Forsting Brown County Grammar School number one that is still standing and currently in my possession. Brainard Township was one and one-half size township and it included five schools with the intent to serve grades one thru eight. The reason for the one-half is because there was a refuge project during the dry years and that was included as the extra one-half township today

The Forsting Brown County Grammar School #1

Grade school teachers were paid Seventy-five dollars per school month, and of that, fifteen per month was given to those who could room and board them for the year. My family provided these accommodations whenever possible. Sometimes schoolteachers would have to buy some of their own teaching materials. They were just like part of the family and whenever possible they were invited into the family activities. I remember one time we had a family spell down (spelling bee) including the teacher. My Irish Mother won the spell down because I couldn't spell "circus." She did! But more importantly than this spelling feat, she was known by all, as a fine mother, friend, a great cook for all who lived in and visited our humble abode.

Saturday night baths were a must and my Mother was a stickler on that. A big tin tub full of heated water was staged in the middle of the kitchen floor. My Mother instructed us to wash up and down as far as possible and when we were done, she would check in and behind the ears for anything else. If we checked out, we were out of there in a flash.

Sometimes tragedy strikes. In 1924 our hip roof barn, which housed hired hands, caught on fire after a long day of threshing. We lost fourteen horses, the hay and the barn. Thank God, we never lost a human life. A neighbor threatened my dad pay back on the crops he lost because of this fire. My Dad considered bankruptcy. All the other neighbors said, "Hank, we will stand behind you." They all chipped together and paid off the loss to the neighbor.

At the end of the 1930s, no mechanical corn pickers were available. For extra money, my Dad gave me and my brother a team of horses and an old wagon to hire out for picking corn by hand. We were paid ten cents per bushel and we might get ninety bushels per day between us. Of course, we went through about four pairs of gloves a day and when we returned home to Mom and Dad, we were so hungry; we ate them out of house and home.

My Dad, Henry bought a Farm-all tractor before the drought. It had steel-cleated wheels. Dad missed one payment to the implement dealer and they said it was going to be repossessed. An ex-sheriff said that if a family member was with the tractor it couldn't be hauled off. I was the lucky one to sit on the tractor for half the day but no one showed up.

We kept the valuable implement.

Okay, in 1941 another disaster struck us. There was a tornado that swept through Brainard Township. It took our windmill that we had for the well water. The top wheel, that my Dad had many times climbed the steps to the top to secure the gears from the wind, was whisked away and driven into the field east of us. My Mom and us kids were trying to hold the doors and windows to keep them from leaving. The force was so great that we dove for shelter. The next day, other than some damage to the house and our "spirits," most everything seemed to be intact. One interesting fact, we found a one hundred gallon barrel of fuel oil that was lifted and set down unharmed one-half mile from our home.

Preceding electricity, the years at home and in grammar school were provided with kerosene lamp light and sunlight. We only had a battery radio to listen to. When the Amos & Andy half hour show was on the radio, we would run in the house from milking the cows and listen intently to their delivery of comedy and drama. Wind-up record players were so valued that if you could afford to purchase a record or find a record, every verse that came out of the box was so loved!

I remember most educational tests were graded by the County Superintendent Staff. We were then notified by mail if we passed to the next grade. That was always a moment of suspense, to see if someone might be held back or excels a grade or two.

For school and recreational activities, we and other grade schools got together for plays and sports competition, such as setting up the bases and creating a ballpark in the pasture. We needed to invent out own entertainment and sometimes the adults would participate.

Another incident remembered in my life very well is the usual occupation of snaring gophers. The bounty was five cents per tail, which was good money to me so I was getting pretty good at it. It was a way to reduce the number of gophers and keep them from digging holes and deteriorating the land. I used a fine copper wire as they stuck their heads out of the hole. One day I was out snaring and was startled by an aircraft that was right above me. I could see the pilot as he wagged the tail and wings by me. Other farmers around identified it as a mail carrier transporting mail to Minneapolis. I made

a promise to myself that when I grew up, I would own one of those flying objects. I have not fulfilled my promise, but I have at least flown on those airborne monsters.

In these times, it was not uncommon for punishment to come from a teacher. Well, I received my first school spanking. We had to ask permission to be excused from class to use the outside toilet (one for boys/one for girls-and only for seven-eight minutes.) I asked to be excused, and as I mentioned above, I was intrigued in snaring gophers. I forgot all about the school time and returned sometime quite later than the seven–eight minutes; I was informed that my punishment was three whacks, with a yardstick on my behind. Well. I was spared by my roll of copper wire in my back pocket that I used for snaring; two whacks with the yardstick and it broke. I was spared the third whack and was set free.

As time went on, the Barnard High School was built. Students who went on from eighth grade rode horses to a stable attached to the grade school to catch the bus to Barnard. Before the bus came, there was a competition to race their horses to see who could be the fastest.

Another memory was when several students from surrounding grade school territories were chosen to compete in a declamatory contest. I was chosen from Brainard School to give the Virginia Militia Colonel Patrick Henry's speech, which I related to "Give Me Liberty or Give Me Death." It wasn't very long, but as soon as I concluded, I jumped from the stage as not to be found. I guess I got the liberty and even survived this community competition ordeal.

Special occasions, such as dances, were held at the schools and the ladies "special committees" always brought lunch. In those days, minced ham sandwiches were a special treat and were put in a special place. They were stored in the cool basement "coal room" and later served to the community with the rest of the fixin's Well as you would imagine, there was a special plan that involved some of us. A special neighbor boy named "Gerb" short for Gerber would always volunteer for a particular mission. "Us Boys" slid him down and pulled him up the coal chute to retrieve a few sandwiches before lunch was served. They always seemed to taste better to "Us Boys" when we taste-tested them before the rest.

Our neighbor, Bill, who was nearly blind, would always play the fiddle for good time music at the dances. He only knew two songs and they were "Good Night Ladies" and: Springtime in the Rockies." All was enjoyed when anyone could bring the music for enjoyment.

Some troublemakers would sometimes attend these township/school special occasions. A set of farming parents were chosen to help keep order. The rough-ins, if causing trouble, would meet face to face with a farmer and found out why they were chosen to keep order. The answer had something to do with their muscular bodies. They got their muscles from hard work, such as pitching hay, manure and milking cows by hand. The rough-ins soon were evicted from the school property after a warning-maybe two.

Even after grade school and entering into a more mature youth hood, I remember some incidents that weren't too laughable at the time.

We, being Catholics, had a choice of three churches (when the Priest could make it.) They were Westport, Frederick, or Hecla. Also, during this time a child movie star-was a rarity. But one did rise to fame by the name of Jackie Coogan. A Jackie Coogan hat was a must for my brother and me. How my parents ever raised enough money to buy me and my brother's "Jackie Coogan" hat is beyond me. Anyhow, church was a must and going toward Westport Church, we had to go down a steep hill and cross the Elm River Bridge. A gust of wind hit our open canvas top model T and lofted both our hats and deposited them in the Elm River. My poor Father needed church that day, as all of us wanted him to wade in the river and retrieve our special hats. He refused and a bad day was had by all-HA! HA!

During the late 1920s and early 1930s, John Dillinger was a well-known Depression "Desperado/Bank Robber." He had a history of partners and gangs in the Midwest. Supposedly, he was becoming more famous and wanted by the authorities. Communities were becoming concerned at to his travels. Our teacher, Mr. Ramsey, had a small radio in the school for himself. It was announced over the radio that Dillinger had actually made it into South Dakota and robbed a local bank. They didn't confirm if a woman was a hostage, but Dillinger may be heading into Canada. Mr. Ramsey had a single barrel rifle to protect us from harm. Well, one day a car stopped across from our schoolhouse and a lady jumped out and tried to run. The driver got our and caught her. The teacher made all of us lay down on the floor, and was pointing his gun out the window to defend us. The car fit the description of Dellinger's car but we don't know if it was him. State Highway 10 was located south of the schoolhouse and it would have made sense to travel for a fast and easy get-away.

I liked sports and heroic athletes. One was Gene Tunney who won back the boxing heavyweight championship from Jack Dempsey. My dad told me if I was awake when he returned from watching the fight at the neighbors, he would tell me the winner. My dad rode the horse back in the dark to give this wide awake boy the greatest news that I had ever heard. It is said that he ate the potato peelings so his family could get their fill with whole potatoes, and that he would not engage in vulgar language and would pray and exit the training premises. Who would not cheer for him as a family and world champion?

Shrine Circus
By Paul Mardian, Aberdeen, South Dakota
Born 1939

I was no different than any kid in that I wanted to see the annual edition of the Shrine Circus when it performed in Aberdeen, South Dakota in the month of April each year. My home was the small town of Roscoe, which is located about 40 miles west of Aberdeen. It was policy at that time that the Shrine Circus organization provided tickets to the area schools at no charge. I suspect this maneuver was to capitalize on the sale of hot dogs and cotton candy. Back in 1948, forty miles was a long trip, so, getting to Aberdeen for the circus was many times quite a challenge. In April of 1948, many of us kids were still not assured of a way to Aberdeen for the circus performance, in spite of having free tickets available to us.

Enter the good Samaritans, the Schneider family owned and operated a cattle and freight trucking business in Roscoe at that time. They came up with a generous plan to accommodate us kids. They proposed their idea to the school for approval and all was given the OK to go with the plan. The morning of this great venture arrived and we kids were all at school early, ready to go, with a free ticket in hand. Schneider's great big semi-trailer rig, which was actually a cattle hauler, pulled up and parked at the curb right in front of the main entrance to the school. The long loading ramp was extended out and down and soon the critters, I mean kids, were piling into the trailer. I do not remember ever hearing a total count, but I will tell you there was at least fifty of us. The trip got under way down Highway 12, headed for the Shrine Circus in Aberdeen. I remember that up front of the trailer and over the top of the cab there was a vent opening, maybe twelve to fifteen inches square, or round. It was great fun for us kids to stand on the benches and stick our head through this opening and take in the sights along the way. I now can only wonder what was in the minds of oncoming vehicle drivers who saw that kid's head sticking out up there. Well, about an hour into this venture and Aberdeen was in sight. The Schneider rig pulled up to park parallel to the curb at the front door of the Aberdeen Civic Arena. Once again, the ramp was lowered into place and we all piled out and headed inside the arena, ready to see the lions, elephants, and all the glorious sights and sounds of the circus. Too soon, it was over, back into the trailer and the one-hour return trip to Roscoe.

John Deere Day was a time set aside in many small farm communities of the upper Midwest back in the 1940s and early '50s. The day was sponsored by the John Deere Company and the local JD dealer. It was a day of appreciation to the area farmers for their patronage through the year. The day was celebrated with the dealers showing off their new line of farm equipment for the season and providing a meal for all to enjoy. The local and rural children looked forward to this day also because the JD dealer did not forget them

Shrine Circus in 1948

in the planning. We kids were excused from school early afternoon so we could take in the festivities. We were treated to bags of candy and trinket toys. Along about mid-afternoon everyone gathered into the local all-events hall where we were treated to a movie on the theatre screen. The popular movies of the time, which we might have enjoyed, would have been maybe The Lone Ranger, Gene Autry or Roy Rogers. Back in those days, the cowboy shoot'em up movies were the most popular and commonly offered movie at the theatres of those days. You must remember this was before TV for most folks in the 1940s.

I was born, grew up and graduated from High School in Roscoe in 1958. I have so many good memories of my days as a kid growing up in a small town of about 500 people at that time. Today, my wife, Arlene, and I are retired, living in Aberdeen. I still enjoy time spent with many friends who still live in Roscoe and cherish all the memories dearly. I am also still an active member of the Roscoe American Legion Post #259. Today I can but wish my grandchildren could have experienced the 1940s in a small farming community like I did, even if only a few days or weeks. I truly believe we kids then grew up at the best of times.

To my good fortune at the time, my father operated the local salvage yard business. I was the fourth born of nine children. At the time, we had only one bicycle to share, not near enough, in my opinion. Summer 1951, I told my dad that I really would like to have my own bike to ride around Roscoe and the countryside. He said, "Ok, but you need to earn it on your own." Now it happened he had hundreds of old scrap electric motors, auto starters and generators which needed to have the copper wire stripped out of them. He went on to say he would pay me five cents per unit. The funds would be held in escrow, his back pocket, until I had the amount needed.

The bike I wanted was the nicest Schwinn of that time and cost $53. At that time, we had no store like Wal-Mart of today. The bike would be mail ordered from a catalog. I think it was Spiegel's and would be delivered by freight truck. Calculation by myself determined that I would have to strip out over 1000 of those things. Dad and I agreed to the deal and I went to work. Well, all was going good and by late summer, the escrow account was gathering dollars. As I neared the total amount, which I needed, I asked dad if we could go ahead with ordering the bike since it is going to take a week or two for delivery to arrive. He said ok to that, but all terms of the deal, we made still apply. The day the truck came by with my bike, in a box in many pieces, I got very excited. Problem, however, I was short of the full amount needed. Dad said he would put the box in the garage until I had the money in the account. Man, the generators started to fly at record speed. This is truly how it happened. That very evening, I had reached the necessary goal. Dad helped me with the assembly of my Schwinn bike and before dark set-in that evening, I was riding around Roscoe on MY OWN BIKE, bought and paid for by maybe sixty-five or seventy-five days of hard work for a twelve-year young kid with a dream.

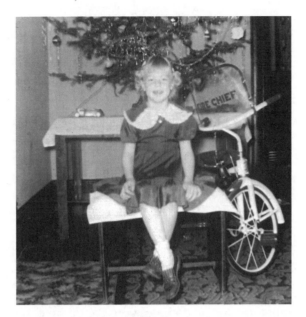

Donna (Heald) Pack in 1956

Woonsocket
By Donna (Heald) Pack, Spring Valley, Illinois
Born 1949

I was born in Wessington Springs, South Dakota. My parents are Marion and Martha Heald. We lived in Woonsocket, South Dakota. I came from a large family. My parents had thirteen children. I'm the third oldest. My dad was the hardest working person I knew. He worked at Van Dyke's east of town, eight hours a day five days a week. Every day one of us kids would stop my Dad's red truck on his way to town to do his other jobs and give him a grocery list my mom made up. He hauled café water for two restaurants in town. He hauled garbage. My dad never had machines do his work, like they do today. He did everything by shovel and hand. He also worked for the funeral home. He dug graves,

winters were the worst. He hauled coal from the trains to the two schools and our home for heating them in the winter.

I remember laundry days. We had a wringer washing machine. We hung the clothes outside on the clothesline my dad put up. After they dried, we had to take them down, fold them, and put them away. In the wintertime, we hung them in the basement. My dad put clothesline down there also. I don't remember how old I was but I do remember how excited we were when they built a laundry mat in town.

My favorite Christmas was the year I got a red tricycle. It had a windshield with Fire Chief wrote on it and a bell to ring. I took it outside and rode it up and down our street. I felt so special. We never got an allowance, so we had to figure out how to make money. So we would take our wagon and walk east toward the three-mile corner, and pick up pop bottles in the ditches. We walked on one side and came back on the other side of the road. We went on into town to turn the bottles in. We got two or three cents a bottle. We thought we were rich. It didn't take long to spend the money; we could get two pieces of candy for a penny. So we walked out of the store with a bag of candy.

In the summer, we spent a lot of our time at the swimming hole. Lake Prior was the best lake. You could swim, go fishing, have picnics, play on the playground equipment, ice skate in the winter, or just hang out.

413

Marion and Martha Heald's family in 1980

Saturday matinees at the Rex Theatre was great. You could go to the movies for twenty-five cents, get a bag of popcorn for ten cents, and a soda for ten cents. We usually got fifty cents from my dad, so you could save the extra five cents or spend it on candy. We never needed to go out of town; we could always find something to do.

School days was rough for my parents. Can you imagine putting ten kids out of thirteen in school every year? Paying all the fees, buying supplies, clothes, and shoes. We never had a Wal-Mart to go to. Whatever we got came from uptown Woonsocket. I hated getting shots and going to the dentist.

We lived on the east end of town and school was on the west end of town. We walked to school, came home for lunch and back to school and home again after school. No matter what the weather was, you did what you had to do. I remember the winters were the worst. I always thought I'd freeze to death; piles of snow everywhere.

The school was a three-story building. When you entered it, you had to go upstairs to get to your classes. Second floor classes first through eighth grades, third floor, more stairs to go up, for classes ninth through twelfth grades. You went downstairs for first floor. It was the restrooms, some classrooms, lunchroom, and the furnace and maintenance rooms. We had an old fire escape in the back of the school. It was a long, big tube like thing. We weren't allowed to play in it. But my friend and I would wait until everyone left the school then we would go back and crawl in and up the fire escape and slide down it. Our voices would echo. We got caught a few times but that never stopped us. We were just having fun.

Some of the most enjoyable times for me was our field trips at the end of the school year. We got to take the school buses and ride to Huron, South Dakota for the Big Circus (Ringling Brothers Barnum and Bailey). When I got older, we got to take bus trips to Forestburg, South Dakota to Ruskin Park, roller-skating.

The biggest yearly event for Woonsocket was and is the fourth of July. We had big celebrations all weekend. It started with Alumni Dances, Class Reunions, Big Parade, picnics at Lake Prior, games for everyone swimming and boat rides. Family and friends came from everywhere to be a part. Finally came the big event, everyone gathered around the lake to watch the best fireworks display I'd ever seen.

I moved away from back home around 1964. I talked my parents into leaving also. I was afraid for my dad's health. He worked so hard with all the many jobs he had. He wasn't getting any younger, just worn out. We all ended up in Illinois. My dad started ordering the Woonsocket newspaper. He wanted to keep up with what was happening back home. After my dad died, I decided to keep the newspaper coming to me. I miss my old stomping grounds where I grew up as a kid. I sometimes wonder what would have been different in our family's lives if we would have never left. I've been back home about four times in the past fifty years. The first time I went back I was so surprised to see how much everything had changed. Our home was gone. Someone put a welding shop on it. Everything looked so much smaller. Main Street really changed. Most of the businesses are gone. I

Donna with her dad, Marion in 1988

414

thought of a ghost town. We hardly seen any people. The old school was still there. It's in bad shape. They built a school next to it, with a gymnasium. It is really nice. My brother and I took our kids back one year. We got pictures of them sitting at our old school desks, and we got to tour the old school building. The kids enjoyed that so much. Just to walk those floors again and reminisce of the good old days was great.

I'm going back this Fourth of July 2014. It's been six years. I'm looking forward to seeing the people I know who are still there, and enjoy all the activities the town does on the weekend of the fourth of July, to also see the town come alive again.

Old Stories from Bradley, South Dakota
By Bonni Jean (Peterson) Glock, Bozeman, Montana
Born 1928

My dad, Marv Peterson, owned and operated a small café in Bradley back at the end of World War I. He served short order meals, had a nice soda fountain and a draft beer tap. My mother Florence drove very early in the mornings to bake the pies, which sold for five cents a slice back in those days.

There were no bathroom facilities at that time, so Dad had a small washstand with a bowl for water and a pitcher of water for customers to wash their hands. One afternoon a local young man, Willie Peek, came into the café and asked my mother for permission to just wash his hands. Mother said, "Yes, of course." Willie finished washing his hands and walked out of the café. Mother went to empty the washbowl and collect the towel, noticing both were stained with a lot of blood. Not until a week later the story came out that Willie found out he had impregnated a local young girl, then he murdered her, hiding her body in a haystack and setting it on fire to hide the evidence. It became a big story even being a cover story for a national crime magazine. Willie was apprehended and taken to the state prison in Sioux Falls for life. He was paroled when he was seventy years old. This happened in the late 1920s.

My Dad, Marv Peterson and a buddy of his, when they returned home from California after being discharged after World War I, were sort of small time entrepreneurs in the town of Bradley, South Dakota. They arranged for and hired inexpensive small time bands to play for dances in local, nearby halls situated on the shores of Bailey's or Round Lake close to Bradley. Once they hired a couple of unknowns, Lawrence, and his brother Larry Welk to play their accordions. Since the Welk brothers Lawrence and Larry, were just starting out, they weren't very good. They didn't draw a large enough crowd, so they were not asked back!

Back in the 1930s pheasant hunting was very popular in the fall and many hunters flocked to the Bradley, Crocker, and Garden City area because of the large bird population. My dad, Marv Peterson, sold gun shells in his store in Bradley, although no guns until later when he acquired the hardware store. One year a couple of "out of towners" drove into Bradley and came into Dad's store to purchase some shells and inquire where the best hunting area was. As folks in small towns seem to know everybody, they were curious to know who this attractive couple were; they were well dressed in nice hunting clothes. Dad directed them down the road to Carson's slough. A couple of weeks later the Webster newspaper reported that Clark Gable and Carol Lombard had flown into Webster by private plane to hunt for pheasants. When my Dad found out he mentioned it to some of his customers and their response was Clark who?

My dad owned and operated a grocery store for many years in Bradley, South Dakota. A graduate of a small business college in California after his discharge from the Army after World War I, he promoted many creative and interesting events to attract customers. During the winter, he offered free coffee and pancakes on Saturday mornings to promote Nash coffee. I was in grade school in the 1930s and my friends and I would go up to Dad's store for pancakes before heading down to Keller's slough for ice skating. The pond was always covered with snow, of course, but Mr. Kinyon, our school janitor, would come down and shovel a sizeable patch of ice for us to skate on. There was an old, rusty barrel, which we used to make tomato soup. Kids would bring all the stuff we needed, grill, wood, paper cups and spoons and crackers. That was always our major form of entertainment on a cold and frozen weekend.

My Dad and a group of friends would drive to the Black Hills for their yearly ritual of deer hunting in the fall. When he was lucky enough to bag a deer, he would dig a pit by the side of the store building and roast the deer, offering free buns, barbequed venison, and coffee to everyone.

He also showed free movies on the side of the store building every Wednesday and Saturday night throughout the summer when all the farmers would come into town for their weekly shopping. Two of the exciting serials I can remember were "The Perils of Pauline" and Frank Buck and Osa Johnson in "Bring Em Back Alive" African adventure. These kept customers coming back every week to see he next installment.

My Dad once put up posters all over town inviting people to come into his store on Saturday for free peanuts in the shell. They could eat all they wanted so long as they would eat them in the store and throw the shells on the floor. I remember this well, because my sister and I helped clean up the mess!

Mark Bender, the wild and wooly scion of a local farmer, would get drunk and ride into the town of Bradley on his really spirited horse, whooping and hollering and waving his big hat to frighten his horse. He would ride up and down the sidewalks of Bradley's two little main streets creating as much noise and commotion as he could, scaring all the people in town for their weekly shopping. I remember my Dad telling us about the time when the drunken Mark rode his horse right into my Dad's store, his horse slipping and sliding around on the ceramic tile floors. The local sheriff and a couple of his deputies grabbed Mark off his wild horse and hauled him off to the local jail, a sturdy little building a block from Main Street where Mark Bender was usually the only occupant!

During the 1930s, my sister and I delivered groceries for our Dad with our Shetland pony "Muggy." Customers would call in their order and Betts and I would hitch up Muggy to a little cart and off we would go. One of our favorite families were Mr. and Mrs. Rook, they were from England, Mrs. Rook would tell us to tie up our pony and tell us to come into their house for tea and cookies.

One of Bradley's truly unforgettable couples during the 1940s was the "Goatman" and his wife, or sister; no one was ever quite sure who she was. I don't remember their names, but the two had a goat farm right outside of Bradley. When the couple would drive into town for shopping on Saturday night, the whole area would wreak with goat smell. The Goat people obviously never bathed or were bothered by the smell, but we all knew when they came to town. I always sort of "took" to strange or perhaps I should say different people, and I hit it off with the Goatman. He liked to have me wait on him because I was kind to him. He was always dirty, unkempt, and so smelly, but I put that aside. He had quite a long beard and he seemed to be a personable fellow.

When I became engaged to be married, the Goatman would tease me and ask me if I were going to send him an invitation to Ron's and my wedding in the Lutheran Church in Bradley. Maybe I thought he was just teasing and didn't say anything. After our wedding, my Dad told me how disappointed the Goatman was that he wasn't invited. Dad said the Goatman took a bath and shaved off his long beard for the occasion!

After fifty-four years later and now living in Bozeman, Montana, as I am recalling this, I still feel guilty that I didn't invite the Goatman!

Flying Over Raymond
By Dean R. Bymers, Raymond, South Dakota
Born 1931

I "dang near died" I was told, about when I had my appendicitis in 1935. I was four years old and spent nineteen days in a local hospital. My folks were told I had a slim chance to live, but I made it through. I had a big tube in me for nineteen days. Gangrene had set in and there was no penicillin back then. I think the bill for the hospital was $180 bucks.

I was born in April of 1931 in a bedroom in our house, as all of us were in those days, on a farm near Conde, South Dakota. We moved eight miles away when I was one year old to a farm near Turton. I had four older sisters Valois, Pat, Iris, and Ramona. In the next seven years, my brothers Duane and Marvin were born. My youngest sister Karen was born in what they called a midwife home. My folks' names were Pete and Gladys. That's my family.

Most of our travel was with horse and buggy or wagon or a sled in the winter. In the early years, all the farm work was done by horses. Dad was an efficient farmer. Our first tractor was a 1931 John Deere "D" and later a John Deere "G.P." was added to the farm.

With eight kids in the family, and no running water in the house, it was all the kids' jobs to haul water in from the windmill. For washdays on Mondays, we'd fill a big tank on a wagon to bring to the house. Sometimes in the winter, we'd use a sled on the snow and if it was uneven snow, it would tip over, and then it'd be back to the pump to fill it once again.

All of us milked cows by hand, fed the pigs with buckets, and fed the chickens. We lived off cream and eggs. We'd take them to town on Saturdays and buy groceries with the egg and cream money. Sometimes we'd get to go to the movies in Clark. They had one of the nicest movie theatres around back in those days I thought. Dad and Mom and we boys would go to the movies, and my sisters usually went to the regular dances on Saturday nights.

Rolling old used tires around the farm and playing in the dirt were things we did just for fun. We had to make our own entertainment. We made our own toys using old wheels and extra parts from around the farm that had served their purpose like wheels, tools, sprockets, whatever we could find. Some of our old creations ended up in the barn that the nieces and nephews played with in later years until all were lost in time.

The teacher couldn't stop us, I remember, when those big military bombers flew in formation over our schoolhouse in Raymond, SD. All the school kids would run outside to see them. We could hear them coming before they got there. Hardly any of us had ever seen an airplane before. There were about 15 or 20 of them and they'd be in formation like a flock of geese, in a big "V." This was in the fall of 1941.

It was two and a half miles to my first school, 50 yards to my second, and five miles to high school in Raymond. I went to three schools growing up, the Barrie school, which had eight grades, one teacher, and 21 students, a country school right across the road from our farm and the Raymond High School since the 7th grade. When I was eleven, I remember I would light the fires for the teacher at the school at 7:30, before school started. We played games like Fox and Goose and softball at recess.

When picking corn in the fall, Dad could pick two rows to our one. I recall walking along the cornrows with my brother Duane, and Dad, picking the corn by hand and flinging it into the wagon being pulled alongside by horses. The wagon had one side three feet higher than the other called a "bang board." We'd throw the corn against that and it would fall in the wagon. "You didn't even have to aim!" The horses would be smart enough to stay along the rows and would move just far enough when dad told them to.

We relied on our horses; most of our travel was with them in the winter. Dad had an old 1928 Chevy, but we didn't use it much in the snow and cold weather. I remember one storm incident when we left school in a white out blizzard. Dad always said that "Old Rosie" would find her way home. But that day, she took us to the neighbor's yard about half of the way home. They used the old crank phone to call dad and he rode a horse over to lead us home.

I remember while in high school I was on the Raymond Redwing basketball team. We practiced basketball after school for a

American Legion Farm Day

417

half hour and after the coach went home, we were told we could play a little more if we wanted to, so we would play a game against each other. Sometimes we would get home after dark much to my dad's dismay. "I'm not doing your chores, you're doing them in the dark!" we were told. We'd end up doing our chores with a lantern in our hands when time got away from us playing basketball.

World War II started in December of 1941. All the young men went to war, which caused no hired farm hand. The whole family, girls, and all did half the chores and in the fall of the year, we shocked grain bundles. Then later we worked pitching them into the threshing machines at harvest.

We drove our own cars to high school. We had interesting experiences, when driving to basketball games in the winter, after the snow fell, half the time, our heaters didn't work... but we made it through with no serious problems.

A few years after I graduated in 1949 with ten students in my class from Raymond High School, I joined the Navy during the Korean War. I was in for four years. Two and a half years I was on the naval ship called the USS Raymond. It was a destroyer escort, protecting the bigger ships as they policed the Atlantic Ocean during the European Occupation. "Going to Gitmo" would be the slang for heading to Guantanamo Bay, a destination often visited.

I got married in 1954 in Boston to a gal I met while on a four month stateside stay in Boston, Massachusetts. Three days later, I was back out to sea.

When I was discharged in 1955, one of the

Dean Bymers's family in 2001

first things I did was take the bus to Detroit and buy the family a 1952 two door sporty looking turquoise colored Chevy for 900 dollars and I drove it home.

I've been a farmer up until retirement in 1999. I farmed for a lot of years with my brother Duane and we also bought a Cessna 172 airplane together. I'd always had a passion to fly since a ride in a neighbor's two-seater airplane when I was younger. I still own that plane long with my nephew Dean and enjoy flying.

I enjoy getting together with friends and family, and my three kids, LeeAnne, Albert "Buddy", and Judy and I've always kept track of all of my graduating class, and also many of my Navy buddies, but as we get old, we are losing some quite regular. All of my siblings are still alive. My oldest sister is now in a nursing home. We are all 73 to 80 years old now and really enjoy our family reunions when we can all get together. There is never a lull in the conversations.

What More Could One Ask?
By Patricia Brown Hanson, Watertown,
South Dakota
Born 1933

Although I was born in 1933 in the middle of the "Great Depression," I was too young to understand its devastating effect on our economy. My father was a physician/surgeon who had completed his medical education in 1929, the year of the "crash." I was the fifth child and the fourth consecutive girl born to my parents so I assume they weren't too excited, although it never became apparent! They came to Watertown in 1930 where Dad went into partnership with a local doctor. They ultimately had seven children and my mother was hospitalized for two weeks with each one.

We needed and lived in large homes but they were all rentals until 1940, people then did not take out large mortgages. Dad designed and had our home built and they spent the rest of their lives there. The home was on the Historical Homes Tour last year.

I'm quite sure people in the early 1930s had very little money to pay their medical bills. However, they still got sick, needed surgery, and had babies. My father took care of them

418

Patricia's family in 1941

regardless. I remember him and his nurse often going out into the country on house calls and to deliver babies, even in blizzard conditions. In fact, my husband's mother gave birth to all four of her children at home on the farm. Many of the farmers paid their bills in produce, chickens, and eggs. One lady brought us eggs every week for years! Local business people often paid their bills in products, such as our refrigerator, range and our Maytag wringer washer (from which I still have scars from running my hand through).

My mother didn't like to go shopping! She had almost everything delivered to the house. Each morning she called the grocery store and the bakery with her order. They would deliver them, bringing them into the kitchen. A neighbor who owned the dry cleaners stopped every Monday and picked up the cleaning- he would deliver them and hang them in the back entry. Everyone walked in whether we were home or not. Our doors were never locked. Mother bought all of her stationary, gift cards, and wrappings from a lady who came to the house. The Fuller Brush man came regularly with cleaning supplies etc. The couple who lived behind us owned a women's clothing store and would bring clothes over for Mother to try on.

My father was an avid waterfowl hunter and so we had Labradors, which he personally trained, they were not house pets. All were named Thor. Our first one was hit by a car. Dad took him to the clinic where he operated on and clamped his broken leg. It healed perfectly. A few years later, there was a woman whom my Dad, as County Health Officer, had committed to the state mental hospital. When she was released, she came back to town and tossed arsenic-laced hamburger into our yard. Of course, our dog ate it, went into convulsions, and died. My sister and I witnessed this as he foamed at the mouth and leaped several feet into the air. The woman did the same to other doctors in town and was returned to the mental hospital. After that, Dad kept his dog on a farm.

Although Dad was a very busy man, he took time to do several special things with us. In summer, he took us swimming on Lake Kampeska in the evenings. He also took us to the city band concerts in summer on the courthouse lawn.

My husband Jim, two years older than I, remembers the "dirty thirties" well. The farmers were the ones deeply affected by the dust bowl and the crop failures. His parents didn't own their own farm until 1940 and very few of the farm homes had indoor plumbing and electricity. They pumped all of their own water. Jim attended a one-room country school for eight years. Even in the early '50s, they still had party line phones with all the neighbors on the same line. Everyone listened in on your conversations- there were no secrets!

We had several young women who came in from the farm and worked for their room

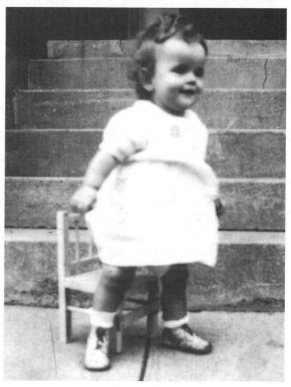

Patricia Brown Hanson at age 2 in 1935

419

and board and spending money. We called them maids but they were basically baby-sitters. Mother did all the cooking. World War II changed all that- the men came home and the girls got married. Thus began the "Baby Boom."

Of course, we had no television. I have memories of Dad sitting next to the huge console radio in the living room. He liked the news and Notre Dame football when Knute Rockne was coach. He also listened to baseball games, especially the World Series. I remember my Grandmother listened to all her soap operas on radio. We kids played outside winter and summer, when possible. We were very creative in our games. On weekends we went to the movies, which we called shows. They cost a dime and you could stay all day, which we did. Popcorn and candy cost a nickel. I bought my first bicycle when I was ten; it was used and cost $5.00. I had to borrow the money from Dad and pay it back out of my allowance.

My siblings and I all attended parochial school and the nuns were definitely in control! They were there to teach and we to learn, and learn we did. If you couldn't keep up, you repeated the grade, and many did. We walked over a mile each way, there was no busing, and rarely did they cancel school due to weather. I got into trouble only once, my friends and I decided to skip school and go fishing on May 1st. We were in eighth grade and the next day our teacher had us fashion fishing poles from tree branches, string, and safety pins. We stood in the corners with our fishing poles all day!

Going into public high school was quite an adjustment, but academically we were very prepared. We also had a lot of fun. There were dances on Friday nights in the gym, after the sporting events. We also had a recreation center in the city auditorium. Everyone went there after school and on weekends.

My husband was a year ahead of me in school. He was my first "true love" and our first date was Homecoming. We had Native-American royalty and he was chosen Chieftain, I was so proud. He drove an old Studebaker car, painted silver! Another of his cars was an old Ford with a rumble seat, his family was into cars. We were married when he was at USD and lived in trailer houses, courtesy of Uncle Sam's war surplus. We had an actual "ice-box" and the iceman came every other day, so did the milkman. Our rent was $30 a month, which Jim also received from ROTC. He had a part-time job, studied hard and graduated with honors. Our parents helped us out with tuition and books. We had two children by 1953.

After his graduation, Jim had to put in two years with Uncle Sam. The children and I were able to be with him and fortunately he never saw combat, even though many were sent to Korea. He served in Georgia, Colorado, and Texas. All through these years we had great times and made many lasting friends. Television and computers didn't dominate our lives. We had dinner parties, played cards, and the children played outside.

The most memorable people in my life besides family were some of my teachers and a very special couple who were our neighbors in the 40s. At age seven, I began cutting through their driveway on my way to school. They would talk to me from their window. They had no children and I spent as much time with them as I did at home. He was a wholesale candy salesman. She was a saintly woman, as well as a gifted pianist and artist. I studied piano at school for nine years and did my practicing at their home. She was my mentor. We lost her to cancer right after I graduated high school. You rarely hear of cancer in those days.

In retrospect, I feel we have lived in the best of times, in spite of experiencing the Great Depression, World War II, the Korean conflict, and Vietnam. The Bible tells us there will always be wars. It is the nature of man and his quest for power.

We did our best to raise six productive children. Parenting is "on the job" training. I feel blessed that I was able to stay at home and care for them. Very few mothers worked outside the home in those days.

My husband was successful because he made sacrifices, got a good education, and worked hard. He ultimately became one of the top executives of four different insurance companies in as many states. Upon his early retirement at age 63, we returned to our "roots" in South Dakota. We left children in Michigan, Indiana, Texas, and California. They love coming here to visit and escape the big city congestion, traffic, and accelerated pace.

Life has been truly good to us. We enjoy

the three important "Fs," faith, family, and many friends. We live in the best place, South Dakota! What more could one ask?

Grandmother Melva Witthoeft's Memories
By Christian H. Grottke, Eau Claire, Wisconsin
Born 1973

Pa's first Model T had no windows, but side curtains with a square of "eising glass" so we could look out. There was no heater. I was very small. If the car didn't start, Pa jacked up one hind wheel so that the motor would turn over easier.

When I was quite young, Wilfred Miller (Uncle Al and Aunt Lorena's son) would come to help Ma shock grain. We girls stayed in the car or its shade. We spent the afternoon "testing tires" by letting air out of the stems like we'd seen at the garage. Wilfred was more than peeved when he came to drive home after a long day of hot, backbreaking labor, and had to pump up every last tire with his hand pump.

When I was a little girl, there were few hangers at our house. Pa had one for his suit and Ma had one for her best dress. We kids covered sticks with colored paper and tied strings on them to hang our dresses on a nail.

Mrs. Russell was my first teacher. No teacher was supposed to be married but she was. She told Ma, but Ma let her stay because the teacher was poor and needed the pay check, and we needed the boarding rent. I took first and second grade in one year and graduated from eighth grade at age twelve.

Ma had an old James Way washing machine that operated by pushing a lever back and forth. Before Delpha and I could walk to school, we each had to do two loads of wash. We had to push the lever for about 10 minutes per load while we watched other school mates walk to school.

One fourth of July, we girls really wanted to sleep in. Pa tolerated no such foolishness. He lit a firecracker and threw it up the steps. We thought the house had exploded! We were not long getting downstairs! Pa sure laughed.

One other July 4th, Pa climbed to the top of the windmill and attached sparklers to the fins. Then he gathered us and lit them while the windmill was going around. It was truly spectacular!

We ran barefoot all summer long. The soles of our feet were really calloused. We learned to walk on grain stubble by shuffling our feet to push over the sharp stubbles. When school started again, our shoes certainly pinched.

Most everyone packed family lunches for the fair. Rows and rows of blankets were spread in the shade of the cars. Ma always served fried chicken, butter sandwiches, potato salad, and pork and beans.

One year at the dairy building at the fair, they were distributing little salt cubes to replace the salt lost by sweat in the intense heat. For the rest of the day, Ma took one or another of us to the water fountain. We didn't see much more of the fair that year!

When Ma canned tomatoes, she told us to

Melva M. Rawstern

421

Oaklie (Otto) Traver, Ruby (Otto) Rawsten, and Lorena (Otto) Miller

rub the skins on our arms to take out the tan. Young ladies should have creamy white skin.

When the feet of long stockings wore out, they were cut off and the leg part pulled on our arms and pinned to our sleeves to protect them from tanning. We were expected to wear sunbonnets too. We hated them.

There are few trees on the prairie. For winter heat, we depended on coal and corncobs. We sisters collected dry cow chips. If someone came along the road, we pretended to be out for a walk.

When I was eleven or twelve, one of Ma's half-grown chicks got wet. She wrapped it in flannel and laid it on top of the warming oven. There was a big pot of asparagus soup on the stove. Just as she reached to refill someone's bowl, the chick, now dried, warmed and lively, wiggled out of the flannel and toppled from the warming oven into the soup. The bird was scalded to death. No one ate any more soup.

Ma only drove the old Model T once. Taking lunch to Pa in the hayfield, she had to turn left by Borah school and go south one mile to the field. She didn't slow down as she neared the corner, but she turned anyway, going lickety split! Just around the corner, the township road scraper was parked. She was going too fast to go around it, so the grader blade struck both front and rear tires on the passenger side. She had to carry Pa's lunch that last mile. I don't think she ever told him how she got those two flat tires.

About 1933, Pa, Delpha, and I went to Huron. On the way home, we stopped to visit Aunt Oaklie and Uncle Harold Traver about five miles west of Huron. We saw a dark dust cloud rise in the west. We tried to make it home in the old Model T, but at the junction

with Broadland Road, dust killed the engine. We stayed until I started to cough. Pa said we had to get out and walk to the filling station a half mile away. Many cars were there. As we walked through the door, I collapsed in a faint.

When dust storms would come up, it would get so dark that the chickens would go to roost, the cows came bellowing home, and we lit the lamps. We used a knife to stuff rags in cracks and crevices in the house, but the dust was so fine it would still cover everything with a fine film. The wind moved so much dirt that it drifted over fences like snowdrifts. The cows could walk right over them. Because the dust was so fine, it packed together really solid.

During the "Dirty Thirties," the only feed for the cattle were Russian thistles, which had to be cut and stacked at the tender stage. We turned the cattle to the stack to keep the thistles tender enough for the cattle to eat. They had constant diarrhea. The cattle lived, but they gained no weight.

In 1934, we made a two-day trip back to Iowa to visit Grandpa Herman and Grandma Alice Otto. Cars would pass and honk because Pa was still driving an old Model T. Coming to a big hill by Sioux Falls; they barely made it to the top. We camped out and in the predawn; Pa got up and crawled under the car to tighten the rods. On the way home there was no food left for supper. We stopped by a cornfield and ate roasting ears.

Lacking commercial hair setting gel or the money to buy it, young women boiled flax seed and used the mucilage as gel. It dried stiff as a board, but it brushed out soft and it held the curl without any bad odor.

Our 4-H once had a bake sale and ice cream social. We also had a shadow social where Art and I had a secret sign; I would reach up to smooth my hair.

In October, we held a box social. Aunt Oaklie Traver and I made our boxes together. Mine was black with yellow ruffles around and yellow cats and pumpkins in the corners of the top, and a big pumpkin and cat in the center. Somehow, Art found out which box was mine. At the social, the other men caught on when an older man began to bid on my box and Art hadn't bid on any. They ran the price up from twenty-five cents to a dollar fifty.

The first years we were married, Art and

I lived on the correction line. The depression and drought made money scarce. Two gunnysacks of coal a week was all we could afford.

One winter we went to borrow something from Pa. Ma talked us into staying for supper. When we got home, the house was so cold that all my houseplants had frozen. I'm sure that little two-room house had no insulation. During the day, we kept the bedroom door shut. At night when we went to bed, we could see frost had accumulated on the walls.

One summer evening I was leaning on the gate watching Art feed the calves. I glanced over and saw the cats had something cornered. Suddenly there was a frantic race and their "prey" ran up my bare leg, under my dress, up to my waist. I grabbed, screamed, hollered, and danced around in absolute panic! Art could not figure out what was wrong! He ran over grabbed the animal around the neck and squeezed until it was limp and dead. It was a RAT!

Arthur and Melva Witthoeft

For some reason we had to haul water from a well a couple of miles from us. It was such cold good tasting water. When the barrels were full, we each took a long drink, until a dead mouse popped out of the spout.

On one Saturday night when Ma and Pa were going to town, they did the chores early. When they were ready to leave, Doris could not be found. She was throwing rotten eggs against a rock watching them explode. Ma could not get the awful stink out of her hair and clothes, so they both had to stay home.

During the late 1930s, the drought was easing and the crops were much better. Then the grasshoppers came. They plastered the north side of every fence post to get out of the hot sun. They ate holes in the laundry on the clothesline, and ate into fork and shovel handles because of the saltiness from our sweat.

Frank Bootz sold ice in Wolsey, east on Church Street. We'd get a big chunk for the icebox on Saturday nights. It would last most of the week until Thursday or so.

After Art's folks died in 1941, we bought their farm. World War II brought gas rationing in 1943. Art had only enough gas to get to my folks for Easter. Pa told us to come early and use his car to go to church. We drove with the doors open on the way home because the windows didn't roll down in the Model T and the manifold generated a lot of heat!

One time Art was out handpicking corn with the horses. When he got to the west end of the field, he hollered "whoa" but the team was feeling frisky. One jumped the fence. They galloped south, breaking off every fence post for nearly a quarter mile. When they reached the corner post by the gate, they stopped. Art freed them and drove them back to the buildings at full gallop. Those horses had never done anything like that before and they never did it again.

During World War II, Art and I located a corn picker at Willow Lake, SD. On the way home, a tire blew out. We had no spare due to rationing. Art went to the rationing board to get a tire. They said they would meet on such and such a day, but Art told them his car was sitting beside the road. They hemmed and hawed because he was out of the county, but they finally gave him a tire.

The Monster Storm
By Joyce Krokel of Mound City, South
Dakota
Born 1942

Growing up one mile from town shouldn't be constricting, but in the early 1950s, it was. My two siblings, parents, and I spent one particular winter storm being housebound.

When the weather forecast was predicting this monster storm, we went to town for groceries. Mom, bless her heart, let us pick out crafts to entertain us after we did schoolwork. Was it for our pleasure or to keep us busy so we wouldn't drive her to pulling out her hair? Probably both. We chose to make seashell jewelry, paint ceramic figurines, and of course, color in coloring books. We couldn't get to school for two weeks.

Because snow and wind made it impossible for Dad to see beyond his feet, he tied ropes together in order for him to get to the barn to feed animals. Then he followed the rope back to the house.

As the wind and snow calmed down, Dad bundled up and, pulling a sled, walked so slowly across the pasture to town. My nose pressed to the frosty window, I finally saw him returning. Stomping through high drifts and sled bearing groceries, he finally reached the house. He surprised us with a candy bar for each of us.

The snowbanks reached the top of the barn, allowing us to walk over the roof and roll, joyfully, to the bottom of the snowbank.

Finally, after two weeks, the sound of snowplows was heard in the distance. It took four plows, one behind the other, the entire day to plow the road, which was only a mile from town. The classroom never seemed as inviting as when I returned to school after that snowstorm!

Hard Work and Good Days
By Gail Vrchota of Veblen, South Dakota
Born 1929

I was born in 1929, the year the stock market crashed. Thing went from bad to worse. My father passed away in 1931, leaving my mother three children to raise. She had 80 acres of hills, trees, and grass surrounded by tribal land. Because of the location, no driveway could be built. We had only a trail, but also we had no car. We depended on relatives for transportation, plus our feet. Five or six milk cows and a few chickens provided our income. Surrounded by trees we burned wood for heat and cooking. We got warm chopping the wood. Years of drought and invasions of grasshoppers and jackrabbits followed.

My two brothers and I walked to our country one-room school, crossing three creeks, up and down hills, and through pastures, often through snowbanks. One teacher taught eight grades. On cold days, we moved our desks around the heater. In the winter, my mother wrapped two long woolen scarves around my neck and head so only my eyes were visible. In the summer, I cut insoles from waxed butter boxes to put in my shoes to cover the holes in the soles and make them last until I got new shoes in the fall for school.

Radios were powered by batteries, which had to be taken into town to be recharged from time to time. When power was low, we sat close to the radio for reception. Elders listened to some of Joe Louis' fights. Younger folks listened to *Jack Armstrong, All America Boy*; *Little Orphan Annie*; and mysteries. Listening time was limited, as we always wanted power to hear news and weather reports.

Wednesday and Saturday nights during the summer months provided a lot of the social activities in our small town. Businesses stayed open in the evenings to accommodate their rural customers. Farmers brought in their eggs and cream to town to sell and then buy supplies they needed. Pool halls were open so the men could socialize there. Women visited in the grocery stores and then enjoyed pie and coffee at one of the cafes. The young folks chased each other up and down the streets and also enjoyed delicious ice cream cones. Merchants held a drawing on Wednesday nights for cash, which helped bring in customers. No drawing was needed on Saturday nights, as people would come in on their own.

These were good days in northeast South Dakota but also involved a lot of hard work and concerns for our elders.

Small Town Fun
By June Comstock of Milbank, South Dakota
Born 1920

We are each proud of our own school. The cheerleaders' songs at all sport events were special. Each town tried to be more clever. Fun was the name of the game. I played a trombone in the school band. I wasn't very good, but I filled the space and it was fun.

Growing up when you know almost every family is very precious. Our large family was taught to be helpful to others. If someone was ill, we would run errands or clean for them. Likewise, when my father was very ill we had help from neighbors and relatives.

Summer fun was a playhouse in the back shed. We spent hours making furniture from boxes and curtains and table covers from cast off clothing. We also put on plays and tried to put on a circus. Cats and dogs became huge animals. Our imaginations helped us become creative.

My first job away from home was working in a General Merchandise Store, dry goods, shoes and groceries. They took eggs from farmers to trade for food. In the summer, they stayed open until ten or eleven on Wednesday and Saturday nights so the farmers could get to town after their farm work was done. I earned five dollars a week. I was fourteen and very happy to get the money.

When I was sixteen, I was hired to sell tickets at the Paradise Theater. On Tuesday and Wednesday nights, the manager had all tickets for ten cents. In spite of hard times in the thirties folks were able to enjoy those movies. A serial that was continued each week, usually a wild west excitement, was also shown for ten cents. I had learned to make change quickly, which helped me get the job. I felt rich.

A summer event in our family was to attend baseball games. My father was a pitcher and a good hitter. My dear mother packed fried chicken and potato salad for picnic lunches when we went to other towns to watch the baseball games. It is amazing no one became ill. There was no refrigeration then but chunks of ice from the icebox were packed in a bushed basket! My father did have his picture and name in the South Dakota Amateur Baseball Hall of Fame.

On summer, evenings we played kick the can or run sheep run. We always had some neighbor kids join us. It was fun!

Grandma's Scary Tales
By Irene J. Anderson of Brandt, South Dakota
Born 1918

Four-year-old Mike in the early '40s came from a modern home in that day with a bathroom. The small town neighborhood consisted mostly of outside "biffies." Ours was a "special" we thought, with a two holer regular height with a smaller and lower one for little folks. I happened to be looking out the window one morning and what did I see? Little Mike had trudged across the alley to our yard and came out of our biffie stark naked except for his shoes and stockings!

Saturday night was time to get in the big tub. There were five of us. The youngest went first. We never even thought twice about the last one and the dirty water!

Christmas presents in the '20s consisted of new underwear and stockings and pajamas made by Mom, and a plastic toy of a sort. Plastic toys were very new then and lasted maybe a day or so!

Dolls were scarce and expensive in the '20s so Mom went to the ragbag and formed a cuddly, soft, lovable doll. I called the doll Mollie.

Not many now remember the day of the dust storms in the early '30s. The days were dark like late evening or dark. Our windowsills had layers of fine dirt. I can remember the neighbor boy coming across the street with black, wet streams of dirt running down his face!

My grandma told me these tales: in those days of the early 1800s, they didn't embalm people after death. If they came to again after the doctor said they were dead, they called it "skin death." On one occurrence, a man sat up in his casket during his funeral! Another time, a man was in the next room making a woman's burying box and she stood in the doorway and asked what he was doing. At another incident, the pallbearers bumped against a pillar with the casket and the man inside woke up. The wife of the man said, "Be more careful next time." lastly, a man was so bereaved by his wife's death that he dug her up and found she had come to and pulled all her hair out. He arranged to have a pipe buried down to his face so he could get air if he came to. Grandma told a lot of scary things!

My twin brother, his friend, and I were drowning out gophers and got a snake with a big bulge. Having no idea what it was, one of the boys slid his shoe across it. Out came a huge toad; the snake had swallowed it whole which surprised us.

Wednesday and Saturday nights were special in our little town. All the farmers and families brought in their cream to the cream station and the money they received for the cream was spent for groceries. If the kids were lucky, they would get a nickel for an ice cream cone. If they only got a penny or two, there was a variety of goodies to choose from. In later years there were outside movies to attend for ten cents if you could afford it. I can remember hearing the music but had no dime to go! Dad would bring home a pint of ice cream and the five of us would share it!

I remember the excitement when gypsies came to town. They weren't exactly friendly. They were dark skinned and wore bright colored clothes. I remember one time a little girl had only part of her face. We were told a horse had kicked her. They traveled with horses and wagons.

Louie the Attack Rooster
By Dee Melicher of Denver, Colorado
Born 1928

In the late 1930s, things were finally getting back to normal after recovering from the 1929 financial crash and years of drought. Things were usually quiet but busy on our quarter section farm located in Argo Township in Brookings County, South Dakota.

My family consisted of Dad, Mom, an older sister, Lois, and me. A younger sister, Marlys, arrived in 1940. On our farm - besides girls - we raised small grains, corn, vegetables, chickens, hogs, and cattle. We also had two teams of workhorses.

Farm life without electricity, running water, or a telephone was common during this era. Social life centered around visiting with neighbors and relatives, church activities, and occasional get-togethers at the district

Dee and her sister, Lois

one room schoolhouse. During the summer, Saturday evenings were the highlight of the week. The area farm families would motor to the town of White (population 500) to do their weekly shopping, visiting, and catching up on all the news.

One summer in the later 1930s, when I was about eleven years old, we had to put up with a very odd situation by the name of Louie. Louie was the largest rooster ever seen. He was the size of a Thanksgiving turkey. He was a tough, mean bird. When my sister, Lois, and I would gather the eggs, Louie would sneak up behind us and attack us as we were leaning over the nests. The backs of our legs were rarely without black and blue bruises.

As I have mentioned, we had no indoor plumbing. Therefore, the outhouse was a necessary part of every farm. What a challenge to exit the outhouse on our farm this particular summer. Big Louie would be waiting to charge at full throttle. We kept weapons such as branches and sticks stashed in the outhouse so we could be armed as we exited. This did not deter Louie in the least.

One sunny afternoon Lois was sent to the well to fetch a pail of water for household use. As she was returning to the house, Louie came toward her at full speed. The only weapon available was her foot. She gave Louie a swift kick squarely in the head. Louie crumpled to the ground. Lois rushed to the house to summon Mom. Mom immediately severed Louie's head from his body. The only way the meat could be made edible was to make poor, tough Louie into soup. We enjoyed chicken noodle soup, chicken vegetable soup, or chicken dumpling soup for days.

With the demise of Louie, we were

no longer in constant fear of fowl attack. However, we actually missed him for a period of time.

Did I mention that Louie never, ever attacked Dad? Just the females in the family were targeted. Would that be called discrimination?

The Rocking Chair
By Harlan F. Olson of Arlington, South Dakota
Born 1939

Memories for each of us, young or old, the age makes no difference as they are recorded in our minds. From time to time, it is good to push the recall button and reflect on them. Many families whose roots are tied here to the Hamlin/Brookings County area go back to the first settlers who came here. Of course, others can trace their families back to places in all directions of our nations. If you look hard enough nearly all will find an old wood rocking chair! Practically every home had one. Some were homemade by a man now long forgotten. Many others came to their first home from an order made to the *Sears and Roebuck Catalog* nearly 100 years ago now. If your family still owns such a rocking chair, I encourage you to appreciate it for the memories of the people who sat in it.

Just such a chair sits in the corner of our living room with a small homemade rug thrown over the back. Today it's just an old antique oak rocker. Not so! It's like ones still found in homes scattered all over the country now. They are the survivors of another time.

Men and women looked at the rocking chair entirely differently through their eyes. Grandpa and Dad both commented they had much to do before taking up the rocking chair! The meaning was obvious – old men of little use anymore belonged in that rocking chair. It was a place to be avoided as long as possible! Today people make Bucket Lists of tasks and adventures to complete before time puts them in a rocking chair. That's probably a good idea. All too often we'll do that later when we have time. How much time do we have?

Women saw that old rocking chair much differently in their eyes. Grandma saw it as a much more personal place! It was comforting because she had sat there many times in her life. Over a span of nearly a hundred years she rocked three babies of her own, more than a half a dozen grandchildren, and a few great-grandchildren before her time was up to leave. She nursed both her son and the neighbor boy through the winter of 1913 in that rocker. I'm sure she shed many a tear in that rocker just a few years later when the flu epidemic took the boy and his granddad. Cemeteries all over the country mark the devastation that epidemic brought to many families. The double funeral was held on the farm in the same house where my dad and I were born. Now only a grove of trees marks that spot. Contagion was much feared before medicine or cures came along for diseases like diphtheria or the flu! To try to control the spread of disease most deaths went from the home directly to the cemetery. In the 1930s, she was rocking a baby boy born during the winter in that chair in her sod house home by the light of a kerosene lamp.

How very different our world is today! Can that old rocking chair talk? No, but it sure brings to mind a lot of memories. The sewing basket sat on the floor. The clicking needles as the wool socks were darned so cleverly you could not see or feel where the repair had been made. Sunday company sat on the sofa; the rocker was her place while they visited. How much more could a world change in one lifetime? She came to South Dakota in a horse drawn wagon as many others did in those early years. Today we drive our air-conditioned cars hundreds of miles a week without a thought of how we got here. We owe our very lives to those survivors who both tried to avoid the rocking chair and to those who found comfort in them! If you remember an old rocker in your past, remember the folks who sat there!

Times Were Tough but We Endured
By Fred Maxwell of Wilmot, South Dakota
Born 1922

I came to the Wilmot area with my mother and sister when I was a year and a half old, and I will soon be 92. My father passed away when I was very young, and we had relatives here. My first home here was two miles east and one and a fourth miles north of Wilmot.

I went to school through the eighth grade in a one-room school and to high school in Wilmot. Back then many boys and some girls too went to high school to age 16 years, which was required and then had to stay home and help with the work on the farm, making a living for the family.

My typical after school time was to eat an afternoon lunch and then go to the barn for the nighttime chores, cleaning and feeding the horse and the cattle, which were kept there in winter.

Due to the lack of trees on the open prairie, blizzards were very common in the winter and because of no radio communication and they came on very sudden sometimes it was necessary to tie a string from the house to the barn during these times. The only light we had was a kerosene lantern, which was hard to keep lit in a strong wind.

In the barn one section was used with horse stalls and the other section was penned for the cows and the young livestock. The cows were trained so there was no need for tying them when they were milked.

The first tractor was bought in 1928, a Farmall, which was used for plowing. All the other farm work was done with horses, and I either walked behind the drag or cultivator or rode where a seat was provided.

I also did some work on construction. At the time many roads had to be built and my job was driving a Caterpillar tractor, pulling an elevator grader, which elevated the dirt to the roadbed from the ditch as it was pulled forward.

In the 1930s there occurred a bad drought in my area of South Dakota which left no feed or grass growing for the cattle to eat except for Russian thistles and some slough weeds. Most ponds dried up. We pastured the cattle we milked about one and three fourths miles from home near Bullhead Lake. That meant going that distance morning and evening to milk the cows in the pasture.

There were also very bad dust storms that would come up without warning. The light of day became like the dark of night, piling up drifts of soil like snowbanks.

I got married in 1943 to my wife, Erma Hicks. We lived about four miles northeast of Wilmot.

On June 10 of 1944 a very bad tornado came from the southwest about one mile south of Wilmot. I had an H Farmall and was cultivating corn about 5:00 p.m. in its path. My wife came to the field and said I should come home. I had just a little left to finish the field so I wanted to stay. The clouds were looking dark. I was two miles from home, and it looked threatening so I drove my tractor to a neighboring farm. No one was home so I parked the tractor and went to the house porch. Soon the owner came home and said let's go in the house. We got in the house and I looked out the window and saw a small building come rolling by. Then I could see all the outbuildings start blowing apart. The next thing the house we were in started moving. The next thing I remember I was summersaulting through the air halfway across a forty-acre field and then the wind let up. I got my bearings and saw the other fellow I was with standing on the edge of his farmstead with no buildings standing. I was near Wilmot so the first thing I did was walk to town. I was covered with dirt and straw and had a cut on my head. There were more people in town. Some were hurt quite badly and some not as bad. The community was badly damaged because it stayed on the ground for many miles. There were seven people in the Wilmot area killed.

Looking back, times were tougher, but we took life as it was handed to us and endured.

Battle with a Rabid Skunk
By Jeanne Carstens of Kalamazoo, Michigan
Born 1952

I grew up on a farm in South Dakota. The nearest small town was 15 miles away. It was very quiet and peaceful and the clear, night sky was white with stars. Sometimes I would lie on my horse's back at night and watch for falling stars while she walked along eating the sweet alfalfa in the ditches.

My brother, Dennis, my sister, Joni, and I always had a lot of animals to raise, play with or care for; horses, cows, sheep, pigs, rabbits, chickens, geese, ducks, cats, and dogs. Occasionally, Dad would bring home a baby raccoon for us to raise. Once he brought us a beautiful, baby fox whose mother had been killed. Mom always encouraged our love for animals. There was one particular animal we would not find much love for and that was skunks.

Early one Sunday morning we were awakened by our dog, Skip. Skip was a beautiful border collie and he never barked without a reason. I got up and looked out the window wondering if we had company. Our nearest neighbor was two miles away, and we rarely had company this time of day. I was shocked to see a skunk right in front of our house! Skip was barking at it, and it was running after Skip a few feet, and then it would run back to the house. Back and forth, they went, but the skunk would not leave.

"SKUNK!" I screamed. My sister, Joni, and I scrambled to get dressed as fast as we could. My brother had left to go work for one of the neighbors very early that morning. My dad rushed to get his rifle and Mom was getting the bullets, which were always hidden in a safe place.

I opened the window and looked down again to see Skip panting, barking, and laying on the ground. Not far away from Skip was our gray and white mother cat. She had a litter of kittens a couple weeks before, and we had not found the kittens yet.

All of a sudden, I saw the skunk. Our old farmhouse had thick vines along the front of it, and the skunk was coming out from under the vines. It did not come out alone. A very tiny, white kitten was staggering out, also, with the skunk attacking it.

My sister and I ran down the stairs and

Dennis, Jeanne, and Joni Ransom

out the door as fast as we could go. The skunk had the kitten down and all I could think of was what could I do to help that kitten. I ran to a nearby shed, grabbed an old fence post and ran back to hit that skunk with it. The skunk turned its attention to me. It ran after me for about ten feet and then turned around to go back after the kitten. We did that three times. A dangerous game just like the skunk had played with Skip a few minutes before. Once again, I ran back and hit that skunk for the third time. This time it died. This all took place in less than ten minutes.

My Dad had to use that rifle, but not on that rabid skunk. He had to shoot the injured kittens and their mother who had fought to save them. We were very thankful our brave and beloved old dog, Skip never got a scratch.

A Deep Appreciation for What We Had
By Dorothy Clites of Mitchell, South Dakota
Born 1924

I was born on a South Dakota farm in the mid-twenties, so I endured the dust storms and grasshopper infestations with crop failures. I remember my mother putting towels on the windowsills and rugs rolled up by doors in an attempt to keep the dirt out, but with the constant high winds, we could hear the gritty sound as we walked on the floors.

Jeanne's parents, LaVerne and Dorothy Ransom in 1998

My father built a sand wagon and pulled it many miles by horses each day as he helped build roads on a WPA project.

In our home, we lived only in the kitchen in the winter, heating it with a cooking stove called a range. If we knew company might be coming, we heated the dining room. We were so happy when we were able to buy a heating stove called a Warm Morning. We played cards and games at the kitchen table.

Our upstairs bedrooms had no heat, so we had a frozen chamber pot in the morning. The outhouse, complete with a *Sears and Roebuck Catalog* stood some distance from the house. Peach wrappers were a luxury enjoyed only in the summer.

We had our baths in a washtub early on Saturday night, several of us using the same water. After all, it was Saturday, our main social time and everyone went into town.

Somehow our family of five managed to squeeze into the Model T, along with a five gallon can of cream and a 12 dozen crate of eggs. The cream was taken to the creamery and the eggs to Thomas Store, where they were traded for groceries. Mother read the store ads very carefully, finding Thomas Store to be a little cheaper than the larger more modern stores of Hendrick and Brewer and Ingalls. In my memory, I can see the Thomas Store. There were two wooden steps to enter and a well-worn wooden floor inside. A heating stove sat near the back in the center of the store. A chair sat on each side of the stove. Barrels of crackers, cookies, beans etc. stood upon the floor.

Our town had a large creamery, and it was very busy on Saturday night. When my parents sent me to pick up the cream check, I lingered to watch Pete Ewert run the huge churn, take out the butter, and then pack it in wooden pails to be shipped out of the area. There also were pound packages, which were sold at the creamery and in local stores. There was no air conditioning, so I can only imagine how hot it was in there, but Mr. Ewert always seemed jolly. He had a job to do and he did it.

The movie theater was packed on Saturday night; two shows were shown, and the price was ten cents. Men stood around in groups on the street visiting. The women did their "trading," then sat in cars visiting with other women. A special was a band concert, presented in the gazebo-like bandstand on the southeast courthouse lawn.

We hastened home late on Saturday night to hear the WLS *National Barn Dance* on the radio as we sat around the kitchen table with homemade bread and ham from Thomas Store. There was no eating in cafes for us!

I went to a one-room country school for eight years. We girls wore skirts over bloomers with elastic at the knees. I remember sitting unladylike in my desk in first grade and my uncle, who was the teacher, said to me, "Would a nice young lady sit that way?" I adored my uncle and it was painful to hear what he said.

The teacher and students worked hard to prepare a nice Christmas program and all the parents and neighbors packed the schoolhouse to hear it. A visit from Santa always followed.

We looked forward to the annual Valentine's Day party, but the highlight of the year was the last day of school picnic. There was a lot of food and real lemonade. Ice cream was brought in, in well insulated kegs. What a treat it was! Young and old participated in the kitten ball game. Drop the handkerchief and hopscotch were popular among the girls.

Dorothy Clites

430

We managed to get into mischief when our parents were away. We were cautioned not to play the wind up record player. It was stored away in a closet. As soon as we saw the car lights turn and go north toward Woonsocket, out it would come. It was a table model with a crank on the side. It was too heavy for us girls, but we managed to persuade our brother to get it from the closet. It was so much fun to play it. We stayed up late and always got it back in the closet before our parents returned.

Sunday was a day to make ice cream. Dad would chop the ice and pack it and the salt as we children turned the crank. It never seemed like work when we did it together. Sometimes company came to help us eat it.

If we were deprived of entertainment, we didn't know it. We found many things to do that didn't cost money. We had a much deeper appreciation for what we had than we do now.

Go Out and Play!
By Harriet Otto of Cheyenne, Wyoming
Born 1936

It's time for recess. Now we could go out and play! We really knew how to have fun. Of course, it gave our rural schoolteacher a chance to catch up on the lessons of the day. But what went on sometimes would have surprised her.

One recess, we were playing kick the can. We all scattered. Carefully, I watched as everyone hid. I watched and chose a spot in the corner of the playground where the fences met. You can imagine that places to hide were hard to find. Peeking out, I saw that "it" had finished counting to 100 and was ready to search. Well, sure enough, I was the first one caught. Trying to make friends with the person who was "it," I reveled the spot where Robert was hiding, but he had moved while I was hidden to the spot I now identified. You can imagine how angry he was. As a first grader, the older kids, fifth and sixth graders, decided I needed to be punished. They ran me "through the mill." I was forced to crawl between their legs and everyone had a chance to swat me. I'm sure I must have cried, but certainly knew not to tell the teacher!

I'm not sure where all the games came from, I think they must have been passed on to the younger students by the older kids. There was crack the whip. I was usually at the end, and I usually ended up being thrown down. Sometimes we would play softball where the older kids invented rules.

Pom, pom, pull away was played with two lines facing each other. Actually, we started with one person, who would approach a person in the line and shout, "Pom, pom, pull away, if you don't come away, I'll pull you away." Of course, you would run and hopefully make it to the facing line without being caught. If you were caught, you would have to help the person who was "it" catch the others challenged. The last one caught would begin the game as "it."

In fact, it was usually games of tag that occupied our recess fun. Anti-I-over was another favorite. We would toss a softball over the roof of the schoolhouse, calling "Anti-I-over." The kids on the other side would catch the ball and attempt to tag the players before they reached the other side of the building. We all would pretend we had the ball but only one would have it. Of course, if you would be caught, you would be a member of the other team. I wonder what that game sounded like at the teacher's desk inside the building.

I know we enjoyed playing Captain, may I? A game where we would instruct someone to take three giant steps. They could do that, but only after they asked, "Captain, may I?" After their answer, they were told if they could or could not take the three giant steps. If they failed to ask, they had to go back. The first person to the goal line was the winner, of course.

We also were sure to have a swing set and spent time pumping up as high as we could, and if we were daring, we would jump out. I can remember jumping out only to discover that my skirt had partially remained in the swing. Thankfully, the teacher had a few safety pins.

Our school was on the highway, and we would often stand at the gate and shout at cars passing by, "What's cooking, good looking?" "Candy, want a kiss?" or "Chicken, want to neck?" I'm afraid we were reprimanded for that activity.

Of course, it wasn't always warm enough to go out and play. On those days we would play Monopoly, Old Maids, Authors, musical chairs, hide and seek, and my favorite, I spy.

Of course, the object had to be hidden in plain sight by one of the class. If you found it you were to whisper to the person who was "it" where it was, not looking at the object and returning to your desk. The game would continue until all had found the object. Hints were given to the last searcher such as, "You're getting hotter."

In the winter, we brought our sleds and trudged up the hill and slid down. The other favorite was fox and geese. It was played when fresh snow allowed us to create a course in the snow to chase each other around. Of course, to make the game more difficult, we would put in traps, which were a dead end. You would certainly be tagged there. We would also slide across the ice of a shallow pond of water in the winter. Once when the ice was quite thin, we slipped in the water and had to wait for our clothes to dry by the center potbelly heater.

Well, about the time we were having the most fun, the teacher would appear on the front porch with the school bell in her hand. Recess was over. But you know when Mom would tell us to go out and play, we had a complete catalog of games to play. Then again, there was shadow tag, poison ivy, etc.

Nothing Grew but Thistles and Weeds
By Marion Ritter Perman Goehring of
Herreid, South Dakota
Born 1934

I can only imagine how parents and families felt in the Dirty Thirties when they knew they were going to have another mouth to feed. I was born on Good Friday, March 30, 1934. There were now two girls and three boys in our family. The oldest was nine. We lived on a farm one and a half miles west of Mound City, South Dakota. Our house was small, with no water, electricity, insulation, or closets. To me it was the best place in the world.

I remember looking out the window and watching the dust and sand blow around; sometimes it was so dark we couldn't see the garage or anything else. My mother would wet rags and lay them on the windowsills to help keep the dust out.

We always had a few milk cows, pigs, chickens, and horses. This gave us milk, cream, butter, meat, eggs, and lard. Nothing except thistles and weeds grew some years. Sometimes we didn't even put in a crop or garden. The Mormon crickets were so bad the roads were slippery. And the grasshoppers even chewed up the few fence posts we had.

My dad would take a load of wheat to Bowdle, South Dakota and have it ground into flour. That took three days. In the fall, we would butcher a pig, make sausage, liver sausage, and head cheese. We had to clean the intestines, inside and out, because that's what we used to put the sausage in. The pork bones were cooked or used for soup. Mother canned some of the meat, sausage, and liver sausage. All winter we would eat pork, dumplings, knoepfle, strudla, kiekla, homemade butter, bread, and ice cream.

In the spring, we got little chickens. They were kept in the house until they were big enough to live in the chicken coop. When they were ready to butcher, we had chicken every day. Mother and I would catch and butcher them in the morning and eat them at noon.

We rode horseback two and a half miles to school in any kind of weather. It was a one-room school with one teacher for all grades. There was no water or electricity. Our mother would put our lunch, which was peanut and syrup sandwiches and pickles, in a paper bag and then in a cloth one, tie it around us, and put us on the horse and send us off. Sometimes the snow was so deep the horse could hardly get through. There were only party line phones in those days so no one knew where anybody

One-room schoolhouse

Ralph, Floyd, Vernon, and Marion

was.

Everybody had a toilet, at home and school. We used catalogs and corncobs for toilet paper. The index of the catalog was the best. The shiny pages had to be crumpled until they were a little soft.

We all took a bath in the same water. In the winter, we melted snow and heated it on the coal stove. In the summer, we caught rainwater in a barrel and let the sun heat it. There was about an inch of water in a small round tub in the kitchen. I was the youngest, so I went first. Mom or Dad was last. Sometimes we went to Lake Campbell to swim and cleanup.

My sister, the oldest, would not go to school when she was six because they had a man teacher, and she was scared. She and my brother started the next year. They graduated from Herreid High School in 1943. All the neighborhood kids who went to high school would pile into one or two cars and drive to school until the roads got blocked. Then we had to stay in town. Sometimes we wouldn't get home for weeks. One year I didn't even get home for Christmas. When they did get the roads open enough so I could walk, home the snowbanks were so high I could walk on the roof of the garage.

When World War II broke out in 1941, there were blackouts and food and gas shortages. We had to have stamps to buy sugar and gas. We could only buy so much. It was during this time that I saw the first airplane. The teacher would let us out of school to see it. My dad was on the Draft Board. He had to draft his own three sons, two in the Navy and one in the Army. That's just the way it was. Almost everybody's boys had to go. When they came home on furlough in their uniforms, I thought they were the best looking brothers anybody could have.

The older I got the poorer we were. I didn't know we were poor then, but now I know God takes care of His people and supplies all their needs.

A Salute to the Two-Room School
By Helen M. Prater of Cleveland, Georgia
Born 1931

On a hill in a small village in Marvin, South Dakota stood a two-story schoolhouse. It was quite advanced in design as well as functions, and the single seats were nicely spaced to eliminate the overcrowding of three in a seat the previous generation had experienced. Forethought also had been given in providing adequate teachers, with one for the twenty or twenty-five students in the first four grades in the downstairs room. Another teacher was provided for the upstairs, fifth through eighth grades. Attached to the upstairs room was a long narrow room that had a separate entrance and that was a first year high school. They also had a teacher. High school was discontinued when I was in the second grade.

The school was equipped with the latest in modern ideas. For the lower grades, a square sand table was provided in which a number of different scenes could be constructed according to the imagination of the children. A new planetarium with all the planets arranged on a chain revolving around the sun an inspiration to all the scientific minded students was placed nearby. The upper grades were not blessed with such visual aids. Their sole attraction was a long table that held a huge dictionary and was used alternately to work on or display art objects.

I need to describe the inside physical structure of this wonderful schoolhouse. As I said, the first four grades were on the first floor and in the room; we had a door that led to the basement. Also we had a narrow hall that led to the downstairs room and large outside doors that also led to a wide stairway that led to the upstairs classroom. We had long stately windows upstairs and down along the south and west walls. They were situated about three feet from the floor and extended almost to the ceiling. Not willing to waste space but to provide the best in heating, we had steam radiators. These radiators, sporting a broad metal protecting cover, were multi-useful. They not only provided heat but they also helped thaw out our socks and mittens and boots and even our very cold bodies. Another feature was that they eliminated boredom because when the teacher became a bit tedious the radiators would begin to knock and spew out steam, and it would be almost impossible to hear above the din. These radiators did not always work properly, especially for the upstairs room. They were powered by a coal furnace in the basement and sometimes the steam pressure didn't make it to the second floor when the temperature was 20 to 30 below zero.

I mentioned the basement; oh yes, you know we didn't need a principal or superintendent because most of us had learned discipline at home, but that basement; it had multiple uses, too. The main use was to store the coal for the entire winter months, and when it was too cold to go out for recess, it provided a place to play if we chose. But that was not the only use; if we didn't pay attention or whispered too much we were sent to the stairs of the basement for punishment. I mentioned the long, narrow hall that led to the downstairs room. That was the other place for the lesson of learning to obey orders. I found myself once in the stairway but twice in the hall. Of course, I didn't think it was fair that I got sent to the hall when I wasn't the one that had turned around and was whispering but one of those times the teacher forgot I was out there without a coat and the temperature was very cold and I caught a cold and was out of school for a week or more.

We had a wonderful large playground and several swings, a monkey bar, and a beautiful "Ocean Wave." This pivoted from the top and had wooden seats all around and it could be pushed to go around in a circle or up and down and around. Some of the older children were able to accomplish this, and many children could ride it at one time. We learned to play many outside games like fox and geese and Anti-I- over and softball and mainly how to get along with our classmates and help to take care of the younger children.

Since I have spent time describing the physical amenities of the school I need to tell you about our restrooms. Since, of course, we didn't have running water, our drinking water was a crockery "bubbler," and someone went to a well and fetched a pail of water and poured it in the cooler. Then everyone took their turn drinking from the bubbler. Our toilets were outside about 100 feet from the schoolhouse and were two outside privies. There was one for the boys and one for the girls. It wasn't a place we lingered long if we had asked permission to go. If someone had used up the paper in the dispenser there wasn't room for a catalog so you learned from experience to bring paper from home.

If I remember right, the government allotted an acre of ground for each school in a section so ours was nicely situated and had a barn on it and a well and was within the town. Of course, there were no school buses so you either walked, rode a horse, or if you were lucky, someone in your family had a car. I was one of the lucky ones. We lived on a farm about three miles from the school so my Uncle Bud took me to school and, since my Aunt Olga, who taught school five to six miles south of Marvin, picked me up. One boy who lived about three miles in a different direction rode a pony. He told me years later how embarrassed he was to ride that pony when he was a really tall boy and his legs hung almost to the ground, but he put the pony in the barn while he was in school.

These small inconveniences only enhanced our learning process. We didn't think we were short of anything. Most of us had a lunch pail with a couple of sandwiches to eat and water to drink and when the blizzards raged and the schools were closed we didn't have to go all summer to make up the days we missed. We just doubled up our lessons and had them made up before the next snow.

We lived through the dust storms and the grasshoppers and always God was good to us and helped us through the trials and made us strong.

Our teachers taught us, even though they had a lot of students and had to teach each grade all of the subjects and they recited in front of the class. We not only learned our lessons but a great share of theirs. And there was not a one of us that came from that school that couldn't read and write.

This old-fashioned school, although modern for its day, has long since been closed and sadly, torn down to make room for more modern education and school consolidation. But from our two-room school came a bank president, nurses, teachers, farmers, and homemakers. We had a record of no slum areas, no juvenile delinquents, and very few jail records.

I would like to salute the old schoolhouse that holds so many fond memories and the capable teachers who excelled in at least some of the many subjects they were called upon to teach and to a community who loved and cared for their young people: Marvin, South Dakota.

Old Radio Program Memories
By Avis Elenz of Jefferson City, Missouri
Born 1931

"Who is that masked man anyway?" While listening to the strains of "The William Tell Overture" we hear, "Hi Ho, Silver, away!" Of course, these quotations exist in the radio program *The Lone Ranger*. It was a favorite story of my brother and I. It was on the air from 6:30 to 7:00 p.m. on Monday, Wednesday, and Friday nights on WNAX 570.

Daily Morning Shows
Aunt Jenny was a 15-minute serial program. Short stories were presented, followed by *Stella Dallas*. Arthur Godfrey had a daily program that lasted one and one half or two hours. It featured the McGuire Sisters and the singing of Julius LaRosa. Arthur even fired Julius on a live program! Saturday mornings on WCCO 830, my cousin and I loved listening to *Let's Pretend*. It was various fairytales sponsored by Cream of Wheat. On *Big Sister* on WNAX, the main character was Ruth Wayne, sponsored by Rinso Laundry Soap. *Hymns of All Churches* with George Beverly Shay was a five-minute program. Kate Smith also had a five-minute show. She always said, "What's up, Ted?" He was her sidekick. She sang "God Bless America" with such gusto, and it became our patriotic anthem. *Ma Perkins* was another soap, with a main character whose name was Shuffle. The show was sponsored by Oxydol Laundry Soap.

Afternoon Programs
Judy and Jane, sponsored by Folgers

Avis and her brother in 1938

mountain grown, was on WNAX. Another soap, *When a Girl Marries* was on WOW, Omaha 590. *Scattergood Banes* had the theme song of a concertina playing "Funicale Funicula," followed by *Portia Faces Life*. *The Neighbor Lady* on WNAX was a program my mom couldn't miss, featuring recipes and domestic tips. She always had a notebook and pen to copy recipes! The lady, Lynn Speece, seemed like a family member to us. We followed the program when she graduated from college, her engagement, and marriage. She shared the birth of her children through their grown up years. My brother and I had a favorite 15-minute serial show, *Jack Armstrong, the All American Boy*, sponsored by breakfast of champions, Wheaties. They had activities; for instance, send in Wheaties box tops and receive a coded ring. We also liked *Sky King*. We liked the show *The Shadow* on Sunday afternoons. "Who knows who lurks in the hearts of men, the shadow knows." My brother would rush home to my grandma's to hear Myron Floren play the accordion on KSOO in Sioux Falls, South Dakota at noon.

News Programs

Every night from WOW Omaha had a 15-minute news program at 5:45. From WNAX national news was Walter Winchell on Sunday at 8:00 p.m. "Good evening to you and all the ships at sea," with background erratic tapping of a telegraph. Local news was also reported nightly. Elmer Davis had a five-minute news report at 7:55 every evening during World War II. No matter what we were listening to, my grandpa would change the station to the news of the war. When Norway was invaded by the Germans, my grandpa just cried and cried.

Programs in the Evenings

Cecil DeMill's *Lux Radio Theater* on Monday night was sponsored by Lux hand soap. Tuesday evening aired *Inner Sanctum*. My dad had to agree to sit with me in the dining room during this spooky program that scared me from the very beginning when the squeaking door was detected. Also on Tuesday night was *The Bob Hope Show* at Omaha, WOW. *Fibber McGee and Molly* entertained us on WNAX. Fibber McGee would open up a closet and everything would fall out. The radio sound effects were great. Thursday was *Major Bowes Amateur Hour*. He would ring the gong if contestants should be cut off due to a less than perfect presentation. *The Aldrich Family* amused us also on Thursday evenings. The main character, Henry, was similar to Dennis the Menace. Every weekday evening, *Amos and Andy* had a 15-minute program. Kingpin was a main character. Friday evening was *Call for Phillip Morris*. It represented a theater program of various content. My dad listened to boxing on Friday night. Joe Louis was his hero. He would even judge every round. Another evening show was Edgar Bergen and Charlie McCarthy. *Hit Parade* was presented on Saturday evening. The girls listening would swoon when Frank Sinatra sang. *G Men* was a thrilling Saturday night event. I remember it was similar to *The Untouchables*. Sunday evening schedule included the Jack Benny program. Don Wilson spoke for the sponsor, Jell-O. It was followed by the *George Burns and Gracie Allen Show*. A polka band show was broadcast nightly. I can still remember their theme song.

WNAX characters were featured at various times of the day or evening. Some of these were: George B. German, who sang with his guitar. In our humble opinion he was not our favorite; Happy Jack O'Malley, whose main song was "I'm Going to Buy You a Rubber Dolly;" and Ben and Jessie Mae, who played and sang. Willie Dean appeared on their program as a special guest.

My dad listened to Major League baseball games and he listened to state baseball tournaments featuring our hometown team. The family listened to regional state basketball tournaments. Another show on WNAX in later years was *Jolly Joe from 570*. He was a disc jockey.

Radio was an important medium during the years before television. The charger resembled a car battery with two clamp hook ups. Remember, we had no electricity, only a battery, and had to travel to town to Lloyd Webster's gas station to have it charged. Radio was practically our only entertainment.

These are my old radio program memories. I was born and raised on a farm in Sanborn County, South Dakota.

Schoolhouse Memories
By Jean P. Olson of Elk Grove, California
Born 1932

Still sits the schoolhouse by the road,
A ragged beggar sunning;
Within…
    John Greenleaf Whittier

For most of a century, the one-room schoolhouse provided the education, social

Happy Hill country school

436

Y.C.L. County Meeting in 1944

life, and chance for adventure for hundreds of boys and girls on the prairie. My two schools were in Jerauld County, South Dakota.

Students arrived at school in and on all sorts of conveyances: by team and wagon, on ponies, on foot, sometimes on a bike, maybe in a car. In the winter, getting to school might involve pouring a teakettle of boiling water onto the car radiator to thaw it out or putting the wagon box on sled runners. Dad made sure we got there; he thought school was very important.

The teacher was sometimes a young high school girl who took "normal" courses at a local college during the summer after she had graduated from high school. When I was twelve years old in seventh grade, my teacher was not yet eighteen! My other teachers included a farmer's wife, a serviceman's wife who had to leave in the middle of the school year when her husband was transferred, and a 70-year-old woman who came out of retirement during World War II because of the teacher shortage.

The curriculum was guided by outlines published by the State Department of Education for each grade and was followed faithfully because at the end of each six week period tests came from this same department. Subjects on the report cards were Reading, Writing, Arithmetic, Language, Grammar, Spelling, History, Geography, Civics, Science and Health, Art, and Music. Percentage grades were given to the nearest one fourth of a point, for example, 80 ¼, 87 ½, or 73 ¾. The teacher taught all subjects, sometimes to all eight grades. Seventh and eighth graders studied review manuals to pass state tests. Sometimes they stayed in school two extra weeks in the spring to prepare for and take these tests. We had to pass every test with 75% accuracy to graduate into high school.

The end of the school year usually found one sad girl who realized that her eighth grade boyfriend wouldn't be returning to school with her in the fall.

Older students helped the younger students, who might also be their siblings. Each grade was called up to the "recitation bench" by the teacher's desk to be instructed in a new concept or to be quizzed about their lessons. An alert student could listen to the older students recite and sometimes could skip a grade.

Our library was a cupboard shelf in the back of the room with a few dog-eared books that were read over and over as each grade used them. Sometimes we brought books from home that we had checked out from the Wessington Springs Andrew Carnegie Library.

Everyone had duties. Cleaning the chalkboard erasers was a prize job. That lucky student could clap them together and generate clouds of chalk dust. We didn't have environmental protection laws then. Raising and lowering the flag was for older students. Filling the water pail was hard. The schools I attended didn't have wells. Sometimes the

Jean is in the back row on the left and her brother, Lynn Powell (of the cut head) is in the front row-middle in 1945

teacher brought a pail of water with her from her home or boarding place.

One day my brother and his friend decided to go on horseback rather than to walk to the farmhouse across the road to fetch a pail of water. They put a stick through the pail's handle and each boy held one end as he sat on the back of his pony. On the way back, with the water splashing, they passed too closely to the mailbox and my brother's leg caught on it. He scooted right off the rear of his horse and onto the ground. The friend's pony stepped on his head and cut it open. I had to go back to the farmhouse and call Mother to come take him to the doctor for stitches.

Games at recess involved a lot of running and very little equipment. Ante Over the Barn; Pum, Pum, Pull Away; Base, Squat, and Statue Tag; Steal Sticks; Jump Rope, and our brand of Baseball filled our playtime. One day my brother and another hard-running student collided and my brother broke his leg. Inside games included Tic, Tac, Toe, and hangman played on the chalkboard. Sometimes the teacher called out math problems to see who could solve them the quickest. For Musical Chairs we reacted to music played on a wind up phonograph.

Lunch consisted of whatever we brought from home. Bread and butter or fried egg or homemade jam sandwiches were the rule. There were no peanut butter or cheese sandwiches; those required store bought items. Once we baked potatoes on top of the heating stove. We covered them with the upside down washbasin. They were burned on the bottom, raw on the top and somewhat baked in the middle – delicious! One mother sent a pot of boiled beans and ham to be warmed on the stove. "Keep them stirred," she said, "and not too hot or they'll burn." They did. The burned taste went all through the beans, but we ate them anyway. There were few trades of lunch items because most kids had the same things: bread, eggs, pickles, cookies, sometimes an orange or apple. We played a game of guessing the brand of someone's orange.

Once a month was Young Citizen's League (YCL) meeting. Sometimes the County Superintendent of School would visit. In the spring students from another school might come for a baseball game and picnic lunch. A basket social was always well attended and earned a little money for extras.

The girls decorated a box or basket containing food items. The boys bid on them and ate with the girl whose basket he had bought. Of course, the baskets had to be smuggled into the schoolhouse sight unseen. There were some happy pairs and some unfortunate ones. Christmas brought out the stage curtains for a play. We recited our "pieces" and acted out some skit that the teacher had found, probably in the *Grade Teacher* magazine.

Field trips consisted of nature hikes to a nearby pond, visiting another school, going to town to the county spelling contest or play day, or to the YCL county meeting. Our family usually went to the South Dakota State Fair in Huron to see the art projects that we had submitted to compete for ribbon awards.

Neither of my schoolhouses had a telephone. I'm not sure how the teacher got emergency help. I suppose she sent an older student to a nearby farmhouse to get help or to use a telephone. My two brothers and I had emergencies at school that included a bad head cut that required stitches, a broken leg, onset of appendicitis, which required surgery, and a persistent nosebleed.

We survived it all and grew up with a good basic education, some lifelong friends, and happy memories.

The Brightest Stars in America
By Milo I. Harpstead of Stevens Point, Wisconsin
Born 1930

I was born on our farm in Lee Township near Wilmot, South Dakota on September 28, 1930. I was delivered by Mrs. Gunhild Stensing, the local midwife and the grandmother of several of my schoolmates. I'm quite sure that she learned her skill in Norway. I believe that Dr. Harris came out soon and confirmed that I was okay.

Our farm was like that of most of our neighbors. There was no electricity or running water. For most of those early years, we had one single wick lamp. If the lamp was needed in the kitchen, the rest of us sat in the dark in the dining room/living room. We grew up not being afraid of the dark. I have never lived in another place where the stars were so bright and the Milky Way was so clear. Similarly, I recall the remarkable display of the Aurora Borealis one evening in the summer of 1938.

On a moonless night with cloudy skies, a lantern was usually carried to find the way to the outdoor toilet. However, if you could see lamp light in the window of the house you could progress in the darkness with a hand outstretched until you felt the toilet door. To go upstairs to sleep, I usually carried a lighted candle.

This brings up another memory. Nobody in our family smoked, but we used fire all the time in the house and outside. We learned to respect fire and never burned anything down. There were a couple of times when a prairie fire got started, and all the neighbors rushed to put it out with just hand tools or wet grain sacks. There was a charred area on the base of our old barn. The story was that there was a terrific bolt of lightning during the night. Mom got up and saw light coming from around the corner of the barn, and she alerted Dad. He hurried out and extinguished it with buckets of water from the stock tank. That was a close call!

Every farm had its own well that could be a problem to maintain. They produced excellent water for drinking but not for washing clothes due to the water's hardness. As a result, most farm homes had a cistern to collect rainwater from the gutters along the edge of the roof. Our cistern was built into a corner of the basement when the house was built. The kitchen had a pitcher pump by the sink in the corner that delivered water from the cistern if the water level was high enough. There was a problem of keeping the cistern walls leak free. We had to paint on black water proofing to seal it up as best we could. A covered hole was in the kitchen floor so that with a rope and a bucket water could be pulled up. Probably due to leakage, I don't think that the cistern water supply ever lasted through the winter. As a result, the only source of soft water was snow. On washday, Mom used to fill a washtub and other containers with as much snow as they would hold and

Milo's home place in 1950-51

melt it on the kitchen stove. The melt water, together with the lye soap that she made by rendering fat from butchered hogs, provided a combination that got our clothes clean. First she had a scrub board, later a foot and arm powered washer, and finally a "One Minute" washer with a Johnson Iron Horse engine that I still have in my collection of antiques.

One advantage of having a windmill and tall buildings was that we learned as children to be comfortable in high places as we climbed up to fix a roof or whatever was needed to be done with the windmill. Whenever the well had to "be pulled," a pulley system was attached high on the tower. This was not natural to me, but I learned to work up there as though I was on the ground. One time I was hired by the owner of the hardware store to attach lightning rods and copper cables to a roof.

All milking was done by hand. To keep the milk in the pail pure was virtually impossible. Straw and worse would sometimes drop from udder into the pail and had to be plucked out with your finger, which could not be clean. Some people used the "wet hand" method of milking in which they started by squirting milk on their hands. Drips were inevitable. An effort was always made to keep the cream separator clean. There were strainers with filters to remove particles from the milk as it was emptied into reservoir, but most people tied a piece of cotton cloth over the top and strained the milk through it. I believe that our exposure to so many microorganisms throughout our childhood helped us to build up resistance to the health risks to come.

The cream separator was normally secured to the kitchen floor, at least in the cold seasons. Cream was usually collected in either a five or eight gallon can that was delivered to the creamery on the floor of the front seat of the car or in the rear if somebody was there to hold it from tipping on a corner. Our creamery had a drive-through corner from where the can was picked up. It was wise to have your name painted on the can to avoid confusion as to who brought in which can. The cream and eggs checks were the income to buy groceries and whatever else was needed that week.

As an aside, I recall a couple of times when one of my baby teeth was slow to come free. My solution was to loop a string around the tooth and tie the other end to the cream separator handle and give it a swing backwards. It happened too quickly to hurt.

In the spring of 1936, we moved to a rented small farm a mile north of our home farm. I believe that it was largely because the folks wanted me to be closer to our country school, Lee #5. This was when an increasing number of farmers were shifting from totally horsepower to small tractors. During this transition, many farmers converted used cars into tractors. Mail order companies sold conversion kits for Model T and Model A Ford cars. These were called "doodle bugs" and now they are collector items. We had one made from a 1924 Dodge car and a Ford truck rear axle. In Albert City, Iowa, the Thieman Company sold a tractor complete with everything but the engine. The farmer could complete it himself with a Ford, Chevrolet, or Dodge car engine. Our doodlebug was not very successful for fieldwork, and the following year (1937), we got our first tractor, a new red Farmall F-12 from the Al Pierson dealership in Peever.

Going back to before I was born, Dad bought a steam threshing rig from a loaning agency that got it on a foreclosure. I was told that it was a Minneapolis engine and a large threshing machine with a 44 inch cylinder. After a few years, it was left immobile just to the west of our farm building, never to be used again. The steam engine was sold for scrap iron in the late 1930s because the Japanese were buying all they could get in preparation for World War II. I recall playing in and around the rig when I was very young.

Before the widespread seeding of hybrid corn farmers planted what is called opened pollinated seed from the previous year's crop. One of the winter jobs was to select nice looking ears of corn from the crib and shell them by hand. That seed was then transferred a handful at a time into a corn grader. Dad held it on his lap and shook it. This action sorted the kernels according to size and provided uniform kernels for the corn planter in the spring.

Even after hybrid corn became popular, corn was planted in what was called a checked pattern with a two row planter. The two planter boxes and the planting mechanism were a fixed distance apart, commonly about 42 inches. A planter wire had what were called "buttons," also spaced at 42 inches, and was stretched the length of the field and the planter wire was placed in a slotted lever on the planter. As the planter was pulled forward a fixed number of kernels were dropped when a button on the wire drew the slotted lever back. This caused the corn to be planted in a square pattern. Cultivation of the crop could then be done in the direction it was planted as well as across the field for better weed control. Appropriate herbicides were not yet available.

Neither my brother nor I considered ourselves "cowboys" but even after we had a tractor a team of horses was kept for the threshing season and other jobs, such as mowing. We had one workhorse that was pretty good for riding. She came in handy for driving cattle from the pasture to the barn. We never owned a saddle, but we could ride bareback at full gallop. I recall one time when a young cow darted out to the side, and I kicked my mount into high gear. The vegetation was about two feet high and neither the mare nor I saw the old wheel ruts. Down she went with me going over her head and sliding nose first through the plants. I took a quick look around, and the rear end of the mare was right at my heels. There was no injury, and we were soon on our way again.

Our farm was a couple of miles east of the hills called the Cateau du Prairie. That is where the Whipple Ranch is located. Frank Whipple and Dad bought a young Herford bull for $110.00 and split the cost. Once when it was time for the bull to service some of our cattle, Frank's hired man, Ervin Swayze, was assigned to deliver it. He saddled a horse and attempted to lead the bull to our place. The bull was stubborn and wasn't about to be led. Ervin's solution was to ride the bull and lead the horse. All went well.

The Changes in My Community
By Alyce Howard of Huron, South Dakota
Born 1925

I have lived most of my 88 years in Huron, South Dakota and have observed many changes in our community.

Milk was delivered to our home every day except Saturday and Sunday. The daily newspaper was called the Huronite and then changed to Daily Plainsman and was also delivered to our home.

My father worked for the Chicago-Northwestern Railroad and we (my parents, my sister, and I) traveled to many states to visit relatives and we had free passes, which was great.

My favorite teachers were Helen Buchanan, Byrne Smith Griffith, and Ruby Matson. Helen taught music in the high school, Byrne taught me voice lessons (she was a graduate of the Julliard School of Music in New York City) and Ruby was a piano teacher and choir director at the American Lutheran Church for thirty years.

We had a swimming pool west of the fairgrounds and my dad would take us there to go swimming. It closed and then we went to a place called Pearl Creek a few miles out of town. Pearl Creek was part of the Jim River, which ran through east part of the town of Huron.

We had an icebox and ice would be delivered to the house. When we moved to our new home at 650 Simmons Avenue, my parents bought a Kelvinator refrigerator so we no longer had ice hauled. We could make our own ice.

Our telephone was on a party line for a few years and then we switched to a one party line. That was much better. Before you could pick up the phone and someone would be talking and you couldn't use the phone until they were through using the phone.

We had great family get togethers with aunts, uncles, cousins who lived close by, and we would often celebrate Thanksgiving and Christmas together.

I also remember the Carnegie Library as I used to go there after school to check out books. I loved to read and I enjoyed going there often.

I could go on and on about memories from the good old days. Memories of friends, relatives, ten-cent movies at the theaters, also radio programs like Jack Armstrong, the All American Boy that I would listen to when I got home from school.

One-Room School and Daily Chores
By Paul W. Patton of Mitchell, South Dakota
Born 1929

We walked to school and carried our own lunch. I had two brothers and a sister in a one-room schoolhouse in Hand County, South Dakota. Our teacher was Helen Upton. She was around five feet two inches. The first thing in the morning we sang songs and gave the flag the Pledge of Allegiance while someone put up the flag. We then had a prayer. There was a 15-minute recess at about 10:30. There was one hour off at noon to 1:00 PM. As we finished lunch, we went out to play till 1:00. We then did our lessons with a 15-minute break and school was dismissed at 4:00 PM. We would then walk home.

We had chores to do when we got home. We had to feed the pigs, gather eggs, and milk cows. Then we would have supper. Our home was lighted by kerosene lamps. Our school was heated with a coal-burning stove. Sometimes in winter, we would bake potatoes in the ashes. There was no dismissal for snow days; if people could get there, we had school. Extra entertainment was a battery-powered radio. We got electricity in 1950. Saturday was a trip to town for groceries. We sold eggs and cream which helped to buy our groceries.

In 1936, we moved to Oregon, as it was so dry we couldn't raise a thing. We lived there for 14 months. In 1941, we moved to a farm near Alpena. The youngest boys drove the cattle the whole way, which was 25 miles. Farming was raising corn, wheat, barley, and rye. Mother had a garden with rhubarb. We always had lots of sauce and pies from that.

We also had potatoes, vegetables, and apples.

My first car was a '35 Ford and I bought it for $200.00. In 1949, I was married. We started our family, but lost our first child. I spent two years in the army and was stationed in Germany as a tank mechanic. I had a wrecker truck which I serviced tanks, trucks, etc.

We moved to Seattle in 1955 and had a service station. When several more opened up, we closed ours. I went to Alaska as a promise of a good job, but it never got started. We moved back to South Dakota to Mitchell and had several businesses here. I had a salvage yard, which a tornado took in 1962. Later I had a service station and did trucking with my own trucks.

After 65 years of marriage, we have several wonderful children, and four of them still live near us. One is in Texas. We have lots of grandchildren and great-grandchildren. We've had a very blessed life.

The Joys of Farm Life
By Selmer N. Anderson of Cresbard, South Dakota
Born 1930

I was born on my grandfather's homestead in the same house my father was born. It was 1930, Edmunds County South Dakota.

I began my education as a first grader in a one-room school with 11 pupils in five different grades and one teacher. The school was 2 miles from home. My father was my transportation with a 1934 Ford sedan until I got old enough to walk or ride a horse.

Since I was an only child, I enjoyed the recess time playing games with the other kids. To this day, I'm still in contact with a couple of those families.

At the end of the eighth grade, I was given a choice to board away for high school or ultimately have the farm. The latter was of the greatest appeal to me.

When I was 17, an opportunity came for me to attend Agriculture College at the State University for 3 winters. That was a special time for me.

Eventually I met and married a girl who would come share my love for tilling the land and raising livestock. We had two girls and a boy. Unfortunately, we lost our boy in a baler accident at the age of 26 working away from home.

I was drafted into the army for two years and spent one of those years on Okinawa during the Korean conflict.

Some of my greatest joys of farm life

Selmer seeding flax

Selmer N. Anderson

was working with horses and working on threshing rigs. As a family, we participated in many parades with our horses.

Today my wife and I of 61 years live in a small town not far from our farm and still attend the same country church.

My hobbies of collecting farm toys and relics from years gone by were a great pleasure as was belonging to a threshing association for 40 some years.

The Life of a Groundhog Day Baby
By Dorothy J. Patton of Mitchell, South Dakota
Born 1931

I was born in 1931 on Groundhog Day, which is in the month of February and is usually very cold. My dad would never let me forget the day I was born. It was a warm day. Dr. Foster came out from the town of Wessington Springs to deliver the new baby. He was walking out in short sleeves. My dad and grandfather were building a new chicken house.

I was the oldest in the family, so at ten years old I drove the tractor. I had a brother who was four years younger. I drove a John Deere Model B. I drove the tractor to pull the binder as Dad sat on it watching it cut and tie bundles. Later the bundles were put together in shocks. If we had to stop, I walked in the uncut grain, Dad said, "Don't trample all the grain down." I also drove a tractor as it pulled a horse-drawn cultivator as Dad sat on the seat guiding it. I had to stop to move the rocks or pull a cocklebur out. We had a hired hand who was doing it for Dad. He got tired of moving the rocks, so he told me to do it. I drove right over the rock and nearly threw him off of the cultivator.

I learned to do the milking. Mom and I usually did milking as Dad was doing other farm work. We raised chickens, turkeys, and a few geese. Mom had a garden but everything was so dry. I only remember green beans. We had a few storms that we lost a barn in. Our two horses were under the rubble. Dad thought he would have to shoot them, but they survived. I went on to high school and graduated in 1948. I then went to the junior college in the summer and taught school at 17 years old because there was a shortage of teachers. A college teacher came out and observed my teaching. It was counted as a credit. With just my summer school, in two years I got a credit the same as a one-year college.

Teaching school at 17, I had 11 students the first year, with three seventh grade boys. The boys thought they would scare me. One asked to go to the outhouse. Another was in the library, in a long, narrow closet. I went in for a book and a garter snake was looking at me. I took him by the tail and carried him through the room and threw him outside. One of the boys, Doug, said, "Teacher, you should have been a clown!" If he was acting out of order, I caught his eye and made some face so the other students didn't realize I was correcting him.

Those boys could come up with some pranks. I usually got on top of them. One day during a blizzard, only the boys went out for recess. There were big snowdrifts. I saw the phone company out on the road. I wondered what they were doing. The boys had hooked wire to the phone lines and put it out of order. Well, Doug said, "We had to do something to keep the old bags off the phone!" It was his mother that used it the most! His mother said I was the first teacher he ever wanted to give a Christmas present to. I may still have it—a satin box for silk stockings. I taught three or four years. When one little first grader's straps came undone on his bib overalls, he said, "Teacher, hook my gate!"

While Paul was in service and when school was out, I went to Germany for six weeks and lived with an old couple in their three-room apartment. We had their living room and cooked on her stove. Across the road were the train tracks. It was in Mannheim, Germany. We rode the streetcar to downtown where big stores were. It was a very memorable trip. While we were over there, I saw Holland, Switzerland, and France. I came back on the Queen Elizabeth and back to South Dakota by train.

We then started a family of five children in five years. Now we have lots of grandchildren and great-grandchildren. That's a whole new story and adventure, but God has given us a very blessed life!

Silly Stories of my Past
By Merle (Nick) Kneebone of Colorado
Springs, Colorado
Born 1922

On a warm summer evening in our little South Dakota town, some of us boys decided to go to the movies. We had ten cents among us, which was the price of a ticket. We went to the popcorn stand run by Les Rieshie (Later my first sergeant in the army). He would give us a sack of "old maids" (unpopped corn). We walked a block east to the lone theater in town—the Chrystal Theater. We walked around to the dark east door of the theater and waited for our one paid-for friend to unlatch the door. It was dark, so we would get in for free—about five of us for ten cents. We did this a few times and never got caught.

During my eighth grade year, I was 13 years old. Our music teacher, Miss Maniss, was auditioning all the kids to select entries for the town music contest. When my turn came, I declined, until Miss Maniss whacked me across the knuckles. I recall all the students staring at me, very unhappy to be there. The piano played and I sang "My Country 'tis of Thee." I was watching the girls in the front row. I remember Mary Francis Hove staring with her mouth wide open. I was selected to compete in the contest. I sang, "Home on the Range" and won first place.

My father, Reuben Kneebone, was a truck driver. He worked very hard for $125 per month, raising five kids. One night he brought home a large Philco radio—our first. We sat around that radio in our front room, amazed at this wonderful device. I remember a scary program, Inner Sanctum.

A small group of white boys, maybe four or five, including me, built a small shack on Kenny's Island" in the middle of the Sioux River. A small group of Sioux Indian boys "attacked" our shack. They threw a burning cigarette onto the roof, which we managed to put out. They managed to make off with some of our stuff, which we later recovered. I became friends with some of the Native Americans later—Red Wing, Wakeman, and Cloud. We have great memories together.

During the 1920s, we would gather at my grandfather's homestead. We called it "Over Home." The boys would play in the barn. We would try to ride calves, chase the girls—in general just try to get in trouble. All of the women (my mother had seven sisters and three brothers) would gather in the kitchen, talking and cooking. The men would gather in Grandfather's room playing cards, on special days, Grandfather would appear on the front porch with a cigar box filled with pennies. He would throw these all out on the front yard. Kids would race to find them. Toward the evening, lanterns would be lit and we followed the grownups to the barn to milk the cows. I joined in milking. I squirted milk to cats who lived in the barn. My mother, Hazel Belle Anderson, told me stories of hardship and adventure. I recall her story about a group of mounted Sioux Indians riding into the yard. They were not warlike—they just wanted to trade for eggs.

On Halloween, we would gather to get into mischief. A primary target was outhouses in everyone's backyard. After dark on a particular Halloween, we were busy trying to tip one of these structures over. The backdoor of the house flew open and the man yelled and fired the shotgun into the air, destroying the electric wires going into his house. Over went the outhouse, and one of our group almost fell in.

We lived a block or so from the dam on the Big Sioux River. We would skinny dip there. We'd also play in the old mill house and fish below the dam. On one occasion, while we were skinny-dipping, we were taunting some Indian girls camping on the other side of the dam. They became increasingly mad and one of them challenged us. My brother Virgil took the challenge. He stepped out on the dam—naked—and she knocked him off the top of the dam: Man's first loss to woman!

Memories of Days Gone By
By Vivian Lundgren of Ankeny, Iowa
Born 1934

I so remember growing up poor and living life with an outdoor toilet—which I totally despised—in a world where all of my friends had indoor bathrooms. I always prayed when my friends visited me they wouldn't have to use our "facility." It was FREEZING in the winter, and hot and SMELLY in the summer, and of course, flies made it additionally pleasant at that time. (I was living in Salem, South Dakota at this time, a small town with nearly a thousand population.)

I lived with my single mom and a brother who was three years older than I was. We coped with many things that were inconvenient, and didn't complain, as we knew it wouldn't make our life any happier. My mother had a quirky sense of humor, and as a result, my brother and I did too. We laughed a lot, and loved a lot. I always said we were poor, but we were never poor in spirit.

One summer evening, my mother had been visiting a friend, and walked home after dark. (We didn't have a car, so walking was our mode of transportation.) Before she came into the house, she "squatted" out by our garden to relieve herself—a thing she often did, when no one could see her. One of my friends, Ila, lived just down the alley from us, and she was coming to see me that night. She saw a person by the garden in a very ungraceful position, so she rushed up, and thinking it was me in the dark, she pushed my mother to the ground, saying, "Ha ha Vivian—I caught you that time!" Poor mom tried to scurry to her feet, a task not easy with her drawers down around her knees. Ila was mortified, as was my mother. Needless to say, Ila never did that again. Fortunately, outside of being quite embarrassed, my mom thought it was hilarious, as did we. Ila and I, friends these 75 years, continue to laugh about it to this day.

A Box of Eight Crayons

I went to a small WPA sponsored kindergarten class two days a week when I was four years old. We lived in Montrose, South Dakota at this time. Montrose was a village of about 500 people, striving to survive what is now known as the Great Depression. I was excited to go to "school," which offered arts and educational opportunities to the poor, which all of us were. There were no kindergartens in school, and this was actually more like a pre-school. My teacher was Mrs. Duffy, and I loved her.

Men in the community had built crude chairs for the students, each of them painted a different bright color, and we thought they were wonderful. It didn't take much to please us as we had so little. It was so much fun to get together with friends! One of these friends had a birthday party, and I was excited to be invited.

Mother and I went together. My gift to her was a box of eight crayons. I had never had a new box of my own, so I was quite envious. From that day on, whenever I saw her at kindergarten or Sunday school, I would ask her how "my" crayons were doing. She would report if any of them had broken—and I would
be SO MAD at her for not being more careful. I never reconciled to the fact they were hers, and not mine!

Dreams of Being Trapeze Artists and Calf Ropers
By Don Markeseth of Havana, North Dakota
Born 1924

I am a North Dakota farmer. I farmed from ten years old to today. I am now 89 years old. I was born, raised, and spent my entire life near Havana, North Dakota. Dr. Seniscall was contacted to help deliver me. He came and stayed 12 hours because my mother wasn't ready to bring me into the world. They did all the usual things like boil water to sterilize the scissors to cut the umbilical cord and other tools had to be prepared also.

Did you know that your belly button was part of the cord fastened to your mother? That cord brought you food from your mother's body, which kept you alive until you were old enough to make it alone outside your mom's body. I watch the mother bird feeding her little chicks with food from her body. The chicks open their mouths real wide, and she crams that food of mashed earthworms down their little throats and flies back to the ground to chew up more worms to feed the little gluttons so they won't perish.

By watching birds, I learned to appreciate my mother who was always there. She had no babysitter to help, no daycare to take me to, and no one to make baby food. I bet she got sick of me and putting up with me until I was six years old and could waddle off to school with my syrup pail for a dinner bucket. I walked to school across the field and met some other kids. We walked, rain or shine. We had no school buses. No one told us it was too cold to go to school. Sometimes it was 20 degrees below and we still walked the mile and a half. We had no telephone, so no one checked if we got there.

My dad was busy working the farm and had at least ten cows to milk twice a day, so he couldn't help my mother. In fact, she had to wash all the clothes by hand and pick corncobs to keep the stove from going out. They were easy to start. Sometimes we used coal, but coal was expensive, so we used recycled cobs from the corn. I guess you would call that "going green." We never saw a paper towel until we were 30 and we've never used Styrofoam cups on the farm to this day. We always had a windmill and no electricity until I was 25.

We got our first car when I was six. My favorite friend was my German shepherd dog named Pal. I put up with my sister Ruby and she expected to be taught all my favorite games. She was good at climbing trees and milking cows, but absolutely terrible at catching a ball. I taught her to ski by taking her out in the dark and going over the ski jump. She didn't fall when she couldn't see the jump. After several nights of this, we tried it in the daylight. She had finally learned. I was kind of proud when she could ski better than my boy friends. They didn't happen to have hills in their pastures, so there was no place for them to practice.

My sister was a real mess after we went to Ringling Brothers and Barnum and Bailey Circus. She convinced my dad that she must have a trapeze on the clothesline post. Dad spoiled her and life wasn't the same. She dyed her underwear bright red and practiced hanging by her legs and swinging on that trapeze that whole summer of 1941. Our little brother Roger had died of scarlet fever the winter of 1940, and my dad spoiled my sister from then on. She wouldn't play softball anymore and I didn't know how to get her to give up her dream of being a famous trapeze artist. How could I tell her she had legs too big to look interesting on the trapeze?

I'm tired of writing, so you will have to find out what happened on North Dakota ranches and especially 4-H rodeos with barrel racing and calf roping. I thought I'd do well with these sports, but really, I wasn't any better at them than my sister was with being a trapeze artist. Now my great nephew plans to be a tattoo artist. I wonder what will happen to his dream!

Little Brother, David, and his Water Tower Adventure
By Georgene Erickson of Scottsdale, Arizona
Born 1936

I grew up, in South Dakota, mostly in Milbank, having moved there, when I was in the third grade, with my parents Abraham and Bernardine Mosey, my older sister Charlene and my younger brother, David. Prior to that, we had lived in Veblen, where I started school and attended the first two grades. Dad had a barbershop and Mom operated the Home Cafe. For a while, we had living quarters, in the back of the cafe. Later, we moved to a house, right alongside Doc and Gay Brinkman's home, the top level of which was also the local hospital.

It's the time that we lived in the rear of the restaurant, that I want to recount here, today. We kids were about three years apart, with me being the middle child and David the "baby." I think he was about three years old, at the time of this incident. Our cafe and Dad's barbershop were along Main Street, next to or across the street from all the other businesses, in town. In back of the cafe, there was a water tower (which seemed enormous, to us kids, never having seen anything taller than a silo, before). One day, Mom just happened to be looking out back and spied David climbing the water tower, he was almost to the railing or ledge that circled around the mid-section. In retrospect, I think Mother almost had a heart attack. She yelled just as loud as she could, "David Lee Mosey, you come down from there right now! On hearing Mother's voice David looked down and by now, we had quite

Georgene, David, and Charlene in 1942

446

a crowd of onlookers, out back, shading their eyes and peering up at the speck, that was my brother. He let go with one hand, so he could grandly wave, to all assembled. That about did it, for Mother. She yelled at my Dad, who incidentally had a fear of heights, and told him in no uncertain terms, to go up there and get David.

Up until that point, I think I had thought it was kind of funny. Once my Dad started up that long ladder rung by rung, I didn't think it was any laughing matter at all. Telling David to, "Just hang on," Dad made it all the way up and holding David made it all the way down. I thought my Dad was the bravest man, in the world and my brother was the biggest brat. I couldn't wait to see Mom give him a spanking or at least a good bawling out. She didn't though; I think she gave him ice cream. Dad became a kind of local folk hero, for a while, until the next big exciting thing happened in Veblen. For the life of me, I can't remember what that was. My brother climbing the water tower, though. Well, I'll never forget that, as long as I live.

The Original
By Orpha D. Bensen of Eureka, South Dakota
Born 1931

My memories and what I have learned being the youngest of nine children born to Henry A and Katie (Losing) Brenneise, I, Orpha D. (Brenneise Zumbaum) Bensen had many questions to ask my mother and siblings. I was told that Emil, the fourth child born who drowned in a stock-watering tank, was the only one who did not have a biblical name. When I was two years and two months old, my dad died. My mother told me she thought she was pregnant again. They were both relieved when she was able to tell him (while lying on his hospital bed) that she was not pregnant. He died February 10, 1934.

Those were some of the dry years in the Spring Creek Township of McPherson County in South Dakota. No grass grew. The government bought cows for a small amount, and just south of Greenway, a big trench was dug by the WPA and the cows were chased in

The Brenneise family in 1953

there, shot, and covered up. Grandpa Johannes died in 1935, the same year as Uncle John's tornado. I am told that Uncle Jacob and John were made guardian of Katie and our family of eight—and we all grew up following the traditions of men.

Many years later, my mother's prayers had followed me and I began to read and study the bible more and found out how it was in the beginning, "The Original." I prayed for wisdom and understanding, and this is what I learned: that God created this world in six days and rested on the seventh. He created Adam and Eve on the sixth day as his companions and placed them in the Garden of Eden to dress and keep it, which was man's work. In this garden was everything Adam and Eve needed—Genesis 1:29: God said, "Behold, I have given you every herb bearing seed which is upon the face of all the earth and every tree, in which is the fruit of a tree yielding seed; to you it shall be for meat." Meat here means

The Brenneise family in 1968

our food. Then I read in Psalms 104:14: He causeth the grass to grow for the cattle. The herb for the service of man; that he may bring forth food out of the earth. I also learned that the bible is an instruction book—a roadmap to eternity. I read II Chronicles 20:20: Believe in the Lord your God, so shall ye be established. Believe his prophets so shall ye prosper (a prophet is a person supernaturally called and qualified as a spokesman for God) and through the prophets were given the laws of health or nature's doctors.

There are eight natural laws of health, and if obeyed, the result is true health. These eight laws are expressed in the phrase, "God's Plan."

God's sunshine: Malachi 4:2
Open air: Genesis 2:7
Daily Exercise: Genesis 2:15
Simple trust: Proverbs 3:5-6
Proper rest: Ecclesiastes 5:12
Lots of water: Ezekiel 4:11
Always temperate: I Corinthians 9:25
Nutrition: Genesis 1:29

In Exodus 20:1-17, you can read God's ten laws of life. James 2-10 says, "For whosoever shall keep the whole law and yet offend in one point, he is guilty of all. And in II Timothy 2-15, it says, "Study to show thyself approved unto God a workman that needeth not to be ashamed, rightly dividing the word of truth. Our modern day prophet Ellen G. White says that, step by step, God is trying to get us back to the original!

5-Cent Gopher Tails and Firehouse Mischief
By Aloyce "Al" Menzia of Mukwonago, Wisconsin
Born 1942

My name is Aloyce Menzia, Born April 9, 1942. The name Aloyce is very confusing to almost everyone, it is pronounced Al-oyce, and most people think that I am a female—wrong, I've been a male for over 72 years. I go by the name "Al" for the past 54 years. Born number eight of nine children in the small town of Roscoe, South Dakota.

Growing up I remember the water pump outside, pumped by hand and make sure that you have gloves on in the winter and don't lick the pump—tongue sticks to it, the outhouse with two holes (seats). At night in the winter, our parents use to setup a 5-gallon pail on the porch for us to use if we needed to go potty.

When we took a bath, we would heat water on the wood stove and take a bath in a galvanized tub.

Every fall we would butcher at least one large pig and we would eat everything except the squeal. We would clean all the intestines for sausage casings, the stomach for headcheese and then our dad would smoke the hams, sausage, and bacon. Whatever wasn't smoked was canned and put into our cellar to keep cool.

We didn't have a refrigerator until the late '40s but our parents did whatever they had to do to feed their nine kids. All of my brothers and two sisters would work for farmers for food or money for the family.

Every spring we would order chicks via the post office, feed them, raise them for their eggs, and then butcher as needed.

When I was about 10 yrs. old, I would go gopher hunting with a single shot 22 rifle. When I would run out of shells I would take a piece of binder twine out of my pocket, make a loop on one end and when I saw a gopher go into their hole, I would put the loop end around the hole, sit back about 10-12 ft. Then I would make a squeaking noise with my lips and when the gopher got curious, it would stick its head out of its hole and I would pull real hard and snag it! Use to get 5-cents per tail but I use to cut them in half when they were really long for 10-cents.

When I was a little older, about 13 yrs. I would go pheasant hunting and continued hunting until I was 18. When I talk to pheasant hunters in Wisconsin, I always tell them that I shot more pheasants than they ever saw!

Another activity while growing up was to tip over outhouses during Halloween—interesting—one time we were in the process of tipping over an outhouse and there was a person using it and he yelled "Hey, what the h— are you doing?" We got the heck out of there. What we needed to do was to watch out for those people that would be one-step ahead of us. What they would do is to move the outhouse over and cover the hole with some light material and when guys like us would attempt to tip the outhouse—OH, S—t!

We also would play around with our

local law enforcement officer (Ed). We had a firehouse, jail building in the center of town that had a bell tower on it. We would take a bail of binder twine and tie the twine to the bell clap, move away for the length of the bail of twine and ring the bell until Ed would go the firehouse to see what was making the bell ring. As soon as he showed up, we would drop the string and run away. Ed followed the twine but no one was there. HA! HA! For fun, we use to play ditch 'em which is like hide and seek.

We also would play "Ante I Over," Marbles, and Kick the Can. Our Mother used to bake bread at least twice a week for us and she would also give bread to people that were in need. When I was still under 6 years old I used to help my mother bake, I used to take a piece of dough and try to stick it on the kitchen ceiling, didn't use it in the bread! We used to buy the flour in 50# bags and used the bag to make clothing for us kids. Ironically, my wife's mother used to use the flour bags for clothes also.

We as a family did not drink very much milk; I used to eat cereal, Corn Flakes, Puffed Wheat, and Puffed Rice in a cup of coffee with cream and sugar. We used to buy cream from farmers and make our own butter out of it; we had a butter churn and would take turns turning it until the butter was made. Now our children and grandchildren get tired of my wife and I saying, "Well, when I was your age, I etc."

Growing up in those times taught me and my brothers and sisters that we can do whatever it takes to make a living and survive.

While in grade school if we did something wrong the teacher would reprimand us with a slap or spanking. You didn't dare go home and tell your parents because they would say what did you do wrong and then spank you again. In high school I was in track and ran the high and low hurdles on a cinder track, played 6 man football, played basketball, sang solos, and sang with the school glee club.

I moved to Milwaukee, WI after graduation in 1960, married in 1963 and have three children and six grandchildren. I am now enjoying my retirement after working for over 40 years.

The Old Brown House in the Thirties
By Dorothy Lichty of Miller, South Dakota
Born 1922

In 1925, the Oliver Johnson family moved from Lyons, Nebraska to Miller, South Dakota. Times were booming and it was easy to borrow money and become a big farmer. In our case, my father loved to speculate—a term used by those too optimistic for the time and desiring to get rich quick by investing their money in any business they thought would be a quick turnover—from rags to riches. Buying land was an option. Money was easily borrowed from the bank. The interest was high, maybe 15 or 20 percent.

All that speculating, with availability of getting hands on the money, was what my father loved, so he went overboard by borrowing and speculating. The result was losing all and the farm as collateral. One option was to move to South Dakota with his family of six children and wife. We came by rail. A few pieces of furniture were also shipped by rail. They consisted of a four-poster bed with weak springs and a worn-out mattress, which was Mom and Dad's bed. There were two sanitary cots—one for the boys and one for the girls, and the baby's crib was no more than a peach crate and blankets.

Finding enough bedding during the cold, blizzardy nights was a challenge. As the family grew, more beds were needed and more bedding was needed. The only part of a pair of old work overalls that was usable was the back of the leg. That was cut into squares and sewn together for a quilt top. The old worn out blankets were used for filling for the quilt. If we didn't have enough quilts, we piled our winter coats on top of the quilt. We were happy to sleep three in a bed just for warmth. A fire was built in the heater in the morning but the house of course wasn't warm except right by the heater. Our bowl of oatmeal was eaten as we huddled close to the heater with our coats on. Our dinner pail was a gallon pail with a sandwich made of homemade bread and many times only butter, sugar, and cocoa was the filling. We bundled up in snow pants, coat, stockings, cap, muffler, mittens, and buckle overshoes, Mother made the mittens from part of any old garment of warmth. They had many layers and were lined with cotton blanket scraps.

We walked to school although the school bus drove right past our house. We and our neighbors weren't allowed to have free transportation because we were considered to be in the city limits. All those who rode the bus and who walked to school carried their lunches and ate at the school in a specified room. We were well supervised with no goofing off! The threat that we would be sent to the superintendent's office if we misbehaved was scary enough to keep us on good behavior. We sure didn't want two spankings! Any school authority—teacher, coach, or superintendent had full authority on school premises. One could be expelled and sent home for a few days for disobedience at school. Both parents were in sync with the school authority, so we couldn't lie our way out of the situation. The superintendent was the strong arm of discipline.

Recess was at 10:15 to 10:30 in the morning and at 2:15 to 2:30 in the afternoon. The teacher went out with her group and supervised the games, which included Dare Base, Pum Pum Pull Away, softball, or you could just watch or stand around. We had a game called Squash. A sturdy fellow or girl would line up all facing the same direction, and as the leader would say "squash" the line would all lean hard backward. The one against the building would feel the pressure of the entire line as with the others in the line. Their feet never moved; all just leaned backward and said squash. Anti-I-Over was another fun game. If there was a building small enough to throw a ball over, we'd play it. We played that at home over our house, which was just a plain house with two long sides and two ends with a roof. If you caught the ball on the other side, the one with the ball would quickly run to the other side and tag as many players as he could before they escaped to the other side. The object was to get all players on one side to be the winner team captain. To begin, they had two captains who chose up sides.

We had to milk two cows. One was a Holstein and the other was a Guernsey. The Holstein was black and white with a good set of horns. She gave a good pail of milk—two or three gallons twice a day. The Guernsey was a gentle and slow moving cow. In the summer since our pasture was only ten acres with a creek running through it, we utilized the railroad right-of-way as a summer pasture, but they had to be herded. That is, someone had to be with them to see that they stayed off the tracks and the highway, which of course was alongside the railroad. My brother and I usually traded off doing the herding. I carried a big stick for protection and authority. When Leo did the herding, he simply climbed on the back of the cow and rode along in the warm sunshine. One sunny afternoon he dozed off and fell off the gentle cow, Pied. She just stopped and waited for him to get off the ground. Clarabel took advantage of the situation and tried to run off. A passerby on the road came to the rescue. He turned Clarabel around and sent her back to the grazing area again. Of course, a passenger train was coming, blowing the whistle furiously. This excited Clarabel more. Pied tossed her head and trotted toward home. Leo was duly scolded. He had learned his lesson, I think. And the cows did, too!

Growing Up on the Prairie
By Geraldine Starkey of Brainerd, Minnesota
Born 1926

I grew up on a farm on the prairie with two sisters and three brothers. We invented most of our toys. We lived one half mile from a one-room schoolhouse called the Red Star School. In the summer, we went down there to explore and play. We crawled in a window and snooped around rather breathlessly, as it was a scary adventure for sure. Then we sometimes walked through our pasture. I still wonder what we discovered. It was a big pasture with roads on two sides and all fenced in. My dad had sheep in that pasture. In one corner, we came to a big sinkhole. You could stand in it on a huge rock in the middle and not be seen on the road about 25 feet away. There were smaller rocks all around it like a table set for company. I don't know if my folks even knew it was there, but it was about a half mile from our farm buildings. I have lived in Minnesota since I'm married, but would check on the rock when I went home for a visit on our old farm. Erosion I think had filled the hole and the rocks had sunk somewhat, but it is still there, as no one can lift it for sure. It was about 30 feet in circumference.

Our farmhouse was old and cold in the

winter. My sister and I slept upstairs. In the living room below, our room was a woodstove. It was fancy in its day. There were lots of chrome decorations and fancy little windows. One or two were broke by one of us kids. I think that glass was called Isinglass. I backed up to get warm one day and caught my dress on fire. My mother grabbed a baby blanket and put the fire out. Well! The stovepipe went through a hole in the ceiling and through our room up to the chimney. One day I went to go upstairs and thick smoke rolled out. We had left our door open and it touched the hot stovepipe and was smoldering. I screamed for Mom. She grabbed the slop pail and dashed up the stairs. She used the pail on the smoking door. It was bitter cold winter and Mom saved our lives for sure with potato peelings and all.

We had two outdoor biffies at school—a boys and a girls. My sister found a ruby ring on the path—that was the engagement ring back then. Our teacher was engaged, so we traded it back and forth over the years. We finally lost it. Back then, they put feed for sale in printed sacks with pretty flower prints and such. My mom made all kinds of things out of them, including kitchen curtains. One day she needed a dress to wear to see the doctor. She took down the curtains and made herself a dress from them.

We made our own entertainment and my two little brothers were tricky, too. We had a hired man and he slept on the bottom floor of our grain elevator. One day it was a hot summer day and he laid down and took a nap. The boys quietly went up the ladder to the upstairs grain bins. There were chutes to empty grain into trucks to take to town. Those rascals scraped dust, shucks, and bird droppings into a big pile over the chute where the hired man slept. Then they pulled the cover off and it all fell down on him. He went roaring up the steps, but he was very heavyset and couldn't get through the hole. The kids hid up there till he left. They then came down, smothering their giggles.

I was a child during the depression and the dust storms, which piled up on fences where thistles blew in. It was easy to get over a fence. I loved it when it finally rained so I could splash around through the puddles. I loved the prairie with its meadows and larks singing. At night, I'd run like the wind as I'd hear coyotes howl in the distance to our biffy.

Geraldine Starkey

I still love rainbows and dandelions. Oh the feeling to go to town on Saturday night! There was an owl sitting on a fence post watching us when we went down the lane to chase the cows home. Dad said if we'd keep walking around the post, we could twist his head off. We almost believed him!

The North Dakota Hills

By Ruby (Markeseth) Chelgren of Peoria, Illinois
Born 1929

I grew up on a homestead farm in Tewaukon Township just a mile and a half into North Dakota, about 13 miles from Veblen, South Dakota where I graduated from high school in 1947. My family milked about a dozen cows, raised 30 pigs to market in the fall, fed and watered a couple hundred baby chickens each summer, raised the roosters until they were big enough to eat, and butchered 65 for my aunt and uncle and their family. My uncle was the family doctor at Wahpeton, North Dakota and the doctor for the Native American school at Wahpeton.

My story begins in the depression years, often called the "dirty thirties." We processed our roosters very early in the morning. They had to be butchered, quickly cooled, and packed so they could be brought to Wahpeton

451

to be quick-frozen before noon. What a relief to know they were safely frozen in the town's locker plant. No one had deep freezers at home. You rented your space and stopped there for your meat a couple of times or more each week. We didn't get money for those roosters. Nearly everything was bartered in those days and the roosters covered our family doctor bills.

My dad had badly damaged lungs from working in the constant dust storms in the mid-thirties and also from living in a bunkhouse in his early teens. The building was heated with lignite coal, which was dirty and loaded with smoke. I suppose the boys also smoked and chewed tobacco, which were equally bad for the lungs.

My dad had to find a job at an early age because his family was large. Their house at home was small and it was time to find employment elsewhere. These newcomer kids from Norway and Sweden didn't get much education and really didn't know they could expect to be trained for some kind of trade. They got what the majority received—a few clothes and a kick in the pants. They were expected to bring home some money for the rest of the family. No one knew about an allowance in the twenties or thirties and the GI's were expected to send some money home when they were in World War II and the Korean Conflict. That wasn't even called a war; and my confirmation class friend became a paraplegic on his second day at the front lines of Korea. He never walked again.

My dad was the last sibling to work at Munson's ranch. The last three siblings stayed at home and ran the farm. No one thought much about it; that's just the way it was!

I began my life away from home at the beginning of my sophomore year at 15 years old. I lived with a nice, widowed grandma who wanted companionship. A friend soon came, too, and we shared a room and did light housekeeping. We went home on weekends, made a few things to eat for the next week, and our moms baked some extra cookies, cupcakes, and other groceries for us to take with us. It was hard to keep something to last for the end of the week. Our Thursday suppers were rather bleak and we loved going home on Friday. My mom usually made Swiss steak—my favorite.

We had lots of wind in the North Dakota hills, so I went to Veblen even though I was a North Dakota resident. The two states absorbed U.S. border rats and never charged extra tuition. I'm sure that doesn't happen today. Our rural schools used the same rules with Native Americans. They attended our country schools in September and October and again in early spring. They went to reservation schools at Wahpeton and Flandreau the rest of the year. I had no classmate in elementary school until the sixth grade when Hannah joined me. I felt sorry for her. She was 15 and I was ten. What a dumb thing to do! Who could expect a 15 year old to want to have class with a ten year old? It didn't last long. Hannah left for Flandreau earlier that year.

The farm required lots of long hours. We didn't have REA until I was 18 so we used gas lanterns or kerosene lamps or went to bed early, which all kids hate. We read with a flashlight under the covers; but that wasn't real successful.

4-H Club and Farmer's Union were high points for my brother Don and me. We both liked to sing and we sang for many funerals. It's hard to find singers for funerals because no one is free to go on short notice. My mom accompanied us. Next, we were invited to enter singing contests in Rutland. Rutland always had amateur contests and I was fortunate enough to win first place three years in a row. That gives a skinny kid a big ego. Now, I wish I was still skinny and still had a good voice. Hay fever and asthma have ruined that talent. I'm sure glad to be able to play the piano. I'm happy to entertain in nursing homes in the Dakotas and Illinois where I live.

We were ice cream fiends at our house. There was no problem in the winter because we made our own ice cream with a one and a half gallon hand-crank freezer. My mom cooked a great custard and she was known as the best ice cream cook in the neighborhood. She used very rich cream and it never lasted after the day it was made. Our problem was to get enough ice cream in the summer. We had no refrigerator, so my dad or brother would go to Rutland. It was 13 miles and they had to speed home before the quart would melt. We tried buying half gallons, but we couldn't eat fast enough to keep it from melting.

Our neighbors were good about visiting new neighbors. One spring evening, we visited some new folks. We kids went to play hide-and-seek in the pasture; it had lots of rocks quite close together. One stone was bigger than the rest and it had carvings. If you crossed your hands, you could put them on the carvings. I told my parents about the rock, but they didn't seem interested and I forgot about it. Our pasture at home had tent rings from early Indians of North Dakota.

Several years went by and I was back in Britton and had heard about its museum. I had some time, so I decided to see it. What a surprise! There in the display was a rock I had seen before! How did it get here? How did they get my/our North Dakota neighborhood rock? I don't know the whole story, but I could show you where it is laid in my neighbor's pasture!

Measles
By Ellen Jean Anderson of Mitchell, South Dakota
Born 1924

We lived in a small town in east central South Dakota. We had a new little brother born on Groundhog Day of 1930. This was a big deal in a farming state, especially after three girls. My mother was busy with wood-burning stoves and an outdoor well. She not only had to keep fires going, but she also had to keep clothes clean. She had to carry in the water and the baby boy needed formula in sterilized bottles and diapers washed and dried.

In those days, the end of winter was the season for "catching" diseases—two kinds of measles, mumps, chicken pox, and whooping cough. I was the oldest in the first year of school, so we had not been exposed before. I liked to go to school for recess with kids my age to play with. Get up, dress, eat oatmeal, and walk two blocks to school.

This particular morning was different. Mother told me later that I had said, "My cock-a-doodle head hurts." There was probably some discussion. Then I remember that I had vomited into the slop bucket. We had no bathroom or kitchen sinks. A parent said, "Aren't you glad you didn't go to school?" Not especially, as I did not see why my mother would say, "vomited". My father

Margie and Richard Hinde in 1930

called it "puke." Once we had talked about this at school, the teacher was with my mother on the subject.

After I had been put to bed, a car drove into the yard and a knock came at the back door. The storekeeper's wife had called the doctor in Mitchell—a small city 26 miles away on a gravel highway. Her little girl was in my grade and was also sick. The doctor had said we should have oranges and poached eggs. There was always an orange in our Christmas stocking and poached eggs were given to someone sick, so this seemed special to me. The lady had driven to every affected house in town to tell this to the mothers. Perhaps there was other advice I did not hear.

It seemed red measles meant a darkened room to protect the eyes of the afflicted. I did not like this after I felt better with less fever and cough, though the rash remained. My father carried mail into the country and he told me of a little girl out there whose room was kept completely dark. This was like the usual parent comment—not fun.

I was in a double bed in the big northwest bedroom. Now I felt better and was playing with a catalog paper doll. I liked her lavender dress. My two younger sisters in the other big bed were both crying loudly. Mama had built up the fire in the small woodstove and was piling blankets and quilts on the girls. When I asked why, she said the measles would break out sooner and they would feel better. Margie, the two year old, sat up and pushed the covers off with a sad, "Oh, dear me!" The baby in the basket in the kitchen did not catch the measles. He still had immunity from his mother.

My next memory is of my teacher coming to our house. I was clear of the rash and playing in the front room. Spring had come and it was time for the end of year school picnic. The teacher talked my mother into letting me go. It was to be on a sandy crick bank south of town. I was not to take off my shoes. Parents worried about complications of measles, more cough and temperature. Several days later, I was ready and waiting to go. Mama was dressing the little sisters, Mary and Margie, who were both crying as she tried to put on their long underwear. I had been allowed to go without for the picnic, so I said, "Oh, let them leave it off." Mama said, "Why? Your dad never leaves his off until he hears the firecrackers the morning of the Fourth of July." Usually a very hot day, so this seemed funny (strange) and I felt very grown up- as she did give up on the long underwear

There was not a happy ending to the picnic story. The teacher told me to go barefoot in the sand. A second grade girl waded in the crick

Ellen Jean and Mary Hinde in 1930

and said a crab bit her toe. When I got home, my folks realized my shoes had been off and I was in trouble, though I had a good reason. There was an ugly red sign on our front door that read: MEASLES. Even so, it was nice to be out in the yard without a coat and without the measles!

Multiple Generations in South Dakota
By Margaret Gjerde of Watertown, South Dakota
Born 1928

I am writing the story of my life in Northeastern South Dakota, where I have lived all of my life. I was born April 3, 1928, the second child of Edwin and Cletus (Schaefer) Robish in a farm home of rural Hazel, South Dakota, joining a sister, Ila Mae, less than a year old. In the fall, we moved one mile up the dirt road north to a small four-room house. Our family increased with two more sisters and two brothers.

Thanksgiving Day—November 28, 1935—they were expecting their sixth child. Their original doctor was gone, so my dad called another doctor form Bryant. He came to our house from a home where they had diphtheria and delivered our baby brother Maynard. My mother was 29 years old on December 9. She got this dreaded disease, diphtheria, and passed away on the 14th with the funeral on the 15th, leaving my dad with a family of six kids ranging from eight years to two weeks old. We were quarantined and no one could come in our house, so she was placed in front of the kitchen window and people walked up on the porch to view her. My dad, Ila Mae (eight), and I (seven), could go to the cemetery, but couldn't get out of the car. A memorial service was held at the church later in the spring. My sister Ramona (five) and my brother Wesley (four) also got the disease, but lived.

Grandma Bertha Robish came and lived with us at the age of 64 and was so proud of that baby. She eventually attended all of the church and sports events for all of us. She said, "If the car goes, I go." My dad, the kindest man there ever was, went to talk with his Aunt Rose Feind for some support and

Guy and Bertha Gjerde in 1901

she said, "Every morning you ask the Lord to take you through the day and thank him every night." I'm sure he did.

My cousins, Dorothy and Lucille Yahn, would come and help my grandma. They would ride their horse over. One day I was riding and went under the clothesline. It caught me below my chin and pulled me off. One day us girls were on the tree across the road and was walking on a big shiny tree that was laying down. Where the branch was broken off, I fell and cut my leg. We came home and as Grandma was cleaning up my leg, she had Ila Mae go to the barn and bring her the Raleigh's Salve they used for the cows' teats. I was reading on the can and I started to cry. Grandma said, "Now, what's the matter?" I said, "It says for man or beast, and I'm not either one!" Another time, Pa and some of the others were going fishing and I never cared to get on the water, so I stayed home and carried

water to the gopher holes in the pasture and snared them. I got 21 that day.

Our aunts and uncles, Albert and Mildred Krueger and George and Verna Redlinger, helped us so much. Verna would get our clothes ready and Mildred would curl our hair by heating the curling iron down in the kerosene lamp. I had the whooping cough, so I was staying with Albert and Mildred and I forgot my teddy bear out by the windmill. When I was getting ready for bed and crying, Uncle Albert went out to get it. Albert and Mildred always called us "The Poodies." We would call them on the telephone and sing, You Are My Sunshine.

In those days, Pa would take us visiting to our extended families. We would go over to Cousin Dorothy and Lucille's place and we would ride the manure bucket out of the barn. It was there that I learned to ride the bicycle, but yes; I fell over too and skinned my knees.

We always had programs on Christmas Eve at church. Pa was always the last one out to the car, but when we got home, Santa Claus had already been there. Guess we were good kids!

One time Pa was going to go visiting, when he felt something down the back seat of the car. Well, he must have guessed I was

Edwin and Cletus Robish holding Ila Mae and Margaret

455

Maurice, Margaret, and Bertha Gjerde

there, and before we got out the driveway, he stopped and I had to get out. I guess I was like Grandma—"When the car goes, I go." I am still ready to go places.

I remember watching when the WPA made our dirt road into a gravel road. When I was 13, Pa bought a farm place two miles down the road with a big house, which we were so happy for. The next spring we had a bad tornado and it took the top half off the barn when Pa and Ila Mae were milking. They just laid in the manger.

We all helped Pa on the farm, and one day he was cutting grain with the binder and we were shocking some on one side of the field and some on the other. I was getting on the binder to ride to the other side and my foot went around with the chain. I was afraid to take my shoe off.

I went to two different one-room schoolhouses through the eighth grade. During my freshman year in high school, I lived with George and Verna that ran a garage in Hazel. When it was my 16th birthday, I stopped after school and he wanted to give me a spanking. He had me lean over the water tank where they would fix tires. He took a rubber hose and gave me 16 swats. I tell you, it was hard sitting in school the next day, but on Saturday, he took me to Watertown and bought me a red spring coat with a black velvet collar.

The summer before my sophomore year, I started working for the Gjerde family and worked there until the fall after my high school graduation. Grandma Gjerde was a mother to me and a lot of fun. She saved goose feathers, so we were making pillows and she said, "Margaret, go get the berry spoon." Well, you know how that would work in feathers, and we would laugh. One day the cows got out, so I got a tool and she and I went to fix the fence. It turned out to be the hoof nippers, but we got

the cows in and the fence fixed. I remember it well the very first day I went to work there; I was so nervous. They milked cows, and the first job was washing the cream separator. Grandpa washed and I wiped. He had six sons and he always said, "No dishwashing would hurt any man." He also was a fun guy—Guy Gjerde. He died during my junior year; I was so sad.

After my senior graduation, I went to work at the J.C. Penney Co. in Watertown and again lived with George and Verna who had sold their garage and moved to Watertown. It was then that Maurice, the youngest of the Gjerde family, came to see me—lonesome I guess. We were married two years later and raised three children on the farm—Bryce, Renae, and Cleo. We have been blessed with ten grandchildren and 15 great-grandchildren. It was very sad when Bryce and Kay lost their daughter Nicole with meningitis at nine and a half months old. All ten of the grandchildren were baptized in Our Savior's Lutheran Church of rural Henry. All nine were confirmed there and a great-grandchild was baptized there, making the sixth generation in that church of Maurice's family. He was so proud of it. The small country church closed two and a half years ago, which was so sad.

Maurice and I had many fun times together and with the family. He passed away just four days before our 58th wedding anniversary. I cherish all of the fond memories very much. We had an M&M Travel Bus Tours that was a lot of fun and I am still doing it now 29 years later. I am so proud to say our whole family of 39 all live in South Dakota and all my sisters and brothers live in South Dakota along with all of my aunts and uncles. All of us were born in Northeastern South Dakota We love South Dakota and blessings for the 125th year: 2014.

Early Family Immigrants
By Mary Jane Patchin of Mankato, Minnesota
Born 1936

As single persons, Uncle Chris and Aunt Anne (aunt to our father) emigrated from Denmark to USA in the late 1890s and early 1900s. Chris had purchased 80 acres of railroad land, which had been deeded to the railroad for potential funds to develop a railroad system. He later purchased the adjacent 80 acres, which is now a public hunting area. Chris and Anne lived on this farm and farmed in a subsistence manner until moving to town in 1947. They had a dog and cats, some chickens, some cattle, some hogs, and horses. He had a horse-drawn hay loader. Behind the house was a very large garden and some apple trees. For most of their lives, they lived without electricity. The windmill provided water from the well to a large wooden tank in the barn upstairs. Gravity then supplied water to the animals. Anne had a wooden, hand-operated washing machine in the entry for her laundry. The original house was the entry and one room to serve as kitchen, living, and sleeping. For instance, Danish newspapers covered the kitchen table to protect the oilcloth on the table. This part of the house had a cool, deep basement for food storage. The addition without a basement comprised of first story living room and bedroom, and the second story had two more bedrooms. In the living room were a beautiful round, glass, china hutch with Sunday dishes, a dining table with wooden chairs, and a rocking chair. They lived well but frugally.

The township un-graveled road past the farm was grass covered. Two wheel tracks on the dirt seemed to be the "driving lane." The road was not graded or raised above field level. The road must not have been passable in winter snows or summer rains. Uncle Chris had a 1929 Dodge sedan. I often have thought of all the shoveling of snow to get that car to the road from the garage—what a job even with the use of horses.

Uncle Chris was very upset with me, a preschooler, one time when I used a paintbrush to "paint" mud all over his chicken waterers. But with their frugal life style, they had enough money to last their lifetimes without seeking "Old Age Pension."

They were proud of that fact.

Drammen Hall

When I was in the first grade, we moved from Chris and Anne's farm in Diamond Lake Township to a farm in Drammen Township. Drammen Hall was a Farmers' Club on the same piece of property that our school District 17 was located. The Hall was a social place. The neighbors met to share potluck meals and play cards. They had vaudeville shows and music here for entertainment. Whole families gathered; and when we children were tired, we would sleep across several chairs or on the stage while our parents socialized. These activities were begun before the days of electricity. The Hall was a place for meetings and the place for voting.

District 17 County School

I attended District 17 from grades 1 through 8. My sister, being younger, attended from grades 1 through 4. A special event each year was the Christmas program. Several students practiced and sang solos or duets. Most of us were assigned speaking parts in short plays. Our mother spent many evenings going through the readings of the plays to be sure we knew our lines. The mothers shared bed sheets so that a "stage" could be created at the front of the school. The entry area was the dressing room for the costumes and for the students. The parents sat in the normal student desks—full house capacity. "Santa" also made an appearance and each child received a small sack with an apple, some peanuts, and hard candy.

Some country school boards provided swimming lessons to be held in the local lakes during the summers. My sister and I both taught Red Cross swimming lessons. Conditions for teaching swimming were ideal in that the mothers car-pooled and sat on the shore watching the activities. All students were well behaved and interested in learning to swim for the fun and the safety. The county superintendent of country schools, Mr. Adrian Little, was adamant about safety and first aid in our state of many lakes—Minnesota. He was our swimming teacher when we were young.

Here's What's Cookin'
By Lisa Langenfeld Buche of Watertown,
South Dakota
Born 1947

This letter was sent to my oldest brother, Joe, along with a box of cookies. December 2010.

This weekend sister Paula spent the day with me in my kitchen mixing up and baking Christmas cookies. All or most of the recipes were family favorites I spent time baking with Grandma Nash so many years ago. It became

Grandma Nash's Cookbook dating back to the 1930s

our tradition. The cookies were her holiday gift to all of us.

I was her number one assistant at a young age. Her apartment was small but our routine was down pat and we managed well with the project. This "job" carried on through most of my early-married years of living in Gregory. We picked Grandma up in Mitchell and the baking continued in my home. For three days, we would use my antique electric oven and stove top in my cracker box kitchen brightly painted with gold and green cupboards and walls. Favorite colors of the '60 s!

We mixed, stirred, and cooled at least a dozen different cookie and candy recipes. Remember her homemade fudge? Grandma would tell me to watch the boiling bubbles of the ingredients while stirring them in the pot on the stove burner and then time them once it came to a full boil... overcooked it would be sugary and undercooked the fudge wouldn't set up. I know how to do both.

In between the process of baking and checking on RF, who was a baby at the time, we played cards and cribbage with scoring carried over throughout each of the three days. The coffee pot was always on and the mixture of scents still makes me smile.

Once our process was completed, we arranged our entire labor of love on individual trays, packaged them securely, boxed them and then wrapped them in brown paper and tied the box with string. Names and addresses neatly penned by Grandma. Kitchen clean, we loaded the packages in the car and headed to the Main Street post office to deliver them for mailing to her many grandchildren.

Grandma typed and gifted me with so many of the recipes. With arthritic fingers, she typed them individually with her old manual gray typewriter. The "hunt and peck system" she called it. The recipe card designs say, "Here's what's cookin'" and "Kissin' wears out...cookin' don't."

I still look through and use many of her recipes, adding my own along the way. So many of them old family recipes. Many she received also from her early years of living in Lake Andes. Thumb print cookies recipe from Marie Ransom, mocha cakes from Aunt Hazel and date cookies (yours and my favorite!) from Sarah Jones. Their names typed at the top of the card. I've spattered bits of egg or dough on the obviously most used cards. But I still keep them. I wouldn't even think about retyping them into my computer and punching up buttons to call them up. Nope, open my recipe box and touch the memories. A gift of love. My fingers more agile, the love still rolled into the dough but the taste not quite, as I remember Grandma's. Hers was a special touch.

I am continuing this baking tradition with my grandchildren. I'm guessing Grandma Nash would have said aloud, "The perfect bonding time. One that passes along love and memories to fill an attic."

Wishing you and your family the season's best. And, as Grandma always signed off on her letters, with lots of love, Lisa.

A Busy Life on the Farm
By Barbara Shawl Campbell of Letcher,
South Dakota
Born 1935

I was born in 1935 on a farm near Letcher, South Dakota. I remember that when I was 12 years old, I was plowing on a Fordson Tractor pulling a 2-bottom plow. Since I was too young to drive and pull the release rope, my younger brother Rodney rode with me and he pulled the rope. I remember that I could just push the clutch in long enough to get it into neutral but could not hold it long enough to put it into gear so my father had to stand on it to get me started and then jump off. I know that it seemed like a lot of work but it was much better to have 2 plows going in the field. So I plowed with this one and he had another plow going at the same time.

As we grew older, we graduated to a Massey Harris tractor. You had to adjust the magneto on it first and then crank it to get it started. I do not ever remember cranking it, I was not big or strong enough to do it, and my dad had to. We mowed hay with a 7-foot sickle mower and rake the hay into rows with a dump rake. Initially, one person was on the tractor to drive and one person on the dump rake to release when it was time. Eventually we got a dump rake that had a rope to release the rake so that only one person was necessary to do the work. Even better was when we got a front mounted 4-wheel rake to make things even easier. The hay had to be windrowed and then bunched up in small stacks so that it could be picked up more easily to make a haystack.

Stacking hay was quite a project. At first, we used a hay buck to bring the hay to a stacker, which then dumped hay on the haystack. There were also 2 people on top of the haystack with pitchforks to arrange the hay so that it was a nice straight tall stack topped off well so that rain would just run off and not pool and ruin it. Later we had a unique stacker called a Jay Hawk. It was an elevator platform that was raised by horsepower. The hay buck would bring the hay and put it on the Jay Hawk, which the horses lifted the hay to the top of the stack and then it was ejected onto the stack. It was really something to watch.

After the fields were plowed, the corn needed to be planted. At first, my father would use a horse drawn two-row corn planter. Later we were able to get a 4 row planter pulled by a tractor. First though, we had to lay planter wire down to space each individual corn stalk so that it could be cross cultivated properly. The worst weed we had to deal with were the native cockleburs. They had to be pulled out by hand and we did a lot of that work for my maternal grandfather. We would walk a mile to his farm and then walk the corn for a couple of hours pulling weeds and then walk back home again. We were paid 25 cents an hour.

I also cultivated corn with a Ford tractor and a 2-row cultivator that had an auto lift at the end of the row. After that we got a 4-row cultivator, which was pulled by our Massey Harris tractor. It had kick pedal auto lifter. I also drove a John Deere at my grandfathers

and you had to use a lever to lift the blades out of the ground at the end of the row. There was kind of a trick to it and I had to hang out over the back to get enough leverage to pull it out.

Another adventure on the farm was using a Buzz Saw to cut wood for the wood burning furnace. We collected dead wood on the river bottom. Dad had mounted a 36-inch blade in front of the tractor that was belt driven and attached to the pulley of the tractor. Dad fed the log on an extended beam to the saw blade. My sister Dvonne would catch the stub and throw it onto the trailer. The rest of my siblings would bring logs to the tractor and help to hold the end up so that it could be fed into the saw blade. When we had filled the trailer up, we would take it home and unload it into the basement through a basement window. That furnace was used to heat the entire house.

When oats and wheat were ready for harvesting, Dvonne and I really went to work. I drove the tractor and she operated the grain binder, which bound the grain into small bundles, which were unloaded 3-4 at a time into windrows. In the evening when it was cooler, the entire family went out into the field to put the bundles into a larger bunch called a shock. There were 8-10 bundles per shock. Wheat was much worse than oats because it had prickly heads and we had to make sure we wore a long sleeved shirt when we did it to keep from getting scratched up. Often after we did this we would all go to the river and jump in and cool off and to wash the dirt off.

When it was time to thresh the grain, this was a community project. My father would operate the threshing machine. Dvonne and I and some others would drive the tractor while the men loaded the bundle onto hayracks. After the racks were full, we took them to the threshing machine and we stayed and helped out dad to unload bundles into the machine. The other men would go back out into the fields to get more bundles to be threshed. When we got older, we would help haul grain to the grainery and unload it using an elevator. This consisted of a front jack to lift the front of the wagon to allow the grain to fall down to the door.to make unloading so much easier. Men and women brought the afternoon lunch and also brought coffee to all the workers. They fed the entire crew dinner. Everyone was busy; there was something to do for everyone. Our gang was Albert Zoss, Kenny

459

Reagen, Emery Patterson, Lyle Shawd, and James Keen.

I did not get into corn picking very much because I and the other children were in school during that time. I do remember though that when all of were younger, we all would help unload the corn from the wagon. We had to do it ear by ear by hand. Later Dad bought an elevator wagon, which made the job so much easier. We also had to scoop ear corn out by hand from the wagon to feed the brood sows (pigs) and then after they were finished eating all the corn off the cob, we went to collect cobs for my mother so that she could burn them in her cook stove. They made a really nice hot fire for cooking. We had to use almost everything we had on the farm, very little was ever wasted.

I remember one time when we lived by the river; we were awakened by this thunderous roar. There was so much water, the dam was not well built, and the force of it had burst the dam. Fortunately, we were high enough that it did not affect us but it made a tremendous noise. There are still remnants of that dam today.

When we lived by the river on the Rainbow Ranch, a train of Gypsies came through town, driving 3 teams of horses and wagons and a long string of saddle horses. They were looking for a place to camp and my dad offered them a place by the river with plenty of timber for fires. They were also trading horses with the locals. I remember that we had a 3/4 thoroughbred stallion that they took a shine to and since all of our mares were related to him, Dad decided we needed a different stallion and he traded for a nice dappled grey that was almost white. It was Dvonne's duty to break him to ride and my dad put a Frasier saddle on him and a halter with a long rope. He took him to a plowed field and Dvonne got on him, he did buck a little but the plowed field made it difficult for him to keep his footing so she was able to ride him. We decided to name him Buck. Our neighbor, Tom Campbell, who lived 1 1/2 miles west of us, traded on of his horses for a nice young gelding of ours. Well he did not like it at Mr. Campbell's farm and escaped and came looking for his old friends. We left the door on the top side of the barn open and even though where he went in it was ground level, he saw the area where the other horses were that was about a 12-foot drop,

and he jumped out that door to that pen. It was incredible that he landed without injury!

My mother was an exceptionally good piano player and our house was a very popular place to get together with friends and neighbors and sing some of the popular songs of the day. My mother loved sheet music and would buy about one piece each week so we always had a nice variety to choose from.

The Moon Landing and the Outhouse
By Corinne Jameson of Ipswich, South Dakota
Born 1950

I will always remember the first moon landing on July 20, 1969. I was 19 years old and my family lived on a "West River" ranch. We had an adorable little dog, "Fritzie," who weighed about 10 pounds and was truly part of our family. That day, we had a houseful of company. My mother and I had cooked a big meal, including home-fried chicken. We had the meal ready and had just set our huge platter of fried chicken on the table when my father called loudly, "Everyone, hurry to the living room. Apollo astronauts are just landing on the moon!" (Our one-and-only television set

Fritzie in 1970

460

was located there.) We all rushed to cluster around and watch with amazement and pride as Neil Armstrong and Buzz Aldrin walked! We remained there for some time, the meal all but forgotten.

Finally, we made our way back to the table. There, to our horror (especially my mother's) stood our beloved "Fritzie" in the MIDDLE of the platter of chicken! He had all four feet planted in the chicken pieces and he was taking bites in all directions! I don't think there was even one piece untouched.

So, "Fritzie" was lifted off the table and banished, and the platter of half-chewed chicken was removed.

I do not remember what was served in place of the chicken, but I do remember that our guests carefully inspected each dish that was passed to them. Who could blame them? (Maybe "Fritzie" walked on other things besides the chicken!) I also remember that not much was said about this until our guests had departed. Then, I remember that our family had a great laugh about it and brought our dear "Fritzie" back from exile.

To this day, when I think of the first moon landing, I automatically associate it with our "Fritzie" standing in the platter of fried chicken.

The Outhouse

When I was about eight years old, our family moved to a "West River" ranch that had been my grandfather's homestead. The unfinished house had no running water or sewer system. At age 8, this seemed like quite an adventure to me. There was a windmill hooked into a well, which supplied our water. We carried the water into the house, as needed, one pail at a time. Then we had a chamber pot, to use as a toilet during the night. In the daytime, we used an outdoor toilet, called an "outhouse." It was nothing more than a small wooden shack with a walk-in door and a wooden floor. Inside, it had a bench with a hole cut in it and that was where you sat. The shack was positioned over a deep hole in the ground. Every so often, my father put lime in the hole to destroy the sewage. A metal coffee can was nailed to the bench and toilet paper was stored inside the covered can. (That seemed very modern to us at the time!) Also, our outhouse had two holes cut in the bench, so it was called a "two-seater!"

I have one very vivid memory of our outhouse days. I was about ten years old. It was in late summer, and an extremely hot day. My mother and I went to the outhouse together. Living "West River" meant that rattlesnakes were native to the area. Mother and I settled in our "two-seater" which was very hot and quite smelly. I was the first to leave. I opened the door and there lay a rattlesnake, stretched out in front of the door. I jumped over it and hollered, "There's a rattlesnake by the door!" Then I ran as fast as I could back to the house. My poor mother, a city girl, was absolutely terrified of snakes. She shut the outhouse door, and stayed in there until my father came home, several hours later. He rescued her from the outhouse. Of course, the snake was long gone. I remember that my mother used the chamber pot, inside the house, most of the time after that traumatic day.

In 1965, a new house was built on the ranch and the running water and bathroom facilities were SO appreciated.

The Olson Girls
By Nancy Olson Burkey of Lakewood, California
Born 1951

I now live in the LA, area of California, but still call Watertown, South Dakota my home, even though I have moved from there nearly 38 years ago. My roots are strong there, as I spent the first 25 years in that great little city.

I grew up on South Broadway in Watertown; I was the 3rd daughter to Hannah and Mervin Olson with older sisters being Kathleen and Phyllis. The town knew us as 'the Olson girls' for the most part. My mother did private duty nursing in town and as a grade school age girl, I would tag along with my mother as she went to peoples home to give them insulin injections. She also worked some in my father's stores.

My father had an appliance store. The first store was uptown on the NW corner of Kemp Ave. and Maple right after WWII that he had the first coin operated laundry mat invented.

The part that I knew about was when he built his own store at 808 South Broadway to be nearer to home at 609 so that he could walk to work.

461

I would think that quite a few people would remember his store (it now sits as the VFW building) as he sold appliances, had a frozen food plan (if you bought an Amana freezer you could join in the frozen food plan), and sold bottle propane gas to farmers. His store was called OLSON'S APPLIANCE AND GAS

He converted his trucks to propane, a man ahead of his time, in the early 1960s. The farmers had those BIG 'ole propane tanks on their property that my dad's truck would come out to refill. In his store, he sold stoves, refrigerators, freezers, window air conditioners, and radiant heaters. I used to have to dust all those appliances! On meat cutting day, which was Tuesdays, we had a man named Lee Opitz come in to butcher meat, and dad would make them into the correct size of steaks or ground up the beef. My mother would wrap the meat and double wrap each piece (to keep out the freezer burn) and I would put a stamp of what was in each package and take them to the freezers that dad kept ready for this. He had a way to FLASH FREEZE them so that they would freeze the fastest. Every piece had to lay flat on a freezer shelf. Then later in the week, my dad and I (after school) would take the meats around to the customers that had ordered and deliver them in his truck that had a cooling/freezer area. I still have some note pads from this part of his business life! He even had a way to dress pheasants, and freeze them to be mailed out on dry ice to the pheasant hunters from out of state. Whew, I remember those pheasant feathers every fall. I believe my father retired in 1968.

My parents were residents there from 1934-1997, and passed 3 weeks apart from each other with the upper NE South Dakota flood of spring 1997 in-between their deaths. My time there was 1951-1976 and still LOVE to go back home.

I grew up going to hear the outside band concerts put on by the city band. I learned how to swim in the 'then' brand new outside swimming pool by highway 212. I used to have Whiz's pizza that was served in little squares.

The interstate that goes to Sioux Falls did not use to exist, so travel to Sioux Falls was always down highway 81, and you took the same highway to go north to Fargo. Harry's Dairy sat at the end of my block on South Broadway and 7th Ave., use to get sent there a lot to pick up milk.

Nelson Park was MY park, use to have craft times there in the summers. The Watertown mall did not exist, we had a bustling downtown that mom use to LOVE to go and park our car on Friday nights uptown and sit and watch the people go by as stores were open late on Friday nights. My dad, one time took his little motor boat up the Sioux River from Pelican Lake as far as he could go, which was up to Riverside park that was one funny and a fun thing we did, ONE TIME only!

Childhood Games and Activities in 1920s and 1930s
By Pauline Lloyd-Davies of Aberdeen, South Dakota
Born 1918

Rose Hoadley was born in Brooklyn, NY in 1920. I was born in South Dakota in 1918, but when we met when we were in our 70's, we discovered that as children we had both played the same games, with only a few differences here and there.

My seven brothers and I had a 'hill' behind our house. It was a water reservoir with earth packed up around the sides. It was ideal for sledding when there was snow. And after my brothers iced the earth with pails of water from our kitchen, it was ideal for our sleds. My brothers made snow forts and had snowball fights with the neighborhood children. In the snow, we played "Fox and Geese," made snow angels and it seemed like every house had a snowman in the yard.

Ice-skating and roller skating were both fun, although the roller skates had to be clamped to our leather-soled shoes and often came off, resulting in skinned knees. The city provided free ice-skating rinks, but only one with a warming house. My brothers often went to the "Mog" (still common slang for the Moccasin Creek that runs through town) to skate. His gang had to clear the snow and build a bonfire.

Because she lived in a large city, Rose and her brother sat on the front step of their home to play taxi and took turns counting cars. If it was a taxi when it was your turn, you got

Building a snow fort in 1936

points.

With South Dakota's constant wind, kite flying was a popular diversion. Of course, our kites were homemade, using laths and wrapping paper or newspaper.

We played several kinds of tag, including tree tag. "Captain May I" depended on memory to correctly ask permission to take steps 1 to 10; the first person to make it through all ten steps got to be the next Captain. Many variations of baseball were played, depending on the equipment available and the number of players. Rose said they used discarded broomsticks to play ball. The broomstick also came in handy for a game called "Pusho." For this, wooden orange crates were fitted with roller skate wheels on the underside and pushed with a broomstick.

We always had wagons and bicycles. The wagons came in handy to have a parade. We put on costumes from the costume box in the attic, put a portable hand-wound record player in the wagon, and listened to opera on our tour around the block.

Dominoes, card games such as "Rummy" and "War," checkers, "Pickup sticks," "Ante I Over" and "Red Light/Green Light" were all popular. We could even use a 'dead' tennis ball for "Ante I Over," which we played by throwing the ball over the garage for the other player to catch. A piece of string was always good for "Cat's Cradle," an ancient game.

"Kick the Can" involved kicking a tin can all the way to school. We also clamped our shoes on empty evaporated milk cans and clumped down the sidewalk.

On the school playground, "Pom Pom Pullaway" was a favorite. We also played "Jacks" on the concrete and counted by onesies and twosies.

Paper dolls have always been a favorite. Some girls drew dresses on paper and cut them out. The Sears and Montgomery Ward catalogs were gold mines of dolls to cut out; we could make clothes for them out of any paper.

Rose made what she called "horse reins," using spool knitting. My husband made bathrobe cords that way. We could also coil the cord and sew it together for a rug for a dollhouse.

Water coloring and crayon work were always good for fun. These supplies seemed to last forever and the backs of letters and other scrap paper were used for the coloring.

My brothers made a game with a cigar box by cutting a hole in the top just large enough for a marble. They challenged a friend to drop a marble into the hole. If successful, he got his marble and another; if not, he had to give up his marble.

Rose said they threw Coke bottle caps toward a wall. Whoever got closest without touching the wall was the winner.

Gum was 5 cents a pack and it seemed everyone chewed gum. The wrappers were thin, strong, pretty paper and were easy to fold and link together into a gum belt. (Read "An Occasional Cow" by Polly Horvath to learn about the long gum belt some children made.)

Most kids had a yo-yo and could do intricate tricks like "walking the dog."

There was no television when I was growing up. Even in the coldest winters, we spent a lot of time outside. I remember those times playing with my brothers and the neighborhood children as wonderful, fun years of my life growing up in South Dakota.

5-Cent Gopher Tails and Firehouse Mischief
By Aloyce "Al" Menzia of Mukwonago, Wisconsin
Born 1942

My name is Aloyce Menzia, Born April 9, 1942. The name Aloyce is very confusing to almost everyone, it is pronounced Al-oyce, and most people think that I am a female— wrong, I've been a male for over 72 years. I go by the name "Al" for the past 54 years. Born number eight of nine children in the small town of Roscoe, South Dakota.

463

Growing up I remember the water pump outside, pumped by hand and make sure that you have gloves on in the winter and don't lick the pump—tongue sticks to it, the outhouse with two holes (seats). At night in the winter, our parents use to setup a 5-gallon pail on the porch for us to use if we needed to go potty.

36 pupils of Geneseo #3 in 1937

When we took a bath, we would heat water on the wood stove and take a bath in a galvanized tub.

Every fall we would butcher at least one large pig and we would eat everything except the squeal. We would clean all the intestines for sausage casings, the stomach for headcheese and then our dad would smoke the hams, sausage, and bacon. Whatever wasn't smoked was canned and put into our cellar to keep cool.

We didn't have a refrigerator until the late '40s but our parents did whatever they had to do to feed their nine kids. All of my brothers and two sisters would work for farmers for food or money for the family.

Every spring we would order chicks via the post office, feed them, raise them for their eggs, and then butcher as needed.

When I was about 10 yrs. old, I would go gopher hunting with a single shot 22 rifle. When I would run out of shells I would take a piece of binder twine out of my pocket, make a loop on one end and when I saw a gopher go into their hole, I would put the loop end around the hole, sit back about 10-12 ft. Then I would make a squeaking noise with my lips and when the gopher got curious, it would stick its head out of its hole and I would pull real hard and snag it! Use to get 5-cents per tail but I use to cut them in half when they were really long for 10-cents.

When I was a little older, about 13 yrs. I would go pheasant hunting and continued hunting until I was 18. When I talk to pheasant hunters in Wisconsin, I always tell them that I shot more pheasants than they ever saw!

Another activity while growing up was to tip over outhouses during Halloween—interesting—one time we were in the process of tipping over an outhouse and there was a person using it and he yelled "Hey, what the h— are you doing?" We got the heck out of there. What we needed to do was to watch out for those people that would be one-step ahead of us. What they would do is to move the outhouse over and cover the hole with some light material and when guys like us would attempt to tip the outhouse— OH, S—t!

We also would play around with our local law enforcement officer (Ed). We had a firehouse, jail building in the center of town that had a bell tower on it. We would take a bail of binder twine and tie the twine to the bell clap, move away for the length of the bail of twine and ring the bell until Ed would go the firehouse to see what was making the bell ring. As soon as he showed up, we would drop the string and run away. Ed followed the twine but no one was there. HA! HA! For fun, we use to play ditch 'em which is like hide and seek.

We also would play "Ante I Over," Marbles, and Kick the Can. Our Mother used to bake bread at least twice a week for us and she would also give bread to people that were in need. When I was still under 6 years old I used to help my mother bake, I used to take a piece of dough and try to stick it on the kitchen ceiling, didn't use it in the bread! We used to buy the flour in 50# bags and used the bag to make clothing for us kids. Ironically, my wife's mother used to use the flour bags for clothes also.

We as a family did not drink very much milk; I used to eat cereal, Corn Flakes, Puffed Wheat, and Puffed Rice in a cup of coffee with cream and sugar. We used to buy cream from farmers and make our own butter out of it; we had a butter churn and would take turns turning it until the butter was made. Now our children and grandchildren get tired of my wife and I saying, "Well, when I was your age, I etc."

Growing up in those times taught me and my brothers and sisters that we can do whatever it takes to make a living and survive.

While in grade school if we did something wrong the teacher would reprimand us with a slap or spanking. You didn't dare go home and tell your parents because they would say what did you do wrong and then spank you again. In high school I was in track and ran the high and low hurdles on a cinder track, played 6 man football, played basketball, sang solos, and sang with the school glee club.

I moved to Milwaukee, WI after graduation in 1960, married in 1963 and have three children and six grandchildren. I am now enjoying my retirement after working for over 40 years.

The Outhouse Turkey Guard
By Colleen A. Anderson of Cresbard, South Dakota
Born 1934

My mother was an industrious farm wife in the early 1940s. She raised several types of poultry, including turkeys, to supplement the family income.

In those days, the bathroom was located in a little building out behind the house. One fine summer day when I was about 6 years old, Mother Nature called and I went to visit the 'outhouse'.

I was just ready to open the door when I heard the old turkey gobbler raising his voice in front of the 'outhouse'. I was now a hostage to a belligerent old tyrant! I started yelling for my mother but the old gobbler gobbled louder. He strutted a short distance from the 'outhouse', giving me a chance to open the door slightly, stick my head out and yell for mom.

My dear mother finally came out of the house to look for me and heard my cries from the 'outhouse'. She immediately grabbed a broom and took after the gobbler! I was never so happy to see my mom.

Later that fall, the 'ole gobbler went to the happy hunting ground when he was sold.

We Were Farmers
By Merlon Kotila of Aberdeen, South Dakota
Born 1924

I was born August 26, 1924 at the Kotila home place in Frederick, Brown County, and Richland Township, South Dakota.

My first recollection of life was when we farmed the Lamport farm between Frederick and Houghton, South Dakota.

The house had one bedroom and an unfinished second floor-we children slept in the living room on the first floor. The farm had an artesian well so we had running water in the house. We heated with a hard coal heater that had icing glass so one could see the glowing coals.

There were two quarters of land, 320 acres. We lived on that farm from 1923 to 1929. My dad bought a Fordson tractor and a new 1926 model "T" Ford while living there.

In 1929, we moved to the Kotila home place. In the spring of 1930, Grandfather Kotila died of pneumonia. Dad took over management of the farm. There were four quarters of land, 640 acres. There were three tractors, a TITON, a 15-30 McCormick Deering, and the Fordson. There were 30 horses. Only about 1/2 were used for fieldwork. This farm was purchased in 1905; the new house was built in 1914. The farm had an artesian well so we had running water at the house, barn, and chicken house. There was a coal-burning furnace in the basement with a large radiator on the living room floor. In the teens, a 32V Delco generator was installed in the basement. It had a large bank of glass batteries. Most of the buildings were wired for lights and power.

As six year olds, we were taught to start the generator by pouring a little gas into a well and how to switch the carbonator to kerosene for its fuel supply. Electrical appliances included an iron, motors to turn grain cleaners, and a large butter churn in the basement. The family there included grandmother, dad and mom and we four children, dad's youngest sister and brother, Aino and Reino (popular Finnish names) and dad's brother Ed, a bachelor.

I started school in the fall of 1930. The

465

Merlon in 1942

corn with a two-row cultivator pulled by four horses. When I was 15 years old I joined the Kotila-Jarvi threshing crew. I had dad's team and bundle rack. We pitched bundles 10 hours a day for .20cents an hour paid for me and .10cents an hour for the team. No wonder that at 15 we thought we were grownups. !

We moved to the Wiltala farm in 1940. This farm is just west of the Savo Church. There were 3 quarters of land and we rented another quarter and an 80. The water supply included an old artesian well that supplied the house with water but due to old age it couldn't supply enough for livestock. A new artesian well was drilled immediately. This new well supplied a lot of water, but was not good for human use due to high sulfur content. It was ideal for livestock because it was warm and kept the cattle tank thawed out in winter.

The house was a large beautiful home with a bathroom, hot water, radiators for heat, and a Delco electric system. Very nice. The original barn had burned in 1936 due to green hay stored in the loft. A new barn was built, so it was a dream place. Dad and mother lived there for 10 years, until he bought his own farm.

The rains had returned and grain prices were good due to the looming war in Europe. This is the first time that dad had money after the summer farming bills were paid. The last time for a profit was in the 1920s. They had been hard years. We were farming with one Farmall tractor and needed another tractor for this many acres. That is when we got a 1935 used Minneapolis Moline tractor. There were three of us sons, ages 12 to 17 years. We could

school was only three years old. A one-room with a basement, and a coal furnace in the basement. It had a horse barn and two out houses beside it.

Due to the drought and depression, the farm and livestock were deeply in debt, so in 1935 we left the farm and moved to a rent farm owned by an insurance company. It was a terrible place. The house had four rooms, two upstairs, and two down. The water came from a surface well with windmill and pump. We were back to kerosene lamps, carrying water and an outhouse. A huge backward step for us.

The school was an old one-room with space heater and a barn and two out houses again. I finished 8th grade there. The woman teachers had to come extra early to a cold room to start a fire in the space heater. This period of time was not good!

In 1936, there was no crop at all, so dad went to Hood River, Oregon to pick apples. While we lived on the rent farm, I learned to drive the Fordson in the field and to cultivate

Merlon Kotila the postmaster from 1967 to 1987

466

do a lot of the work and enjoyed life. Mom and sister were happy to be in a nice home. My sister and I drove dad's car nine miles to Frederick High School.

When I was 17 years old I was plowing in a field between the buildings and Savo Church. The heavy rains had filled ponds in the field so I had to take the plow out of the ground and travel around the water. One of these times I was driving the Moline tractor and pulling a 3-bottom plow. As I was going around a pond, I took the plow out of the ground and put the tractor into a higher gear. I was on the seat with a steering spinner in my hand when the seat assembly main bolt broke. I fell under the plow moving at 5-6 mph, so I took hold of part of the top of the plow frame. I could not pull myself forward and could not slide out the back because a plowshare caught my overalls. I was hoping that the tractor would go into water and get stuck and give me time to get out. But as luck would have it, my father was cleaning a fence line about 100 yards away and saw the tractor travelling without a driver and rushed there and stopped the tractor. By then a pile of dirt had built up in front of my chest so large that the main wheels were off the ground. After he got me out of the dirt, I saw the church and decided, "There is a God." My belief became real. I tried to roll a cigarette to calm down but I shook so bad that I couldn't. Dad said, "I think you had better take the rest of the day off."

I remained on the farm until age 20 when Mary and I were married, and then I volunteered to be drafted into the army.

After I got out of the army, in 1946, I did wiring work with my Uncle Reino getting farms ready for Rural Electric service to all the farms.

Midnight Solitaire
By Duane W. Laufmann of Huron, South Dakota
Born 1951

The winds whipped the snow into high, hard-packed mounds. It spared no corner, no crevice; snow banks were everywhere; where the snow didn't rise in feet, it merely strayed over the wind-swept ground.

Winter came with a snowstorm, blocking our long driveway and one-mile gravel road to the county road; to take my ACT college entrance exam on the day after the storm, I walked over the snow-covered fields to the county road, getting a ride with several other seniors. Walking was interesting, not having done anything quite like that before for anything but hunting or messing around. By the time we were on our way home, the roads had been plowed.

My dad was injured for part of the winter and was hospitalized, and with my oldest brother, Curtis, in the Army, the responsibilities of the farm weighed on me and my siblings and our mom. We were constantly fighting the snow, and the snow was gradually winning. My oldest sister, Linda, came home from working in Washington D.C. around Christmas, and received an engagement ring by mail from her boyfriend in Vietnam. Before the time for her to go back, a major snowstorm forced her to leave early.

From then on, the winter gradually became brutal, with the snow walls made by plowing the roads getting ever higher, until just a high wind would drift the roads closed. One school day the wind rose and my siblings and I skedaddled for home; Dad met us somewhere in the beginning of our mile homestretch with a tractor and a loader without a cab to open the snow drifts quickly blocking the road. One of the tires of the tractor's narrow front end went flat and Dad had to hold on for dear life to get the tractor loader to push snow. At one time, it was so bad he climbed off the tractor and came into the car to warm up and to relieve his sciatic nerve pain, then quickly going back to the tractor to push snow. He got us to the end of the driveway before the pain and cold got to him and we traveled the driveway ourselves. From that desperate effort, Dad had hurt his back so bad the sciatic nerve pain drove him to the Veteran's Hospital in Sioux Falls to recover.

Missing weeks from school because of road closures, the farm became our daily challenge; having to find ways to feed the livestock, keep the driveway clear, whatever it took to keep the farm functioning. One day the struggle took my brother, Byron, with the aid of our younger siblings, Marla, Susan, and Bob, to haul ear corn across the snow banks with an upside down car hood, for the pigs. Snow rose high around a haystack, forcing us to throw the hay upward to the cattle over the fence. One disaster came when a bunch of feeder pigs smothered under the piling of other pigs to keep warm, in the pole shed. Dad sold the rest before it could happen again, which was discouraging to Byron and me, as we were trying so hard to keep up. Throwing silage down the silo chute became a race to get more from the sides, as the sides were freezing fast; high, broad battlements of silage grew in the silo, until one day a couple uncles, Gideon and Arnold, came to break down these encircling walls, as well as getting a load of manure out of the barn.

Still we had some free time, not being in school for most of a week or so at a time with the blocked roads; while hunting jackrabbits one day I ventured onto a neighbor's land, the farmstead uninhabited. I crawled over a small ridge and the shallow crater abounded with rabbits, a valley out of the wind; within a pleasant refuge, the rabbits seemed content. If I shot, I didn't get any; the rabbits scattered at my intrusion. At home when the evening's dark approached, jackrabbits from all directions came to get a meal at the ear corn piles left over from the filled corncribs by the driveway. It was easy to shoot them as a missed shot went unnoticed; they didn't get startled by the little fluff of snow thrown up.

Midway through winter on a Saturday night, I drove down our gravel road, finding a number of semi-tractor trailers blocking the road. They were loading the cattle that belonged on the farm across the road; the owner had tried farming after a successful career elsewhere, and had hired two men to feed and water the cattle for the winter, while the owner left for the winter. One farmhand quit, leaving a one-armed man to do the work, which he couldn't, so the cattle were slowly starving and thirsting to death, along with some horses about a mile away. Cattle need fresh water, as they can't eat snow; the horses were starving to death, though they could eat snow for moisture. I tried to go around a semi-trailer, but got stuck, being pulled out by one of the truck drivers, eventually getting back on my way to my girlfriend's.

For my birthday in January, Mom made me cream puffs, a delectable treat after the long afternoon of chores. When I watched Richard Nixon's first presidential inauguration Mom was surprised that, I was interested in that, but it was an event I was becoming more aware of; also it, possibly was a diversion from the drudgery of fighting the snow.

One afternoon my mother asked if I would try to get chores done a little earlier, because we were always eating supper late because of all the work. I tried to rush feeding the cattle silage with the unloader wagon, but pulling away from the silo hurriedly I accidentally drove a wagon wheel on a large snow bank, with the wagon tipping over on its side, breaking the wagon tongue. I had to unload the wagon by hand where it had fallen as the cattle were crowding around the wagon. Getting it tipped upright, I chained the broken tongue to the tractor, and hauled it out of the cattle yard to the garage where the welder was. I had only dabbed at welding a little before, but I tried to weld the pieces together; finally, after many attempts I managed to weld an extra iron piece, which was strong enough to hitch the wagon back on the tractor. It wasn't pretty but it was solid. Needless to say, we were even later that night for supper.

When we made it to school, we might be there for a couple of days or more, but the snow would put a stop to that. I didn't know it until years later that some farm kids stayed with families in Canova, S.D., where school was. It would not have worked for me and my siblings. I don't resent this in anyway, because it had to be this way. I was tops in my class even though I missed quite a few assignments; some of my classmates asked why I was allowed to miss so much, while they had to complete everything, plus possibly wondering why I was still permitted to retain my standing; but fortunately we had an understanding school superintendent.

Finally, the winter was fading. We still had the 8-10 foot high snowdrifts in the farmyard, on which we had strung an electric wire on steel posts, to keep the cattle from wandering off. But the days were getting longer, not that winter was releasing its hold on us; something was in the air though. Finally, after being snowbound again, with the driveway and roads snow-blocked, with our spirits flagging I'm sure as the days dragged on, one Sunday night we saw the lights of some vehicle from a half mile or more away on the road, from the living room (carpet room, that is, used for entertaining guests), which meant somehow that vehicle must have been pushing snow.

Mom asked me to go to the end of the driveway to wait for whatever was moving the snow, to ask if the driver would open our driveway, before opening the rest of the gravel road. I went and waited and waited at the driveway end, leaning on an electric pole, as the snow machine slowly cleared the road. I went back to the house to warm up and steady my nerves, being anxious. Going out again, it being around midnight, I waited quite a while again, but the pay loader, as it turned out to be, finally came—I stopped the driver, asking him to clear our driveway, which he did right away.

In the morning, we went to school between the huge snow piles on either side of the roadway. Dad just happened to be at the school, to confer with the superintendent as Dad was on the school board; Dad was healed and ready to go home, being kept away by the closed roads; so he went home after being away possibly a couple months. After that, I don't think we missed any more school; we still had to wait for the snow to melt which left huge ponds, streams, but it was on the downside, and we had survived. It had been a record snowfall in quite a few places, I imagine our area too.

We've had many rough winters since then, but nothing quite like that winter of 1968-9.

The Wringer Washing Machine
By Edna Angerhofer of Milbank, South
Dakota
Born 1933

True facts from a city girl farm wife:
  Haul the water
  heat water
  fill washing machine
  start machine
  put in white clothes
  run through wringer
  rinse and wring again
  put in colored clothes
  hang white clothes outside
  wring colored clothes
  rinse and wring again
  put in underwear
  hang colored clothes outside
  wring underwear,
  rinse and wring again
  put in work shirts
  hang underwear outside
  wring work shirts
  rinse and wring again
  put in work socks
  hang work shirts outside
  wring socks
  rinse and wring again
  put in jeans
  hang work socks outside
  wring jeans
  rinse and wring
  put in overhauls
  hang jeans outside
  wring overhauls
  rinse and wring again
  hang overhauls outside
  prop up clothesline
  fix dinner
  carry out wash water
  use rinse water to
  mop floor and porch
  carry out rinse water
  bring in dry clothes
  iron, fold and put away
  fix supper.
This was a good summer day, It did not rain, a flock of geese did not fly over, and the cows did not get out and run through the clotheslines, tearing them down. Winter was a time of frozen fingers to hang the clothes and then taking them down, giving a whole different meaning to freeze-dried!

Playhouse Days to be Remembered
By Deloris Bertram of Rosholt, South
Dakota
Born 1929

When I was a little girl, playhouses were popular. Playhouses were not the manufactured ones you might purchase now days. Mine was put together outside, likely in a grove near the house, and made of boxes, tree trunks, old cast-off chairs and/or tables, a pretend stove, and cast-off dishes, pots and pans.

And we made mud pies. Mud pies were made of dirt and water and decorated with pretty stones, torn up leaves, or seeds. We did a pretty good job of that. And of course, they were sun baked in an old cover, a cracked dish from Mom's cupboard, or whatever.

One day as I set off to make a pie, I went to the kitchen part and, in getting things ready to bake, I lifted an old zinc jar cover to view a batch of pink, hairless, "creepy" looking, crawling baby mice. I did scream and took off to the house to report to my mother what a terrible trick my little brother had played on me! Oh my, I was so mad and unduly upset with my sibling for such trickery! My only compensation for the event was the pretty stiff scolding Mother gave my kid brother. It was not physical, but it was a stern scolding.

My playhouse days were fun, but that day was one not to be forgotten for various reasons, such as "Ha, ha, I got you in trouble, didn't I" of my kid brother!

Outhouse Trips
By Jim D. Huff of Detroit Lakes, Minnesota
Born 1941

I remember my childhood days living in the country in South Dakota. We had no indoor plumbing. Our running water meant running out to the well and getting a pail of water. Our bathroom was a little unheated outhouse with two holes. This was located, of course, a short distance from the house because of summer time smell.

As we would get deeper into the winter a pyramid of you know what built up in each hole. We would take care of this problem with a piece of 2x4 on one of those below zero days. If you would ram the 2x4 against the top of the pyramid, you could knock the top off. This would give you room for a while.

Our toilet paper was represented by the *Sears Roebuck* or *Montgomery Ward Catalog*. Of course, the first pages to be used was the index pages. The colored sheet pages would always be the last pages used. We always looked forward to canning season in the fall. Our ma would buy peaches by the crate. Each peach would come individually wrapped in a tissue type paper. This was a time of year the whole family appreciated.

I remember my nighttime trips to the outhouse, winter or summer. When the job was all done, I would open the door, go out, and latch the door. Then I would sprint as fast as I could the twenty yards or so to the house.

All the years of racing to the house it seems I always beat the footsteps I could hear running behind me.

In case you didn't make the connection with the peach wrappers, they were used for toilet paper.

Onions behind the Outhouse
By William A. Schumacher of Milbank,
South Dakota
Born 1949

I, William A. Schumacher, spent the first 18 years of my life on a farm three miles east of Milbank. I was born to Alvin and Alma Schumacher on November 22, 1949.

In the fall of 1956 I went to Big Stone #3, a rural one room school about one and a half miles east of the Alvin H. Schumacher farm. There were ten kids in the school: myself and my sister Judy, Dick, Don, and Dale Camus, Don and Dwight Harrison, and their younger brother - his name escapes me. Oh well. And Georgette Holquist and Veroh Bucholtz.

In the spring of the year, it didn't take long for the boys to raise their hands for the bathroom. Behind the boys' outhouse, a crop of wild onions grew. When the boys returned to the schoolroom, everyone knew why he had gone out.

Old Drugstore Display Cases and Old Phonographs
By Beth Will of Watertown, South Dakota
Born 1954

As a child (four to eight years old), I remember going to Greening Drug. It was the drug store my grandparents owned in Dell Rapids, South Dakota. Grandma would always give us kids a generous handful of tasty mixed nuts from the nut case. How warm, crunchy and special! The penny display case was also cool and delightful for this young girl. The bubble gum, Tootsie Rolls, and other treats all danced in my head!

Today I treasure the memories and heritage of the 1890s display case as it sits proudly in our home! An Edison phonograph also rests on top of the display case. Sweet melodies are treasured from my great-great-

1890s display case

grandmother Pinkert who purchased the nostalgic phonograph in 1905in Brown's Valley, Minnesota.

The winter of 1968-69 was awesome for a young teen. It was a blizzard that took us away from school for almost a month. We tunneled our way to the barn. The snow was way up past the barn doors. When we got there, we scooped the door open to feed and milk the uncomfortable cows. Sadly, Daddy dumped milk or fed the pigs with the milk because the bulk tank driver couldn't get in to get our milk. When spring finally came, we had flooding. We missed more than a month of school, which they wrote off the books, as it was too much to make up. What a memorable winter!

The Grasshopper Dilemma
By Mabel Dockter Freitag of Leola, South Dakota
Born 1928

It was the summer of 1936. My sister, Arlyne, was six years old and I was eight. We lived on a farm in McPherson County, South Dakota. The air was thick with grasshoppers.

One hot day, at noon, we were sent out to the well to get some fresh water to drink. On our way back to the house, a large grasshopper decided to take a swim in our water pail. We emptied out the polluted water and went back to the well for a refill. Halfway back to the house, again, a grasshopper jumped in to the water pail. We went to the house and told our mother about our dilemma. She gave us a lid from one of her pans. On the third try, we made it back to the house with clean, fresh, cold water to drink on a very hot summer day.

Plane Crash Memory
By Darleen Brace of Douglas, Wyoming
Born 1931

We lived on a farm four miles southwest of Fedora, South Dakota. It was my parents, Lester and Lizzie Waters; my brothers, Lavern and Delmer; my sisters, Delores and Audrey; and me, Darleen. I was twelve years old, and Delores was ten years old.

Sunday, June 13, 1943, was a clear and sunny day. In the afternoon, it was after dinner, my cousin, Frank Eller, his wife, Martha, and their two children, Arlene and Merl, came to visit. Frank was driving his bright orange school bus, as he was a bus driver for the Fedora School. We were all standing in the shade of the house on the east side, visiting. We heard this loud noise and saw three bombers just to the northwest of Fedora, flying in formation, so low!

The bombers flew just to the southeast of Fedora, and when they were almost to the east of us, we saw one bomber drop to the ground, engulfed in black smoke and flames.

Frank said, "Let's all get in the bus and go over there, as that looks like the plane crashed close to our place." Frank and Martha lived where Bob and Nance Banks live now. It probably took us 20 minutes to get to the crash.

When we got there, we had to crawl through a barbed wire fence in the southeast corner of this field. There were a few people standing there. I remember the grass or weeds had burned a black circle around where the fuselage was and to the back of the wreckage. There must have been a fire inside the plane because Delores and I could see the wood frame partially burned black. My most remaining picture was of the dead soldier lying on the ground, alone, and seeing the parachuter coming down out of the clear blue sky and land so close to us!

This happened so many years ago, but remembering it is like opening a door that has been closed for so many years. All of the people named are dead now, of course, except me. I met my love of my life when I was sixteen. We dated for four years and then got married in October of 1951. We had a girl and then a boy in our family. Our daughter became an English teacher, and our son a computer technology engineer.

The mystery of which plane that parachuter came from has never been told. The people didn't discuss this unfortunate plane crash, not my folks or the neighbors, no one!

Embarrassment in the Outhouse
By Mary Louise Lechner of Leola, South
Dakota
Born 1932

My mom, Fern, was a very pretty woman and always wanted to look nice. On a Sunday, most of us could dress ourselves for church. We would all be in the car waiting for her, and we had a small porch on the house, which had an old pail. We'd see her come out and then squat over the pail, her hat always in place. Then she would come out to the car and say, "Well, you know I had to get you kids all ready for church. That's why I'm so late."

When we were in grade school and living on the farm, my family consisted of our parents; me, the oldest; Arlan; my sister, Shirley; and Keith, my youngest brother. My mom heated water on a kerosene stove in our basement. Every Saturday night, we all got a bath from the youngest to the oldest, with my dad being last. All in the same water with a little hot water was added when needed.

In the early 1950s, we returned to South Dakota to live with my in-laws near Leola on a farm. We had been Air Force people. Anyway, one day the men were all in the fields, and my mother-in-law went to town for supplies.

Mary Louise's family

Mary Louise's father and his children

We had no indoor plumbing in those days. So, having to go to the bathroom, I went to the old outdoor toilet, and as I was in the toilet, I heard the farm dog barking. So I stood up with my panties on the floor and tried to see out of a little window. As I did this the door burst open, and a man stood there. I don't know who was more embarrassed. Anyway, he was gone, and later I found out he was with the Jehovah's Witnesses, who were going about with their visiting homes in the area.

Arnold Mundhenke: Rural Mail Carrier
By Lorna Mundhenke Perkins of Colorado
Springs, Colorado
Born 1939

My father, Arnold Mundhenke, became a rural mail carrier in 1920. At that time, no one wanted the job, as a team of horses had to be used in the winter. He had two teams and would change horses halfway around his route. He paid the farmer $1.00 per day for stabling and feeding the horses. In addition, this $1.00 included a hot noon meal.

One summer day he arrived at a patron's

472

mailbox. The mother of a small child met him in tears and pointing to near the top of their windmill. Her three-year-old daughter had climbed the windmill. My father immediately started climbing to get her down. My dad and the mother kept shouting at her to hang on. When my father reached her, she wouldn't let go. My dad had to hang onto her, the windmill, and pry her little fingers loose. Finally, they both arrived safely on the ground. My dad was afraid of heights but managed to save the little girl. All in the days work of a rural mail carrier!

Many years later, Willow Lake was having to city reunion. A beautiful lady walked up to me and asked if Arnold Mundhenke was my dad. She asked me if he had ever told me the story of rescuing a little girl who climbed to the top of a windmill. When I replied, "Yes, many times," she told me that she was that little girl! I then said, "Did you know he was afraid of heights?"

My father loved his job and the people on his route. Infrequently, a patron would meet him at the mailbox wondering if medicine had arrived. If it hadn't, my dad would take it out in the afternoon if it had come in on the morning train. He would also deliver baby chicks if they arrived on the morning train. Many of the baby chicks would die without food or water if they would have to wait until the next day. It also was not the nicest smell if they stayed in the post office.

My father retired in 1963 after 43 years of service. The interesting part is after 43 years when no one wanted the job, the superintendent of schools applied for the job! What started out as a job no one wanted became a job that was sought after!

Changes in my Lifetime
By Nadine Jones of Aurora, South Dakota
Born 1921

Hi. My name is Nadine Jones and I am an old woman of 92 years old. I live on a farm south of Aurora, South Dakota in the same house I have lived in all but about seven years of my life. I was born in a house in Lincoln County in this great state of South Dakota. My folks were Robert and Blanche DeMint. They moved on to this farm in 1925, so I grew up in the 1920s and 1930s.

I have witnessed many changes in my lifetime. Many amazing things have happened. I lived through the Great Depression, dust storms, droughts, grasshopper plagues, blizzards, several wars, W.P.A years, rationing of gas, sugar, tires, etc. but there has been lots of years of good times, too. I received my eighth grade education in a one-room schoolhouse a half-mile south of my home where I learned all grades and all eight subjects. Not many pupils were fortunate enough to be able to attend high school in those years.

I have lived through several decades of miracle things that have occurred. We went from kerosene lamps and lanterns to gas lamps and Aladdin lamps then onto our electric lights many years later. I also remember our first icebox that we could keep our cream and butter in so it would keep better. We churned our own butter from the cream we separated from milk from our cows, which we milked by hand.

My mother was a wonderful cook and baker. Everything was cooked and baked on a wood and coal range. Cobs and wood were used to provide the heat. It had a reservoir on one end of it filled with water from a well. We carried it up the hill in a water pail. That was also our drinking water. We had a dipper in the pail and we all drank out of the same dipper. No one was worried about germs in those days. I believe we were all healthier then than we are now. My dad was a farmer; he farmed with horses—using all horse-drawn equipment. What a great day it was when he got his first tractor. He also raised Hereford cattle and hogs, which he butchered for our fresh pork to eat. That happened only in the winter when it was cold enough to keep it frozen. Then along came the locker in town where we could rent a locker and have meat the year round and other great treats.

I only had one brother and he was killed in World War II in France. He is buried in St. James, France. My husband is a World War II veteran. He is 93 years old and we are still living on our home doing most of the things we have always done—only a lot slower.

When I was growing up, we always had plenty of things to do. We were never bored as kids are today. We provided our own entertainment. We had three neighbors that had ten children apiece, so all of our activities

473

took place in our schoolhouse. We played ball on the school grounds. We had dances, basket socials, plenty of good picnics, and parties there also. No one had a car that could be driven too far from home. One of our neighbors had a stock truck and he would take us to ballgames, dances, etc. we even went as far as Huron to the State Fair. We were a little windblown when we got there, but we had fun. We later got R.E.A and what a thrill that was to be able to turn on a switch and do all our washing clothes, cooking, and all the luxuries we now have. Also, rural water has improved our quality of life.

My Life Began in 1940
By Arlene Parsley of Watertown, South Dakota
Born 1940

My life started in 1940. My father lost part of his hand in a corn picker in the fall of 1940. I didn't have any brothers or sisters, so I mostly played alone. I did have a rat terrier dog was born around the time that I was. We were good friends and it really did protect me so that no one could hurt me. My dog would snip at my dad's heels and anyone else who tried to play with me.

My parents and grandparents were all a good part of my life growing up. It was good that I had a few years with my father as he was killed in an automobile accident when I was 18 years old. I remember the outhouse and the pots. On Saturdays, we had baths. We had a high sink that the young ones got a bath in. Summer meant that we went to the barn and bathed in the hot water in a bucket hanging from posts where the cows were milked. In winter, we washed in a large wash pan.

Mom made many of my clothes. As I got older, I made many of my own clothes. We had a black and white TV later in the fifties. Party lines were at times hard to get on the phone because other people were on it. On the party lines, many people listened to other conversations. We listened to the old radio stories like Fibber McGee and Molly.

My first four years of school was in Oxford #6 country school. I liked my teacher and she was my favorite of the 12 years. The schools were then consolidated and I was

transferred to a much bigger school in town, but the town was still small. Usually we had one or two blizzards a year and if it got too bad then school got called off.

I remember the old icebox in the house as the fridge. When it was no longer used inside, it went outside to play house and make mud pies and cake. Dad's nephew came to visit one afternoon and Mother asked him if he would like several things. He didn't care for anything she had. So she said, "Maybe a piece of chocolate pie?" "Yeah, sounds good," he replied. So Mom had to eventually tell him what it was—my mud pie from the chocolate pudding she had given me!

I had four or five calls to go out on a date with men. None of them ever really worked out. The call came one day and a man asked me over for supper. I went and it was a very good evening. We had several more dates. I guess it was meant to be because we were married in 2002 and are still together. I guess it was because we went to school as freshmen in school. It is unusual that all of the others that called me have all passed away. I guess I just saved the best for last!

Paper Dolls and Blizzards
By Jewel Aeilts of Carthage, Illinois
Born 1927

My cousin, Iva Mae Carson-Aeilts and I loved to play paper dolls, but we cut them out of catalogs! My mother always raised chickens. Baby chickens came to the post office and there was always a lot of peeping when they arrived! She started them in the house in a cardboard box. They were so cute! When they got older and jumped out of the box, she took them to a brooder house. She put a cot out there and slept several nights there, as she was so afraid of fire. She had a little stove in there, keeping the chickens warm. We kids often gathered the eggs, but if a hen was setting on eggs, Mother had to get those. The hen would peck at us and we were afraid! Selling eggs and cream bought many of our groceries.

When I was seven or eight years old, my father took us to town, Langford, to see Santa Claus. We didn't get a chance to see Santa

Claus very often. It was my little brother, Floyd, about five years old, and my older brother, Dale, who was about 12 years old. I had been invited to a birthday party, too, but in the middle of the party, my dad came and got me, as it was snowing so hard! I didn't want to leave!

We lived along a railroad track, one mile from Langford. About halfway home, the car got stuck, so Dad said we had to walk the rest of the way home on the railroad track. He put the sweet potatoes in his pockets. He carried my little brother and I walked beside him. My older brother ran ahead, and every once in a while, Dad would holler at him, as it was snowing so hard and he wanted to be able to see him. Mother was so glad to see us when we got home. She rubbed snow on our cold feet and hands!

That night was supposed to be the SS Christmas program at the little Methodist Church in town. Of course, we didn't go. Several nights later, we did go in a bobsled. Mother had heated soapstone to help keep our feet warm. It was a clear night and the stars were very bright. All the way to town, we kept asking Mother, "Which star is the star of Bethlehem?" (Later, we heard a woman did freeze to death in that blizzard. She had taken shelter in a barn. I didn't know her.)

We had a good garden during the depression years, as it was watered by an artesian well. Artesian water ruined the soil, so we could not have a garden there again. But many people were thrilled to see such a lush garden in those dry, dusty years. The dust storms were horrible in the '30s. I'm sure it was very depressing for the adults, especially. I remember making Canadian thistle houses. We made them pretty big or otherwise, if we got too near them, we would get pricked! One year we were to have a picnic at the end of school. The dust was blowing so badly outside that our teacher said we had to eat our picnic lunch inside. I was disappointed!

There was a movie at the town hall in Langford. I had never seen a movie! It was a clear, spring night, so my mother walked with my brother, Dale, and I along the railroad track the one mile to see the movie. I remember it was about animals. Sometime later, when my older sisters, Carol and Hazel, were going to college, they asked me to come and spend the weekend with them. They took me to see my second movie, "Rebecca of Sunnybrook Farm." I thought that was the most wonderful movie—with Shirley Temple, of course!

Ozzie's Bake Shop
By Vickie (Veeder) Marotz of Watertown,
South Dakota
Born 1950

It is 1958 and I am riding in my dad's bakery delivery truck. We are stopping at most of the little "Mom and Pop" groceries all over Watertown with our fresh baked goods. Each one of the groceries was so unique and the penny candy in the glass jars always appealed to this eight year old. Our delivery stops included these groceries: Belatti, Brewster's, Graham HiWay (Kemps) Home Grocery, Hunter's, Linden Park, Reliable and Star Grocery, and also Skagg's Uptown Grocery.

I am the oldest of four kids, so my dad is okay to trust me alone in the truck while he pulls the large silver trays out of the back of the truck loaded with fresh baked goods, all hand-wrapped and sealed with red twists. He usually gave me a penny to spend at the store of my choice and I usually chose a Tootsie Roll. They were so big back then.

Back at Ozzie's Bake Shop on 7th St. S.E., my mom (Fran) is busy waiting on customers, packaging bread and rolls, and frosting cakes and donuts while watching my three younger siblings—Mike, age six, Gary, age four, and Cindy, age two. Mom and Dad started their day at 3:00 A.M. Dad would mix the dough for bread and rolls in the largest mixer named "Big Bertha." One of their largest orders was

Vickie's dad's delivery truck

Vickie's dad, Ozzie

250 dozen buns, each one rolled out by hand by our dad. Mom would carefully put the bread through the slicer after it had cooled and then wrap it on the spot. They baked and decorated many wedding and birthday cakes, fried donuts, and baked rolls every day.

They were members of the Watertown Baking Association along with Balsiger and Oven Gold bakeries. They owned and operated Ozzie's Bake Shop from 1954-1968. As the neighborhood kids grew into teens, they would work at the bakery and our first and longtime employee was Janice Stricherz.

It was a good life. The neighbors were great and faithful customers and the 7-Up/Pepsi workers bought rolls on their lunch breaks every day. There was a screen door on the back door of the bakery and the neighbors (mostly dirty barefoot kids) would be most welcome to come in and watch the everyday baking and frying of the fresh donuts. Mom or Dad would place a fresh, warm donut hole

Vickie's mom, Fran

rolled in sugar into each little extended mud pie-making hand. Life was good at Ozzie's Bake Shop.

Saturday Night Baths and Wringer Washers
By Carol Pevestorf of Huron South Dakota
Born 1932

I was born in 1932 (the dirty thirties) and lived on a farm with my parents and three older brothers. When I was six months, my dad died from a busted appendix. There was no electricity in our house, with the exception of a wind charger that charged three large batteries in the cellar. When the batteries were charged, due to some wind, we could listen to the radio for the news and maybe a program such as Ma Perkins, The Lone Ranger, the Neighbor Lady, and some musicians. We had two wells—one pumped water for the animals in a stock tank, and the other was drinking water. We also used this water for laundry and bathing, it had a hand pump on it and I pumped plenty of water and hauled it in the house in buckets. Afterwards we would have to haul it out, also.

Saturday was bathing night. We hauled the water in and heated it up on the stove in a boiler, then poured in a round metal tub. I was the youngest, so I got to bath first. Then it was my mom's turn and then more water was added to that and my brothers bathed. They had to haul it out. Sunday night, water was carried in and put in the boiler, ready to be heated up for washday on Monday. The first washer that I remember was one that was run by a gasoline engine that had to be exhausted outside or we could be gassed. Then the next one had its own engine. They both had wringers and always two tubs for rinsing. At that time, you started the wash with the whites, the colored clothes, and then the dark stuff and ending with the rugs. We hung them out all the time, even in the winter.

Being we had no running water, of course there was no indoor bathroom. During the winter nights I got to use the chamber pot, but all the rest of the time we all had use the outdoor biffy with the wind blowing up as you sat there. Believe me; it was mighty cold sitting there in the winter!

The chores were many on the farm. The eggs had to be gathered, and if you were lucky, the old hen would let me put my hand under her to get the egg without getting pecked. I remember helping my brother pick corncobs up in the hog pen. Mother would use them in the cook stove. When I got a little older, I helped with the milking, I had a pet cow, and in the summer, we always milked them outdoors. If you didn't milk her, first she would bother the other cow until she was milked. Of course, in the cold weather they were put inside to be milked.

I attended a country one-room schoolhouse for eight years. The first three grades were in one schoolhouse and the teacher boarded with us. She and I drove a horse and buggy to school. Then the rest of the grades were in three different districts. I walked home most of the time in the nice months, which were around two to three miles. Most of the time at recess we played hopscotch and "kitten ball" in the summer and "fox and goose" in the snow. Just about every Saturday we would go to town, which was about nine miles. Mother would take the eggs and cream to the creamery to be sold and then go to the grocery store for the week's food. She had a big garden, so she mostly bought sugar, flour, yeast and fruit.

After shopping, we would go to the movies. Usually on Saturday, they would run westerns, like Roy Rogers, Gene Autry and Tim Holt. It cost 12 cents to go. By now, my brothers were either married, in the service, or working out, so my mom had a farm sale and moved to town so that I could go to high school. That was the first time to live in a house with electricity and running water. It was also the first time to have milk in a bottle that the milkman delivered.

I wasn't around television until I got married in 1951. Also at time, we had a rotary phone. The most famous person at time was Herbert Humphrey; he owned a drugstore in our town. When I was small and also in high school, my mother made all my dresses and even coats on an old Singer treadle sewing machine. The toys I remember playing with were mostly paper dolls, and I would also cut them out of old catalogs.

Herding cows on the ditches was another chore I did. I would start them out and then walkway ahead. When they caught up with me, I would turn them around to go back home. That would take about two or three hours. I also remember in the winter the boys would put up ice in the icehouse. They would go to the river, cut big chunks of ice with a saw, take it home, and pack it in an icehouse with straw around each chunk. Then, in the summer, we would use it in the icebox in the cellar and also to make homemade ice cream. Seems like we had lots of blizzards and snowstorms back in the '30s and '40s. I know my brothers made a cave in a big snow bank one year; that was fun to play in.

A Country School, Waverly #1 and its Teacher, Jennie Hagen
By Anna (Hansen) Chesser of Canby, Oregon
Born 1937

This is a tribute to a one-room country school, Waverly #1 and its teacher, Jennie Hagen (Mrs. Duane Roehr). Several years ago, many of Miss Hagen's students received this wonderful letter and old photos from her. In her letter, she related her thoughts and memories of her first four years of teaching at Waverly #1, which led to a fulfilling career of many years in education. The following is the letter written to all of the first year students at Waverly #1:

In May of 1949, I graduated from Britton High School. I went to Lambert Bauer, chairman of the school board, and applied for the job of teaching Waverly #1. I remember his asking, "There are some big boys there; are you sure you can handle them?" Why, when you are 18 you can handle anything, so I answered, "Yes, I think I can." I was hired at a salary of $125.00 a month, I think.

I attended Northern State College for ten weeks, which qualified me to teach rural school. In the fall of 1949, I began teaching Waverly #1. There were 16 to begin with: Marian and Bernetta Bauer; Anna, Eva, and Ollie Hansen; Karen Hartman; Marianne, James and Karen Mettler; Lois, Caroline, Marjorie and Steven Price, and the three Fisher boys. The last two years, Larry and Charlotte joined us.

I remember leaving home the first day of school and running back to tell my mom, "Mom, I'm scared." She said, "Go ahead and do the best you can." And so, I became a teacher.

But the strange thing was—I was the one who learned from all of you. I remember going to Celina Gronseth, our County Superintendent of Schools and saying, "I don't have the foggiest idea of what I'm doing." She smiled and replied, "We sometimes find that those who think that become our best teachers." I grew to love teaching. I still do and when I find time, I still sub in Britton Elementary. I taught for four years in Waverly: 1949-1950, 1950-1951, 1951-1951, and 1952-1953. I then taught Waverly #4, Spain School, and Hamilton School. I taught first grade in Britton for four years and quit when our first son Richard was born. Richard died at 21 months and our second son Alan was born in 1972. When Alan was in the third grade, Britton Elementary began asking me to sub kindergarten through sixth grades, Special Ed. and music. I subbed for a total of 16 years straight. For a few years, I averaged about three days a week.

The children I teach all become very important to me, but there has always been a special place in my heart for all of you at Waverly #1, the first school I taught.

Anna, Eva, and Ollie Hansen in 1948

I did some good teaching and some not-so-good teaching. I hope that you will forgive me for all my errors. I also hope that you have some happy memories as I do of our time together. The Valentine and Halloween parties, the school programs, the baseball and other games we played, the school picnics, the Y.C.L. conventions and just being together. How proud I was of all of you when we went to the county Y.C.L and you all knew the songs and all behaved so well! Would you believe I still have some of the artwork that you did? Our country schools are now a part of our history. I still believe that some good things came from our rural schools and that we lost something good when they had to close.

I do not have any pictures of our first year together. I think that I could not afford a camera that year. I hope that you will enjoy the pictures as much as I have as I have taken a trip down Memory Lane.

I would love to hear from you as to your families and the life you now lead. To me, you will always be a special group of people. I forgot to add that the Fordham boys, Leonard, Donald, and John were a part of our school the last year.

Special thoughts and love to you all,
Jennie (Miss Hagen) Roehr

Waverly #1 School

The Waverly schools in Marshall County, South Dakota were built between 1884 and 1890. Our school, Waverly #1, closed in 1959. It was sometimes in earlier years known as the Bauer School. My sisters and I attended country school at Waverly #1 as children and Miss Hagen was one of our teachers for several years. Reading her letter brought back a lot of memoires of our country school days and a special teacher and later on a good friend. What a challenge at 18 teaching children ages six through 18 must have been! Classroom teaching was a full day, but her day also included many other responsibilities and duties. She would need to arrive early before the children to get the potbellied coal stove heated up on a cold South Dakota morning, as the school had no insulation or storm windows. My teacher in the fourth grade Eleanor Severson burned a hole in her dress as she leaned too close to the stove. She had to wear her coat the rest of the day. We did get an oil-burning stove in 1948.

Miss Hagen always greeted us every morning with a smile, ready to begin the day teaching us to read, write, and all other subjects as we progressed in grade levels. She found time to join her students at recess for games and activities. Recess was time for games like Pump-Pump-Pull-Away, Annie-I-Over, and softball games. We had a small entrance to the one-room school where our coats were hung and the water cooler kept. We could play hopscotch there in the winter months and a lot of games on the blackboard like Hangman's Noose and Tic-Tac-Toe.

When you needed to use the outhouse, you had to sign out on the blackboard, which ran the full length of the front of the school. Occasionally two students would be outside as only one signed out. Once noticed by the teacher, they could be found outside playing on the swing set and in trouble. It was hard to play some games outside at recess because of such a difference in ages and sizes between first and eighth graders, as there were always some big boys.

We had basket and pie socials. A lot of mothers were known as good cooks and pie makers. The bidding went up on these pies and baskets and the school got more money for some much-needed items. The pies and baskets were eaten at the school and the student whose mother brought them had to sit with the buyer.

Every morning started with the Pledge of Allegiance to the flag and a song. We participated in many Y.C.L. (Young Citizens League) projects. A small bookcase stood in back of the room and every couple of weeks the county superintendent of school would come by with new books to read.

The Christmas program was the highlight of the year. A makeshift stage was made with yards of blue cotton print made in to curtains that were hung on a wire across the front of the classroom. After practicing for weeks on skits, songs, and poems, we were ready for the big production. The small school was filled to capacity with anxious and proud family members ready to watch their children perform. The night ending with the appearance of Santa Claus who passed out candy for all.

A classmate, Wayne Fisher, reminded me of this story. One winter when he and his brother were helping his dad haul hay from the haystack to the barn, they found a hibernating gopher in the haystack. They picked it up and left it outside until the next morning. It was Monday and still hibernating, so of course, what fun it was to take it to the school and put it in the teacher's desk drawer! By noon, the school was starting to warm up

and the gopher warmed up enough to start stirring. The teacher heard something in her desk drawer and opened it up where upon the gopher jumped out and scared her to death. Needless to say, she knew exactly who would have done that. Wayne knew he was in trouble when she told his dad.

We would also like to honor other past teachers from Waverly #1 from 1943 to 1957. They include: Mrs. Roy (Alma) Anderson, Stella Hildreth, Lucille Mitchell, Jennie Hagen, Mrs. Ambrose (Eleanor) Gronseth, Mary Ann Johnson, Dorothy Debele, Lena Eisenlar, and Mrs. Frank (Cora) Jaspers.

Families in the area who had children attending school were the Morris, Junker, Bauer, Price, Mettler, Fisher, Hansen, Orr, Hartman, Fordham, Martin, and Thayer families. School board members for a number of years were Albert Bauer, Mrs. Ed (Helen) Carlson, and Art Jones. Waverly #1 closed in 1959. It still stands lonely and deserted in Waverly Township. Its walls are no longer filled with voices and laughter of children and dedicated teachers who started them all on their paths of education. The era of country schools and its teachers have now ended. I hope this glimpse into the past will bring back memories of your own schools and special teachers.

My Story
By Ruby Johannsen of Huron, South Dakota
Born 1933

I was born on January 3, 1933 at home near Carpenter to Otto Richard McMillan and Hannah Christina Iverson McMillan. I was named Ruby Lillian McMillan. Dr. Fleeger delivered me at the house. My Aunt Carolina helped with the delivery. That house was known as the Baker's Farm. Later we moved to my Grandparents Iverson's home built in 1919-1920. My parent rented the home after my grandparents died within a couple months of each other. My grandmother (Anna Bergette Saboe: 1859-1934) had gone blind from glaucoma. I don't remember my grandparents, as they died shortly after I was born. (Tollef Iverson: 1857-1934) was born in Sand, Norway. He came to the United States when he was 17 as a sailor but then jumped (left) ship and stayed in the States. I was born with brown hair and blue eyes. My hair soon became blond and my eyes brown. My family included at that time: Florence Albertha (11), Charles (Bud) Richard (9), Eugene (Gene) Edward (7), Irwin Leonard (4), Keith Thomas (2), Mom and Dad, and assorted pets, as well as the normal farm animals: cows, horses, sheep, pigs, turkeys, chickens, guineas, ducks and geese.

One of the stories my family told was I picked up just about every germ that came along. Of course, my older brothers and sister brought everything home to me from school. We lived in the basement of the house because it was too hot and dusty upstairs. It was the "Dirty Thirties"—no rain, lots of dust, no crops, and lots of grasshoppers. I guess I liked to eat the grasshoppers, I am told.

One of my earliest childhood memories is of going to Aunt Carolina's for Christmas dinner and it was always cold because she wore long underwear and was always warm. She wasn't a very good cook, but everyone brought something to eat. I started school at age four. I remember my early school days as fun but hard. I went to school (first grade) because the teacher wanted two neighbor girls (Rhoda and Sylvia Tschetter) and me in the same class. They were five and six. But I enjoyed school. They moved away when we were in the third grade. Their father was a preacher.

The things I liked best about school then were that it was fun to learn and I had someone to play with. I went to a one-room schoolhouse. I remember one time the weather was so bad they had to come after us and the teacher had to stay at our house several days. We were only about a quarter mile from the school. We lived at the big house my grandfather had built (Tollef Iverson). I am told he went back to Norway while the house was being built. Before then, they lived in a small shanty (two rooms). He added two bedrooms at one time. There were seven children. They used trundle beds (a bed slid under another bed). One bedroom was for the girls, and one for the boys.

I liked to read and draw as a pastime. My sister (Florence) was 11 years older than me, so we didn't have much in common. Then there were four boys. Keith was just two years older than me. Then Lyle (six years younger)

and Vivian (eight years younger) came along. I really just babysat and played with them. Some of the games and toys we had were checkers, cards, jump rope, dolls and paper dolls. At school, we played ball, Pum, Pum Pull Away, and Giant Strides (chains on a tall pole. We would run around the pole and swing.) That game is probably too dangerous today.

I remember our home as busy and fun with lots of work on the farm. I was spoiled. The boys had to work harder. We all rode horses. We all had chores to do. Milk cows, feed the animals, and gather the eggs. On Sundays, we would play softball with my cousins from across the road. The only girls around were the two Tschetter girls, but they lived a mile away. The only books I had were Brenda and Girls Scouts that I can remember. I only remember one movie we went to: "The Little Colonel" starring Shirley Temple. Mom played the piano some and we sang some; I don't remember what, but it was hymns mostly. Irwin and I took some piano lessons. Florence took lessons, too, before the depression and all the money ran out. Florence started high school, but there wasn't enough money to keep her going. Bud and Gene each started high school but didn't continue.

I remember there were school plays at Christmastime. All the neighbors came and we all had a good time. I was very shy. I remember my teenage years as happy. Going to visit friends, staying overnight and on weekends. We went to Carpenter on Saturday night and had a chance to visit with other people; that was the highlight of the week. We took eggs to town and traded them for groceries.

The Depression: 1930-1936
In the Depression years, everyone was in a bad way. No one had much for money to buy food and other things. It wasn't bad enough that no one had any money, but there was dust everywhere and no water. There weren't any crops—nothing but dust and wind blowing it around. The women had to try to take care of the kids and the men had to work on the WPA (Workmen's Projects Administration). They had to go to work in the morning, taking teams of horses and wagons if they had them, then they had to drive them home at night. The men and the animals were both tired, then back to work in the morning. They worked on roads, dams, and anything else the government could

think of. They didn't get much pay, about a $1.00 a day, more if you had a team of horses and a wagon. Our dad was one of them. This was how they fed their family.

There also were people who were artists or craftsmen that couldn't work on the roads, so they were paid to paint pictures, or as at the Dakotaland Museum, make model buildings. At least they did something to earn their pay so they could feed their families.

This went on until about 1936-37 before it started to rain, the dust went away, and they started to get crops again and start to make a living. I don't remember any of this, but I remember that we lived in the basement of the big house because it was too hot and dusty upstairs. Mostly I remembered that there were shelves and dishes in the basement.

Florence said that when all this started, "She was just creeping and she got so dirty on the floor. We tried to keep Ruby's clothes clean, but couldn't. It was really hard to go to school, and it got so dark with dust that we could hardly read. We were glad it snowed so the dust didn't blow. You didn't have to worry about what dress you were going to wear; if you had a clean one you wore it. As soon as I got out of the eighth grade, I started working for the neighbors, cooking for threshers and taking care of kids. Anyway we learned how to work for a living."

Florence worked for Floyd's mother, cleaning house and helping with washing etc. She later married Floyd on January 3, 1941 in Watertown. They always teased Floyd about wearing two pairs of socks to keep his feet warm. (They always wore silk socks for dress then, so they were not very warm.) But he wore a blue on the outside on one foot and brown on the outside of the other foot.

They lived in the same house as his mother until her death. They separated two rooms off from the rest of the house and Rose Batien lived there. Of course, they took care of her. I am sure this was not easy, but you did what you had to back then. After her death, they finished raising their family of four boys there. Eventually they moved to Willow Lake where Floyd worked for the school as janitor and Florence was the school cook for a number of years. Florence now lives in Watertown an apartment complex.

Christmas 1934 in Bristol
By Mary Anne Clark of Groton, South Dakota
Born 1931

I was three years old when I got my first dolls, and I have loved dolls ever since. It was near Christmastime, and I was still recuperating from a near-death illness of scarlet fever and my father had been laid off from his railroad job. We faced a bleak Christmas, when one afternoon the three baby dolls appeared on our doorstep! They didn't come in a basket with a note, but they were in a doll crib (on wheels), along with a tea table and doll dishes and other toys.

I acquired other dolls during my childhood (and better days) and when I was older, we passed on this same gift to another little girl in hard times. However, we did keep one doll. I still have her, and my mother (who died at age 98) sewed her a little dress on her old treadle sewing machine (at age 96) and wanted the doll's face repaired. I had the doll restored and she proudly wears the simple little dress my mother made for her.

I'm sure we had a wonderful Christmas that year long ago. My parents talked of it many times. God gave me a second chance

Mary Anne's mother, Lena Erwick in 1934

on life, someone gave us the most wonderful gift of the dolls, and my dad got enough work so that we never had to go on government relief—something these proud Norwegian immigrants did not want to do.

We never found out who left this most memorable Christmas gift on our doorstep. It remains a mystery to this day. I named my little doll "Dolly" but she is really a "Look-alike Patsy." She is a reminder to me to be more aware of the needs of others, while we are so blessed. Many years later, I became a porcelain doll maker and also an antique doll collector. "Dolly" started it all.

Mary Anne Clark and her dolls

Sunshine Days and Soft Summer Evenings
By Muriel Reeve Sorbel of Yankton, South Dakota
Born 1949

I spent my summer vacations growing up at Medicine Lake in northeast South Dakota near Florence. I have great memories of long, hot summer days swimming and playing in the water. Not only did we swim, but we made

rafts of boards and car tire inner tubes. We packed our picnic lunches and paddled around "the point" to a huge rock where we spreads out a blanket and ate our lunches. When I say "we", I mean my cousins, Doug and Darla, who would come spend the summer with us, and my brother, Dallas. My brother, who is redheaded and freckled, almost always won the prize for most sunburned. I never remember putting on sunscreen as a kid fifty years ago, but I guess I do remember being sunburned occasionally.

The cousins, brother, and I would get up in the morning and put on our swimsuits. We would be in the water playing right after breakfast, so why get dressed in play clothes, only to change to swimsuits right away? We would play in the water games we made up or build sand communities. We would wait for the local folks to come swimming after a day of baling hay or harvesting crops. We got so we recognized family cars and pickups coming down the road to go swimming.

I have fine memories of sunshine days and cool evenings of playing under the yard lights and under the lilac bushes. To this day, the smell of lilacs brings back pleasant memories of soft summer evenings.

While we were all having fun, my grandparents were operating the summer resort. There were dances with real bands in the dance hall. My grampa would let me help him sprinkle sawdust on the floor so folks could slide their feet smoothly over the wooden floor while dancing. I always had to go to bed before seeing the adults dance the waltz or the polka, but the dance hall windows would be open, catching a lake breeze, and I used to fall asleep listening to the music.

My grandfather played the violin, which we called his fiddle. With a certain amount of begging, he would play his fiddle. I remember "Blueberry Hill." Besides fiddling and arranging dances, my grandfather organized community auctions. Local farmers and others would bring household goods and farm equipment to the resort on a Saturday or Sunday and, as I remember, my grampa would hire an auctioneer. How I loved to hear the auctioneer "sing" his tune!

Another memory of the summer is of my grandmother renting swimsuits and towels to folks who came to the resort. Not everyone owned a swimsuit then or there was the occasional "spur of the moment" swim. She would mend and wash the swimsuits, buying a few new ones each year to have varied sizes. When someone needed a suit, she would find the right size, hold it up, and say, "I'm sure this will fit." People just were not so picky then about looks, as they just wanted to swim.

Ed, When Will It Snow?
By Marlyce Peterson of Willow Lake, South Dakota
Born 1933

Some say he was a bum, a hobo who rode the rails to the Dakota prairie. Others said he'd studied to be a priest, but gave up his calling when he fell in love, only to have his sweetheart jilt him. Others said his wife and little girl died and in his heartache, he lost himself to the prairie.

I would prefer the latter, because I was the little girl Ed became fond of, and I cherish the memory of a man every one called Dirty Ed. The nickname was appropriate because he gave the appearance of a tramp, yet Ed Kelbough was a very intelligent man.

Through a child's eyes, Ed was part mystery, and he was fascinating to me. I liked him and he liked me.

Ed moved into a vacant building, which adjoined my father's land. He drove his team and buggy to town, crossing our pasture. From the top of his voice, I could hear him singing, "spring time in the Rockies" as he passed our gate. I remember standing by the well, wearing red and white pinafore dress with my blonde pigtails blowing in the Dakota wind and waving to Ed until the melody disappeared in the breeze.

Ed shoveled grain for my father at harvest time. It was my task to run across the pasture to tell Ed to come to work. I remember his shanty, not because of how dirty it was but how bare it was. It contained only a stove, a dark cupboard, a table, one chair, and his bed.

My mom packed a huge basket of lunch for the harvest crew, but I got to bring lunch to Ed. He loved ripe tomatoes, so I always took two of the biggest ones to him. While he ate them, I skipped rope in the alleyway of the granary. He told me of faraway places in my geography book.

Once when he was shoveling grain, he was so hot and thirsty so we went to the windmill for water. I ran ahead and filled the dipper with cold water. Handing it to Ed, who was dripping with sweat, I said out of the blue, "Ed, when will it snow?" He laughed from the very bottom of him and said, "You ask when it's going to snow on the hottest day of the year!"

In South Dakota inevitable, it snowed. As a child, I though the whole world must be covered with snow, just as mine was.

When the snow was too heavy for Ed to walk to town, he would come to our place for supplies. He'd carry a gunnysack over his shoulder. My mom would fill the sack with coffee, potatoes, rutabagas, beans, and slabs of salt pork, and my dad put in some chewing tobacco.

I don't know if Ed had a calendar, but he came at dusk on a snowy Christmas Eve. There were ten children in our family so the house was full of gaiety. We were singing carols and getting ready for the traditional lute fish supper. Ed was out of coffee, and Mom filled his sack, adding a few extra goodies. Actually, we had very little, but Mom always managed to give. I realize now even love freely given returns a hundred fold.

I asked if he would like to stay and eat with us, but he declined, saying he wanted to get home before dark.

His mittens lay steaming on the giant hard coal stove. I ran to get them, stopping to see the reflection in the panes of icing glass. Gazing back was a blonde, dimpled little girl and behind her stood a be-whiskered old man. I turned, pigtails swinging, handed him the mittens and said, "Merry Christmas, Ed." He left.

I ran to the window to wave goodbye to him. I saw Ed standing with the snow falling down all around him, looking back at the lighted house. He brushed his arm across his face, then turning, he pulled his worn coat tighter around him and walked into the night.

Postscript: Ironically, Ed died in a state hospital on a Christmas Eve. No one knew of his death and no one came to his burial. The plot of ground where Ed is buried is unmarked, but every spring there grows a tomato plant.

Child of the Prairie
The roses still grow in profusion
Untended.

Yellow petals scatter in the wind
A reminder of days gone by.

She was young then with yellow gold hair
She and the yellow rose were the only spot
Of beauty here on the lonely prairie.

Then, a girl child with a
Wisp of yellow hair came.
Her eyes, a dreamy blue.
Reflected skies she gazed upon.

Then, prairie's hand, knotted, bony
Grasped, until Life was gone.

He left knew prints where he knelt
Upon the snow…vowed to hate this land
That took all that he had loved.
Then he shuffled into the log house
Where wind and love would touch him no
more.

Now, remaining on the prairie
Upon a grassy knoll
Are two hand-carved crosses
And a yellow rose
To scatter petals in the wind.

Linoleum Floor Coverings and Crocheted Bedspreads

By Janet Hoglund Johnson of Lake Norden,
South Dakota
Born 1937

Such happy memories I have as the fifth out of six children. Here are some things I remember:

Horses – We had three horses on the farm when I was little in the '40s. One was used for riding. I think Gene was the only one who rode May. We also had two big plow horses that were used during threshing at harvest time. They pulled the wagons and hayracks to pick up the grain shocks. I remember Sander, who was the man who we called the spike pitcher.

Daddy and three or four other farmers would work together during threshing time. Shirley and Janet would help in the grain wagon. We kept the grain shoveled to the front of the wagon as it came out of the threshing machine spout. I think we thought it was fun.

Ha.

We also helped in the fields to shock the grain. We brought water with us, which we kept in quart jars and placed in the shock to keep it cool.

When the linoleum floor coverings in the dining and living rooms got worn out, Mother would get new rugs downstairs and put the old ones upstairs in the bedrooms. She painted them a color that would match the cream/white crocheted bedspreads that covered a brightly colored sheet, which set off her wonderful handiwork. Beautiful! She would then take many different shades of paint and, using the brush, she'd stipple paint on the whole rug. That's the only kind we ever had at our humble farmhouse. I just saw a rug you could buy today that had that type of pattern on it.

Mother always wore bib-type aprons, which she had made. If company came to the house, the housewife would always have extras so they could put on clean ones, never to be caught with a dirty apron. Her aprons were mostly made out of flour sacks. When we were little, our dresses were also made out of feed sacks. They bought flour and feed in 50-pound cloth sacks and were careful to pick out materials that matched.

As little children, we would build tents over the clotheslines with sheets and handmade quilts. We would lie out in the grass and look up at the sky and watch the stars, waiting for shooting stars and trying to find the Big and Little Dipper and the Milky Way. The Northern Lights were frequent and colorful; they were very beautiful, to watch. I remember going up on the hill to watch them to see them better.

Daddy always had many cattle, pigs, chickens, ducks, and turkeys. The pigs and our wonderfully patient Mother didn't get along too well, as they would root under the fences and get into her vegetable and flower gardens. In the spring, we kids would help when they moved the cattle from the barns down the dirt road to the pasture, which was on the land by the creek a mile away. Daddy raised a lot of turkeys, too. Jo Ann, Shirley, and I also helped with the turkey chores. We had black and blue marks on our bodies where they picked at the medal rivets on the pockets of our jeans.

We did not get electricity on the farm until

1945 when our area welcomed the REA. In earlier years, there were kerosene lamps, gas lanterns, and an Aladdin lamp for the house. It was our job to keep the globes clean and shiny. A kerosene lantern was used for the many trips to the barn, especially in the middle of the night during calving season.

There were always pets: We had one goat, which we claim butted Mother and pushed her over. Always there was a dog, and many cats, which provided us with a good supply of kittens. They were kept outside except for one mother cat who usually managed to get in the house and have her kittens upstairs in a box in Mother's closet.

When we were kids, Daddy planted large fields of potatoes. I remember him hiring boys to come and help hand pick the potatoes. I suppose the horses pulled the wagons. My memory is that Daddy did have a potato picker for one year, but the next year he no longer planted this crop. I remember large trucks coming in the yard to haul the potatoes to potato houses for sale. Ruby remembers going with Dad to Bryant to sell potatoes. It was in the hard times, and nobody had any money to buy them so he ended up giving them away.

Shirley and I spent a lot of time out in the corncrib playing house. We made make-believe rooms and, of course, made meals out of corn, mud, leaves, weeds or anything else that would be around. A lot of hamburgers made with mud pie between two lilac leaves were sold in our restaurant. Corn cobs picked from the pigpen were used in the kitchen stove for heat. We learned to do that chore early while the cobs were nice and clean and dry.

Mother did a lot of sewing and crocheting. Her hands were always busy. When we were little children, she made most of our clothes and also taught us to sew on the treadle Singer sewing machine. She made our sister, Carol's, wedding dress out of heavy white slipper satin. It had a long train and the tiniest hand-covered satin buttons all down the back and up the tapered long sleeves. Jo Ann, Janet, and Shirley all wore this same beautiful gown. Mom and Daddy would drive us to school every day, morning and afternoon. They would give us a nickel to buy a candy bar after school. Even there, she had her crochet hook with her in her black purse.

Every once in a while Daddy would sit down and play the fiddle. He also played the piano. Songs like "Oh My Darlin, Oh My Darlin". Get the picture? Mother and Dad saw to it that we all had piano lessons. One of the best times, almost every day, were when we gathered around the piano, with our sister, Jo Ann, playing for us, and we all sang as loud as we wanted to. This was also a memorable part of our many lively cousin and neighborhood parties.

One of the fun things we did as kids was to go down to the creek and go swimming with the Koisti kids. I, for one, did not enjoy picking the blood suckers off our skin when we got through swimming. Mother never took her eyes off of us when she took us there and also to the nearby lake. "Don't go out too far, girls," she would say over and over. We also would go down to the creek for ice skating. Sometimes there would be enough ice behind the barn where we could use our strap-on ice skates. A friend, Joan Jorgenson Jacobsen, reminded me of the time Mother brought us corn on the cob with melted butter when we were roller skating up in the haymow of the new barn. Wonderful memories!

After the snow storms we always had huge snow banks in the yard by the lilac bushes. We would dig long tunnels in the snow and play until we got too cold. Sometimes the snow got so deep we could almost touch the top of the telephone pole. That's when the Model A car had to be left at the end of the driveway and we walked home the rest of the way. We remember carrying our many groceries, along with a live Christmas turkey that we had won in our small town Saturday afternoon Christmas drawing. Our oldest sister, Ruby, told us that during the terrible, hot dry years, she rode a horse across our big dry lake, lake Norden. Our dad said that's when they played neighborhood baseball almost every day, as there were no crops or fields to work.

Wash day was a hard day's work for Mother. First, she had to haul the water from the well to the house and then heat it on the kerosene stove. In the winter, she would hand all the wash on clotheslines that were strung between nail pounded into the top of the door frames. Can you imagine?

I could go on and on…

My Dad and Mother

By Alice M. Olson of Aberdeen, South
Dakota
Born 1930

Greetings! I would like to tell you about my dad, Frank Fletcher LaDue. Frank was born February 22, 1888 to Frank Albert LaDue and Clara Albertine Fletcher of Sisseton Township of Marshall County.

My dad's dad was born in Brockton, New York and came to Sisseton Township in 1883. His mom came over in 1884. They met in South Dakota and fell in love. They were married in 1885. Their families back East were very upset that they came to South Dakota. They were afraid that they would be scalped by Indians, as they had heard stories of such happenings! They, however, were intrigued by the state and were ready for adventure.

My dad's parents were well educated. In fact, his mom received the Noyes Medal, which is the highest honor of scholarship offered in her school. She became an excellent teacher and was anxious to make a difference in education in South Dakota. In 1884, she ran for the position of County Superintendent of

Frank and Hattie Marske LaDue in 1917

Schools on the Independent Ticket and won. She didn't care for the views of either the Republican or Democratic Party at that time. She served two terms, spending long hours holding workshops and helping teachers in any way she could to promote good education in Marshall County when the county was young.

Dad's mom had a sister, Lillian Moore, back east who taught in Dr. Howe's School for the Blind. She taught Laura Bridgeman and her best friend, Ann Sullivan, taught Helen Keller.

One weekend, Lillian Moore and Ann Sullivan came to visit Dad's mom, Clara. Ann Sullivan had brought Helen Keller along. Helen Keller was so excited over the baby and wanted to hold him. Ann placed my dad in her arms, and Helen got to hold him for a short time. Afterwards she bragged that she had babysat! That was a pretty exciting time for my dad's family. Who knew at that time how famous Helen Keller would be?

Another thing I would like to tell you about my dad is when I was going to country school and how my dad often took me the five miles with horses. A neighbor girl, Betty Price, would walk over two miles to my place, and we would go together. On wintry, stormy days, my dad took us in a bobsled. It had an enclosed box on the front end with a window to see out of and for holding the reins.

On one stormy school day, my dad came back early to get us. Other dads had the same idea, as the weather was getting worse. Our teacher let us all go early. By the time Dad got us loaded and covered with heavy quilts, you could hardly see across the road. Betty and I were afraid but my dad said, "Don't be afraid, God is with us and Juell and Daisy know the way home." He let the reins hang loose and told the horse to go home, and they did!

My mother was so glad to see us. She thought my dad looked like Santa Claus with icicles hanging down his chin. We giggled and my dad laughed. Then he took the horses to the barn while my mother made hot cocoa for us and fed us some cookies while we huddled around the stove to warm up. Later, Dad came in and got some hot cocoa, too. He told us girls not to eat all of the cookies, as he needed the most! Betty's mom stayed overnight. The storm lasted for five days.

Another important person I would like

Miss Lillian Fletcher's kindergarten class

you to know is my mother, Hattie Marske, and later Hattie LaDue, because she married my dad. She came over to America on a boat when she was three years old. Her parents were looking for a better, safer life here. They settled in the little town of Andover, South Dakota in a small, three-bedroom house across the railroad tracks. She had three sisters and four brothers. In those days, people made do. The girls had one bedroom and the boys another.

Ever since my mother was little, she loved music, especially piano. She never missed Sunday school on Sunday and would always sit in the front row so she could watch where the teacher put her fingers on the keys. Her parents didn't have a piano and didn't like noise, so she would wait until they took their daily nap, and then she would quietly leave the house, cross the railroad tracks to the little church, and practice and practice until she had them learned perfectly! She had excellent pitch and great determination. From her daily visits to the little church, she learned to play the piano beautifully.

My mother excelled in her schoolwork by

Alice (LaDue) Olson and her husband, Bernard

getting straight A's and going to college and becoming a teacher!

South Dakota was a great state. Our ancestors knew it. With great determination, a good work ethic, strong faith in God, and great love for one another, they knew they would succeed. Families in those days always helped each other, shared what they had, encouraged one another, and never, ever gave up! Church on Sunday was a must! What a great heritage we have!

Farming Along the James River
By Dvonne Pearl Shawd Hansen of Letcher,
South Dakota
Born 1934

I was born in January of 1934 on my grandparents' farm northeast of Letcher, South Dakota. My parents' names were Lyle Shawd and Vanetta Halling. Shortly after I was born, they moved north of Letcher to a ranch located on the James River, where we lived from 1936 to 1941. My father farmed with mules, and he also bought us a Shetland pony for a pet. My mother told me that during that time they received $2.90 each week as a living allowance from the government. My father also worked for the Works Project Administration and helped to build roads.

We did not have an indoor toilet and used an outhouse. I remember one time I asked to be excused from supper to use the outhouse, and when I did not return in a timely fashion, my father went looking for me. Like most children, I loved to play in the water, and he found me playing in the water with my hands. He snuck up behind me and threw me in the river. That was not very deep, but I did not know that and I was kicking and splashing for all I was worth. As you can imagine, that was the last time I did that.

In 1942, we then moved from that location to a farm that was south of the town of Cuthbert and lived there for about a year and a half. We then moved back to another ranch near the James River that was known as the Russian Ranch. A rich senator had built that place up, and it was known as Richards Landing when he finished. Eventually, he grew tired of that place and sold it to the Hutterites. At that time, it was very large and fancy and had servant's

487

quarters, exquisite living quarters. There were two bathrooms, two fireplaces, one upstairs and one downstairs, cut glass doorknobs, and a big open stairway.

When we lived there we were two miles from school, and the only road to our home was a dirt trail. Sometimes we would ride our pet Shetland pony to school, but we also were able to get a car ride to school and then we would walk home. We went fishing and swimming almost every day.

At that time, the Russian Ranch was owned by Jack Fairfield. We lived there for about a year, and then moved to another farm that was known as the Alt place. Unfortunately, the time that we spent at the Russian Ranch ended up being a very expensive endeavor because we ran our cows with Jack Fairfield's cows and they were infected with brucellosis.

Because my father knew the threshing machine, he would go to each farm and help harvest the oats, wheat, and barley. There was a good spirit in people then, and everyone helped everyone else out with threshing their crops until everything was in the granary.

We had quite a few milk cows, and all of us kids were given the responsibility of seeing that it was done properly. Not only did we have to milk the cows by hand, but we also had to use a machine that was cranked by hand that separated the cream from the milk. The milk was fed to the pigs and the calves, and some of it was set aside to use in the home. The cream was taken to Letcher and sold for cash.

Letcher also had a bandstand. This was a large open building with a roof. Every Wednesday night there was a main band that performed there, and there were also other bands that would perform too.

Chickens were a major commodity for the farm. They provided eggs to sell and meat to eat. Since there was no refrigeration, we butchered them and ate them the same day. One day we came home from school after a big rainstorm, and our parents were nowhere to be found. We decided to walk a mile to our grandparents' home and try to find them. They were checking cows in another pasture, got stuck in a washed out ditch, and ruined the car. The first thing they wanted to know was how the young chickens were doing. Unfortunately, we had not checked on them and instead of going into the brooder house for shelter, they had piled up on each other and suffocated.

It was time to move again, and we found ourselves back to life by the James River. A man came from Illinois to hunt pheasants and asked my father if he could run this ranch on the James River if the man bought it. My father agreed to the arrangement and they began a 50/50 partnership. We had a big house with running water and 32-volt electricity. There was a flow well located uphill from the house, and it conveniently ran into the house and was connected to a box with shelves that acted like a cooler. It also traveled downhill and was connected to the water tanks for the cattle and hogs. There was also a huge barn built into the side of a hill, and you could drive right into the second story. We stored all the grain and hay there. The cows and horses were kept in the lower level in two main parts, one with stalls for the horses and one with milking stanchions for the cows. The grain was conveniently stored on the second level, and there was a trap door that you could just back a wagon up to and fill it by gravity. The barn was a wonderful place to play, and we and the neighbor kids spent a lot of time there. We always had horses and colts, and it was up to us kids to break them to ride.

We went fishing for bullheads almost every day, and this became a staple food in the summer because they were so easy to catch. In the winter, we had big ice-skating parties with a large bonfire and would play with a stick and tin can. We also spent considerable time at Ruskin Park near Forestburg, roller skating and going to different dances. When it snowed in the winter, we all had two runner sleds, and we always had contests to see who could break the record of how far we could go on them.

We had to walk a mile and a half to a one-room schoolhouse. When we started high school, we still had chores to do, and we had to make sure we milked the cows before we caught the bus to go to school. By this time, we did not have to take the eggs and cream to Letcher to sell but instead the Armour Creamery would send a truck to the country to pick up the eggs and cream from different farmers.

We had a very hilly pasture where we kept the cows, and I would always saddle up a horse a couple of times a week, ride through, and check the herd out. One time I decided to cross the river with my horse by the ford. But I missed the crossing; we were in deep water and I could only see the ears of the horse, and then I decided to bail off and swim. She was walking on the bottom and eventually came out, and I got back on her and rode home. One time I was close to the area and I heard a noise while I was looking for cows to bring home, and I heard a baby pig squealing. I looked and finally found him in a hole in the ground. I retrieved the pig but was really wondering what on earth that hole was for. Later I read that the Native Americans would make these holes to store things in and then retrieve them later, which was known as a cache.

Another very popular thing we did in the summer was to have picnics. We had a spot next to the river where we used to have them. The picnic tables were placed there permanently, and we would use any excuse to have a picnic. We fished, swam, and played softball and horseshoes.

We used a dump rake to place hay in windrows to pick up with a hay buck and make a haystack. Grain had to be put in bundles and shocked and then threshed. Corn was picked with a one and two row corn picker and shelled with a corn sheller. Not much grain was sold because everyone had pigs, chickens, milk cows, stock cows, and horses to feed it to. Everyone would gather at a farm when it was time to haul manure. One person loaded the manure spreader with a loader and the rest hauled it to the fields with their manure spreaders and spread it out as natural fertilizer. Everyone plowed fields that were planted to corn as it had to be cultivated to keep down the weeds. As we usually ran two or three plows, we could get done before everyone else, and then we would go help the neighbors. All of us kids were hired out to our grandfather to walk the corn and pull out cockleburs, which was a major weed then. We earned 25 cents an hours.

Our neighborhood also started up a 4-H Club and as a result of that, I taught myself leather carving and design. As people in the neighborhood learned of my craft, I started to get orders to make name belts, purses, billfolds, and other types of leather craft. I even won a trip to Chicago for my 4-H participation.

Then the owner of the ranch died, and the heirs offered it to my father to buy. He told them that he was tired of keeping up fences on a big ranch like that, and he decided to buy the farm owned by my mother's parents instead. We did not know at that time that this big ranch along the river with the huge barn and modern conveniences was previously owned and built up by our maternal great-grandfather, James Keen.

I married Richard Hansen, who served in the Air Force during the Korean War Conflict, and we first lived in a small house near my grandparents that had no modern conveniences. My husband helped the owner of that place with various chores to pay for the rent. Furs were a very good price, and he also trapped beaver and mink to help support us. He also hunted deer and venison became a staple of our diet. Our refrigerator that first winter was a five-gallon pail that we kept outside. I cooked on a wood burning stove, and we made a heating stove out of a 50-gallon barrel. We also got some extra money when my husband received $125.00 a month to attend a school for veterans to learn how to become a good farmer. We later moved and lived on my maternal grandparents' farm, which was known as the Halling farm, until my parents bought it.

We later found a farm for sale north of Mitchell. Since my husband was a trained lineman, we thought we could afford to buy it while he worked for Rural Electric Cooperative. We sold everything we could and were able to make the down payment. We raised our four children on that farm. This farm was also located along the James River, and it also became a neighborhood place for family and friend get-togethers. We had picnics and played softball and had overnight trial rides. I am still living on that farm and running a herd of cows, and I still have my leather shop where I do all kinds of leather crafting and saddle repair and restoration.

Recess at District # 45
By Jane Jensen Pierce of Belcamp, Maryland
Born 1953

"I get Little Joe, you take Hoss," and another recess of make believe began at our one-room schoolhouse. A small mound of dirt, "the hill," became a log cabin with the

District #45 schoolhouse

top of the hill being upstairs. We had to cross a two-foot wide irrigation ditch to get to the hill, and balancing on that board to get across became another adventure. Until I was in the third grade, our little school "Bonanza," was very popular, and Little Joe was often married by the end of our fifteen-minute recess. However, we played many games to develop our athletic prowess, too. "Annie Over the Schoolhouse" was a favorite with teams chosen and each team going to an opposite side of the schoolhouse. One would throw a softball over the schoolhouse, and someone on the other side was supposed to catch it, hide it behind her back, and the whole team would run to the other side to try to touch members with the ball and capture them. I only remember once that the ball didn't quite make it over the roof, and Little Sue (there were two Sues) broke one of the windows. We played softball rather awkwardly, and something called, "Pom. Pom, pull away," which involved yanking on arms and being "safe" while standing on the cistern cover. Our playground included a swing set and teeter-totter, but I don't remember spending much time on them.

We didn't have indoor plumbing in our little school, so there were two outhouses behind the schoolhouse. Since we were a majority of girls, we had to switch which outhouse we used each year to keep things even. Heaven forbid if one forgot which outhouse was "ours" and used the boys' territory. We had a large crock for drinking water, and on Monday, we received a new paper cup to use for that week. We didn't have an easy way to wash our hands after going out to the outhouse, and perhaps that accounts for the many colds and flu we shared especially during the winter. An old oil burner heated the room, and those who had desks near the stove were usually too warm while others wished

they were closer to the heat. We all brought our lunches, and setting a jar of soup or a potato on the stove to heat during the morning was a real treat. We had three rows of desks to accommodate the ten or twelve students, and a wooden cabinet at the back of the room held our small library. A family of mice made their home in the space between windows one winter, and that made for a merry mouse chase with a broom, screeching, and climbing on desks.

Our teacher taught at least five subjects to eight grades each day, which meant forty preparations for every day of teaching. Our assignments were written on the blackboard, and we were to work while our teacher spent a few minutes teaching a particular subject to a class. We overheard all the lessons, so next year when dinosaurs were scheduled for my class, we already knew the material. I can't remember ever having homework unless I had been sick and stayed home for a day or two. Seldom was school called off because of weather, even in the deepest of winter. Parents took us to school enabling the community to gather twice a day while transporting their students. I don't recall having a telephone in the schoolhouse, but I do remember someone coming to the school to announce that the president had been shot. Our teacher turned on a small radio to hear the news, and we all heard when President Kennedy died. This was the first time I ever saw my parents cry. School was cancelled until after his funeral, and I remember watching our black and white television nonstop during those dark days.

We were all members of YCL, the Young Citizens League, and we had duties to perform each week including cleaning the erasers and sweeping the wooden floor with some smelly red compound. At least once a year, we put on a "show" for the surrounding community. This involved learning songs and memorizing plays and poems. We changed venues to the town hall in Hetland that had a real stage complete with oil-painted backdrops. Games like the "fish pond," musical chairs, and the cakewalk kept the entertainment going long into the evening. The annual visit of the county superintendent of schools provided additional excitement. This imposing dignitary came to judge us all, and we were to work diligently while we glanced at her making notes in the back of the room. We all breathed a sigh of relief when she got back into her car. We were also academically judged by the Iowa Test of Basic Skills, and I often wondered why Iowa? Weren't we in South Dakota? Would there be trick questions that only kids in Iowa would know?

We were coaxed into class by our teacher's reading to us every day after noon recess. We discovered Laura Ingalls Wilder and Nancy Drew, and our teacher was an expert at the concept of "cliff-hangers" to keep us all anxious to hear what would happen in the next day's episode. I trace my love of reading to these wonderful moments. Each school year would end with a picnic. Many times, we traveled to Lake Campbell where our families would have a potluck dinner together and roller skate for the rest of the day. One year we all rode our bikes to a nearby grove of trees for our celebration. Later we heard our mothers worrying about our teacher who was newly pregnant and shouldn't be riding a bike. I believe that was our last year at District # 45, as the concept of consolidation became a reality. Some of us were bussed into Lake Preston and others to Arlington, and our little school house began its final journey back into the prairie. The bell, books, and desks were all auctioned off, but our memories will last a lifetime.

Wilmot, South Dakota Snowstorm of March 1962
By Russell H. Payne of Kenosha, Wisconsin
Born 1937

According to *The Wilmot Enterprise* of Wilmot, South Dakota issue dated Thursday, March 15, 1962, the following snowstorm hit the Wilmot area, starting with a one-inch snowfall on Thursday, March 8. Sunday, March 11, Wilmot received three inches of snow with blizzard conditions. Five inches of additional snow fell on Monday, March 12. Schools were closed on Monday and Tuesday, March 12 and 13.

I was a teacher at the high school in Wilmot, and I was dating a young lady, Carol Howell, at that time. I was invited to her home for dinner after church on Sunday, March 11. Carol's mother, Lorene Howell was an excellent cook. Sometime in the afternoon,

the snow began and the winds came up, and blizzard conditions had arrived.

Late afternoon I decided I should leave and drive into Wilmot, three miles to town where I had a room rented. I had a good car with excellent snow tires, but my attempt to drive into town almost cost me my life. Highway 15 was only one mile south of Howells, but I barely made it halfway before I was off in the ditch. I tried shoveling around the car, but soon found that was a waste of my energy.

I knew I had to walk back to Howells, and I had enough sense to get back in the car and warm up before I headed back to their home. Cell phones were not invented yet, so the only option was for me to start walking north.

I almost did not make it back to the Howell farm, as it was very difficult to move my legs. I have no idea what the chill factor was, but it was very cold along with a hard wind. The Howell family was surprised to see me. Francis (Pete) Howell had to pull my Levis off, and they were so frozen that he leaned them against the wall, and they stood up by themselves.

I taught several subjects at Wilmot for two and one-half years, but mainly English. Other classes were economics and math, and I was school librarian, responsible for ordering and cataloguing all new material for the library. I also directed the junior class play.

Carol and I were married at the First Presbyterian Church on Easter Sunday, April 14, 1963, and we just marked fifty-one years of marriage this past April 14, 2014. We came to Kenosha, Wisconsin on our honeymoon for a job interview with the Kenosha School System. A contract was offered to me as a full-time librarian in a high school with about 3,300 students.

Carol's mother, Lorene, was not pleased that we were moving so far away, six-hundred miles, from Wilmot. Carol went to school, and became a Licensed Practical Nurse and spent several years in her profession.

I was employed in the Kenosha Unified School System for thirty-three years, and retired early due to a heart attack and open-heart surgery.

One of the memories that I remember very well of South Dakota was the date of March 11, 1962 when I came very close to losing my life to a South Dakota Blizzard.

The Farm Then and Now
By Mark Arnold of Watertown, South Dakota
Born 1948

In 1879, my great-grandfather, Stephen Killen Johnston, came to Dakota Territory. He came from Jefferson, Ohio and had also lived in several places in Iowa and Minnesota. He started living on a farm in Kilborn, Grant County, and Dakota Territory in that year.

In June 1888, he filed for a homestead farm at the Watertown Land Office. The homestead certificate was signed by President Grover Cleveland and was for a homestead of one hundred and sixty acres. He lived on the farm with his wife and children. Stephen built a home, a barn, a hog house, a granary, and two chicken coops. He planted 300 apple trees, along with rose bushes, raspberry bushes, gooseberry bushes, plum trees, and many shade trees.

As the family grew, Stephen built a second house. It was a typical two story square house with porches on three sides and an attic. A basement under part of the house had cement and stone walls. Each story had four rooms. This home was built for $2,000.00, probably quite a sum at that time. Some of the tax receipts showed that he paid $15.00 taxes some years ago, quite different from taxes that are paid for property now.

My mom lived across the road at another farm until she was seven. Then my grandfather, F. Lyle, moved the family to the Johnston farm. This was after his dad had passed away and his brother, Robert, had moved away. In the center of the farmyard was an artesian flowing well. The well was said to be 365 feet deep. It had a valve so that water could

The Johnston farmstead

be pumped to three places: a water tank by the barn, a sink in the kitchen, and the hog barn. In the early 1930s, the shallow wells on the nearby farms went dry. So many neighbors hauled water from the Johnston farm for their family and livestock use.

My grandfather farmed with horses named Bird and Nell. He plowed with the horses, as well as loaded hay and grain. My mom also helped with the farm work and used the horses. She told how when Grandpa got a John Deere tractor he pulled a grain binder behind the tractor, and my mom had to ride on the binder to trip the bundle carrier every so often. The binder would put the grain into bundles, and the bundles were lined up in rows so it was easier to shock the grain. When the shocks were cured long enough they loaded the bundles into a hay rack pulled by the horses and hauled them to the farmyard where they could be threshed for the grain. One of their neighbors had a threshing machine and threshed grain for all the neighbors. Neighbors helped each other with harvesting.

Mom told me stories about how she had to herd the cows along the ditches and in fields after grain was harvested. She told of one time when Grandpa and Grandma were working in a field away from the farmyard. The cows got out of their fence area. Mom told how she had to get her little sister in the car they had just gotten and drive to where her parents were working. Her little sister cried all the way, because she was so scared. Their parents came back to the farmyard to get the cows herded back in the fence.

Many years later, my parents were farming about four miles away from my grandparents' farm. My grandparents had retired to Milbank,

Ella Johnston feeding the chickens

and they had rented the farmland out to neighbors. This worked really well for many years until the neighbors moved to another area of the county. Then one day, my mom came home and told Dad that she had bought a farm! Surprise!

In the first few years that my parents farmed the Johnston farm, the United States Farm Administration listed the farm under Dad's name. It wasn't until years later that this farm administration recognized that women were land owners, too. It was then listed under Mom's name.

My siblings and I helped our parents farm the land and take care of the cows, chickens, turkeys, and pigs on our home place. I remember helping to pick rock every spring after the snow was gone. Those were the rocks that came up on top of the soil after natural erosion. Dad would drive the tractor and pull a trailer behind. He had a loader on the front of the tractor to dig out the bigger rocks, and the 'kids' walked by the trailer picking up the smaller rocks. This was an important job, since the rocks could damage the expensive tractors and equipment.

We never had to milk cows by hand as our mom and dad did when they were growing up. Mom told us how after the cows were milked by hand, the milk was separated with a milk separator machine. The milk was poured into a round tank on top, and a handle had to be turned at the right speed. The milk went through a set of disks, and then cream came out one spout and the remaining milk or whey came out the other spout. Milk was put into ten gallon milk cans to sell it.

Then the cream was put into a butter churn. The handle of the churn had to be turned until the cream turned to butter. Salt was added for taste. Then the butter could be put into decorative molds in one or two pound sizes. The decorative molds were made out of wood and consisted of the outer shell and a design plunger that pushed the butter out onto a plate.

Lucky for us, our parents put in milking machines and a milk room with a bulk tank so it was a lot easier for everyone. And now, butter comes in convenient packages.

The Johnston farm has remained in our family for over 126 years, and the memories of farm life will always be with us.

Visits to My Grandparents on the Farm
By Kathy Jo Haugan of Monticello,
Minnesota
Born 1962

My memories of the Martin and Goldie Rovang (maternal grandparents) farm are from the 1960s to the 1990s. The farm is still in the family and enjoyed.

Driving to South Dakota was usually a four to six hour drive, depending on where I lived. I remember driving down the road, and we played a game called, "Who can see the church steeple first?" That was the sign that we were almost to Grandma's and Grandpa's. As we drove down the gravel road from the church to the farm, we would then look for the mailbox. Grandpa had the mailbox cemented into a cream can.

Garfield Lutheran Church was very important to my grandparents. My grandparents and parents were married there. One time we were at a church function and I was a bit bored. My grandpa saw me sitting in the car. He came and sat with me and taught me a Norwegian table prayer that I can still remember:

"I Jesu navn gar vi til bords, a spise, drikke pa ditt ord. Deg Gud til aere, oss til gaven, sa vi har mat I Jesus navn. Amen."

In English this means, "In Jesus' name to the table we go, to eat and drink according to His word. To God the honor, us the gain, so we have food in Jesus' name. Amen."

When you drove down the driveway, the crab apple trees were on the north side. In the late summer or the early fall, we would pick the apples. That was always so much fun. Grandma would make all kinds of goodies with those apples. In the basement, there were shelves with quart jars of applesauce and pickled apples. She also did a lot of canning of meat and vegetables.

The barn, windmill, and garden were straight ahead. The barn was enormous and had a beauty all of its own. The cistern with a hand pump was between the corncrib and the barn. The corncrib was a wire one, which was great for climbing. The windmill was another source of attraction. In the front of the barn, Grandma had a flower and vegetable garden. Even after she was using a walker, she managed to plant her vegetable garden. She had a bag tied on her walker with the seeds.

Kathy and her grandfather, Martin Rovang in 1978

She used the hoe to make the hole. Then she dropped in the seed.

One time we got a ladder, and we climbed up on the windmill. As we got a little older, Grandpa would let us drive the car around the yard. Then we would park the car by the cistern and wash it for him. In the fall, after the grain was out of the fields and was in the granary, we used to jump off the rafters into the grain.

The house was white with a small porch on the front, and it had a pantry. Grandma kept her sewing machine in there with the kerosene stove. Grandma was always busy making something. Her sewing machine was not electric; it was a treadle sewing machine. She used foot power to run it. She made use of everything, never wasting a thing! She would remake old clothes, did patching, and spent a lot of time sewing old clothes cut into squares to make quilts.

My grandparents did not get running water or a bathroom in the house until 1974. Even at that time, my grandmother did not think it was necessary to have running water in the kitchen. So water was carried from the bathroom sink or tub. The kitchen sink always looked so funny to me, because it had holes in it for the faucet but no faucet.

In the kitchen was the cook stove used for heat and cooking. My grandma knew how many corncobs she needed to bake bread or cookies or make lefse. You could really make a lot of lefse on there. Of course, you will never eat lefse as good as that. Making lefse was a family project. Grandma usually rolled and Grandpa and the grandchildren would cook the lefse. I always admired how she could take any leftover potatoes and make lefse quickly. To this day, I only like oatmeal cookies that were made by my grandmother. I tried one once and have never had the desire to taste another one.

Grandma's beautiful upright piano was in the living room. He father bought it for her in 1896 when she was one year old. Sometimes Grandma would play for me. That piano is now in the Hayti Historical Society Museum in Hayti, South Dakota.

Off the kitchen was the bathroom. There was a throw rug, and when you removed, the rug there was a trap door to the dirt cellar. I could not believe that their cellar was dirt. The canned goods were kept in the cellar.

The stairs to the second floor were very steep. As you climbed the steps in the farmhouse to the upstairs there was another little door on the right side that led to the attic. I was small enough to fit inside the opening. My brother, Rodney, and sister, Heidi, would push me in there, which would scare me. But if you were brave, enough to move through the attic there was a bigger door that opened into the bedroom. There were two rooms upstairs. There were always a lot of quilts on the beds. Those quilts were so heavy you could hardly move, but I loved that feeling. Most months it was cold up there so the quilts were welcome.

I was a town girl, and I loved to answer the farm phone. They were on a party line. I think their phone rang two shorts (rings). Another neighbor might have one long ring or two longs or a one long a short. Grandma would let me know when I could pick the phone up. Sometimes when Grandma wasn't in the kitchen, I would pick up the phone very quietly and listen to the other conversations.

We made trips to Bryant from the farm. We went to see great aunts Isabelle and Mabel,

Kathy's family making lefse

Martin Rovang's sisters. Their houses were back to back, and I always thought it was neat that two sisters lived so close together. Mabel worked at the post office, and on her break, she would take me to the café for a soda pop. I was fascinated with the way they served it, with the glass upside down over the top of the bottle.

When I got my driver's permit, my grandparents would save all their big errands for my visit, so I could drive. We drove to De Smet to get the clock fixed. We went to Bryant or Watertown for the groceries. We would also go to Lake Norden with its drive-in, so I could have a fish sandwich and ice cream. The lake was the big meeting place. We also drove to Estelline and Lake Poinsett. I got a lot of driving time in and time alone with Grandma and Grandpa.

My grandpa was always very quiet, which was very comforting to me. He was just one of those people you just liked being around. I went to a baseball game with him and Mr. Burham in Lake Norden. My mother told me the Burham's thought I was a very special girl, because I always called him Mr. Burham. We also visited Alice Jaeger, and she would always have pudding for us. I liked all of their friends, and they were always kind to me.

My grandma showed me how to put a marble in a hot oven and then drop it in a pan of ice water; the marble would crack and would look like a piece of jewelry. Then you could glue it onto a piece of metal to make a necklace. She taught me how to embroider and to sew on her sewing machine.

We purchased eggs from another farmer. I think they were something like 20 cents a dozen. I always thought farm eggs were strange, because sometimes they were brown.

My grandparents were very good people. They were always kind to me and loved me, and I learned a lot from them. When I think of them, it is always with great admiration and love. Grandma would say, "I don't believe in luck. You are fortunate" …and I am.

The Short and Long of It
By Joyce J. Poppen of Castlewood, South Dakota
Born 1952

Being one of six siblings, life was always interesting. Being the middle child, I was the first member of our family to attend kindergarten at Estelline Public School. That same spring of 1958 my brother, Paul, 14 months older than myself, started first grade and the age rules of being born before a certain date did not apply, so I was always the youngest one in our class. The school had many memories for our family, as my mother was so blessed to be able to attend by staying in town and doing housework for an elderly lady starting in 1936. My mother graduated from Estelline High School in 1940 and I graduated from there in 1970, my husband in 1964, and my daughter was a graduate in 1994. My two older sisters attended the country school two miles from our farmhouse for three years. The small one room country school opened in 1905 and closed in 1956. At the time of its closing, it was called Hamlin County School of Estelline #9. Prior names were the Peyton School and Gilligan, named after families from the area. It was named the Peyton School when my mother-in-law, Katie Rust, attended as a young girl through eighth grade in the 1920s. In these years, the small country schools dotted the townships only about a mile apart. Teachers roomed with families close by, and thus the marriages of some of our neighbors took place with a young teacher who came looking for work.

Our driveway on the farm we lived on was a quarter of a mile long. During the winters of the late '50s and '60s we had a lot of very cold, snowy winters. On the windiest, coldest days, my father would wrap a quilt around each of us, accompanying us down the driveway so we were warm, and the wind and the cold were kept off our faces. It was my father's way of showing us love and security, and knowing that he walked along side us gave us great comfort. Such sweet memories of my father. I can still visualize in my mind those cold days. When looking out the bus window, I could see his big strides as he headed home with a pile of five big quilts in his arms, pressed against his face to keep it warm and the wind from freezing it.

I can clearly visualize myself sitting in those small desks in the kindergarten room that eventually became the lunchroom as years passed. After all, it was my first time away from the sheltered life of a farm girl. Being away from my family made it feel very strange and lonely. The days seemed so long.

Many of my classmates who I started with in those simple times of learning, coloring, and writing our names ended up graduating with me from high school. Parents were from a very agricultural setting in eastern South Dakota. Rarely

Public school in Estelline, South Dakota

did anyone move at that time. Children from town whose parents owned businesses in Estelline were also prosperous and stayed. New children moved into our small town over the course of the twelve years, but only a few ever moved away.

The most unusual changes that happened at school then verses now were something that would never happen today. My third grade teacher would always send me from the classroom and tell me to go downtown to Zafft's Grocery Store and buy her cigarettes. I was to charge them to her paper written account. Not only could teachers smoke at that time, but at the age of eight years old I also could legally buy my female teacher her tobacco of choice. Some other things were permitted, like hitting an unruly student over the top of the head with a book or making copies for the teacher away from the classroom. We were only in the third

and fourth grade but often missed class time.

It was also very common to notice that teachers did not stay for very many years. Many were only there for a year. Either very young teachers in elementary grades left to find a mate or more elderly teachers who taught the higher grades left because they couldn't handle discipline situations, especially with the boys.

The exception to that common occurrence of teachers leaving was Mrs. Mary Clarke. She was my favorite teacher and the strictest but the most memorable person. I'd have to say she was my best teacher of all. My daughter ended up having her for her sixth grade teacher as well. She always took the time every half hour after our lunch break to read us all the series of Laura Ingalls Wilder books about the prairies of Minnesota and South Dakota, near De Smet. We listened intently to her expressive ways of telling Laura's life, her trials, her joys, and her sadness. As we listened, we moved right into the story as if we were with Laura through a snowstorm, doing the chores, gardening, and preparing food to store up for the winter months. By reading to us, Mrs. Clarke taught us how to take ourselves to a different world. She did it over and over, year after year. She must have had the books memorized. We were rewarded a lot with gold stars in the sixth grade. Mrs. Clarke emphasized map drawing, her way to teach us geography. Each week, she would pick a gold star winner from all the different maps drawn. From that she picked out a number one winner who also received a full sized Snickers candy bar. They were big and cost only a nickel. I was so happy that I was a good map drawer, because a lot of weeks I would win that special Snickers bar, and it was such a treat for me.

We entered two different doors to go to our

high school classes. By the time, I attended Estelline High School it did not matter which door you went in, but at one time, it was essential that you entered the proper door. In the front of the brick school building there were two doors with steps leading up to them that were balanced across the front view equally at each side. Above them framed in doors on one side was written "Boys" and above the other door on the opposite end of the school it read "Girls." I do not know at what time entering the proper door ended, but it always seemed so strange to me, reading the words above the doors even in the '60s.

But a factor that entered our lives was when we attended school was that the girls all had to wear dresses. No jeans were allowed. If we wore jeans, it was because our mothers made us put them on underneath our dresses on cold days. I always felt so embarrassed to have to wear them. I just hated it and would run to the bathroom as fast as I could to take them off. The handbook writers never dreamed of the fact that the styles of the sixties, the short dresses and the mini skirt, were all going to hit the market. Not a dress would be knee length for a long time to come. The rulebook stated that all our dresses had to be touching the floor when we were on our knees. Being a fashion lover, I bought a skort skirt right away on my senior year. I was on my knees as if praying to God a lot that year, but my prayers were really always, about whether my skirt would meet dress code. That skort was a full six inches off the floor when I wore it that day, and being from the country they never sent me home, and I continued to wear it again and again.

A lot of us girls attended home economics and learned to sew and to cook. Fond memories flood my heart over the plaid gold and grey wool skirt I cut out and sewed on the diagonal with matching the plaids on both sides of the skirt. Another match was needed where the zipper went down the middle of the back. A solid gold colored jacket made of fabric to match the plaid with a collar, pockets, lining, buttonholes, and a perfect match on the plaid earned me an A+ on the project and it fit and felt so good on.

We enjoyed the school plays and dances, attending the Prom on our junior and senior years. We also had a dance where the girls asked the boys called the Sadie Hawkins Dance. A king and queen were picked to be crowned each year for the dance. The year I was chosen as queen, we had a blizzard, the dance was cancelled, and I never felt the thrill of being a queen for a night.

Such wonderful times and memories for a young farm girl growing up in rural eastern South Dakota. Short or long, they were all good times. My stories could go on and on.

Adventures on the Prairies
By Ellen Lehmkuhl Kub of Cheyenne, Wyoming
Born 1949

Little House on the Prairie by Laura Ingalls Wilder was one of Ellen's favorite books when she was growing up on the prairies of central South Dakota. This was because Ellen grew up on a farm/ranch south of Onida and could relate to many of Laura's adventures in South Dakota.

Ellen was born to Elmer Lehmkuhl and Marian Thomas Lehmkuhl on September 29, 1949 in Pierre, South Dakota. She is the fourth of five children. Ellen's dad had worked for Bill Asmussen, who farmed near Agar, in the 1930s. Elmer served in the Army during World War II and was injured at the Battle of the Bulge. Elmer returned home, met Marian, fell in love, and they were married. Thanks to Mr. Asmussen, Elmer obtained a loan and was able to purchase a farm six miles south and four miles east of Onida. Ellen had three older siblings, Sharon, Connie, Chuck, and one younger sibling, little brother Dave.

The Lehmkuhl family lived in a two-story farmhouse, which did have running water by the time Ellen was born. After Elmer passed away in 1978 at the age of 70, Marian rented the farm out to Johnny Gross, and in 1983, she sold it to the Gross family. When Ellen's mother passed away in 2012, Ellen and all her siblings and their families took a nostalgic drive from Pierre to Blunt and up the gravel road to the old farm and then on to Onida for Marian's memorial service at the First Presbyterian Church. It was quite a sight when they stopped at the end of the driveway and now saw a beautiful brick ranch house surrounded by many grain bins and a lot of farm equipment. This was quite a

Ellen and her dad, Elmer

contrast from the old farmhouse, which was surrounded by a couple grain bins, the old red barn, a chicken coop, a couple sheds, and Elmer's red Farmall tractor. It was a thrill to see this positive transformation that had taken place at the old farm. It brought back so many fond memories about living in that old house that no longer existed.

The house had only one bathroom for the family of seven. Several memories of that little bathroom still remain in Ellen's mind. Ellen was about the age of six when she went in to use the bathroom, lifted the toilet seat, and to her surprise, a little garter snake was swimming in the toilet bowl. Yikes! To a little girl, this was rather scary. Ellen went to the refrigerator, came back with an orange, flushed the snake down the toilet, and stuffed that orange in the toilet so the snake would not surface again. Needless to say, Ellen's dad wasn't too happy when he came in that afternoon, took the toilet apart, and found the orange. Ellen did confess so her siblings wouldn't get blamed and punished for her wrongdoing.

When Ellen was a little older, the age when she started to shave her legs, she nicked her leg pretty bad with the old-style razor. When she got out of the tub, the blood oozed down her leg and dropped onto the floor. Evidently, the floor was a little uneven, since the blood was dropping into the next room. Ellen's brother, Chuck, was the first to discover the blood and told their parents Ellen was dying in the bathroom. Ellen's dad was quite fond of Mercurochrome, so he applied a little of that and a Band-Aid and all was good.

One more crazy memory in this little bathroom occurred when some of Ellen's friends had brought her home from a dance. She had tasted some beer on the way home, which she did not like, and it had left an awful taste in her mouth. She was trying to be quiet since she realized her mother was sleeping on the rollaway in the playroom next to the bathroom. When Ellen went into the bathroom to brush her teeth to get rid of the taste of the beer she did not turn on the light so she wouldn't wake her mom. Ellen opened the medicine cabinet, reached for a tube, and put the paste on her toothbrush. Ellen quickly discovered she was using Ben-Gay (another of Elmer's favorite products) to brush her teeth. Forget trying to be quiet so she wouldn't disturb her mom! After a lengthy explanation, Ellen's mom finally believed her, which brought many laughs every time the story was told.

There were a couple of other unique features in the farmhouse where Ellen lived as a child. Since it was a two story and the furnace system wasn't too high tech at this time, there was a hole about the diameter of a basketball in one of the upstairs bedrooms. The three girls slept in the bigger bedroom where the hole was, and the boys slept in the adjacent bedroom. This hole was there to allow the warm air to get to the bedrooms. This hole was also a great way to drop dirty clothes downstairs on laundry day. It was also great fun for all five of the kids to look down and try to see Santa on Christmas Eve. It seems, though, that they always fell asleep before Santa made his rounds to their house.

On the main floor, there were two large furnace vents on the floor – one in the kitchen and the other between the dining room and the master bedroom. Money, small toys, or something seemed to always fall into these floor furnace vents. The kids got creative and soon discovered by taking gum, which was a real treat; they could stick it to the end of a yardstick and retrieve the fallen object. After thinking about it, Ellen is pretty certain many objects were dropped intentionally!

The Lehmkuhl kids all attended North

Lincoln School in Sully County for all eight of their elementary years. Ellen was the only student in her grade throughout her primary years. Ellen and her siblings rode to school with their dad in his 1949 pickup, since he was the one who brought buckets of water to fill the cooler at school. The school had no indoor plumbing so the bathroom was an outhouse near the school. The highlights of going to a country school were the declam contests and field days held at Blaine School, which was just up the road from North Lincoln School. This was an exciting time for Ellen, since she finally met kids from other schools and realized there were a lot of other students her age that actually existed. Besides going to church on Sunday mornings and to the grocery store on occasion, Ellen's social life was primarily living in that little house on the prairie with her family.

When Ellen was little, she always loved making paper dolls, creating mud pies, making a tent out of sheets on the clothesline, and playing with the kittens in the haymow. Since Ellen's dad usually worked outside all day, working in the fields, tending to livestock or fixing equipment, Ellen's mom made Saturday night's special by making homemade fudge and popcorn. It became even more extra-special when the Lehmkuhl family got their first television when Ellen was ten. Watching *Gunsmoke* on Saturday nights became a favorite. Ellen will never forget February 9, 1964, getting to watch The Beatles debut on the *Ed Sullivan Show*. Before the kids were allowed to watch this show or any program, all their homework had to be done. Homework was always done around the kitchen table. Neither Ellen's mother nor father went to college so this was a special goal that they wanted for all their kids.

4-H was a major activity for rural families in South Dakota and the Lehmkuhl kids were no exception. This was not only where they learned how to sew, can meat and produce, cook, bake, and learned to take care of livestock, but also how to keep a record book and especially learned responsibility. The best part of being in 4-H were the once a month meetings and entering your projects at the Sully County Fair. This was a real social event for Ellen and her entire family.

Once the fair was over and before school started after Labor Day, the Lehmkuhl family took their annual trip to the Black Hills. It was fun to get away but seven people all packed in a Ford Galaxy, three in the front and four in the back, with no air conditioning, no seatbelts, legs rubbing against each other, and keeping one's hands to themselves proved to be an experience that would get on each other's nerves.

Ellen started dating Joe Kub during her junior year in high school. Joe put many miles on his El Camino driving to and from Ellen's place to take her on dates. It was the night of their Senior Prom; their parents had agreed to let them meet some friends and drive to Pierre after the dance. Joe had already changed out of his suit and was taking Ellen to her house to change out of her dress. The rain was coming down pretty hard so Joe, not knowing, missed the intersection to turn to Ellen's house and was on the wrong road. Joe knew he was on the wrong road when they ended up in Sig Severson's stock dam. Fortunately, only the front end of the El Camino with Ellen sitting on the passenger side was in the dam. Joe walked in the dark of night and in the rain to wake up Sig. Sig was able to pull the car and Ellen, without too much damage, out of the stock dam. Oh what a night!

You might be surprised that Ellen continued to date Joe after the stock dam incident. Well, they did continue to date. Ellen was attending South Dakota State in Brookings and Joe was going to the School of Mines in Rapid City

The Lehmkuhl children entertaining themselves

when they met back in Onida in January of 1969 for semester break. Ellen's mom was in Rapid City with Sharon, who was having a baby. This was Ellen's second year in college and she was homesick a lot. Joe agreed to meet her in Onida and take her out to the farm. The snow was coming down quite heavy, but Joe thought he could make it. Well, near the home of Clarence and Hazel Ludwig they got stuck in a big snowdrift and couldn't get out. It was now after 10:00 p.m. and Joe and Ellen walked to the Ludwig residence and knocked, but no one answered. Most people didn't lock their doors back then, so they let themselves in. Ellen called her brother, Chuck, who was staying in Onida that night. While they waited for Chuck to arrive, they heated coffee and wrote a note to let the Ludwigs know they had been there. The next day they made it to Ellen's little house on the prairie buried in the snow. This was one of the last weekends Ellen spent time on the farm with her dad. It was a special time, savoring so many special memories of growing up in that little house on the prairie in South Dakota.

Ellen did marry Joe in 1971 and they moved to Rapid City, where he completed his engineering degree. He took a job in Cheyenne, Wyoming. It was hard for them to move out of South Dakota and start a new life where they didn't know a soul. After 40 years of living there, they now call it home.

After reading all of Laura Ingalls Wilder's books as a child, Ellen loved the qualities of Laura's character and her spirit. Ellen hopes in some small way her story has given another perspective of life in rural South Dakota during a different time and place, but still on the prairies of South Dakota.

Hometown Memories from the "Good Old Days"
By Betty Roggenbuck of Eugene, Oregon
Born 1935

I, Elizabeth "Betty" (Reents) Roggenbuck was born in Twin Brooks, South Dakota in 1935, the tenth and youngest child of Casjen and Eliza "Lizzie" Reents. Like others around us we lived on a farm, had no electricity, running water, or telephone. We lived two miles from the Twin Brooks # 2 County Schoolhouse; where one teacher taught eight children and eight grades. My classmates at the time were Lillian, Dwayne, and Kenneth Reiner, my friend Rosemary Barledge, Darwin Doctor, my brother, Casper, and myself, plus one other boy.

The school was one large square room with the teacher's desk in front and a bookcase behind her; there was a side room for our coats and the bathrooms. There was a bell outside but no one dared to ring it, I believe the cord was missing! We had assigned seating; our chairs and desk were connected, in straight lines and faced the teacher. We always said the pledge to the flag, had reading and writing class and then recess. During recess on really cold days, we would sit around the large grate in the floor with the furnace under us and talk' we'd hang our feet over it to keep warm. We'd generally bring peanut butter and jelly sandwiches on homemade bread for lunch and the County would supply large Red Delicious apples, they were a real treat for us but we had to eat them at school.

I would walk to school from my home and sometimes bring along my pet wolf. I would lay my coat on the floor in the hallway near the entrance and "Wolfie" would lay there and sleep until we went outside. The boys liked throwing things for "Wolfie" to fetch but she never brought them back to us. During extremely bad weather, instead of walking home, I would stay with my brother, Bernie and his wife, Dorothy (Erickson) who lived near the school; the teacher, Carolyn Nisonger also boarded with them.

When we had to go to the bathroom, we would raise our hand with one or two fingers up to indicate if we had to pee or do a big job. The teacher would excuse us and also time us; she would get mad if we took too long. All I had to wear to school were boy hand-me-downs from my sister, Pearl who got them from Curtis Seide. I had on so many layers; I took a long time in the bathroom. I had to take the outer clothes off, pull the bib overalls and the long johns down, as well as the long socks with suspenders and underpants. And by that time, I would inevitably have to go # 2, which would take longer and then I'd have to get redressed and readjust everything. I was always afraid I would get in trouble for being in the bathroom too long.

Although I never did get in trouble at school' the Reiner boys did and had to sit in the corner and face the wall. Kenneth always said he liked to get in trouble because then he didn't have to do his schoolwork until later.

School Day Snowstorm
By Lowell Seymour of Pollock, South Dakota
Born 1939

"Dad, why do we have to get up so early?"

"Son, today seems to be a nice day, and last night some of us neighbors decided to go to town."

"OK, but I'm tired."

"I couldn't tell you last night because it was late and you were sleeping."

"I don't know why we have to do all of the chores in the winter. Can't Mary and Mom do them like they do in the summer?"

"In the summer you and I, Les, and the hired men do the field work and don't have time for chores!"

"Okay, Dad."

Dad and some neighbors left with filled cream cans and filled egg crates to sell so that groceries, coal, and other supplies could be bought. Mary, Les, and I walked to our small one-room country grade school. The students at the school ranged in age from six to 13 years old. The school had no phone or electricity. The school was cold in the morning, and all of the students huddled near the stove. As the room warmed, the students gradually took their seats.

The weather was fine until noon when the wind increased, the temperature dropped, and the snow began to fall. Our teacher, Mr. Putnam said, "We will all stay inside today." After our lunch pails were emptied, we played basketball. We used wads of paper for our basketballs and used the wastebasket for a hoop.

By midafternoon, snow was blowing into the school through the ill-fitting windows. A hush fell over the students as the wind again increased. Suddenly the door opened, and Mr. Fetterley appeared. "Your fathers are stranded halfway home. I want all of you to get into my sleigh. I will take you to my house for safety." Mr. Fetterley had a huge two-story sod house, so there was room for all.

Getting a dozen scared kids into a wooden wagon with two adults was not easy. But being close together gave warmth. Phylis Fetterley said, "I am happy to get into the sleigh!" She crawled to the front of the sleigh and her Dad put his strong arm around his eight-year-old daughter. Several blankets covered the crowded group of frightened children and adults. There was no back or top covering on the wagon, so the snow swirled around and covered the faces and clothing of the passengers as the powerful horses pulled the sleigh home. Mr. Fetterley gave the horses their heads, and they pulled us to safety through the trackless snow.

The trip of about a mile seemed to go quickly. Joy and laughter erupted as we entered the huge house. The walls of the house were two feet thick and covered with stucco inside and wood on the outside, so the house was warm. The large front room of this house was used by Lutheran families for church services. Mina had fresh cinnamon rolls for us to eat and hot cocoa to drink when we arrived. After we finished our snack, Gene and Ralph yelled, "Let's play basketball."

Mabel, Ella Jean, and Bonnie said, "No!"

So Mina said, "Girls, let's sing some songs around the piano!"

I said, "Let's play basketball, where is your wastebasket?"

Gene said, "We have a real basket, basketball and indoor court in the hay mow of our barn." We played basketball with joy and enthusiasm. The snowstorm was forgotten. The girls decided later to go to the barn to watch the game. While the game was going on, Judy and Sylvia suddenly screamed, "That cat is going to catch those birds!" The birds (sparrows) were roosting high on the steel rail used to transport hay into the haymow. When we came back to the house, Mina washed our faces. After riding in the dirty wagon and playing basketball in the dusty haymow, our faces were covered with dust.

Mina fed us a good supper of canned beef and potatoes around a large rectangular table. We slept at the Fetterley home that night. In the morning, the weather cleared, and we were brought to the school. Our father picked us up with the sleigh pulled by draft horses. Mr. Fetterley (Sid) said, "Albert, are we having church tomorrow?"

"Yes, and it will be at the larger one-room country school. It is your turn to get the preacher, (Rev. J.H. Ford) and the organ for Mrs. Jones so she can accompany the hymns." After the snowstorm and the long isolation of winter, the people enjoyed a long joyful church service.

(Note: This is a true story. It happened in the late 1940s when I was about nine, Les, 12, and Mary was seven.)

Ed Sonnenschein in 1916

Homesteading
By LaVern Papka of Waterstown, South Dakota
Born 1922

Louise, Bertha, and Edward Sonnenschein were siblings. Louise was my Mother, and I am LaVern Hallauer Papka. I was always curious about my bachelor Uncle Ed, who came to

Bertha Sonnenschein in 1916

South Dakota when he was an older man and claimed to have lived in a dugout home in the side of a hill on land he had homesteaded in the early 1900s, in the state of Montana.

One day, Mother and I were looking at old post cards and pictures, and we found this picture of him seated outside just such a dwelling and I realized that his story was true! He looks quite dapper in his black suit, white shirt, and fedora, posing for the camera. To think, how awful it must have been to live in such a place with the rats, mice, gophers, coyotes, and probably rattlesnakes.

Bertha and her husband homesteaded in Montana also. The picture of the two ladies, Bertha's Mother on the left, and a visiting friend, is taken outside of a lath and tarpaper house on their homesteaded land.

My mother, Louise, and her younger sister, Bertha, married Hallauer brothers and my parents stayed in South Dakota. Those old homesteaders are all gone now as are my parents, but they must have been hardy, hardworking people to endure such hardships.

I am now ninety-two years old and I live in an assisted living facility in Watertown. I have loved to dance since I was a teenager and after I lost my husband, I continued to go to dances in the area, often riding with a member of the band. It was great fun while it lasted, but I use a walker now, which doesn't seem to work on the dance floors so I no longer dance as I did for so many years. I love music and still enjoy listening to those old music makers. Even now, in 2014, some of the members of those old bands often entertain us here at Stoney Brook Suites, which makes it a very special day!

The Good Old Days in Roscoe, South Dakota

By Catherine R. Crisp of Milwaukee,
Wisconsin
Born 1928

I am Catherine R. (Mengia) Crisp. I lived in Roscoe, South Dakota for 24 years. I came from a family of nine. I had one sister and seven brothers. We weren't rich and we weren't poor, but we were family and lived a simple life

I remember the dust storms. It blew in the windows. The grasshoppers—you couldn't help but step on them. They were hard on the crops. The tumbleweeds—when it was so dry we would have a bonfire in the fall with them. The blizzards in the winter were many. One year the banks were as high as a light pole. We as children had a good time sliding down the banks. We used shovels and just cardboard and one sled.

We had an outhouse with two holes and a catalog. In the summer when we got a crate of peaches, we would save the tissue paper for a treat. We had a nice outhouse. My father built it and bolted it down so the trick-or-treaters couldn't tip it over, which they tried but were unsuccessful at. My dad put an air vent in it. We had linoleum floor in the summer and we would scrub it every Saturday. We did have a chamber pot for nights.

Wash day was Monday for clothes and Thursday was for bedding. We had to pump all the water and heat it on the cook stove. We had a wringer washer. I remember it well. We always hung out the clothes. It was pretty cold in the winter, but it helped the clothes to dry faster. We didn't have a basement, so we would hang the clothes in the front room and kitchen when it rained. I was five years old and I was taking out my doll clothes when I got my finger in the wringer. I still have a scar from that to this day. My parents took me to the shoemaker, Mr. Wudel. He checked it out to see if my bone was broken. I had a cousin who was helping my mother when she got her hair in the wringer. My mother noticed her red hair and got it out.

Saturday was bath night. We put the tub in the middle of the kitchen. One by one, they got in and out. We kept adding water as each child got out. In the summer it was easier; we had the sun warm the water and took our baths in the summer kitchen.

We had a radio; when my dad was home, he would listen to Amos and Andy, Fibber McGee and Molly, Jack Benny, and Gabriel Heater for the news. The boys had their shows like boxing and the Lone Ranger. Myself, I liked music, so I would listen to Lawrence Welk and other music. During the depression, my dad would pipe it out so the neighbors could hear the radio; not everyone had a radio back then. We did not have a telephone until 1950. It was hard when my brother would call and was called up to the store, especially when my brother called home when he was in the services.

We made up games. I liked Kick the Can, Anti-I-Over, Who's got the Button, and a deck of cards were always available. We played many games—Pig, Hearts, War, Five Hundred Rummy. The older people always played Whist. We played Cops and Robbers and made guns out of wood and used an old tire tube to cut the rubber band. We made stilts and tried to walk on them. We always had a ball. We would play 500. We never had a football; guess they weren't popular at that time. We had one wagon, one sled, one pair of skates, and one bicycle, all of which we had to share. I don't remember us fighting over these things.

Shoes—if they were worn out before it was our turn to get a pair, we would cut a sole out of cardboard. We just kept replacing that until we got a new pair of shoes. If the shoe would flop, we would use a rubber band. In the summer, we were barefooted most of the time. My cousin's wife was a seamstress, so she did all of our sewing. I had to wear my sister's hand-me-downs, which didn't fit me, so they put some tucks on the shoulders. I did get a new dress for church. I wore it until it got too small then I got another. Our coats were always made out of old coats. I got my first coat when I was 13 and it was purple. My slips were made out of flour sacks. Nothing went to waste and they were so creative.

We didn't have a clothes closet, so that meant we didn't have that many clothes. When school started, the boys each got two pairs of jeans and two shirts. When summer came, they would make short-sleeved shirts. There was always one set in the wash and one set they wore. The girls had a big spike in their room to hang clothes.

I get together with my brothers every New Year's Day and we always reminisce about South Dakota. My brothers have a lot of stories; they are younger than myself. There are five of us left out of nine.

Tic'em
By Dorothy Reyelts of Mount Vernon,
Missouri
Born 1935

I was born Dorothy Mae Janssen, October 2, 1935 at 12:30 a.m. in the Geneseo Township, Roberts County, South Dakota. My parents, three brothers, and one sister lived on a farm about three and a half miles east of Corona, South Dakota. They had no phone and no electricity.

On October 1, my mom told my dad to go to Corona, South Dakota and call Doctor Flett at Milbank South Dakota. The car was not used, as money was scarce so dad hitched the team of horses and made the call. It was arranged that the doctor would come by train that evening. (The train ran from Milbank to Sisseton morning and evening, I think) stopping at Corona. So that evening my dad again hitched up the horses, he took my brothers and sister to my maternal grandparents to stay at their farm about one mile out of Corona. My grandmother went with my dad to pick up the Doctor from the train. My grandmother would be my nurse

Dorothy age 1 with her dog Tic'em

Dorothy, her brother Edward, and driving the load of hay is Dorothy's brother Norbert

and stay with us till mother was able to care for the family again. (Back then new mothers stayed in bed for a week to ten days.)

Next morning my dad hitched the team and took the doctor to the train at Corona to return to Milbank.

My brothers and sister were taken to the one-room school they attended one and one-half miles from our farm, by my uncle still living at home, also three aunts still at home, cared for that family.

Later that day, dad came to the school to talk with the teacher, when she came back to her desk; she announced that the Janssen family had a new baby sister and that the Janssen children should again walk back home that afternoon.

When my siblings returned home from school, grandma was sitting by the kitchen wood burning stove, with the oven door open for warmth, holding me, when they saw the new baby sister for the first time. (I am the youngest one in the family.)

I went to the same one-room schoolhouse. We always walked no matter what kind of weather we had.

The next summer and fall of 1936, my mother carried me on her hip as she herded the milk cows along the road, as the pastures were ate down to the dirt. She was training a new cattle dog, telling him to sic'em. My mom told me my first word was tic'em not being able to say the "s" sound. The dog's name was Ted, a big dog, that was part Saint Bernard and part Collie.

Growing Up in Hetland
By Donna Steenson of Brookings, South Dakota
Born 1933

I grew up in and around the small town of Hetland, South Dakota in the eastern part of the state. My life began on a farm. I was born at my grandparents' home as was common those days. My mom told me she thought she had eaten too much watermelon and laid down to rest. I was born shortly after that. She said she did not like that melon any more.

My parents lived on several farms when I was young. I had one sister who was 18 months older than I and we grew up inseparable. Work was our play and we never complained. Of the two of us, I was the one who followed behind our dad and did what he said. My sister helped Mom in the house. One time we were both out watching the men on the threshing run. It went from farm to farm and the women and children went also to help with the cooking and take morning and afternoon lunches to the fields. One time when we were out with them at lunch, a man on top of the thresher wanted a hammer. My sister went to get it for him and another man reached for it also and hit my sister in the head. She passed out and got a cut on her forehead.

It was hard times those days, so when it was cold enough for the radiator to freeze on the car, my dad drained it and we were on foot till spring. No money for antifreeze, and who knew what the roads would be like. Our school was ¾ of a mile west of us and our mailbox ¼ mile east. We walked to school at temps as low as negative 40 degrees. Mom would put thin scarves completely over our faces, but we could see through enough to find our way. Otherwise our faces would have frozen. The teacher walked, too. Our

Donna Wonsbeck Steenson and her sister, Doris Wonsbeck Kjellsen in about 1940

parents never knew if we or the teacher got there or not until we came home at night. No telephones! We would walk right past our driveway, continue on to get the mail from the box, and return home. Dad would walk across the fields carrying the cream can to town to sell our cream so he would have money to buy supplies. At one time, my dad worked on the WPA (Works Progress Administration). It put food on the table and we got commodities.

We moved from the farm we had rented into the town of Hetland after I finished fourth grade. Dad bought a gas station and feed store and made our living that way. Mom worked in the hardware store. We finished grade and high school in Hetland until the high school closed in 1949 because of lack of students. We had 12 girls and 4 boys, but we had a basketball team. A boy in the fifth grade made the fifth player. If one or more fouled out, the rest had to go on. We had some really good players and they did win some games.

The whole town of Hetland was our

playground. We had a lot of friends, including two special ones who would stay overnight with us a lot. Four in a double bed was crowded, so sometimes we slept crossways. Now days they advertise you should get a new mattress every eight years. Back then, mattresses were passed on to the next generation. I don't remember one ever being thrown away. Our old mattress sloped so badly toward the middle that the ones on the edge really had to hang on!

Every Saturday my sister and I helped Mom clean the whole house. Back then, we didn't have so much stuff, so cleaning was easier. Our folks had first a potbellied stove, which burnt wood and coal, and a cook stove heated in the same way. It sure was hot cooking and baking in the summer! On the farm, we picked cobs from the pigpen to burn and we had coal in the cellar.

In the winter, we would put on our snowsuits and take our strap-on roller skates up to the town hall and roller skate. There was no heat in there on cold winter days, but it lacked wind and snow. Since there was no toilet there, we had to go home to use the outdoor toilet. One time I waited too long and I stood there dancing trying to get the hook off the door. I had to go tell Mom I wet my snow

Donna Wonsbeck Steenson and her sister, Doris Wonsbeck Kjellsen in 1945

pants. I suppose we had to dry them by the oil burner.

My sister and I had a paper route, and every night we went to wait for the train. If the train didn't have to stop for passengers or supplies, they just threw the papers off and we picked them up and delivered them. We made a little money doing it, but we had to collect from our customers. We rode the school bus to Lake Preston when the high school closed in Hetland. The bus would stop at "Bill and Dot's" grocery store before it left town, so if anyone wanted to get a treat for the ride home we could. We didn't spend foolishly and really considered if we wanted to spend a nickel for an apple. Imagine a nickel for an apple, bottle of pop or a double dip ice cream cone! We were the last to get on the bus and the last to get off.

There were very few phones anywhere, so if news had to be spread about upcoming activities, us four girls would take a note from house to house and tell them to read it. We always hated to go to the house where the old man lived that tried to hit us with his cane, but we went. There was a man everyone called "Frank Carty" who was sort of a cripple who sat on the bum bench a lot. We hated to go there, too. We weren't afraid of her but a lady with purple hair lived over the pool hall and we would go there with the notes and also to sell poppies for the American Legion. She always told us "I already have bought a poppy and I will show it to you." She would bring a faded old one she purchased a long time ago.

The pool hall was a mysterious place. Our good friend's Uncle "Sig" ran the place and we dared not look in. I'm sure it was a place for pool and perhaps a beer. If we were out walking and he saw us girls he would put some roasted peanuts in our hands if we stuck them towards his door. When it was warm enough for movies to be shown in the town hall, even when we lived back on the farm, Dad saw to it we had a nickel to go to the movies on Saturday night.

Most of the original buildings are gone now, even Dad's Feed Store. The American Legion building and the old bank building which is now a museum still stand, as does the schoolhouse. It is a big, white, two-story building whose fate is pending. The bell has been removed from the top and placed on the school grounds near the old playground equipment. Children still go there to play.

I met my future husband when I transferred to the nearby Lake Preston School. I was a junior and he was a senior. Both of us graduated high school with honors but used common sense, the knowledge of right and wrong, and a couple of classes for college. We have 6 children, 15 grandchildren, and 13 great-grandchildren. My husband made a living as a farmer, auto mechanic, plastics worker, and maintenance for a storm door and window company. I babysat, worked in a hardware store, grocery store, and fast food store (Taco John's). My last raise brought me to $6.10 an hour. I love our church and the Senior Center. We worship at First Lutheran and take part in other things there. Technology has taken over the world, some for good and some for bad. Most kids are on some type of iPad, cell phone, or such. Believe it or not, I saw a snowman last winter!

Out on the Farm
By Connie Lehmkuhl Larson of Joliet,
Illinois
Born 1947

Growing up on the farm in South Dakota had (as I remember it) its blessings and challenges. I was born in 1947 to Elmer and Marian Lehmkuhl, the second of five children: Sharon, Connie, Charles, Ellen and David. We didn't get indoor plumbing with running water until the 1950s. For several years, we used the outhouse for our bathroom with the Sears and Roebuck catalog as our toilet paper. You never knew for sure what lurched in yonder outhouse hole, and my sister says Dad had to remove a nest of snakes in the outhouse at school. This was one of my least favorite places to be, and it gave me an uneasy feeling when I was there. When we did get indoor plumbing, I remember Saturday nights were bath night, so we took baths according to age, youngest to oldest. Yep, I was next to last in the five or six inches of water we were allotted in the tub.

Each of us had our jobs to do on the farm, and my mom was a meticulous housekeeper, so she passed on this trait to each of us. On Saturdays we would scrub the old farmhouse floors, dust and vacuum.

Mondays were "warsh day" at the Lehmkuhl farm—"all day." I put the "warsh" in quotations, as I still get teased to this day for pronouncing it wrong. So I just say that's how they pronounce it in South Dakota "down on the farm." And the "all day" meant just that—sun up to sun down. So, early Monday morning at sun up, we would sort out all the clothes into piles according to color in the back porch area of the house where the old "wringer washer" presided. Then Mom would crank up the old wringer washer and we would add a load at a time, starting with the whites. After agitating for a few minutes and putting through the rinse, on occasion I would have the honor of feeding the clothes through the wringer, getting all the water out and ready to hang on the line outside. It was "key" to keep your fingers and hands out of the way of the wringers or you could have a "pancake shaped" hand. Although I never had a limb or hand removed, I remember a few close calls with the fingers engaging the wringers.

I remember even in the winter on a sunny day we would put the clothes in a laundry basket and head for the open skies (and hopefully a nice sunny day) to hang the clothes to dry with clothespins on the wire clothesline. We had traditional wood clothespins with springs and round, slotted wooden clothespins. For most jobs I preferred the springed "pinchers" as I called them. After the clothes dried (and sometimes came in frozen and stiff as a board) we would sprinkle the clothes that needed ironing and roll them into balls and place in the clothesbasket. And most of the clothes back then did need ironing, as they didn't have the "no wrinkle permanent press." So that meant sheets, pillowcases, underwear, handkerchiefs, shirts, jeans, etc. all had to be ironed. Our sprinkler consisted of a glass Coca-Cola bottle with an aluminum sprinkler head with cork stopper. So by this time it was "sun down." Now we're already for Tuesday and ironing day. And on it goes!

Another memorable "job" we had was helping to "dress" the chickens. You know that saying, "You're running around like a chicken with your head cut off?" Well that saying is literally true. The chickens would dance around the yard behind the old bottle gas tank for literally three or four minutes after they had their heads cut off. Mom or Dad had the job of actually wringing the chicken's

507

Elmer and Chuck Lehmkuhl ready to combine

neck and cutting its head off. Then my job and my siblings' jobs were to dip the chickens in boiling water and pluck their feathers, as they called it. Mom always said she liked the back, neck and wings of the chicken to eat, but I later realized she said that because those were the only pieces left with such a big family.

Helping Dad with the combining in the summer and milking the cows was always a memorable experience. I would bring the milk cows in from the pasture, usually on foot. I still remember sitting on the three-legged stool milking the cows while they would switch their tail to keep the flies off, occasionally giving me a switch of the tail right in the face. We would bring the milk pail (full of milk, hopefully, if you were lucky enough not to have the cow spill it for you while you were milking) to the house and put it through the milk separator so we could have milk and cream. Then we would churn the cream into butter.

In the summer, we kids would climb in the old metal water tank in which the cows drank from to cool off. That's what we called the "ole swimming hole." I can still see the "slimy green algae" along the edges of the tank. Starting fires to burn weeds on a windy day behind the haystack in July with 90 degree plus weather is NOT a good idea! Well, when you get the neighbor kids together, you can come up with all kinds of great ideas! So when the neighbor lady came to give Mom a permanent, we thought it would be fun to burn weeds. We sent little sister Ellen to get the matches. Well, it didn't take long for the small little fire to become a roaring blaze, with the fire department showing up, and Mom's quick

thinking to open the gate to keep the barn from burning to the ground. Thank God everything turned out okay and no one was hurt. Moral of the story: Don't play with matches!

Living ten miles from Onida and seven miles from Blunt with six miles of gravel roads to Onida and seven miles of gravel roads to Blunt had its challenges. I always tell my children and grandchildren, "I was just like Laura Ingalls on "Little House on the Prairie and went to a one-room schoolhouse, North Lincoln, with outhouses for bathrooms and no running water." We were about a half mile from the school, so lots of times we would walk home at night, but Dad usually took us to school in the morning in his old black Ford pickup (The kind you see in Terry Redlin's paintings). We always carried a container for drinking water for the day.

At the front of the room was a big blackboard with the alphabet printed out on green above. We had a big potbelly stove for warmth and we would bring a thermos of soup and other casseroles to keep warm on the stove. One memorable event for me was that all classes being in the same room, the teacher would be having class for another student while the rest of us were studying. Usually there were only one or two students per class. So one day I commented to the teacher that I couldn't concentrate on my reading while she was conducting another class and talking. I guess that didn't last long because when she called me for my class time, I was so engrossed in my reading that I didn't hear her call me for class.

Other fun memories were spending the night with one of our teachers, Joy Lehman, in the cold winter—sleeping in a feather bed

The 4-H East Sully Cobblers and their float in 1957

508

with no heat, but being toasty warm. We also had speech contests at Blaine School, the largest of the rural schools, where I presented a flannel graph story, I don't remember for sure, but I think it was the Three Billy Goats Gruff and I received a first place. What a talent!

I still remember 4-H and the Sully County Fair. When I think of all the things we did growing up on the farm, I just want to give my mom and dad credit for all they did to help us experience a memorable childhood. My dad allowed each of us to have a baby beef and enter it in the Sully County Fair each year. We would then get the money from the sale of the beef at the end of the fair. During the year we helped care for the calf by feeding, grooming and cleaning the stalls in the barn. My mom helped each of us girls with sewing projects for the county fair, so three of us girls had to take turn using the sewing machine. We also made a dress or suit and modeled it in the "Make it With Wool Contest."

One of my memorable experiences at the county fair was entering an old picnic basket I redid with matching napkins and placemats for a set. I didn't feel it was that great, so I tried to hide it when I brought it to enter in the fair. Much to my amazement, I received a purple ribbon and got to send it to the State Fair! This was a self-confidence builder for me.

Mr. Ron Lawrence, an excellent teacher and basketball coach at Onida High School, taught my government and history class. My mischievous ways got me in trouble with Mr. Lawrence for talking in class, so my punishment was cleaning the basketballs for the team after school one day.

Every week we would attend the Onida Presbyterian Church, with all five of us kids piling in our 1958 Ford Fairlane. It was always a challenge to get to church without having a few "encounters" in the back seat on the way. Mom and Dad sent us to church camp at Thunderhead Falls in the Black Hills of South Dakota and also to the Mennonite church camp. It was later after I married that I accepted Jesus as my Savior and Lord, but am grateful for the introduction to Him as a child.

Living in the country with its gravel roads had its challenges. I remember when my sister Sharon was learning to drive; Mom put her behind the wheel one day as we were coming home from Pierre. We met a car which put Sharon in a tailspin and we went from one ditch to the other and back again with the door opening, and a few bangs here and there. Thankfully, no one was seriously hurt. Then when it was my turn to learn to drive, Dad asked me if I wanted to drive home from town one night. Thank goodness, it was just the two of us. I had been sitting in the driveway for weeks practicing shifting the straight stick up and down so I knew how to put the car into the different gears, so I was ready! And really, I did pretty well on the gravel roads until we got to our driveway, and took the corner a little short and cut across through the ditch, but landed right side up on the road in our driveway.

The biggest challenge of the gravel roads was when I was dating my husband. He had a 1964 red Corvette convertible. This wasn't our first date, but one of the times he came to pick me up he told me I would need to have my brother, Chuck, drive me six miles to the highway because he didn't want to drive his Corvette on the gravel roads. It was "true love" because we've been together almost 45 years now! It was worth the trip!

A Wonderful Life
By B. Violet (Heber) Grapp of Boise, Idaho
Born 1921

I had a wonderful life with my parents, Mike and Lula Heber, six brothers; John, Marion, William, Forrest, Robert, and (one stillborn), and three sisters; Margaret, Fannie Mae, and Katherine.

I am now 92 years old and the last living member of our family.

We were poor (my family were farmers) but we always had enough to eat, clothes to wear, and always felt very loved. On the farm, we had many pets including dogs, cats, ponies, cows, horses, and chickens.

I will always remember on the Fourth of July each year we would go to Faulkton (a small town nearby) and on that day, each of us would have a bottle of pop and didn't have to share it with anyone else. That was a special treat!

We lived in South Dakota, and one of the elementary schools we attended was the

Sievers Elementary School. It was a one-room schoolhouse and had only one teacher for all eight grades.

I then went on to high school in the nearby town of Faulkton and graduated in 1939. Next, I attended college in Aberdeen, South Dakota, and from there went on to a business college and graduated in 1942. I received a good education and became very successful in life.

I got married and have lived in Boise, Idaho since 1956. I have four children, Pamela, Gary, Larry, and David. I also have four grandchildren, and many nieces and nephews.

I am a widow, live on my own in own house, and am in good health. I have lots of family and friends that live near and watch over me. I am very thankful and blessed for the life and longevity that has been given to me.

Lightning Strikes
By Duane Ellis of Brookings, South Dakota
Born 1930

My name is Duane Ellis. I saw the first light of day in August 1930. I am now eighty-three and a half years old and live with Parkinson's disease.

I started school in 1936 as a first grader. We lived one and a half miles north of school. In good weather, we walked to school. It started at nine a.m. and walked home when school was out at four p.m.

It was a one-room school with eight grades and thirty students. I carried a lunch bucket every day for twelve years, which included high school. We had a recess midmorning and midafternoon. During these times, we played different games like "Anti I Over," "Pump Pump Pull Away," "Jacks," "Jump Rope," a lot of softball and even some wrestling. There was no electricity; water was from a cistern, which collected water from the schoolhouse roof. A chain link pump was used to retrieve the water.

In the spring, we would drown out gophers. We would pour water down their holes and trick them with a baseball bat, when they came out.

As I got older, I was given a horse and cart for transportation to and from school. Cows had to be milked before and after school. We had no electricity at that time. We had Aladdin Lamps for light in the house. Outside it was kerosene lanterns we carried with us.

There were two things that happened to me I never told anyone about. One was when I was a freshman in high school. I came home one night and no one was home. A thunderstorm was in the area with lightning, as I walked 30-feet to the door of the house, I heard a loud crack. The next thing I remember was getting up from the concrete pad, which we called the porch, a ten feet south of the house door. I do not know to this day how I got there. I was frightened of lightning for a long time after that.

The second thing was a runaway with six horses and a harrow. I was harrowing the field after it was planted. I was a junior in high school. We were going through a soft spot in the field. The horses begun to sink in the soft ground, got scared and started to run. They were headed at a diagonal to the pasture fence. They were so excited I could not stop them or turn them away from the fence. It looked like tragedy for the end of the evener-would go under the fence, stop, and really wreck things. I was going to get thrown off and the horse hurt.

But they stopped dead still as the evener touched the post. I did not know what to do. I was a flat mile from any help. I could not call for help and scare the horses.

The only thing I could do was lay down the lines, get down, and unfasten the tugs. There were twelve of them. I did that, picked up the line, drove them away, and turned away so they couldn't see what I was going to do. Then I unhitched one horse led him to the end of the harrow and he pulled it out of the fence, returned him to the others. Drove them over and backed them up to the harrow, hitched all twelve tugs up, got up in the seat, and said, "Git up and finish the job."

Yes, we lived through what was known as bad times such as "The Dust Bowl," and "The Great Depression." We didn't know it was tough. We just lived it and have many fond memories.

Chicken Butchering Days
By Tim Dewald of Bowdle, South Dakota
Born 1946

It's a lost art. No one does it anymore. And why should we? It was a grueling, stinking, task detested by everyone who participated. Now we can go to the grocery store and buy our chicken meat-cheap. But there was a time when butchering chickens was a ritual performed on virtually every Midwest farm for at least a few days each year.

The process began the night before butchering day. Dad would herd us three kids to the chicken coop shortly after dusk. By then, the unsuspecting chickens would be perched for the night on a roost, a series of thin boards nailed near the roof for the hens' sleeping quarters. Dad would quickly reach up to the roost and pull each chicken down for her examination. He would press his fat, stubby fingers into her pelvic bone opening, if two of his fingers fit in her pelvic opening, that meant she was presently earning her keep by laying eggs, and she was tossed aside to live a few more months. Less than two, fingers fitting in meant she was not presently laying eggs, and by dusk the next day, she would be canned soup. Those hens that were to meet their doom were handed to us, and we would dash to another, nearby shed, throw in the chickens, and run back, always mindful that he did not want to wait even one second for us to return. We would repeat the process until all of the hens on the roost had been examined and their fate for the next day determined. Dad's job was now finished. He hated butchering chickens as much as we did, and we could bet that the next day, when the actual butchering occurred, he would find oil to change, or some fieldwork that could just not be put off even one more hour.

Then for us, it was off to bed because mom's mother, Grandma Schoch (Don't even try to pronounce it unless you've spoken German-Russian for at least twenty years because you'll never get the o-o-o-c-h in Schoch to sound just right,) was coming down from the neighboring town of Hosmer, in the morning to help us butcher. To us, Grandma Schoch, who doted on her grandchildren, was a kind, gentle, woman three hundred and sixty days out of the year. But, on butchering days, she was a dictatorial fiend; fifty chickens a day was her goal, and forty-nine would certainly not do.

Grandma Schoch was an imposing woman, almost twice as big as Grandpa, with strong, broad shoulders, and just a little too much blue in her gray hair. She always wore a dress, never pants, with an apron, and thick black high-heeled shoes that tied in the front. To cover her legs, she wore long cotton stockings. When she bent over, we could see that roll of stocking just above her knees. And people around Hosmer secretly whispered that it was no wonder Felix Schoch drank too much since he had that bossy Margaret waiting for him at home.

At dawn the next morning, Mom would roust us out of bed. By then she had water boiling in two big copper oblong tubs on the bottle gas stove. We'd eat our Cheerios, listening intently for Grandpa's old 1949 Ford to come rumbling up the drive. When we heard our dog, Hundy's first warning bark, we'd drop our spoons and run out to the porch. Before Grandpa could turn off the engine, the passenger door would swing open. Wielding her amazingly sharp butcher knife and greeting us merely with "Let's go, kids," Grandma went striding off to the chicken coop with us running to keep pace.

My job was to go inside the shed where the earmarked chickens had spent the night. I'd grab my homemade chicken catcher, a stiff, thick, six-foot-long wire with a hook on one end and a corncob handle on the other. I'd place the hook on the scaly, straight part of the chicken's foot, below the drumstick, but above the claw, and then jerk toward me. Before the dull-witted chicken realized what was happening, I'd have her feet in my hand, open the door, and hand her to my sister, Susan stationed outside the door. She, in turn, would hand the chicken to Grandma. With one quick motion, Grandma would put the chicken's wings under one of her feet, the chicken's feet under her other foot, grab the chicken's head in one hand, and ruthlessly cut the chicken's head off with her butcher knife. She would then release the headless chicken, which would jump and flop around for several minutes, bleeding profusely. Once they had stopped jumping, my sister, Joanne would gather them onto a pile, ready to be carried to the butchering shed.

Chickens, which are not noted for their

high I.Q.'s, were easy to snare at first. But after I had caught about five, they seemed to sense that someone was after them. Stirring up dust and feathers, they'd begin to mill around the shed, just out of reach of my outstretched chicken catcher. And as I'd chase them around and around, I could see Grandma right through the walls with her bloody hands on her hips, impatiently tapping her brogan high-heeled shoes.

Finally, we'd have one batch butchered. Grandma and we kids would carry the carcasses to the butchering shed where Mom was waiting with two five-gallon pails of boiling water. It was time to scald the chickens. This was one job only for adults. Not only was it too dangerous for us kids to work with the scalding water, but we hadn't yet learned the art of scalding. Leaving the chickens in the scalding water too long would result in the chicken's skin breaking when we plucked the feathers. Not leaving the chickens in the scalding water long enough would result in the feathers being too tough to pluck. Somehow, Mom and Grandma just seemed to know the exact number of seconds to keep the chicken in the scalding water. They'd grab the chicken by the feet and dunk her in the water for a few seconds; then they'd turn her upside down, grasp her by the neck, and dip her in the water for a few more seconds.

Now the scalded hen was ready to pluck. This was the worst part for us. The scalding water mingled with the feathers gave the chickens a smell unduplicated by any other smell on earth. Trying to hold our breath so that we wouldn't choke each of us reluctantly grabbed a chicken and started delicately picking feathers. Luckily for us, Grandma was an expert at this too. A few deft moves with her giant paws at lightning speed resulted in a plucked chicken. Mom, too, who had learned the art of plucking under Grandma's watchful eye for many years, was swift and sure. Each of them could clean five chickens while we labored over one. And if we stalled long enough, they would finally grab our last one with a disgusted look at us for our ineptitude and finish ours.

The mountain of plucked chickens then had to be singed-another indescribable smell. A few newspapers draped in a five-gallon tin pail were lit, and each chicken was briefly held for a few seconds at the top of the flame to burn off the fine hair on the skin. Following the singeing, the chickens were placed in water for a brief washing to remove the soot and burned hairs.

Now the one fun part of the day for me began-ripping out the guts. A quick slit with the knife at the neck of the chicken eliminated the crop and the excess neck skin. Then a slit along the breastbone and breaking the breastbone back revealed the guts, shining and glistening coils with just one more indescribable smell. There is something fascinating to a boy of about twelve about looking down into the cavern of an animal and seeing the entrails. This was also the mystery part of butchering hens because occasionally, upon lifting the guts to remove them from the chicken, we would discover that Dad had been wrong with his diagnosis of a non-laying hen. She would be filled with yokes designed to be eggs, and often she would even have a hard-shelled egg still inside her.

After the gutting of the chickens, my job was completed. Mom and Grandma would wash and cut up chickens far into the night, and when they had finished, they would can the chickens for soup. The next morning when we awoke, we would see the rows and rows of jars of canned chicken, our supply for the next winter.

An Old Adage Proven True
By Freda Poyet of Sisseton, South Dakota
Born 1932

It was the summer of 1938, and South Dakota was recovering from the worst drought in the history of the Mid-West. It was the year I entered the first grade. I was six-years-old, when I learned the true meaning of, "You can lead a horse to water, but you can't make him drink."

It was a hot, muggy day in July, as only one could be in South Dakota. My dad and two older brothers were going out to the field to try to get the corn cultivated before the July Fourth.

We had a big black stallion, "Prince" that was very gentle. I loved horses and spent a lot of time tending to our horses, to the point that my dad trusted me to do this special task, "water Prince at noon and make sure he drinks." They were going to work the field till it was finished which would be way past noon.

I untied Prince and lead him to the water tank. He just stood there not drinking. My dad's words echoing in my mind, I tried to remind Prince that he needed to drink. I took a hold of each side of his halter and started to pull his head down, he suddenly jerked it up high, and since I was attached to it, I went up as well. What goes up must come down. He put me right smack into the water tank. Which was quite a surprise to both of us.

It was a soaking wet "me' that crawled out of the tank after having let go of the halter. He stepped back as if to say, "You lead me to water, but you couldn't make me drink." I'm sure he had a horse grin on his face, seeing me all wet.

I lead Prince back to the barn, gave him a measure of oats, filled his manger with hay, and proceeded to sneak into the house, to change into dry clothes. My very watchful, now irate mom, at the sight of her wet soaked daughter demanded, "Were you playing in the water tank?" You know the rule, "No one plays in that water tank! When my mom heard what had really happened, she turned away from me and I'm sure, my mother, who wasn't one to laugh easily, had a good laugh.

When I grew up, I became a teacher, taught for forty-five years, and told the story and lesson Prince had taught me many times at the beginning of each school year. Only I gave it a new twist, "I can try to teach you, but only you can make up your mind to learn." Prince is long gone, but the lesson, "You can lead a horse to water, but you can't make him drink," lived on and motivated many boys and girls.

Yes, teacher can teach, but we must want to learn.

My Story about Life in Bradley, South Dakota
By Beverly Phelps of White Bear Lake, Minnesota
Born 1927

I was born in Bradley, South Dakota on December 11, 1927, and was named Beverly. My parents were Roy and Inez Peterson. The attending doctor was Dr. McIntire; there was not another doctor nearby nor was there a

Beverly's dad, Roy Peterson

hospital. The Doctor wasn't "on call," as there were no phones. He was brought to the house by my dad and rested on the daybed until my hour of arrival. Mom wanted me to be born on her sister, Jean's birthday, which was no problem…the tenth lost a couple of hours and the eleventh gained a couple of hours.

My first five years were spent in Bradley in a little three-room house about a block from my grandparents, Mattie and Anton Peterson, who settled there when they emigrated from Norway. Grandpa ran a little grocery store down by the railroad tracks and Grandma was the town dry cleaner. She cleaned clothes with Naptha on the front porch in the winter and outside in the summer. The ironing board was always up.

Dad was a surveyor. He rode the train to his job site and was gone a lot. We moved from Bradley to the hills south of Wallace when I was five years old. My dad had never farmed before but my Uncle Marv owned a farm and somehow we became farmers. The farmhouse had no insulation and was cold and drafty. That year, my folks shut off the upstairs

Beverly's mom, Inez Peterson

and kitchen and we lived in two rooms-the bedroom and the living room.

My first memory of Santa Clause was that same year, when a huge gentleman in a big sheepskin coat knocked on the kitchen door, took apples and oranges out of his deep pockets, and gave them to my brother, Berkeley, and I as Christmas gifts. I later met our neighbor, Tobias Waslund, who lived up the hill about a mile behind us. He had faced the cold and walked through the snow (no road) to give us a memorable Christmas. That year I got a big baby doll that my folks bought at the grocery store, my brother got boxing gloves (which he didn't like at all) and like always, we each got a book.

That spring, Dad bought a pair of mules to start farming. When he couldn't get them to move he came in the house for the BB gun. They still didn't move. Mom was bent over washing clothes on the porch as he questioned the action of the gun. The mules were sold shortly thereafter.

We lived three miles from the country schoolhouse so I went to stay with my Grandma and Grandpa to attend first grade,

however, they had to adopt me in order for me to change schools. The next year when my brother started school, we walked the three miles. Towards winter, Dad bought a little green building (like a fish house) on sleighs. My folks heated a large rock in the oven and we had a nice warm horse-drawn sleigh ride to school. School was never cancelled. The carrier pigeons wouldn't go out in bad weather, few people had access to Western Union or telephones, and the origin of the Internet and texting were a long way off. Parents decided if the teacher was going to make it to school, so were their kids.

I can't remember getting a store-bought Valentine. We made and decorated a big box at school and spent a lot of time making our own valentines. There wasn't much money in the hills of Wallace. Our first car was a Velie-now we could go to Bradley where the action was! My Uncle Marv owned the Peterson Grocery Store in Bradley. Everyone came to town on Saturday nights to shop for groceries, market eggs and cream, visit friends and relatives, and see western movies. The movies were shown on the side of my Uncle Marv's store and they were free, so marketing existed back then too!

The Depression hit and Dad went back to surveying. He worked for the Works Progress Administration, (WPA,) a federal work-relief program. We wore clothes issued by the government and were given some free food, but I never knew we were poor. Franklin Delano Roosevelt, a democrat, was president from 1933 to 1945. We listened to his fireside chats on the radio, and for folks things got a lot better because he gave them hope. WPA was probably the most famous of President Roosevelt's New Deal Programs, because it affected so many people's lives. A poem sent to Roosevelt in February 1936, in block print, read, in part,
"I THINK THAT WE SHALL NEVER SEE A PRESIDENT LIKE UNTO THEE…POEMS ARE MADE BY FOOLS LIKE ME, BUT GOD, I THINK, MADE FRANKLIN D."

We moved to our farm between Florence and Wallace when I was in the fifth grade. School was closer, only a mile. We carried our water and lunch to school. In the wintertime, we could have a hot lunch by baking a potato in the ashtray of the big wood burning stove. Because I was the oldest and my brother had hay fever, I had to carry the water jug. One day I decided he could carry it home, so I left it on the road. I had to go back and get it.

Berkeley hitchhiked a ride from our place to Watertown (about forty miles,) to get shots for his hay fever during the summer months. He would take along a pillowcase and stop at the factory where puffed wheat was made. The workers would fill it for him from the spillover and he would hitchhike back home. The puffed wheat almost made up for the water jug incident.

I was at a classmate's home and we were doing dishes when the news of the attack on Pearl Harbor came over the radio. I ran most of the two miles home to tell my folks.

We moved back to a farm in the Bradley area when I was a sophomore in high school, and most of the school year I stayed at Grandmas. Grandpa had died of a heart attack. Grandma was still the dry cleaner and it was her only income. There was no social security and no Medicare. My folks supplied her with meat, dairy, and vegetables, and my dad's brother, Uncle Marv, took care of the rest. Grandpa at one time owned three homes in Bradley but let them go because he wouldn't or couldn't pay the taxes. When he died, he left a whole lot of stock that was worthless.

We lived in potato country (1940s,) and I earned summer money picking and sacking potatoes. You did that with a partner, one to hold the sack while the other emptied the potato pail. Your paycheck was based on how many sacks you picked. One time the digging machine broke down and the two of us added some "borrowed" sacks; I cashed my twenty-dollar paycheck and went with my folks to the lake that weekend. I accidently left my purse with the twenty-dollar bill in the outhouse (outdoor toilet.) The consequence was someone else got the money that I really didn't earn. It was a lesson I've never forgotten.

My Brother, Brian, was born in 1938. He was four-years-old when we moved back to the farm in Bradley. At the time, my dad had a gasoline tank in the yard that he used to fuel the old Farmall tractor. Brian started then to lie on top of the tank and inhale the fumes. We pulled him away from the barrel very, very often. He went into the military service at an early age and was in a security division. He was quite smart. After military service, he held a good job with the telephone company until he retired. He died an alcoholic in 2001, perhaps his addiction started back when he was four.

My Brother, Berkeley, went to college at the Brookings State College, South Dakota, and after graduating worked for the Federal Fish and Wildlife Division until he retired. He died in 2008.

Not all memories were good ones. There were things I didn't tell my folks because I didn't know how. No one ever talked about the birds and the bees and sex was a dirty word. I was about ten when one of my folk's best friends gave me a ride home, stopped the Model-T and tried to molest me. I got out of the car and ran cross-country for home, where the Model-T couldn't follow. It was only instinct that got me to safety.

I was about twelve, when another neighbor and family friend did the same thing when I was home alone. I was a little smarter but not much fortunately, my folks made a timely appearance. Avoiding people like that is difficult when they are card-playing friends of your folks. Around that same time, Mom took me to a dental appointment in Watertown. The office was upstairs above the dime store. She left to do some shopping. I don't know

Beverly Peterson Phelps

what the job description was but the dentist lay across me as he worked and the pressure wasn't just on my teeth. I never said anything about it then or later, but I never stayed alone with a dentist again in those young years.

When I was about fourteen years old, Mom sent me to the neighbors to help with canning. It took the entire day and I stayed overnight. The neighbor was deaf and she lived alone with her son who was about ten years older than me. He came into my room that night and raped me. Screaming didn't seem to help, remember his mother was deaf. Unbelievably, he had the nerve to write to me and send me pictures when he was in the Army. He lost his life in World War II.

I never told my folks about any of these sexual predators, in fact this is the first time I have revealed the incidents. Except for the dentist, all the men involved were friends of my family all of their lives.

I have no temper and I've never been jealous. I think I can thank Mom for that. Her standard remark was "he has an insane temper or he's insanely jealous." During those times, apparently, being insane was about the worst thing that could ever happen to anyone.

Mom was a city girl before marriage and she learned a lot on the farm! Butter does not come in a chunk after it's churned. Bulls can run really fast, and if you are in a pinch, you can jump a fence. Bed bugs live in old houses, hotels, and at the neighbors. When I stayed overnight with my girlfriend, my mom always washed my clothes that next day. I don't know what they fumigated with, but I sure remember the smell.

I left home following a short trip to the University of South Dakota; got married, raised a family of five, and became an insurance agent for Northwestern Mutual Life. I 'm still active in sales and have a store on eBay, which I work daily. I haven't died yet but I'm working on it.

Life on the Farm
By Martha Deering of Miller, South Dakota
Born 1918

We came from a family of six boys and six girls. As girls, we were pretty close in age ranging from 12, 14, and 16. Seems as we always did crazy things together.

One time our mom said we should go and get the milk cows, which were in a big rental pasture. In this pasture was a big government dam. So, this one time we decided we were not going to let them go across this dam bank. So we forced them to go behind the dam, which was seeping water from the dam and caused the cows to get stuck. We only got about a few cows across; the rest went on the dam bank. Well the three cows went across and got stuck. So we ran home a half mile to tell our mom. So Mom called our dad, but he was in town about five miles away. So he came home and got two horses to pull them out with a chain around their neck. We really got by with that one. Dad didn't know how the cows got their feet stuck. Of course, we sure paid for that. Our milk cow's bags were full of mud so we had to wash the bag.

One time it was time to get the milk cows about a half mile away in a cornstalk field. Well when we got them all together on the road for home, they were walking close together so we tied a couple of cow's tails together. For some reason, they all started running. The tail kept cracking and we thought the tail was coming out. Finally, the tails came apart, only one cow had more tail than the other cow.

Our Beloved Oreo
By Bernice Lemley of Aberdeen, South Dakota
Born 1928

My husband, Oscar, always wanted a dog after we moved to town. I saw this ad in a paper – free puppy to anyone who will give her a good home. We drove to town to look at her, and we both felt she was just what we wanted. It was cold and the rain was coming down hard. She was chained to a tree and she was all wet and muddy. We let her get into the car and took her home to North Roosevelt Street where we lived in the country at that time. We gave her some milk, which she really gulped down. Then I took her outside, where she relieved herself and went right to the door. I let her in, wiped her, and then Oscar put her in the garage, but it was dark and cold in there, and she barked for almost two hours. I told him to bring her into the family room. She lay down and went to sleep. It was warm

Oreo

in the family room. When she woke up, she went outside and relieved herself. I brought her in, wiped her, and gave her water and dog food.

Then I made an appointment for her at a pet grooming place called Noah's Critters. She really needed a good cleaning and a haircut, a bath, and more. When I went to pick her up, I couldn't believe her new look. She got a warm bath. She also had a badly needed haircut, had her nails polished a bright red, and had red ribbons in her hair. And she smelled so nice!

We really loved her, and she never was a problem. She chased other dogs that came into our yard. The squirrels, she always chased out of the yard. She knew at least twelve words when you spoke to her. She was a real smart dog.

My husband, Oscar, passed away in 1998. So I took Oreo with me wherever I went. When I went shopping or visiting a nursing home, she was always with me. She stayed in the car. She was so happy getting a ride in the car.

Oreo's last year on earth, 2001, was really hard. On April 21, she was very sick. She was at the Animal Health Clinic overnight. Dr. Swenson said he was sure that she had pancreatic cancer. On May 15, she was unable to keep any food down. She vomited at least five times, barely sipping water and taking Pepto Bismal and Pedialite. We took her to the vet hospital in Mabridge but they couldn't help her. This was on May 23rd. on May 17, I took her outside but she wanted in the house after 20 minutes. On May 24, she went to be with our Lord at about 6:00 a.m. On May 25,

I called Pastor Steve Meyer and he came to the house and brought communion to Henry, Vonnie, and me. We all prayed for Oreo. In June 2001, we buried her south of the house on Roosevelt Street. I bought a casket from Kevin Spitzer from Spitzer-Miller Funeral Home. Our precious Oreo is gone but not forgotten. May she rest in Peace.

Oreo was 46 years old when we got her. We had her for 14 years. So she was actually 60 years of age when she went to Heaven.

Beloved pet, never forgotten, rest in Peace, dear Oreo.

Memories of My Grandparents
By Audrey R. Pedersen of Pea Ridge,
Arizona
Born 1940

My grandparents, Engebret and Anna Kampen, grew up in Norway and emigrated to the U.S.A. in 1893 and 1902 respectively. They settled in Summit, South Dakota, a small railroad town, as many of their fellow Norwegians did, and were married in December of 1902. Engebret homesteaded at first, but the land was rocky. There was a depression in the 1890s and the weather set records for bone-chilling temperatures as well. So in 1906 he got a job on the Milwaukee Railroad and continued there until his retirement. This story describes a typical day in the life of the Kampen family in the early 1900s.

Days began early at the Kampen house. Engebret would get up at 5:00 AM and take a big lunch in a syrup can with a thermos bottle, and would head out to the railroad for a ten-hour workday. The Milwaukee Railroad had been completed through Summit in 1880, so there was no new track to build. So what did Engebret do all day long? Plenty. As a Section Boss, he was responsible for maintaining the tracks from Summit South Dakota eastward and down a large hill to Milbank South Dakota—a distance of 23 miles. Each morning Engebret and the gang would go out on the tracks in a handcar to look for and replace bad ties, tamp loose spikes, and tighten bolts. They would fix broken rails and build new tracks where needed. By 1905, the tracks through Summit were 25 years old, so much maintenance was necessary. Lives depended on good railroad tracks. A regular gang consisted of three or four men. Extra gangs were sometimes brought in and housed in camp (bunk) cars where they are provided lodging and meals at a nominal cost. At one time, about 300 Chinese workers were brought in and Engebret supervised them as well.

Engebret was also responsible for keeping records in the Pocket Timebook. This was a pre- printed pocket size memo/reference book in which he would write the names of crewmembers, total hours worked, rates of pay, and other information. They worked quite a bit with railroad ties, which were eight to nine feet long and weighing 100-150 pounds each. Engebret was very strong and could lift two at a time if the occasion required. And let's not forget snow removal in the winter, which was a huge job. During the summer, there was a lot of weed control to be done.

At the end of a long day, they would ride the handcar back to the station in Summit. Then it was time to get the cows in the town pasture. Old Mrs. Granberg would go to the pasture first and call the cows by name: "Here, Bessie, Here, Molly," and so on. Then the owners would take their cows and bring them home to be milked. Anna and Engebret both milked the four or five cows and put milk in the separator to get the cream. The cows spent the night in the barn, and in the morning Anna took them back. Later on, their two sons would get the cows and sometimes a grandson went along with them.

They lived in town, but had room for their animals. Besides the cows, they had a whole flock of chickens (40-50) and Anna would gather the eggs. A chicken was killed every Sunday for dinner. They also had three or four pigs and had a slop pail under the kitchen sink for dishwater, potato peels, carrot tops etc. This mixture would be put into the pig trough. The pigs would keep the trough clean, but the drinking water would leak down and cause mud to form, so the little pigs always

Engebret and Anna Kampen in 1902

had something to roll around in!

They would butcher a cow or calf or pig when the time came. Flour and salt were just about the only groceries they bought. Besides the big vegetable garden, they had fruit trees—apples, plums, and cherries. Their grandson Bob said, "Either you or the birds will get those cherries!" In the summer, there would be sales of apricots and peaches. Late in the evening, Anna would shop for fruit and would get a case of very ripe fruit and would can it right away. Everyone got some. Potatoes were kept in a storage bin. Shelled corn costs three cents a bushel. Corn on the cob was free.

When the city mowed the ditches, Engebret and Anna would get the hay and put it in the haymow in the barn. They would also go out and get the cow pies and let them get petrified so they could be used for fuel.

Of course, Anna had her hands full with a new baby every two years! They would eventually have seven children in 15 years. She cooked on a big iron stove that burned coal or wood. There was no hot water, so if she wanted to wash dishes or give baths, the water had to be heated on the stove first. She baked a lot, so the stove was going much of the time.

Water had to be heated to do the laundry, and Anna did the family washing in a large washtub with a washboard, and the iron had to be heated on the stove first. And then there was the cooking and the cleaning. She also did a lot of canning from their big garden. They had a cellar under the house, just a hole in the ground really, where they kept the potatoes and other root crops and extra canned goods. The children would work too, besides working at the Summit Hotel. They would help take slop to the pigs and would also gather eggs, feed chickens and bring in wood for the kitchen stove.

There was always a Sears catalog in the outhouse. For going out to the barn in the dark, they had several lanterns, but they couldn't have them by the bed for fear of starting a fire. Toward the end of the day, Anna would start supper. They would eat about 7:00 or 7:30. Anna and Engebret both worked very long days! Then extra railroad ties would have to be chopped up for kindling or fence posts.

Their sons Gunder and Eddie would fight over getting the cows and hoeing the garden. In the fall, they would have to bank the house's foundation with dried manure to help keep the house warm inside. In the spring, they would put the manure in the garden. They would rent a horse to plow the garden. They had lots of corn and potatoes. The kids helped plant the vegetable garden.

In the spring, they would take a large wagon and store big chunks of ice in the icehouse across the alley. They sold ice all summer for the iceboxes, as there were no refrigerators in those days. They got electricity in the late 1930s.

After his retirement, Engebret could take life a little easier. One of his hobbies was whittling and carving. His grandson Jerry remembers that he made two sticks connected with a cord and a man hanging onto the cord. When the sticks were squeezed, the man would dance. He also made birdhouses with twigs. He would take naps in the yard and rest his head on a flat rock. He would use his railroad cap to cushion his head a little. In the evenings, they both loved to play cards, especially Whist. Engebret would say, "Come where you're really strong now!"

When we grandchildren arrived, Grandpa would balance us on his toes while he sat in his rocking chair and sang, "la, la, la, la, la, la," to the tune of The Irish Washerwoman. We all remember that. Anna and Engebret lived long, worked hard and raised a fine family. May God bless their memory.

Blizzard of 1966
By Clarence A. Senftner of McLaughlin,
South Dakota
Born 1928

I have lived in the McLaughlin area all my life. I farmed until 1968 when I moved to town. I started to work at the Farmer's Elevator in 1967 as manager of the Fertilizer Department. I gave up farming because I couldn't do both.

I went to Roosevelt School for my elementary education. This was a big rural school. There were forty-four students attending this school. We had two teachers. There was a curtain that separated the three grades from the older students. This didn't work very well, so a small school was moved there the next year. This was a good decision. There were students in each grade. I graduated from the local high school. My first two years, I lived in the boys dorm. The last two years, I could live at home, because we moved closer to town.

When I was eleven or twelve years old one of my sisters and I got a little to adventurous. We had an old icebox that we kept for cream that we sold to customers in town or shipped to Mandan, North Dakota. We also kept butter in the top part. It happened to be empty one day. My sisters and I wondered what it would be like in the bottom part. My three-year-old sister and I crawled in it. She closed the door. There we were sitting with our knees up to our chin and no way to get out. Dad was turning the separator and needed the milk pail changed. The other sister left to do that. Then she went to the house because a neighbor girl came. Our sister forgot about us. Dad wondered where we were. It got a bit warm in there. We had a little bit of air from the water drainpipe from the top. Mother was fixing supper. She asked for someone to go get the butter from the top of the icebox. That is when sister remembered where we were. When she opened the door, we fell out like wet noodles. What a happy ending this was. Our curiosity could have been disastrous.

One day I wanted to show my siblings what is done at the sale barn. My parents went to town. I went after our pony. I took him into the kitchen. We had new linoleum on the kitchen floor. When the pony turned around, he took the top off the linoleum. We covered the damage with another piece of linoleum. I

519

told my siblings not to tell, but my youngest sister couldn't wait to tattle on me. I got a scolding; I came out of that situation lucky.

The 1930s brought the Dust Bowl. The wind blew an awful lot, so there was dirt in the air a lot. There was very little or no rain. No matter how tight windows and doors were sealed up, the dust still got into homes. There were times when day was dark like night because of the blowing dirt. The cows ate what green grass they could find and weeds in the summer. There was no hay to put up for winter. Dad took thirty-gallon barrels and cut them in half-lengthwise to make troughs. We put old straw in the troughs and poured black strap molasses over the straw. The cows licked the troughs clean like a kid eating candy. When it was thirty below zero, the molasses had to be warm so it could be poured easily.

Not only did the wind blow the dust a lot, there were grasshoppers to contend with. Anything with a wooden handle had to be put inside. If left outside, the grasshoppers ate the soft grain in the handles. If clothing was left outside very long the hoppers ate holes in them. The chickens didn't need to be fed very much. They had all the grasshoppers they wanted. When the grasshoppers took flight it was like an eclipse there were so many.

My mother baked bread once a week. She used dried cow chips in the cook stove for heat. My siblings and I would take our little wagon and a stick and go to the pasture to get cow chips. The stick was used to check to see if the chips were dry enough and protection from rattlesnakes.

It was a hot day, but mother put the chips in the stove and lit paper to start the fire. The smoke came out of the top of the stove. She tried several times to get the fire started, but nothing but smoke came out. She told us to find Dad.

Dad came with strands of barbed wire with two burlap sacks on one end of wire. He climbed up on the roof and poked the wire down the chimney. The hoppers were solid in there. They had gone there because it was cooler. Mother cleaned the grasshoppers out from the oven. Then she had a fire and we ended up with great homemade bread.

We had a blizzard in March 1963. It was a bad one. We lived beside the main highway. We had so much snow we couldn't get out of our yard. We also had many people that were traveling and ended up in the ditch. They came knocking at our door so we had many overnight guests. One family remembered us every Christmas and Easter for years.

In 1966, we had another blizzard. This was a very bad one that lasted several days. The snowdrifts were higher than the barn and granary doors. When the blizzard was over and we started digging in the snow, we were devastated. We found cows that were dead, and cows near death that had to be shot. Some lost their tails and some lost milking quarters. Some were drifting away with their eyes covered with ice. We lost half the herd. This was a disaster for us.

In February of 1990, I retired from the Farmers Elevator. My wife, Jean and I have done a lot of travelling. Our favorite trip was to Norway. Norway has a lot of mountains and water. It is a beautiful country.

Now I spend my day reading and going to the Senior Citizen Nutrition Site for lunch. After we eat, we play pinochle. We love to play six-handed. My wife still works, so I go alone.

Uecker's Cash Store
By Leonard Uecker of Quitman, Arkansas
Born 1931

In the early 1900s, the beginning of a new town often began with the establishment of a General Store. In 1911, my father and family moved from Elgin, Minnesota to Raymond, South Dakota and started both a bank and a general store. After my father's death in 1935, my brother, Wilmont continued the store with the help of my mother, my sisters, and me. Many childhood memories are centered around helping out in the family store. I learned math counting out change for customers No computer was available to calculate the amount. Silver dollars were still in limited use for purchases. When World War II came along ration stamps and tokens were needed to purchase scarce items like sugar, coffee, meat, and butter. We had to paste the stamps in a booklet to turn in to authorize replenishing store stock.

Flour was sold in cloth sacks that were printed in colorful patterns. The housewife would look for the same sack pattern on her

Wilmont Uecker in the white apron the owner of Uecker's Cash Store in 1938

farmers brought in on Saturday nights. The cream had to be tested for butterfat content to determine the price paid. The eggs had to be transferred from the farmer's small crate to the thirty dozen crates picked up by the produce buyer. That was my Saturday night job, which kept me from roaming the streets and enjoying visiting with all the boys in town for the evening. One night, I arranged for some fun with the help of my friend Harold. I had him suggest to the boys that they go and steal apples from Uecker's trees. He assured them, that I was still working at the store and that no one would be home to catch them. In reality, it was late enough that all the farmers had already come to town, and I was relieved of my chore. I was waiting on the open porch of our house with my .410 shotgun. Soon I could hear the rustling in the grass under the apple trees and the sound of apples being pulled off the trees. That was my clue to stand up and holler, "Who's stealing those apples?", followed quickly by the blast of my shotgun into the air. Speed records may have been set by boys' running back to town. Harold, who was with them, told me later that some of them swore they heard the buckshot whistle right by their heads.

Many homes still had barns on their property from the horse and buggy days. We kept a cow in our barn to provide milk for sale in the store. After milking, the milk was strained, cooled, and put in glass bottles. I delivered milk around town to a few regular customers. Cost was eight cents a quart. In the summer, after the morning milking, I would take the cow down the road to where there was a nice grass filled ditch. The cow would be staked out for the day on a long chain to enjoy the lush grass until time for the evening milking.

Uecker's Cash Store that burnt down in 1939

next purchase so she could finish the dress she was making. Coffee beans came in burlap bags and were ground in a big hand-cranked mill. Dried apples, pears, prunes and apricots came in wooden boxes and were sold by the pound. A glass hinged cover was used to display the box of bulk cookies for sale. My brother's wife would carefully count out the cookies that she included in the lunches she would send with my brother and me when we worked on the farm. He had a sweet tooth that she was trying to curb. I never gave away the secret of the box of bulk cookies hidden in the combine toolbox.

The store carried a limited stock of clothing; overalls, shirts, gloves, socks, work shoes and caps or straw hats. A special glove marked with a metal hook in the palm was available for manually husking corn. Corn was handpicked in the field and tossed into a wagon being slowly pulled along by a team of horses. The wagon had a backstop on one side that the ear of corn was tossed against to then fall into the wagon. The picker walked along the rows as he picked the ears from the stalks.

The store also bought cream and eggs that

Besides being the general store manager, my brother also served as a substitute rural mail carrier. His help was especially in demand in winter when snowdrifts made roads impassable by car. He had a team of horses that were kept in our barn in winter when they were not needed for fieldwork. He built a small plywood cab to mount on the front-runners of a horse drawn sleigh and that would be his transportation to deliver mail over the drifted roads. As the people on his route knew that he ran the store, he would often find a note in the mailbox requesting that he would please bring a pound of coffee, some sugar, or a tin of Prince Albert tobacco on his next trip. Most men rolled their own cigarettes by hand. "Tailor-mades" were expensive and not widely available. I don't think I ever saw a woman hand roll a cigarette. In very cold weather, the horses would come back from the route with long icicles hanging from their nostrils.

Regular customers at the store would run a tab for their groceries, to be paid at the end of the month or when they sold some grain, cattle, or chickens to have some cash money. Coming to town for groceries was also somewhat of a social event. After dropping off their eggs or cream to sell, they would leave a list of groceries they wanted to buy with the store clerk. Then they were off to shop, run errands, or visit with friends, while the clerk assembled their grocery order. When ready to leave for home they would settle up the difference between what they were paid for their produce and the cost of the groceries they bought.

We usually had a large garden and grew enough tomatoes and maybe enough peas or carrots to be able to sell some in the store. Mother would start tomato plants indoors early in spring and have enough to sell tomato plants in the store. I was glad when I became old enough (10) to drive tractor or a team of horses and work on the farm in summer and spend less time hoeing in the garden or mowing lawns around town. There were only rotary push mowers, no gas engine powered motors. I felt that I had reached manhood when I could drive a team of horses on a hayrack picking up bundles of grain to feed into a threshing machine. Combines soon ended the era of the threshing machine.

My brother's first tractor was mostly used to replace a team of horses in pulling farm implements. He would sit on the grain binder just as he had done with the team, while I drove the tractor. My leg was barely long enough to push the clutch all the way in to be able to shift gears. My brother tied a rope on the clutch, ran it forward to a pulley, and then back to the binder where he sat. When there was a problem with the binder, he would pull the clutch in with the rope so I could shift the tractor into neutral.

South Dakota was the last state to require a driver's license. (About 1953) No test was required. When I was in the eighth grade, I did some tractor driving for a man who had farmland in several locations. One day I was working in a field when he and his hired hand drove up in a car and a pickup truck. The farmer said that they were going over to another field and that they were leaving the pickup for me to drive over when I was finished here. I didn't tell them that I had never driven a car. I knew the manual shift pattern for a car so I started out in low gear and carefully drove onto the road. When I thought I had the feel of steering, I shifted into second gear. As I again became confident, I shifted into high and soon was a bonafide motor operator.

Better roads and affordable automobiles caused the decline of many small towns. It was easier to travel greater distances to larger towns for more variety in shopping. Horse and wagon travel was no longer used. Even the school barn that kept the country kids horses during the day now stood empty. My brother sold the store and bought a farm and that was the end of Uecker's Cash Store. The store passed through several ownerships and jointly functioned as store and coffee shop until finally closing after one hundred plus years.

Saturday Night Bath on the Farm
By Leann Fredrickson of Aberdeen, South Dakota
Born 1936

Taking a bath was quite a chore when you lived in the country on a farm that had no running water in the house. Saturday night was bath night (We were all going to town for the evening.) We got out the big round galvanized tub that was used on washday. It

Olive and Hugh Jones with Leann, and Larry in 1944

was set in the middle of the kitchen. We had done the chores early or the last guy for the tub was just finishing the chores. Hot water had been heated in a big white teakettle on the stove. The first one to take a bath had about two inches (if he was lucky) of water. I was tiny enough so I could kneel down in the tub and with a washcloth and soap bath my whole body. The second person to take a bath got more hot water added to the tub. Probably the same washcloth and a clean towel. The third person likewise. So the last person to take a bath got the most water, but you can imagine that the water he was using was "well used" or as we would, say today "recycled" many times.

Saturday nights were looked forward to all week. Earlier on Saturday, we washed the eggs (the eggs did not always come from the nests "squeaky-clean") and put them into egg crates. Our crates were wooden and would hold twelve dozen eggs and the eggs were separated by dividers that held three dozen eggs. Each divider was made of pressed gray paper that had indentions for twelve eggs. Each layer of three dozen eggs was put in the crate until the layers were four-deep.

We all got dressed and climbed into the car. We were off to Ipswich for the evening. On the way, Dad started off the songs. My mother knew all the words and dad knew all the tunes. We sang all the way to town and many times on the way home too. Dad's favorite was The Old Rugged Cross and Mother's was Will

There Be Any Stars in My Crown. Others that were sang was I Want a Girl Just like the Girl that Married Dear Old Dad, Down by the Old Mill Stream and Little Brown Church in the Wildwood.

On arriving in town, we took our eggs to Charlie, the Jew. Mrs. Koehley worked for him. They counted the eggs, checked for cracked eggs and gave us a check.

This check was used for the groceries that we were getting that evening at Don Williams Red Owl Grocery Store. Mother had been making this list all week as she discovered what she needed. Flour and yeast were priority on her list. She baked bread twice a week. The list was given to the store clerk and they would fill the order. While they were filling the order, visits to other stores were made for purchases. When the purchases had been made, we would go to the car. We always tried to park the car on Main Street. We went to the car and watched the people walk by.

We kids sometimes got to go to the show. The State Theater was on the south end of Main Street. It had two movies (the same movie) back to back. In the beginning and in between movies, there was a newsreel and a cartoon. Kids up to high school were fourteen cents and high school was thirty-five cents.

Some of the first movies I remember were The Bells of St. Mary starring Bing Crosby (I cried a bucket of tears!) To Each His Own with Olivia de Havilland and The Sullivan Brothers (the story of five brothers who went to World War II and all went down on the same ship.) Mother (who hardly ever went to the movies,) thought I should see Gone with the Wind. There was a special showing of this movie and she took me. I think this movie was in the middle of the week, so this was very special-just Mom and me!

Back to Saturday night-if we did not go to a movie and went to the early movie, we would meet a friend. My friend was Carol. We would walk from the theater on the south end of Main Street to the Library, which was two blocks north on Main Street. We walked on one side of the street north and the other side coming back. We did this several times on Saturday night.

Don Williams Red Owl Grocery Store filled many orders for the farmers on Saturday night. These orders were put in big paper sacks and set along the front of the store with the name on each bag. We would pick up our bags, pay with the egg check, and take them to the car.

Mother and Dad got to visit with several friends and neighbors, got the items they needed, groceries. When the stores began to close at ten p.m., it was time to head for home. We had had popcorn from Mr. Lass. He had a popcorn cart in front of his cream station. Occasionally an ice cream cone from C and C Café was a real treat! We shared what we had learned in town and sang the rest of the way home. Saturday night in town was wonderful!

Growing Up in the Depression
By Marge Blue of Iroquois, South Dakota
Born 1925

I was born in 1925, the seventh child in a family of ten. When I was just four years old, my mother died, and one of my older brothers and I went to live with an aunt and uncle. My uncle was a farmer. He homesteaded and built the house we lived in. The house was never completely finished however, as he was only able to complete things as money was available. My aunt made all of my clothes, or I wore hand-me-downs. I remember my bloomers were made from flour sacks with rubber strips cut from inner tubes for elastic. We wore whatever ill-fitting shoes were available in the winter, but we were always barefoot in the warm weather. The first dress I ever received was for my eighth grade graduation. My brother bought it for me.

I remember that in the wintertime we lived in the kitchen and did not heat the rest of the house…unless company was coming! When we went upstairs to bed at night, we would sleep in a feather tick with a sad iron

Marge's uncle, Ralph Moser's home place

for warmth. Every fall we would make a new mattress of cornhusks. In the spring when it was extremely hot, we would sleep outside in the wagon box. We couldn't sleep on the ground because of snakes. In the winter, we took our baths in the washtub behind the range. It was nice and warm there. We had no indoor plumbing so used a chamber pot at night.

I had many chores to do starting when I was about five years old. My first chore was picking up chips after wood was chopped. One time the axe came back and cut my nose. My aunt just taped it up…still have a nice scar! My other chores included gathering eggs, milking cows, doing dishes, and dusting…a chore I hate to this day! As I got older, I did other things to earn money and to help the family. I remember babysitting for several children, and ironing clothes all day for twenty-five cents. When I was about twelve or so, I would trap and skin skunks. We sold the hides for five dollars each. One winter I got five of them! When there was a blizzard, we would tie a rope to the house and then to the fence so we could check the cattle, feed the chickens, and get back to the house safely.

My uncle and his friends dug a shallow well. It had no curb, so mice and snakes could get in. Starting when I was about six-years-old, and picked because I was the smallest, they would lower me into the well with a pulley several times each summer so I could clean it out. I remember being terrified each time for fear the well would collapse on me! The well was about a quarter of a mile up the hill behind our house. We would pump water by hand into a tank for forty cows and six horses. We would haul water in a wagon, using cream cans, to water the pigs and chickens. We also hauled all water for household use. Because the water was hard, my aunt would put household water in big crocks and put lye in it. She would let it sit overnight, and then the next morning, we would skim it and have soft water.

My aunt baked all of our bread and we made our own butter. We picked wild berries for making jam. We also picked mushrooms and lamb quarter to eat. We raised chickens for eggs and for meat. We also had a few pigs and would butcher occasionally. There were a couple of winters where I remember we received government commodities such as

Marge and her aunt picking berries in 1934

peanut butter, canned meat, fresh fruit, and rice, which added a bit of variety to our meals. I loved the fresh fruit! My aunt also did her best to have a garden, but the soil and lack of moisture kept it from being very successful most of the time.

My first five years of school, we walked three miles each way. In the wintertime, we often arrived with frost bitten faces. We couldn't ride our horse to school because there was no place to keep it. We always had fun at school and usually had good teachers. I remember one time all of the kids arrived at school safely, but the teacher was unable to get there because of a blizzard. Instead of turning around and walking home again, we all stayed at school for the day without the teacher! A few of the older kids poured water on the floor, and since there was no heat, the water froze and we used the floor for a skating rink! I remember we were punished and each student had to bring six cents to cover the damages. However, it must have been just to teach us a lesson as we all got our money back at the end of the year. At recess time, we would play games like "Anti I Over," "Pump Pump Pull Away," "Red Rover," and "Captain, May I." The closest church was fourteen miles away if we went through the pastures! We didn't go to church often in the winter. We had an old Whippet car with a rumble seat where my brother and I would ride. We usually ended up half-frozen or half-baked depending on the season.

For fun, we would often go sledding on the butte in the winter, or swimming in the stock dam in the summer. I also remember reading behind the range in the kitchen because it was so warm and comfortable there. We played kitten ball with the neighbor kids on Sundays

after church, and after sharing a picnic lunch. I also remember getting to go to the Days of 76 one time. At Christmas time, we always had a present under the tree. Rich relatives from Wisconsin helped Santa, though I didn't know that until I was older!

When I reached high school age, I worked for room and board for two years, and then at the age of sixteen, I moved back to live with my dad, taking lots of memories with me.

Adventures in South Dakota
By Joyce Wieseler of Orient, South Dakota
Born 1940

As a kid, growing up in the middle of South Dakota was memorable. My dad and mom were farmers. I was born in 1940. We had the necessities. We used an outhouse, a two seater, most of the time, also had a chamber pot. There was a bathroom in the house but it didn't work very well, there was running water, but conserved. Dad, mom and us five kids were bathed once a week and used the same water, us kids did anyway. Mom had a wringer washer, used the same water for all the laundry. Dad hauled the water into a cistern that was soft, because our well water was way too hard.

There were always wild turkeys, geese, and chickens running loose, we never went barefoot because of all the droppings. Mom and my sister and I cleaned chickens and geese by the hundreds.

We went to a Catholic school taught by the Benedictine nuns, all twelve years. We lived across the road, about two blocks to walk to school always, rain, shine, or snow. Polo was the name of the village like place where we lived. There was a Catholic Church, and school, grade and high school a boarding school, probably fifty boarding students that came from all over the state. And yes, there were spankings and rulers over the knuckles, the nuns were strict, but they had to be, after all, they were the parents to those students away from home.

I was a high school junior before we got a black and white television. And a telephone didn't come till after I left home for college. It was a party line phone; sometimes we heard some good gossip.

During high school years, an older couple

Polo's church and school complex in 1947

came to the school and called square dances. That was so much fun. We danced in the basement of the school. There was a small town eight miles away, Orient, where we went for regular dances, a great dance hall. In the town of Miller was a movie theater, we didn't get to go except a few times to a MA & PA Kettle movie. Us kids got to go now and then for some shopping.

Us five siblings and cousins, lots of them, made our own entertainment. Lots of outdoor play. We played on the bale stacks and in the barn haymow, snow piles, ice-skating with just enough ice back of the barn. Also, we roller-skated in the basement of our house. Great roller-skating in Orient in the same hall we danced in, such great fun.

As younger kids with the cousins, we went to the hen house and had egg throwing. Now that resulted in a punishment. My brothers tried swimming in the dugout, they wasn't supposed to

Blizzards seemed every winter, like all the time. Snow banks seemed to cover everything; the snow would be piled as high as the phone lines along the road. The roads got plowed eventually. There was a general merchandise store on the corner called the Polo Store. You could get anything there except clothing. What a popular place that was, a fun place for everyone to hangout.

Dad put cows in the barn when it stormed. We had three workhorses, didn't use them. Didn't have a horse to ride either. We played in the haymow and nearly fell down the feeding holes to the cattle below, so we covered them first.

Polo had a baseball team, like legion players, the ball diamond was in my dad's pasture, there was a game nearly every Sunday; we loved to watch the games. The teams traveled to other area towns for games. I think only on Sundays.

My mom made dresses for my sister and I. We always had to wear dresses to school.

In the house, there was an icebox that was sitting in the dining room, no deep freezers then. There was a locker by the Polo store that we rented a couple of boxes for frozen items, or during the winter, we sat food in the porch to keep frozen. I guess the folks went to Orient to get chunks of ice for the icebox.

As for the blizzards, we usually had school, my siblings and I walked to school and with all the boarding students there were enough for school. We just enjoyed playing in the snow. Didn't seem to be so cold as it is now, or maybe it's the age.

In the summer, Dad made grain bundles with the binding machine, then mom and us kids would put the bundles into shocks. The shocks were then pitched with a fork into the threshing machine. Lots of physical labor. The kids would walk up and down the cornrows pulling up weeds that had burrs on them. Mom and my sister and I cooked meals for about a dozen men that helped with the threshing. We butchered young chickens early in the morning and made pie, than washed a ton of dishes in a pan on the table. We would set up washbasins outside for the men to wash. This would probably go on for a week.

We had two milk cows that were milked morning and night; the milk was separated, so we had milk and cream, made our own cottage cheese, butter, and ice cream with a crank machine. Chicken chores too feed and pick up eggs and wash them if they were dirty. All the other foul that ran over the farm was fed with grain on the ground or they forged for themselves.

My uncle that lived in our household came home from World War II when I was probably five; I remember being afraid of him, maybe the uniform or him too.

The pets we had were barnyard cats, but tame ones, most of them; they loved the fresh

Polo High School in 1954

milk warm from the cow. This is the milk we drank after it was separated and cooled.

We had a small terrier dog that got to come into the house only as far as the kitchen. He lay behind the cook stove where it was warm.

We picked wagonloads of corncobs for the cook stove from the hog yard. Dad had lots of hogs. We butchered hogs for our own use then we rendered lard, makes the best piecrust too.

I also remember helping Mom with a huge garden, we did lots of canning, vegetables and fruit, had a wonderful asparagus patch, also strawberries, picked many wild plums and canned them too.
There were nice flowers around that mom loved

One time a sibling and me were swinging on a rope with our hands and my hands slipped off and I fell flat on my face with a bad nosebleed. Mom cut the rope down, that was the end of that.

We had a big two story square house with an attic. Mom, my sister, and I cleaned from top to bottom every spring. We had to polish every piece of wood.

Encounters with snakes weren't so bad. They were usually small. It was the spiders that were really scary. I hated them and I still do today.

We visited every weekend, I think at one of the uncles and aunts place or at our home. The adults played cards and us kids just played, maybe some board games, most fun. But jumping on the beds didn't go over to well.

Don't really remember a favorite singer, but I do remember when Elvis came on the scene, he was awesome. We listened to country music-and still do today.

Coon Babies
By Mary Lou A. Gasper Malli of Arvada,
Wyoming
Born 1947

Far View Farm in Deuel County raised four generations of Gaspers. My grandfather was orphaned when he was four-years-old. Gerhard Gasper died when he was struck by lightning when he was unloading loose hay into the barn loft. The team of horses were knocked down by the bolt but were unharmed.

Grandpa (John) grew into manhood and in 1903 a new barn was built, followed by a new house in 1905. My dad, LeRoy was born to my grandparents in 1910, myself in 1947.

We gardened a lot on the farm carrying water to the plants when the rain was not so plentiful. Our produce was disappearing and the raccoon tracks were plentiful. My brother, Bernie, "the Hunter," tracked the coon to an old threshing machine, finding a mom with four babies and stored garden vegetables. I had to summon help, seeking out my oldest brother, Wally. They worked for a few hours and got mom in the right place to shoot. Bernie promptly crawled into the thresher and retrieved the four babies. We kept them in a box, feeding them now ourselves. They would stand on their hind feet holding their own bottles to nurse. Lots of entertainment for my siblings and myself! They continued to grow and learned to climb. Then Mom was missing a few baby chickens and the raccoons had to leave. A new home was found for them at the Watertown Zoo. We were sad to lose our friends and never ventured back to see them.

District # 27, Pleasant view School (also called the Wattnem School,) was where all of us attended our elementary years. Recess time was fun. We were spies and hid in the horse barn. In my oldest brother's era, they actually kept their horses there out of the storms that they had rode to school that morning. We had no running water at school and bathrooms outside got tipped over every Halloween. Dad's always had to come in and tip them back for school.

Teachers kept the coal furnace full and running and brought our drinking water to a crock that had a spicket on it.

Wintertime was fun too. We bundled up and went outside. I never remember being cold! The oldest grade boys dug a hole in the road ditch and we younger one brought blocks of snow; building a snow fort that was high enough for us to stand up in! Once built, we spent all our recesses in our snow house. We were all family with connection of being from farms in the immediate area.

When I reached the seventh grade in 1959, our school closed for modern times and the lack of money to hire a teacher for eight grades. I was then bussed to Estelline Public School, seven miles away.

Hats off to those who attended District # 27. We learned and had a lot of good times.

The Irish Family
By Emmett Coughlin of Elkton, South
Dakota
Born 1922

The "Good Old Days," were not all grimness and despair. Emmett Coughlin, who was about ten years old during some of these events, loves to tell anecdotes about the Irish in Parnell Township, where he was born and has lived his entire ninety-one years and counting.

There was one Irish family in the neighborhood, consisting of the parents and six children: four boys and two girls, who really livened up the atmosphere of the "Dirty Thirties." We'll call them "Jones," to protect their identity.

The "Jones" boys were all typical Irish-very bright and willing to elaborate a story in the telling. The following are some escapades of theirs that Emmett enjoys telling in his inimitable Irish way.

One of the boys, Bob, was especially bright and daring; so when the government was trying to help people to survive during the 1930s; Bob went to their office in Brookings and managed to talk them into giving him some hens, which he was to have the use of until the little chicks were hatched and growing. Then he was supposed to return the hens for the next family to use. To hear Emmett tell how Bob assured the officials that, "*Someone stole the hens,*" when in truth, the Jones family had eaten them all, is a riot in itself.

Emmett's family had a telephone (which was unusual then,) and many neighbors made use of it, too. Emmett recalls one day, Mrs. Jones came blasting into the kitchen, demanding to use the phone PDQ to call the Sheriff.

It turned out that her umbrage was connected to something some young men had proposed to her daughters at a dance the night before. The Sheriff was a busy man in Parnell.

The boys in any family attended grade school only in the winter months because of the work on the farm. This one family (not the Joneses,) had an eighteen-year-old son in school that winter when Emmett was in second grade. The eighteen-year-old, Leo was particularly obnoxious one day and the teacher told him to go home. She was attempting to lead him out of the schoolhouse, but he wasn't willing to leave, and wrapped one arm around the stovepipe and pulled it down on the way out. School had to be dismissed for the day because of the soot all over everything. Leo became the hero of the day, in the eyes of the rest of the boys.

My Memories

My Memories

Index A (Hometown)

Danna Garber Mercer	Blunt	South Dakota	263
B. Violet Heber Grapp	Boise	Idaho	509
Gail Anderson Winter	Borger	Texas	141
Tim Dewald	Bowdle	South Dakota	511
Bonnie Jean (Peterson) Glock	Bozeman	Montana	415
Geraldine Starkey	Brainerd	Minnesota	450
Irene J. Anderson	Brandt	South Dakota	425
Bonita Dolney	Bristol	South Dakota	45
Doris Wenck Alberts	Britton	South Dakota	175
Paul Bremmon	Britton	South Dakota	357
Betty Jean Fisher	Britton	South Dakota	35
Ray A. Johnson	Britton	South Dakota	360
George Schott	Britton	South Dakota	118
Marjorie Thoelke	Britton	South Dakota	386
Grace Wegleitner	Britton	South Dakota	377
Kathryn Cole Quinones	Bronx	New York	167
Barbara Behrend	Brookings	South Dakota	295
Barbara Booton	Brookings	South Dakota	254
Catherine Hausman Ching	Brookings	South Dakota	280
Carol Langner Dusharm	Brookings	South Dakota	320
Duane Ellis	Brookings	South Dakota	510
Lewayne M. Erickson	Brookings	South Dakota	344
Helen Gottsleben	Brookings	South Dakota	193
Clara Hegg	Brookings	South Dakota	123
Lawrence L. Helwig	Brookings	South Dakota	77
Mary Flemmer Husman	Brookings	South Dakota	129
JoEllen D. Johnson	Brookings	South Dakota	125
Shirley A. Neshiem	Brookings	South Dakota	228
Donna O'Connell	Brookings	South Dakota	388
H. Lynette Olson	Brookings	South Dakota	301
Loran Perry	Brookings	South Dakota	242
Donna Steenson	Brookings	South Dakota	505
Carol Joffer	Brotten	Minnesota	231
Lorraine Peickert	Browns Valley	Minnesota	162
Elaine McDaniels	Bryant	South Dakota	22
Ardis Dragsten	Buffalo	Minnesota	160
Elroy Dragsten	Buffalo	Minnesota	37
Melba Pierce Brown	Cameron	Missouri	46
Anna (Hansen) Chesser	Canby	Oregon	477
Jelene Tilden	Canova	South Dakota	57
Susan Hines	Carpenter	South Dakota	330
Jewel Aeilts	Carthage	Illnois	474
Vincent Leemhuis	Castlewood	South Dakota	24
Joyce J. Poppen	Castlewood	South Dakota	495
Starla Fitzjarrell	Centennial	Colorado	397
Devona J. Simonson	Chamberlain	South Dakota	311
David G. Anderson	Champlin	Minnesota	258
Sheral (Sievers) Morrill	Chandler	Arizona	398
Cynthia Bartels	Charlotte	Iowa	276
Donald G. Steward	Chelsea	South Dakota	124
Ellen Lehmkuhl Kub	Cheyenne	Wyoming	497
Harriet Otto	Cheyenne	Wyoming	431
Margaret L. Grottke	Chili	Wisconsin	324
Stephen J. Grottke	Chili	Wisconsin	404

Virginia Pulfrey	Claremont	South Dakota	369
Beverly Kluess	Clark	South Dakota	237
Margaret McPeek	Clark	South Dakota	200
Les Solberg	Clark	South Dakota	94
Chester Benson	Clear Lake	South Dakota	119
Roger Hovey	Clear Lake	South Dakota	113
Dorothy Moe	Clear Lake	South Dakota	85
Helen M. Prater	Cleveland	Georgia	433
Judy Miles	Colman	South Dakota	298
Merle (Nick) Kneebone	Colorado Springs	Colorado	444
Lorna Mundhenke Perkins	Colorado Springs	Colorado	472
Alma M. Paulson	Columbia	South Carolina	47
Arlowene Hitchcock	Conde	South Dakota	131
Marvin Madsen	Corona	South Dakota	229
Raiden V. Peterson	Covina	California	48
Colleen A. Anderson	Cresbard	South Dakota	465
Selmer N. Anderson	Cresbard	South Dakota	442
Helen Holsing	Cresbard	South Dakota	72
Ann J. Cazer	Custer	South Dakota	45
Harlow H. Rudolph	Dallas	Oregon	389
Rose Grothe	De Smet	South Dakota	284
Thelma Hayden	De Smet	South Dakota	44
Jacqueline Lee	De Smet	South Dakota	191
Evelyn Paulson	De Smet	South Dakota	340
Beverly M. Prostrollo	Deadwood	South Dakota	95
Dee Melicher	Denver	Colorado	426
Nadine TeBeest	DeSmet	South Dakota	305
Jim D. Huff	Detroit Lakes	Minnesota	470
Darleen Brace	Douglas	Wyoming	471
Dorothy E. Beam-Saddler	Dumfries	Virginia	218
Dale D. Harpstead	East Lansing	Michigan	372
Christian H. Grottke	Eau Claire	Wisconsin	421
Mike Drooger	Edgerton	Minnesota	154
Jean P. Olson	Elk Grove	California	436
Emmett Coughlin	Elkton	South Dakota	528
Lois Erschens	Elkton	South Dakota	101
Paul Erschens	Elkton	South Dakota	232
Anastasia Gebhart	Elkton	South Dakota	70
LaJoy Thompsen	Esmond	South Dakota	387
Jim Gloe	Estelline	South Dakota	194
Betty Roggenbuck	Eugene	Oregon	500
Orpha D. Bensen	Eureka	South Dakota	447
Selma Lapp	Eureka	South Dakota	385
Joan I. Oster	Eureka	South Dakota	318
Mary Lou Fluegel Beath	Evansville	Wisconsin	28
Lois B. Warfield	Fairfax	Virginia	250
Joanne Drenkow	Fargo	North Dakota	386
Gayle Charron	Faulkton	South Dakota	312
Wauneta Holdren	Faulkton	South Dakota	40
Rosalia Schmidt	Faulkton	South Dakota	372
Kenneth Wherry	Faulkton	South Dakota	123
Betty Walker Schinkel	Ferney	South Dakota	264
Ed Buck	Flandreau	South Dakota	337
Warren Thomas	Forestburg	South Dakota	103

Joe Malheim	Forman	North Dakota	81
Cheris St. John	Fort Collins	Colorado	234
Lola Gelling	Frederick	South Dakota	17
George M.C. Thompson	Garden City	South Dakota	112
Don Dorsman	Garretson	South Dakota	82
Lucille Ellenbecker	Gettysburg	South Dakota	228
Thelma Norris Hepper	Gettysburg	South Dakota	197
Lona Swanson	Gettysburg	South Dakota	192
Sharon Cole	Gillette	Wyoming	347
Margaret Bradbury Jewell	Grand Junction	Colorado	150
Dorothy Bierwagen	Greenly	Colorado	20
Bob Boardman	Grenville	South Dakota	97
Donna Lewandowski	Grenville	South Dakota	331
Mary Anne Clark	Groton	South Dakota	481
Dorene Nelson	Groton	South Dakota	210
Robert Pray, Sr.	Groton	South Dakota	50
Twila Sanborn Ruden	Groton	South Dakota	262
Emery Sippel	Groton	South Dakota	108
William E. Beastrom	Harrold	South Dakota	393
Don Markseth	Havana	North Dakota	445
Barbara Solsaa	Hayti	South Dakota	156
Peggy Kasten	Hazel	South Dakota	359
Doris Struckman Koisti	Hazel	South Dakota	390
Gail Roe	Hazel	South Dakota	26
Leland Roe	Hazel	South Dakota	44
Donald Erickson	Hendricks	Minnesota	138
Violet Nelson	Hendricks	Minnesota	303
Marion Ritter Perman Goehring	Herreid	South Dakota	432
Vernon Vedvei	Hetland	South Dakota	98
Alice E. Buchheim	Highmore	South Dakota	205
Darlene Konrad	Highmore	South Dakota	224
John Zilverberg	Highmore	South Dakota	233
Phyllis DeJong	Hitchcock	South Dakota	341
Shirley Reed	Holt	Michigan	153
Mary Lynn James	Houghton	South Dakota	367
Calvin C. Huber	Hoven	South Dakota	256
Cheryl Vosburgh	Howard	South Dakota	191
Nila Weidler	Howard	South Dakota	99
Phyllis Arwood	Huron	South Dakota	60
LeRoy P. Gross	Huron	South Dakota	70
Daniel P. Horn	Huron	South Dakota	134
Alyce Howard	Huron	South Dakota	441
Ruby Johannsen	Huron	South Dakota	479
Laura M. Jones	Huron	South Dakota	220
Roger Larsen	Huron	South Dakota	179
Duane W. Laufmann	Huron	South Dakota	467
Nadine Matthews	Huron	South Dakota	127
Eugene McMillan	Huron	South Dakota	275
Alice M. (Stegeman) Mentzel	Huron	South Dakota	348
Lyle L. Meyers	Huron	South Dakota	158
Lois Peterson	Huron	South Dakota	206
Carol Pevestorf	Huron	South Dakota	476
D. Ransom	Huron	South Dakota	219
Steve Riedel	Huron	South Dakota	27

James A. Schmidt	Huron	South Dakota	300
William F. Smith, Jr.	Huron	South Dakota	150
Corinne Jameson	Ipswich	South Dakota	460
Juliana Malsom	Ipswich	South Dakota	183
Marge Blue	Iroquiois	South Dakota	524
Avis Elenz	Jefferson	Missouri	435
Murvin H. Perry	Johnson City	Tennessee	314
Connie Lehmkuhl Larson	Joliet	Illinois	507
Jeanne Carstens	Kalamazoo	Michigan	428
Les Patton	Kenmore	Washington	306
Russell H. Payne	Kenosha	Wisconsin	491
Ileen Groft-Tennyson	Kirksville	Missouri	139
Mary Hymans	Lake Norden	South Dakota	315
Janet Hoglund Johnson	Lake Norden	South Dakota	484
Ronald E. Kangas	Lake Norden	South Dakota	229
John Larson	Lake Norden	South Dakota	172
Clarice Logan	Lake Norden	South Dakota	329
Phyllis E. Nelson	Lake Preston	South Dakota	375
Nancy Olson Burkey	Lakewood	California	461
Charles J. Hendricks	Lakewood	Colorado	216
Darlene Rowderdink	Lancaster	California	42
Margaret Schmidt	Lane	South Dakota	327
Hazel Erickson	Langford	South Dakota	301
Janet Elaine Meehan	Lead	South Dakota	48
Mabel Dockter Freita	Leola	South Dakota	471
Mary Louise Lechner	Leola	South Dakota	472
Barbara Shawl Campbell	Letcher	South Dakota	458
Dvonne Pearl Shawd Hansen	Letcher	South Dakota	487
Alice Clark	Madison	South Dakota	46
Katherine Deremo	Madison	South Dakota	229
Bonnie Funk	Madison	South Dakota	394
Lois Hagemann	Madison	South Dakota	187
Beverly Langner	Madison	South Dakota	330
Nadine Mikel	Madison	South Dakota	336
Thorine "Terry" Weiland	Madison	South Dakota	202
Nancy Stakke Bauer	Mandeville	Louisiana	266
Roberta Hilgendorf	Manitowoc	Wisconsin	76
Mary Jane Patchin	Mankato	Minnesota	456
Howard Roe	Manning	Iowa	138
Mae L. Palmer	Mansfield	South Dakota	191
Delores Beckman	Marshall	Minnesota	385
Clarence A. Senftner	McLaughlin	South Dakota	519
Ruth Overby	Mellette	South Dakota	50
Carleton Peters	Mesa	Arizona	142
Donald R. Bye	Midwest City	Oklahoma	217
Edna Angerhofer	Milbank	South Dakota	469
Norman Barlund	Milbank	South Dakota	214
June Comstock	Milbank	South Dakota	425
Diann Dauwen	Milbank	South Dakota	244
Orville Hilbrands	Milbank	South Dakota	292
Clarice W. Kranz	Milbank	South Dakota	215
Helyn Mertens	Milbank	South Dakota	463
William A. Schumacher	Milbank	South Dakota	470
Marge Stewart	Milbank	South Dakota	375

Suzanne Unzen	Milbank	South Dakota	235
Martha Deering	Miller	South Dakota	516
Dorothy Lichty	Miller	South Dakota	449
Joyce Meyer	Miller	South Dakota	353
Ruth A. Moller	Miller	South Dakota	400
Gene Norton	Miller	South Dakota	45
Donald Schultz	Miller	South Dakota	231
Luella Schultz	Miller	South Dakota	240
Catherine R. Crisp	Milwaukee	Wisconsin	503
Martha Mehlhaff	Mina	South Dakota	277
Shirley Adams	Mitchell	South Dakota	94
Ellen Jean Anderson	Mitchell	South Dakota	453
Dorothy Clites	Mitchell	South Dakota	429
Raeburn Moore	Mitchell	South Dakota	235
Gladys Noack	Mitchell	South Dakota	174
Dorothy J. Patton	Mitchell	South Dakota	443
Paul W. Patton	Mitchell	South Dakota	441
Mike Bezenek	Mobridge	South Dakota	207
Eileen Hoover	Mobridge	South Dakota	123
William W. Klucas	Mobridge	South Dakota	47
Kathy Jo Haugan	Monticello	Minnesota	493
Joyce Krokel	Mound City	South Dakota	424
Dorothy Reyelts	Mount Vernon	Missouri	504
Aloyce "Al" Menzia	Mukwonago	Wisconsin	448
Norm Sparby	Napa	California	200
Ardyce (Steen) Struck	New Effington	South Dakota	96
Arlyn "Butch" Smith	Odham	South Dakota	378
Philipina (Phil) Heintzman	Onaka	South Dakota	279
Roy Heintzman	Onaka	South Dakota	275
Carol Shoup	Onida	South Dakota	140
Marileen Tilberg	Onida	South Dakota	74
Joyce Wieseler	Orient	South Dakota	525
Jerry Otis Peters	Owatonna	Minnesota	331
Audrey R. Pedersen	Pea Ridge	Arizona	517
Ruby Markseth Chelgren	Peoria	Illinois	451
Shirley Kangas	Philip	South Dakota	193
Betty J. Voigt	Phoenix	Arizona	89
Gail A. Perry	Piney Flats	Tennessee	89
Virgil Likness	Plattsmouth	Nebraska	387
Lowell Seymour	Pollock	South Dakota	501
Phyllis A. Bjerke Peterson	Polson	Montana	406
Dorothy Goodspeed O'Neill	Portland	Oregon	338
Leonard Uecker	Quitman	Arizona	520
Lois Marie Hubbard	Racine	Wisconsin	402
Julie Brinkman	Ramona	South Dakota	201
Myrle Sederstrom	Ramona	South Dakota	304
Verna E. Schutt	Rancho Cordova	California	124
Lisa M. Droz	Rapid City	South Dakota	203
Pat La Mee	Rapid City	South Dakota	145
Eleanore R. Moe	Rapid City	South Dakota	169
Nadine Sievers	Rapid City	South Dakota	172
Jerry L. Tracy	Rapid City	South Dakota	62
Dean R. Bymers	Raymond	South Dakota	416
Patricia Anderson	Redfield	South Dakota	68

Dr. Richard Baus	Redfield	South Dakota	92
Evelyn Brand	Redfield	South Dakota	63
Lucille Brindley	Redfield	South Dakota	71
Raymond C. Ernster	Redfield	South Dakota	18
Darwin Jessen	Redfield	South Dakota	227
Edward A. Moeller	Redfield	South Dakota	191
Virginia O'Connor	Redfield	South Dakota	213
Junior P. Bukaske	River Ridge	Louisiana	126
Bonnie Anderson	Roscoe	South Dakota	181
Mathilda Nipper	Roscoe	South Dakota	104
Leroy Sauer	Roscoe	South Dakota	130
Deloris Bertram	Rosholt	South Dakota	469
Helen Johnson	Rosholt	South Dakota	332
Jane Curtis	Santa Fe	New Mexico	185
Lois Chamberlain	Scottsdale	Arizona	93
Georgene Erickson	Scottsdale	Arizona	446
James W. Geditz	Selah	Washington	265
Lorraine Kightlinger	Selby	South Dakota	195
Luella Miller	Selby	South Dakota	277
Ervin Spitzer	Silverdale	Washington	263
Grace Wangberg	Sinai	South Dakota	333
John S.Wangberg	Sinai	South Dakota	49
Darlene Carlson	Sioux Falls	Iowa	293
Kristin Gedstad	Sioux Falls	South Dakota	274
Lucille (Foote) Green	Sioux Falls	South Dakota	177
Burton Horsted	Sioux Falls	South Dakota	88
Alice Mae Bjerke Miller	Sioux Falls	South Dakota	370
Dana Reeve	Sioux Falls	South Dakota	143
John "Matt" Sutton	Sioux Falls	South Dakota	248
Barbara A. Kallstrom	Sisseton	South Dakota	350
Gloria Langager	Sisseton	South Dakota	84
Freda Poyet	Sisseton	South Dakota	512
Jean Hansen	South Shore	South Dakota	236
Donna (Heald) Pack	Spring Valley	Illinois	413
Milo I. Harpstead	Stevens Point	Wisconsin	438
Mr. Jerry Travis	Sun City West	Arizona	66
Lois Nelson	Surfside Beach	South Carolina	80
Dale T.Bussell	Tucson	Arizona	73
Ruth Myrvold	Tucson	Arizona	215
Milton Wolff	Tukwila	Washington	271
Frank Weis	Valley City	North Dakota	44
Karen Borgen	Veblen	South Dakota	370
Delores Henning	Veblen	South Dakota	239
Cindy Neuharth Hofland	Veblen	South Dakota	380
Gail Vrchota	Veblen	South Dakota	424
Ramona Kirkeby	Vienna	South Dakota	196
Roger Goens	Volga	South Dakota	33
Blaine Hoff	Volga	South Dakota	262
Mark Kisely	Volga	South Dakota	125
Mark Arnold	Watertown	South Dakota	492
Donald Becht	Watertown	South Dakota	310
Jeann Bevers	Watertown	South Dakota	267
Lisa Langenfeld Buche	Watertown	South Dakota	457
Dorothy Bull	Watertown	South Dakota	214

Dorothy Even	Watertown	South Dakota	93
Sharon Gill	Watertown	South Dakota	290
Margaret Gjerde	Watertown	South Dakota	454
Melba Gronau	Watertown	South Dakota	128
Donna Groskreutz	Watertown	South Dakota	227
Clark Hanson	Watertown	South Dakota	26
Patricia Brown Hanson	Watertown	South Dakota	418
Pat Herr	Watertown	South Dakota	386
Rick Herr	Watertown	South Dakota	70
Myla Johnson	Watertown	South Dakota	366
Janet Keenan-Hauck	Watertown	South Dakota	282
Jack Kennedy	Watertown	South Dakota	362
Duane J. Knebel	Watertown	South Dakota	55
Vickie (Veeder) Marotz	Watertown	South Dakota	475
Phyllis Meseberg	Watertown	South Dakota	299
Gene Monahan	Watertown	South Dakota	382
Lois (Kannegieter) Monahan	Watertown	South Dakota	367
Edith M. Noeldner	Watertown	South Dakota	147
Marion (Bunting) Nordquist	Watertown	South Dakota	291
Joyce R. Stanislzus Olson	Watertown	South Dakota	172
LaVern Papka	Watertown	South Dakota	502
Francis Parsey	Watertown	South Dakota	330
Arlene Parsley	Watertown	South Dakota	474
Lawrence L. Peterson	Watertown	South Dakota	261
Devon M. Reeve	Watertown	South Dakota	222
Arlo Remmers	Watertown	South Dakota	203
Elaine Ries	Watertown	South Dakota	230
Kathy Scharn	Watertown	South Dakota	287
Virginia Rawlins Skiner	Watertown	South Dakota	65
Nancy Volkart	Watertown	South Dakota	75
Beth Will	Watertown	South Dakota	470
Wilferd (Buzz) Greening	Waubay	South Dakota	321
Ruth Jorgenson	Waubay	South Dakota	70
Bonnie Kirchmeier	Waubay	South Dakota	115
Adeline Rumpza Tracy	Waubay	South Dakota	311
Lyle Berg	Webster	South Dakota	97
Lois B.Carlson	Webster	South Dakota	110
Tom W. Jones	Webster	South Dakota	190
Erma Knutson	Webster	South Dakota	190
James P. Kurkowski	Webster	South Dakota	155
Nadine Huwe Sauer	Webster	South Dakota	24
Gail Torrence	Webster	South Dakota	336
Frances Carmody	Wessington	South Dakota	335
RuthAnn Major	Wessington	South Dakota	116
Jeff (Hub) Keiser	Wessington Springs	South Dakota	51
Edward H. Lamers	W. Browns Valley	Minnesota	100
Joyce Yexley West	Fargo	North Dakota	251
Herbert Lokken	White	South Dakota	228
Rose Lamb	Willow Lake	South Dakota	135
Marlyce Peterson	Willow Lake	South Dakota	483
Helena Townsend	Willow Lake	South Dakota	173
Fred Maxwell	Wilmot	South Dakota	427
Harold G. Thaden	Wilmot	South Dakota	144
Florence Adermann	Wolsey	South Dakota	164

Josephine Christopherson	Wolsey	South Dakota	92
Verla Lindblad	Wolsey	South Dakota	313
Delphine Decker	Yale	South Dakota	132
Sister Kevis Irwin	Yankton	South Dakota	223
Muriel Reeve	Yankton	South Dakota	482
Joseph Nuhsbaumer	Zell	South Dakota	287

Index B (Year of Birth)

Name	Year	No.	Name	Year	No.
Grace Wangberg	1927	333	Ruth Myrvold	1930	215
Nila Weidler	1927	99	Joseph Nuhsbaumer	1930	287
Dorothy Bull	1928	214	Alice M. Olson	1930	486
Darlene Carlson	1928	293	Arlene Randall	1930	261
Josephine Christopherson	1928	92	Twila Sanborn Ruden	1930	262
Ronald D. Cornell	1928	199	Leroy Sauer	1930	130
Catherine R. Crisp	1928	503	Cheris St. John	1930	234
Mabel Dockter Freita	1928	471	David Sveum	1930	31
Margaret Gjerde	1928	454	LaJoy Thompsen	1930	387
Bonnie Jean Glock	1928	415	Jerry L. Tracy	1930	62
Lawrence L. Helwig	1928	77	Nancy Stakke Bauer	1931	266
Helen Johnson	1928	332	Orpha D. Bensen	1931	447
Lorraine Kightlinger	1928	195	Darleen Brace	1931	471
Ramona Kirkeby	1928	196	Dean R. Bymers	1931	416
Bernice Lemley	1928	516	Mary Anne Clark	1931	481
Verla Lindblad	1928	313	Avis Elenz	1931	435
Herbert Lokken	1928	228	Bonnie Kirchmeier	1931	115
Dee Melicher	1928	426	Dorothy J. Patton	1931	443
Edward A. Moeller	1928	191	Les Patton	1931	306
Edith M. Noeldner	1928	147	Helen M. Prater	1931	433
Gene Norton	1928	45	Devona J. Simonson	1931	311
Raiden V. Peterson	1928	48	John "Matt" Sutton	1931	248
Beverly M. Prostrollo	1928	95	Nadine TeBeest	1931	305
Virginia Pulfrey	1928	369	Leonard Uecker	1931	520
Earl Randall	1928	261	Betty J. Voigt	1931	89
Clarence A. Senftner	1928	519	Patricia Anderson	1932	68
Claraa Waldman	1928	342	Dr. Richard Baus	1932	92
Thorine Weiland	1928	202	William E. Beastrom	1932	393
Kenneth Wherry	1928	123	Donald Becht	1932	310
Deloris Bertram	1929	469	Lyle Berg	1932	97
Dorothy Bierwagen	1929	20	Evelyn Brand	1932	63
Ruby Chelgren	1929	451	Lois B. Carlson	1932	110
Shirley J. Dayton	1929	308	Raymond C. Ernster	1932	18
Paul Erschens	1929	232	Mary K. Frazier	1932	138
Thelma Hayden	1929	44	Anastasia Gebhart	1932	70
Sister Kevis Irwin	1929	223	Wilferd Greening	1932	321
Beverly Kluess	1929	237	Charles J. Hendricks	1932	216
Luella Miller	1929	277	Burton Horsted	1932	88
Paul W. Patton	1929	441	Margaret Bradbury Jewell	1932	150
Alma M. Paulson	1929	47	Tom W. Jones	1932	190
Lawrence L. Peterson	1929	261	Beverly Langner	1932	330
George Schott	1929	118	Mary Louise Lechner	1932	472
Verna E. Schutt	1929	124	Elaine McDaniels	1932	22
Norm Sparby	1929	200	Phyllis E. Nelson	1932	375
Marjorie Thoelke	1929	386	Jean P. Olson	1932	436
Warren Thomas	1929	103	Carol Pevestorf	1932	476
Gail Vrchota	1929	424	Freda Poyet	1932	512
Selmer N. Anderson	1930	442	Darlene Rowderdink	1932	42
Chester Benson	1930	119	Marge Stewart	1932	375
Duane Ellis	1930	510	Lois B. Warfield	1932	250
Milo I. Harpstead	1930	438	Bonnie Anderson	1933	181
Calvin C. Huber	1930	256	Edna Angerhofer	1933	469
Darwin Jessen	1930	227	Joanne Brownell	1933	122
Darlene Konrad	1930	224	Lois Erschens	1933	101

Name	Year	No.	Name	Year	No.
Betty Jean Fisher	1933	35	Leann Frederickson	1936	522
Bonnie Funk	1933	394	Virgil Likness	1936	387
Jim Gloe	1933	194	Danna Garber Mercer	1936	263
Rose Grothe	1933	284	Lois (Kannegieter) Monahan	1936	367
Patricia Brown Hanson	1933	418	Glenn Olson	1936	385
Helen Holsing	1933	72	Mary Jane Patchin	1936	456
Ruby Johannsen	1933	479	Loran Perry	1936	242
Marvin Madsen	1933	229	Howard Roe	1936	138
Gladys Noack	1933	174	Dorothy Van Kempen	1936	274
Marlyce Peterson	1933	483	Molly Williams	1936	71
D. Ransom	1933	219	Karen Borgen	1937	370
Nadine Huwe Sauer	1933	24	Anna (Hansen) Chesser	1937	477
Kathy Scharn	1933	287	Janet Hoglund Johnson	1937	484
Luella Schultz	1933	240	Duane J. Knebel	1937	55
Donna Steenson	1933	505	Russell H. Payne	1937	491
Donald G. Steward	1933	124	Bonita Dolney	1938	45
Adeline Rumpza Tracy	1933	311	Don Dorsman	1938	82
Mr. Jerry Travis	1933	66	Lewayne M. Erickson	1938	344
Frank Weis	1933	44	James W. Geditz	1938	265
Florence Adermann	1934	164	Lois Marie Hubbard	1938	402
Colleen A. Anderson	1934	465	Ronald E. Kangas	1938	229
Mary Lou Fluegel Beath	1934	28	Janet Keenan-Hauck	1938	282
Lois Chamberlain	1934	93	John R. Maciejewski	1938	213
Marion R. P. Goehring	1934	432	Joyce Meyer	1938	353
Dvonne P. S. Hansen	1934	487	Larry L. Steele	1938	105
Jean Hansen	1934	236	Harold G. Thaden	1938	144
Jacqueline Lee	1934	191	Milton Wolff	1938	271
Vivian Lundgren	1934	444	David G. Anderson	1939	258
Juliana Malsom	1934	183	Dorothy E. Beam-Saddler	1939	218
Martha Mehlhaff	1934	277	Ileen Groft-Tennyson	1939	139
Lyle L. Meyers	1934	158	Sharon L. Hansen	1939	286
Nadine Mikel	1934	336	Eileen Hoover	1939	123
Raeburn Moore	1934	235	Mary Lynn James	1939	367
H. Lynette Olson	1934	301	Paul Mardian	1939	411
Jerry Otis Peters	1934	331	Alice M. S. Mentzel	1939	348
Donald Schultz	1934	231	Harland F. Olson	1939	427
Shirley Adams	1935	94	Francis Parsey	1939	330
Phyllis Arwood	1935	60	Lorna Mundhenke Perkins	1939	472
Barbara Shawl Campbell	1935	458	Lowell Seymour	1939	501
Frances Carmody	1935	335	Mike Bezenek	1940	207
Delphine Decker	1935	132	Gayle Charron	1940	312
Lois Hagemann	1935	187	Ellen Dinger	1940	364
Delores Henning	1935	239	Daniel P. Horn	1940	134
Lois Nelson	1935	80	Shirley Kangas	1940	193
Shirley A. Neshiem	1935	228	Jack Kennedy	1940	362
Shirley Reed	1935	153	John Larson	1940	172
Dorothy Reyelts	1935	504	Arlene Mardian	1940	53
Betty Roggenbuck	1935	500	Leland Olson	1940	246
Les Solberg	1935	94	Arlene Parsley	1940	474
Dale T. Bussell	1936	73	Audrey R. Pedersen	1940	517
Ann J. Cazer	1936	45	Gail Torrence	1940	336
Jane Curtis	1936	185	Joyce Wieseler	1940	525
Georgene Erickson	1936	446	Joanne Drenkow	1941	386
Ben Fowler	1936	127	Jim D. Huff	1941	470

Nadine Matthews	1941	127	Sheral (Sievers) Morrill	1948	398
Phyllis A. Bjerke Peterson	1941	406	Suzanne Unzen	1948	235
Elaine Ries	1941	230	Julie Brinkman	1949	201
Leland Roe	1941	44	Carol Langner Dusharm	1949	320
Lona Swanson	1941	192	Starla Fitzjarrell	1949	397
Ed Buck	1942	337	Roberta Hilgendorf	1949	76
Sharon Gill	1942	290	Ellen Lehmkuhl Kub	1949	497
Joyce Krokel	1942	424	Joan I. Oster	1949	318
James P. Kurkowski	1942	155	Donna (Heald)Pack	1949	413
Aloyce "Al" Menzia	1942	448	Muriel Reeve	1949	482
Alice Mae Bjerke Miller	1942	370	William A. Schumacher	1949	470
Kathryn Cole Quinones	1942	167	Paul Bremmon	1950	357
Arlene Schneiderman	1942	61	Corinne Jameson	1950	460
Arlyn "Butch" Smith	1942	378	Joe Malheim	1950	81
Caroll Ann Whitman	1942	368	Vickie (Veeder) Marotz	1950	475
Dorothy Graves	1943	29	James A. Schmidt	1950	300
Margaret L. Grottke	1943	324	Marileen Tilberg	1950	74
JoEllen D. Johnson	1943	125	Peggy Westby	1950	173
Peggy Kasten	1943	359	Nancy Olson Burkey	1951	461
Judy Miles	1943	298	Catherine Hausman Ching	1951	280
Ruth A. Moller	1943	400	Duane W. Laufmann	1951	467
Carol Shoup	1943	140	Jelene Tilden	1951	57
Grace Wegleitner	1943	377	Delores Beckman	1952	385
Sharon Cole	1944	347	Jeanne Carstens	1952	428
Blaine Hoff	1944	262	Rick Herr	1952	70
Mary Hymans	1944	315	Susan Hines	1952	330
William W. Klucas	1944	47	Gloria Langager	1952	84
Donna Lewandowski	1944	331	Janet Elaine Meehan	1952	48
Donna O'Connell	1944	388	Joyce J. Poppen	1952	495
Gail Roe	1944	26	Nancy Volkart	1952	75
Barbara Solsaa	1944	156	Roger Larsen	1953	179
Louise E. Beld	1945	299	Mathilda Nipper	1953	104
Diann Dauwen	1945	244	Jane Jensen Pierce	1953	489
Barbara A. Kallstrom	1945	350	Arlo Remmers	1953	203
DoreneNelson	1945	210	Gail Anderson Winter	1953	141
Violet Nelson	1945	303	Joyce Yexley	1953	251
Tim Dewald	1946	511	Barbara Booton	1954	254
Melba Gronau	1946	128	Kristin Gedstad	1954	274
Lois Peterson	1946	206	Roger Goens	1954	33
Harlow H. Rudolph	1946	389	Pat Herr	1954	386
George M.C. Thompson	1946	112	Cindy Neuharth Hofland	1954	380
Bob Boardman	1947	97	Steve Riedel	1954	27
Lisa Langenfeld Buche	1947	457	Beth Will	1954	470
Donna Groskreutz	1947	227	Myla Johnson	1956	366
Terry Jackson	1947	92	Ray A. Johnson	1956	360
Mike Jurgens	1947	319	Mark Kisely	1956	125
Connie Lehmkuhl Larson	1947	507	Gail A. Perry	1956	89
Mary Lou A. Gasper Malli	1947	527	Cynthia Bartels	1958	276
Betty Walker Schinkel	1947	264	Lisa M. Droz	1959	203
Cheryl Vosburgh	1947	191	Jeff (Hub) Keiser	1960	51
Mark Arnold	1948	492	Dana Reeve	1960	143
Clark Hanson	1948	26	Mike Drooger	1961	154
Carol Joffer	1948	231	Kathy Jo Haugan	1962	493
RuthAnn Major	1948	116	Stephen J. Grottke	1969	404

Christian H. Grottke	1973	421
LeRoy P. Gross	Unknown	70
Mary F. Husman	Unknown	129
Ruth Jorgenson	Unknown	70
Erma Knutson	Unknown	190
Doris S. Koisti	Unknown	390
Pat La Mee	Unknown	145
Rosalia Schmidt	Unknown	372
Virginia R. Skiner	Unknown	65
Joyce Steinle	Unknown	391